STRUCTURING TECHNIQUES

STRUCTURING TECHNIQUES

AN INTRODUCTION USING C++

by Andrew C. Staugaard, Jr.
College of the Ozarks

An Alan R. Apt Book

Prentice Hall, Englewood Cliffs, New Jersey 07632

Library of Congress Cataloging-in-Publication Data
Staugaard, Andrew C..
    Structuring techniques : an introduction using C++ / Andrew C.
Staugaard, Jr.
      p.   cm.—("An Alan R. Apt book.")
    Includes bibliographical references and index.
    ISBN 0-13-012576-8
    1. Structured programming. 2. C++ (Computer program language)
      I. Title. II. Series
  QA76.6.S717   1994
  005.13'3–dc20
                            93-34289
                               CIP

Publisher: Alan Apt
Production Editor: Mona Pompili
Cover Designer: Tommy Boy
Copy Editor: Henry Pels
Production Coordinator: Linda Behrens
Editorial Assistant: Shirley McGuire
Cover Art: Paul Klee: *Polyphonically Enclosed White* 1930. Watercolor and pen and India ink on paper,
    mounted on cardboard. $13^{1}/_{8} \times 9^{5}/_{8}$ inches.

© 1994 by Prentice-Hall, Inc.
A Paramount Communications Company
Englewood Cliffs, New Jersey 07632

The author and publisher of this book have used their best efforts in preparing this book. These efforts include the development, research, and testing of the theories and programs to determine their effectiveness. The author and publisher shall not be liable in any event for incidental or consequential damages in connection with, or arising out of, the furnishing, performance, or use of these programs.

Printed in the United States of America

10 9 8 7 6 5 4 3 2

ISBN 0-13-012576-8

PRENTICE-HALL INTERNATIONAL (UK) LIMITED, *London*
PRENTICE-HALL OF AUSTRALIA PTY. LIMITED, *Sydney*
PRENTICE-HALL CANADA, INC., *Toronto*
PRENTICE-HALL HISPANOAMERICANA, S.A., *Mexico*
PRENTICE-HALL OF INDIA PRIVATE LIMITED, *New Delhi*
PRENTICE-HALL OF JAPAN, INC., *Tokyo*
SIMON & SCHUSTER ASIA PTE. LTD., *Singapore*
EDITORA PRENTICE-HALL DO BRASIL, LTDA., *Rio de Janeiro*

PREFACE

This book has been written to provide an introduction to structured programming using the C++ language. The C++ language is ideal for learning structured programming, since it provides all the major control structures and modularity features of any structured language. It is no harder learning good program structuring techniques using C++ than it is using a traditional teaching language such as Pascal. Moreover, since C++ has taken the commercial software development industry by storm, an added benefit is that of learning a language that is widely accepted in the industrial world. Most C++ books assume a prior knowledge of the C language. This text starts from the beginning, assuming no previous knowledge of C, or any other programming language.

Features of this book include:

- Beginning C++ that does not require any previous programming experience.

- Emphasis of algorithms and problem solving using a modular top/down structured approach.

- Comprehensive coverage with a solid introduction to object-oriented programming and ADTs.

- Compatibility with any C++ compiler.

- Over 300 Quick-Check exercises at the end of the chapter sections with answers in an appendix.

- Over 300 questions and programming problems at the end of the chapters.

- Over 65 examples that pose problems and give step-by-step solutions.

- Over 15 case studies that present a structured top/down approach to problem solving.

- Debugging Tip, Style Tip, Maintenance Tip, Programming Tip, and Caution boxes.

- A TURBO C++ Jump Start appendix for those using this compiler

- A comprehensive glossary of C++ terms.

To the Instructor

This text has been developed to teach structured programming concepts using the C++ language at the freshman level in a CS1 type of course. In addition, your students will obtain a solid introduction to object-oriented programming and ADTs in preparation for further study of these topics. The transition from structured programming to ADTs is very natural using C++, since ADTs are easily implemented using C++ classes.

Some will say that you can't teach structured programming using C++, since the language is too complicated. I disagree. There is no need to teach every detail of the language in a beginning course. I have used a subset of C++ to teach fundamental structuring and object-oriented concepts and have found that beginning students do not have any more difficulty using C++ than Pascal with this approach. In addition, learning C++ has the added benefit for the student of learning a very widely used industry standard, as opposed to Pascal.

The text begins with a general overview of computer hardware and software technology in the first part of Chapter 1. This material is rather basic and can be covered rapidly or skipped entirely if students have already had some programming experience. However, the latter part of Chapter 1 discusses what I call "The Programmer's Algorithm" and should be covered thoroughly. The programmer's algorithm is a step-by-step process that I have used to get students started on the right programming track by considering problem definition, step-by-step solution planning via algorithms, and good documentation. Algorithmic development, prior to coding, is stressed throughout the text. I have employed a pseudocode algorithmic language that is generic, simple, and allows for easy translation to the coded C++ program.

Chapter 2 introduces the concept of data typing and modular top/down program structuring using C++. Then, in Chapters 3–6, students learn about program I/O, decision making, and iteration.

In Chapter 7, students really get the flavor of a structured language when they learn how to write their own functions in C++. From this point on, the idea of a modular top/down design approach to problem solving is emphasized. Such an approach is mandatory if the student plans on tackling complex programming tasks like those they would encounter in industry.

One-dimensional arrays are discussed in Chapter 8 and multidimensional arrays are discussed in Chapter 9. Chapter 9 can easily be skipped if time is a factor.

The important topic of pointers is "addressed" in Chapter 10. This material is fundamental to programming in C++ and should be covered thoroughly.

Furthermore, subsequent chapters employ pointers throughout so that the student becomes comfortable with their use.

A sound introduction to object-oriented programming is provided in Chapters 12 and 13. Chapter 12 introduces a whole different way of problem solving through the use of classes and their associated objects. Chapter 13 is devoted to the related topics of inheritance, polymorphism, and dynamic binding. I should emphasize that it is *not* the intent of this book to teach object-oriented programming. The intent is to teach structured programming techniques using C++, while providing a solid introduction to OOP. Students will have to take an additional course in OOP if they wish to become competent object-oriented programmers.

Chapter 14 provides an introduction to ADTs in preparation for an advanced course in data structures. The classic stack, queue, and linked list ADTs are covered thoroughly. In this chapter, ADTs are covered at two levels: The purely abstract level using the black box interface approach, and at the implementation level using C++ classes. Here is where the student really appreciates object-oriented programming, since ADTs are naturally implemented using C++ classes.

The text closes with a chapter on File I/O (Chapter 15). Here, the student will learn how to read, write, append, and change disk files using C++. In addition, the student learns how C++ employs a class hierarchy to implement file streams.

The text can be taught in one or two terms, depending on the ability of the students. In a two term sequence, I would suggest coverage through the topic of one-dimensional arrays (Chapters 1–8). Then, begin the second term with multidimensional arrays and finish out the book (Chapters 9 – 15). This sequence will allow you to thoroughly cover the important topics of pointers, structures, classes, objects, inheritance, polymorphism, and ADTs.

Although the code in the text has been developed using Borland's TURBO C++ compiler, I have attempted to employ only those language features that are common to all C++ compilers. In other words, the text material is very portable and can easily be taught using any C++ compiler. In the few cases where I use code that is specific to TURBO C++ or the DOS platform, I have clearly indicated this fact and suggest that the student research his/her compiler documentation to implement similar operations. The code has been tested using both the DOS and UNIX platforms. If you are using TURBO C++ for DOS, I suggest that you refer students early to Appendix A which provides an overview of this compiler. In specific, you should assign the "Hello World" program exercise in Appendix A the first week of the semester.

To the Student

This book has been written to provide you with an introduction to structured programming using the C++ language. In other words, it will not only teach you the C++ language, but more important, it will teach you how to define problems and plan their solution so that they can be easily coded using the C++ language, or any structured language for that matter. The text emphasizes problem solution using a modular top/down structured approach. You will learn to attack problems using a "divide and conquer" strategy. By the end of the text you will have the knowledge required to solve complicated problems using this modular top/down structured approach that today's computer solutions require. In addition, you will get a solid introduction to *object-oriented programming (OOP)* and *abstract data types (ADTs)* to prepare you for further study of these topics.

Make sure that you go through all the examples and case studies. These have been written in short, understandable modules that stress the fundamental concepts being discussed. Case studies are included at the end of many of the chapters in an effort to tie things together and present a top/down design approach to problem solving using the C++ language.

Finally, above all, get your hands dirty! You cannot become a competent programmer by just reading this book and listening to your instructor's lectures. You must get your hands dirty at the machine by developing *your own* C++ programs.

Acknowledgments

Contributions to this text have come from many circles. From the academic world I would like to thank Buster Dunsmore of Purdue University, George Luger of The University of New Mexico, and Keith Pierce of The University of Minnesota. All have reviewed the manuscript and have made valuable contributions. Special thanks to Buster Dunsmore and his colleagues who taught their CS1 course at Purdue using an early draft of the manuscript.

From the industrial world, I would like to thank Bjarne Stroustrup of Bell Labs who reviewed the manuscript and made many valuable suggestions relative to teaching C++ to beginning students as well as the language philosophy and details.

From the student world, I would like to thank my own students who have inspired the creation of this text and have made many valuable suggestions. In particular I would like to thank Brenda Snider, a former student and now colleague, who developed the appendix material and reviewed the text from a student's perspective.

CONTENTS

CHAPTER 1: *GETTING ACQUAINTED WITH COMPUTERS, PROGRAMS, AND C++*

CHAPTER 2: *GETTING ACQUAINTED WITH C++*

CHAPTER 3: GETTING THINGS IN AND OUT ⇒ READING AND WRITING

CHAPTER 4: WRITING SIMPLE C++ PROGRAMS

CHAPTER 13: CLASS INHERITANCE

CHAPTER 14: ADTs

CHAPTER 15: FILE I/O

APPENDIX A: TURBO C++ JUMP START

APPENDIX B: QUICK CHECK SOLUTIONS 701

GLOSSARY 730

INDEX 739

STRUCTURING
TECHNIQUES

1

GETTING ACQUAINTED WITH COMPUTERS, PROGRAMS, AND C++

INTRODUCTION

In this first chapter you will begin your learning journey in the important topic of structured programming using C++. This chapter has been written to provide you with an introduction to computers, computer programs, and C++ in general. You will learn about the relationship between the computer system and the computer programs that operate the system. In particular, you will study the steps required to solve just about any programming problem using a top/down structured approach. Even though some of the material contained in this chapter might be familiar to you, it's always a good idea to review the high points.

The last section of this chapter teaches you how to develop algorithms. Make sure you understand this material and work the related problems at the end of the chapter. As you become more experienced in programming, you will find that the "secret" to successful programming is good planning through the use of structured algorithms. In the chapters that follow, you will build on this knowledge to create workable C++ programs.

Any computer system, regardless of its size, can be broken down into two major components: hardware and software. We begin with an overview of each.

1-1 THE HARDWARE

You undoubtedly have seen some of the hardware components of a computer. These are the physical devices that you can see and touch, such as those shown in Figure 1-1a. This typical microcomputer system obviously has a keyboard for user input, a display monitor for output, and magnetic disk drives for program and data storage. Two very important parts of the system that cannot be seen, because they are inside the console, are the ***central processing unit*** and its ***working memory.***

The block diagram in Figure 1-1b shows all of the major hardware sections of the system. From this figure, you see that the system can be divided into five functional parts: the central processing unit (CPU), main working or primary memory, secondary memory, input, and output.

The Central Processing Unit (CPU)

The central processing unit (CPU) is the brain and nerve center of the entire system. This is where all of the calculations and decisions are made. In a microcomputer system, the entire CPU is contained within a single integrated circuit (IC) chip called a ***microprocessor.***

A *microprocessor* is a single integrated circuit (IC) chip that contains the entire central processing unit (CPU) for a microcomputer system.

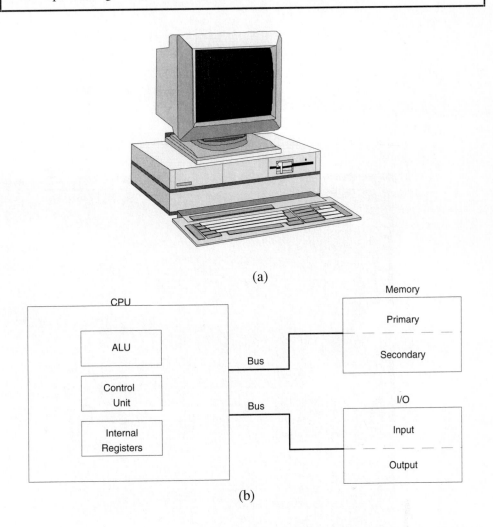

(a)

(b)

Figure 1-1 (a) A typical microcomputer system and (b) its hardware structure, or architecture.

In fact, a microprocessor is what distinguishes a microcomputer from a mini or mainframe computer. In mini and mainframe computers, several ICs make up the CPU, not just one as in a microcomputer. A typical microprocessor IC is pictured in Figure 1-2, along with a magnified view of the chip itself.

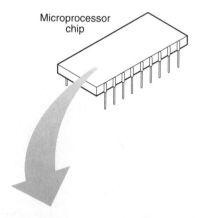

Figure 1-2 A microprocessor chip is the CPU of a microcomputer system. (Copyright by Motorola, Inc. Used by Permission).

There are three functional regions within the CPU. They are the ***arithmetic and logic unit (ALU)***, the ***control unit***, and the ***internal registers*** as shown in Figure 1-3.

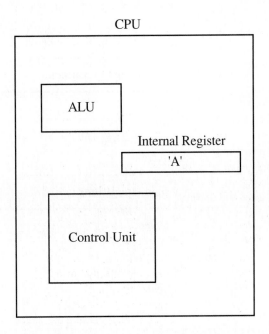

Figure 1-3 The CPU consists of an ALU, Control Unit, and Internal Registers.

The Arithmetic and Logic Unit (ALU)

As its name implies, the arithmetic and logic unit performs all of the arithmetic and logic operations within the CPU. The arithmetic operations performed by the ALU include addition, subtraction, multiplication, and division. These four arithmetic operations can be combined to perform just about any mathematical calculation, from simple arithmetic to calculus.

Logic operations performed by the ALU are *comparison* operations that are used to *compare* numbers and characters. The three logic comparison operations are equal (==), less than (<), and greater than (>). Notice that a double equals symbol (==) is used to denote the equals operation. More about this later. These three operations can be combined to form the three additional logic operations of not equal (< >), less than or equal (<=), and greater than or equal (>=).

Take a look at Table 1-1. It summarizes the arithmetic and logic operations performed by the ALU. The symbols listed in the table are those that you will use later to perform arithmetic and logic operations when writing C++ programs.

TABLE 1-1 A SUMMARY OF ARITHMETIC
AND LOGIC OPERATIONS PERFORMED
BY THE ALU SECTION OF THE CPU

Arithmetic Operations	Symbol
Addition	+
Subtraction	−
Multiplication	*
Division	/

Logic Operations	Symbol
Equal to	==
Not equal to	!=
Less than	<
Less than or equal to	<=
Greater than	>
Greater than or equal to	>=

The Control Unit

The control unit section of the CPU directs and coordinates the activity of the entire system. This section interprets program instructions and generates electrical signals to the other parts of the system in order to execute those instructions. The control unit communicates with other sections of the CPU via internal signal paths called *buses*. The control unit often is likened to a traffic cop or orchestra leader, because it directs the activity of the entire system.

Internal Registers

The internal register section of the CPU contains temporary storage areas for program instructions and data. In other words, these registers temporarily hold information while it is being processed by the CPU. In Figure 1-3, the internal register shown is holding the character 'A' in preparation for processing this character or as a result of some previous processing step. Be aware that a CPU contains several internal registers, even though only one is shown in Figure 1-3.

Primary Memory

Primary memory often is called main working memory. The reason for this is that primary memory is used to store programs and data while they are being "worked," or executed, by the CPU. As Figure 1-4 shows, there are two types of primary memory: *random access memory (RAM)* and *read-only memory (ROM)*.

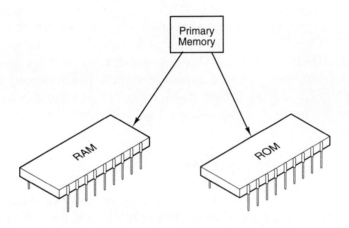

Figure 1-4 Primary memory consists of RAM and ROM.

Random Access Memory (RAM)

Random access memory is memory for you, the user. When you enter a program or data into the system, it goes into RAM. This is why the amount of RAM often is quoted when you buy a computer system. You most likely have heard the terms 640 Kilobytes (640K), 1 Megabyte (1M), 2 Megabyte (2M), and so on, when describing a microcomputer system. This is the amount of RAM, or user memory, that the system contains. Here, the letter K stands for the value 1,024, and M for the value K^2, or 1,024 × 1,024. Thus, a 640K system has 640 × 1,024 = 655,360 bytes of RAM, a 2M system has 2 × 1,024 × 1,024 = 2,097,152 bytes of RAM, and so forth. The more bytes of RAM a system has, the more room there is for your programs and data. As a result, larger and more complex programs can be executed with larger amounts of RAM.

By definition, RAM is ***read/write memory***. This means that information can be written into, or stored, into RAM and read from, or retrieved, from it. When writing new information into a given area of RAM, any previous information in that area is destroyed. Fortunately, you don't have to worry about this when entering programs, since the system makes sure that the new program information is not written over any important old information.

Once information has been written into RAM, it can be read, or retrieved, by the CPU during program execution. A read operation is nondestructive. Thus, when data are read from RAM, the RAM contents are not destroyed and remain unchanged. Think of a read operation as a "copy" operation.

One final point about RAM: It is ***volatile***. This means that any information stored in RAM is erased when power is removed from the system. As a result, any programs that you have entered in main working memory (RAM) will be lost when you turn off the system. You must always remember to save your programs on a secondary memory device, such as a disk, before turning off the system power.

Read-Only Memory (ROM)

Read-only memory often is called ***system memory*** because it stores system-related programs and data. These system programs and data take care of tasks such as reset, cursor control, binary conversions, input/output (I/O), and so on. All of these system programs are part of a larger operating system program that is permanently stored in ROM or on a disk. In IBM PC and compatible systems the system software stored in ROM is called ***BIOS***. The operating system, ***DOS*** or ***OS/2***, is stored on disk and works with BIOS to perform ***transparent*** system operations. The term *transparent* means that the user in not aware of the underlying system operations being performed.

As its name implies, read-only memory can only be read from and not written into. Consequently, information stored in ROM is permanent and cannot be changed. Since the information is permanent, ROM must be ***nonvolatile***. This means that any information stored in ROM is not lost when power is removed from the system. Due to this feature, ROM programs often are called *firmware.*

Secondary Memory

Secondary memory, sometimes called ***bulk*** or ***mass storage***, is used to hold programs and data on a semipermanent basis. The most common type of secondary memory used in microcomputer systems are magnetic disks shown in Figure 1-5. Floppy disks, like those shown in Figure 1-5a and 1-5b, get their name from the fact that they are flexible, rather than rigid, or hard. The disk is coated with a magnetic material and enclosed within a 5 1/4" soft plastic jacket or 3 1/2" hard plastic cover. When inserted into a disk drive the disk is spun on the drive at about 300 rpm. A read/write recording head within the drive reads and writes information on the disk through the access slot, or window, in the disk jacket. Most systems today include a built-in hard disk drive like the one shown in Figure 1-5c. In fact, a hard drive system is a must when working with professional-level integrated program development software like you find with most C++ compilers.

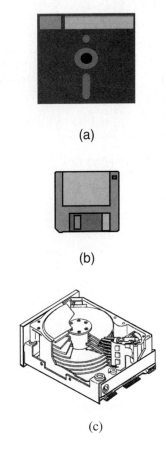

(a)

(b)

(c)

Figure 1-5: The common (a) 5 1/4 inch disk, (b) 3 1/2 inch disk, and (c) exposed hard disk.

When writing programs, you will first enter the program code into the system primary memory, or RAM. When *saving* C++ programs, you must create a work file name for the program. This work file name creates an area, or file, on the disk where your program will be saved. As you enter and work with your program in RAM, you will periodically save the program on the disk so that it is permanently stored. When you save the program, the system simply copies the program from RAM and saves it on the disk under the work file name that you created. This process is illustrated in Figure 1-6a.

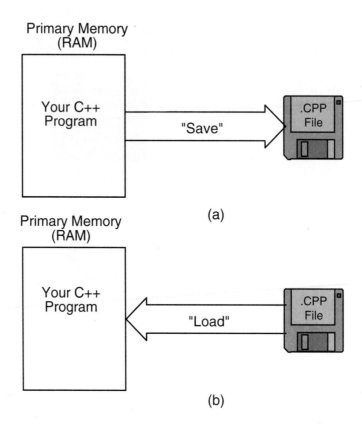

Figure 1-6 (a) Saving a program on disk, and (b) loading a program from disk.

Saving a program on disk allows you to retrieve it later. To read a program from a disk, you simply *load* the work file name assigned to the program. This tells the system to read the work file and transfer it into primary memory (RAM), as illustrated in Figure 1-6b. Once it is in working memory, the program can be compiled/linked, executed (run), or changed (edited). Of course, if any changes are made the program must be saved on disk again so that the changes are also made on the disk. If you are using the TURBO C++ compiler, you can refer to Appendix A for details on how to enter, save, and load programs. Otherwise, consult your compiler reference manual for details on how to enter, save, and load programs.

Input

Input is what goes into the system. Input devices are hardware devices that provide a means of entering programs and data into the system. The major input device for a microcomputer system such as the one pictured in Figure 1-1a is the keyboard. The computer keyboard contains all of the characters that you will need to write a program. In addition, there are also special control functions and special control keys that provide for system operations such as cursor movement. You should study the operating manual of your particular system so that you understand the function of all of the keyboard keys.

The disk drive is another form of input device, since it also provides a means of loading programs and data into the system. There are many other types of input devices used with computer systems, but the keyboard and disk drive are the only two devices that you will be using when learning how to write C++ programs.

Output

Output is what comes out of the system. Output devices are hardware devices that provide a means of getting data out of the system. The three major output devices that you will be concerned with are the display monitor, printer, and disk drive. The display monitor is just the screen in front of you. It allows you to observe programs and data that are stored in primary memory (RAM).

A printer provides you with a hard copy of your programs and data. During a printing operation, the system actually copies information from primary or secondary memory to the printer. Thus, any information to be printed must be stored in primary or secondary memory.

Finally, a disk drive is also an output device, since information stored in primary memory can be written to the disk. You could say that a disk drive is an input/output (I/O) device, since it provides a means of getting information both in and out of the system.

The Fetch/Execute Cycle

The fetch/execute cycle is what takes place when you *run* a program. To run a program, you must first enter it into primary memory via the keyboard or load it from disk. Once in primary memory, the program must be *compiled* and *linked*.

The compiling/linking process is performed by a C++ compiler. The compiler converts the C++ instructions into a binary machine code that can be executed by the CPU. In addition, the compiler checks the program for errors and generates error messages and warnings to you via the display monitor. Your program cannot be run, or executed, until it is free of errors and completely compiled. After a C++ program is compiled, it is **linked** with any additional programs that are required for execution. As you will learn shortly, a completed C++ program is actually comprised of several separate programs that are linked together.

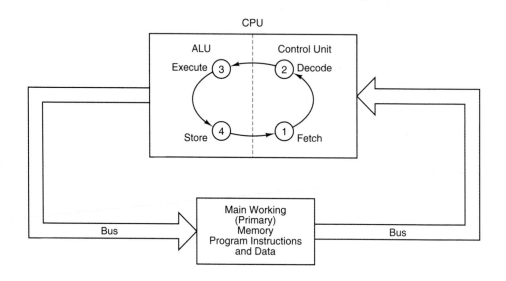

Figure 1-7 The fetch/execute cycle between the CPU and main working memory.

Once a C++ program has been compiled and linked, the machine instructions are **fetched** from primary memory and **executed,** or **run,** as shown in Figure 1-7. Observe the **fetch/execute** cycle within the CPU. The control unit first fetches a given program instruction from primary memory. The instruction is then decoded, or translated, to determine what is to be done. Next, the control unit makes available any data required for the operation and directs the ALU to perform the operation. The ALU executes the operation, and the control unit stores the operation results in an internal register or primary memory. The resulting data is temporarily stored in an internal register or primary memory until it is used for another operation or sent to an output device such as a disk or printer. In summary, you can see from Figure 1-7 that the four basic fetch/execute cycle operations are *fetch, decode, execute,* and *store.* That's it in a nutshell!

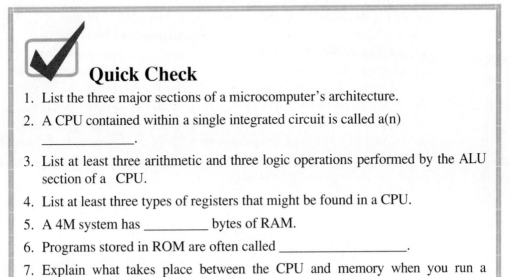

Quick Check

1. List the three major sections of a microcomputer's architecture.
2. A CPU contained within a single integrated circuit is called a(n) _____.
3. List at least three arithmetic and three logic operations performed by the ALU section of a CPU.
4. List at least three types of registers that might be found in a CPU.
5. A 4M system has _____ bytes of RAM.
6. Programs stored in ROM are often called _____.
7. Explain what takes place between the CPU and memory when you run a program.

1-2 THE SOFTWARE

If computer hardware can be likened to an automobile, computer software can be likened to the driver of the automobile. Without the driver, nothing happens. In other words, the computer hardware by itself can do nothing. The hardware system requires software that provides step-by-step instructions to tell the system what to do. A set of software instructions that tell the computer what to do is called a computer program. To communicate instructions to the computer, computer programs are written in different languages. In general, computer languages can be grouped into three major categories: *machine language, assembly language,* and *high-level language.*

Machine Language

All of the hardware components in a computer system, including the CPU, operate on a language made up of binary 1s and 0s. A CPU does not understand any other language. When a computer is designed, the CPU is designed to interpret a given set of instructions, called its **instruction set.** Each instruction within the instruction set has a unique binary code that can be translated directly by the CPU. This binary code is called **machine code**, and the set of all machine coded instructions is called the **machine language**.

A typical machine language program is provided in Figure 1-8a. To write such a program, you must determine the operation to be performed, and then translate the operation into the required binary machine code from a list of instruction set machine codes provided by the CPU manufacturer. As you might imagine, this is an extremely inefficient process. It is time consuming, tedious, and subject to a tremendous amount of error. In addition, simple operations, such as multiplication and division, often require several lines of machine code. For these reasons, machine-language programming is rarely used. However, remember that high-level language programs are always translated to machine language to enable the CPU to perform the fetch/execute cycle.

01001100	mov bx, offset value	x = 2;
11101001	mov ax, [bx]	if (x<=y)
10101010	add ax, 5	x = x + 1;
10001110	add bx, 2	else
00001111	add ax, [bx]	x = x − 1;
(a)	(b)	(c)

Figure 1-8 (a) Machine language (b) assembly language, and (c) high-level language.

Assembly Language

Assembly language is a step up from machine language. Rather than using 1s and 0s, assembly language employs alphabetic abbreviations called **mnemonics** that are easily remembered by you, the programmer. For instance, the mnemonic for addition is ADD, the mnemonic for move is MOV, and so forth. A typical assembly language program is listed in Figure 1-8b.

The assembly language mnemonics provide us with an easier means of writing and interpreting programs. Although assembly language programs are more easily understood by us humans, they cannot be directly understood by the

CPU. As a result, assembly language programs must be translated into machine code. This is the job of another program, called an **assembler**. The assembler program translates assembly language programs into binary machine code that can be decoded by the CPU.

Although programming in assembly language is easier than machine-language programming, it is not the most efficient means of programming. Assembly language programming is also tedious and prone to error, since there is usually a one-to-one relationship between the mnemonics and corresponding machine code. The solution to these inherent problems of assembly language programming is found in high-level languages.

This does not mean that assembly language is not useful. Because of its one-to-one relationship with machine language, assembly language programs are very efficient relative to execution speed and memory utilization. In fact, many high-level language programs include assembly language routines, especially for those tasks requiring high-speed software performance.

High-level Language

A high-level language consists of instructions, or statements, that are similar to English and common mathematical notation. A typical series of high-level statements is shown in Figure 1-8c. High-level language statements are very powerful. A typical high-level language statement is equivalent to many machine code instructions.

High-level languages were developed in the early 1950s to take some of the work out of programming. When programming in a high-level language, you do not have to concern yourself with the specific instruction set of the CPU. Rather, you can concentrate on solving the problem at hand. Once you learn a given high-level language, you can program any computer that runs that language.

You must be aware that, even when programming in a high-level language, the system must still translate your instructions into machine code that can be understood by the CPU. There are two types of system programs that can be employed for this purpose: a **compiler** or an **interpreter**. A compiler is a program that accepts a high-level language program and translates the entire program into machine code all at one time, before it is executed by the CPU. On the other hand, an interpreter translates and executes one high-level statement at a time. Once a given statement has been executed, the interpreter then translates and executes the next statement, and so on, until the entire program has been executed. Although interpreters do have their advantages, especially during the debugging stage, and are used with many microcomputers, C++ employs a compiler. For this reason, let's look closer at the operation of a compiler.

The diagram in Figure 1-9 illustrates the basic function of a compiler. The compiler acts as the interface between your program and the machine. Here's how a typical C++ compiler works. Once you have entered a C++ program into the system, you must execute the C++ compiler to translate your program. Your C++ program is referred to as a ***source program*** and the machine language program that is generated by the compiler is called an ***object program***. C++ source programs usually have a .CPP file name extension, while the corresponding object program has a .OBJ extension.

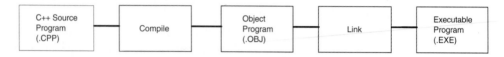

Figure 1-9 The C++ compiler and linker translate source code into machine code that can be executed by the CPU.

A ***source program*** is the one that you write in the C++ language and normally has a DOS file extension of .CPP. An ***object program*** is the binary machine language program generated by the compiler and always has a DOS file extension of .OBJ.

As the program is being translated, the compiler checks for errors. After the program is compiled, the compiler displays a list of error messages and warnings. In addition, some compilers, like TURBO C++, place the cursor on the display monitor at the point in your program where a given error was detected. After you correct all the errors, you must execute the compiler again until you get a successful compilation.

Once compiled, your program must be ***linked***. As mentioned earlier in this chapter, the linking step integrates your program with any additional routines that are required for proper program execution. These routines can be other high-level programs, assembly language programs, or operating system routines. The linking step produces an executable file with a .EXE file name extension. Errors can also occur during the linking step, especially if any required routines are not available or cannot be located. Your C++ software will also report any linking errors.

Finally, when the entire program has been successfully compiled and linked, you can execute, or run, your program. When you run your program, you actually are executing the machine-language program generated by the compiler.

As you are probably aware, there are several popular high-level languages, including COBOL, Pascal, FORTRAN, BASIC, LISP, Ada, and C++, among others. Each has been developed with a particular application in mind. For instance, COBOL, which stands for COmmon Business Oriented Language, was developed for business programming. FORTRAN, which means FORmula TRANslator, was developed for scientific programming. LISP was developed for artificial intelligence programming, while Pascal was developed primarily for education to teach the principles of software design. C++ was developed for efficient implementation of complex high-level structures that are required for software solution of today's complex problems. Let's take a closer look at the C++ language in general.

Why C++?

First there was the B language, then C, then C++. All were developed at Bell Telephone Laboratories and, like all high-level structured languages, have their roots in ALGOL. The B language was developed by Ken Thompson at Bell Labs in an effort to develop an operating system using a high-level language. Prior to B, operating systems were developed using the assembly language of the particular CPU on which the operating system was to run. Using the B language as a basis, Dennis Ritchie developed the C language at Bell Labs. The main purpose for the C language was to develop an operating system for the DEC PDP-11 mini computer. The resulting operating system became known as UNIX. In fact, most versions of UNIX today are written almost entirely in C. The C language was originally defined in the classic text *The C Programming Language*, written by Kernighan and Ritchie. In fact, the C language became such a popular commercial language that an ANSI (American National Standards Institute) standard for C was released in 1989. A programming language standard is a document that describes the details of a programming language so that programs written to the standard specifications are "portable" between systems.

The C++ language is an extension of the C language. Bjarne Stroustrup of Bell Labs enhanced the C language by adding ***object-oriented programming (OOP)*** capability. Object-oriented programming allows complex programs to be developed using simpler constructs called ***objects*** which can communicate by exchanging messages. More about this later. The obvious goal of Mr. Stroustrup was to maintain the efficiency of C while providing the power of OOP to the language. The resulting language became known as C++. You will realize where the ++ came from when you learn about the C++ *increment* operator. Because C++ is an enhancement of C, any C program is also a C++ program; however the opposite is not true.

Like C, C++ is taking the software development industry by storm. The reason for this is that both languages offer all the advantages of a high-level language, but also provide low-level access to system hardware and software just like assembly language. For this reason, C and C++ are often referred to as *mid-level* languages. In fact, most of the commercial software developed today is written using C or C++. As a result, an ANSI standard for C++ will soon be released.

The design of C++ lends itself to the idea of *structured design* and *structured programming*.

> *Structured design* is a methodology that requires software to be designed using a top/down modular approach and *structured programming* allows programs to be written using well-defined control structures and independent program modules.

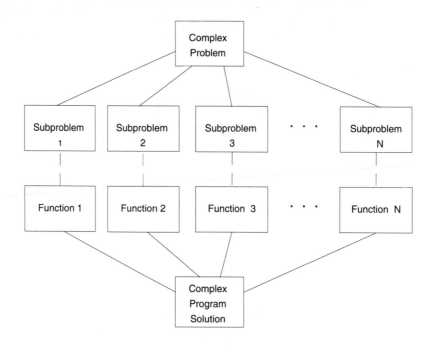

Figure 1-10 The "divide-and-conquer" idea behind a structured programming language, like C++.

As you will soon find out, the rules that apply to C++ encourage you to write well-organized, modular programs that are easy to read, understand, modify, and maintain. Structured, modular programs allow you to "divide and conquer" a large complex programming problem. The idea is to break down the complex problem into a group of simpler subproblems, or modules. Individual program modules, called *functions*, are then written to solve the simpler subproblems. The function modules can then be easily combined to solve the overall complex problem. This idea is illustrated by Figure 1-10. A non-structured language, such as BASIC, provides simple solutions to simple problems. However, non-structured languages require complex solutions to complex problems due to the lack of modularity, or structure.

 Quick Check

1. Why is C++ often referred to as a mid-level language?
2. List the steps that must be performed to translate a C++ source code program to an executable program.
3. What type of file is produced by the compile step?
4. What type of file is produce by the linking step?
5. What is the purpose of the linking step?
6. What is the major difference between the C language and the C++ language?

1-3 THE PROGRAMMER'S ALGORITHM

Before we look at the programmer's algorithm, it might be helpful to define what is meant by an algorithm. In technical terms:

An *algorithm* is a series of step-by-step instructions that produce a solution to a problem.

Algorithms are not unique to the computer industry. Any set of instructions, such as those you might find in a recipe or a kit assembly guide, can be considered an algorithm. You will learn how to develop precise computer program algorithms in Section 1-4. However, before you do this, let's look at a step-by-step procedure that you, the programmer, must use when developing computer programs. For obvious reasons, I have chosen to call this the *programmer's algorithm*. The algorithm is as follows:

Step 1: Define the problem.
Step 2: Plan the problem solution.
Step 3: Code the program.
Step 4: Test and debug the program.
Step 5: Document the program.

Defining the Problem

You might suggest that this is an obvious step in solving any problem. However, it often is the most overlooked step, especially in computer programming. The lack of good problem definition often results in "spinning your wheels," especially in more complex computer programming applications.

Think of a typical computer programming problem, such as controlling the inventory of a large department store. What must be considered as part of the problem definition? The first consideration probably is what you want to get out of the system. Will the output information consist of printed inventory reports or, in addition, will the system automatically generate product orders based on sales? Must any information generated by a customer transaction be permanently saved on disk, or can it be discarded? What type of data is the output information to consist of? Is it numerical data, character data, or both? How must the output data be formatted? All of these questions must be answered in order to define the output requirements.

Careful consideration of the output requirements usually leads you to deciding what must be put into the system in order to obtain the desired system output. For instance, in our department store inventory example, a desired output would most likely be a summary of customer transactions. How are these transactions to be entered into the system? Is the data to be obtained from a keyboard, or is product information to be entered automatically via an optical character recognition (OCR) system that reads the bar code on the product price tags? Does the input consist of all numerical data, character data, or a combination of both? What is the format of the data?

The next consideration is processing. Will most of the customer processing be done at the cash register terminal, or will it be handled by a central store computer? What about credit card verification and inventory records? Will this processing be done by a local microcomputer, a minicomputer located within the store, or a central mainframe computer located in a different part of the country? What kind of programs will be written to do the processing, and who will write them? What sort of calculations and decisions must be made on the data within individual programs to achieve the desired output?

All of these questions must be answered when defining any computer programming problem. In summary, you could say that problem definition must consider the application requirements of output, input, and processing. The department store inventory problem clearly requires precise definition. However, even with small application programs you must still consider the type of output, input, and processing that the problem requires. The application will always dictate the problem definition. I will discuss problem definition further, as we begin to develop computer programs to solve real problems.

Planning the Solution

The planning stage associated with any problem is probably the most important part of the solution, and computer programming is no exception. Imagine trying to build a house without a good set of blueprints. The results could be catastrophic! The same is true of trying to develop computer software without a good plan. When developing computer software, the planning stage is implemented using an algorithm. As you already know, an algorithm is a series of step-by-step instructions that produce results to solve problems. When planning computer programs, algorithms are used to outline the solution steps using English-like statements, called *pseudocode*, that require less precision than a formal programming language. A good pseudocode algorithm should be independent of, but easily translated into any formal programming language.

Pseudocode is an informal set of English-like statements that are generally accepted within the computer industry to denote common computer programming operations. Pseudocode statements are used to describe the steps in a computer algorithm.

Coding the Program

Coding the program should be one of the simplest tasks in the whole programming process, provided you have done a good job of defining the problem and planning its solution. Coding involves the actual writing of the program in a formal programming language. The computer language you use will be determined by the nature of the problem, the programming languages available to you, and the limits of the computer system. Once a language is chosen, the program is written, or coded, by translating your algorithm steps into the formal language code. In this text, you will code programs using the C++ programming language. Appendix A provides you with a quick introduction to writing C++ programs using the TURBO C++ environment.

I should caution you, however, that coding is really a mechanical process and should be considered secondary to algorithm development. In the future, computers will generate their own program code from well-constructed algorithms. Research in the field of artificial intelligence has resulted in "code generation" software. The thing to keep in mind is that computers might someday generate their own programming code from algorithms, but it takes the creativity and common sense of a human being to plan the solution and develop the algorithm.

Testing and Debugging the Program

You will soon find out that it is a rare and joyous occasion when a coded program actually "runs" the first time without any errors. Of course, good problem definition and planning will avoid many program mistakes, or "bugs." However, there always are a few bugs that manage to go undetected, regardless of how much planning you do. Getting rid of the program bugs (debugging) often is the most time-consuming job in the whole programming process. Industrial statistics show that over 50 percent of a programmer's time often is spent on program debugging.

When programming in C++, there are three things that you can do to test and debug your program: ***desk–checking*** the program, ***compiling*** the program, and ***running*** the program.

Desk-Checking the Program

Desk-checking a program is similar to proofreading a letter or manuscript. The idea is to trace through the program mentally to make sure that the program logic is workable. You must consider various input possibilities and write down any results generated during program execution. In particular, try to determine what the program will do with unusual data by considering input possibilities that "shouldn't" happen. Always keep Murphy's law in mind when desk-checking a program. If a given condition can't or shouldn't happen, it will!

For example, suppose a program requires the user to enter a value whose square root must be found. Of course, the user "shouldn't" enter a negative value, since the square root of a negative number is imaginary. However, what will the program do if he or she does? Another input possibility that should always be considered is an input of zero. This is especially important if the input value is to be used in a division operation.

When you first begin programming, you will be tempted to skip the desk-checking phase, since you can't wait to run the program once it is written. However, as you gain experience, you soon will realize the time-saving value of desk-checking.

Compiling and Linking the Program

Now you are ready to enter the program into the computer system. Once entered, the program must be compiled, or translated, into machine code. Fortunately, the compiler is designed to check for certain program errors. These usually are *syntax* errors that you have made when coding the program. A syntax error is any violation of the rules of the programming language, such as using a period instead of a semicolon. There might also be type errors. A *type error* occurs when you attempt to mix different types of data. It is like like trying to add apples to oranges.

During the compiling process, the C++ compiler will generate error and warning messages as well as position the display monitor cursor to the point in the program where the error was detected. If you cannot understand a given error message, you will need to consult your C++ reference manual for further explanation of the message. The program will not compile beyond the point of the error until it is corrected. Once an error is corrected, you must attempt to compile the program again. If other errors are detected, they must be corrected, the program must be recompiled, and so on, until the entire program is successfully compiled. After the program is successfully compiled, it must be linked to other routines that might be required for its execution. Linking errors will occur when such routines are not available or cannot be located in the designated system directory.

A *syntax* error is any violation of the rules of the programming language. A *type error* occurs when you attempt to mix different types of data. A *run-time* error is when the program attempts to perform an illegal operation as defined by the laws of mathematics or the particular compiler in use.

Running the Program

Once compiled and linked, you must execute, or run, the program. However, just because the program has been compiled and linked successfully doesn't mean that it will run successfully under all possible conditions. Common bugs that occur at this stage include *infinite loops* and *run-time* errors. An infinite loop occurs when the program tells the computer to repeat an operation, but does not tell it when to stop repeating. Such a bug will not cause an error message to be generated, since the computer is simply doing what it was told to do. The program execution must be stopped and debugged before it can run successfully.

A run-time error occurs when the program attempts to perform an illegal operation, as defined by the laws of mathematics or the particular compiler in use. Two common mathematical run–time errors are division by zero and attempting to take the square root of a negative number. A common error imposed by the compiler is an integer value out of range. Most C++ compilers limit integers to a range of $-32,768$ to $+32,767$. Unpredictable results can occur if an integer value exceeds this range.

Sometimes, the program is automatically aborted and an error message is displayed when a run-time error occurs. Other times, the program seems to execute properly but generates incorrect results, commonly called garbage. Again, you should consult your compiler reference manual to determine the exact nature of the problem. The error must be located and corrected before another attempt is made to run the program.

DEBUGGING TIP

A word from experience: Always go about debugging your programs in a systematic, common–sense manner. Don't be tempted to change something just because you "hope" it will work and don't know what else to do. Use your resources to isolate and correct the problem. Such resources include your algorithm, a program listing, your integrated C++ debugger, your reference manuals, this textbook, and your instructor, just to mention a few. Run–time errors usually are the result of a serious flaw in your program. They will not go away and cannot be corrected by blindly making changes to your program. One good way to locate errors is to have your program print out preliminary results as well as print messages that tell when a particular part of the program is running.

Documentation

This final step in the programmer's algorithm often is overlooked, but it probably is one of the more important steps, especially in commercial programming. Documentation is easy if you have done a good job of defining the problem, planning the solution, coding, testing, and debugging the program. The final program documentation is simply the recorded result of these programming steps. At a minimum, good documentation should include the following:

- A narrative description of the problem definition that includes the type of input, output, and processing employed by the program.

- An algorithm.

- A program listing which includes a clear commenting scheme. Commenting within the program is an important part of the overall documentation process. Each program should include comments at the beginning to explain what it does, any special algorithms that are employed, and a summary of the problem definition. In addition, the name of the programmer, date the program was written and last modified should be included.

- Samples of input and output data.

- Testing and debugging results.

- User instructions.

The documentation must be neat and well organized. It must be easily understood by you as well as any other person who might have a need to use or modify your program in the future. What good is an ingenious program if no one can determine what it does, how to use it, or how to maintain it?

One final point: Documentation should always be an ongoing process. Whenever you work with the program or modify it, make sure the documentation is updated to reflect your experiences and modifications.

 Quick Check

1. English-like statements that require less precision than a formal programming language are called _____.

2. What questions must be answered when defining a computer programming problem?

3. What can be done to test and debug a program?

4. Why is commenting important within a program?

1-4 PROBLEM SOLVING USING ALGORITHMS

In the previous section, you learned that an algorithm is simply a sequence of step-by-step instructions that will produce a solution to a problem. It is now time for you to learn how to develop algorithms in preparation for coding C++ programs.

You could say that just about any sequence of step–by–step instructions can be classified as an algorithm. For instance, consider the following series of instructions:

> Apply to wet hair.
> Gently massage lather through hair.
> Rinse, keeping lather out of eyes.
> Repeat.

Look familiar? Of course, this is a series of instructions that might be found on the back of a shampoo bottle. But does it fit the technical definition of an algorithm? In other words, does it produce a result? You might say "yes," but look closer. Since the algorithm requires that you keep repeating the procedure an infinite number of times, theoretically you would never stop shampooing your hair! A good algorithm must terminate in a finite amount of time. The repeat instruction could be altered easily to make the shampooing algorithm technically correct:

> Repeat until hair is clean.

Now the shampooing process can be terminated. Of course, you must be the one to decide when your hair is clean.

The foregoing shampoo analogy might seem a bit trivial. You probably are thinking that any intelligent person would not keep on repeating the shampooing process an infinite number of times, right? This obviously is the case when we humans are executing the algorithm, because we have some common–sense judgment. But what about a computer? Most computers do exactly what they are told to do via the computer program. As a result, a computer would repeat the original shampooing algorithm over and over, an infinite number of times. This is why the algorithms that you write for computer programs must be precise.

Now, let's develop an algorithm for a process that is common to all of us—mailing a letter. Think of the steps that are involved in this simple process. You must first address an envelope, fold the letter, insert the letter in the envelope, and seal the envelope, right? Next, you need a stamp. If you don't have a stamp, you have to buy one. Once a stamp is obtained, you must place it on the envelope and mail the letter. The following algorithm summarizes the steps in this process:

> Obtain an envelope.
> Address the envelope.
> Fold the letter.
> Insert the letter in the envelope.
> Seal the envelope.
> If you don't have a stamp then buy one.
> Place the stamp on the envelope.
> Mail the letter.

Does this sequence of instructions fit our definition of a good algorithm? In other words, does the sequence of instructions produce a result in a finite amount of time? Yes, assuming that each operation can be understood and carried out by the person mailing the letter. This brings up two additional characteristics of good algorithms: each operation within the algorithm must be ***well-defined*** and ***effective***. By well-defined, I mean that each of the steps must be clearly understood by the person or machine executing the algorithm. By effective, I mean that some means must exist in order to carry out the operation. In other words, the person mailing the letter must be able to perform each of the algorithm steps. In the case of a computer program algorithm, the machine must have the means of executing each operation in the algorithm.

In summary, a good computer algorithm must possess the following three attributes:

1. Employ well-defined instructions that can be understood by the machine executing the algorithm.

2. Employ instructions that can be carried out effectively by the machine executing the algorithm.

3. Produce a solution to the problem in a finite amount of time.

In order to write computer program algorithms, we need to establish a set of well-defined, effective operations that are generally understood within the industry. The set of pseudocode operations listed in Table 1-2 will make up our algorithmic language. We will use these operations from now on, whenever we write computer algorithms.

TABLE 1-2 ALGORITHMIC OPERATIONS USED IN THIS TEXT

Sequence	Decision	Iteration
Square	If/Then	While
SquareRoot	If/Then/Else	Do/While
Set or Assign (=)	Switch/Case	For
Read		
Write		
Calculate		
Add (+)		
Subtract (−)		
Multiply (*)		
Divide (/)		
Increment		
Decrement		

Notice that the operations in Table 1-2 are grouped into three major categories: *sequence*, *decision*, and *iteration*. These categories are called *control structures*. The sequence control structure includes those operations that produce a single action or result. As its name implies, the decision control structure includes the decision-making operations. Finally, the iteration control structure includes those operations that are used for looping, or repeating, operations within the algorithm. Many of the operations listed in Table 1-2 are self-explanatory. Those that are not will be discussed in detail as we begin to develop more complex algorithms.

Now, let's develop some algorithms for real programming problems through the following series of case studies:

CASE STUDY: PYTHAGOREAN THEOREM

Problem:

Develop an algorithm to find the hypotenuse of a right triangle using the Pythagorean theorem depicted in Figure 1-11. Construct the algorithm using the algorithmic instructions listed in Table 1-2.

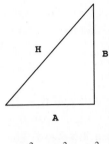

$$H^2 = A^2 + B^2$$

Figure 1-11 Solving the hypotenuse of a right triangle using the Pythagorean theorem.

Problem Definition

When defining the problem, you must consider three things: *output, input,* and *processing* as related to the problem statement. Recall that a right triangle has two right-angle sides and a hypotenuse. Let's label the two sides A and B, and the hypotenuse H. The problem requires us to find the hypotenuse (H), given the two sides (A and B). So, the output must be the hypotenuse (H). We will display the hypotenuse value on the system monitor. In order to obtain this output, the two sides (A and B) must be received by the program. Let's assume that the user must enter these values via the system keyboard.

The Pythagorean theorem states that the hypotenuse squared is equal to the sum of the squares of the two sides. In symbols,

$$H^2 = A^2 + B^2$$

This equation represents the processing that must be performed by the computer. In summary, the problem definition is:

Output: The hypotenuse (H) of a right triangle displayed on the system monitor.

Input: The two sides (A and B) of a right triangle to be entered by the user via the system keyboard.

Processing: Employ the Pythagorean theorem: $H^2 = A^2 + B^2$

Now that the problem has been defined in terms of output, input, and processing, it is time to plan the solution by developing an algorithm.

The Algorithm

In Table 1-2, you will find two sequence operations called *Read* and *Write*. The *Read* operation is an input operation. We will assume that this operation will obtain data entered via a keyboard. The *Write* operation is an output operation. We will assume that this operation causes information to be displayed on the monitor. With this in mind, the algorithm for the right triangle problem is:

```
BEGIN
    Write a program description message to the user.
    Write a user prompt message to enter the first side of the triangle (A).
    Read (A).
    Write a user prompt message to enter the second side of the triangle (B).
    Read (B).
    Square(A).
    Square (B).
    Assign (A² + B²) to H².
    Assign square root of (H²) to H.
    Write (H).
END.
```

STYLE TIP

The foregoing case study illustrates some operations that result in good programming style. Notice that the first *Write* operation is to write a program description message to the person running the program—the user. It is good practice always to include such a message so that the user understands what the program will do. In addition, the second *Write* operation will display a message to tell the user to "enter the first side of the triangle (A)." Without such a prompt, the user will not know what to do. You must write a user prompt message anytime the user must enter data via the keyboard. Such a message should tell the user what is to be entered, and in what format the information is to be entered. (More about this later.)

CASE STUDY: SALES TAX

Problem

Develop an algorithm to find the amount of sales tax and the total cost of a sales item, including tax. Assume the sales tax rate is 5 percent and the user will enter the cost of the sales item.

Problem Definition

The problem requires us to find two things: the amount of sales tax and the total cost of the item, including sales tax. However, only the total cost of the item needs to be generated by the program.

Since the sales tax rate is given (5 percent), the only data required for the algorithm is a user entry of the item cost.

Finally, the processing must calculate the amount of sales tax and add this value to the item cost to obtain the total cost of the item. In summary, the problem definition in terms of output, input, and processing is:

Output: The total cost of the sales item, including sales tax to be displayed on the system monitor.

Input: The cost of the sales item to be entered by the user on the system keyboard.

Processing: $Tax = 0.05 \times Cost$
$TotalCost = Cost + Tax$

The Algorithm

Using the above problem definition, we are now ready to write the algorithm as follows:

```
BEGIN
    Write a program description message to the user.
    Write a user prompt to enter the cost of the item (Cost).
    Read (Cost).
    Assign (0.05 × Cost) to Tax.
    Assign (Cost + Tax) to TotalCost.
    Write (TotalCost).
END.
```

CASE STUDY: CREDIT CARD INTEREST

Problem

The interest charged on a credit card account depends on the remaining balance according to the following criteria:

Interest charged is 18 percent up to $500 and 15 percent for any amount over $500. Develop an algorithm to find the total amount of interest due on any given account balance.

Let's begin by defining the problem in terms of output, input, and processing.

Problem Definition

Output: According to the problem statement, the obvious output must be the total amount of interest due. We will display this information on the system monitor.

Input: We will assume that the user will enter the account balance via the system keyboard.

Processing: Here is an application where a decision–making operation must be included in the algorithm. There are two possibilities as follows:

1. If the balance is less than or equal to $500, then the interest is 18 percent of the balance, or

$$Interest = 0.18 \times Balance$$

2. If the balance is over $500, then the interest is 18 percent of the first $500 plus 15 percent of any amount over $500. In the form of an equation:

$$Interest = (0.18 \times 500) + [0.15 \times (Balance - 500)]$$

Notice the use of the two *If/Then* statements in these two possibilities. Translating these words to an algorithm you get:

The Algorithm

BEGIN
    Write a program description message to the user.
    Write a user–prompt to enter the account balance.

Read (*Balance*).
If *Balance* <= 500 Then
    Assign *(0.18 × Balance)* to *Interest*.
If *Balance* > 500 Then
    Assign *(0.18 × 500)* + *[0.15 × (Balance − 500)]* to *Interest*.
Write(*Interest*).
END.

As you can see, the two decision-making operations stated in the problem definition have been incorporated into our algorithm. Notice the use of indentation to show which calculation goes with which *If/Then* operation. The use of indentation is an important part of pseudocode since it shows the algorithm structure at a glance.

How might you replace the two *If/Then* operations in this algorithm with a single *If/Then/Else* operation? Think about it, as it will be left as an exercise at the end of the chapter!

 Quick Check

1. Why is it important to develop an algorithm prior to coding a program?
2. What are the three major categories of algorithmic language operations?
3. List three decision operations.
4. List three iteration operations.

CHAPTER SUMMARY

Any computer system can be broken down into two major components: hardware and software. Hardware consists of the physical devices required to make up the machine, while software consists of the instructions that tell the hardware what to do.

There are five functional parts that make up the system hardware: the CPU, primary memory, secondary memory, input, and output. The CPU directs and coordinates the activity of the entire system as instructed by the software. Primary memory consists of user memory (RAM) and system memory (ROM). Secondary memory is usually magnetic and is used to store programs and data on a semipermanent basis. Input is what goes into the system via hardware input devices, such as a keyboard. Output is what comes out of the system via hardware output devices, such as a display monitor or printer.

There are three major levels of software: machine language, assembly language, and high-level language. Machine language is the lowest level, since it consists of binary 1s and 0s that can only be easily understood by the CPU. Assembly language consists of alphabetic instruction abbreviations that are easily understood by the programmer, but must be translated into machine code for the CPU by a system program called an assembler. High-level languages consist of English-like statements that simplify the task of programming. However, to be understood by the CPU, high-level language programs must still be translated to machine code using a compiler or interpreter. C++ is often referred to as mid-level language, since it has all the English-like structures of a high-level language, while at the same time it is extremely memory and execution efficient like assembly language.

The five major steps that must be performed when developing software are: (1) define the problem, (2) plan the problem solution, (3) code the program, (4) test and debug the program, and (5) document the program. When defining the problem, you must consider the output, input, and processing requirements of the application. Planning the problem solution requires that you specify the problem solution steps via an algorithm An algorithm is a series of step-by-step instructions that provide a solution to the problem in a finite amount of time. Once an algorithm is constructed, it must be coded into some formal language that the computer system can understand. The language used in this text is C++. Once coded, the program must be tested and debugged through desk-checking, compiling, and execution. Finally, the entire programming process, from problem definition to testing and debugging, must be documented so that it can be easily understood by you or anyone else working with it.

QUESTIONS AND PROBLEMS

Questions

1. Name the three operational regions of a CPU and explain their function.

2. Explain the term *volatile* as it relates to computer memory.

3. Another name for software located in read-only memory (ROM) is _____.

4. A floppy disk is a form of _____ memory.

5. Name the three levels of software and describe the general characteristics of each.

6. Explain the operational difference between a compiler and an interpreter.

7. An interpreter or compiler translates a source program into a(n) _____ program.

8. What is a structured language and what advantages does such a language have over a non-structured language?

9. Define an algorithm.

10. List the five steps of the programmer's algorithm.

11. What three things must be considered during the problem definition phase of programming?

12. What vehicle(s) are used for planning the solutions to a programming problem?

13. The writing of a program is called _____.

14. State three things that you can do to test and debug your programs.

15. List the minimum items required for good documentation.

16. What three characteristics must a good computer algorithm possess?

17. The three major control structures of a structured programming language are _____, _____, and_____.

18. Explain why a single *If/Then* operation in the credit card interest case study won't work. If you know the balance is not less than or equal to $500, the balance must be greater than $500, right? So, why can't the second *If/Then* operation be deleted?

Problems

Least Difficult

1. Develop an algorithm to compute the sum, difference, product, and quotient of any two integers.

2. Revise the above algorithm to protect it from a divide-by-zero run–time error.

More Difficult

3. Develop an algorithm to read in an employee's total weekly hours worked and rate of pay. Determine the gross weekly pay using "time and a half" for anything over forty hours.

4. Revise the algorithm in the credit card case study to employ a single *If/Then/Else* operation in place of the two *If/Then* operations.

5. A dimension on a part drawing indicates that the length of the part is 3.00 +− 0.25 inches. This means that the minimum acceptable length of the

part is $3.0 - 0.25 = 2.75$ inches, while the maximum acceptable length of the part is $3.00 + 0.25 = 3.25$ inches. Develop an algorithm that will display "ACCEPTABLE" if the part is within tolerance or "UNACCEPTABLE" if the part is out of tolerance. Also, show your problem definition in terms of output, input, and processing.

6. Develop an algorithm to calculate voltage from input current and resistor values using Ohm's Law.

7. The resistance of a conductor can be calculated based on its material composition and size using the following equation:

$$R = \rho\, \frac{l}{A}$$

where: R is the conductor resistance in ohms.

     ρ is the resistivity of the conductor.

     l is the length of the conductor in meters.

     A is the cross-sectional area of the conductor in square meters.

Develop an algorithm to calculate the resistance of any size copper conductor, assuming that the user enters the conductor length and cross-sectional area. (*Note*: The resistivity factor for copper is 1.72×10^{-8}.)

8. Revise the algorithm in problem 7, assuming that the user enters the conductor length in inches and the cross-sectional area in square inches.

9. Develop an algorithm that will allow the entry of three integer coefficients of a quadratic equation and generate the roots of the equation. Provide for an error message if complex roots exist.

2

GETTING ACQUAINTED WITH C++

INTRODUCTION

Now you are ready to begin learning the building blocks of the C++ language. As you already know, C++ is a structured language, from the top down. Although it might seem cumbersome at first, this structure makes C++ programs very readable, efficient, and powerful.

You will get your first exposure to the structure of C++ in this chapter as you learn about the various data types of the language. Data is any information that must be processed by the C++ program. However, before C++ can process any information, it must know what type of data it is dealing with. As a result, any information processed by C++ must be categorized into one of the legal data types defined for C++.

The simple data types that you will learn about in this chapter are the *integer*, *floating point*, and *character* data types. It is important that you understand this idea of data typing, since it is one of the most important concepts in C++. Once you learn the general characteristics of each data type, you will learn how to declare and define different types of data for use in a C++ program.

In addition to the simple data types employed by C++, this chapter will introduce you to complex data structures called ***structs*** and ***classes.*** The class structure is particularly important for you to learn, since it forms the basis for ***object-oriented programming (OOP)***. As you are aware, OOP is what separates C++ from many other languages.

Finally, you will be introduced to ***functions*** and see how they are employed to form the overall structure of a C++ program.

2-1 THE IDEA OF DATA TYPES

Just as C++ programs are highly structured and modular, so are the data that the programs operate upon. You might be thinking: "Data are data, how can there be different types of data?" First, you must think of data as any information that the computer might perform operations on or manipulate. So, let's define a ***data element*** to be any information item that is manipulated or operated on by the computer. Now, think about the types of information, or data elements, that the computer manipulates. Of course, a computer manipulates numbers, or ***numeric data***. One of the primary uses of a computer is to perform calculations on numeric data, right? But what about letters, called ***characters***? Isn't the computer operating with character data when it prints out your name? Thus, numeric data and character data are two different ***types*** of data. What makes them different? Well, numeric data consists of numbers, while character data consists of alphanumeric symbols. In other words, each data type (numeric or character) consists of a set of data elements that more or less "belong with each other." This will form our definition of a *data type*.

> A *data type* is a set of data elements that more or less belong with each other. That is, numbers belong with numbers and characters belong with characters. Even more specifically, a given integer should belong with the set of integers and a given decimal number (real) belongs with the set of reals.

Now for the big surprise: There are more than just numeric and character data types defined for C++. The diagram in Figure 2-1 shows all of the various types of data that can be used in C++ programming. First, observe that there are three major data-type categories: *scalar, structured*, and *pointer*.

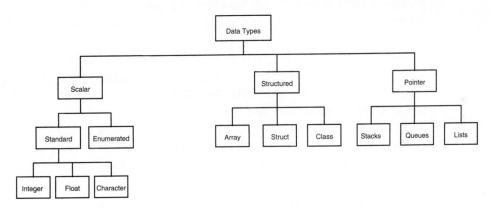

Figure 2-1 Data organization of a structured language.

Scalar data types are those whose data elements are ordered. By ordering, I mean that given two elements in the data type, one element is either equal (=), greater than (>), or less than (<) the other element. Numeric data, such as integer and real numbers, are clearly scalar data types since all numbers have this ordering property. You will soon find out that characters are also ordered, and thus considered a scalar data type.

Observe also from the diagram that scalar data types can be *standard* or *enumerated*. Standard data types are those that are predefined, or "built-in," to the C++ language. These consist of integer numbers and floating point numbers, as well as character data. The enumerated data type is one that you, the user of

C++, must define to meet a given application problem. In other words, an enumerated data type is a set of related data elements that you will create within your C++ program for a specific purpose. For example, you might want to define the set of all the days of the week (Sun, Mon, Tue, Wed, Thur, Fri, Sat) as an enumerated data type in your program. Here, the data elements are the individual days and are ordered from Sun through Sat. As a result, these elements can be manipulated within your program in a similar way as the standard data types. At first, the idea of creating your own set of data elements might seem foreign to you, but you will soon see how this can be a powerful tool when programming in C++. You will learn more about enumerated data types shortly.

The structured data-type category consists of data structures called *arrays,* *structs,* and *classes.* These data types are complex data types, in the sense that they are made up of other data types. As an example, your name, address, and telephone number can be combined to form a *struct.* This struct obviously consists of integers and characters, both of which are simple data types. In other words, structured data types are formed using combinations of the simpler scalar data types as building blocks.

Pointer data types are used to form data structures called stacks, queues, linked lists, and binary trees. The use of pointers is fundamental to the C and C++ languages and you will learn about them in Chapter 10. In addition, you will be introduced to stacks, queues, and lists in Chapter 14.

The *class* data type provides the foundation for object-oriented programming (OOP) in C++. Like the *struct* data type, the *class* data type is comprised of simpler data types. In addition, the *class* data type includes subprogram modules, called functions, that operate on the *class* data. You will begin learning about the *class* data type and object-oriented programming in Chapter 12.

 Quick Check

1. A set of data elements that more or less belong with each other is called a

   _____.

2. Data types that are predefined within a programming language are called_____ data types.

3. User-defined data types defined to meet a given application are called

   _____ data types.

4. The three major data type categories in a structured programming language are the _____, _____, and _____ data categories.

2-2 STANDARD DATA TYPES

Recall that standard data types are built into the C++ compiler. This built-in feature simply means that the C++ compiler recognizes any legal elements contained in a standard data type. There are three standard data types that we need to discuss: *integer, floating point,* and *character.*

The Integer Data Type (int)

As you know, integers are the whole numbers. They may be positive, negative, or 0. In an algebra course, you most likely learned that there are no theoretical limits to the integers. They can range from minus infinity $(-\infty)$ to plus infinity $(+\infty)$. However, there are practical limits in the real world of computers. In C++, the largest and smallest possible integer values depend on the particular type of integer and compiler that is being used.

So, you're thinking that integers are integers, how can there be different "types" of integers? Well, the C++ language defines four separate types of integers that define four separate integer ranges. They are *int, unsigned int, long,* and *unsigned long.* As you can see from Table 2-1, each integer type defines a legal range of integer values for that type.

You might be wondering why there are different types of integers. Why not just define one type that will provide enough range for most applications? For instance, why not use the **long** integer type all the time, since it provides the largest range of values? Well, recall that an advantage of C++ is its efficiency relative to execution speed and memory utilization. Each of the above integer types employs a predefined number of memory bytes to represent an integer value. For example, **int** requires two bytes of memory to represent a value while **long** requires twice as many, or four bytes, to represent a value. Thus, it takes twice as much memory space to represent **long** integers as it does **int** integers. In addition, it would take twice as long to fetch a **long** as an **int.** So, the idea is to use the type of integer that has enough range to satisfy a given application. For most applications **int** will do the job and provide for efficient execution and memory utilization.

TABLE 2-1 INTEGER TYPES AND CORRESPONDING RANGES

INTEGER TYPE	RANGE	BYTES
int	−32768 to +32767	2
unsigned int	0 to +65535	2
long	−2147483648 to +2147483647	4
unsigned long	0 to 4294967295	4

Example 2-1:

Which of the following are *not* legal **int** data type elements according to Table 2-1?
a. +35
b. 35
c. −247
d. 0
e. 3.14
f. 32,767
g. 32768

Solution:

The values in a, b, c, and d are all legal **int** elements in C++, since they are all whole numbers within the defined range of **int**. Notice that + 35 and 35 are both legal representations of the integer value 35.

The values in e, f, and g are not legal **int** elements in C++. The value 3.14 is not an integer because it is not a whole number. The value 32,767 is an integer within the predefined range, but is not legal in C++ since it contains a comma. Commas are not allowed as part of numeric values in C++. Finally, the value 32768 is not a legal **int** element in C++, since it is outside of the predefined **int** range.

You must be especially aware of the integer range limits imposed by C++ when performing integer calculations within your C++ programs. For example, multiplying two integers could easily produce an integer result beyond this range, resulting in an incorrect result. This is called an *overflow* condition. Depending on where it occurs, an overflow condition might or might not generate an error message during program compiling or execution. Even if no overflow error message is generated, the operation will produce an incorrect result.

Example 2-2:

Which of the following **int** operations will generate an overflow condition in C++? (Use Table 2-1 to determine the legal **int** range and assume that the * symbol means multiplication and the / symbol means division.)

a. 32 * 1000

b. 100 * 1000

c. (100 * 1000) / 5

Solution:

a. 32 * 1000 = 32000, which is within the predefined **int** range. No overflow condition exists.

b. 100 * 1000 = 100000, which is outside of the predefined **int** range. The overflow condition will result in an incorrect integer result.

c. (100 * 1000) / 5 = 100000 / 5 = 20000. Although the final result is within the predefined **int** range, an overflow condition will occur, thereby generating an incorrect result. Why? Because the multiplication operation in the numerator results in a value outside of the **int** range.

The Floating Point Data Type (float)

Floating point numbers include all of the whole number integers as well as any value between two whole numbers that must be represented using a decimal point. Examples include the following:

$$3.14$$
$$-2.56$$
$$0.0$$
$$1.414$$
$$-3.0$$

All of the foregoing numbers have been written using *decimal-point* notation. Decimal-point notation requires a sign, followed by an integer, followed by a decimal point, followed by another unsigned integer. This format is shown below:

DECIMAL FORMAT FOR A FLOATING POINT NUMBER

(+ or − sign) (integer) . (integer)

Another way to represent very large and very small floating point numbers is with scientific notation, sometimes called *exponential format.* With this notation, the floating point number is written as a decimal point value multiplied by a power of 10. The general format is:

EXPONENTIAL FORMAT FOR A FLOATING POINT NUMBER

(+ or – sign) (decimal point value) E (integer exponent value)

In both the foregoing formats, the leading + sign is optional if the value is positive.

Examples of floating point numbers using this format include:

$$1.32E3$$
$$0.45E{-}6$$
$$-35.02E{-}4$$
$$-1.333E7$$

Here, the letter E means "times 10 to the power of." The letter E is used, since there is no provision on a standard computer keyboard to type above a line to show exponential values. Again, the + sign is optional for both the decimal point value and the exponential value when they are positive.

Example 2-3:

Convert the following exponential values to decimal values.
a. 1.32E3
b. 0.45E–6
c. –35.02E–4
d. –1.333E7

Solution:

a. $1.32E3 = 1.32 \times 10^3 = 1320.0$
b. $0.45E{-}6 = 0.45 \times 10^{-6} = 0.00000045$
c. $-35.02E{-}4 = -35.02 \times 10^{-4} = -0.003502$
d. $-1.333E7 = -1.333 \times 10^7 = -13330000.0$

You might be wondering if there is any practical limit to the range of floating point numbers that can be used in C++. As with integers, C++ defines different types of floating point data that dictate different legal value ranges. Again, the value range is determined by the C++ compiler that you are using. As an example, Table 2-2 summarizes the floating point data types defined for the TURBO C++ compiler.

TABLE 2-2 FLOATING POINT TYPES AND CORRESPONDING RANGES

FLOAT TYPE	RANGE	BYTES
float	3.4×10^{-38} to 3.4×10^{38}	4
double	1.7×10^{-308} to 1.7×10^{308}	8
long double	3.4×10^{-4932} to 1.1×10^{4932}	10

As you can see from Table 2-2, it costs you more memory space to achieve greater precision when using a float data type. Again, the application will dictate the required precision, which in turn dictates the type of float data type to use. For most applications, the *float* type will provide the required precision.

Example 2-4:

In electronics, you often see quantities expressed using the prefixes in Table 2-3. Given the following quantities:

> 220 picoseconds (ps)
> 1 kilohertz (kHz)
> 10 megahertz (MHz)
> 1.25 milliseconds (ms)
> 25.3 microseconds (μs)
> 300 nanoseconds (ns)

a. Express each of the listed quantities in exponential form.
b. Express each of the listed quantities in decimal form.

Solution:

a. To express in exponential form, you simply convert the prefix to its respective power of 10 using Table 2-3. Then, use the E notation to write the value like this:

> 220 ps = 220E−12 seconds
> 1 kHz = 1E3 Hertz
> 10 MHz = 10E6 Hertz
> 1.25 ms = 1.25E−3 seconds
> 25.3 μs = 25.3E−6 seconds
> 300 ns = 300E−9 seconds

b. To express each in its decimal form, simply move the decimal point according to the exponent value.

220 ps = 220E–12 seconds = 0.000000000220 seconds
1 kHz = 1E3 Hertz = 1000.0 Hertz
10 MHz = 10E6 Hertz = 10000000.0 Hertz
1.25 ms = 1.25E3 seconds = 0.00125 seconds
25.3 μs = 25.3E–6 seconds = 0.0000253 seconds
300 ns = 300E–9 seconds = 0.000000300 seconds

TABLE 2-3 COMMON PREFIXES USED IN ELECTRONICS

PREFIX	SYMBOL	MEANING
pico-	p	10^{-12}
nano-	n	10^{-9}
micro-	μ	10^{-6}
milli-	m	10^{-3}
kilo-	k	10^{3}
mega-	M	10^{6}
giga-	G	10^{9}

Example 2-5:

C++ includes several *standard functions* that you can call upon to perform specific operations.

A *standard function* is a predefined operation that the C++ compiler will recognize and evaluate to return a result.

One such function is the *sqrt()* function. The *sqrt()* function is used to find the square root of a floating point number. As an example, execution of *sqrt(2)* will return the value 1.414. On the other hand, an operation *not* included as a standard function is the square function. You must write your own user-defined function to perform the square operation. More about this later. Now, given the standard *sqrt()* function determine the result of the following operations:
a. sqrt(3.5)
b. sqrt(–25)
c. sqrt(4E–20)

Solution:

a. sqrt(3.5) = 1.87
b. sqrt(–25) is imaginary and will generate a run-time error when encountered during a program execution.
c. sqrt(4E–20) = 2E–10

The Character Data Type (char)

All of the symbols on your computer keyboard are characters. This includes all the upper- and lowercase alphabetic characters as well as the punctuation, numbers, control keys, and special symbols. Most C++ compilers employ the American Standard Code for Information Interchange (ASCII) character set shown in Table 2-4.

As you can see from the table, each character has a unique numeric representation code. The reason for this is that, in order for the CPU to work with character data, the individual characters must be converted to a numeric (actually binary) code. When you press a character on the keyboard, the CPU "sees" the numeric representation of that character, not the character itself. Table 2-4 provides decimal equivalents of the ASCII characters. Many times you will want the hexadecimal (hex) equivalents of the characters. A more complete table that includes both the decimal and hex equivalents can be found on the inside cover of this text for quick reference purposes.

Example 2-6:

C++ includes a standard function called *toascii()*. This function is used to generate, or return, the decimal representation for any character. Determine the result of the following operations using Table 2-4.
a. toascii('A')
b. toascii('Z')
c. toascii('a')
d. toascii('z')
e. toascii('#')

Solution:

Using Table 2-4, you get the following:
a. toascii('A') = 65
b. toascii('Z') = 90
c. toascii('a') = 97
d. toascii('z') = 122
e. toascii('#') = 35

TABLE 2-4 ASCII CHARACTER CODE TABLE

DEC	CHAR	DEC	CHAR	DEC	CHAR	DEC	CHAR
0	^@ NUL	32	SPC	64	@	96	
1	^A SOH	33	!	65	A	97	a
2	^B STX	34	"	66	B	98	b
3	^C ETX	35	#	67	C	99	c
4	^D EOT	36	$	68	D	100	d
5	^E ENQ	37	%	69	E	101	e
6	^F ACK	38	&	70	F	102	f
7	^G BEL	39	'	71	G	103	g
8	^H BS	40	(	72	H	104	h
9	^I HT	41	)	73	I	105	i
10	^J LF	42	*	74	J	106	j
11	^K VT	43	+	75	K	107	k
12	^L FF	44	,	76	L	108	l
13	^M CR	45	−	77	M	109	m
14	^N SO	46	.	78	N	110	n
15	^O SI	47	/	79	O	111	o
16	^P DLE	48	0	80	P	112	p
17	^Q DC1	49	1	81	Q	113	q
18	^R DC2	50	2	82	R	114	r
19	^S DC3	51	3	83	S	115	s
20	^T DC4	52	4	84	T	116	t
21	^U NAK	53	5	85	U	117	u
22	^V SYN	54	6	86	V	118	v
23	^W ETB	55	7	87	W	119	w
24	^X CAN	56	8	88	X	120	x
25	^Y EM	57	9	89	Y	121	y
26	^Z SUB	58	:	90	Z	122	z
27	^[ESC	59	;	91	[	123	{
28	^\ FS	60	<	92	\	124	|
29	^] GS	61	=	93	]	125	}
30	^^ RS	62	>	94	^	126	~
31	^-- US	63	?	95	--	127	DEL

The foregoing example points out several characteristics of character data. First, each character has a unique numeric representation inside the computer. Since each character has a unique numeric representation, the characters are ordered. This is why they are classified as a scalar data type. For instance, 'A' < 'Z', since the numeric representation for 'A' (65) is less than the numeric representation for 'Z' (90). Likewise, '#' < 'a' < 'z', since 35 < 97 < 122. Next, notice that whenever a character is specified, it is always enclosed in single quotes like this: 'a'. This is a requirement of the C++ compiler.

TABLE 2-5 CHARACTER DATA TYPES AND
CORRESPONDING RANGES

CHARACTER TYPE	RANGE	BYTES
char	−128 to +127	1
unsigned char	0 to +255	1

Recall that there were different types of integers and floating point values defined by the C++ compiler. These different types determine the range of values that are legal for a given type. Well, the same is true of characters. There are two different types of characters defined for C++: **char** and **unsigned char,** both shown in Table 2-5.

The **char** type allows for all the ASCII characters shown in Table 2-4. In addition, small negative integer values can be represented with this data type. The **unsigned char** type also allows for all the ASCII characters shown in Table 2-4 but, in addition, allows for an extended character set as defined for the IBM PC. (See your PC documentation for this extended character set.) Again, the application will dictate which character type to use. The **char** type will satisfy most of the applications in this text.

CAUTION

C++ will allow you to perform arithmetic operations on character data. However, be careful since the results can be sometimes difficult to predict. What do you get when you add the character 'A' to the character 'B', or multiply these two characters?

Since characters are stored in the machine as integer values, you can perform arithmetic operations on character data. For instance, you can add 1 to the character 'A' and get the character 'B'. This is an example of the flexibility built into the C++ language. However, with this flexibility comes responsibility. Other structured languages, like Pascal, will not allow you to perform arithmetic operations on characters.

Strings

A string is simply a collection of characters. Examples of strings include your name, address, and phone number, as well as the sentence you are now reading. When operating on strings, you must keep in mind that you are still operating with individual characters.

Figure 2-2 illustrates how strings are stored in memory by C++. As you can see, each individual character is placed in a one byte memory cell. The collection of cells holding the string is called an ***array***. We will discuss arrays in more detail later, but for now it is only important that you understand how they are used to store string data.

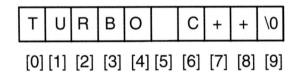

Figure 2-2 C++ stores character strings in memory arrays which are terminated by a null terminator.

The individual cells in the array are referenced via a position number, beginning with position [0]. The last position in the string array always contains the character '\0' to terminate the string. This '\0' character is referred to as a ***null terminator*** character. The null terminator tells C++ where the string ends in memory.

As you see from Figure 2-2, the character 'T' is located at position [0] of the array, while the null terminator is located at position [9] of the array. Notice that the array requires ten cells to store a nine character string due to the null terminator requirement.

One final point: Strings in C++ are always enclosed in double quotes like this: "TURBO C++." Recall that individual characters are enclosed in single quotes. Thus, 'a' denotes an individual character, while "a" denotes a string of one character.

Example 2-7:

Given the following strings, determine how many bytes are required to store each string and show how the strings appear in memory.

a. "This text is great!"
b. "x"
c. "1234"

Solution:

a. This string requires 20 bytes of storage. The corresponding string array is shown in Figure 2-3a.
b. This sting requires 2 bytes of storage. The corresponding string array is shown in Figure 2-3b.
c. This string requires 5 bytes of storage. The corresponding string array is shown in Figure 2-3c. Note that the double quotes indicate that "1234" is a string of four characters and *not* numeric data. In fact, the string "1234" requires 5 bytes of storage, while the **int** 1234 only requires 2 bytes of storage. In addition, arithmetic operations cannot be performed on the string "1234". For these reasons, numeric data should be represented using a numeric data type and not the string data type.

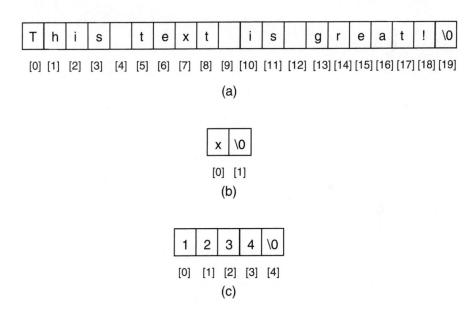

(a)

(b)

(c)

Figure 2-3 Solutions for Example 2-7.

Quick Check

1. What range of values can be provided via the standard **int** data type?

2. What type of error occurs when, as a result of a calculation, a value exceeds its predefined range?

3. The two ways that floating point values can be represented in a C++ program are using either _____ or _____ format.

4. What will be returned when the following functions are executed?

   toascii('B')

   toascii('?')

5. What characters must employ the **unsigned char** data type?

6. A character string is stored in a data structure called a(n) _____.

7. How many bytes of storage are required by the string "The United States of America"?

2-3 CONSTANTS AND VARIABLES

From mathematics, you know that a constant is a value that never changes, thereby remaining a fixed value. A common example is the constant Pi (π). Here the Greek symbol π is used to represent the floating point value 3.14. This value of π never changes, thus remaining constant regardless of where and how it might be used in a calculation.

On the other hand, a variable is something that can take on different values. In mathematics, the symbols x and y are often used to denote variables. Using the equation $y = 3x + 2$, you can substitute different values of x to generate different values of y. Thus, the values of x and y in the equation are variable.

The values of variables are stored in main working memory for later use within a program. Each variable has a symbolic name that locates its value in memory. This idea is illustrated in Figure 2-4. The memory contents located by the symbols x, y, and *Count* might change during the execution of the program. As a result, these symbols are called variables.

In C++, the values of constants are not stored in memory as in other languages. The value of a constant is substituted for the constant identifier wherever it appears in the C++ program during compile time. This is just one of many reasons why C++ is more efficient than other languages, like Pascal , since no memory access is required to obtain constant values during the program execution. For instance, if the identifier *PI* is to be used as a constant with the value 3.14, this value will be substituted for the word *PI* when the program is compiled. As a result, the value of *PI* can never be altered during program execution, thereby making it constant.

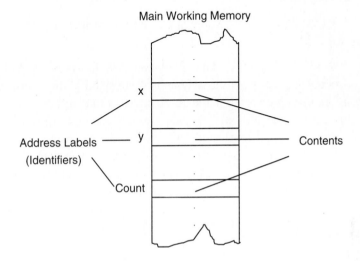

Figure 2-4 Each variable has a label, or identifier, that locates its value in memory.

DECLARATIONS VERSUS DEFINITIONS

The words *define* and *declare* are often used interchangeably in connection with programming languages. Actually, a declaration specifies the name and attributes of a value, but does not reserve storage. On the other hand, a definition is a declaration which also reserves storage. This is why we declare constants and define variables in C++.

The reason the we must declare constants and define variables in a language is twofold. First, the compiler must know the value of a constant before it is used and must reserve memory locations to store variables. Second, the compiler must know the data type of the constants and variables. Now, let's see how both constants are declared and variables are defined in C++.

Declaring Constants

To declare a constant, you must use the word **const** like this:

CONSTANT DECLARATION FORMAT

const <data type> <identifier > = <constant value>;

Notice the syntax: The word **const** is followed by the data type of the constant. The constant data type is followed by the constant *identifier*. The constant *identifier* is the name of the constant that will be replaced by the constant value during compile time. So that you can identify constants easily within your program, I suggest that your constant identifiers always be in all capital letters. This way, it makes it much more clear that no statement should attempt to alter the constant value. An equals sign (=) is used to separate the constant identifier from its declared value. Finally, each constant declaration must be ended with a semicolon.

Example 2-8:

Suppose you wish to use the price of 29 cents for a first-class postage stamp in your C++ program. In addition, your program must calculate the sales tax required for a given sales item based on a sales tax rate of 5 percent. Declare appropriate constant identifiers to represent the price of a stamp and the sales tax rate.

Solution:

Using the format given above, the postage price and sales tax rate could be declared as follows:

```
const float POSTAGE = 0.29;
const float TAX_RATE = 0.05;
```

With these declarations, you would simply use the words *POSTAGE* and *TAX_RATE* when performing calculations within the program. For instance, to find the tax on an item that costs $100 you would simply write the expression:

```
SalesTax = 100 * TAX_RATE;
```

When the program is compiled, the compiler simply substitutes the constant value 0.05 for the *TAX_RATE* identifier.

What about the word *SalesTax* in this expression? Is it a constant or a variable? You're right—it's a variable identifier, since its value will change, depending on the sale price of the item. What data type must *SalesTax* be? In other words, what type of data is generated as a result of the operation: integer, floating point, or character? Right again--floating point, since the *SalesTax* might often result in a decimal value. Thus, *SalesTax* must be defined as a floating point variable. You will find out how to do this shortly.

STYLE TIP

Notice in Example 2-8 that the constant identifier *TAX_RATE* is made up of two words, *TAX* and *RATE*. The C++ compiler will not allow you to separate multiword identifiers using spaces. Thus, I have chosen to separate the two words with the underscore symbol (_). Also, notice that the variable identifier *SalesTax* is made up of two words. Here, the two words are run together with the first letter of each word capitalized. These two techniques will be used throughout the text when using multiword identifiers. How long can an identifier be? This depends on the version of C++ that you are using. For instance, TURBO C++ identifiers can be up to any length, where the first 32 characters are significant. Here are some other rules that govern the use of identifiers in any C++ compiler:

- All identifiers must start with a letter or an underscore symbol (_).
- No spaces or punctuation, except the underscore (_) character are allowed.
- Identifiers in C++ are *case sensitive*. Thus, the identifiers *Tax* and *TAX* are seen as two different identifiers by the compiler.

You are probably wondering why we should declare constants using identifiers. Why not just insert the constant value into the expression whenever it is needed, like this:

SalesTax = 100 * 0.05;

Have you ever known postage or sales tax rates to change? Of course you have! You might say that these types of "constants" are not constant forever. So, when using constants such as these that might be subject to change in the future, it is much easier to define them in one single place at the beginning of the program. Then if they need to be changed, you only have to make a single change in your program. Otherwise, a change must be made in each place that you use the constant within the program.

One final point: You probably have noticed that the word **const** is set in bold type. Such a word in C++ is called a *keyword*. Keywords have a specific meaning to the C++ compiler and are used to perform a specific task. You cannot use a keyword for anything else other than the specific operation for which it is defined. C++ contains about 64 keywords, including **const**. You will learn about other keywords in subsequent chapters. In any event, from now on all keywords will be printed in bold type so that you can recognize them.

String Constants

Recall that a string in C++ is formed using an array of characters. Thus, to declare a string constant, you must apply the **char** data type to an array identifier using the following format:

STRING CONSTANT DECLARATION FORMAT

const char <identifier>[ ] = "string value";

As you can see, the two key words **const** and **char** are followed by the array identifier. A set of *empty* square brackets must follow the identifier to denote an array. The square brackets are followed by an equals sign, which is followed by the string value enclosed within double quotes. Finally, a semicolon must be used to terminate the declaration. Let's look at an example to illustrate this idea.

Example 2-9:

Define three constants that can be used to represent your name, address, and phone number.

Solution:

Using the keyword **const**, the appropriate declarations might be:

```
const char NAME[] = "Andrew C. Staugaard, Jr.";
const char ADDRESS[] = "Box 999, C++ City, USA";
const char PHONE_NUMBER[] = "(012)345-6789";
```

When a string constant is compiled, an array is created that contains one byte for each character in the array, plus a final byte for the null terminator. Thus, the *NAME* constant in Example 2-9 will occupy 25 bytes of program code each place it appears in the program. Count the characters and add one for the null terminator to see if you agree. Remember that spaces and punctuation must be counted as characters.

You probably are wondering how and where string constants are used. One common use of a string constant is to represent information that must be printed often, such as header information. For instance, each time you need to print your name in a report, you would simply insert an instruction into the program to print the constant identifier *NAME*. Since the value of *NAME* is your name, the computer will print your name. You will see how this works when you learn about input and output operations in Chapter 3.

Defining Variables

Before you can use a variable in a C++ program, it must be defined. When you define a variable, the compiler reserves a location inside the computer memory for the variable value. Variables should be defined at the beginning of your C++ programs. However, unlike C, C++ allows you to define a variable anyplace within a program as long as it is defined before it is used. To define a variable, you must specify its data type, its name, and an optional initializing value. Here's the format:

VARIABLE DEFINITION FORMAT

<data type> <identifier> = <optional initializing value>;

The foregoing format requires that the variable data type be listed first, followed by the variable identifier, or name. You can terminate the definition at this point with a semicolon, or you can add an optional equals symbol, =, followed by an initializing value, then the semicolon to terminate the definition. Here's the idea:

Example 2-10:

There is a simple relationship in electronics, called *Ohm's law*, that allows you to find either voltage, current, or resistance, given the other two quantities. Ohm's law simply states that voltage is equal to the product of current times resistance. In symbols:

$$V = I \times R$$

where: *V* is voltage in volts.

I is current in amperes

R is resistance in Ohms

Suppose that you must write a C++ program to calculate voltage from current and resistance values using Ohm's Law. Define the three variables (*V*, *I*, and *R*) that will be used in the program for the calculation.

Solution:

The variable identifiers are given to be *V*, *I*, and *R*. Now, the question is: What data type must these variables be? You know that *V*, *I*, and *R* will be used to represent numeric data, so your decision as to their data type reduces to integer or floating point. If you define *V*, *I*, and *R* as integers, you will be limited to using whole number values for these variables within your program. However, this might create a problem since voltage, current, and resistance values often are decimal values. So, let's define them as floating point variables like this:

```
float V;
float I;
float R;
```

STYLE TIP

Most C++ compilers allow variable identifiers, or names, to be any length, where the first 32 characters are significant. Thus, your programs will become much more readable and self-documenting if you use words, rather than letters and symbols, to represent variable values. For instance, the variable definition in Example 2-10 would be much more readable to a non-technical user if you were to define voltage, current, and resistance like this:

```
float Voltage;
float Current;
float Resistance;
```

Using this definition, the actual words (*Voltage*, *Current*, and *Resistance*) would be used within your program when applying Ohm's law. So, the statement required to calculate voltage would appear in your program as follows:

```
Voltage = Current * Resistance;
```

Notice the use of the equals symbol, =, in this equation. This is the way that you must assign quantities in C++. Also, notice the use of the star symbol, *, for multiplication.

A word of caution: When using names as variable identifiers, you cannot use any punctuation within the name. For instance, the variable identifier *Total(Sales)* to represent total sales is an illegal identifier in C++ because of the parentheses. Two legal identifiers would be *TotalSales* or *Total_Sales*. In the first case, the two words are connected together with the first letter of each word capitalized. In the second case, the underscore symbol, _, is used to separate the two words instead of a space. This symbol is okay to use within C++ identifiers. You will see both of these techniques employed for identifiers throughout the remainder of this text.

Example 2-11:

You must write a program to calculate the sales tax of a sales item using a sales tax rate of 5 percent. Declare the appropriate constants and define the required variables.

Solution:

First, you must decide what identifiers to use. Always use word identifiers that best describe the related constant or variable. Let's use the word *SalesTax* to identify the resulting calculation, the word *Price* to identify the cost of the item, and the word *TAX_RATE* to identify the sales tax rate. So, using these identifiers, the sales tax calculation would be:

SalesTax = Price * TAX_RATE;

Now, the question is: Which are variables and which are constants? Obviously, the *SalesTax* and *Price* identifiers are variables, since they will change depending on the cost of the item. However, the *TAX_RATE* will be constant, regardless of the cost of the item. So, we will define *SalesTax* and *Price* as variables and *TAX_RATE* as a constant like this:

const float TAX_RATE = 0.05;
float SalesTax, Price;

Notice that both the variables are defined as floating point, since both will be decimal values.

Suppose that you were to define *TAX_RATE* as a variable rather than a constant and initialize it to the value 0.05 like this:

float TaxRate = 0.05;

There is no problem with this definition. The compiler will reserve storage for the variable *TaxRate* and place the initial value of 0.05 at this storage location. However, the value of *TaxRate* could be changed by the program, whereas it could not be changed if declared as a constant.

Example 2-12:

Choose an appropriate name and define a variable that could be used to represent the days of the week. Assume that the days of the week are represented by the first letter of each day.

Solution:

Let's pick a meaningful variable identifier such as: *DaysOfWeek*. Now, since the days of the week will be represented by the first letter of each day, the variable must be a character variable. When defining character variables, you must use the keyword **char** in the variable definition as follows:

char DaysOfWeek;

Do you see any problems with the definition in Example 2-12? There are no syntax errors and it is perfectly legal as far as C++ is concerned. But are there any problems associated with the usage of this variable? A character variable is limited to representing a single character at any given time. This is why each day of the week must be represented by a single letter. However, using the first letter of each day creates a problem. Does an 'S' represent Saturday or Sunday? Likewise, does a 'T' mean Tuesday or Thursday? The solution to this dilemma is found in string variables.

String Variables

The C or C++ languages do not include a built-in string data type like some other languages. In C or C++, a string must be stored in an array of characters. So, to define a string variable, you must define a character array. There are two ways to do this: Defining a string variable without an initializing value or with an initializing value. Here are the required formats:

STRING VARIABLE DEFINITION FORMAT WITHOUT AN INITIALIZING VALUE

char <identifier>[<maximum size of string + 1>];

STRING VARIABLE DEFINITION FORMAT WITH AN INITIALIZING VALUE

char <identifier>[] = "string value";

In the first case, the compiler must know the maximum size of the string, plus 1. The size must be specified so that the compiler knows how much memory to set aside to store the string. You must specify a size that is one greater than the maximum string size to allow room for the null terminator character.

In the second case, you do not need to specify a string size, since the compiler can determine how much memory to set aside from the initializing string value. A maximum string size can be specified, however, it must be at least as large as the length of the initializing value, plus 1. Initializing a string variable to a value is basically the same as defining a constant string value; however, the keyword **const** is not employed. Remember, a constant string value can never be changed within the program, whereas a variable string can be changed at any time during the program execution. You will learn how to change the value of a string variable later in the text.

Example 2-13:

Using the character variable definition in Example 2-12 presents a usage problem when representing the days of the week, because a character variable can only represent a single character at a time. Solve this problem by using a string variable definition. Define an appropriate string variable without an initializing value, then rewrite the variable definition to initialize it with the value "Wednesday".

Solution:

A string variable can be used to represent any number of consecutive characters. So why not define *DaysOfWeek* as a string variable like this:

char DaysOfWeek[10];

With this definition, the variable *DaysOfWeek* can be used to represent the entire day of the week word (Sunday, Monday, Tuesday, etc.). Why did I choose 10 as the maximum length of the string? Because the longest day of the week word is Wednesday, which has 9 characters. However, you must leave room for the null terminator character, making the size of the string 10.

You can initialize the string to Wednesday with the following definition:

char DaysOfWeek[] = "Wednesday";

With this definition, the string "Wednesday" is stored in memory and located by the identifier *DaysOfWeek*. The compiler automatically inserts the null terminator character after the last character, 'y' .

Example 2-14:

Suppose that you must write a C++ program to instruct the user of the program to enter his/her name, address, and telephone number. Choose appropriate variable identifiers and define three string variables to represent this information.

Solution:

Let's call the variables *Name, Address,* and *PhoneNumber*, respectively. Now, you must decide the maximum length of each string variable. Don't forget to include spaces, special symbols, and the null terminator character. A length of 31 should be sufficient for *Name*, 31 for *Address*, and 14 for *PhoneNumber*. If you are not sure, it is better to overestimate, rather than underestimate its length. Using the foregoing variable identifiers and string lengths, the proper definitions are:

```
char Name[31];
char Address[31];
char PhoneNumber[14];
```

Quick Check

1. What are the two reasons for declaring/defining constants and variables in a C++ program?
2. Declare a constant called *PERIOD* that will insert a period wherever it is referenced in a program.
3. Declare a constant called *BOOK* that will insert the string "Structuring Techniques: An Introduction Using C++" wherever it appears in a program.
4. Given a string variable that must store a string of up to 25 characters, what array size must be specified in the variable definition?
5. Define a string variable called *Course* that will be initialized to a string value of "Digital Circuits".

2-4 ENUMERATED DATA TYPES

One distinct advantage of using C++ is that it allows you, the programmer, to create your own types of data. Up to this point, you have been using the standard data types of integer, float, and character. As you have seen, these data types have been adequate for many programming applications. Although these predefined data types can be used for just about any programming task, they often are insufficient to describe a problem clearly. You will soon discover that enumerated data types enhance the readability of your program by making it clearer and application oriented, something we are especially concerned about in problem solving. The more clearly we can express a problem as related to its application, the easier it is for us and others to understand and solve the problem.

Enumerated data types consist of a set of data elements that you, the programmer, define for a particular application. The idea of defining your own data type might seem awkward to you at first, but you will soon discover that it provides a convenient means of working with real-world problems. There will be times when none of the standard data types will work conveniently for certain applications. For example, suppose an application problem required the manipulation of the days of the week. Since none of the standard data types include the days of the week as elements within their predefined range, you might suggest that each day of the week be set to an integer value using the **const** definition like this:

```
const int SUN = 0;
const int MON = 1;
const int TUE = 2;
const int WED = 3;
const int THU = 4;
const int FRI = 5;
const int SAT = 6;
```

Then, using this definition, you could actually manipulate the days within your program. For instance, assuming the variable *Day* is defined as an integer, a program might include the following pseudocode operations:

If Day == FRI Then
Write ("It's pay day!")

Since you have set the days of the week to integer values, the above **if** statement is simply comparing the value of *Day* to the integer value assigned to *FRI* (5). If *Day* equals 5, then the message is generated. Notice here that double equals (==) are employed in the pseudocode to indicate a logical test, while the single equals (=) is used to make an assignment. This notation will be employed throughout the text since it is consistent with C++ code.

C++ allows a more convenient way to work with non-standard data through the use of an enumerated definition. Rather than using numeric assignments as above, you can define the set of days using the keyword **enum** like this:

enum DaysOfWeek {Sun, Mon, Tue, Wed, Thur, Fri, Sat};

Here, the keyword **enum** defines the data type *DaysOfWeek* to include the set of seven elements *Sun*, *Mon*, *Tue*, *Wed*, *Thur*, *Fri*, and *Sat*. *DaysOfWeek* is called a user-defined data type since you, the user, have defined it.

Defining Enumerated Data

The general format and syntax for defining enumerated data is:

ENUMERATED DATA DEFINITION FORMAT

enum <data type identifier> {element #1, element #2, . . . , element #n};
<data type identifier> <variable identifier>;

As you can see, enumerated data requires a two-part definition. First, you must define the data elements using the keyword **enum** followed by a data type identifier and a list of the elements that make up the data type. Notice that the element list is enclosed within curly braces, { }, and a semicolon terminates the definition. Second, one or more variables are defined for the enumerated data type. The variable(s) provide access to the data type elements. The variable identifier, or name, is listed after the same data type identifier used in the **enum** definition. For instance, let's go back to our days of the week data type. The days in the week are first defined as an enumerated data type definition like this:

enum DaysOfWeek {Sun, Mon, Tue, Wed, Thur, Fri, Sat};

Then, a variable must be defined for the data type like this:

DaysOfWeek Day;

Any operations with the enumerated data in your program will then use the variable identifier (*Day*) as follows:

If Day == Fri Then
Write ("It's pay day!")

DEBUGGING TIP

It is important to realize that the enumerated data type elements are *not* variables or strings. Thus using the data element *Sat*, for example, as a variable in a program will cause an error. An enumerated data element must never appear on the left side of an assignment operator like this:

Sat = Fri + 1;

Another common source of error is to inadvertently declare the enumerated data elements as strings like this:

enum DaysOfWeek {"Sun", "Mon", "Tue", "Wed", "Thur", "Fri", "Sat"};

This will always cause a compile error. Again, the individual data elements are *not* strings, they are actually constant identifiers.

The Ordering of Enumerated Data

An enumerated data type is also a scalar, or ordered, data type. In fact, the word *enumerated* means "numbered with order." As a result, the C++ compiler assigns an order to the enumerated elements such that element #1 < element #2 < . . . < element #*n*. This means that, in the *DaysOfWeek* data type, *Sun < Mon < Tue < Wed < Thur < Fri < Sat*. As a result, relational operations involving the enumerated data type are perfectly legitimate. For instance, consider the following pseudocode:

> If (Day > Sun) AND (Day < Sat) Then
> Write ("It's a weekday")

Here, the value of *Day* is compared to *Sun* and *Sat*. Using the above enumerated definition for *DaysOfWeek*, *Day* must be a weekday if it's between *Sun* and *Sat*, right? How does it work? The C++ compiler actually assigns integer values to the enumerated data elements in the order that they are listed, beginning with the value 0. Thus, in the above example, *Sun* is assigned the value 0, *Mon* the value 1, *Tue* the value 2, and so on. Therefore, the above **if** statement reduces to a comparison of integer values.

Example 2-15:

Define the following as enumerated data types. Provide an appropriate variable to go along with the type definition.

a. *MonthsOfYear* consisting of the 12 months of the year.

b. *TestGrades* consisting of the five common letter grades.

c. *ArmyRanks* consisting of the eight common ranks found in the army.

Solution:

a.
```
enum  MonthsOfYear  {Jan, Feb, Mar, Apr, May, Jun, Jul, Aug, Sep, Oct,
                     Nov, Dec};
MonthsOfYear  Month;
```

b.
```
enum  TestGrades  {F, D, C, B, A};
TestGrades  Test;
```
c.
```
enum  ArmyRanks {Private, Corporal, Sergeant, Lieutenant, Captain,
                 Major, Colonel, General};
ArmyRanks  Rank;
```

Observe the syntax in the foregoing definitions. First, the data type name must be all one word. No spaces or punctuation are allowed. Also, notice that individual words within the data type name begin with a capital letter. This is not a requirement of C++, but has been done for clarity. Next, you see that the elements are listed inside of curly braces and separated by commas. Finally, a semicolon is required at the end of the element listing to mark the end of a given data type definition.

Look at the *TestGrade* data type a little closer. Notice that there are no quotes around the character symbols. A common mistake when defining character symbols as enumerated data is to enclose the data symbols in single quotes as you would characters. In an enumerated data definition, the character symbols are not treated as characters, but unique elements of the enumerated data type.

You should also note the ordering of each definition. The *TestGrade* data type is ordered such that an $F < D < C < B < A$. This represents a natural ordering, when you consider the application of grading. If the test grades were defined as characters, the ordering would be the opposite due to the relative ASCII values of the given characters. In addition, the *ArmyRanks* data type is ordered according to the natural order of ranks from the lowest rank (*Private*) to the highest rank (*General*). Finally, notice that an appropriate variable has been defined for each data type.

Example 2-16:

Given the courses Assembler, C++, COBOL, Architectures, Numerical Analysis,

Algebra, Trig, Calculus, English, Literature, and Theater, define a data type called *Courses* to include these courses. Define an appropriate variable.

Solution:

Using the **enum** definition, the above set of courses would be defined as follows:

```
enum Courses {Assembler, CPP, COBOL, Architectures,
              Numerical_Analysis, Algebra, Trig,
              Calculus, English, Literature, Theater};
Courses Course;
```

You might take note that the C++ course element had to be designated as *CPP*, since the plus symbol, +, cannot be used as part of an identifier in C++.

 Quick Check

1. Why would you want to create an enumerated data type in your program if a standard data type could be used to do the job?
2. Define an enumerated data type called *Automobiles* which consists of at least ten popular automobile brands.
3. What numeric value does the compiler assign to the first element in an enumerated data type?

2-5 THE STRUCTURE OF A C++ PROGRAM

You now have some of the basic ingredients to begin writing C++ programs. You will be doing this shortly, in the next chapter. However, before we leave this chapter, let's put things into some perspective and take an initial look at the overall structure of a C++ program.

Recall that the C++ language is a modular, structured language. This idea is evident from the overall appearance, or structure, of a C++ program. Look at Figure 2-5. Observe that any C++ program consists of two sections: a *preprocessor* section and a *main function* section.

First, you should always include a comment at the top of your program to explain the purpose of the program. Notice that comments in C++ are inserted into a program using a double *forward* slash (//). The double forward slash tells the compiler to ignore the rest of that particular line. Thus, a comment on any given line must begin with the double forward slash. The double forward slash can appear anyplace on a given line, but anything after // on a given line is ignored by the compiler. I will be making extensive use of comments within programs in this text to *self-document* the C++ code. I suggest that you do the same in your programs. Commenting your programs makes them much easier to read and maintain.

```
//*********************************************************************************
// A GENERAL COMMENT ABOUT THE PURPOSE OF THE
// PROGRAM SHOULD GO HERE
//
//*********************************************************************************

// PREPROCESSOR SECTION

#include <filename.h>
#include <filename.h>
#define value #1
#define value #2
// CONSTANT AND VARIABLE DEFINITIONS GLOBAL TO
// THE ENTIRE PROGRAM GO HERE

// MAIN FUNCTION SECTION
void main()
{       // BEGIN MAIN FUNCTION BLOCK

        // CONSTANT AND VARIABLE DEFINITIONS LOCAL TO
        // main() GO HERE

        // STATEMENT SECTION OF PROGRAM GOES HERE

}       // END MAIN FUNCTION BLOCK
```

Figure 2-5 The general structure of a C++ program.

The Preprocessor Section

The **preprocessor** in a C or C++ program can be viewed as a smart text editor which consists of **directives** that always begin with a pound (#) symbol. The two preprocessor directives that you will use the most are the *#include* and *#define* directives.

The #include Directive

The *#include* directive tells the compiler to copy, or include, the given file name into the C++ program at the point where the directive is found. You will see later that C++ programs are *built* by merging several files into one. A file referenced in the *#include* directive is called an ***include file*** or a ***header file.*** I will refer to them as header files in this text. In C++ it is common practice to indicate a header file by using a *.h* file name extension as shown in Figure 2-5. Header files are employed when a given set of routines might be common to many different C++ programs. Rather than typing the routines into each program in which they must appear, you simply create a header file containing the common code and include that header file in each program, using the *#include* directive. A C++ compiler will contain several standard header files that contain routines that are common to many programs. Consult your compiler reference manual for a complete listing of these files and the routines that they contain. Standard header files that we will use extensively are the *stdio.h, stdlib.h, math.h, string.h*, and *iostream.h* files. We will also be creating our own header files, especially when we work with object-oriented programming.

There are two ways to tell the C++ compiler how to locate a header file: by enclosing the header file name within double angle brackets, < >, or double quotes, " ". When angle brackets are used, the preprocessor looks in the primary system default directory and not the current working directory. The system default directory is where the standard header files included with your compiler will be located. The use of double quotes will tell the preprocessor to look for the indicated header file *first* in the same directory where your C++ program is located. This directory is often referred to as the ***working directory.*** So, whenever we include a standard header file in our program we will specify the include file name within double angle brackets like this: <filename.h>. Later on when we write our own header files and place them in the working directory, we will specify the include file name within double quotes like this: "filename.h".

The #define Directive

The *#define* directive tells the preprocessor to define a data item or operation for the C++ program. For example, the directive:

#define LINE_SIZE 65

will substitute the value 65 everywhere the identifier *LINE_SIZE* appears in the program. Thus, the code **char** Line[LINE_SIZE] is translated to the code

char Line[65]. It's as if you actually typed-in the value 65 into the program source code. Thus, using the *#define* directive to define a data item has the same effect as defining a constant for that item.

Example 2-17

Use the *#define* directive to create the following:
a. A string substitution of "C++" for the identifier *CPP*.
b. A character substitution of '.' for the identifier *PERIOD*.

Solution:

a. Simply define CPP like this: #define CPP "C++" Note that you *do not* use a data type or equals sign in a *#define* directive as you must in a constant declaration.
b. The required directive is #define PERIOD '.'

One final point: You *do not* terminate a preprocessor directive with a semicolon, since a preprocessor directive is not an executable C++ statement. Remember, a directive simply acts as a smart substitution editor for the compiler.

The Main Function Block

The main function block of the program is where all the C++ code appears. As you will see later, a C++ program is simply a collection of *function* blocks.

> A *function* in C++ is a subprogram that returns a single value, a set of values, or performs some specific task such as I/O.

Notice the syntax shown in Figure 2-5. The main function identifier is *main( )*. The main function identifier is preceded by the keyword **void**. The reason for this will become apparent in Chapter 7. This identifier must appear immediately after any preprocessor directives. A left curly brace, {, must follow the main function identifier prior to any other statements. This brace defines the beginning of the main function block and normally appears directly below *main( )*. At the bottom of Figure 2-5 you see a right curly brace, }. This brace is used to define the end of the main function block. You must always use a set of curly braces, { }, to define a block of code in C or C++. Thus, the set of curly braces in Figure 2-5 define the main function block, which includes the entire C++ program.

You must declare/define any *global* constants and variables prior to *main( )*. *Global* constants and variables are those that are accessible to the entire program, versus *local* constants and variables which are only accessible to a localized block within the program. Local constants and variables can be declared/defined anywhere in a program block as long as they are declared/defined prior to their use. More about global versus local values later.

The statement section of the program is the main executable body of the program. The program instructions, or statements, go here. Each statement must be terminated with a semicolon. Since C++ is a modular language, the statement section of the program consists of additional function blocks, whose combined execution performs the overall program task.

Example 2-18:

Using the program structure shown in Figure 2-5 and the definitions in Example 2-11, write a program that will calculate the sales tax of a sales item. Assume that you must include a system file named *iostream.h* for the program to perform some future I/O task.

Solution:

In Example 2-11, we used the following relationship to calculate the sales tax of a sales item:

$$SalesTax = Price * TAX\_RATE;$$

where *SalesTax* and *Price* were defined as floating point variables and *TAX_RATE* was declared as a constant value of 0.05.

Putting this information into the required C++ program structure shown in Figure 2-5, you get:

```
//*******************************************************************************
//
// THIS PROGRAM WILL CALCULATE THE SALES TAX
// OF A SALES ITEM
//
//*******************************************************************************
#include <iostream.h>

void main()
{
// DEFINE LOCAL CONSTANTS AND VARIABLES
   const float TAX_RATE = 0.05;
   float SalesTax;
   float Price;

// CALCULATE SALES TAX
   SalesTax = Price * TAX_RATE;
}
```

The program begins with a brief comment about its purpose. Observe the structure: The program is very readable and everything used within the program is clearly defined. Note that the program statements are indented about three spaces within the main function block. Such indentation is permissible, since C++ ignores spaces. In addition, the indentation clearly shows that the statements are part of the function block *main( )*. Indentation is used to "set-off" a block of code so that it is not confused with other blocks of code. We will make extensive use of indentation within our C++ programs to make them easier to read and understand. That's all there is to it! We have just written our first C++ program!

The simple program in Example 2-18 will calculate the sales tax of an item, given the item price. But how does the actual price of the item (*Price*) get into the program so that the calculation can be performed? Then, once the calculation is performed, how do you get the resulting sales tax value (*SalesTax*) out of the program and displayed on a monitor or printed by a printer? Getting things in and out of a C++ program is called reading and writing—the topic of the next chapter.

 Quick Check

1. Any C++ program consists of two sections called the _____ and _____ sections.

2. Write a **#include** directive to include a standard header file called *stdlib.h* into a program. Assume that the header file is located in the system default directory.

3. Write a **#define** directive to substitute the string "PROGRAM 2-3" every place that the identifier *Prog* appears in the program.

4. A subprogram that returns a single value, a set of values, or performs some specific task in C++ is called a _____.

5. Where must global constants and variables be declared/defined in a C++ program?

6. Where must local constants and variables be declared/defined in a C++ program?

CHAPTER SUMMARY

C++ is a typed language. This means that all of the data processed by a C++ program must be part of a given data type that is defined within the program. There are three major data type categories: scalar, structured, and pointer.

Scalar data elements are ordered and consist of standard and enumerated data. Standard scalar data types include the integer, floating point, and character data types. The integer data type in C++ includes the **int, unsigned int, long,** and **unsigned long** types, each of which defines a given range of integers.

The floating point data type consists of decimal values that can be represented in either decimal or exponential form. Floating point constants and variables can be declared/defined as **float, double,** or **long double** data types, each of which defines a given range of floating point values.

Character data includes all of the symbols on your computer keyboard. Characters are ordered, since they are represented internally using a numeric ASCII code. In C++, there are two character data types: **char** and **unsigned char.** The former is used to represent small integer values and the ASCII character set. The latter is used to represent the ASCII character set as well as the extended PC character set.

A string is a series of characters. C++ implements strings as character arrays, where each element in the array contains a character in the string, with the last string element being the character '\0', called a null terminator.

Enumerated data types are those that you, the programmer, define when constructing a program. Enumerated data types can be employed in your C++ programs to make them more understandable and application oriented. These data types are defined using the keyword **enum.** Since enumerated data types are scalar, the elements defined as part of a given data type are ordered in ascending order from the first element in the element listing to the last element in the listing.

All constants and variables used in a C++ program must be declared/defined prior to their use in the program. Constants are declared using the keyword **const.** The constant identifier is simply set equal to its constant value. Variables are defined by listing the variable data type followed by the variable identifier. An optional initializing value can be included in the definition. Like string constants, string variables must be defined as character arrays.

C++ programs consist of two sections: the preprocessor section and the main function section. The preprocessor section contains preprocessor directives that provide editing tasks on the program. Two directives commonly used are the *#include* and *#define* directives. The *#include* directive is used to copy C++ header files into the source program The *#define* directive is used to substitute data values into the source program.

The statement section of the program is the main executable body of the program and is called the *main function block*. This section begins with *main()*, followed by a left curly brace, and closes with a right curly brace. All program statements must appear within this main function block. Global constant and variable declarations/definitions must be made prior to *main()*. Local constants and variables can be declared/defined anyplace in the program prior to their use.

QUESTIONS AND PROBLEMS

Questions

1. Name the three standard scalar data types defined in C++.

2. What feature does a scalar data type have over a non-scalar data type?

3. Which of the following are *not* legal integer values in C++? Explain why they are not valid. Assume the **int** data type.

   a. −32.0

   b. +256

   c. 256

   d. 3,240

   e. 32000

   f. 40000

4. What is an integer overflow condition, and when will it generate incorrect results in C++?

5. Which of the following are not legal floating point values in C++? Explain why they are not valid. Assume the **float** data type.

   a. 35.7

   b. −35.7

   c. 0.456

   d. 1.25E−9

   e. −2.5−E3

   f. −0.375E−3

   g. 25

6. Convert the following decimal numbers to exponential notation:

    a. −0.0000123

    b. 57892345.45

    c. 1.00004536

    d. +012.345

7. Convert the following exponential values to decimal notation:

    a. 3.45E–7

    b. −2.25E–5

    c. 2.22E6

    d. −3.45E4

8. Three values in a electronics problem are: 15.3 kHz, 2.2 MHz, and 10 ps.

    a. Express each as a floating point value in decimal form.

    b. Express each as a floating point value in exponential form.

    c. Express each as an integer value.

9. The following current and voltage values are measured in a circuit: 1 milliampere, 32 millivolts, 100 microvolts, and 125 nanoamperes.

    a. Express each current and voltage value in decimal form.

    b. Express each current and voltage value in exponential form.

10. What is the data type of each of the following?

    a. 250

    b. −250.0

    c. −16

    d. −3.5E–4

    e. 'x'

    f. '$'

    g. "2"

    h. "175"

    i. "1.25E–3"

11. Enumerated data are defined using the keyword _____.

12. Given an enumerated data definition, how are the elements ordered within the data type?

13. Write definitions for the following enumerated data types. Make sure to provide an appropriate variable to go along with each data type.

a. *This_Semester_Courses* consisting of the courses you are taking this semester.

b. *Major_Courses* consisting of the courses required in your major program.

c. *My_Family* consisting of all the members of your immediate family.

d. *Weekdays* and *Weekends* consisting of those respective days of the week that occur in these subranges.

e. *Spring, Summer, Fall,* and *Winter* consisting of those respective months that make-up these seasons.

14. Given the following definition:

```
enum Colors {Blue, Green, Yellow, Red, Orange};
Colors Color;
```

Which of the following are TRUE and which are FALSE?

a. Blue < Yellow

b. Red > Orange

c. (Green < Yellow) AND (Yellow > Blue)

d. (Yellow > Orange) OR (Yellow > Blue)

15. Using the definition in question 14, which of the following are valid statements? Explain why a particular statement is not valid.

a. Color = Black;

b. Colors = Red;

c. Color = Blue + Green;

d. Color = "Yellow";

Problems

Least Difficult

1. Write a #define directive to substitute the ':' character for each place the identifier *COLON* appears in a program.

2. State the difference between a character and a string variable.

3. Choose appropriate names, and declare constants to represent each of the following:

a. A maximum value of 100.

b. The value required to represent the prefix milli-.

c. The value required to represent the prefix kilo-.

    d. Your age.

    e. A period.

    f. Your birth date.

    g. Your school.

4. Declare a series of constants using a single **const** declaration that would represent the months of the year.

5. Choose appropriate names and define variables for each of the following:

    a. Grade point average (GPA).

    b. The grade for a course.

    c. Gross pay on a paycheck.

    d. Student name, course name, and course number. Assume that the student and course names require 25 characters and the course number is a seven-position alphanumeric number such as ENG-103.

6. The = symbol is used in C++ to denote an assignment operation. For now, you can think of it as an equals operation, but you will find out later that it actually has a different meaning than just equals. Given the following:

```
// PROBLEM 2-6
#include <math.h>
void main()
{
    const float VALUE = 2.5;
    int x;
    int y;
    float a;
    float b;
}
```

Determine the results of each of the following program statements:

    a. x = 25;
        b = sqrt(x);

    b. y = 5;
        a = sqrt(sqrt(y));

    c. x = 1;
        x = x + 1;
        y = sqrt(x);

    d. x = 2;
        y = x + x;
        a = (y + 1) * VALUE;

e.   x = 2;
     y = x + x;
     a = y + 1 * VALUE;

More Difficult

7. The *cout* instruction is used in C++ to display a value on the display monitor. The format for this instruction is:

cout << variable or value to displayed;

Notice that the << symbols direct the variable or value to the *cout* instruction. Thus, to display the value of the variable x in a program, you simply use the following statement:

cout << x;

Add a *cout* statement to each of the program segments in problem 6 that will display the final results of the program.

8. Write a C++ program that will find the sum of three variable decimal values and display the sum on the system monitor. Let's call the variables *A, B,* and *C* and assume that they have initial values of 95.3, 78.5, and 85.2, respectively. Make sure to use the program structure given in Figure 2-5. (Note: You must include the *iostream.h* header file to use the *cout* statement.)

9. Expand the program you wrote in problem 8 to calculate and display the average of the three values. (Note: The / symbol is used for division of floating point values in C++.)

10. Write a C++ program that will find the total resistance of three series resistors whose values are of 3.3k, 2.2k, and 1M. (Note: The total resistance of resistors in series is simply the sum of the individual resistances.) Display the total resistance on the display monitor using a *cout* statement. You must include the *iostream.h* include file in your program to use the *cout* statement. Make sure to use the program structure given in Figure 2-5.

3

GETTING THINGS IN AND OUT: READING AND WRITING

INTRODUCTION

You are now ready to begin getting your hands dirty. In this chapter, you will learn how to get information in and out of your system via C++. Getting data into the system is called **reading** and generating data from the system is called **writing**. You will discover how to write information to your display monitor and printer. Then, you will learn how to read information from your PC keyboard. Armed with this knowledge, you will be ready to write some simple C++ programs. Make sure that you do the programming problems at the end of the chapter. You **must** get your hands dirty with some actual programming experience to learn how to program in C++.

At the end of this chapter you will be asked to write, enter, and execute your first C++ programs. As a result, it's probably a good idea for you to familiarize yourself with the operation of your system at this time. You should know how to load the C++ compiler, enter and edit programs, compile programs, debug programs, and run programs. A summary of the TURBO C++ integrated development environment (IDE) is provided in Appendix A, should you need a reference to this product. Now, let's get down to business.

3-1 GETTING THINGS OUT: WRITING ⇒ *cout*

When executing your C++ programs, you usually will want to generate information to one of two hardware devices: a monitor or a printer. In fact, there will be occasions when you will need to generate information to both of these devices during the execution of a program.

You can write information to a display monitor using a *cout* (pronounced as "c-out") statement. The word *cout* is not considered a keyword within C++ and, therefore, is not set in bold type. Rather, *cout* is part of the *iostream.h* header file that invokes pre-defined routines to accomplish the output task. In fact, *cout* is actually an **object** defined in the *iostream.h* header file. Objects are at the core of object-oriented programming and you will learn how to define and apply your own objects in C++ programs later in the text. For now, let's learn how to use the pre–defined *cout* object to write data to the display monitor.

The *cout* Statement

The general format for the *cout* statement is:

cout FORMAT

cout << item #1 << item #2 << item #3 << . . . << item #n;

As you can see, *cout* is followed by a list of the items to be written. The items within the listing must be separated by double left angle brackets, <<. These brackets are referred to as an ***operator***. In addition, the item listing must be terminated with a semicolon. In terms of object-oriented programming, we say that the items listed in the *cout* statement are being passed to the *cout* object to be acted upon by that object. You don't really need to know the inner workings of the object if you know what it does and how to pass information to it. The idea that the inner workings of the object are hidden from the programmer is an extreme advantage of object-oriented programming, since it allows software developers to develop commercial programs without revealing the inner workings of those programs.

The best way to understand how *cout* works is to look at the output generated by several different *cout* statements. Probably the simplest use of the *cout* statement is to write fixed, or constant, information. There are two types of fixed information that can be written: numeric and character.

Getting Out Fixed Numeric Information

When you want to write fixed numeric information, you simply pass the numeric values to the *cout* object. Thus, the statement:

```
cout << 250;
```

generates an output of:

```
250
```

The statement:

```
cout << -365;
```

generates an output of:

```
-365
```

The statement:

```
cout << 1 << 2 << 3 << 4;
```

generates an output of:

```
1234
```

The statement:

```
cout << 2.75;
```

generates an output of:

```
2.75
```

When several individual items are passed to the object, the output does not generate any spacing between the items. This is why the statement:

```
cout << 1 << 2 << 3 << 4;
```

generates an output of:

```
1234
```

Next, notice that when a floating point value is passed, you get its decimal equivalent on the output, not the exponential equivalent. Both of these conditions (item spacing and decimal output) can be altered using special formatting options within the *cout* statement. Output formatting will be discussed shortly.

Getting Out Fixed Character Information

To write character information, you must enclose the output information in double quotes. Consequently, the statement:

```
cout << "Hello";
```

generates an output of:

```
Hello
```

The statement:

```
cout << "This text is great!";
```

produces an output of:

```
This text is great!
```

Example 3-1:

Construct *cout* statements to generate the following outputs:
a. 3.14
b. 1 2 3 4

Solution:

a. cout << 3.14;
b. cout << 1 << ' ' << 2 << ' ' << 3 << ' ' << 4;

To get spacing in the output, use blank characters between the output values. Remember that blanks are also characters. As a result, the above statement generates blanks, or spaces, where they are inserted within the double quotation marks.

Getting Out Variable Information

The next thing you must learn is how to write variable information. Again, this is a simple chore using the *cout* object: You simply pass the variable identifier(s) to the *cout* object. For instance, if your program has defined *Voltage, Current,* and *Resistance* as variables, you would write their respective values by listing them in the *cout* statement like this:

cout << Voltage << Current << Resistance;

The foregoing statement would write the values stored in memory for *Voltage, Current,* and *Resistance,* in that order. The order of the output will be the same as the listing order within the *cout* statement. However, there would be no spacing between the values. Blank characters must be inserted within the *cout* statement to provide spacing. Let's see how this statement might be used within a complete program.

Example 3-2:

Remember Ohm's law from the last chapter? Ohm's law states that voltage is equal to the product of current and resistance. Write a C++ program that will write a voltage value, given a current value of 0.001 amperes and a resistance value of 4700 ohms.

Solution:

Let's define three variables to represent voltage, current, and resistance. We will initialize the given current and resistance values and use Ohm's law to calculate the voltage. The resulting voltage will then be written using the *cout* object. Here's the program:

```
// EXAMPLE 3-2 (E3-2.CPP)
#include <iostream.h>

void main()
{
  float Voltage;                    // VOLTAGE IN VOLTS
  float Current = 0.001;            // CURRENT IN 40 ERES
  float Resistance = 4700;          // RESISTANCE IN OHMS
  Voltage = Current * Resistance;   // CALCULATE VOLTAGE
  cout << Voltage;                  // DISPLAY VOLTAGE
}
```

The output produced by the program is:

4.7

STYLE TIP

The output generated in Example 3-2 is simply the number 4.7. What a bore! You need to "dress up" your program outputs so that the user of the program understands what's going on. First, you should always use a series of *cout* statements at the beginning of your program that tell the user what the program is going to do. This is called a ***program description message.*** A program description message does two things:

1. It tells the user (the person running the program) what the program will do.

2. It provides documentation within the program listing as to what the program will do. As a result, the program listing becomes self-documenting.

A program description message for the program in Example 3-2 might be coded something like this:

```
cout << "This program will calculate voltage, given a current of .001 amps \n"
        "and a resistance of 4700 ohms. \n";
```

This one *cout* statement will generate the following output:

This program will calculate voltage, given a current of .001 amps
and a resistance of 4700 ohms.

Observe that one *cout* statement is used to write two lines of character information. The trick is to break up the output sentence into two strings on two separate lines. Notice that each string item must be enclosed within double quotes. Also, notice the symbol \n at the end of each line. The \n symbol is treated like a character and is called an **escape sequence.** It tells the *cout* object to generate a carriage return/line feed (CRLF) wherever it appears. Thus, the first string item is written on one line, a CRLF is generated to move the cursor to the beginning of the next line, and the second string item is written. Another CRLF is generated at the end of the second line to position the cursor at the beginning of the next sequential line for any subsequent output. Even though the *cout* statement comprises two lines of code, it is not terminated until the semicolon appears at the end of the second line. Figure 3-1 illustrates how the \n escape sequence character controls the location of the cursor when used in the *cout* statement.

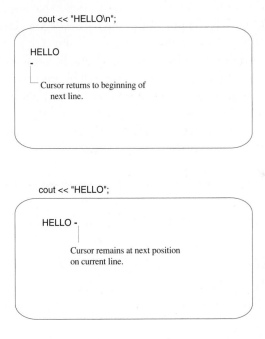

cout << "HELLO\n";

HELLO
  ▪
      └─ Cursor returns to beginning of
          next line.

cout << "HELLO";

HELLO ▪
      │
         Cursor remains at next position
         on current line.

Figure 3-1 Using the \n escape sequence forces the cursor to the next line.

STYLE TIP

Good style would dictate that output information should be descriptive. In other words, the output information should be self-documenting. In Example 3-2, the voltage output statement could be modified like this:

```
cout << "Given a current value of " << Current << " amperes and a \n"
        "resistance value of " << Resistance << " ohms, the \n"
        "resulting voltage is " << Voltage << " volts.\n";
```

This one *cout* statement will generate the following output:

```
Given a current value of .001 amperes and a
resistance value of 4700 ohms, the
resulting voltage is 4.7 volts.
```

Let's analyze this output. First, observe that a \n escape sequence has been inserted after each output string. This generates a CRLF after each output string, thereby creating a single spacing effect on the display. Next, look at the output lines themselves. See how an output sentence is constructed using three separate string items. The sentence is formed by three separate character strings enclosed within double quotation marks. The current, resistance, and voltage values are inserted in the sentence by listing the variables (*Current*, *Resistance*, and *Voltage*) when they are needed as part of the output. Notice that the character strings and variable items are separated by left angle brackets from each other in the listing. It is important that you see that the quotation marks are around the string information and *not* around the variables.

Example 3-3:

Insert the *cout* statements given in the previous style tips into the program developed in Example 3-2 to form a complete program.

Solution:

```
// EXAMPLE 3-3 (E3-3.CPP)
#include <iostream.h>

void main()
{
```

```
// DEFINE AND INITIALIZE VARIABLES
   float Voltage;                  // VOLTAGE IN VOLTS
   float Current = 0.001;          // CURRENT IN AMPERES
   float Resistance = 4700;        // RESISTANCE IN OHMS

// GENERATE PROGRAM DESCRIPTION MESSAGE
cout << "This program will calculate voltage, given a current of .001 amps \n"
        "and a resistance of 4700 ohms.\n\n";

// CALCULATE VOLTAGE
   Voltage = Current * Resistance;

// DISPLAY RESULTS
   cout << "Given a current value of " << Current << " amperes and a \n\n"
           "resistance value of " << Resistance << " ohms, the \n\n"
           "resulting voltage is " << Voltage << " volts.\n\n";
}
```

As you can see from Example 3-3, the general idea of using the *cout* statement is simple: You insert the *cout* statement in your program whenever you want to display information on your system monitor.

Monitor versus Printer Output

All of the output operations that you have seen up to this point will cause the information to be displayed on your system monitor. So how can you get the information to be printed by your system printer? Well, to perform printer output in C++, we must write code to create our own object, a *print* object. Here is a print object that I developed for the DOS platform:

```
//*********************************************************************
// THIS SEGMENT OF CODE DEFINES "PRINT" AS AN OUTPUT FILE
//              POINTING TO YOUR PRINTER PORT (PRN)
//
//*********************************************************************

   ofstream print;          // DEFINE PRINT AS AN OUTPUT FILE STREAM
   print.open("PRN");       // OPEN PRINTER FILE AND POINT TO PRN
   if (!print)              // MAKE SURE PRINTER IS READY
   {
     cout << "There is a problem with the printer.\n";
     exit(1);
   }
```

This code will only work on DOS platforms due to the specific reference to the printer file, PRN. However, a similar object could be created for other platforms and used in the same way. At this point, it is not important that you understand the above object-oriented code. This will come in time. For now, it is only important that you know how to use the *print* object that I have created. You will use this object just like you did the *cout* object. Thus, the print statement format is:

print FORMAT

print << item #1 << item #2 << item #3 << ... << item #n;

As you can see, the items to be printed are passed to the *print* object using the same syntax as was used for displaying information with the *cout* object. Here's an example to illustrate the use of *print*:

Example 3-4:

Revise the program in Example 3-3 so that the output information is printed on your system printer rather than to the monitor.

Solution:

Here's the revised program:

```
// EXAMPLE 3-4  (E3-4.CPP)
#include <iostream.h>
#include <fstream.h>
#include <process.h>

void main()
{
//********************************************************************************
// THIS SEGMENT OF CODE DEFINES "PRINT" AS AN OUTPUT FILE
//           POINTING TO YOUR PRINTER PORT (PRN)
//
//********************************************************************************
  ofstream print;              // DEFINE PRINT AS AN OUTPUT FILE STREAM
  print.open("PRN");           // OPEN PRINT FILE AND POINT TO PRN
  if (!print)                  // MAKE SURE PRINTER IS READY
  {
    cout << "There is a problem with the printer.\n";
    exit(1);
  }
```

```
    float Voltage;              // VOLTAGE IN VOLTS
    float Current = 0.001;      // CURRENT IN AMPERES
    float Resistance = 4700;    // RESISTANCE IN OHMS

    // GENERATE PROGRAM DESCRIPTION MESSAGE
    cout << "This program will calculate voltage, given a current of\n"
         " .001 amps and a resistance of 4700 ohms.\n\n";

    // CALCULATE VOLTAGE
    Voltage = Current * Resistance;

    // PRINT RESULTS
    print << "Given a current value of " << Current << " amperes and a \n"
             "resistance value of " << Resistance << " ohms, the \n"
             "resulting voltage is " << Voltage << " volts.\n";

    print.close();       // CLOSE PRINT FILE
}
```

Now the program output will be generated on your system printer rather than on the monitor. Notice that the print object code has been integrated into function *main()* of the program. In addition, for this code to compile properly we must include the *fstream.h* and *process.h* header files. Once the print object is created, you simply use it like the *cout* object to write information to the printer. Finally, the last statement in *main()* must be inserted to close the print file.

Actually, we could have redefined the *cout* object to write to the printer. However, there will be times when you will want to write simultaneously to both the display monitor and the printer. As a result, we will employ the pre-defined *cout* object for display output and our own *print* object for printer output.

By now, you are probably wondering why the C++ language doesn't include a built-in print command like you might find in other languages? Well, the C++ language does not include any standard input/output commands. Input/output operations are *not* defined as part of the original C or C++ language, but have been added as separate routines by the compiler manufacturers. This is why they are part of header files and libraries that come with your compiler. Many of these routines have been incorporated into the ANSI standard for C and therefore are more or less accepted as a standard part of the C or C++ language.

Formatting the Output

By formatting an output, I mean to structure it to meet a given application. C++ allows output formatting using special commands within the output statements.

These commands are referred to as ***escape sequences*** and ***I/O manipulators.*** Before discussing the details, let's learn how the computer "sees" a display screen or printed page.

Many systems, including the IBM PC, divide a page of output into 25 rows and 80 columns as shown by the layout chart in Figure 3-2. Layout charts are used to lay out, or format, your output. The layout chart allows you to align output information so that:

- Proper margins are provided for header information.

- Numeric and character data are properly aligned under column headings and evenly spaced across the page.

- The output looks professional.

The first thing to do when using a layout chart is to fill in the chart with the information to be written. For instance, suppose you must create three columns of output: the first for a person's name, the second for the person's address, and the third for a person's phone number. Figure 3-3 shows how these three columns might be laid out on a layout chart. Looking at the figure, you can make the following observations:

- There are three headings located on row 4.

- There are dashes in row 5 to underscore each column heading.

- The NAME heading has a field width of 15.

- The ADDRESS heading has a field width of 22.

- The PHONE heading has a field width of 23.

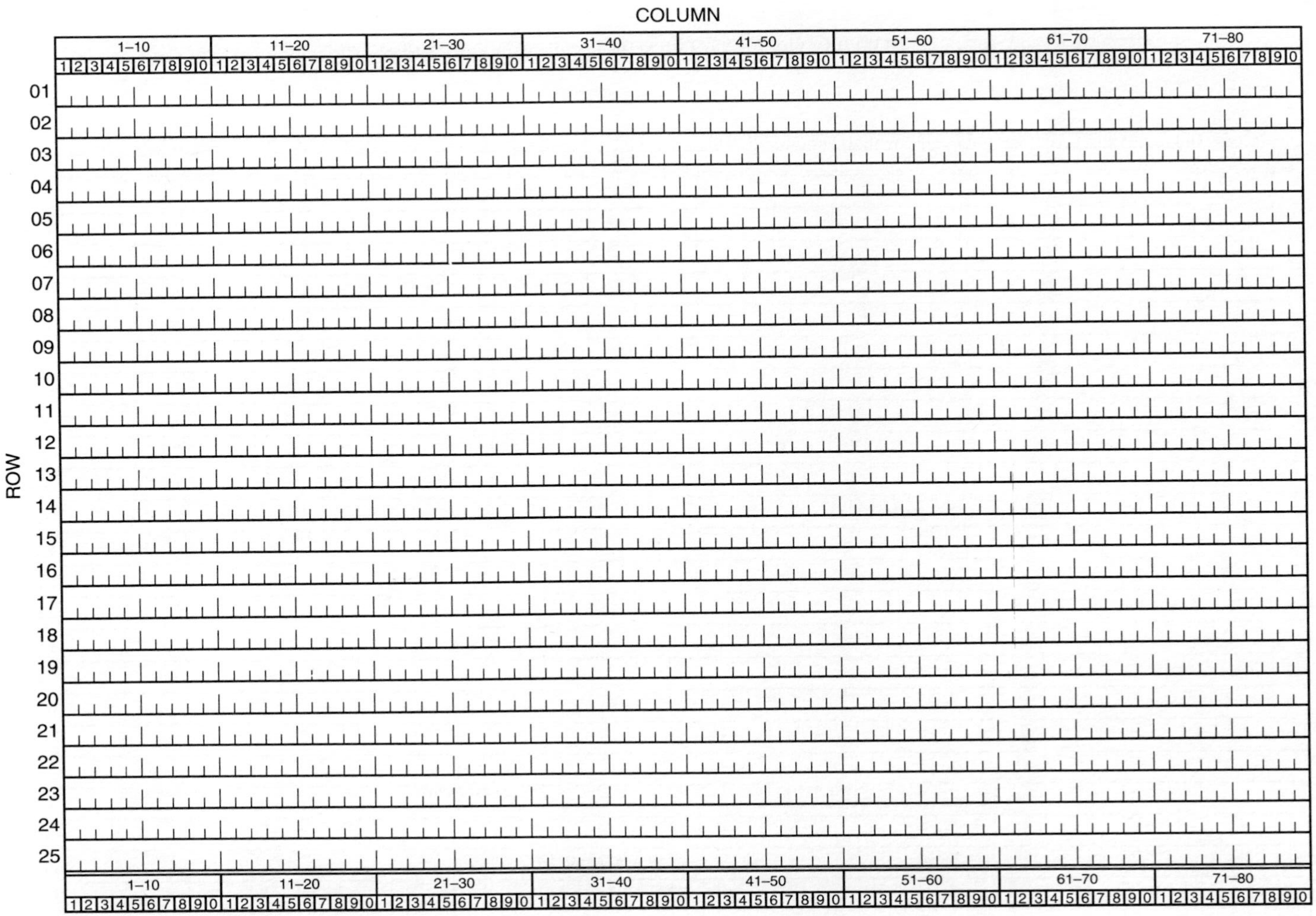

Figure 3-2 A typical layout chart.

91

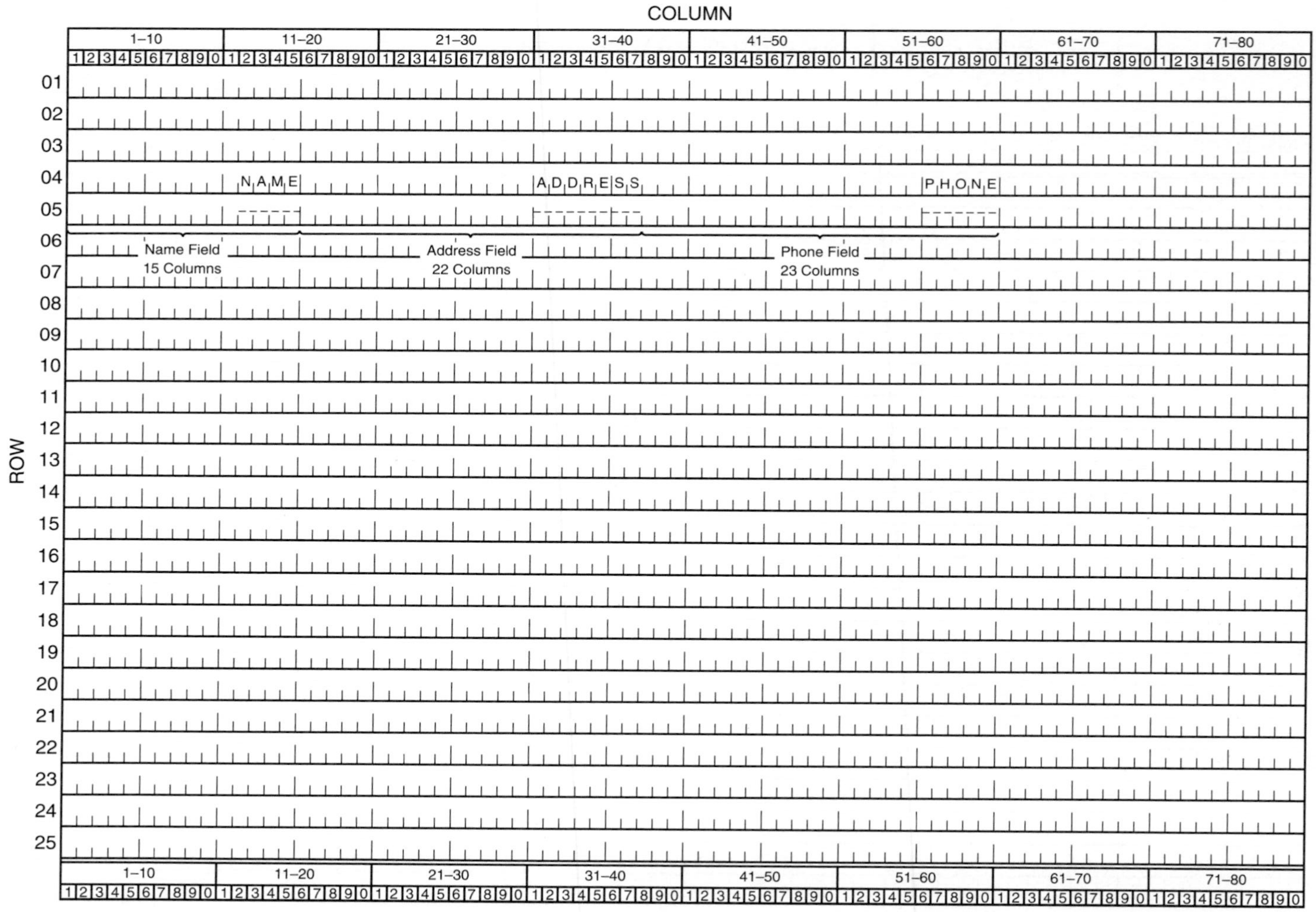

Figure 3-3 Laying out an output using a layout chart.

Using this information, let's write a program that will display the headings just as they appear on the layout chart. Here it is:

```
// PROGRAM TO GENERATE OUTPUT SHOWN IN FIGURE 3-3
#include <iostream.h>
#include <iomanip.h>
#include <conio.h>

void main()
{
  clrscr();        // CLEAR THE SCREEN - DOS ONLY

// SKIP FIRST THREE LINES AND DISPLAY HEADER INFORMATION.
  cout <<"\n\n\n"
         << setw(15) << "NAME"
         << setw(22) << "ADDRESS"
         << setw(23) << "PHONE\n"
         << setw(15) << "----"
         << setw(22) << "-------"
         << setw(23) << "-----\n";
}
```

The first thing you see in *main()* is the statement *clrscr()*. This is an abbreviation that means "clear screen." It does exactly what it says: It clears the monitor screen. C++ compilers that run on the DOS platform include this standard function to clear the screen. The *clrscr()* function is located in the *conio.h* header file. This is why there is a **#include** directive to include *conio.h* in the program. You should be aware, however, that *conio.h* is only available in compilers that run on DOS platforms. After the *clrscr()* function is executed in *main()*, you see a single *cout* statement with seven output items. The first item passed to *cout* is a series of three CRLF escape sequences. These three escape sequences generate the three blank lines in rows 1, 2, and 3, respectively.

Now, looking at the layout chart in Figure 3-3, you see that each heading is designated by a field width which indicates the number of columns that a given output item will occupy. To communicate the field width to the *cout* object, you must use an ***I/O manipulator*** contained in the *iomanip.h* header file. A list of several I/O manipulators is provided in Table 3-1. Notice that I/O manipulators allow you to manipulate the output stream to obtain some desired effect, in our case using the *setw(n)* manipulator to set the field width of a given output item. Consult your C++ reference manual for more information on these and other I/O manipulators. Remember that in order to use any of these manipulators, you must include the *iomanip.h* header file in your program.

TABLE 3-1 I/O STREAM MANIPULATORS FOR C++

Manipulator	Action
setw(n)	Set field width to n
setprecision(n)	Set floating point precision to n
setfill(n)	Set fill character to n
dec	Decimal output
hex	Hexadecimal output
oct	Octal output
ws	Extract whitespace characters
endl	Inserts a new line in the output stream then flushes the output stream
ends	Adds a null terminator to the output stream.
flush	Flushes the output stream.

Any of the manipulators in Table 3-1 can be inserted in the *cout* statement just like any other item. The following format shows how the *setw(n)* manipulator will set the field width for the next item to be output.

FIELD WIDTH FORMAT

cout << setw(field width) << output item;

In Figure 3-3, observe that the first output, "NAME", has a field width of 15. Thus, *setw(15)* tells C++ to assign a field width of 15 columns to the next item to be written, which as you can see from the program, is "NAME". When "NAME" is written, it will be right justified within this field width. Since it is right justified, NAME is positioned at the extreme right-hand side of the field. And, since the word "NAME" only requires four columns of output, C++ generates $15 - 4$, or 11, spaces prior to "NAME".

Next, count the number of columns from the "NAME" field to the last 'S' in the "ADDRESS" field. You get 22, right? Thus, the "ADDRESS" field width is 22. Therefore *setw(22)* is passed to *cout* prior to passing the item "ADDRESS".

Finally, counting the number of columns from the "ADDRESS" field to the last letter ('E') in "PHONE" field you get 23. Consequently, the "PHONE" field width is set to 23. Notice that the CRLF escape sequence is passed at the end of the "PHONE" item so that the cursor will be positioned at the beginning of the next output line. The same basic idea is then repeated on the next output line (row 5) to generate the dashes which provide underscoring for the headings.

Example 3-5:

Write a program segment that will format a three-column table for *RESISTANCE, CURRENT*, and *VOLTAGE*. Underscore each column heading.

Solution:

Using a layout chart, you must first lay out the output headings. Such a layout is shown in Figure 3-4. Here, the table headings are located in row 5 and each heading has a field width of 20. In addition, each heading is underscored by using dashes in row 6. The dashes must also have a field width of 20 to locate them under their respective headings. The resulting program is:

```
// EXAMPLE 3-5 (E3-5.CPP)

#include <iostream.h>
#include <iomanip.h>
#include <conio.h>

void main()
{
  clrscr();                             // CLEAR SCREEN - DOS ONLY
  cout <<"\n\n\n\n"                     // SKIP FIRST FOUR LINES
       << setw(20) << "RESISTANCE"      // DISPLAY HEADINGS
       << setw(20) << "CURRENT"
       << setw(20) << "VOLTAGE\n"
       << setw(20) << "----------"
       << setw(20) << "-------"
       << setw(20) << "-------\n";
}
```

Example 3-6:

Given a current value of 0.001 amperes and a resistance value 4700 ohms , write a program to calculate voltage using Ohm's law. Write the current, resistance, and voltage values using the format developed in Example 3-5.

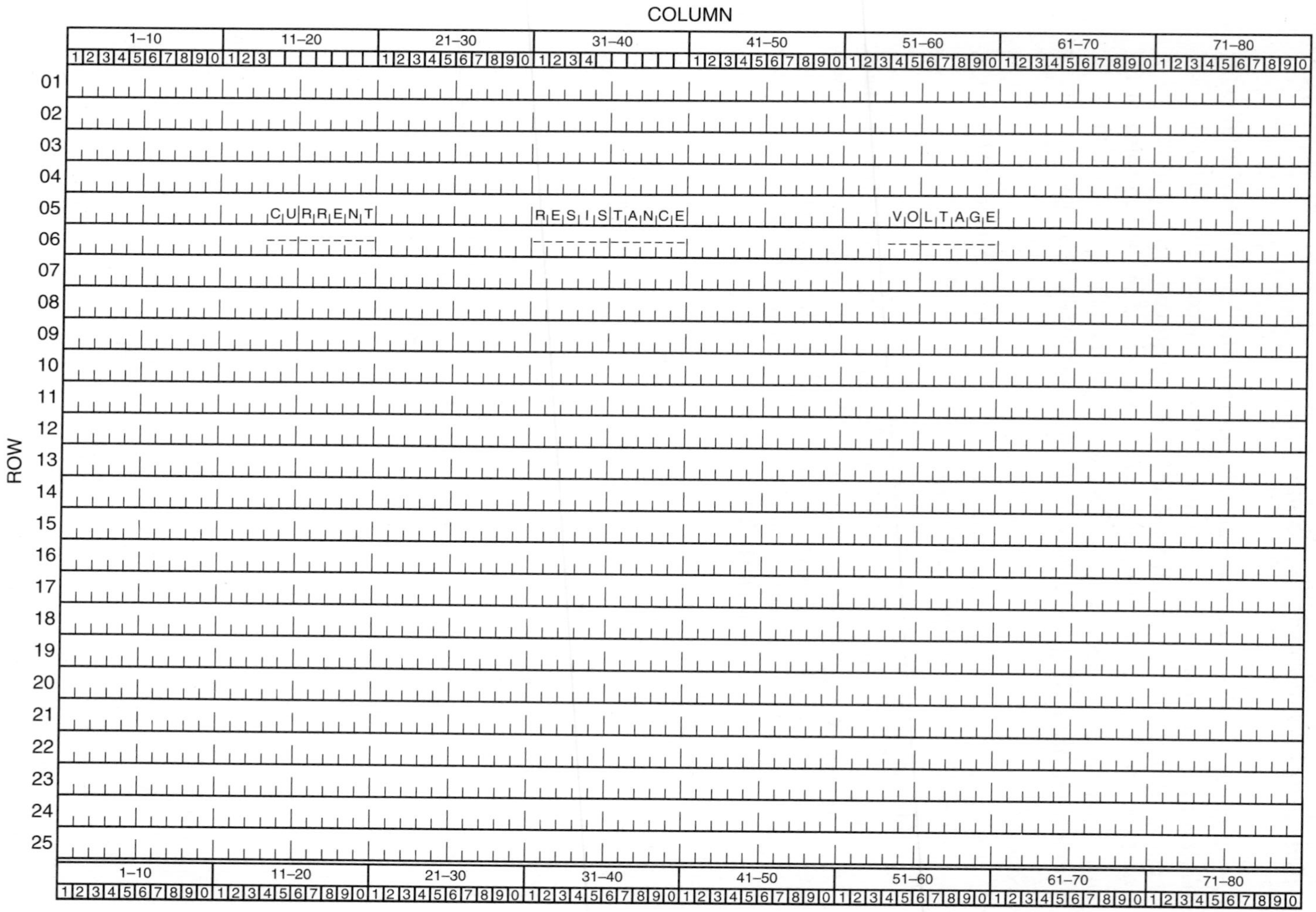

Figure 3-4 Layout for Example 3-5.

Solution:

The following program will do the job:

```
// EXAMPLE 3-6 (E3-6.CPP)

#include <iostream.h>
#include <iomanip.h>
#include <conio.h>

void main()
{

// DEFINE AND INITIALIZE VARIABLES
   float Voltage;                        // VOLTAGE IN VOLTS
   float Current = 0.001;                // CURRENT IN AMPERES
   float Resistance = 4700;              // RESISTANCE IN OHMS

// CALCULATE VOLTAGE
   Voltage = Current * Resistance;

// DISPLAY HEADINGS
   clrscr();                             // CLEAR SCREEN - DOS ONLY
   cout  <<"\n\n\n\n"
         << setw(20) << "RESISTANCE"
         << setw(20) << "CURRENT"
         << setw(20) << "VOLTAGE\n"
         << setw(20) << "----------"
         << setw(20) << "-------"
         << setw(20) << "-------\n";

// DISPLAY VALUES
   cout  <<'\n'
         << setw(20) << Resistance
         << setw(20) << Current
         << setw(20) << Voltage;
}
```

Here, I have simply combined several things that we have done previously. The headings program segment from Example 3-5 was inserted to generate the required CURRENT, RESISTANCE, and VOLTAGE headings. Notice that the last *cout* statement in the program writes the actual values of current, resistance, and voltage, respectively. Here, the variable identifier is listed after the field width specifier required to locate the value under the respective heading. You might note that two *cout* statements are used for clarity, one to write the header information and another to write the variable information. Actually, a single *cout* statement could have been used to do both.

Up to this point, you have seen the use of the \n escape sequence (CRLF) to control cursor positioning. There are others that you might need to use from time to time, some of which are listed in Table 3-2.

TABLE 3-2 ESCAPE SEQUENCES DEFINED FOR C++

Sequence	Action
\a	Bell
\b	Backspace
\f	Formfeed
\n	CRLF
\r	CR
\t	Horizontal Tab
\v	Vertical Tab
\\	Backslash
\'	Single quote
\"	Double quote
\?	Question mark
\O	O = a string of up to three octal digits
\xH	H = a string of hex digits

To use any of these escape sequences, simply include them as part of a string or enclose them within single or double quotes in the output stream.

 Quick Check

1. The file that must be included to use *cout* is the _____ header file.
2. The operator that must be employed to send information to the *cout* object is the _____ operator.
3. Write a *cout* statement to display your name as a fixed string of information.
4. Write a *cout* statement to display your name when it is stored in a string variable called *Name*.

5. The escape sequence that must be used to generate a CRLF is the
_____.

6. The file that must be included to use the *setw()* field width manipulator is the
_____ header file.

7. Write a *cout* statement that will display the value of a variable called *Number*
with a field width of 10 columns.

3-2 GETTING THINGS IN: READING ⇒ *cin*

Getting information into a program for processing is called *reading*. In most
present-day systems, information is read from one of two sources: from a
keyboard or from a disk file. In this section, you will learn how to read
information that is being entered via a keyboard by the system user. Reading from
a disk will be covered in a later chapter.

The primary C++ statement that we will use for reading keyboard data is the
cin (pronounced "c-in") statement. Like *cout, cin* is a predefined object in C++
and is part of the *iostream.h* header file. Before you can understand how this
statement works, you must know a little bit about how C++ sees a line of data.
Suppose you wish to enter a line of data consisting of three numeric values as
follows:

74 92 88.⏎

When typing in the foregoing data on a keyboard, you would type each
number consecutively, separating them with one or more spaces. At the end of the
line, you must press the ENTER (⏎) key. How do you suppose the system knows
where one data item ends and another begins? You're right--the spaces, or blanks,
define the separate data items. Next, how do you suppose the system knows where
the line of data ends? Right again—by pressing the ⏎ key you are defining the end
of the line. This operation places an end-of-line (eoln) marker at the end of the
line. In fact, as you might guess, the system does not actually take in any data
until it sees the end-of-line marker produced by pressing the ⏎ key.

Now back to the *cin* object. The general format for using *cin* is:

cin FORMAT

cin >> variable#1 >> variable#2 >> variable#3 >> . . . >> variable#n;

Notice that the word *cin* is followed by a variable listing separated by the double right angle bracket operator, >>. Of course, the variables must be defined using a legal data type prior to using them in the *cin* statement.

DEBUGGING TIP

A common source of error when first writing *cout* and *cin* statements is to use the wrong operator. Remember that the << operator is used in the *cout* statement, while the >> operator is used in the *cin* statement.

Suppose, for example, that you have defined three integer variables called *TestScore1, TestScore2*, and *TestScore3*. Then, to read three scores into the system, you would insert a *cin* statement into your program like this:

cin >> TestScore1 >> TestScore2 >> TestScore3;

When C++ encounters the foregoing statement in your program, it halts execution until the user enters a line of data. Now suppose the user enters the following via the system keyboard:

75 92 88.↵

What do you suppose happens? You're right again—the value 75 is assigned to *TestScore1*, the value 92 is assigned to *TestScore2*, and the value 88 is assigned to *TestScore3*. Thus, you can think of the *cin* operation as an assignment operation. The values entered on the keyboard are assigned on a one-to-one basis to the variables listed in the *cin* statement. The assignment order is the order of the respective data and variable listings. Once you press the ↵ key, the system knows that the line has ended. It then makes the assignments and execution of the program continues.

You're probably wondering what happens if the number of variables in the *cin* statement does not equal the number of data items entered by the user. The general rule is that the *cin* statement will not terminate until you enter *at least as many* variables as are listed in the statement. For instance, suppose the user entered just two scores for the foregoing *cin* statement like this:

75 92.↵

The *cin* statement will not terminate until the user enters as least as much data as is required by the statement. Even if the user presses the ENTER key, the *cin* statement will not terminate until the user enters another value.

Next, suppose the user enters more data than is required by the *cin* statement. In this case, only the required amount of data is used. Any *excess data items are ignored*. For instance, suppose the user enters four scores like this:

75 92 88 67↵

This results in the values 75, 92, and 88 being assigned to *TestScore1*, *TestScore2*, and *TestScore3*, respectively. The value 67 is ignored by this *cin* statement.

Reading Different Data Types

The two cardinal rules that apply when reading any data are:

1. All variables listed within the *cin* statement must be defined prior to its use in the statement.

2. The type of data entered for a given variable should match the data type defined for that variable.

By now, the first rule should be obvious. You cannot use a variable in a C++ program unless it has been previously defined in the program. The second rule needs to be explored a bit further. Consider the following program:

```
// THIS PROGRAM DEMONSTRATES THE cin OPERATION.
#include <iostream.h>

void main()
{
  int TestScore1;
  float TestScore2;

  cin >> TestScore1 >> TestScore2;
}
```

Now, suppose the user enters the following line of data when the *cin* statement is encountered:

98.5 78 ↵

What happens? Notice that the program defines *TestScore1* as an integer and *TestScore2* as a floating point value. However, the user has entered a decimal value for *TestScore1* and an integer value for *TestScore2*. Thus, C++ attempts to assign a decimal value (98.5) to an integer variable (*TestScore1*). This is called a **data type mismatch** and will result in an error in many strongly typed languages, like Pascal. However, recall that C++ is not as strongly typed as some other structured languages. When the user presses the ENTER key, C++ will actually assign the integer portion of the first value to *TestScore1* and the decimal portion of the first value to *TestScore2*. Thus, *TestScore1* takes on the value 98 and *TestScore2* takes the value 0.5. The input value of 78 is ignored. This clearly illustrates the reason you should define a variable so that it has the same data type as the data that is expected to be entered for that variable. Otherwise, you are very likely to obtain invalid data.

Next, using the same program, suppose the user enters the following line of data:

98 78.↵

Now there is no problem. But, how can this be, since the computer assigns an integer value (78) to a floating point variable (*TestScore2*)? This is okay, since the integers are a subset of the real numbers. The computer simply converts the integer value to the floating point format. Thus, the integer value 78 is converted to the floating point value 78.0 for storage within main working memory.

Reading Character Data

Reading numeric data is straightforward, as long as you adhere to the two rules for reading data. However, there are several things that you will want to keep in mind when reading character data using *cin*.

1. Only one character is read at a time.

2. **Whitespace** (blanks, tabs, new lines, and form feeds) are ignored by *cin* when using the >> operator. However, whitespace can be read using a different *cin* operator.

3. Numeric values can be read as characters, but each digit is read as a separate character.

DEBUGGING TIP

When you initially code a program, it is always wise to echo an input value back to the display. This assures you that the program has performed the read operation and made the correct variable assignment. To echo an input value back to the display, you simply insert a *cout* statement after the *cin* statement. Within the *cout* statement, you list the same variables that are listed within the *cin* statement. For instance, to echo the test scores in the foregoing program, you would add a *cout* statement like this:

```
// THIS PROGRAM DEMONSTRATES HOW TO ECHO
// INPUT VARIABLES DURING PROGRAM DEVELOPMENT.

#include <iostream.h>

void main()
{
  int TestScore1;
  float TestScore2;

  cin >> TestScore1 >> TestScore2;
  cout << '\n' << TestScore1 << '\n' << TestScore2;
}
```

Once the program has been debugged and is completely operational, you can remove the echoing *cout* statements.

Let's look at a simple program that illustrates most of these concepts. Consider the following:

```
// THIS PROGRAM DEMONSTRATES READING
// OF CHARACTER DATA.

#include <iostream.h>
```

```
void main()
{
  char TestScore1;
  char TestScore2;
  char TestScore3;
  cin >> TestScore1 >> TestScore2 >> TestScore3;
  cout << TestScore1 << TestScore2 << TestScore3;
}
```

The foregoing program defines three variables (*TestScore1, TestScore2, TestScore3*) as character variables. The program then reads the three character variables from the system keyboard and echoes the variables back to the system display. Now let's see what the program will do for several input cases.

Case 1:

User types in: **Grade⏎**
System displays: Gra

Here, the user has typed in the word "Grade" and pressed the ENTER key. However, the system displays only the first three letters (Gra) of the entered word. The reason is that character data are read one character at a time. Only the first three characters are echoed back, since only three character variables are read. The Character 'G' is assigned to *TestScore1*, the character 'r' is assigned to *TestScore2*, and the character 'a' is assigned to *TestScore3*. The remaining two characters ('d' and 'e') are excess and ignored.

Case 2:

User types in: **A B C⏎**
System displays: ABC

Here, the character 'A' is assigned to *TestScore1*, the character 'B' is assigned to *TestScore2*, and the character 'C' is assigned to *TestScore3*. Notice that there are spaces between the 'A' and 'B' and the 'B' and 'C' characters. This is referred to as **whitespace** and is ignored by the *cin* object when using the >> operator.

Case 3:

User types in: **ABC⏎**
System displays: ABC

Notice that the output here is identical to that of Case 2. This is due to the fact that the *cin* object ignores whitespace.

Case 4:

User types in: **75 92 88.⌐**
System displays: 759

In this case, the user has typed in three numeric test grades rather than letter grades. However, since the variables are defined as character variables, the system treats the digits as characters during the read operation. Each digit within a number is seen as a separate character. Thus, the character '7' is assigned to *TestScore1*, the character '5' is assigned to *TestScore2*, and the character '9' is assigned to *TestScore3*. The remaining data (2 88) are excess and ignored by the program. The lesson to be learned here is to always use numeric variables (integer or floating point) to read numeric data. As you can see, data can be lost when using character variables to read numeric data.

Case 5:

User types in: **97.5 73 84.⌐**
System displays: 97.

Again, the user has typed in three numeric test scores, which are treated as character data by the program. Thus, the first three characters are assigned and the remaining information is ignored. As you can see from the echo, the character '9' is assigned to *TestScore1*, the character '7' is assigned to *TestScore2*, and the decimal point is assigned to *TestScore3*.

As you can see, reading only one character at a time imposes a severe limitation on entering character data. A separate variable is required for each individual character to be entered. This is why we need to have a way to read string data.

Reading String Data

You will have difficulties when trying to use the *cin* object with the >> operator to read string data. Let's see what happens when we try to do it via the following program:

```
// THIS PROGRAM SHOWS HOW cin READS STRING DATA
// USING THE >> OPERATOR
```

```
#include <iostream.h>
void main()
{
  char Name[30];           // DEFINE CHARACTER ARRAY

  cin >> Name;             // READ THE NAME STRING
  cout << '\n' << Name;    // WRITE THE NAME STRING
  }
```

This program defines *Name* as a 30-element character array. After the definition, *Name* is read via a *cin* statement and subsequently echoed to the display via a *cout* statement. Here's how the program works:

User types in: **Jane Doe⏎**
System displays: Jane

What happened to Jane's last name? Well, when reading string data, the >> operator causes the *cin* object to terminate the read operation whenever any whitespace is encountered. So, the *Name* character array only includes the string "Jane". Here is what you would see if you were to inspect the *Name* character array in memory using a debugger.

Name

[0]	'J'
[1]	'a'
[2]	'n'
[3]	'e'
[4]	'\0'
[5]	
.	
.	(random memory data)
.	
[29]	

As you can see, array positions [0] through [3] contain the string "Jane" formed by the individual characters 'J', 'a', 'n', and 'e'. Array position [4] contains the null terminator character, '\0'. The *cin* object inserts the null terminator and terminates its execution when it encounters the blank character. Thus, the remaining input characters are ignored as reflected by the remaining array positions containing random memory data. In fact, if another *cin* statement were to follow this one, it would contain Jane's last name ("Doe"), since the user has already typed in the full name thereby placing "Doe" in the keyboard buffer.

There are several ways around this dilemma. One way is to define a separate character array variable for each whole word to be entered. In this case, you could create a *FirstName* character array and a *LastName* character array and use two *cin* statements to read in the first and last names, respectively.

Another, more preferred method is to use a function called *getline()* in conjunction with *cin* rather than the >> operator. The *getline()* function will allow *cin* to read the entire string, including any whitespace. Recall that *cin* is an object of the *istream* class. Since *getline()* is a member function of the *iostream* class, *cin* can call upon *getline()* to read an entire line, including any whitespace, Here's the general format:

READING STRINGS WITH *cin*

cin.getline(<string var.>, <max. string length + 2>, <'delimiting character'>);

Notice that a dot is used between *cin* and *getline()*. This dot notation is used to invoke the *getline()* function. The *getline()* function uses three **arguments.** An argument is something that must be passed to a function in order for it to perform its designated operation. The first argument is the string variable identifier. This is the name of the character array defined to store the string. The second argument is the maximum string length. This is the maximum number of characters that will be read. The length value should be at least two greater than the actual string length to allow for the '\n' CRLF character and the '\0' null terminator character. Finally, the delimiting character tells the *getline()* function when to terminate the read operation. The delimiting character is read and stored as the next to last character in the string. The *getline()* function automatically inserts the null terminator as the last string character. If no delimiting character is specified, its value defaults to the '\n' escape sequence character. Let's look at an example program:

```
// THIS PROGRAM SHOWS HOW TO USE cin AND getline() TO READ
// STRING DATA.

#include <iostream.h>
```

```
void main()
{
  char Name[32];                    // DEFINE CHARACTER ARRAY
  cin.getline(Name,32);             // READ THE NAME STRING
  cout << Name;                     // DISPLAY THE NAME STRING
}
```

The program works like this:

User types in: **Jane Doe.⏎**
System displays: Jane Doe

If you were to use the integrated debugger to display the *Name* array you would see this:

Name

[0]	'J'
[1]	'a'
[2]	'n'
[3]	'e'
[4]	' '
[5]	'D'
[6]	'o'
[7]	'e'
[8]	'\n'
[9]	'\0'
[10]	

.

.   (random memory data)

.

[29]

You see here that the array now holds the entire string, including the blank between the first and last names. Also notice that since no delimiting character is specified for the *getline()* function, the default of '\n' was read and stored just prior to the null terminator.

Example 3-7:

Write a program that will read and write the user's name and address.

Solution:

Obviously, the data to be entered will be string data. So, you must define several character arrays to accommodate the input strings. How must the input information be partitioned? Should you define one character array for the user's name and another for his/her address? But, what if our program needs to access just the users zip code? It might make more sense to break up the address into several character arrays that could be individually accessed. So, let's define one character array to store the user's name, then define five character arrays to store the user's street, city, address, state, and zip code, respectively. Then we will insert individual *cin* and *cout* statements to read the required information. Here's the program:

```
// THIS PROGRAM WILL READ AND WRITE THE USER'S
// NAME, ADDRESS, AND PHONE
#include <iostream.h>

void main()
{
// DEFINE CHARACTER ARRAYS
    char Name[32];
    char Street[32];
    char City[22];
    char State[4];
    char Zip[12];
    char Phone[15];

// READ NAME AND ADDRESS STRINGS
    cin.getline(Name,32);
    cin.getline(Street,32);
    cin.getline(City,22);
    cin.getline(State,4);
    cin.getline(Zip,12);
    cin.getline(Phone,15);

// DISPLAY NAME AND ADDRESS STRINGS
    cout << Name;
    cout << Street;
    cout << City;
    cout << State;
    cout << Zip;
    cout << Phone;
    }
```

First, notice that each of the required strings have been defined as character arrays. I have defined each array length to be *two* characters longer than need be. This is to leave room for the '\n' CRLF escape sequence character and the '\0' null terminator character. For instance, the *State* array is four bytes long to provide for a two character state abbreviation along with the CRLF and null terminator characters. Once the character arrays are properly defined, the program reads each string with a separate *cin* statement, then writes each string with a separate *cout* statement.

Here is what will happen when the program is executed:

User types in:

        Jane M. Doe.⏎
        999 Programmer's Lane.⏎
        C++ City.⏎
        WY.⏎
        12345.⏎
        (000)123-4567.⏎

System displays:

        Jane M. Doe
        999 Programmer's Lane
        C++ City
        WY
        12345
        (000)123-4567

A Problem When Using *getline()*

Although *getline()* will work when reading consecutive string data, you will have trouble when trying to use it to read a string variable after you have used *cin* to read a character variable or a numeric variable. For instance, suppose that you read the string variable *Name* after you read the integer variable *Number* like this:

```
// THIS PROGRAM DEMONSTRATES THE PROBLEM OF
// USING cin.getline() TO READ A STRING AFTER YOU
// HAVE READ A NUMERIC VARIABLE.

#include <iostream.h>
void main()
{
```

```
      char Name[20];
      int Number;

      cout << "Enter an integer:  ";
      cin >> Number;
      cout <<Number;

      cout << "Enter a name:  ";
      cin.getline(Name,20);
      cout << Name;
   }
```

When this program is executed, it seems as if C++ skips over the *cin.getline()* statement. How could this be? Well, if you use your debugger to look at *Number* and *Name*, here is what you see after the program is executed. Assume you entered the integer 123 for *Number*.

	Number	
int		123

	Name	
[0]		'\n'
[1]		'\0'

Notice that the string variable, *Name*, contains the CRLF escape sequence at position [0] and the null terminator at position [1] of the array. The reason for this is that when you enter the number 123, you must press the ENTER key. This inserts a CRLF character in the keyboard buffer. However, the *cin >> Number* statement does not read the CRLF character and it remains in the buffer. When the *cin.getline(Name,20)* statement is executed, it reads the keyboard buffer and sees the CRLF character. Since, by default, this is the delimiting character, it stops reading and inserts the null terminator character in the array. Thus, the user never gets an opportunity to enter a name. There are basically three ways around this problem. One way is to specify a different delimiting character in the *getline()* function. However, the user must enter this character and it will be stored as the last character, prior to the null terminator, in the array.

A second way is to clear the keyboard buffer by reading the CRLF character into a *trash* variable after reading any numeric or character data and prior to reading any string data. To do this, you must define a *trash variable* as a two-character array like this: char Trash[2];

After using *cin* to read any numeric or single character data, we will use the statement *cin.getline(Trash,2)* to read the remaining CRLF character in the keyboard buffer, thus clearing the buffer. Here's how the preceding program would be modified to employ this trash operation:

```
// THIS PROGRAM SHOWS HOW TO USE A TRASH
// VARIABLE TO CLEAR THE KEYBOARD BUFFER
// AFTER YOU HAVE READ A NUMERIC VARIABLE.
#include <iostream.h>

void main()
{
  char Trash[2];
  char Name[20];
  int Number;

  cout << "Enter an integer:  ";
  cin >> Number;                        // READ NUMERIC DATA
  cout <<Number;
  cin.getline(Trash,2);                 // CLEAR KEYBOARD BUFFER
  cout << "Enter a name:  ";
  cin.getline(Name,20);                 // READ STRING DATA
  cout << Name;
}
```

A third, more preferred way, is to use a different read statement. There is a collection of string I/O functions defined in both C and C++ for reading and writing string data. Two of these functions are listed in Table 3-3.

TABLE 3-3 STRING I/O FUNCTIONS IN C AND C++

Function	Description
gets()	Reads input string. CRLF converted to null terminator.
fgets()	Reads input string. CRLF is read and null terminator is added.

The string I/O functions shown in Table 3-3 are provided in the *stdio.h* header file. In fact, there are many other I/O functions in this header file, but we will only need to employ the string I/O functions in this text. The *gets()* or *fgets()* functions will solve the problem we have with *getline()*. To use *gets()* or *fgets()*, you must include the *stdio.h* header file and pass one or more arguments to the respective function. Here's the format for both functions:

gets() FORMAT

gets(<string variable>);

fgets() FORMAT

fgets(<string variable>,<max. chars + 2>, stdin)

The *gets()* function only requires that the string variable identifier be passed to the function. The *fgets()* function requires the string identifier, the maximum number of string characters to be read plus two, and the word "stdin".

From Table 3-3, you see that *gets()* will convert the CRLF character (produced by the ENTER key) to a null terminator. Thus, no CRLF is stored in the string with *gets()*. However, *fgets()* reads the CRLF character and adds the null terminator. As a result, the CRLF and null terminator characters will always occupy the last two bytes of the string.

As an example, suppose you use *gets()* and *fgets()* in a program like this:

```
// THIS PROGRAM DEMONSTRATES THE USE OF gets() AND fgets()

#include <stdio.h>
#include <iostream.h>
void main()
{
// DEFINE STRING ARRAYS
  char Name[21];
  char Address[32];

// OBTAIN USER INPUT
  cout << "Enter your name:  ";
  gets(Name);
  cout << "Enter your address:  ";
  fgets(Address,32,stdin);
}
```

Suppose that you make the following entries when executing the program:

Enter your name: **Jane Doe.**⏎
Enter your address: **C++ City**⏎

If you use your debugger to inspect *Name* and *Address* you will see:

Name

[0]	'J'
[1]	'a'
[2]	'n'
[3]	'e'
[4]	' '
[5]	'D'
[6]	'o'
[7]	'e'
[8]	'\0'

Address

[0]	'C'
[1]	'+'
[2]	'+'
[3]	' '
[4]	'C'
[5]	'i'
[6]	't'
[7]	'y'
[8]	'\n'
[9]	'\0'

You see that *Name* does not include the CRLF character, while *Address* does. You can always use *cout* to write string data. The *cout* object will write all the characters stored in the string until it encounters the null terminator. Thus, no CRLF is generated if a string is read using *gets()* and subsequently written using *cout*. However, the same string read using *fgets()* will generate a CRLF when subsequently written with *cout*.

DEBUGGING TIP

You have undoubtedly noticed the use of program comments in the previous example programs. Program comments in C++ are inserted using double forward slashes, //. When the C++ compiler encounters double forward slashes, it ignores the remainder of the line in which the slashes appear. In this text, program comments will appear in all caps so that they can be readily distinguished from the program code.

Program comments are an important part of the program documentation and should be used liberally. At a minimum, the program should include the following comments:

- The beginning of the program should be commented with the programmer's name, date the program was written, date the program was last revised, and the name of the person doing the revision. In other words, a brief ongoing maintenance log should be commented at the beginning of the program.

- The beginning of the program should be commented to explain the purpose of the program which includes the problem definition. This provides an overall perspective by which anyone, including you, the programmer, can begin debugging or maintain the program.

- Major sections of the program should be commented to explain the overall purpose of the respective section.

- Individual program lines should be commented when the purpose of the code is not obvious relative to the application.

- All major subprograms (functions in C++) should be commented just like the main program function.

Remember, someone (including you) might have to debug or maintain the program in the future. A good commenting scheme makes these tasks a much more efficient and pleasant process.

Quick Check

1. The operator that must be employed to send information to the *cin* object is the _____ operator.

2. Write statements to prompt the user to enter a value for an integer variable called *Number*. Use *cin* to read the user entry.

3. Provide some examples of whitespace.

4. True or False: When reading character data, *cin* will read only one character at a time.

5. When does the *cin* statement terminate when using the >> operator to read string data?

6. What function can be employed with *cin* to read string data, including whitespace?

7. When should you use *gets()* or *fgets()* in lieu of *cin* to read string data?

8. Employ the *gets()* function to read a string of up to 25 characters and store it in a variable called *Name*.

9. How is the CRLF character treated with *gets()*?

10. How is the CRLF character treated with *fgets()*?

3-3 USER-FRIENDLY AND INTERACTIVE PROGRAMMING

You must always strive to make your programs as user-friendly as possible. By a user-friendly program, I mean a program that is easy to use and does not confuse the user. Such a program should always include the following (at a minimum):

1. A program description message that tells the user what the program is going to do.

2. Prompting messages prior to any read operations. These user prompts must tell the user what information to enter and how to enter it in clear, unconfusing terms.

3. Output information that is well formatted and whose meaning is easily understood by the user.

Let's see how we can make the name, address, and phone number program developed in Example 3-7 more user-friendly. Suppose we revise the program as follows:

```cpp
// THIS PROGRAM WILL READ AND WRITE THE USER'S
// NAME, ADDRESS, AND PHONE
#include <iostream.h>

void main()
{
// DEFINE CHARACTER ARRAYS
    char Name[32];
    char Street[32];
    char City[22];
    char State[4];
    char Zip[12];
    char Phone[15];

// DISPLAY PROGRAM DESCRIPTION MESSAGE
cout << "This program will ask you to enter your name, "
            "address, and phone \n number.  Please press the "
            " ENTER key after each entry.";

// READ THE NAME AND ADDRESS STRINGS
    cout << "\n\nPlease enter your name (first, "
            "middle initial, last):  ";
    cin.getline(Name,32);
    cout << "\nPlease enter your street address:  ";
    cin.getline(Street,32);
    cout << "\nPlease enter your city:  ";
    cin.getline(City,22);
    cout << "\nPlease enter your two character state abbreviation:  ";
    cin.getline(State,4);
    cout << "\nPlease enter your zip code:  ";
    cin.getline(Zip,12);
    cout << "\nPlease enter your phone number:  ";
    cin.getline(Phone,15);

// WRITE NAME AND ADDRESS STRINGS ENTERED BY THE USER
    cout << "\nThe information that you entered is:\n\n";
    cout << Name;
    cout << Street;
    cout << City;
```

```
cout << State;
cout << Zip;
cout << Phone;
}
```

Here is what the user sees on the display after the program has run:

This program will ask you to enter your name, address, and phone number. Please press the ENTER key after each entry.

Please enter your name (first, middle initial, last): **Jane M. Doe**↵

Please enter your street address: **999 Programmer's Lane**↵

Please enter your city: **C++ City**↵

Please enter your two character state abbreviation: **WY**↵

Please enter your zip code: **12345**↵

Please enter your phone number: **(000)123-4567**↵

The information that you entered is:

Jane M. Doe
999 Programmer's Lane
C++ City
WY
12345
(000)123-4567

Notice that the information entered by the user is set in bold type so that you can distinguish it from the output information generated by the program. As you can see, the program description message tells the user what the program is about to do, as well as providing some general data-entry instructions.

Next, the program prompts the user to enter his or her name, indicating the required name format. A CRLF escape sequence is *not* used at the end of the prompt so that the user's name will be entered on the same line as the prompt. Remember this little trick! It makes for good interactive programming style. A *cin.getline()* statement is required after the prompt to read the user entry and assign the entry to the string variable *Name*. The program then prompts and reads the user address and phone information. Finally, all the entries are displayed to allow the user to verify the information.

One final point: Notice how the '\n' CRLF escape sequences are used to provide output line spacing. This separates the output information making it clear and easy to read, all in an effort to make the program more user-friendly.

CASE STUDY: USER FRIENDLY PROGRAMS

Problem:

As an overall program summary to the material presented in this chapter, let's write a user-friendly program that will calculate voltage from different values of current and resistance entered by the user. We will format a three-column table for current, resistance, and voltage and underscore each column heading. The final program output will be a printed table showing the current, resistance, and voltage values.

Let's first define the problem in terms of output, input, and processing as follows:

Problem Definition

Output: The final program output must be a printed table showing the calculated voltage value along with the current and resistance values used in the calculation. In addition, user prompts should be provided on the monitor to direct the user to enter the required values.

Input: The input must be a current and a resistance value entered by the user. Appropriate user prompts must be generated to instruct the user to enter the values.

Processing: Ohm's Law: Voltage = Current × Resistance

The next step is to construct an algorithm from the problem definition. The following algorithm will do the job:

The Algorithm

BEGIN
   Write a program description message to the user.
   Write a user prompt to enter the current value (*Current*).
   Read(*Current*).
   Write a user prompt to enter the resistance value (*Resistance*).
   Read (*Resistance*).
   Calculate the voltage: $Voltage = Current \times Resistance$.
   Print table headings for current, resistance, and voltage. Underscore the headings.
   Print the current, resistance, and voltage values under the respective headings.
END.

   Now, using the foregoing algorithm and your knowledge of C++, the program is coded like this:

```
// CASE 3-1 (CASE3-1.CPP)

// OUTPUT:
// THE PROGRAM OUTPUT MUST BE A PRINTED TABLE
// SHOWING THE CALCULATED VOLTAGE VALUE ALONG
// WITH THE CURRENT  AND RESISTANCE VALUES USED
// IN THE CALCULATION.
// IN ADDITION, USER PROMPTS SHOULD
// BE PROVIDED ON THE MONITOR TO DIRECT THE USER
// TO ENTER THE REQUIRED VALUES.

// INPUT:
// THE INPUT MUST BE A CURRENT AND
// A RESISTANCE VALUE ENTERED BY THE
// USER. APPROPRIATE USER PROMPTS MUST BE
// GENERATED TO INSTRUCT THE USER TO ENTER THE VALUES.

// PROCESSING:
// OHM'S LAW:  VOLTAGE = CURRENT * RESISTANCE

#include <iostream.h>
#include <iomanip.h>
#include <fstream.h>
#include <process.h>
```

```cpp
void main()
{
//****************************************************************************
//
// THIS SEGMENT OF CODE DEFINES "print"  AS AN OUTPUT
//  FILE POINTING TO YOUR PRINTER PORT (PRN)
//
//****************************************************************************
  ofstream print;                  // DEFINE PRINT AS AN OUTPUT FILE
  print.open("PRN");               // OPEN PRINT FILE
  if (!print)                      // MAKE SURE PRINTER IS READY
  {
    cout << "There is a problem with the printer.\n";
    exit(1);
  }

// DEFINE THE REQUIRED OHM'S LAW VARIABLES
  float Voltage;                   // VOLTAGE IN VOLTS
  float Current;                   // CURRENT IN AMPERES
  float Resistance;                // RESISTANCE IN OHMS

// DISPLAY PROGRAM DESCRIPTION MESSAGE
  cout << "\n\nThis program will calculate voltage from current"
          "\nand resistance values that you enter.";

// GET THE CURRENT AND RESISTANCE FROM THE USER
  cout << "\n\nEnter a current value in amperes:  Current = ";
  cin >> Current;
  cout << "\nEnter a resistance value in ohms:  Resistance = ";
  cin >> Resistance;

// CALCULATE VOLTAGE USING OHM'S LAW
  Voltage = Current * Resistance;

// PRINT THE OUTPUT TABLE
  print   <<"\n\n\n\n"
          << setw(20) << "RESISTANCE"
          << setw(20) << "CURRENT"
          << setw(20) << "VOLTAGE\n"
          << setw(20) << "----------"
          << setw(20) << "-------"
          << setw(20) << "-------"
          << flush;
```

```
print   <<'\n'
          << setw(20) << Resistance
          << setw(20) << Current
          << setw(20) << Voltage
          <<  '\f'
          << flush;
print.close();
}
```

Notice how *cout* and *print* are being used to perform both display and printer output. In particular, you see the *flush* I/O manipulator being used in the print statement to flush the print buffer prior to sending another output stream. This is always good practice to assure reliable printed information. You now should have no trouble understanding the remainder of this program with the material presented in this chapter.

 Quick Check

1. What should you do in order to make a program more user friendly?

2. What I/O manipulator should be used after a printer output operation to assure reliable printed information?

3. The symbol used to insert comments in your program is the _____ symbol.

4. State at least four places where your program should include comments.

Now, make a serious effort to complete all of the questions and problems that follow. It is time to get your hands dirty and to program your system to apply the program exercises that follow. This is where you will really learn how to program in C++.

CHAPTER SUMMARY

Getting information into your system is called *reading*, while getting information out of your system is called *writing*. The C++ statement used for reading is the *cin* statement, while the statement used for writing is the *cout* statement.

Each *cout* statement must include a listing of the items to be written. The items in the listing must be separated by double left angle brackets, <<. The *cout* statement can be used to write either fixed or variable information. Fixed numeric information is written by simply listing the numeric values within the *cout* item listing. When writing fixed character information, the information to be written must be enclosed within single quotes for single characters, or double quotes for strings. When writing variable information, the variable identifier must be listed within the *cout* statement. Information can be written to the system monitor or printer. You use the built-in *cout* object for writing to the monitor, but you must define your own *print* object for writing to the printer. To format an output, you must often include an I/O manipulator in the item listing. As an example, the *setw(n)* field width manipulator must be included prior to the item to be written to adjust the item field width. The field width manipulator value specifies the number of columns of output that will be allocated to the item being written. You must always include the *iomanip.h* file when using I/O manipulators. In addition, always use a layout chart to lay out your output and determine the correct field width values.

The statements used for reading in C++ are the *cin* object, *gets()* function, and *fgets()* function, among others. Like *cout* , *cin* is a predefined object in C++. The *cin* statement must include a listing of the variables to be entered, or read. Input data are assigned sequentially to the variables listed within the *cin* statement as the data are entered on the system keyboard. All variables listed within the *cin* statement must be defined prior to their use in the program. Moreover, the type of data entered for a given variable should match the data type defined for that variable. The double right angle bracket operator, >>, is used within the *cin* statement between numeric and single character variables to be read. Since the >> operator ignores whitespace, you should use the *getline()* function along with *cin* when reading character arrays, or strings. However, *cin.getline()* should not be used to read a string after numeric or single character information is read by *cin*, since it might be prematurely terminated by a '\n' character in the keyboard buffer. The *gets()* and *fgets()* functions contained in the *stdio.h* header file are also used for reading strings. The *gets()* function converts CRLF to a null terminator when the string is stored, while *fgets()* reads and stores CRLF while adding the null terminator at the end of the string.

User-friendly programs require interaction between the program and the user. At a minimum, a user-friendly program must:

- Write a program description message to the user.

- Prompt the user prior to any read operations.

- Generate well-formatted outputs whose meaning is easily understood by the user.

QUESTIONS AND PROBLEMS

Questions

1. Indicate the output for each of the following:

    a. cout << "\n\n";

    b. cout << setw(40) << "HELLO";

    c. cout << setw(12) << -36.2;

    d. cout << 3.75;

    e. cout << '\n'<< "   " << 1 << setw(5) << 2 << '\t' << 3
               << setw(5) << 4;

    f. cout << setw(20) << "My test score is: 97.6/n/n";

    g. cout <<"\n\t\tTEST SCORE\t\t97.5";

    h. cout <<"\n\t\tTEST SCORE\n\t\t97.5";

    i. print <<"\t\tTEST SCORE\n\t\t97.5\f";

2. Suppose that you define a constant as follows:

    const char SPACE = ' ';

    What will the following statement do?

    cout << '\n' << setw(20) << SPACE << "HELLO";

3. What will the following statement do?

    cout << '\n' << setw(20) << ' ' << "HELLO";

4. What is the difference between the output produced by the following two statements?

    cout << "\n#\n#\n#";

    cout << "\n###";

5. Consider the following program segment:

    char A;
    char B;
    cin >> A >> B;
    cout << A << B;

    What will be displayed for each of the following user entries?

    a. AB

    b.   3.14

    c.   A B   (Note: There is a space between the 'A' and the 'B')

6. What header file must be included in order to use the *setw(n)* field width specifier?

7. What function must be used with *cin* to obtain string data?

8. Define an appropriate variable and write statements to read and then display your school name.

9. Suppose that you must generate two separate pages of output on a printer. How do you make the printer advance to the second page, once the first page is printed?

10. Explain what happens when the user enters a string that is longer than the array variable defined for that string.

11. Explain what happens when the user enters a string that is shorter than the array variable defined for that string.

12. What arguments must be provided when using *getline()* to read string data?

13. What is the relationship between *iostream, cin*, and *getline()*?

14. Why should you define a string two bytes longer than the maximum string length if you are using *cin.getline()* to read the string?

15. Explain the difference between an escape sequence and an I/O manipulator.

16. When should *gets()* or *fgets()* be used in lieu of *cin.getline*?

17. What header file must be included to use *gets()* or *fgets()*?

18. Explain how the operation of *gets()* differs from that of *fgets()*.

19. Why is *getline()* unsafe for reading string data after it is used to read numeric or single character data?

20. Describe three methods for solving the *getline()* problem referred to in question 19.

Problems

Least Difficult

1. Using the layout chart in Figure 3-2, write a program to display your first name in the middle of the monitor screen.

2. Using the layout chart in Figure 3-2, write a program to display your first name in the upper left-hand corner of the display using characters that are six lines high.

3. Write a program that will generate a rectangle whose center is located in the middle of the display. Construct the rectangle using X's 8 lines high and 20 columns wide.

4. Write a program that will generate the following output in the middle of the display:

STUDENT	SEMESTER AVERAGE
--------------	---------------------------------
1	84.5
2	67.2
3	77.4
4	86.8
5	94.7

More Difficult

In the problems that follow you will need to employ several arithmetic operations. In C++, a plus symbol (+) is used for addition, a minus symbol (−) is used for subtraction, a star symbol (*) is used for multiplcation, and a slash symbol (/) is used for division. When a problem requires a decimal point output you will need to employ the setprecision() I/O manipulator located in the iomanip.h header file.

5. Write a program to calculate simple interest on a $2,000 loan for two years at a rate of 12.5 percent. Format your output appropriately, showing the amount of the loan, time period, interest rate, and interest amount.

6. Write a program that will prompt the user to enter any four-letter word. Then display the word backwards. (Keep it clean!)

7. Electrical power in a direct current (dc) circuit is defined as the product of voltage and current. In symbols, *Power = Voltage × Current*. Write a program to calculate dc power from a voltage value of 12 volts and a current value of 0.00125 amperes. Generate a tabular display of input and output values in decimal form.

8. Write a user-friendly program that will calculate power from voltage and current values entered by the user. Generate a tabular display of input and output values in decimal form.

Most Difficult

9. Write a user-friendly program that will calculate the weekly gross pay amount for an employee, given his/her rate of pay and number of hours worked. Assume the employee is part-time and, therefore, works less than 40 hours per week. Generate a display showing the employee's name, rate of pay, hours worked, and gross pay. Provide the appropriate display headings.

10. Write a user-friendly program to calculate the circumference and area of a circle from a user's entry of its radius. Generate a tabular display showing the circle's radius, circumference, and area. Note: Circumference of a circle $= 2 \times pi \times r$. Area of a circle $= pi \times r^2$.

11. Write a user-friendly program that will allow a student to calculate his/her test average from four test scores. Generate a display of the student's name, course name, individual test scores, and test average.

12. The "4 Squares" bowling team has four bowlers. On a given bowling night, each team member bowls three games. Write a program that will read the date, each bowler's name, and the individual game scores for each bowler. Using the input information, generate a bowling report on a printer: The printed report should show the date at the top of the page, then a table for each bowler showing his/her scores, total, and average.

13. Write a user-friendly program that will calculate the equivalent resistance of a series circuit from five resistances entered by the user. Generate a tabular display of input and output values in decimal form.

14. Write a user-friendly program that will calculate the equivalent resistance from two parallel resistances entered by the user. Generate a tabular display of input and output values in decimal form. Use the following product over sum rule to calculate the equivalent resistance value:

$$R_1 = (R_1 * R_2) / (R_1 + R_2)$$

Observe the use of parentheses to group the quantities in the above equation. Why do you suppose this is necessary?

4 WRITING SIMPLE C++ PROGRAMS

INTRODUCTION

You are now ready to begin learning how to write simple straight–line programs in C++. By a straight-line program, I mean a program that does not alter its flow, it simply executes a series of statements in a straight line, from beginning to end.

In order for your programs to perform meaningful tasks, you must be familiar with several standard, or built-in, operations available to you in C++. The simplest of these are the standard arithmetic operations. By definition, an arithmetic operation generates a numeric result. Such operations are the topic of the first section of this chapter.

The second section of the chapter deals with the C++ assignment operators. Assignment operators assign a value to a variable in memory. There are compound assignment operators in C++ that allow you to combine an arithmetic operation with the assignment operation.

In addition to arithmetic operations, there are logical operations available in C++ that generate a TRUE or FALSE result. These operations are covered in the third section of the chapter.

In order to simplify the programming task, C++ employs several standard functions. These functions allow you to easily implement many common operations, such as square root, sine, and cosine without writing special routines. Standard functions are discussed in the fourth section of the chapter.

Finally, the last section of this chapter applies the material in the first four sections to several real-world case studies. Here you will learn by example. I encourage you to study these cases very closely, since they employ many of the ideas and concepts presented in these first four chapters. Now, let's get to it!

4-1 ARITHMETIC OPERATIONS

Arithmetic operations in C++ include the common add, subtract, multiply, and divide operations, as well as increment/decrement operations. The basic add, subtract, multiply, and divide operations can be performed on any numeric data type. Recall that the standard numeric data types in C++ are the integers and reals (floating point). In addition, you can perform arithmetic operations on character data in C++, since characters are represented as integers (ASCII) within the computer.

Table 4-1 lists the four basic arithmetic operations and the C++ symbols used to represent those operations. The addition (+), subtraction (−), and multiplication (∗) operators are straightforward and do not need any further explanation. However, you might note that an asterisk (∗) is used for multiplication rather than a times symbol (×) so that the computer does not get multiplication confused with the character 'x'.

TABLE 4-1 ARITHMETIC OPERATORS
DEFINED IN C++

Operation	Symbol
Add	+
Subtract	−
Multiply	∗
Divide	/
Remainder (Modulus)	%

The division operator needs some special attention. This operator will generate a result that is the same data type of the operands used in the operation. Thus, if you divide two integers you will get an integer result. If you divide one or more decimal floating point values, you get a decimal result. Thus, 10 / 3 = 3 and 10.0 / 3 = 3.333333. Here, the former is integer division and generates an integer result. The latter is floating point division and generates a floating point result.

Finally, the remainder, or modulus, operator is only defined for integer operands. You will get a compile error if you try to apply it to floating point values. The modulus operator (%) simply generates the remainder that occurs when you divide two integers. For example, the result of 5 % 3 is 2, 5 % 4 is 1, and 5 % 5 is 0.

Let's look at a couple of examples that illustrate these operations. Example 4-1 shows several arithmetic operations on integers, while Example 4-2 deals with arithmetic operations on floating point values.

Example 4-1:

What value will be computed as the result of each of the following operations?
a. 3 ∗ (−5)
b. 4 ∗ 5 − 10
c. 10 / 3
d. 9 % 3

e. −21 / (−2)

f. −21 % (−2)

g. 4 * 5 / 2 + 5 % 2

Solution:

a. 3 * (−5) computes the value −15.

b. 4 * 5 − 10 computes the value 10. Note that the multiplication operation is performed before the subtraction operation.

c. 10 / 3 computes the value 3, since this is integer division.

d. 9 % 3 computes the value 0, since there is no remainder.

e. −21 / (−2) computes the integer quotient, 10.

f. −21 % (−2) computes the remainder, −1.

g. 4 * 5 / 2 + 5 % 2 = (4 * 5) / 2 + (5 % 2) = 20 / 2 + (5 % 2) = 10 + 1 = 11. Notice that the multiplication, *, division, /, and remainder, %, operators are performed first, from left to right. The addition operation is performed last.

Aside from showing how the individual operators work, the foregoing example illustrates the priority, or ordering, of the operators. When more than one operation is performed in an expression, you must know the order in which they will be performed to determine the result. C++ performs operations in the following order:

- All operators within parentheses are performed first.

- If there are nested parentheses (parentheses within parentheses) the innermost operators are performed first.

- The *, /, and % operators are performed next, from left to right within the expression.

- The + and − operators are performed last, from left to right within the expression.

Arithmetic operations on floating point values are basically the same as those on integers, with the exception of division. Remember that the / operator will return a floating point value if either of its operands are floating point. The remainder operation (%) is only defined for integers and will generate a compiler error if you attempt to apply it to floating point values.

When performing several floating point operations within an arithmetic expression, division and multiplication have the same priority. Thus, operators within parentheses are performed first, followed by multiplication and division, followed by addition and subtraction.

Example 4-2:

Evaluate each of the following expressions:
a. 4.6 – 2.0 + 3.2
b. 4.6 – 2.0 * 3.2
c. 4.6 – 2.0 / 2 * 3.2
d. –3.0 * ((4.3 + 2.5) * 2.0) – 1.0
e. –21 / –2
f. –21.0 % –2
g. 10.0 / 3
h. ((4 * 12) / (4 + 12))
i. 4 * 12 / 4 + 12

Solution:

a. 4.6 – 2.0 + 3.2 = (4.6 – 2.0) + 3.2 = 2.6 + 3.2 = 5.8
b. 4.6 – 2.0 * 3.2 = 4.6 – (2.0 * 3.2) = 4.6 – 6.4 = –1.8
c. 4.6 – 2.0 / 2 * 3.2 = 4.6 – ((2.0 / 2) * 3.2) = 4.6 – (1.0 * 3.2) = 4.6 – 3.2 = 1.4
d. –3.0 * ((4.3 + 2.5) * 2.0) – 1.0 = –3.0 * (6.8 * 2.0) – 1.0 = –3.0 * 13.6 – 1.0 = –40.8 – 1.0 = –41.8
e. –21.0 / –2 = 10.5
f. –21.0 % –2 = "Illegal use of floating point error" since % is only defined for integer values.
g. 10.0 / 3 = 3.333333
h. ((4 * 12) / (4 + 12)) = 48 / 16 = 3
i. 4 * 12 / 4 + 12 = 48 / 4 + 12 = 12 + 12 = 24

Notice that I have used parentheses in the solutions for the preceding examples to indicate the order of the operations. As you can see, the parentheses clarify the expression. For this reason, I suggest that you always use parentheses when writing arithmetic expressions. This way, you will always be sure of the order in which the compiler will execute the operators within the expression. Keep in mind, however, that the compiler will always perform the operators within parentheses from inside out, as shown in part (d) of Example 4-2. In particular, notice how the evaluation of part (h) of Example 4-2 differs from part (i). The parentheses in part (h) force C++ to perform the division operation last, after the addition operation. In part (i) the division operation is performed prior to the addition operation, generating a completely different result. This is why you should always use parentheses when writing expressions. It is better to be safe then sorry!

The Increment and Decrement Operators

There are many times in a program when you will need to increment (add 1) or decrement (subtract 1) a variable. The increment and decrement operators shown in Table 4-2 are provided for this purpose.

TABLE 4-2 INCREMENT AND DECREMENT OPERATORS

Operation	Symbol
increment	++
decrement	--

Increment/decrement can be applied to both integer and floating point variables, as well as character variables. An increment operation adds 1 to the value of a variable. Thus, $++x$ is equivalent to $x + 1$. Conversely, a decrement operation subtracts 1 from the value of a variable. As a result, $--x$ is equivalent to $x - 1$. Here's a short example to illustrate increment/decrement:

Example 4-3

Determine the output generated by the following program:

```
// EXAMPLE 4-3 (E4-3.CPP)
#include <iostream.h>

void main()
{
  int x = 5;
  int y = 10;
  cout << " x = " << ++x << '\n';
  cout << " x = " << --x << '\n';
  cout << " y = " << (y = ++x - 2) << '\n';
  x = 5;
  cout << " y = " << (y = x++ - 2) << '\n';
  cout << " x = " << x << '\n';
  x = 0;
  cout << " y = " << (y = x-- -2) << '\n';
  cout << " x = " << x << '\n';
}
```

Solution:

Here is the output that you will see on the monitor:

$$x = 6$$
$$x = 5$$
$$y = 4$$
$$y = 3$$
$$x = 6$$
$$y = -2$$
$$x = -1$$

Notice that the variable x is initialized with the value 5 at the start of the program. The first *cout* statement simply increments x to the value 6. The second *cout* statement then decrements x back to the value 5. Next, the third *cout* statement **pre-increments** the value of x, then subtracts 2 from its value. We say that x is pre-incremented since the increment symbol appears before x and the increment operation is performed *before* x is used in the expression. Thus, the expression reduces to $x + 1 - 2 = 5 + 1 - 2 = 4$. Finally, the fourth *cout* statement involves a **post-increment** operation on x. A post-increment operation is indicated by the increment symbol following x. So, what's the difference between a pre-increment and a post-increment operation? Well, a pre-increment operation increments the variable *before any expression involving the variable is evaluated.* On the other hand, a post-increment operation increments the variable *after any expression involving the variable is evaluated.* Now, looking at the fourth *cout* statement in the program, you find that x starts out with the value 5. Thus, the expression reduces to $x - 2 = 5 - 2 = 3$. *After* the expression is evaluated, x is incremented to the value 6 as shown by the next *cout* statement. Finally, the last two *cout* statements show the result of a post-decrement operation. Here, x is assigned the value 0 to be used in the expression. Thus, $y = 0 - 2 = -2$. *After* the expression is evaluated, the value of x is decremented to a -1, as shown by the last output value.

From Example 4-3 you see that a variable can be pre–incremented or post-incremented. Likewise a variable can be pre-decremented or post-decremented.

Quick Check

1. List the order in which C++ performs arithmetic operations. Be sure to mention how parentheses are handled.

2. Write a statement using the decrement operator that is equivalent to the statement $x = x - 1$.
3. True or False: The division operator will produce an integer result when either of the operands is an integer.
4. True or False: The modulus operator is only defined for integers.
5. What is the difference between using the pre-increment operator versus the post-increment operator on a variable, especially when the variable is used as part of a compound expression?

4-2 ASSIGNMENT OPERATIONS

An assignment operation stores a value in memory. The value is stored at a location in memory which is accessed by the variable on the left hand side of the assignment operator. As a result, a C++ assignment operator assigns the value on the right side of the operator to the variable appearing on the left side of the operator. Another way to say this is that the variable on the left side of the operator is set to the value on the right side of the operator. The C++ assignment operators are listed in Table 4-3.

TABLE 4-3 ASSIGNMENT OPERATORS
USED IN C++

Operation	Symbol
Simple Assignment	=
Compound Addition Assignment	+=
Compound Subtraction Assignment	−=
Compound Multiplication Assignment	*=
Compound Division Assignment	/=
Compound Remainder Assignment (integers only)	%=

First, let's say a word about the simple assignment operator, =. Although an equals symbol is used for this operator, you cannot think of it as equals. Here's why: Consider the statement $x = x + 1$. If you put this expression on an algebra exam, your professor would mark it wrong, since x cannot be equal to itself plus

1, right? However, in C++ this expression means to add 1 to x, then assign the resulting value to x. In other words, set x to the value $x + 1$. This is a perfectly legitimate operation. As you will soon find out, equals is a logical operator and uses the symbol == in C++.

The compound assignment operators shown in Table 4-3 simply combine the assignment operator with an arithmetic operator. Suppose that we define x and y as integers, then:

$x \mathrel{+}= y$ is equivalent to $x = x + y$

$x \mathrel{-}= y$ is equivalent to $x = x - y$

$x \mathrel{*}= y$ is equivalent to $x = x * y$

$x \mathrel{/}= y$ is equivalent to $x = x / y$

$x \mathrel{\%}= y$ is equivalent to $x = x \% y$

As you can see, both the increment/decrement operators and the compound assignment operators provide a short-hand notation for writing arithmetic expressions. Get used to this notation, since it will be used extensively in programs throughout the rest of this text.

Quick Check

1. Write a statement using the compound addition assignment operator that is equivalent to the statement $x = x + 5$.

2. Write a statement using the compound division assignment operator that is equivalent to the statement $x = x / y$.

4-3 BOOLEAN OPERATIONS

Boolean operations are those that will generate a logical, or Boolean, result of TRUE or FALSE. In C++, a logical FALSE is equated to a 0 and a logical TRUE is equated to a 1. Actually, *any non–zero* value is considered TRUE when applied to a Boolean operation in C++. There are two categories of Boolean operators: *relational* and *logical* operators.

Relational Operators

Relational operators allow two quantities to be compared. The six common relational operators available in C++ are listed in Table 4-4.

TABLE 4-4 THE SIX RELATIONAL OPERATORS USED IN C++

Mathematical Symbol	C++ Operator	Meaning
=	==	Equal to
≠	!=	Not equal to
<	<	Less than
≤	<=	Less than or equal to
>	>	Greater than
≥	>=	Greater than or equal to

The relational operators in Table 4-4 can be used to compare any two variables or expressions. In general, you should only compare data of the same data type. This means that integers should be compared to integers, floating point to floating point, and characters to characters. The one exception to this rule is that floating point values can be compared to integers, since integers are reals. In all cases, the operation generates a Boolean result of TRUE or FALSE. Let's look at some examples.

Example 4-4:

Evaluate the following relational operations:

a. $5 == 5$
b. $0.025 >= 0.333$
c. $3 \; != 3$
d. $-45.2 < -3$
e. 'A' < 'Z'
f. $x = 25, y = -10$
   $x <= y$

Solution:

a. TRUE , since 5 equals 5.

b. FALSE, since 0.025 is not greater than or equal to 0.333.

c. FALSE, since 3 equals 3.

d. TRUE, since −45.2 is less than −3.

e. TRUE, since C++ is actually comparing the ASCII value of 'A' to the ASCII value of 'Z'.

f. FALSE, since the value assigned to x (25) is not less than or equal to the value assigned to y (−10).

Relational operators can also be combined with arithmetic operators, like this:

$$5 + 3 < 4$$

Now the question is: How does the computer evaluate this expression? Does it perform the addition operation or the relational operation first? If it performs the addition operation first, the result is FALSE. However, if it performs the relational operation first, 3 is less than 4 and the result is TRUE. As you might suspect, the addition operation is performed first, then the relational operation. Consequently, the result is FALSE, since 8 is not less than 4. Remember, when relational operators are combined with arithmetic operators within an expression, the relational operators are always performed last.

In the next chapter, you will see how relational operators are used within a C++ program to test data prior to making decisions.

Example 4-5:

Both arithmetic and relational operators can be part of an output statement to evaluate an expression. Determine the output generated by the following program:

```
// EXAMPLE 4-5 (E4-5.CPP)
#include <iostream.h>

void main()
{
   cout << (3 + 4) << '\n';
   cout << ('J' > 'K') << '\n';
   cout << (3 * 10 % 3 - 2 > 20 / 6 + 4) << '\n';
}
```

Solution:

The output generated by the above program is:

7
0
0

The first output line is obvious, since 3 + 4 = 7. The remaining output lines are logical values based on the evaluation of the respective relational operations. Remember that a logical FALSE is represented by a 0 and a logical TRUE by a 1 in C++. Thus, the result of 'J' > 'K' is 0 (FALSE) since the ASCII value for 'J' is not greater than the ASCII value for 'K'. Finally, the result of the last expression is 0 (FALSE). Here, the evaluation process goes like this:

$$(((3 * 10) \ \% \ 3) - 2) > ((20 \ / \ 6) + 4) =$$
$$((30 \ \% \ 3) - 2) > (3 + 4) =$$
$$0 - 2 > 7 =$$
$$-2 > 7 =$$
$$0 \ (\text{FALSE})$$

Notice that the multiplication operation is performed first, followed by the % and / operators, from left to right. Then the addition/subtraction operators are performed, and finally the greater-than operation is performed.

Logical Operators

Logical operators also generate logical results. The three logical operators used in C++ are given in Table 4-5.

TABLE 4-5 LOGICAL
OPERATORS USED iN C++

Operation	Symbol
NOT	!
OR	‖
AND	&&

From the table you see that the exclamation symbol (!) is used for NOT, the double vertical bar symbols (‖) for OR, and the double ampersand symbols (&&) for AND. The NOT operator is used to negate, or invert, a logical value. Since there are only two possible logical values (TRUE and FALSE), the negation of one results in the other. For example, suppose we define a logical variable A. Then the variable A can take on only two values, TRUE or FALSE. If A is TRUE, then $!A$ is FALSE. Conversely, if A is FALSE, then $!A$ is TRUE. This operation can be shown using a truth table, as follows:

A	!A
0	1
1	0

As you can see, the 0 and 1 representations for FALSE and TRUE are employed in the truth table.

The OR operation is applied to multiple logical variables. For instance, suppose that A and B are both defined as logical variables. Then A and B can be either TRUE (non-zero) or FALSE (zero). The OR operator dictates that if either A or B are TRUE, the result of the operation is TRUE. In terms of a truth table:

A B	A ∥ B
0 0	0
0 1	1
1 0	1
1 1	1

Notice from the table that $A \parallel B$ is TRUE whenever A is TRUE or B is TRUE. Of course, if both A and B are TRUE, the result is TRUE.

The AND operator also operates on multiple logical values. Here, if A and B are logical variables, then the expression $A \;\&\&\; B$ is TRUE (non-zero) only when both A and B are both TRUE (non-zero). In terms of a truth table:

A B	A && B
0 0	0
0 1	0
1 0	0
1 1	1

The logical operators can also be applied to logical expressions. For example, consider the following:

$$(-6 < 0) \;\&\&\; (12 >= 10)$$

Is this expression TRUE or FALSE? Well, $-6 < 0$ is TRUE and $12 >= 10$ is TRUE. Consequently, the expression must be TRUE, thereby generating a result of 1. How about this one?

$$((3 - 6) == 3) \;||\; (\;!\;(2 == 4))$$

You must evaluate both sides of the expression. If either side is TRUE, then the result is TRUE. On the left side, $3 - 6$ is equal to -3, which is not equal to 3. Thus, the left side is FALSE. On the right side, $2 == 4$ is FALSE, but NOT ($2 == 4$) must be TRUE. Consequently, the right side of the expression is TRUE. This makes the result of the ORing operation TRUE, which would generate a result of 1 in C++.

Observe in the two foregoing expressions that parentheses are used to define the expressions being operated upon. Remember to do this whenever you use a logical operator to evaluate two or more expressions. In other words, always enclose the things you are ORing and ANDing within parentheses.

You will see in Chapter 5 how these logical operators are used to make decisions that control the flow of a program. For example, using the AND operator, you can test to see if two conditions are TRUE. If both conditions are TRUE, the program will execute a series of statements, while skipping those statements if one of the test conditions is FALSE.

Finally, you should be aware that C++ also includes *bitwise* logical operators that perform the respective logical operations on the individual bits of one or more operands. These bitwise logical operators will be introduced later in the text when an application requires their use.

 Quick Check

1. Operators that allow two values to be compared are called _____ operators.
2. In C++, a logical FALSE is equated to the value _____.
3. What is the difference between the = operator and the == operator in C++.
4. What value is generated as a result of the following operation?

   $4 > 5 - 2$

5. What value is generated as a result of the following operation?

   $(5 \;!= 5) \;\&\&\; (3 == 3)$

4-4 THE STANDARD FUNCTIONS IN C++

In Chapter 3, you were acquainted with several standard functions such as *sqrt()*, *getline()*, etc. Standard operations such as these are so common in programming that C++ includes them as built–in functions. There are literally hundreds of standard functions available in the various C++ header files. The tables that follow list some of the more commonly used functions. I should caution you, however, that different versions of C++ have different standard functions available. In this text, we will use the functions available in the TURBO C++ compiler. Check your C++ compiler reference manual for functions that might be available in your compiler, if you are not using TURBO C++.

As you progress through this text, you will be using some of these functions and they will be discussed in more detail at that time. As a result, do not worry about learning them now. Simply scan each table to get an idea of what functions are available. The tables that follow simply list the function, its header file, and a short description of its operation. Space does not permit a detailed discussion of each function. However, a detailed discussion of each function is provided in your compiler reference manual. If you are using TURBO C++, you can get on-line descriptions of each function. All you have to do is press Ctrl F1 from within the TURBO edit mode and select the function of interest from the on-line help index. Other compilers also provide this on-line help feature.

Mathematical Functions

Mathematical functions perform an arithmetic operation. As a result, these functions require a numeric argument and return a numeric result. For this reason, they are sometimes called numeric functions. Some standard mathematical functions are listed in Table 4-6.

Most of the operations in Table 4-6 should be familiar to you from your background in mathematics. When using any of these functions in C++, you must make sure that the argument is the correct data type as specified by the function definition. In addition, any variable assigned to the function must be defined as the same data type returned by the function.

TABLE 4-6 SOME STANDARD MATHEMATICAL FUNCTIONS AVAILABLE
IN C++

Function	Header File	Operation
abs()	math.h	Returns the absolute value of the argument.
acos()	math.h	Returns the arc cosine of the argument (radians).
asin()	math.h	Returns the arc sine of the argument (radians).
atan()	math.h	Returns the arc tangent of the argument (radians).
complex()	complex.h	Creates a complex number.
cos()	math.h	Returns the cosine of the argument (radians).
hypot()	math.h	Returns the hypotenuse of a right triangle.
imag()	complex.h	Returns the imaginary portion of a complex number.
log()	math.h	Returns the natural log of the argument.
log10()	math.h	Returns the base 10 log of the argument.
polar()	complex.h	Returns a complex number for a given magnitude and angle.
pow()	math.h	Returns x raised to the power of y.
pow10()	math.h	Returns 10 raised to the power of y.
rand()	stdlib.h	Generates a random number between 0 and $2^{15}-1$.
random()	stdlib.h	Returns a random number between 0 and (argument $-$ 1).
randomize()	stdlib.h	Initializes random number generator and should be used prior to *rand()* or *random()*.
real()	complex.h	Returns the real portion of a complex number.
sin()	math.h	Returns the sine of the argument (radians).
sqrt()	math.h	Returns the square root of the argument.
tan()	math.h	Returns the tangent of the argument (radians).

Conversion Functions

The conversion functions listed in Table 4-7 convert one type of data to another
type, usually between integer and character data types.

TABLE 4-7 SOME STANDARD CONVERSION FUNCTIONS
AVAILABLE IN C++

Function Name	Header File	Operation
atoi()	stdlib.h	Converts a string to an integer.
itoa()	stdlib.h	Converts an integer to a string.
toascii()	ctype.h	Converts a character to its ASCII value.
tolower()	ctype.h	Converts a character to lowercase.
toupper()	ctype.h	Converts a character to uppercase.

String Functions

The standard C++ string functions are used to manipulate strings. Since string processing is a large part of many application programs, these functions are often very useful. The functions listed in Table 4-8 provide some of the more common string manipulation routines.

TABLE 4-8 SOME STRING FUNCTIONS AVAILABLE IN C++

Function Name	Header File	Operation
strcat()	string.h	Appends one string to another.
strcmp()	string.h	Compares two strings.
strcpy()	string.h	Copies a string.
strlen()	string.h	Calculates the length of a string not including the null terminator.

A string function of special interest is the *strcpy()* function. This function should be used when assigning strings to string variables. As an example, consider the following string variable definition:

char Name[31];

Now, suppose that you wish to assign a string value to the *Name* string. The following statements *will not* compile:

Name[] = "Brenda";   or   Name = "Brenda";

The reason that these assignments will not work is that the string variable, *Name*, is actually a memory address. Thus, you are attempting to assign a character string value to an address value. This is called a ***data type mismatch*** and will not compile. To assign string data, you must use the *strcpy()* function to copy the string value into the string storage area like this:

strcpy(Name,"Brenda");

Of course, you must include the *string.h* header file in the program for this statement to compile.

Example 4-6

The string compare, *strcmp()*, function should be used when comparing strings rather than the Boolean relational operators. The reason is that the Boolean relational operators are not reliable when comparing strings. Let's see what happens when the following program is executed:

```
// EXAMPLE 4-6 (E4-6.CPP)

#include <iostream.h>
#include <string.h>

void main()
{
   cout << strcmp("Janet","Janet") << '\n';
   cout << ("Janet" == "Janet") << '\n';
   cout << strcmp("JANET","Janet") << '\n';;
   cout << strcmp("Janet","JANET") << '\n';
}
```

Solution:

The foregoing program first uses the *strcmp()* function to compare the string "Janet" to the string "Janet". The second line of the program also compares "Janet" to "Janet" using the == relational operator. If you look up the operation of *strcmp()* you will find that it returns a 0 if the two strings are equal, a negative value if the first string argument is less than the second string argument, and a positive value if the first string is greater than the second string. How are the two strings compared? Well, recall that each character in the string is represented by an ASCII value. The *strcmp()* function simply compares the individual ASCII values one character at a time from left to right until an unequal condition occurs or it runs out of characters. Here is the output of the program:

0
0
−32
32

Notice that the output of the first statement is a 0, correctly indicating that according to the *strcmp()* function, the two strings are equal. However, the output of the second statement, which uses the Boolean relational operator == , is also 0. As you know, this means FALSE, thereby erroneously indicating that the two strings are unequal. In the third statement, the *strcmp()* function generates a negative value of −32, correctly indicating that "JANET" is less than "Janet". Finally, in the last statement, the *strcmp()* function generates a positive value of 32, correctly indicating that "Janet" is greater than "JANET".

I/O Functions

The C++ language includes a wide range of functions that can be used for I/O, some of which are shown in Table 4-9. Most of these functions are included in the *stdio.h* and *conio.h* header files. The I/O functions in these header files were developed early in the life of the original C language to facilitate different specialized forms of I/O. Be aware, however, that *conio.h* is only available on compilers that run on the DOS platform.

TABLE 4-9 SOME COMMON I/O FUNCTIONS DEFINED FOR C++

Function Name	Header File	Operation
cgets()	conio.h	Reads a string from console and stores string length.
cprintf()	conio.h	Writes formatted output to text window.
cputs()	conio.h	Writes string to the text window.
cscanf()	conio.h	Scans and formats console input.
getc()	stdio.h	Gets one character from a stream.
getch()	stdio.h	Gets one character from the console without echo.
getche()	stdio.h	Gets one character from the console with echo.
gets()	stdio.h	Gets a string from the stdin file.
printf()	stdio.h	Sends formatted output to the stdout file.
putc()	stdio.h	Writes one character to a stream.
putch()	stdio.h	Writes one character to the text window.
putchar()	stdio.h	Writes one character to the stdout file.
puts()	stdio.h	Writes a string to the stdout file and add a new line.
scanf()	stdio.h	Gets formatted input from the stdin file.
ungetc()	stdio.h	Pushes one character back to the input stream.
ungetch	conio.h	Pushes one character back to the keyboard buffer.

You should be aware that many of these functions, especially the input functions, are tricky to use and are referred to as "unsafe," since you often get unpredictable results. This is why I have attempted to stay with *cin* and *cout* where possible when performing I/O operations. Recall that *cin* and *cout* are objects, not functions, and therefore are only defined for the C++ language and not the C language. Up to this point, we have only used the *gets()* function because *cin* was not reliable for reading strings under certain conditions. We will also use other I/O functions in the future, should the need arise.

Graphics Functions

One reason that C and C++ are very popular commercial languages is the inherent flexibility of the operations that can be performed through the use of the functions available in the various header files. These functions provide the ability to operate on everything from single bits, as you might in assembly language programming, to screen graphics, as you might in a very high-level language. The graphics functions listed in Table 4-10 illustrate the latter.

As mentioned earlier, these are just a few of the many standard functions available in the various C++ header files. Remember that different C++ compilers provide different built-in functions. Consult your compiler reference manual for a complete listing of all available functions.

TABLE 4-10 SOME GRAPHICS FUNCTIONS AVAILABLE IN C++

Function Name	Header File	Operation
circle()	graphics.h	Draws a circle at (x,y) of a given radius.
ellipse()	graphics.h	Draws an eliptical arc.
fillellipse()	graphics.h	Draws and fills an ellipse.
fillpoly()	graphics.h	Draws and fills a polygon.
getx()	graphics.h	Returns the x-coordinate of the cursor position.
gety()	graphics.h	Returns the y-coordinate of the cursor position.
gotoxy()	conio.h	Positions the cursor at coordinate (x,y).
textbackground()	conio.h	Sets the text background color.
textcolor()	conio.h	Sets the text color.

Quick Check

1. In order to use a standard function in your program, you must include its _____.

2. Explain how you can get an on–line description of a standard function using your compiler.

3. What function must be employed to assign string data to a string variable in your program?

4. Write a statement that will assign the string "C++" to a string variable called *Compiler*.

5. Why should the *strcmp()* function be used instead of Boolean relational operators when comparing string values?

Now, read over the following case studies, since they illustrate many of the concepts discussed up to this point in the text.

CASE STUDY: INVENTORY CONTROL

Problem:

The following is an partial inventory listing of items in the sporting goods department of Ma and Pa's General Store:

Item	Quantity	Units Sold This Month
Fishing line	132 spools	24 spools
Fish hooks	97 packages	45 packages
Sinkers	123 packages	37 packages
Fish nets	12 ea.	5 ea.

Write a program that will print a monthly report showing the item name, beginning quantity, units sold this month, ending quantity, and percent of quantity sold.

The problem solution begins with the problem definition phase.

The Problem Definition

Output: The program must generate a printed monthly report of the item name, beginning quantity, units sold this month, ending quantity, and percent of quantity sold. Now is a good time to develop the printout format. Suppose we use a tabular format like this:

<u>ITEM</u> <u>BEGIN QTY</u> <u>UNITS SOLD</u> <u>ENDING QTY</u> <u>% SOLD</u>

Input: Ma or Pa must enter the inventory data shown in the above table. Therefore, the program must be *very* user-friendly.

Processing: Since the item, beginning quantity, and units sold are entered by Ma or Pa, the program must use this information to calculate two things: the ending quantity, and the percent sold. The ending quantity is found by simply subtracting the units sold from the beginning quantity, like this:

$$Ending\ Qty.\ =\ Beginning\ Qty.\ -\ Units\ Sold$$

The percent sold is found by dividing the units sold by the beginning quantity and multiplying by 100% like this:

$$\%\ Sold\ =\ (Units\ Sold\ /\ Beginning\ Qty.)\ \times\ 100\%$$

Now for the algorithm:

The Algorithm

BEGIN
    Write a program description message.
    Write a user prompt to enter the month.
    Read (*Month*).
    Print the header information.
    Write a user prompt to enter the item name.
    Read (*Item*).
    Write a user prompt to enter the beginning quantity.
    Read (*Beginning Qty*).
    Write a user prompt to enter the number of units sold.

Read (*Units Sold*).
Calculate *Ending Qty. = Beginning Qty. – Units Sold*
Calculate *% Sold = (Units Sold / Beginning Qty.) × 100 %*
Print *Item, Beginning Qty., Units Sold, Ending Qty.*, and *% Sold.*
Repeat the above processing for the remaining sales items.
END.

Given our problem definition, the foregoing algorithm is straightforward. Ma or Pa must enter the beginning inventory information. Then, the program will make the required calculations and print the report. In developing the algorithm, you would quickly realize that the processing is the same for each sales item. As a result, a single *repeat* statement is added at the end of the algorithm, rather than actually repeating all of the algorithm statements five more times. This has been done to make the algorithm more efficient.

Now the job is to code this algorithm in C++. With your present knowledge of C++, coding most of the algorithm should not present a problem. But what about the repeat statement at the end of the algorithm? Well, notice that this statement requires that you go back and repeat many of the previous statements over and over until all the items are processed. Such a repeating operation is called an **iteration**, or **looping**, operation. To date, you do not have the C++ tools to perform such an operation. So, we will have to repeat all of the processing steps four times in our program for each of the four sales items. In Chapter 6, you will learn how to perform iterative operations in C++, thus making the code much more efficient.

Here's the straight line program:

The Program

```
// CASE 1 (CASE4-1.CPP)

// OUTPUT:    A PRINTED MONTHLY REPORT OF THE
//            ITEM NAME, BEGINNING QUANTITY,
//            UNITS SOLD THIS MONTH, ENDING
//            QUANTITY, AND PERCENT OF QUANTITY
//            SOLD

// INPUT:     MA OR PA ENTER THE INVENTORY DATA SHOWN
//            IN THE ABOVE TABLE.

// PROCESSING:   THE PROGRAM MUST CALCULATE TWO THINGS:
//               ENDING QUANTITY AND THE PERCENT SOLD.
```

```cpp
#include <iostream.h>
#include <stdio.h>
#include <iomanip.h>
#include <fstream.h>
#include <process.h>

void main()
{
  char Month[10];          // MONTH OF REPORT
  char Item[20];           // SALES ITEM
  float Begin_Qty;         // BEGINNING QUANTITY OF SALES ITEM
  float Units_Sold;        // NUMBER OF UNITS SOLD THIS MONTH
  float End_Qty;           // ENDING QUANTITY OF SALES ITEM
  float Percent_Sold;      // PERCENT OF SALES ITEM SOLD


//*******************************************************************************
//
// THIS SEGMENT OF CODE DEFINES "print" AS AN OUTPUT
// FILE POINTING TO YOUR PRINTER PORT (PRN)
//
//*******************************************************************************

  ofstream print;          // DEFINE PRINT AN OUTPUT FILE STREAM
  print.open("PRN");       // OPEN PRINT FILE AND POINT TO PRN
  if (!print)              // MAKE SURE PRINTER IS READY
  {
    cout << "There is a problem with the printer.\n";
    exit(1);
  }

// DISPLAY PROGRAM DESCRIPTION MESSAGE
  print << setprecision(2);
  cout << "Dear Ma or Pa\n\n"
          "You will be asked to enter four sales items, one at\n"
          "a time.  With each item you will be asked to enter\n"
          "the item name, the beginning quantity, and the quantity\n"
          "sold this month.  The computer will then print a monthly\n"
          "inventory report for the sales items.\n\n\\n";

// GET THE MONTH AND PRINT HEADINGS
  cout << "Please enter the month:  ";
  gets(Month);
  print << "\n\nMONTH:  " << Month;
```

```
        print << "\n\n\n" << setw(15) << "ITEM" << setw(15) << "BEGIN QTY"
               << setw(15) << "UNITS SOLD" << setw(15) << "ENDING QTY"
               << setw(10) << "% SOLD";
        print << '\n' << setw(15) << "----" << setw(15) << "---------"
               << setw(15) << "----------" << setw(15) << "----------"
               << setw(10) << "------\n";

     // GET ITEM INFORMATION, CALCULATE, AND PRINT RESULTS
        cout << "\nPlease enter the item name:  ";
        gets(Item);
        cout << "\nPlease enter the beginning quantity of " << Item << " :  ";
        cin >> Begin_Qty;
        cout << "\nPlease enter the number of units of " << Item
               << " sold in " << Month << " :  ";
        cin >> Units_Sold;
        End_Qty = Begin_Qty - Units_Sold;
        Percent_Sold = (Units_Sold / Begin_Qty) * 100;
        print << setw(15) << Item << setw(15) << Begin_Qty
               << setw(15) << Units_Sold << setw(15) << End_Qty
               << setw(10) << Percent_Sold << '\n';

     // GET ITEM INFORMATION, CALCULATE, AND PRINT RESULTS
        cout << "\nPlease enter the item name:  ";
        gets(Item);
        cout << "\nPlease enter the beginning quantity of " << Item << " :  ";
        cin >> Begin_Qty;
        cout << "\nPlease enter the number of units of " << Item
               << " sold in " << Month << " :  ";
        cin >> Units_Sold;
        End_Qty = Begin_Qty - Units_Sold;
        Percent_Sold = (Units_Sold / Begin_Qty) * 100;
        print << setw(15) << Item << setw(15) << Begin_Qty
               << setw(15) << Units_Sold << setw(15) << End_Qty
               << setw(10) << Percent_Sold << '\n';

     // GET ITEM INFORMATION, CALCULATE, AND PRINT RESULTS
        cout << "\nPlease enter the item name:  ";
        gets(Item);
        cout << "\nPlease enter the beginning quantity of " << Item << " :  ";
        cin >> Begin_Qty;
        cout << "\nPlease enter the number of units of " << Item
               << " sold in " << Month << " :  ";
        cin >> Units_Sold;
```

```
End_Qty = Begin_Qty - Units_Sold;
Percent_Sold = (Units_Sold / Begin_Qty) * 100;
print << setw(15) << Item << setw(15) << Begin_Qty
      << setw(15) << Units_Sold << setw(15) << End_Qty
      << setw(10) << Percent_Sold << '\n';

// GET ITEM INFORMATION, CALCULATE, AND PRINT RESULTS
cout << "\nPlease enter the item name:  ";
gets(Item);
cout << "\nPlease enter the beginning quantity of " << Item << " : ";
cin >> Begin_Qty;
cout << "\nPlease enter the number of units of " << Item
     << " sold in " << Month << " : ";
cin >> Units_Sold;
End_Qty = Begin_Qty - Units_Sold;
Percent_Sold = (Units_Sold / Begin_Qty) * 100;
print << setw(15) << Item << setw(15) << Begin_Qty
      << setw(15) << Units_Sold << setw(15) << End_Qty
      << setw(10) << Percent_Sold << '\n';

// CLOSE PRINT FILE
print.close();
}
```

Using the sales data provided, this program will generate the following inventory report:

MONTH: May

ITEM	BEGIN QTY	UNITS SOLD	ENDING QTY	%SOLD
Fishing Line	132	24	108	18.18
Fish Hooks	97	45	52	46.39
Sinkers	123	37	86	30.08
Fish Nets	12	5	7	41.67

Again, notice how a whole block of C++ code is repeated four times to process the four sales items. Wouldn't it be nice to simply code the processing steps once and then tell the computer to repeat these steps the required number of times? Such a repeating operation would make our coding much more efficient, wouldn't it?

You should be able to understand the above C++ code, given the material presented up to this point in the text. However, there is one small, but important, point that needs some discussion. Look at the *Percent_Sold* calculation in the program. Notice that it is obtained by dividing the *Units_Sold* by the *Begin_Qty* and multiplying by 100. Now, you see that in the definition section at the top of the program that both *Units_Sold* and *Begin_Qty* are defined as floating point values. Well, why couldn't they be defined as integers, since both will always be whole number values, right? The reason that you can't define them as integers is that if you divide two integers using the / operator you will get an integer result. Thus, if the units sold were 10 and the beginning quantity were 100, the *integer* quotient would be 10 / 100 = 0. As a result, the *Percent_Sold* would be 0 which is obviously incorrect. So, the solution is to define *Units_Sold* and *Begin_Qty* as floating point values. Then dividing the two will yield a floating point result. Using the values above you would get 10 / 100 = 0.1, resulting in a correct value of 10% sold.

One final point: Since the inventory report is a printed output, all of the processing for one sales item can be performed and then printed before processing the next sales item. As a result, there only needs to be one set of variables instead of four sets. Could this be done if the output were a display rather than a printout? Why?

CASE STUDY: DATA COMMUNICATIONS

Problem:

In the field of data communications, binary digital computer data are converted to analog sine wave data for transmission over long distances via the telephone network. This idea is illustrated in Figure 4-1. Here, a binary 1 is represented by a sine wave of a high amplitude, while a binary 0 is represented by another sine wave of a lower amplitude. This is called **amplitude modulation**. Since binary data are represented using a sine wave, the study of data communications often requires the analysis of a sine wave. One such analysis is to find the amplitude, in volts, of a sine wave at any given point in time. This is called the **instantaneous value** of the sine wave and is found using the following equation.

$$v = V_{peak} \, Sin(2\pi \, ft)$$

where:

v is the instantaneous voltage at any point in time, t, on the waveform.
V_{peak} is the peak amplitude of the waveform in volts.

π is the constant 3.14159.

f is the frequency of the waveform in Hertz.

t is the time, in seconds, for v.

Write a program to find the instantaneous voltage value of the sine wave in Figure 4-1. Have the user enter the peak voltage in volts, the frequency in kilohertz, and the time in milliseconds.

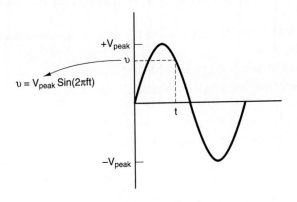

Figure 4-1 A sine wave for Case 2

The Problem Definition

Output: The program must display the instantaneous voltage value, v, resulting from the above equation.

Input: The user must enter the following information:

- The peak amplitude of the waveform, V_{peak}, in volts.

- The frequency of the waveform, f, in kilohertz.

- The point in time, t, in milliseconds for which the instantaneous voltage must be calculated.

Processing: The program must calculate the instantaneous voltage value using the given equation.

The Algorithm

BEGIN
Write a program description message.
Write a user prompt to enter the peak amplitude of the waveform, V_{peak}, in volts.
Read (V_{peak}).
Write a user prompt to enter the frequency of the waveform, f, in kilohertz.
Read (f).
Write a user prompt to enter the time, t, in milliseconds.
Read (t).
Calculate $v = V_{peak} Sin (2\pi \ ft)$.
Write the instantaneous voltage value, v.
END.

Following the algorithm, the coded program is:

The Program

```
// CASE 2 (CASE4-2.CPP)

// OUTPUT:     THE PROGRAM MUST DISPLAY
//             THE INSTANTANEOUS VOLTAGE VALUE, V,
//             RESULTING FROM THE ABOVE EQUATION.

// INPUT:      THE USER MUST ENTER THE FOLLOWING:
//             THE PEAK AMPLITUDE OF THE WAVEFORM, VPEAK,
//             IN VOLTS.
//             THE FREQUENCY OF THE WAVEFORM, F,
//             IN KILOHERTZ.
//             THE POINT IN TIME, T, IN MILLISECONDS FOR WHICH
//             THE INSTANTANEOUS VOLTAGE MUST
//             BE CALCULATED.

// PROCESSING:  THE PROGRAM MUST CALCULATE THE
//              INSTANTANEOUS VOLTAGE VALUE.

#include <iostream.h>
#include <math.h>
#include <iomanip.h>
```

```
void main()

{
// DEFINE CONSTANT AND VARIABLES
    const float PI = 3.14159;
    float V_Peak;              // PEAK VOLTAGE IN VOLTS
    float f;                   // FREQUENCY IN KILOHERTZ
    float t;                   // TIME IN MILLISECONDS
    float v;                   // INSTANTANEOUS VOLTAGE IN VOLTS

// DISPLAY PROGRAM DESCRIPTION MESSAGE
    cout << setprecision(2);
    cout << "This program will display the instantaneous voltage\n"
            "value of an AC signal.  You must enter the following\n"
            "three quantities:\n\n";
    cout << "\tPeak voltage of the signal, V_Peak.\n\n"
            "\tFrequency of the signal, f.\n\n"
            "\tThe point in time, t, for which the voltage\n"
            "\tmust be calculated.\n\n\n";
    cout << "Enter the peak signal voltage in volts:  V_Peak = ";
    cin >> V_Peak;
    cout << "\n\nEnter the signal frequency in kilohertz:  f = ";
    cin >> f;
    cout << "\n\nEnter the time in milliseconds:  t = ";
    cin >> t;
    v = V_Peak * sin(2 * PI * f * t);
    cout << "\n\nThe instantaneous voltage at " << t << " milliseconds is\n"
         << v << " volts.";
}
```

It's probably a good idea to take a closer look at some of the features of this program. Here is what you will see on the display after the program has been run:

This program will display the instantaneous voltage
value of an AC signal. You must enter the following
three quantities:

Peak voltage of the signal, V_Peak.

Frequency of the signal, f.

The point in time, t, for which the voltage
must be calculated.

Enter the peak signal voltage in volts: V_Peak = **10.**⏎

Enter the signal frequency in kilohertz: f = **1.**⏎

Enter the time in milliseconds: t = **.125.**⏎

The instantaneous voltage at 0.13 milliseconds is
7.08 volts.

As you can see, the program description message describes the purpose of the program. In addition, it tells the user what values must be entered and identifies the variables to be used for the entered values. Another observation from the above program output is that the user must enter the waveform frequency in kilohertz and the time in milliseconds. These are typical units found in data communications. Notice that the user prompts indicate this entry requirement.

The calculation of the output voltage, *v*, is performed with the following program statement:

$$v = V\_Peak * sin(2 * PI * f * t);$$

The equation does not have to be altered to accommodate *f* in kilohertz and *t* in milliseconds, since the product of these two units cancel each other out (10^{+3} cancels 10^{-3}). Another thing you see from the program statement is the use of the word *PI* to represent the value 3.14159. As you can see, this identifier is declared as a constant at the beginning of the program. One final point: The *sin()* function in C++ is defined to evaluate angles in *radians*. Fortunately, the quantity *(2*PI*f* t)* produces radians and not degrees. If the value to be evaluated by the *sin()* function is in degrees, it must be converted to radians to obtain a correct result. You will see this shortly. To use the *sin()* function you see that the *math.h* header file has been included at the beginning of the program.

CASE STUDY: POLAR AND RECTANGULAR COORDINATES

Problem:

Many times in trigonometry problems you are required to convert between rectangular and polar coordinates. This is especially true in vector analysis, when applied to physics. The vector diagram in Figure 4-2 summarizes the conversion process. As you can see, a vector can be represented in one of two ways.

1. Polar coordinate:

$$M\angle\theta$$

where:

> M is the magnitude, or length, of the vector.
> θ is the angle the vector makes with the horizontal axis.

2. Rectangular coordinate:

$$x + jy$$

where:

> x is the real axis, or horizontal coordinate, for the tip of the vector.
> y is the imaginary axis, or vertical coordinate, for the tip of the vector.
> $j = \sqrt{-1}$, an imaginary number.

Using right angle trigonometry, you can convert between polar and rectangular coordinates. The conversion equations are shown in the figure.

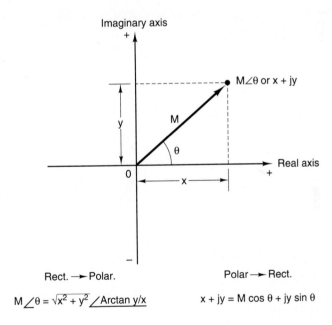

Rect. → Polar.

$$M\angle\theta = \sqrt{x^2 + y^2} \angle \text{Arctan } y/x$$

Polar → Rect.

$$x + jy = M \cos\theta + jy \sin\theta$$

Figure 4-2 Polar/rectangular conversion for Case 3.

Let's write a C++ program that will convert from polar to rectangular coordinates using values supplied by the user. (A program to convert from rectangular to polar is left as a problem for you at the end of the chapter.)

The Problem Definition

Output:
The output will be in tabular form, showing the input polar coordinate and the corresponding rectangular coordinate. The polar coordinate will be displayed in the format M @ θ. The values of M and θ will be displayed as variables and the @ symbol will be displayed as a fixed character. The rectangular coordinate will be displayed using the format: $x + jy$. The values of x and y will be displayed as variables using two decimal places. The $+$ symbol and j character will be displayed as fixed character information.

Input:
The user must enter the magnitude of the vector and the angle it makes with the horizontal axis.

Processing:
The program must calculate x and y as follows:

$$x = M\ Cos\theta$$
$$y = M\ Sin\theta$$

The angle must be converted to radians during the calculation.

Using this problem definition, an appropriate algorithm is:

The Algorithm

BEGIN
   Write a program description message.
   Write a user prompt to enter the vector magnitude, M.
   Read (M).
   Write a user prompt to enter the vector angle, *Angle*, in degrees.
   Read (*Angle*).
   Calculate $x = MCos(Angle)$.

Calculate *y = MSin(Angle)*.
Write the table headings.
Write the polar coordinate, *M @ Angle*.
Write the rectangular coordinate *x + jy*.
END.

Following this algorithm, the coded C++ program is:

The Program

```
// CASE 3 (CASE4-3A.CPP)

// OUTPUT:      THE OUTPUT WILL BE IN TABULAR FORM, SHOWING
//              THE INPUT POLAR COORDINATE AND THE
//              CORRESPONDING RECTANGULAR COORDINATE.
//              THE POLAR COORDINATE WILL BE DISPLAYED
//              IN THE FORMAT M @ ANGLE
//              THE VALUES OF M AND ANGLE WILL BE DISPLAYED
//              AS VARIABLES AND THE @ SYMBOL WILL
//              BE DISPLAYED AS A FIXED CHARACTER.
//              THE RECTANGULAR COORDINATE WILL
//              BE DISPLAYED USING THE FORMAT: X + JY.
//              X AND Y WILL BE DISPLAYED AS VARIABLES USING
//              TWO DECIMAL PLACES.  THE + SYMBOL AND
//              J CHARACTER WILL BE DISPLAYED AS
//              FIXED CHARACTER INFORMATION.

// INPUT:       THE USER MUST ENTER THE MAGNITUDE, M,
//              OF THE VECTOR AND ITS ANGLE.

// PROCESSING:  THE PROGRAM MUST CALCULATE X AND Y AS
//              FOLLOWS:

//              X = M * COS (ANGLE)
//              Y = M * SIN (ANGLE)

//              THE ANGLE MUST BE CONVERTED
//              TO RADIANS DURING THE CALCULATION.

#include <iostream.h>
#include <iomanip.h>
#include <math.h>
```

```
void main()
{
// DEFINE CONSTANT AND VARIABLES
   const  float PI = 3.14159;
   float x;                     // RECTANGULAR X-COORDINATE
   float y;                     // RECTANGULAR Y-COORDINATE
   float M;                     // POLAR MAGNITUDE
   float Angle;                 // POLAR ANGLE

// DISPLAY PROGRAM DESCRIPTION MESSAGE
   cout << "This program will convert polar vector coordinates\n"
           "to rectangular vector coordinates.\n\n\n";

// GET MAGNITUDE AND ANGLE OF VECTOR
   cout << "Enter the magnitude of the vector:  M = ";
   cin >> M;
   cout << "\n\nEnter the vector angle in degrees:  Angle = ";
   cin >> Angle;

// CALCULATE RECTANGULAR COORDINATES
   x = M * cos(PI/180 * Angle);       // (PI/180 * Angle) CONVERTS
                                      // DEGREES TO RADIANS
   y = M * sin(PI/180 * Angle);

// DISPLAY POLAR AND RECTANGULAR VALUES TO USER
   cout << "\n\n\n" << setw (25) << "POLAR COORDINATE"
        << setw(40) << "RECTANGULAR COORDINATE\n";
   cout << setw(25) << "----------------"
        << setw(40) << "----------------------\n\n";
   cout << setprecision(2);
   cout << setw(10) << M << " @ " << setw(6) << Angle << " degrees"
        << setw(23) << x << " + j" << << y;
}
```

This program will generate the following display when executed.

This program will convert polar vector coordinates
to rectangular vector coordinates.

Enter the magnitude of the vector: M = **5**↵

Enter the vector angle in degrees: Angle = **53.13**↵

<u>POLAR COORDINATE</u>   <u>RECTANGULAR COORDINATE</u>

5 @ 53.13 degrees   3 + j4

You should now have the knowledge required to write such a program. One thing that you should note is the conversion from degrees to radians within the *cos()* and *sin()* functions. You must multiply the *Angle* by the quantity (*PI*/180) to get radians. Remember that the *cos()* and *sin()* functions will only evaluate radians, not degrees.

Let's write another program for this task using functions available in the *complex.h* header file. In Table 4-6 you will find three functions called *polar()*, *real()*, and *imag()*. These functions are only available for use on DOS-based compilers. Check your reference manual for similar functions if you are using a compiler that runs on a different platform. The *polar()* function will convert a polar value to a complex rectangular value, given the magnitude and angle of the polar coordinate. The *polar()* function returns a complex value and fortunately C++ includes a *complex* data type. So, we can define a complex variable, say *z*, and assign the complex value returned by *polar()* to *z* like this:

```
complex z;
z = polar(M,Angle);
```

Next, we can use the *real()* and *imag()* functions to extract the real and imaginary portions of *z* like this:

```
real(z);
imag(z);
```

Here's the entire program:

```
// CASE 4-3B  (CASE4-3B.CPP)

#include <iostream.h>
#include <iomanip.h>
#include <complex.h>

void main()
{
// DEFINE CONSTANT AND VARIABLES
   const float PI = 3.14159;
   double M;                        // POLAR MAGNITUDE
```

```
    double Angle;                  // POLAR ANGLE
    complex z;                     // RECTANGULAR COORDINATE

// DISPLAY PROGRAM DESCRIPTION MESSAGE
    cout << "This program will convert polar vector coordinates\n"
            "to rectangular vector coordinates.\n\n\n";

// GET MAGNITUDE AND ANGLE OF VECTOR
    cout << "Enter the magnitude of the vector:  M = ";
    cin >> M;
    cout << "\n\nEnter the vector angle in degrees:  Angle = ";
    cin >> Angle;

// CALCULATE RECTANGULAR COORDINATES
    z = polar(M,PI/180 * Angle);

// DISPLAY POLAR AND RECTANGULAR VALUES TO USER
    cout << "\n\n\n" << setw (25) << "POLAR COORDINATE"
         << setw(40) << "RECTANGULAR COORDINATE\n";
    cout << setw(25) << "----------------"
         << setw(40) << "----------------------\n\n";
    cout << setprecision(2);
    cout << setw(10) << M << " @ " << setw(6) << Angle << " degrees"
         << setw(23) << real(z) << " + j" << imag(z);
}
```

Here you see the power of C++. First you find the variable *z* defined as a complex data type at the beginning of *main()*. To convert the polar value, you simply call the *polar()* function, using the magnitude and angle (in radians). The *polar()* function requires that its arguments be defined as double floating point values. This is why *M* and *Angle* are defined as *double*. The final *cout* statement calls the *real()* and *imag()* functions to obtain the real and imaginary parts, respectively, of *z*. Notice that the *complex.h* header file must be included to use these complex functions. This program will produce the same output as the previous program. That's all there is to it!

CASE STUDY: BOOLEAN LOGIC

Problem:

A common Boolean logic operator that is not available in C++ is the NAND (NOT AND) operation. Given two variables, *A* and *B*, the NAND operation is defined as follows:

A B	*A* NAND *B*
0 0	1
0 1	1
1 0	1
1 1	0

Notice that the NAND operation is simply the opposite of the AND operation. In symbols, *A* NAND *B* = NOT(*A* AND *B*). Write a C++ program that will display the NAND result of two logical values entered by the user.

Let's begin by defining the problem in terms of output, input, and processing.

The Problem Definition

Output: The program must display the logical result of the NAND operation as defined by its truth table.

Input: The user must enter logical values for the input variables, *A* and *B*.

Processing: Although the NAND operation is not available in C++, you can implement it by using the NOT and AND operators like this:

$$A \text{ NAND } B = \text{NOT } (A \text{ AND } B) = !\ (A\ \&\&\ B)$$

Now, the idea is to prompt the user to enter two logical values for *A* and *B* and apply the above relationship to generate a logical result. However, there is one minor difficulty. You cannot read logical values from the keyboard. Instead, you must read character information, test the information for TRUE or FALSE, then make an assignment to the variables, *A* and *B*. Here's an algorithm that will do the job:

The Algorithm

BEGIN
    Write a program description message.
    Write a prompt to enter a logical value of 'T' for TRUE or 'F' for FALSE.
    Read (*Entry*).
    If *Entry* is 'T' then assign TRUE to *A*, else assign FALSE to *A*.
    Write a prompt to enter a logical value of 'T' for TRUE or 'F' for FALSE.
    Read (*Entry*).
    If *Entry* is 'T' then
     Assign TRUE to *B*
    Else
     Assign FALSE to *B*.
    Assign NOT (*A* AND *B*) to NAND.
    Write NAND.
END.

The algorithm shows that a character ('T' or 'F') is read in, then tested to see if it is a 'T' or 'F'. An assignment is then made to the logical variable, depending on the test. If the character is a 'T', then TRUE is assigned to the logical variable, else FALSE is assigned to the variable. This testing operation is called an *If/Else* operation, for obvious reasons. You will learn more about this in Chapter 5. Once the logical values have been assigned, the NAND operation is performed and the result is displayed. Here's the program:

The Program

```
// CASE 4-4 (CASE4-4.CPP)

// OUTPUT:    THE PROGRAM MUST DISPLAY THE
//            LOGICAL RESULT OF THE NAND OPERATION
```

```
// INPUT:       THE USER MUST ENTER LOGICAL VALUES FOR
//              THE INPUT VARIABLES, A AND B.

// PROCESSING:  A NAND B = NOT (A AND B) = ! (A && B)

#include <iostream.h>

void main()
{
  char Entry;        // USER ENTRY
  int NAND;          // RESULT OF NAND OPERATION
  int A;             // BOOLEAN VALUE
  int B;             // BOOLEAN VALUE

  cout << "This program will generate a NAND (not AND) result\n"
          "from two Boolean values that you must enter.\n\n\n";
  cout << "Enter a Boolean value (T for TRUE or F for FALSE):  A = ";
  cin >> Entry;
  if ((Entry == 'T') || (Entry == 't'))
     A = 1;
  else
     A = 0;
  cout << "\nEnter a Boolean value (T for TRUE or F for FALSE):  B = ";
  cin >> Entry;
  if ((Entry == 'T') || (Entry == 't'))
     B = 1;
  else
     B = 0;
  NAND = !(A && B);
  if (NAND != 0)
     cout << "\n\nThe NAND result is:  TRUE";
  else
     cout << "\n\nThe NAND result is:  FALSE";
}
```

This program will generate the NAND (NOT AND) result, given two logical values entered by the user. One thing you will notice is that the variables (*A* and *B*) are defined as integers. This is required since the logical FALSE and TRUE values are represented in C++ as the integers 0 and 1, respectively. You see that the variables (*A* and *B*) are assigned a 1 *if* the user enters a 'T' or 't', *else* the variables are assigned a 0. Notice also that the logical OR operator, ||, is employed to accept either a 't' or 'T' input character. Once the variable assignments are made, the NAND expression is evaluated and assigned to the integer variable *NAND*. Finally, *NAND* is tested using an *if/else* statement to produce the correct output. Don't worry about the *if/else* statement syntax now, since it is covered in the next chapter. At this time, it is only important that you understand the program logic.

CHAPTER SUMMARY

Arithmetic operations in C++ include the common add, subtract, multiply, and divide operations that can be performed on any numeric data type. Addition, subtraction, multiplication, and division are basically the same for both the integer and floating point data types. However, when you divide two integers you will get an integer result. If you need a floating point result, the operands must be defined as floating point values and not integer values. The remainder (%) operator is only defined for integers and will generate a compile error if used with floating point values.

There are increment/decrement operators defined in C++. The increment operator, ++, adds one to a variable and the decrement operator, —, subtracts one from a variable. You can pre-increment/decrement a variable or post-increment/decrement a variable. There's a big difference when the increment/decrement is used as part of an expression to be evaluated by C++. A pre-increment/decrement operation on a variable is performed before the expression is evaluated while a post-increment/decrement operation is performed on the variable after the expression is evaluated.

The simple assignment operator in C++ is the = operator. A value on the right side of the = operator is assigned to a variable on the left side of the operator. There are compound assignment operators such as +=, *=, etc. that combine an arithmetic operation with the assignment operation. These operators are used as a form of short hand notation within a C++ program.

Logical operators are those that generate a logical result of TRUE or FALSE. In C++, a logical value of FALSE is represented by the integer 0, while a logical TRUE is represented by the integer 1, or any non-zero value. The two categories of logical operators in C++ are relational and logical operators. Relational operators allow two quantities to be compared. These operators include ==, != , > , < , <=, and >=. Logical operators perform logic operations on logical values to generate a logical result. The standard logical operators available in C++ are ! (NOT), || (OR), and && (AND).

Finally, the C++ header files include several standard functions that can be used to perform common tasks. There are mathematical functions, conversion functions, I/O functions, and graphics functions, just to mention a few categories. Consult your C++ compiler reference manual for a categorized listing of all the standard functions available with your compiler.

QUESTIONS AND PROBLEMS

Questions

1. What value will be returned for each of the following integer operations:
   a. 4 – 2 * 3
   b. –35 / 6
   c. –35 % 6
   d. –25 * 14 % 7 * –25 / –5
   e. –5 * 3 + 9 – 2 * 7
   f. (–13 / 2) % 6

2. Evaluate each of the following expressions:
   a. 0.5 + 3.75 / 0.25 * 2
   b. 2.5 – (1.2 + (4.0 – 3.0) * 2.0) + 1.0
   c. 6.0E–4 * 3.0E + 3
   d. 6.0E–4 / 3.0E + 3

3. Evaluate each of the following expressions:
   a. 5.0 – (6.0 / 3)
   b. 200 * 200
   c. 5 – 6 / 3
   d. (5 – 6) / 3
   e. 1 + 25 % 5
   f. –33000 + 2000

4. Evaluate each of the following expressions:
   a. int i = 0;
      int j = 10;
      ++i + j++;
   b. float k = 2.5;
      k-- * 2;

    c.   char Character = 'a';
        ++Character;

    d.   int x = 1;
        int y = -1;
        int z = 25;
        ++x + ++y - --z;

5. Evaluate each of the following relational operations:

    a.   7 != 7

    b.   −0.75 <= −0.5

    c.   'm' > 'n'

    d.   2 * 5 % 3 − 7 < 16 / 4 + 2

    e.   "Andy" == "Andy"

    f.   strcmp("Andy","Andy")

6. Determine the output generated by the following:

    a.   cout << ((2 % 5) / (5 % 2));

    b.   cout << (3 * 6 / 3 + 6);

    c.   cout << ((3 * 6) / (3 + 6));

    d.   cout << (!(1 || 0));

    e.   cout << ((2 - 5/2 * 3) <= (8 % 2 - 6));

    f.   int x = -7;
        int y = 3;
        cout << (!(3*x < 4*y) && (5*x >= y));

    g.   3.5 && 0

    h.   3.5 || 2.0

7. A common logic operation that does not have a standard operator in C++ is the *XOR* operation. Given any two logic variables, *A* and *B*, here is how the *XOR* operation is defined:

A	*B*	*A* XOR *B*
FALSE	FALSE	FALSE
FALSE	TRUE	TRUE
TRUE	FALSE	TRUE
TRUE	TRUE	FALSE

Do you see a pattern in the above table that gives a hint to how *XOR* works? Well, the *XOR* operation will always produce a TRUE result if there are an odd number of TRUE variables. Now for the question: Which of the following logical expressions will produce the *XOR* operation?

   a.   !A || !B

   b.   (A && !B) || (!A && B)

   c.   !(A && !B) || (!A && B)

   d.   !(!A && !B)

8. What standard logical operation is performed by the expression in question 7d?

9. Develop a truth table for the following logical expression:

                       !A || !B

10. Which of the following is equivalent to the logic operation in question 9?

   a.   !(A && B)

   b.   !(A || B)

   c.   !A && !B

   d.   None of these

11. Explain how to get information on how to use a standard function available in your compiler.

12. Determine the output generated by the following functions. Use your compiler reference manual or on–line help feature to make sure that you understand how the function operates.

   a.   abs(-5)

   b.   sin(1.57)

   c.   log(2.73)

   d.   log10(100)

   e.   pow(2,5)

   f.   pow10(3)

   g.   cos(0)

   h.   toascii(' ')

   i.   tolower('A')

   j.   strlen("C++")

13. Explain what happens as the result of executing the following functions:

   a.   strcpy(Name,"Brenda");

   b.   gotoxy(80,25)

   c.   textbackground(CYAN)

      d.   textcolor(BLACK)

      e.   strcmp(Name1,Name2)

  14. Prove or disprove via truth tables that:

$$!A \ \&\& \ !B == !(A \ \&\& \ B)$$

Problems

Least Difficult

1. Write a program that will allow a user to convert a temperature in degrees Fahrenheit to degrees Centigrade using the following relationship:

$$C = 5/9 \times (F - 32)$$

2. Write a program that will allow a user to convert a measurement in inches to centimeters.

3. Write a simple test program that will demonstrate what happens when you use an illegal argument within a function. For example, what happens when you use a character argument in an arithmetic function?

4. Write a program that will allow a user to find the hypotenuse of a right triangle using the Pythagorean theorem. (Hint: Try using the *hypot()* function in the *math.h* header file.)

5. Write a program to solve the following equation for x:

$$3x - 5y + 2 = 35$$

Assume that values for y will be entered by the user.

6. Write a program to generate a truth table for a NOR operation. A NOR operation is a NOT OR operation. Thus,

$$A \ NOR \ B = NOT \ (A \ OR \ B)$$

Assume that logical values for A and B will be entered by the user.

More Difficult

7. Write a program to convert from rectangular to polar coordinates. Generate a tabular output of the rectangular versus polar coordinate.

8. The kinetic energy of a moving object is found using the following equation:

$$K = 1/2(mv^2)$$

where:

K is the kinetic energy in kgm/s.

m is the mass in kilograms.

v is the velocity in meters per second.

Write a program that accepts inputs of mass and velocity of an object and determines its kinetic energy.

9. Here is the inventory and price list of the Health and Beauty Aids department in Ma and Pa's General Store.

Item	Price
Grandma's Lye Soap	0.49
Bag Bahm	1.29
Chicken Soup	0.29
Liniment	2.35
Baking Soda	0.63

Ma and Pa want to run a "big" sale and reduce all Health and Beauty Aid items by 5 percent. Write Ma and Pa a program that will print a listing of all the Health and Beauty Aid items showing the regular and sale price. Assume that Ma or Pa will enter the above item price list.

10. Revise the program in problem 9 to allow Ma or Pa to enter any percentage sales discount they desire.

Most Difficult

11. Ma and Pa were so elated with the programs you have written so far that they want to expand their computer operations to the payroll department. Write Ma and Pa a payroll program that will calculate Herb's (their only employee) net pay given the following information:

Employee's name

Number of weekly hours worked

Hourly rate of pay

FICA (7.15%)

Federal withholding (16%)

State withholding (4.75%)

Assume that Ma or Pa will only be required to enter the first three items when running the program. Provide a printed report using the following format:

Employee Name: XXXXXXXXXXXXXXXXXXXXXXX

Rate of Pay: $XXX.XX

Hours Worked: XX.X

Gross Pay: $XXXX.XX

Deductions:

    FICA $XXX.XX

    Fed. Withholding   XXX.XX

    State Withholding   XXX.XX

                                ————

    Total Deductions $XXX.XX

Net Pay: $XXXX.XX

12. The diagram in Figure 4-3 illustrates how triangulation is used to find the distance to an object. Here's the idea: Two triangulating devices are positioned a certain distance apart and both devices get a "fix" on an object as shown in the figure. The two triangulating devices and the object form a triangle whose one leg, d, and two angles $\theta1$ and $\theta2$ are known. The third angle is easily found by subtracting the two known angles from 180 degrees. The distance form each triangulating devices to the object is then found using the Law of Sines, which states"

$$r1 \ / \ Sin\theta1 = r2 \ / \ Sin\theta2 = d \ / \ Sin(180 - (\theta1 + \theta2))$$

Write a program to find the distance that the object is from each triangulation device. Assume that the user will enter the distance (d) between the devices and the two angles ($\theta1$ and $\theta2$) that the object makes with the triangulating devices.

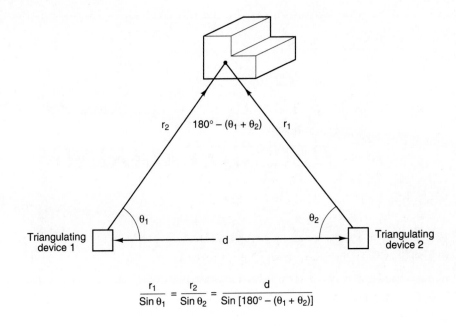

$$\frac{r_1}{Sin\,\theta_1} = \frac{r_2}{Sin\,\theta_2} = \frac{d}{Sin\,[180° - (\theta_1 + \theta_2)]}$$

Figure 4-3 A triangulation diagram for problem 12.

5

DECISION MAKING

INTRODUCTION

As stated earlier, C++ is a structured programming language. As you will begin to find out, structured programming languages, such as C++, make programs easier to write, check, read, document, and maintain. A major reason for this is the modularity feature of a structured programming language. *Program modularity* means that any program, no matter how complex, can be broken down into simpler independent program modules. In fact, any complex program can be broken down into modules that conform to one of three fundamental patterns called *control structures*. A control structure is simply a pattern for controlling the flow of a program module.

The three fundamental control structures of a structured programming language are *sequence*, *selection*, and *iteration*. The sequence control structure is illustrated in Figure 5-1. As you can see, there is nothing fancy about this control structure, since program statements are executed sequentially, one after another, in a straight-line fashion. This is called *straight-line programming* and is what you have been doing in C++ up to this point.

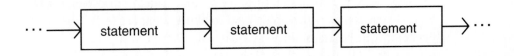

Figure 5-1 The sequence control structure is a series of sequential step-by-step statements.

The second two control structures, selection and iteration, allow the flow of the program to be altered, depending on one or more conditions. The selection control structure is a decision-making control structure. It is implemented in C++ using the **if**, **if/else**, and **switch** statements. These are the topics of this chapter.

The iteration control structure is a looping control structure. It is implemented in C++ using the **while, do/while,** and **for** statements. These operations are discussed in Chapter 6.

Now, let's explore the selection control statements available in C++.

5-1 THE *if* STATEMENT

The operation of the **if** statement is illustrated by the diagram in Figure 5-2.

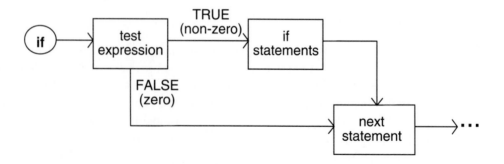

Figure 5-2 The flow of the **if** operation.

Observe that the flow of the program is altered, depending on the result of a test expression. The **if** test can be TRUE (non-zero) or FALSE (zero). Remember that C++ equates a non-zero value to TRUE and a zero value to FALSE during a test operation. If the test expression is TRUE (non-zero), the **if** statements are executed. However, if the result of the test is FALSE (zero), the **if** statements are bypassed and the program flow continues. This is known as a ***selection***, or ***decision–making***, operation, since the program selects, or decides, between one of two possible routes depending on the conditions that are tested. In summary, the **if** operation can be stated in words like this: "If the test is TRUE, execute the **if** statements." Of course, this implies that the **if** statements are not executed and bypassed if the test is FALSE.

Before we look at the C++ format for the **if** statement, let's take a closer look at the test expression. The test expression is a conditional test. This means that one or more conditions are tested to generate a TRUE or FALSE result. To test a single condition, you will use the relational Boolean operators of ==, != , < , > , <=, and >=. For instance, a typical test might be **if (x == y)** . Here, the single condition, $x == y$, is tested. If x does in fact equal y, the result of the test is TRUE and the TRUE statements will be executed. If x does not equal y, the TRUE statements are bypassed and the next sequential statement is executed.

To test multiple conditions, you must use the logical Boolean operators of OR and AND. For example, a test such as **if ((x != y) && (a < b))** tests two conditions. If x does not equal y and if a is less than b, the test result is TRUE and the TRUE statements will be executed.

The C++ format for the **if** statement is:

if STATEMENT FORMAT

```
if (test expression)
{
   statement 1;
   statement 2;
              .                    // COMPOUND STATEMENT

              .

              .
   statement n;
}
```

First, notice the overall structure of this format. The word **if** and its associated test expression is written on the first line of the statement. The word **if** is a keyword in C++. The test expression follows the **if** keyword and *must* be enclosed within parentheses. The first line is followed by the statements that will be executed if the test is TRUE. This statement block is "framed" by curly braces. A left curly brace, {, signals the beginning of the statement block and the right curly brace, }, denotes the end of the block. Notice that the beginning curly brace is placed on a separate line, directly below the keyword **if**. The ending curly brace is placed on a separate line immediately after the last statement in the block and in the same column as the beginning brace. In addition, you should always indent all the block statements two or three spaces in from the curly braces for readability. When this structure is part of a complex program, there is no question which statements belong to the **if** operation.

If there is more than one statement to be executed within this block, the entire group of statements is referred to as a ***compound statement***. When a compound statement is encountered within a C++ program, the entire group of statements is treated like a single statement. Compound statements must always be framed with curly braces. However, framing is optional when there is only a single statement within the block.

Finally, look at the punctuation syntax of the **if** statement. Notice that there is no semicolon after the test expression in the first line. However, each statement within the statement block is terminated by a semicolon.

It's probably a good idea to look at some example exercises and programs at this time to get a "feel" for the **if** operation.

Example 5-1:

Determine the output for each of the following program segments. Assume that x and y have the following assignments prior to the execution of each **if** operation:

```
x = 2;
y = 3;
```

```
a.  if (x < y)
    {
       cout << "x = " << x << '\n';
       cout << "y = " << y << '\n';
    }
b.  if (x)
    {
       cout << "The value of x is non-zero. \n";
    }
c.  if (x < y)
    {
       Temp = y;
       y = x;
       x = Temp;
       cout << "x = " << x << '\n';
       cout << "y = " << y << '\n';
    }
d   if ((x < y) && (y != 10))
    {
       Sum = x + y;
       cout << "x = " << x << '\n';
       cout << "y = " << y << '\n';
       cout << "Sum = " << Sum << '\n';
    }
e.  if ((x > y) || (x - y < 0))
    {
       ++x;
       --y;
       cout << "x = " << x << '\n';
       cout << "y = " << y << '\n';
    }
```

f. if ((x > y) || (x * y < 0))
    {
      ++x;
      --y;
      cout << "x = " << x << '\n';
      cout << "y = " << y << '\n';
    }
    cout << "x = " << x << '\n';
    cout << "y = " << y << '\n';
g. if (x % y == 0)
      cout << "x is divisible by y." << '\n';
      cout << "x is not divisible by y." << '\n';

Solution:

a. The value of *x* is less than the value of *y*. Thus the output is:

    x = 2
    y = 3

b. Here, the test is on the value of *x*. If *x* is zero, the test is FALSE, If *x* is non–zero, the test is TRUE. Since *x* is a non-zero value, the test is TRUE and the *cout* statement is executed, producing an output of:

    The value of x is non-zero.

c. The value of *x* is less than *y* so the compound statement is executed and the output is:

    x = 3
    y = 2

    Notice that the values of *x* and *y* have been swapped using a temporary variable called *Temp*. Why is this temporary variable required?

d. The value of *x* is less than y *and* the value of *y* is not equal to 10. As a result, the two values are added and the output is:

    x = 2
    y = 3
    Sum = 5

e. Here, the value of *x* is not greater than the value of *y*, but *x* − *y* is less than 0. Thus, the test result due to the OR operator is TRUE and the compound statement is executed resulting in an output of:

```
x = 3
y = 2
```

Notice that the compound statement increments *x* and decrements *y*.

f. This time the test is FALSE. Thus, the compound statement is bypassed. As a result, the values of *x* and *y* remain unchanged and the output is:

```
x = 2
y = 3
```

g. This is a tricky one. Here, the test is FALSE, since *y* does not divide evenly into *x*. So, what happens? Since there are no curly braces framing the block, the compiler only takes the first *cout* statement to be the TRUE statement. As a result, the first *cout* statement is bypassed and the second one is executed to produce an output of:

```
x is not divisible by y.
```

What would happen if the test expression were TRUE? In this case, both *cout* statements would be executed, generating an output of:

```
x is divisible by y.
x is not divisible by y.
```

But, this logic doesn't make sense. You only want one of the *cout* statements executed, not both. To solve this dilemma we need a different decision control structure called the **if/else** control structure. The **if/else** control structure is discussed next.

Now, let's look at a case study that employs the **if** control structure.

CASE STUDY: MA AND PA'S PAYROLL

Problem:

You need to write a simple payroll program to run on Ma and Pa's new PC. The program must read in an employee's total weekly work hours and rate of pay and determine the gross weekly pay using "time and a half" for anything over 40 hours.

The Problem Definition

Output: The program will write the employee's name, hours worked, pay rate, and gross pay.

Input: The user will be prompted to enter the employee's name, hours worked, and pay rate.

Processing: Case 1 (Hours worked less than or equal to 40)

$$Gross\ Pay\ =\ Hours \times Rate$$

Case 2 (Hours worked greater than 40)

$$Gross\ Pay\ =\ (40 \times Rate)\ +\ [(Hours\ -\ 40)\ \times\ 1.5\ \times\ Rate]$$

The Algorithm

Here is where you must think out the problem in terms of the program logic and flow. Notice from the problem definition that the gross pay is calculated using one of two cases, depending on the number of hours worked. Thus, a decision must be made to use processing case 1 or case 2. One approach is testing to see if the hours worked are less than or equal to 40. If so, use processing case 1. Then test to see if the hours worked are greater than 40. If this is the case, use case 2. This approach suggests two **if** operations. Here's the algorithm:

BEGIN
    Write a program description message.
    Write a user prompt to enter the employee's *Name*.
    Read (*Name*).
    Write a user prompt to enter the *Rate* of pay.
    Read (*Rate*).
    Write a user prompt to enter the weekly *Hours* worked.
    Read (*Hours*).
    If *Hours* <= 40
        Calculate *Gross Pay* = *Hours* × *Rate*.

If Hours > 40
    Calculate *Gross Pay* = *(40 × Rate)* + *[(Hours − 40) × 1.5 × Rate]*
Write appropriate output headings.
Write employee *Name*, *Rate* of pay, *Hours* worked, and *Gross Pay*.
END.

You might be wondering why two **if** operations are required. You say that if the hours worked are not less than or equal to 40, then you know the hours must be greater than 40. However, suppose the second **if** operation were eliminated. In addition, suppose that the hours worked are less than 40. Then the gross pay would be calculated twice, right? This would result in an erroneous gross pay figure. In fact, if you were Ma and Pa's employee I'm sure you would complain, since you would be getting cheated. (Why?)

One final point about the algorithm: Notice how indentation is used to show those steps that are executed if the test is TRUE. Using an indentation scheme such as this makes your algorithms readable. In addition, it makes your C++ programs much easier to code. Now, simply follow the algorithm to code the program like this:

The Program

```
//PAYROLL 1   (CASE5-1.CPP)

// OUTPUT:    THE PROGRAM WILL WRITE THE EMPLOYEE'S NAME,
//            HOURS WORKED, PAY RATE, AND GROSS PAY.

// INPUT:     THE USER WILL BE PROMPTED TO ENTER
//            THE EMPLOYEE'S NAME, HOURS
//            WORKED, AND PAY RATE.

// PROCESSING:    CASE 1 (HOURS WORKED LESS THAN
//                OR EQUAL TO 40)

//                GROSS PAY = HOURS  X  RATE

//                CASE 2 (HOURS WORKED GREATER THAN 40)

//                GROSS PAY = (40  X  RATE) + [(HOURS - 40)
//                                 X  1.5  X   RATE]
```

```
#include <iostream.h>
#include <iomanip.h>
#include <stdio.h>

void main()
{

// DEFINE VARIABLES
    char Name[25];                      // EMPLOYEE NAME
    float Hours;                        // WEEKLY HOURS WORKED
    float Rate;                         // HOURLY RATE OF PAY
    float Gross;                        // WEEKLY GROSS PAY

// DISPLAY PROGRAM DESCRIPTION MESSAGE
    cout << "This program will calculate the weekly gross pay of\n"
            "an employee, given his/her rate of pay and hours"
            " worked.\n\n";
    cout << "Enter the employee's name:  ";

// GET EMPLOYEE DATA
    gets(Name);
    cout << "\nEnter the hourly rate of pay for " << Name << ":  $";
    cin >> Rate;
    cout   << "\nEnter the number of hours that " << Name
           << " has worked:  ";
    cin >> Hours;

// TEST HOURS WORKED AND MAKE APPROPRIATE GROSS PAY
// CALCULATION
    if (Hours <= 40)
       Gross = Hours * Rate;
    if (Hours > 40)
       Gross = (40 * Rate) + ((Hours - 40) * 1.5 * Rate);

// DISPLAY EMPLOYEE SALARY DATA
    cout << setprecision(2);
    cout << "\n\n\nEMPLOYEE:  " << Name << "\n\n";
    cout << "HOURS WORKED\tHOURLY RATE\tGROSS PAY\n";
    cout << "_____\t_____\t_____\n\n";
    cout << setw(12) << Hours << setw(10) << "$" << Rate
         << setw(10) << "$" << Gross;
}
```

When you look at the **if** statements in the program, you will see that no curly braces are used to define the statement block. This is okay when you only have a single statement within the block. However, you should still use indentation as shown for program readability.

Quick Check

1. True or False: A test expression that evaluates to any non-zero value is considered TRUE.

2. True or False: When a test expression in an **if** statement evaluates to zero, the related **if** statements are bypassed.

3. What is wrong with the following **if** statement?

```
if (x = y)
    cout << "There is a problem here";
```

4. What Boolean operator must be employed to test if two conditions are TRUE?

5. What Boolean operator must be employed to test if one of two conditions is FALSE?

6. What Boolean operator must be employed to test if one of two conditions is TRUE?

7. For what values of x will the *cout* statement in the following code be executed?

```
if(!x)
    cout << "Hello";
```

5-2 THE *if/else* STATEMENT

The operation of the **if/else** statement is illustrated by the diagram in Figure 5-3. Here, you see that there are two sets of statements that can be executed, depending on whether the test expression is TRUE or FALSE. If the test result is TRUE, the **if** statements are executed. Conversely, if the test result is FALSE, the **else** statements are executed. In words, "If the test expression is TRUE, then execute the **if** statements, otherwise execute the **else** statements." In C++, an equivalent statement would be "If the test expression is non-zero, execute the **if** statements, otherwise execute the **else** statements." As compared to the **if** operation, you could say **if/else** is a two-way selection process, while **if** is a one-way selection process.

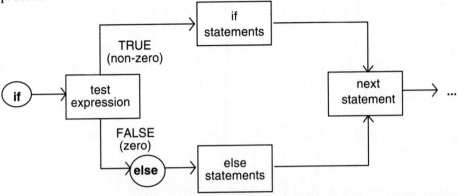

Figure 5-3 The flow of the **if/else** operation.

The C++ format for the **if/else** operation is:

if/else STATEMENT FORMAT

if (test expression)
{
   statement 1;
   statement 2;

    .
    .
    .

   statement n;
}
else
{
   statement 1;
   statement 2;

    .
    .
    .

   statement n;
}

As you can see, the **else** option is included after the **if** option. If the test expression is TRUE, the **if** statements are executed and the **else** statements are ignored. However, if the test expression is FALSE, the **if** statements are ignored and the **else** statements are executed.

A few words about syntax: First, observe that both the **if** and **else** statements are "framed" using curly braces. However, you can eliminate the curly braces in either section when only a single statement is required. Second, notice the indentation scheme. Again, such a scheme makes your programs self-documenting and readable.

Now, let's see how the **if/else** operation can be applied to the gross pay problem.

CASE STUDY: MA AND PA'S PAYROLL REVISITED

Problem:

Revise Ma and Pa's payroll program developed in the previous case study to employ a single **if/else** operation in place of the two **if** operations.

The problem definition does not require any alteration. Only the algorithm and C++ coding must be changed as follows to employ the **if/else** operation.

The Algorithm

BEGIN
    Write a program description message.
    Write a user prompt to enter the employee's *Name*.
    Read (*Name*).
    Write a user prompt to enter the *Rate* of pay.
    Read (*Rate*).
    Write a user prompt to enter the weekly Hours worked.
    Read (*Hours*).
    If *Hours* <= 40
        Calculate *Gross Pay* = *Hours* × *Rate*
    Else
        Calculate *Gross Pay* = *(40 × Rate)* + *[(Hours* − *40)* × *1.5* × *Rate]*
    Write appropriate output headings.
    Write employee *Name*, *Rate* of pay, *Hours* worked, and *Gross Pay*.
END.

As you can see, the **else** operation replaces the second **if** operation of the previous case study. If the hours worked are less than or equal to forty, the test expression is TRUE and the gross pay is calculated without overtime. However, if the hours worked are greater than forty, the test expression is FALSE and the **else** operation is performed to include the overtime calculation. Notice that the indentation scheme clearly shows the two selection options. Now, for the coding:

The Program

```
//PAYROLL 1   (CASE5-2.CPP)

// OUTPUT:      THE PROGRAM WILL WRITE THE EMPLOYEE'S NAME,
//              HOURS WORKED, PAY RATE, AND GROSS PAY.

// INPUT:       THE USER WILL BE PROMPTED TO ENTER
//              THE EMPLOYEE'S NAME, HOURS
//              WORKED, AND PAY RATE.

// PROCESSING:      CASE 1 (HOURS WORKED LESS THAN
//                  OR EQUAL TO 40)
//                  GROSS PAY = HOURS  X  RATE

//                  CASE 2 (HOURS WORKED GREATER THAN 40)
//                  GROSS PAY = (40  X  RATE) + [(HOURS - 40)
//                              X  1.5  X  RATE]

#include <iostream.h>
#include <iomanip.h>
#include <stdio.h>

void main()
{
// DEFINE VARIABLES
   char Name[25];              // EMPLOYEE NAME
   float Hours;                // WEEKLY HOURS WORKED
   float Rate;                 // HOURLY RATE OF PAY
   float Gross;                // WEEKLY GROSS PAY

// DISPLAY PROGRAM DESCRIPTION MESSAGE
   cout << "This program will calculate the weekly gross pay of\n"
           "an employee, given his/her rate of pay and"
           " hours worked.\n\n";
   cout << "Enter the employee's name:  ";

// GET EMPLOYEE DATA
   gets(Name);
   cout << "\nEnter the hourly rate of pay for " << Name << ":  $";
```

```
cin >> Rate;
cout   << "\nEnter the number of hours that " << Name
        << " has worked:  ";
cin >> Hours;

// TEST HOURS WORKED AND MAKE APPROPRIATE GROSS PAY
// CALCULATION
  if (Hours <= 40)
    Gross = Hours * Rate;
  else
    Gross = (40 * Rate) + ((Hours - 40) * 1.5 * Rate);

// DISPLAY EMPLOYEE SALARY DATA
  cout << setprecision(2);
  cout << "\n\n\nEMPLOYEE: " << Name << "\n\n";
  cout << "HOURS WORKED\tHOURLY RATE\tGROSS PAY\n";
  cout << "_____\t_____\t_____\n\n";
  cout << setw(12) << Hours << setw(10) << "$" << Rate
        << setw(10) << "$" << Gross;
}
```

Comparing this program to the program in the previous case study, you find that the second **if** statement is simply replaced by the **else** statement.

 Quick Check

1. True or False: When the test expression in an **if/else** operation evaluates to zero, the **else** statements are executed.

2. Why does the following pseudocode need an **else** statement?

   > If *Day* == *Friday*
   >> Write("It's pay day")
   >> Write("It's not pay day")

3. True or False: Framing with curly braces can be eliminated when an **if** or **else** statement section only has a single statement.

5-3 NESTED *if's*

Up to this point, you have witnessed one-way and two-way decisions using the **if** and **if/else** statements, respectively. You can achieve additional selection options by using nested **if** statements. A nested **if** statement is simply an **if** statement within an **if** statement. To illustrate this idea, consider the diagram in Figure 5-4.

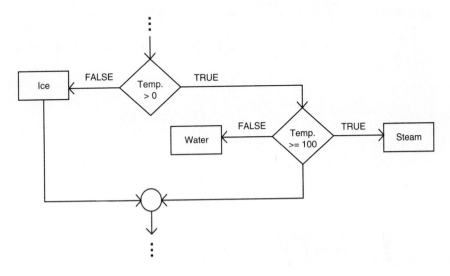

Figure 5-4 A nested **if** operation.

Here, a temperature is being tested to see if it is within a range of 0 to 100 degrees Celsius. If it is within this range, you get water. However, if it is outside the range you get steam or ice, depending on whether it is above or below the range, respectively.

Let's follow through the diagram. The first test expression operation checks to see if the temperature is greater than 0 degrees. If the test result is FALSE, the temperature must be less than or equal to 0 degrees, resulting in ice. However, if the test result is TRUE, a second test is made to see if the temperature is greater than or equal to 100 degrees. If this test result is TRUE, you get steam. However, if this second test result is FALSE, you know that the temperature must be somewhere between 0 degrees and 100 degrees, resulting in water. Notice how the second test is "nested" within the first test. The first test result must be TRUE before the second test is performed.

Let's develop a program to implement the nested decision making operation illustrated in Figure 5-4. We begin with the problem definition.

The Problem Definition

Output: The word "WATER," "STEAM," or "ICE."

Input: Temperature in degrees Celsius from the user keyboard.

Processing: Determine if the temperature constitutes water, steam, or ice.

Now for the algorithm. Here is one that will work:

The Algorithm

```
BEGIN
     Write a program description message.
     Write a user prompt to enter the Temperature in degrees Celsius.
     Read (Temperature).
     If Temperature > 0
       If Temperature >= 100
          Write "STEAM".
       Else
          Write "WATER".
     Else
       Write "ICE".
END.
```

This algorithm is constructed by simply following the diagram in Figure 5-4. Notice how the second **if/else** operation is nested within the first **if/else** operation. If the *Temperature* is not greater than 0 degrees, the nested **if** operation is not performed. However, if the *Temperature* is greater than 0, the nested **if** operation is performed to see if the *Temperature* results in steam or water.

To code the program you simply follow the algorithm like this:

The Program

```
// OUTPUT:      DISPLAY THE WORD "STEAM," "ICE," OR "WATER "
//              DEPENDING ON TEMPERATURE TO BE ENTERED
//              BY THE USER.

// INPUT:       A CELSIUS TEMPERATURE VALUE FROM THE USER.

// PROCESSING:     TEST TEMPERATURE VALUE AGAINST
//                 A RANGE OF 0 TO 100 DEGREES CELSIUS.

#include <iostream.h>

void main()
{
// DEFINE VARIABLE
   float Temperature;              // TEMPERATURE VALUE FROM USER

// DISPLAY PROGRAM DESCRIPTION MESSAGE TO USER
   cout << "This program will evaluate a temperature to see if\n"
           "it produces ice, water, or steam.\n\n\n";

// GET THE TEMPERATURE FROM USER
   cout << "Enter a temperature in degrees Celsius:  ";
   cin >> Temperature;

// TEST IF TEMPERATURE IS  WATER, STEAM, OR ICE
   if (Temperature > 0)
        if (Temperature >= 100)
                cout << "\nSTEAM";
        else
                cout << "\nWATER";
   else
        cout << "\nICE";
}
```

Notice how the program flow can be seen by the indentation scheme.

However, you do not see any curly brace pairs framing the **if** or **else** blocks. Remember that you do not need to frame a code block when it consists of only a single statement. But, you say that the first **if** block looks as if it consists of several statements. Well, the first **if** block contains a single **if/else** statement. Since the compiler sees this as a single statement, it does not need to be framed. Of course, if you are in doubt, it does no harm to frame the block like this:

```
if (Temperature > 0)
{
  if (Temperature >= 100)
     cout << "\nSTEAM";
  else
     cout << "\nWATER";
}
else
  cout << "\nICE";
```

 Quick Check

1. Explain why indentation is important when operations are nested.
2. True or False: Any given **else** always goes with the closest **if**.

   Consider the following pseudocode to answer questions 3 – 5:
```
        If Value < 50
          If Value > –50
             Write ("Red")
          else
             Write ("White")
        else
          Write ("Blue")
```
3. What range of values will cause "Red" to be written?
4. What range of values will cause "White" to be written?
5. What range of values will cause "Blue" to be written?

5-4 THE *switch* STATEMENT

This last category of selection enables the program to select one of many options, or *cases*. The selection of a particular case is controlled by a matching process. A *selector* variable is first evaluated to produce a value. The selector value is then compared to a series of cases. If the selector value matches one of the case values, the corresponding case statements are executed. If no match is made, the program simply continues in a straight-line fashion, with the first statement following the **switch** statement. Here's the C++ format for **switch**:

switch STATEMENT FORMAT

```
switch (selector variable)
{
    case  case 1 value : case 1 statements;
                            break;
    case  case 2 value : case 2 statements;
                            break;
                    .
                    .
                    .
    case  case n value : case n statements;
                            break;
}
```

The format requires the selector variable to follow the keyword **switch.** The selector variable must be enclosed within parentheses and must be an integral data type. By an *integral data type* I mean a data type that is stored as an integer. This basically means that the selector variable must be defined as either an integer or a character variable. Defining the selector variable as a floating point or character string data type will cause a compile error.

The **switch** syntax requires the use of curly braces to open and close the **switch** block of **case** statements as shown. The **switch** block is comprised of several cases which are identified using the keyword **case**. An integral case value must be supplied with each case for matching purposes. The **switch** statement attempts to match the value of the selector variable to a given case value. If a match occurs, the corresponding case statements are executed. Note that a colon separates the case value from the case statements. A given case statement block can be any number of statements in length and does not require framing with curly braces. However, the keyword **break** is often inserted as the last statement in a given case statement block. If **break** is not used, any subsequent cases will be executed after a given case match has occurred until a **break** is encountered. This may be desirable at times, especially when multiple case values are to "fire" a given set of case statements. Again, the idea behind the **switch** statement is easy, if you simply think of it as a matching operation. Some examples should demonstrate this idea.

Suppose the selector variable is the letter grade you made on your last quiz. Assuming that the variable *LetterGrade* is defined as a character variable, a typical **switch** statement might go something like this:

```
switch (LetterGrade)
{
  case 'A' : cout << "Excellent\n";
          break;
  case 'B' : cout << "Superior\n";
          break;
  case 'C' : cout << "Average\n";
          break;
  case 'D' : cout << "Poor\n";
          break;
  case 'F' : cout << "Try again\n";
          break;
}
```

Here, the selector variable is *LetterGrade*. The case values are 'A', 'B', 'C', 'D', and 'F'. The value of the selector variable is compared to the list of case values. If a match is found, the corresponding case statements are executed. For instance, if the value of *LetterGrade* is 'B', the code generates an output of

                                    Superior

Now, suppose you leave out the keyword **break** in each of the previous cases like this:

```
switch (LetterGrade)
{
  case 'A' : cout << "Excellent\n";
  case 'B' : cout << "Superior\n";
```

```
      case 'C' : cout << "Average\n";
      case 'D' : cout << "Poor\n";
      case 'F' : cout << "Try again\n";
  }
```

This time, assuming that *LetterGrade* has the value 'B', the code generates an output of:

```
                    Superior
                    Average
                    Poor
                    Try Again
```

As you can see from the output, case 'B' was matched and its case statement executed. However, all of the **case** statements subsequent to case 'B' were also executed. Surely you can see the value of using **break** in this application.

Are there times where you might want to eliminate the **break** command? Of course! Consider the following **switch** statement:

```
switch (LetterGrade)
{
  case 'a' :
  case 'A' : cout << "Excellent\n";
          break;
  case 'b' :
  case 'B' : cout << "Superior\n";
          break;
  case 'c' :
  case 'C' : cout << "Average\n";
          break;
  case 'd' :
  case 'D' : cout << "Poor\n";
          break;
  case 'f' :
  case 'F' : cout << "Try again\n";
          break;
}
```

Here, multiple case values need to fire the same **case** statement. So, if *LetterGrade* has the value 'b', then a match is made with case 'b'. No **break** is part of this case so the next sequential case is executed which will write the word

"Superior". Since case 'B' contains a break, the **switch** statement is terminated after the output is generated.

What happens if no match occurs? As you might suspect, all the cases are bypassed and the next sequential statement appearing after the **switch** closing brace is executed.

The *default* Option

The last thing we need to discuss is the use of the **default** option within a **switch** statement. The **default** option is normally employed at the end of a **switch** statement like this:

```
default OPTION FORMAT

switch (selector variable)
{
  case  case 1 value : case 1 statements;
                  break;
  case  case 2 value : case 2 statements;
                  break;


          .
          .
          .

  case  case n value : case n statements;
                  break;
  default: default statements;
                  break;
}
```

The **default** option allows a series of statements to be executed if no match occurs within the **switch**. On the other hand, if a match does occur, the **default** statements are skipped. This provides a valuable protection feature within your program. For instance, suppose that you ask the user to enter a letter grade to be used in a **switch** statement. But, what if the user presses the wrong key and enters a character that is not a valid case value. Well, you can use the **default** option to protect against such invalid entries like this:

```
switch (LetterGrade)
{
   case 'a' :
   case 'A' : cout << "Excellent\n";
            break;
   case 'b' :
   case 'B' : cout << "Superior\n";
            break;
   case 'c' :
   case 'C' : cout << "Average\n";
            break;
   case 'd' :
   case 'D' : cout << "Poor\n";
            break;
   case 'f' :
   case 'F': cout << "Try again\n";
            break;
   default  : cout << "No match was found for the ENTRY "
                << LetterGrade;
            break;
}
```

Here, the **default** statement is executed if *LetterGrade* is anything other than the listed case characters. For example, if the user entered the character 'x' for *LetterGrade*, the foregoing **switch** statement would produce an output of:

No match was found for the ENTRY x

You will find that the **default** option in the **switch** statement is extremely useful when displaying menus for user entries. Now, let's take a look at a case study that employs several of the selection operations discussed in this chapter, in particular the **switch** statement.

CASE STUDY: MENU-DRIVEN PROGRAMS

Problem:

The **switch** statement is often used to create menu-driven programs. I'm sure you have seen a menu-driven program. It's one that asks you to select different options during the execution of the program. For instance, suppose you must write a menu-driven program that will allow the user to calculate dc voltage, current, or resistance. By Ohm's law *(Voltage = Current × Resistance)*, you know that any one of these can be found by knowing the other two.

Problem Definition

Output: A program menu that prompts the user to select either a voltage, current, or resistance calculation option.
Invalid entry messages as required.
A voltage, current, or resistance value, depending on the program option that the user selects.

Input: A user response to the menu (V, I, or R).
If V is selected: User enters values for current and resistance.
If I is selected: User enters values for voltage and resistance.
If R is selected: User enters values for voltage and current.

Processing: Calculate the selected option.
Case V: *Voltage = Current × Resistance.*
Case I: *Current = Voltage / Resistance.*
Case R: *Resistance = Voltage / Current.*

The Algorithm

BEGIN
    Write a program description message.
    Display a program menu that prompts the user to choose either a voltage (V), current (I), or resistance (R) option.
    Read *(Choice)*.
    Case V: Write a user prompt to enter a current value.
                Read *(Current)*.
                Write a user prompt to enter a resistance value.
                Read *(Resistance)*.
                If *Resistance < 0*
                    Write an invalid entry message and ask the user to run the program again.
                Else
                    Calculate *Voltage = Current × Resistance.*
                    Write *(Voltage)*.

Case I:	Write a user prompt to enter a voltage value.
	Read (*Voltage*).
	Write a user prompt to enter a resistance value.
	Read (*Resistance*).
	If *Resistance* $<= 0$ then
	Write an invalid entry message and ask the user to run the program again.
	Else
	Calculate *Current* = *Voltage* / *Resistance*.
	Write (*Current*).
Case R:	Write a user prompt to enter a voltage value.
	Read (*Voltage*).
	Write a user prompt to enter a current value.
	Read (*Current*).
	If *Current* $== 0$
	Write an invalid entry message and ask the user to run the program again.
	Else
	Calculate *Resistance* = *Voltage* / *Current*.
	Write (*Resistance*).
Default:	Write an invalid entry message and ask the user to select again.

END.

Taking a close look at the algorithm, you find several protection features. First, the menu-driven options are provided by three cases. If the user selects an option not provided by a case, the default is executed that instructs the user to select again. When a proper option is selected, the **if/else** statements within each case option protect against invalid data entries. A negative resistance value is invalid, since there is no such thing as negative resistance. In addition, you cannot divide by 0. As a result, the algorithm checks for zero entries if the value is to be used as a divisor. Using the above algorithm, the C++ program is:

The Program

```
// OHMS LAW MENU PROGRAM (CASE5-3.CPP)

// OUTPUT:    A PROGRAM MENU THAT PROMPTS THE USER
//            TO SELECT EITHER A VOLTAGE CURRENT,
//            OR RESISTANCE CALCULATION OPTION.
//            INVALID ENTRY MESSAGES AS REQUIRED.
```

```
//              A VOLTAGE, CURRENT, OR RESISTANCE
//              VALUE, DEPENDING
//              ON THE PROGRAM OPTION THAT
//              THE USER SELECTS.

// INPUT:       A USER RESPONSE TO THE MENU (V, I, OR R).
//              IF V IS SELECTED: USER ENTERS VALUES
//              FOR CURRENT AND RESISTANCE.
//              IF I IS SELECTED: USER ENTERS VALUES
//              FOR VOLTAGE AND RESISTANCE.
//              IF R IS SELECTED: USER ENTERS VALUES
//              FOR VOLTAGE AND CURRENT.

// PROCESSING: CALCULATE THE SELECTED OPTION.
//              CASE V:     VOLTAGE = CURRENT X RESISTANCE.
//              CASE I:     CURRENT = VOLTAGE / RESISTANCE.
//              CASE R:     RESISTANCE = VOLTAGE / CURRENT.

#include <iostream.h>
#include <iomanip.h>
#include <conio.h>
#include <stdio.h>

void main()
{
// DEFINE VARIABLES
    char Choice;                // USER MENU ENTRY
    float Voltage;              // VOLTAGE IN VOLTS
    float Current;              // CURRENT IN MILLIAMPERES
    float, Resistance;          // RESISTANCE IN KILOHMS

// DISPLAY PROGRAM DESCRIPTION MESSAGE AND USER MENU
    clrscr();
    cout << "This program will calculate DC voltage, current, or\n"
            "resistance given the other two values.\n\n\n\n";
    cout << "\t\t\tEnter V to find voltage\n\n"
            "\t\t\tEnter I to find current\n\n"
            "\t\t\tEnter R to find resistance\n\n"
            "\tPlease enter your choice:  ";
    cin >> Choice;

// SET MESSAGE COLOR AND OUTPUT PRECISION
    textcolor(RED + BLINK);
    cout << setprecision(2);
```

```
// PERFORM REQUIRED CALCULATIONS
  switch (Choice)
  {
    case 'v':
    case 'V' :    cout << "Enter the current value in milliamperes\tI = ";
                  cin >> Current;
                  cout << "\nEnter the resistance value in kilohms\tR = ";
                  cin >> Resistance;
                  if (Resistance < 0)
                  {
                     cprintf ("\n\nThis is an invalid entry. Press ENTER"
                             " and run the program again.");
                     getch();
                     clrscr();
                  }
                  else
                  {
                     Voltage = Current * Resistance;
                     cout << "\n\nThe voltage value is:  " << Voltage
                             << " volts.";
                  }
                  break;

    case 'i':
    case 'I' :    cout << "Enter the voltage value in volts\tV = ";
                  cin >> Voltage;
                  cout << "\nEnter the resistance value in kilohms\tR = ";
                  cin >> Resistance;
                  if (Resistance <= 0)
                  {
                     cprintf ("\n\nThis is an invalid entry. Press ENTER"
                             " and run the program again.");
                     getch();
                     clrscr();
                  }
                  else
                  {
                     Current = Voltage / Resistance;
                     cout << "\n\nThe current value is:  "
                             << Current<< " milliamperes.";
                  }
                  break;
```

```
        case 'r':
        case 'R' :    cout << "Enter the voltage value in volts\tV = ";
                      cin >> Voltage;
                      cout << "\nEnter the current value in milliamperes\tI = ";
                      cin >> Current;
                      if (Current == 0)
                      {
                         cprintf ("\n\nThis is an invalid entry. Press ENTER"
                                  " and run the program again.");
                         getch();
                         clrscr();
                      }
                      else
                      {
                         Resistance = Voltage / Current;
                         cout << "\n\nThe resistance value is:  " << Resistance
                              << " kilohms.";
                      }
                      break;

     default : cprintf("\n\nThis is an invalid entry, press ENTER "
                       "and run the program again.");
               getch();
               clrscr();
               break;
  } // END SWITCH
} // END MAIN
```

Now look at the program closely and you will find that it incorporates most of the things that you have learned in this chapter. In addition, I have done some things with I/O that you might want to use in writing your own programs. In general, you will find a **switch** statement that contains a **default** option. In addition, notice the **if/else** statements embedded within each **case**. In particular, you should observe the beginnings and endings of the various sections, along with the associated indentation and commenting scheme. As you can see, the program is very readable and self-documenting.

Now for the details. There are six cases, two for each user-selected option. Notice that the first case in each option allows the user to enter a lowercase character. These cases do not have a **break** statement and, therefore, permit the program to fall through to the uppercase character case. Notice that there is a **break** statement at the end of each uppercase case, as well as at the end of the **default** case.

If the user enters an invalid character from the main menu, the **default** statement is executed which displays an error message and asks the user to run the program again. Likewise, if the user enters an invalid value within a given case, it is caught by the **if/else** statement which displays an error message and asks the user to run the program again. As you can see, I have used the **if** part of the **if/else** to catch the invalid entry and the **else** part to proceed with the calculation if the entry is valid. This is typical of the way that many programs are written.

Next, you will note the use of the *textcolor()* and *cprintf()* functions, both of which are part of the *conio.h* header file. These functions, along with the *clrscr()* function, are only available on DOS platforms. If you are not using a DOS machine, check your compiler reference manual for similar functions. The *textcolor()* function will set the color of the text to be displayed by the *cprintf()* function. The argument for *textcolor()* is RED + BLINK. As a result, anything displayed by *cprintf()* will be blinking red text. The words RED and BLINK are constants contained in the *conio.h* header file. See your C++ reference manual for other color constants that are available. The *textcolor()* function has no effect on the *cout* object. Thus, anything generated by *cout* will be standard white text. Notice that the *cprintf()* functions are only used to output the error messages to get the user's attention. I have also inserted a *getch()* function after an error message is generated by *cprintf()*. This simply freezes the given screen output until the user presses the ENTER key.

Finally, as you begin to frame more operations using curly braces it often becomes difficult to determine what a closing curly brace is closing. The indentation scheme helps, but a commenting technique is also used. When several closing curly braces appear in succession, you should insert a comment after the brace as shown to indicate what a given brace is closing. Commenting helps both you and anyone reading your program to readily see the program framing. The following output shows the menu generated by the program as well a sample case execution.

```
This program will calculate DC voltage, current, or
resistance given the other two values.

              Enter V to find voltage

              Enter I to find current

              Enter R to find resistance

          Please enter your choice:  V↵
```

Enter the current value in milliamperes I = **10.**⏎

Enter the resistance value in kilohms R = **5.**⏎

The voltage value is: 50 volts.

 Quick Check

1. The selection of a particular case in a **switch** statement is controlled by a _____ process.

2. Suppose that you have *n* cases in a **switch** statement and there are no **break** statements in any of the cases. What will happen when a match is made on the first case?

3. True or False: There are never any times when a case should not contain a **break** statement.

4. A statement that can be inserted at the end of a switch statement to protect against invalid entries is the _____ statement.

5. A common application for a **switch** statement is _____.

CHAPTER SUMMARY

In this chapter, you learned about the selection, or decision making, operations available in C++. These include the **if**, **if/else**, and **switch** statements. Each of these operations alter the flow of a program, depending on the result of a test expression or matching condition.

The **if** statement executes its statements, or clause, "if" its test expression is TRUE (non-zero). If the test result is FALSE (zero), the program continues in a straight-line fashion. The **if** clause can be a single line statement, or a compound statement composed of a series of single line statements. When using a compound statement, you must frame the entire statement block within curly braces.

The **if/else** statement consists of two separate clauses: an **if** clause and an **else** clause. If the associated test expression is TRUE (non-zero), the **if** clause is executed; otherwise, the **else** clause is executed when the test result is FALSE (zero). Thus, you could say that **if/else** is a two-way selection operation. Again, compound statements can be used within the **if** or **else** clauses; however, they must be framed within curly braces. Additional selection options can be achieved using nested **if** or **if/else** statements.

The **switch** statement achieves selection using a matching process. Here, the value of a selector variable is compared to a series of case values. If the selector value matches one of the case values, the corresponding case statements are executed until a **break** statement is encountered or the **switch** statement terminates. If no match is made, the program simply continues in a straight-line fashion. In addition, C++ provides a **default** option with the **switch** statement. When using the **default** option, the **default** statements are executed if no match is made. However, if a match does occur, the corresponding case statements are executed and the **default** statements are skipped. Remember, you must always frame the body of the **switch** statement using curly braces.

QUESTIONS AND PROBLEMS

Questions

1. When will *x* be written as a result of the following **if** statement?
   ```
   if ((x <= 0) && (x % 5))
      cout << x;
   ```

2. Convert the single **if** statement in question 1 into two nested **if** statements.

3. Consider the following program segment:
   ```
   cout << "Enter a value for x ";
   cin >> x;
   cout << "Enter a value for y ";
   cin >> y;
   if x > 0
   {
     if y > 0
       --y;
   }
   else
     ++x;
   ```
   a. Are there any syntax errors in this code? If so, where are they?

   b. Assuming any syntax errors are corrected, when will *y* be decremented?

   c. Assuming any syntax errors are corrected, when will *x* be incremented?

4. Consider the following segment of code:

```
cout << "Enter a value for x ";
cin >> x;
cout << "Enter a value for y ";
cin >> y;
if (x > 0)
{
  if (y > 0)
    --y;
else
  ++x;
}
```

    a.   Are there any syntax errors in this code? If so, where are they?

    b.   Assuming any syntax errors are corrected, when will y be decremented?

    c.   Assuming any syntax errors are corrected, when will x be incremented?

5. True or False: You must always frame the body of a **switch** statement.

6. Which **if** does the **else** belong to in the following code segment?

```
if (x > 0)
  if (y > 0)
    --y;
else
  ++x;
```

7. True or False: When using a **switch** statement in C++, a no-match condition results in an error.

8. Consider the following segment of code:

```
if (x >= 0)
  if (x < 10)
  {
    y = x * x;
    if (x <= 5)
      x = sqrt(x);
  }
  else
    y = 10 * x;
else
  y = x * x * x;
cout << "\nx = " << x;
cout << "\ny = " << y;
```

What will be displayed by the program for each of the following initial values of x?

a. x = 0;

b. x = 4;

c. x = -5;

d. x = 10;

9. Consider the following **switch** statement:

```
x = 2;
switch (Power)
{
  case 0 :  cout << '1';
            break;
  case 1 :  cout << x;
            break;
  case 2 :  cout << x * x;
            break;
  case 3 :  cout << x * x * x;
            break;
  case 4 :  cout << x * x * x * x;
            break;
  default : cout << "No match exists for this Power.";
            break;
}
```

What will be displayed by the code for each of the following values of *Power*?

a. Power = 0;

b. Power = 1;

c. Power = 2;

d. Power = 3;

e. Power = 4;

10. Consider the following nested **switch** statements:

```
switch (x)
{
  case 2 :
  case 4 :
  case 6 :  switch (y)
            {
                case 1 :
                case 2 :
                case 3 :  x = x + y;
                    break;
                case -1 :
                case -2 :
```

```
                    case -3 : x = x - y;
                        break;
                    }                    // END switch(y)
                break;
        case 1 :
        case 3 :
        case 5 :  switch (y)
                {
                    case 2 :
                    case 4 :
                    case 6 : x = x * y;
                        break;
                    case -1 :
                    case -4 :
                    case -6 : x = y * y;
                        break;
                    }                            // END switch(y)
                break;
        }                            // END switch(x)
        cout << "\nx = " << x;
        cout << "\ny = " << y;
```

What will be displayed by the code for each of the following values of *x* and *y*?

a.   x = 4;
     y = -2;

b.   x = 3;
     y = 6;

c.   x = 1;
     y = -4;

d.   x = 7;
     y = -2;

e.   x = 2;
     y = 5;

Problems

Least Difficult

1. A dimension on a part drawing indicates that the length of the part is 3.00 +−0.25 inch. This means that the minimum acceptable length of the part is 2.75 inches and the maximum acceptable length of the part is 3.25

inches. Write a program to display "ACCEPTABLE" if the part is within tolerance, or "UNACCEPTABLE" if the part is out of tolerance. (Note: In Chapter 1, problem 5, you developed an algorithm for this problem. Why not use this algorithm to code the C++ program?)

2. Use your algorithm from problem 9 in Chapter 1 to code a program that will find the roots of a quadratic equation.

3. Write a program that will display two integer values in numerical order, regardless of the order in which they are entered.

4. Write a program that will display the corresponding name of a month for an integer entry from 1 to 12. Protect for invalid entries.

More Difficult

5. Employ nested **if/else** statements to convert a numerical grade to a letter grade according to the following scale:

$$90 - 100 : A$$

$$80 - 89 : \ B$$

$$70 - 79 : \ C$$

$$60 - 69 : \ D$$

$$\text{Below 60: } F$$

6. Electrical power, in watts, of a direct current (dc) circuit is defined as the product of voltage and current. In symbols,

$$P = V \times I$$

where:

    P is power in watts

    V is voltage in volts

    I is current in amperes

Write a menu-driven program that will allow a technician to find either dc power, voltage, or current, given the other two values. Protect against invalid entries.

Most Difficult

7. Ma and Pa are at it again. This time they need a program that will project the profit of their Sporting Goods department. The items in the department are coded with a 1, 2, or 3, depending on the amount of profit for the item. An item with a profit code of 1 produces a 10 percent profit, a code of 2 produces a 12 percent profit, while an item with a code of 3

generates a 15 percent profit. Write a program that will project the profit of the following inventory:

Item	Quantity	Price	Profit Code
Fishing Line	132 spools	$3.95	1
Fish Hooks	97 packages	$0.89	2
Sinkers	123 packages	$0.49	2
Fish Nets	12 ea.	$8.75	1
Spinner Baits	256 ea.	$2.49	3
Jigs	49 ea.	$0.29	3

The program should generate a printed report of the item, quantity, expected profit in dollars per item, and total expected profit for all items.

8. Besides getting a regular salary, Herb also receives a commission on what he sells at Ma and Pa's General Store. His commission is based on the total dollar sales he makes in one week according to the following schedule:

Sales	Commission (%)
Below $250	0
$250 – $499	5
$500 – $1000	7.5
Over $1000	10

Write Ma and Pa a program that will determine Herb's sales commission from a user entry of his weekly sales. The program should display the total sales dollars and corresponding sales commission in dollars.

9. The value of y is defined as follows:

$$y = x^2 + 2x - 3 \qquad \text{if} \qquad -3 <= x <= 2$$
$$y = 5x + 7 \qquad \text{if} \qquad 2 < x <= 10$$
$$y = 0 \qquad \text{if} \qquad x < -3 \text{ or } x > 10$$

Write a program that will find y, given a user entry for x.

10. Write a menu-driven program that will allow the user to convert between the following units.

   1. Degrees Fahrenheit to degrees Centigrade.

   2. Degrees Centigrade to degrees Fahrenheit.

3. Inches to centimeters.

4. Centimeters to inches.

5. Pounds to kilograms.

6. Kilograms to pounds.

Provide for invalid user entries.

6 LOOPING OPERATIONS: ITERATION

INTRODUCTION

In Chapter 5, you learned about the selection control structure. It is now time to explore the third and final control structure employed by C++: *iteration*. Iteration simply means to do something repeatedly. In programming, this is called *looping* because the iteration control structure causes the program flow to go around in a loop. Of course, there must be a way to get out of the loop or the computer would loop forever! Such a situation is called an *infinite loop*, for obvious reasons. To prevent infinite looping, all iteration control structures test a condition to determine when to exit the loop. *Pretest* loops test a condition each time before the loop is executed. *Posttest* loops test a condition after each loop execution. And finally, *fixed repetition* loops cause the loop to be executed a predetermined number of times.

The three iteration control structures employed by C++ are the **while**, **do/while**, and **for**. As you will learn in this chapter, each provides a means for you to perform repetitive operations. The difference between them is found in the means by which they control the exiting of the loop. The **while** is a pretest loop, the **do/while** is a posttest loop, and the **for** is a fixed repetition loop. Let's begin our discussion with the **while** loop.

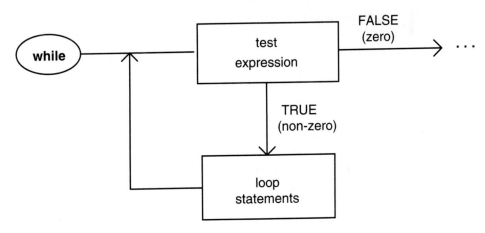

Figure 6-1 The **while** loop operation.

6-1 THE *while* LOOP

You can see from Figure 6-1 that the **while** loop is a pretest loop because a test is made before the loop statements can ever be executed. If the test expression is

TRUE (non-zero), the loop statements are executed. If the test expression is FALSE (zero), the loop statements are bypassed and the next sequential statement after the loop is executed. As long as the test expression is TRUE, the program continues to go around the loop. In other words, the loop is repeated "while" the test expression is TRUE. To get out of the loop, something must change within the loop that makes the test expression FALSE. If such a change does not take place, you have an infinite loop. In addition, the diagram shows that if the test expression is FALSE the first time it is encountered, the loop statements will never be executed. This is an important characteristic of the **while** control structure.

The C++ format for the **while** statement is:

---

while STATEMENT FORMAT

```
while (test expression)
{
    statement 1;
    statement 2;
           .
           .                    // LOOP STATEMENTS
           .
    statement n;
}
```

The first line of the statement contains the keyword **while** followed by a test expression within parentheses. To test a single condition, you will often use the Boolean operators of ==, !=, <, >, <=, >=, and !. To test multiple conditions, you must use the logical operators of OR (||) and AND (&&). Remember, however, that any expression that reduces to zero will be considered FALSE and any expression that reduces to a non-zero value will be considered TRUE.

Notice that the loop statements are framed using curly braces. This forms a compound statement, which consists of the individual loop statements. An indentation scheme is also used so that the loop portion of the statement can be easily identified. Finally, you should be aware that the loop does not have to be framed if it consists of only a single statement. However, the CPU will only execute this single statement during the loop. Any additional statements are considered to be outside the loop structure. Let's see how the **while** loop works by looking at a few simple examples.

Example 6-1:

What will be displayed by the following segments of code? Assume that the variables employed in each segment have been appropriately defined.

a.

```
Number = 5;
Sum = 0;
while (Number)
{
  Sum += Number;
  --Number;
}
cout << "The sum is " << Sum;
```

Here, the variable *Number* is first assigned the value 5 and the variable *Sum* is assigned the value 0. The **while** loop statements will be executed as long as *Number* is greater than 0. You might be thinking that there is no test expression in the **while** statement. But, recall that C++ interprets non-zero values to be TRUE and a value of 0 to be FALSE. Thus, as long as *Number* is greater than zero, the loop statements will be executed. You would get the same result by using *while (Number > 0)*.

Observe that each time the loop is executed, the value of *Number* is added to *Sum*. In addition, the value of *Number* is decremented by 1. Let's trace through each iteration to see what is happening, keeping track of the values of *Number* and *Sum* after each iteration:

1st Iteration:	*Sum* is 5 *Number* is 4
2nd Iteration:	*Sum* is 9 *Number* is 3
3rd Iteration:	*Sum* is 12 *Number* is 2
4th Iteration:	*Sum* is 14 *Number* is 1
5th and Final Iteration:	*Sum* is 15 *Number* is 0

The looping stops here since the value of *Number* is zero which is interpreted by C++ to be FALSE. As a result, the loop statements are bypassed and the *cout* statement is executed, producing a display of:

The sum is 15

In summary, you could say that the program segment computes the sum of integers from 1 through 5.

---

b.

```
Number = 5;
Sum = 0;
while (Number)
{
  if (Number % 2)
     Sum += Number;
  --Number;
}
cout << "The sum is " << Sum;
```

Here, an **if** statement has been included within the loop so that *Number* is only added to *Sum* if *Number* is odd. Why will the calculation be performed when *Number* is odd? Well, the remainder of any odd number divided by 2 is 1, right? In a Boolean test situation, this 1 is interpreted as a logical TRUE result. Thus, the calculation is made. If *Number* is even, the remainder operation generates a 0 result, which is interpreted as a FALSE test expression. As a result, the calculation statement is bypassed. This program segment computes the sum of odd integers from 1 through 5, resulting in a display of:

The sum is 9

---

c.

```
Number = 5;
Sum = 0;
while (Number)
{
  if (!(Number % 2))
     Sum += Number;
  --Number;
}
cout << "The sum is " << Sum;
```

This time, the program computes the sum of even integers from 1 through 5, since *Number* is only added to *Sum* if *Number* is not odd. (Why?) As a result, the display is:

The sum is 6

---

d.

```
MaxNumber = 5;
Number = 0;
Sum = 0;
while (Number != MaxNumber)
{
   Sum += Number;
}
cout << "\nThe average of the first " << MaxNumber
     << "positive integers is :  " << Sum/MaxNumber;
```

This is an infinite loop. Notice that the loop is executed as long as *Number* and *MaxNumber* are not equal. The initial value of *Number* is 0, and the initial value of *MaxNumber* is 5. However, these values are never changed within the loop. Thus, *Number* is always not equal to *MaxNumber*, resulting in an infinite loop. No display is generated, and with many systems you must turn off the computer in order to get out of the loop.

---

e.

```
MaxNumber = 5;
Number = 0;
Sum = 0;
while (Number != MaxNumber)
{
   ++Number;
   Sum += Number;
}
cout << "The average of the first " << MaxNumber
     << " positive integers is:  " << Sum/MaxNumber;
```

Now the loop in part d has been modified so that the value of *Number* is incremented by 1 with each iteration. When *Number* reaches 5, it reaches the value of *MaxNumber*, the iterations stop, and the resulting display is:

The average of the first 5 positive integers is: 3

---

f.

What would happen if *Number* were incremented by 2 in part e?

This modification would also result in an infinite loop, since the value of *Number* would skip over the value of *MaxNumber* and the two would always be unequal.

DEBUGGING TIP

Remember, an infinite loop is the result of a logical error in your program. ***The compiler will not detect an infinite loop condition.*** For this reason you should always desk-check your loop structures very closely prior to coding and execution.

Data Entry Using *while*

There are many situations in which you will want to use a looping operation to read data. One common example is to read strings of data. The idea is to read a singie data element, such as a character, each time the loop is executed. Then break out of the loop when the data string is terminated. For instance, consider the following program:

```
// COUNT THE CHARACTERS
#include <iostream.h>

void main()
{
  const char PERIOD = '.';
  char InChar;                    // USER ENTRY
  int Count;                      // LOOP COUNTER

  cout  << "Enter a string of characters and terminate the input\n"
          "with a period.  Press ENTER when finished.\n";
  Count = 0;
  cin >> InChar;
  while (InChar != PERIOD)
  {
    ++Count;
    cin >> InChar;
  }
```

```
    cout << "\nThe number of characters entered was:  " << Count;
}
```

The general idea of this program is to read a string of characters until a period, '.', is encountered. The period is called a ***delimiter***, since it ends, or ***delimits***, the input string but is not part of that string. The input variable is *InChar*. The **while** loop is executed as long as *InChar* is not equal to a period. With each iteration, a counter (*Count*) is incremented to count the number of characters that were entered before the period. Here is what you will see when the program is executed:

Enter a string of characters and terminate the input
with a period. Press ENTER when finished.

abcd.⏎

The number of characters entered was: 4

Here the user has entered six characters including the delimiter and the CRLF character generated by the ENTER key. The program counts the number of characters entered, excluding the delimiter and the CRLF character.

Now, let's look at the program a bit closer. First, notice that a character is read just prior to the **while** statement. The reason is that the **while** statement tests the variable *InChar* to see that it is not a period. Without the first read operation, *InChar* would not have a value and, therefore, could not be tested. Remember that the variable being tested in the **while** statement must always have a value prior to the first test. This is a common source of error when writing **while** loops. Why didn't the program count the period or the CRLF character? Well, the loop is broken and *Count* is not incremented for the period character, and *cin* ignores the CRLF whitespace character.

Now, let's look at another program that employs a **while** loop to read data. This time, we will use the CRLF character as our delimiter. Here it is:

```
// COUNT THE CHARACTERS

#include <iostream.h>
#include <stdio.h>

void main()
{
  const char CRLF = '\n';
```

```
char InChar;                    // USER ENTRY
int Count;                      // LOOP COUNTER

cout << "\n\nEnter a string of characters and press"
        "ENTER when finished.\n";
InChar = getchar();
Count = 0;
while (InChar != CRLF)
{
  ++Count;
  InChar = getchar();
}
cout << "\n\nThe number of characters entered was:  " << Count;
}
```

The logic of this program is the same as the previous program. However, this time we have used the *getchar()* function in lieu of the *cin* object to read the character data. Since we are testing a whitespace character (CRLF) we need a function that will read it. The function of choice here is *getchar()*, which is provided in the *stdio.h* header file. The *getchar()* function returns any character entered by the user, including whitespace characters. In our program, the returned character is assigned to the character variable *InChar*. The *InChar* variable is tested by the **while** statement to see if it is the CRLF character. When the CRLF character is present, the loop is broken and the value of *Count* is not incremented again. Here is what the user will see when the program is executed:

Enter a string of characters and press ENTER when finished.

abcd.⌐

The number of characters entered was: 5

Notice that the period was counted but not the CRLF character. (Why?)

 Quick Check

1. True or False: A **while** loop breaks when the test expression evaluates to zero.
2. True or False: The **while** loop is a posttest loop.
3. What is wrong with the following code?

```
            x = 10;
            while (x > 0)
                cout << "This is a while loop";
                --x;
```

4. Correct the code in question 3.

5. How many times will the following loop execute?

```
            x = 1;
            while (x <= 0)
                cout << "How many times will this loop execute?";
```

6. How many times will the following loop execute?

```
            x = 1
            while (x >=0)
            {
                cout << "How many times will this loop execute?";
                ++x;
            }
```

6-2 THE *do/while* LOOP

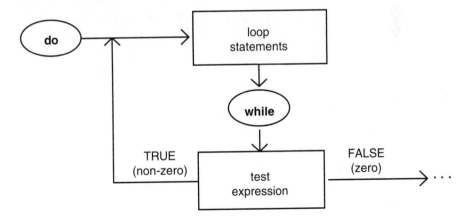

Figure 6-2 The **do/while** loop operation.

The flow of the **do/while** loop can be seen in Figure 6-2. If you compare it to the flow of **while** in Figure 6-1, you will find that the test is made at the end of the loop, rather than the beginning of the loop. This is the main difference between the **while** and the **do/while.** Since the **do/while** is a posttest loop, *the loop statements* *will always be executed at least once.* To break the loop, the test expression must become FALSE (zero). Thus, if the test condition is initially TRUE, something must happen within the loop to change the condition to FALSE; otherwise, you have an infinite loop. Here's the required C++ syntax:

---

do/while STATEMENT FORMAT

```
do
{
   statement 1;
   statement 2;
                              Loop Statements
   statement n;
}
while (test expression);
```

The above format shows that the operation must begin with the single keyword **do**. This is followed by the actual loop statements, which are followed by the keyword **while** and the test expression enclosed within parentheses. You must always frame multiple loop statements with curly braces. However, no framing is required when there is only a single loop statement. In addition, notice that there is no semicolon after the keyword **do** in the first line, but a semicolon is required after the test expression in the last line. Look at the program segments in Example 6-2 and see if you can predict their results.

Example 6-2:

What will be displayed by the following segments of code? Assume that the variables and constants employed in each segment have been appropriately defined.

---

a.

```
Number = 5;
Sum = 0;
do
{
  Sum += Number;
  --Number;
}
while (Number);
cout << "The sum is " << Sum;
```

In this segment, the value of *Number* is initially set to 5 and the value of *Sum* to 0. Each time the loop is executed, the value of *Number* is added to *Sum*. In addition, the value of *Number* is decremented by 1. The looping will end when *Number* has been decremented to 0. The resulting display is:

The sum is 15

Notice that this **do/while** loop computes the sum of integers 1 through 5, as did the **while** loop in Example 6-1a.

---

b.

```
Number = 0;
Sum = 0;
do
{
  Sum += Number;
  ++Number;
}
while (Number != 5);
cout << "The sum is " << Sum;
```

In this segment, both *Number* and *Sum* are initially 0. Again, you might suspect that the loop computes the sum of the integers 1 through 5. But, it actually computes the sum of integers 1 through 4. Why? Notice that *Number* is incremented after the *Sum* is calculated. Thus, when *Number* increments to 5, the loop is broken and the value 5 is never added to *Sum*. The resulting display is:

The sum is 10

How would you change the loop to sum the integers 1 through 5? One way is to change the test expression to *while(Number != 6)*. Another, more preferred way, is to reverse the two loop statements so that *Number* is incremented prior to the *Sum* calculation.

---

c.

```
MaxNumber = 5;
Number = 0;
Sum = 0;
do
{
  --Number;
  Sum += Number;
}
```

```
while (Number != MaxNumber);
cout << "The average of the first " << MaxNumber
       << " positive integers is :  " << Sum/MaxNumber;
```

In this segment, *MaxNumber* begins with the value 5 while both *Number* and *Sum* are initialized to 0. The loop is broken when the value of *Number* equals the value of *MaxNumber*. How many times will the loop execute? If you said "five", you are wrong! Notice that *Number* is decremented each time the loop is executed. Theoretically, the loop will execute an infinite number of times. However, since the range of integers in C++ is normally from −32,768 to 32,767 the loop will execute 65,531 times. How did I get this figure? Well, 32,768 loops will have executed when *Number* reaches −32,768. The next looping operation will decrement *Number* to 32,767. It then takes 32,762 loops to decrement *Number* to 5. Notice that 32,768 + 1 + 32,762 = 65,531. Of course, this is infinite for all practical purposes.

---

d.

```
MaxNumber = 5;
Number = 0;
Sum = 0;
do
{
   ++Number;
   Sum += Number;
}
while (Number != MaxNumber);
cout << "The average of the first " << MaxNumber
       << " positive integers is:  " << Sum/MaxNumber;
```

Here, the loop in part c has been corrected so that the value of *Number* is incremented by 1 with each iteration. When *Number* reaches 5, it equals the value of *MaxNumber* and the loop is broken. The resulting display is:

The average of the first 5 positive integers is: 3

---

e.

```
const char PERIOD = '.';
char InChar;                    // USER ENTRY
int Count;                      // LOOP COUNTER
cout  << "\n\nEnter a string of characters and terminate the input\n"
          "with a period.  Press ENTER when finished.\n";
Count = 0;
```

```
do
{
   ++Count;
  cin >> InChar;
}
while (InChar != PERIOD);
cout << "The number of characters entered was:  " << Count - 1;
```

This program segment shows how a delimiter can be employed to break a **do/while** loop. Notice that each iteration reads a single character from the terminal keyboard until the period key is entered. When this operation was performed using a **while** loop, you had to read the first character prior to the loop structure so that there was an initial value to test. This is because the Boolean test is made at the beginning of **while**. On the other hand, a **do/while** loop performs the Boolean test at the end of the loop. As a result, you do not have to read the first character prior to the loop structure, since the loop statements will always be executed at least once and *InChar* will have a legitimate value before the test is made.

Now, look at the *cout* statement and you see that the value to be displayed is *Count – 1*. Why? Observe that *Count* will be incremented, even for the last loop iteration that reads the period delimiter. Therefore, 1 must be subtracted from the value of *Count* to get the correct number of characters entered, excluding the delimiter. This is required due to the posttest nature of **do/while**. Think about it!

Assuming the user enters the string "abcd.", the display would be:

Enter a string of characters and terminate the input
with a period. Press ENTER when finished.

abcd. ⏎

The number of characters entered was: 4

---

f.

```
const char CRLF = '\n';
char InChar;              // USER ENTRY
int Count;                // LOOP COUNTER

cout << "\n\nEnter a string of characters and press"
        " ENTER when finished.\n";
Count = 0;
do
{
   ++Count;
  InChar = getchar();
}
```

```
while (InChar != CRLF);
cout << "The number of characters entered was:  " << Count - 1;
```

This segment illustrates how the CRLF character can be used to terminate a **do/while** loop. The loop will continue to read in characters until the CRLF character is generated by pressing the ENTER key. Given a user input of "xyz", the output would look like this:

Enter a string of characters and press ENTER when finished.

xyz↵

The number of characters entered was: 3

Quick Check

1. True or False: A **do/while** loop breaks when the test expression is zero.

2. True or False: The **do/while** loop is a post-test loop.

3. What is wrong with the following code?
```
x = 10;
do
   cout << "This is a do/while loop";
while (x > 0);
```

4. Correct the code in question 3.

5. How many times will the following loop execute?
```
x = 1;
do
   cout << "This is a do/while loop";
while (x <= 0);
```

6. How many times will the following loop execute?
```
x = 1
do
{
   cout << "This is a do/while loop";
   ++x;
}
while (x >=0);
```

6-3 THE *for* LOOP

The flow of this final iteration control structure is illustrated in Figure 6-3. The **for** loop is called a ***fixed repetition*** loop because the loop is repeated a fixed number of times.

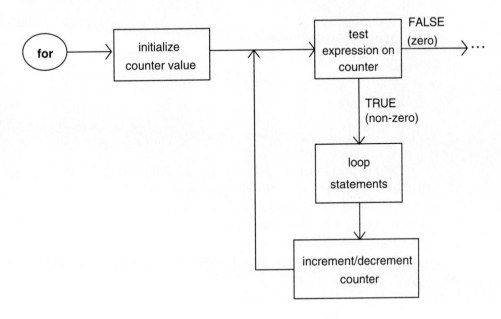

Figure 6-3 The **for** loop operation.

As you can see, the first thing that takes place before the loop statements are executed is the *initialization* of a counter. Initialization simply means to set a counter variable to some initial, or beginning, value. A test expression is then executed to test the counter value. If the result of this test is non-zero (TRUE) the loop statements are executed. Each time the loop statements are executed, the counter value must be incremented or decremented. The test expression is evaluated again before the loop statements are executed another time. The loop is repeated as long as the result of the test expression is a non-zero value. In other words, the counter is incremented/decremented, tested, and the loop is repeated until the test expression is zero. When this occurs, the test is FALSE, the loop statements are not executed again, and the loop is broken. Control of the program then goes to the next sequential statement following the loop. Here's the C++ format:

for STATEMENT FORMAT

for (<data type> *Counter* = initial value; *Counter* test expression;
                                    Increment/Decrement *Counter*)
{
    statement 1;
    statement 2;
              .
              .   // LOOP STATEMENTS
              .
    statement n;
}

The statement begins with the keyword **for**. This is followed by three separate statements: an *initialization* statement, a *test expression*, and an *increment/decrement* statement. The loop counter is initialized by assigning the counter variable an initial value. The counter variable can be any simple data type, except *float*. The counter variable data type can be defined before the **for** statement or within the **for** statement as part of the initialization step like this:

for (int *Count* = 1; ...

If defined within the **for** statement, it is only valid for the function in which it is defined. Thus, as far as C++ is concerned, the counter variable doesn't exist outside of the function in which the **for** loop appears.

The test expression is used to test the value of the loop counter against some predetermined value. The loop statements will be executed until the result of the test expression is zero (FALSE).

The increment/decrement statement is used to change the value of the loop counter so that the test expression becomes zero after a fixed number of iterations. If the value of the loop counter is never changed you have an infinite loop. It is important to note that the increment/decrement statement is not executed until *after* the loop statements are executed in a given iteration. Thus, if the initial test expression is non-zero, the loop statements will be executed at least once. However, if the initial test expression is zero, the loop statements are never executed. This means that the **for** loop acts very much like the **while** loop. In fact, a **for** loop and a **while** loop are really one in the same looping structure just coded differently. Think about it!

One last point about the loop counter variable: *Never* alter the counter variable within the body of the loop. The counter variable can be used within the body of the loop, but its value should not be altered. In other words, never use the counter variable on the left side of the assignment symbol (=) within the loop.

Finally, notice from the above format that the loop statements are framed within the curly braces. This is always required when there is more than one loop statement. The framing can be eliminated when there is only a single loop statement. Here are a few examples; see if you can predict the results.

Example 6-3:

What will be displayed by the following segments of code?

a.

```
for (int Count = 1; Count != 11; ++Count)
    cout << Count << '\n';
```

The loop counter variable, *Count*, ranges from 1 up to 11. How many iterations will there be? Eleven, right? Wrong! The *++Count* statement increments the value of *Count* after each loop iteration. When the value of *Count* reaches 11, the test expression is zero (FALSE) and the loop is broken. As a result, there is no 11th iteration. With each loop iteration, the *cout* statement displays the value of *Count* like this:

```
1
2
3
4
5
6
7
8
9
10
```

b.

```
for (int Count = 10; Count; --Count)
    cout << Count << '\n';
```

Here, the value of *Count* ranges from 10 down to 0. The *--Count* statement decrements the value of *Count* after each loop iteration. When the value of *Count* reaches zero, the loop is broken. Notice that the test expression is simply *Count*. No Boolean relational test operation is needed, since when *Count* reaches zero

C++ interprets the expression to be FALSE. Remember this little trick, since it saves some coding. The output generated by this loop is:

```
10
9
8
7
6
5
4
3
2
1
```

c.

```
for (int Count = -5; Count < 6; ++Count)
   cout << Count << '\n';
```

Here, *Count* ranges from –5 to 6. Since the loop is broken when *Count* reaches 6, the *cout* loop statement is executed for values of *Count* from –5 to 5. How many times will the loop be executed? Ten, right? Wrong! There are 11 integers in the range of –5 to 5, including 0. As a result, the loop is executed eleven times to produce an output of:

```
-5
-4
-3
-2
-1
0
1
2
3
4
5
```

d.

```
cout << "\n\tNumber\tSquare\tCube";
cout << "\n\t------\t------\t----\n";
for (int Count = 1; Count < 11; ++Count)
   cout << '\t' << Count << '\t' << Count * Count
        << '\t' << Count * Count * Count << '\n';
```

This **for** loop is being used to generate a table of squares and cubes for the integers 1 through 10. Notice how the counter variable, *Count*, is squared and cubed within the *cout* loop statement. However, observe that at no time is the value of *Count* altered within the loop. The resulting display is:

Number	Square	Cube
1	1	1
2	4	8
3	9	27
4	16	64
5	25	125
6	36	216
7	49	343
8	64	512
9	81	729
10	100	1000

e.

```
for (char Character = 'A'; Character < 'Z'+ 1; ++Character)
    cout << Character;
```

The counter variable in this loop is the character variable *Character*. Recall that the character data type is ordered such that 'A' is smaller than 'Z'. Notice that the test expression, *Character* < 'Z' + *1* forces the loop to execute for the last time when the value of *Character* is 'Z'. Consequently, the loop is executed twenty-six times as *Character* ranges from 'A' to 'Z'. The value of *Character* is displayed each time using a *cout* statement to produce an output of:

ABCDEFGHIJKLMNOPQRSTUVWXYZ

f.

```
const int MAXCOUNT = 100;
float Sum = 0;
float Average;
setprecision(2);
for (int Count = 1; Count < MAXCOUNT + 1; ++Count)
    Sum +=Count;
Average = Sum / MAXCOUNT;
cout << "\n\nThe average of the first " << MAXCOUNT
        << " positive integers is:  " << Average;
```

Here, the counter value is being added to the floating point variable *Sum* each time through the loop. Thus, the loop adds all the positive integers within the defined range of the counter variable. The range of *Count* is from 1 to *MAXCOUNT + 1*. Notice that *MAXCOUNT* has been declared a constant with a value of 100. Therefore, *Count* will range from 1 to 100 + 1, or 101. However, since the loop is broken when *Count* reaches the value 101, this value is never added to *Sum*. This results in a summing of all integers within the range of 1 to *MAXCOUNT*. After the loop is broken, the value of *Sum* is divided by *MAXCOUNT* to calculate the *Average* of all integers from 1 to 100. Here's what you would see:

The average of the first 100 positive integers is 50.5

Notice that the variable *Sum* was defined as a floating point variable so that the division operator, /, produces a floating point quotient. If both *Sum* and *MAXCOUNT* were defined as integer variables, the division operator would produce an erroneous integer result of 50. Also, you should be aware that constants like *MAXCOUNT* are often used as shown here for the initial or final counter values in a **for** loop. The reason is this: If the constant value needs to be changed for some reason, you only need to change it in one place, at the beginning of the program within the **const** declaration. This changes its value anyplace it is used within the program.

---

g.

```
const int MAXCOUNT = 100;
for (int i = 1; i < MAXCOUNT + 1; ++i)
{
   if (!(i % 17))
      cout << "\nThe value " << i << " is divisible by 17.";
}
```

An **if** statement is used in this loop to determine when the counter value, *i*, is divisible by 17. Thus, the loop displays all the values between 1 and *MAXCOUNT* (100) that are divisible by 17. Do you understand how the test expression is working in the **if** statement? Here is what you would see when it is executed:

The value 17 is divisible by 17.
The value 34 is divisible by 17.
The value 51 is divisible by 17.
The value 68 is divisible by 17.
The value 85 is divisible by 17.

Nested Loops

Many applications require looping operations within loops. This is called *nested looping*. To get the idea, think about the seconds, minutes, and hours of a 12 hour digital timer. Isn't each a simple counter? The seconds count from 0 to 59, the minutes from 0 to 59, and the hours from 0 to 11. For every 60 seconds, the minutes counter is incremented. Likewise, for every 60 minutes, the hours counter is incremented. Thus, the seconds count is "nested" within the minutes count and the minutes count is "nested" within the hours count. Here's how a digital timer might be coded in a C++ program using nested **for** loops:

```
// DIGITAL TIMER

#include <iostream.h>

void main()
// DEFINE VARIABLES
{
  int Hours;
  int Minutes;
  int Seconds;

// DISPLAY HEADINGS
  cout << "\n\n\n\n\t\t\tHours\tMinutes\tSeconds\n\n";

// START TIMER
  for (Hours = 0; Hours < 12; ++Hours)
    for (Minutes = 0; Minutes < 60; ++Minutes)
      for (Seconds = 0; Seconds < 60; ++Seconds)
      {
        cout << "\t\t\t\t\t\r";                  // BLANK DISPLAY
        cout << "\t\t\t" << Hours << '\t'
               << Minutes                         // DISPLAY TIME
               << '\t' << Seconds << '\r';

      }                                           // END SECONDS LOOP
}                                                 // END FUNCTION MAIN
```

As you can see, the seconds **for** loop is part of the minutes loop, which is part of the hours loop. The *outer* **for** loop begins by initializing the *Hours* counter to 0. The statement within this loop is another **for** loop that begins by initializing the *Minutes* counter to 0. This leads to the seconds loop, where the *Seconds* counter is initialized to 0. Once the *Seconds* counter is initialized, the seconds loop is executed 60 times, as *Seconds* ranges from 0 to 59. Each time the seconds loop is executed, the *Hours, Minutes,* and *Seconds* count values are displayed. After the seconds loop is executed 60 times, the *Minutes* count is incremented and the seconds loop is entered again and executed 60 more times.

So, the seconds loop is executed 60 times for each iteration of the minutes loop. Likewise, since the minutes loop is nested within the hours loop, the minutes loop is executed 60 times for each iteration of the hours loop. After 60 iterations of the minutes loop (3,600 iterations of the seconds loop) the *Hours* count is incremented and displayed. The hours loop is not broken until it has been executed 12 times, from 0 to 11. Of course, this requires $12 \times 60 = 720$ iterations of the minutes loop, and $12 \times 60 \times 60 = 43{,}200$ iterations of the seconds loop. We say that the seconds loop is the *innermost* loop, while the *outermost* loop is the hours loop.

Notice that *no* framing is required for the hours and minutes loops. This is because the hours loop consists of a single **for** statement which is the minutes loop and the minutes loop consists of a single **for** statement which is the seconds loop. Here is where an indentation scheme becomes important, since it is the indentation that really shows the nesting. The seconds loop requires framing since it consists of two *cout* statements. The first *cout* statement "blanks" the output values prior to displaying the time values in the second *cout* statement. Blanking is required so that the time values appear correctly on the screen. Notice that the '\r' escape sequence is employed in both *cout* statements so that a given output overwrites the previous output.

To make the digital timer work, the seconds counter must be incremented precisely once every second. This requires a special delay function within the seconds loop to slow down the seconds count accordingly. This will be left as a programming exercise at the end of the chapter.

Before we leave the topic of nested loops, you should be aware that **while** and **do/while** loops can also be nested. You will find examples of this in the questions at the end of the chapter.

Down-to *for* Loops

In most of the **for** loops you have seen so far, the loop counter has been incremented from some initial value to some final value. In C++ it is often more convenient to decrement the loop counter down to zero and simply test the counter value, rather than increment the counter and use a relational test. This is because C++ interprets the test expression to be FALSE when its value is zero. Using this idea, the digital timer program segment could be easily revised to employ down-to loops like this:

```
// DIGITAL TIMER
#include <iostream.h>
```

```
void main()
// DEFINE VARIABLES
{
  int Hours;
  int Minutes;
  int Seconds;

// DISPLAY HEADINGS
  cout << "\n\n\n\n\t\t\tHours\tMinutes\tSeconds\n\n";

// START TIMER
  for (Hours = 12; Hours; --Hours)
    for (Minutes = 60; Minutes; --Minutes)
      for (Seconds = 60; Seconds; --Seconds)
        {
          cout << "\t\t\t\t\r";                    // BLANK DISPLAY
          cout << "\t\t\t" << Hours << '\t'
               << Minutes                          // DISPLAY TIME
               << '\t' << Seconds << '\r';
        }                                          // END SECONDS LOOP
}                                                  // END FUNCTION MAIN
```

The differences here are that the initial and final values of the respective loop counters have been changed so that the timer counts down from 12:60:60 and times out when the count reaches 00:00:00. The test expressions are simply the counter values, and the counters are being decremented rather than incremented. When a given counter value reaches zero, the loop test becomes FALSE and the respective loop is broken. The net effect is still the same: There are sixty iterations of the seconds loop for each iteration of the minutes loop, and sixty iterations of the minutes loop for each iteration of the hours loop. Of course, the timer counts down rather than counting up as in the previous program.

 Quick Check

1. List the three things that can appear in the first line of a **for** loop structure.
2. True or False: The loop counter in a **for** loop is altered after the loop statements are executed in a given iteration.

3. True or False: A **for** loop can always be replaced by a **while** loop, since they are basically the same looping structure, just coded differently.

4. How many times is the following loop executed?

```
for (int x = 0; x; ++x)
    cout << "How many times will this loop execute?";
```

5. How many times is the following loop executed?

```
for (int x = 0; x <= 10; ++x)
    cout << "How many times will this loop execute?";
```

6. When must the **for** loop statements be framed?

7. Suppose that you have two nested loops. The inner loop executes five times and the outer loop executes ten times. How many total iterations are there within the nested loop structure?

8. In a down-to loop, the loop counter is always _____.

6-4 THE *break* AND *continue* OPTIONS

The **break** and **continue** statements can be used to alter the execution of predefined control structures, such as loops, when certain conditions occur. In general, the **break** statement is used to immediately terminate a loop and the **continue** statement is used to skip over a loop iteration.

The *break* Statement

You observed the use of the **break** statement within the **switch** statement in the last chapter. Recall that the **break** statement forced the **switch** statement to terminate. The same is true when you use the **break** statement inside a loop structure. When C++ executes the **break** statement within a loop, the loop is immediately terminated and control is passed to the next statement following the loop. The **break** statement is usually used as part of an **if** statement within the loop to terminate the loop structure if a certain condition occurs. The action of the **break** statement within a **while** can be illustrated like this:

THE **break** *OPTION***

```
while (test expression)
{
    statement 1;
    statement 2;
        .
    if (test expression)
        break;
        .
    statement n;
}
Next statement after while;
```

Consider the following program segment:

```
int Number = 1;                    // LOOP COUNTER
while (Number < 11)
{
    if (Number == 5)
        break;
    cout << "\n\nIn the while loop, Number is now:  " << Number;
    ++Number;
}
cout << "\nThe loop is now terminated and the value of Number is:  "
        << Number;
```

This **while** loop employs a **break** statement to terminate the loop when *Number* reaches the value of 5. Here is what you would see as a result of the loop execution:

```
In the while loop, Number is now:  1
In the while loop, Number is now:  2
In the while loop, Number is now:  3
In the while loop, Number is now:  4
The loop is now terminated and the value of Number is:  5
```

As you can see, even though the final value of *Number* is 5, the *cout* statement within the loop is not executed when *Number* reaches 5 since the **break** statement forces the loop to terminate for this value. Normally, you would not break out of a loop as a result of a natural loop counter value. Doing so would indicate that you have coded your loop test incorrectly. This was only done to illustrate how the **break** statement works. You will primarily use the **break** statement to break out of a loop when the potential for an infinite loop exists. Such an application could be to interrupt the digital timer loops given in the last section as the result of a user entry to stop the timer.

The *continue* Statement

You have not seen the use of the **continue** statement before this, since it is primarily used to skip an iteration within a loop if a certain condition occurs. Like the **break** statement, the **continue** statement is normally employed within a loop as part of an **if** statement. We can illustrate the operation **continue** within a **for** loop like this:

THE *continue* OPTION

for (*Counter* = initial value; *Counter* test expression; Increment/Decrement
                                                                          Counter)
    {
        statement 1;
        statement 2;

                    .
                    .
                    .

        if (test expression)
            continue;

                    .
                    .
                    .

        statement n;
    }
    Next statement after **for**;

Here you see that when the **if** statement test expression is TRUE (non-zero), the **continue** statement is executed, forcing the current iteration to terminate. It is important to remember that *only the current iteration is terminated* as the result of **continue**. All subsequent iterations will be executed, unless of course they are terminated by executing a **break** or **continue**. The following program segment demonstrates how **continue** works:

```
for(int Number = 1;Number < 11; ++Number)
  {
    if (Number == 5)
        continue;
    cout << "\n\n In the for loop, Number is now:  " << Number;
  }
  cout << "\nThe loop is now terminated and the value of Number is:  "
        << Number;
```

Here is the result of executing the above program segment:

```
In the for loop, Number is now:  1
In the for loop, Number is now:  2
In the for loop, Number is now:  3
In the for loop, Number is now:  4
In the for loop, Number is now:  6
In the for loop, Number is now:  7
In the for loop, Number is now:  8
In the for loop, Number is now:  9
In the for loop, Number is now:  10
The loop is now terminated and the value of Number is:  11
```

You see here that the fifth iteration is skipped due to the execution of the **continue** statement. All subsequent iterations are performed and the loop is broken naturally when *Number* reaches the value of 11.

Quick Check

1. The statement that will cause only the current iteration of a loop to be aborted is the _____ statement.

2. The **break** and **continue** statements are normally used as part of a(n) _____ statement within a loop structure.

3. How many times will the following loop execute?

```
x = 0;
while (x <10)
{
    cout << "How many times will this loop execute?";
    if (x)
        break;
    ++x;
}
```

CASE STUDY: PARALLEL RESISTOR CIRCUIT ANALYSIS

Problem:

Let's close this chapter by writing several programs that will allow a user to find the total resistance of a circuit for any number of resistors in parallel as shown in Figure 6-4. We will solve the problem three different ways, using each of the three iteration control structures discussed in this chapter. First, let's define the problem in terms of output, input, and processing. Suppose you are working for an industrial firm and you are assigned a project to write a program that will allow an engineer to find the total equivalent electrical resistance of a resistive circuit for any number of resistors in parallel.

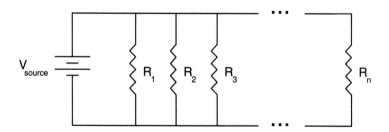

Figure 6-4 The solution of a general parallel resistor circuit is a candidate for iteration.

A simple way to find the equivalent resistance of the circuit is to use the *product-over-sum rule*. To use this rule, you start with the first two resistor values (R_1 and R_2) and calculate an equivalent resistance like this:

$$R_{equiv} = (R_1 \times R_2) / (R_1 + R_2)$$

Notice that the equivalent resistance for the two resistances is found by dividing their product by their sum. Thus, the rule is called the "product-over-sum" rule.

Next, the equivalent value obtained from this calculation is used with the third resistor value (R_3) to find a new equivalent like this:

$$R_{equiv} = (R_{equiv} \times R_3) / (R_{equiv} + R_3)$$

Then, this equivalent value is used with the fourth resistor value (R_4) to calculate a new equivalent value as follows:

$$R_{equiv} = (R_{equiv} \times R_4) / (R_{equiv} + R_4)$$

This process of calculating a new equivalent resistance value from the old one continues until all the resistor values in the circuit have been used. Notice that the same basic calculation must be *repeated* several times. Such a repetition operation would always suggest a loop structure in your program.

Now, do you suppose that you can develop a program to perform the required task? Remember that the program must find the equivalent resistance of any number of resistors in parallel. Let's first define the task at hand in terms of output, input, and processing.

The Problem Definition

Output: The program must first prompt the user to enter the number of resistors in the parallel circuit. A prompt will then be generated to enter each resistor value separately. The final output will be a display of the equivalent parallel resistance.

Input: The number of resistors in the circuit and the individual resistor values.

Processing: Each time a resistor value (R) is entered, the equivalent parallel resistance (R_{equiv}) will be recalculated using the "product-over-sum" rule as follows:

$$R_{equiv} = (R_{equiv} \times R) \ / \ (R_{equiv} + R)$$

Now, using the above problem definition, we are ready for the algorithm. Let's first employ the **while** iteration control structure to repeatedly calculate the equivalent parallel resistance each time a resistor value is entered.

The Algorithm

BEGIN
    Write a program description message.
    Write a user prompt to enter the number of resistors in the circuit.
    Read (*Number*).
    Set *Count* = 0.
    While (*Count* < *Number*)
        Set *Count* = *Count* + 1.
        Write prompt to enter resistor #(*Count*).
        Read (*R*).
        If *Count* == 1 Then
          Set $R_{equiv} = R$.
        Else
          Calculate $R_{equiv} = (R_{equiv} \times R) / (R_{equiv} + R)$.
    Write (R_{equiv}).
END.

As you can see, this is a rather simple algorithm employing the **while** control structure. Each time the loop is executed, an additional resistor value is entered and the equivalent resistance of the circuit is calculated. You probably are wondering why the **if/else** statement is used within the loop. Well, the first resistor value is entered the first time through the loop. Since *Count* = 1 during this first iteration, the **if** clause of the **if/else** statement is executed and R_{equiv} is set to this first resistor value. In subsequent iterations, the **else** clause is executed to calculate R_{equiv} using the product-over-sum rule. Without setting R_{equiv} to the first resistor value the first time through the loop, R_{equiv} would have no beginning value for subsequent calculations and the results would be unpredictable. Think about it!

So, you say to set the value of R_{equiv} equal to zero prior to the loop. But, this will result in the numerator of the product-over-sum equation being zero, which makes the value of R_{equiv} zero in each loop iteration. The easiest solution is to set R_{equiv} to the value of the first resistor during the first loop iteration. Then, the value of R_{equiv} is recalculated with each subsequent loop iteration. Of course, if there is only one resistor in the circuit (*Number* = 1), the loop is only executed once with the value of R_{equiv} being set to this single resistor value.

Notice also that a counter (*Count*) must be initialized to 0 prior to the loop. The value of *Count* must then be incremented with each loop iteration to prevent an infinite loop. The looping continues until the value of *Count* equals the number of resistors in the circuit (*Number*). When this happens, the loop statements are not executed again and the equivalent resistance is displayed.

Following the algorithm, you can easily code a C++ program like this:

The Program

```
// PARALLEL RESISTANCE USING WHILE (CASE6-1A.CPP)
#include <iostream.h>
#include <iomanip.h>

void main()
{
// DEFINE VARIABLES
   int Count;               // LOOP COUNTER
   int Number;              // NUMBER OF RESISTORS IN CIRCUIT
   float R_equiv;           // RESISTANCE OF CIRCUIT IN OHMS
   float R;                 // INDIVIDUAL RESISTANCE VALUES IN OHMS

// WRITE PROGRAM DESCRIPTION MESSAGE AND GET NUMBER
// OF PARALLEL RESISTORS
   cout << "This program will calculate the equivalent resistance\n"
           "of any number of parallel resistors.\n\n";
   cout << "Enter the number of resistors in the parallel circuit:  ";
   cin >> Number;

// CALCULATE EQUIVALENT RESISTANCE USING WHILE
   Count = 0;
   while (Count < Number)
   {
        ++Count;
        cout << "\nEnter the value for resistor #" << Count << ":  ";
```

```
            cin >> R;
            if (Count == 1)
               R_equiv = R;
            else
               R_equiv = (R_equiv * R) / (R_equiv + R);
      }
   cout << setprecision(2);
   cout << "\n\nThe equivalent resistance for the parallel circuit is:  "
         << R_equiv << " ohms";
}
```

Here is what you would see on the display when the above program is executed:

This program will calculate the equivalent resistance
of any number of parallel resistors.

Enter the number of resistors in the parallel circuit: **3**↵

Enter the value for resistor #1: **10**↵

Enter the value for resistor #2: **12**↵

Enter the value for resistor #3: **15**↵

The equivalent resistance for the parallel circuit is: 4 ohms

Next, suppose you want to use the **do/while** control structure to perform the same task. Remember the major difference is that the **do/while** loop statements are always executed at least once.

The Algorithm

BEGIN
    Write a program description message.
    Write a user prompt to enter the number of resistors in the circuit.
    Read (*Number*).
    Set *Count* = 0.
    Do
        Set *Count* = *Count* + 1.
        If Number == 0 Then
            Break

Write prompt to enter resistor #(*Count*).
Read (*R*).
If *Count* == 1 Then
   Set R_{equiv} = *R*.
Else
     Calculate R_{equiv} = (R_{equiv} × *R*) / (R_{equiv} + *R*).
While (*Count* < *Number*).
Write (R_{equiv}).
END.

Here you can see that the only difference between this algorithm and the previous **while** algorithm is the addition of an **if** statement that will cause the loop to break if the user enters a value of zero for the number of resistors in the circuit. Remember that a **do/while** loop is always executed at least once. Therefore, the loop must be broken and no calculation performed if there are no resistors in the circuit. This is an ideal application for the use of a **break** statement within a **while** loop. Here's the resulting program.

The Program

```
// PARALLEL RESISTANCE USING DO/WHILE (CASE6-1B.CPP)

#include <iostream.h>
#include <iomanip.h>

void main()
{
// DEFINE VARIABLES
   int Count;             // LOOP COUNTER
   int Number;            // NUMBER OF RESISTORS IN CIRCUIT
   float R_equiv;         // RESISTANCE OF CIRCUIT IN OHMS
   float R;               // INDIVIDUAL RESISTANCE VALUES IN OHMS

// WRITE PROGRAM DESCRIPTION MESSAGE AND GET NUMBER
// OF PARALLEL RESISTORS
   cout << "This program will calculate the equivalent resistance\n"
           "of any number of parallel resistors.\n\n";
   cout << "Enter the number of resistors in the parallel circuit:  ";
   cin >> Number;
// CALCULATE EQUIVALENT RESISTANCE USING DO/WHILE
   Count = 0;
```

```
do
{
    if (!Number)      // BREAK IF NUMBER IS ZERO
        break;
    ++Count;
    cout << "\nEnter the value for resistor #" << Count << ":  ";
    cin >> R;
    if (Count == 1)
        R_equiv = R;
    else
        R_equiv = (R_equiv * R) / (R_equiv + R);
}
while (Count < Number);
cout << setprecision(2);
cout << "\n\nThe equivalent resistance for the parallel circuit is:  "
    << R_equiv << " ohms";
}
```

The output of this program is the same as that of the **while** program.

Finally, let's rewrite the algorithm and code a program to employ the **for** iteration control structure. Remember that, with the **for** structure, the loop is executed a fixed number of times as the loop counter ranges from its initial to final value. So, why not set the initial counter value to 1 and make a test against the number of resistors in the parallel circuit. Here's the idea in the form of an algorithm:

The Algorithm

BEGIN
    Write a program description message.
    Write a user prompt to enter the number of resistors in the circuit.
    Read (*Number*).
    For *Count* = 1 to *Number*
        Write prompt to enter resistor #(*Count*).
        Read (*R*).
        If *Count* == 1 then
            Set R_{equiv} = R.
        Else
            Calculate R_{equiv} = (R_{equiv} × R) / (R_{equiv} + R).
    Write (R_{equiv}).
END.

Here, the loop executes as *Count* ranges from 1 to *Number*. The counter is incremented and tested as part of the **for** control structure. An **if/else** is used as before to initialize the value of R_{equiv} to the first resistor value during the first loop iteration. Here's the program:

The Program

```
// PARALLEL RESISTANCE USING FOR (CASE6-1C.CPP)

#include <iostream.h>
#include <iomanip.h>

void main()
{

// DEFINE VARIABLES
    int Count;              // LOOP COUNTER
    int Number;             // NUMBER OF RESISTORS IN CIRCUIT
    float R_equiv;          // RESISTANCE OF CIRCUIT IN OHMS
    float R;                // INDIVIDUAL RESISTANCE VALUES IN OHMS

// WRITE PROGRAM DESCRIPTION MESSAGE AND GET NUMBER
// OF PARALLEL RESISTORS
    cout << "This program will calculate the equivalent resistance\n"
            "of any number of parallel resistors.\n\n";
    cout << "Enter the number of resistors in the parallel circuit: ";
    cin >> Number;

// CALCULATE EQUIVALENT RESISTANCE USING FOR
    for (Count = 1; Count <= Number; ++Count)
    {
        cout << "\nEnter the value for resistor #" << Count << ": ";
        cin >> R;
        if (Count == 1)
            R_equiv = R;
        else
            R_equiv = (R_equiv * R) / (R_equiv + R);
    }
    cout << setprecision(2);
    cout << "\n\nThe equivalent resistance for the parallel circuit is: "
            << R_equiv << " ohms";
}
```

Notice how the algorithm statement *For Count = 1 to Number* is coded in
C++ as *for (Count = 1; Count <= Number; ++Count)*. The value of *Count* is
first initialized to 1. Then, to allow *Count* to range from 1 to *Number*, the test
must be *Count <= Number*. This allows the final iteration to occur when the
value of *Count* equals the value of *Number* and forces the loop to break when the
value of *Count* exceeds the value of *Number*. Of course, the value of *Count* is
incremented as part of the **for** statement.

The output of this program is the same as that for the previous two
programs.

CHAPTER SUMMARY

In this chapter you learned about the three iteration control structures employed by
C++: **while**, **do/while**, and **for**. The **while** is a pretest looping structure, the
do/while a posttest looping structure, and the **for** a fixed repetition looping
structure. As a result, the following general guidelines should be considered when
deciding which looping structure to use in a given situation:

- Use **while** whenever there is a possibility that the loop statements will not
  need to be executed.

- Use **do/while** when the loop statements must be executed at least once.

- Use **for** when it can be determined exactly how many times the loop
  statements must be executed. Thus, if the number of loop iterations is
  predetermined by the value of a variable or constant use a **for** loop.

The **break** and **continue** statements can be used to interrupt loop iterations.
Execution of the **break** statement within a loop forces the entire loop structure to
terminate immediately and pass control to the next statement following the loop
structure. Execution of the **continue** statement within a loop only terminates the
current loop iteration.

QUESTIONS AND PROBLEMS

Questions

1. Name the three iteration control structures employed by C++.
2. Which iteration control structure(s) will always execute the loop at least
   once?

3. Which iteration control structure(s) evaluates the test expression before the loop is executed?

4. Which iteration control structure(s) should be employed when it can be determined in advance how many loop repetitions there should be?

5. What will the following loop do?

```
while (3)
    cout << "Hello";
```

6. Explain the difference between the execution of **break** and **continue** within a loop.

In questions 7–17, determine the output generated by the respective program segment. Assume that the appropriate header files have been included.

7.
```
int A = 1;
while (17 % A != 5)
{
  cout << A << " " << 17 % A << '\n';
  ++A;
}
```

8.
```
int B = 2;
do
{
  cout << B << " " << B / 5 << '\n';
  B *= 2;
}
while (B != 20);
```

9.
```
int B = 2;
do
{
  cout << B << " " << B / 5 << '\n';
  B *= 2;
}
while (B != 32);
```

10.
```
int Number = 1;
int Product = 1;
do
{
  ++Number;
  Product *= Number;
}
while (Number < 5);
cout << "The product is:  " << Product;
```

11.    ```
int Count = -3;
while (Count < 3)
{
  if (!Count)
    continue;
  cout << Count << '\t';
  ++Count;
}
```

12.    ```
int Count = -3;
while (Count < 3)
{
  ++Count;
  if (!Count)
    continue;
  cout << Count << '\t';
}
```

13.    ```
int Count = -3;
while (Count < 3)
{
  ++Count;
  if (!Count)
    break;
  cout << Count << '\t';
}
```

14.    ```
cout << "\nAngle\tSin\tCos";
cout << "\n-----\t---\t---\n";
const float PI = 3.14159;
cout << setprecision(3);
for (int Angle = 0; Angle < 91; Angle += 5)
  cout << Angle << '\t' << sin(Angle * PI/180)
       << '\t' << cos(Angle * PI/180) << '\n';
```

15.    ```
for (int Row = 1; Row < 6; ++Row)
{
  for (int Col = 1; Col < 11; ++Col)
    cout << Row << ',' << Col << '\t';
  cout << '\n';
}
```
```

16.
```
int Count = 0;
const int MAXCOUNT = 5;
while (Count < MAXCOUNT)
{
  for (int I = 1; I < MAXCOUNT + 1; ++I)
    cout << I;
  cout << '\n';
  ++Count;
}
```

17.
```
int Times = 3;
do
{
  Count = 0;
  while (Count < MAXCOUNT)
  {
    for (int J = 1; J < Count + 1; ++J)
        cout << J;
    ++Count;
    cout << '\n';
  }
  cout << '\n';
  --Times;
}
while (Times);
```

Problems

Least Difficult

1. Write a program that will compute the average of any number of test scores using a **while** loop.

2. Revise the program in problem 1 to employ a **do/while** loop.

3. Revise the program in problem 1 to employ a **for** loop.

4. Write a C++ program that will find the equivalent resistance of any number of resistors in series. Employ the **while** control structure.

5. Revise the program in problem 4 to employ the **do/while** control structure.

6. Revise the program in problem 4 to employ the **for** control structure.

7. Using the formula $C = 5/9(F - 32)$, generate a Celsius conversion table for all even temperatures from 32 degrees to 212 degrees Fahrenheit.

More Difficult

8. Write a menu-driven program that will calculate the equivalent resistance of any number of resistors in a series or a parallel circuit.

9. Write a program that will calculate the mean ($\overline{x}$) and standard deviation (σ) of a series of numbers. The mean of a series of numbers is the same as the average of the numbers. The standard deviation of a series of numbers is found using the following formula:

$$\sigma = \sqrt{\frac{(x_1 - \overline{x})^2 + (x_2 - \overline{x})^2 + \cdots + (x_n - \overline{x})^2}{n}}$$

10. Some programming languages, like BASIC, allow you to use a STEP command within a **for** statement like this:

FOR Counter = \<initial value\> TO \<final value\> STEP N DO

The STEP command allows the loop counter to increment by some value (N), other than the value 1, with each loop iteration.
Write a **for** loop in C++ that will emulate this STEP operation. Provide for user entry of any desired step value. To demonstrate its operation, use your step loop to display every fifth integer, from 1 to 100.

11. The DOS versions of C++ include a function called **delay()** which allows you to insert a time delay in your programs. The **delay()** function is located in the *dos.h* header file and accesses the system clock via DOS to provide a precise time delay. To use **delay()**, you simply insert the desired time delay, in milliseconds, as the argument within the function. Thus, **delay(10000)** would create a 10 second delay. Add the **delay()** function to the digital timer program given in this chapter to create a precise timer. Compile, execute, and observe the program output.

12. Using the ideas you saw in the digital timer program in this chapter, write a C++ program to display the output of a 4-bit binary counter. A 4-bit binary counter simply counts in binary from 0000 to 1111. The first count value is 0000, the second is 0001, the third is 0010, and so on, until it reaches the final count value of 1111. Insert a delay in the program such that the counter increments once every two seconds. Change the delay

value and observe the effect on the count frequency. (*Hint:* You will need four nested loops, one for each bit within the count value.)

Most Difficult

13. Write a program that will find the equivalent resistance of a series-parallel circuit of any arbitrary configuration. A series-parallel circuit is one in which there are both series and parallel resistor connections. (*Hint:* When combining resistors in such a circuit, you must start with the last resistor, at the end of the circuit, and work towards the first resistor, at the beginning of the circuit.)

7

FUNCTIONS FOR TOP/DOWN DESIGN

INTRODUCTION

Up to this point, you have been working with C++ programs that consist of one main section defined by function *main( )*. The idea of functions is central to C and C++ programming. In fact, it is often said that C and C++ are languages of functions. This is because well-structured C and C++ programs are simply a collection of functions. You have already used built-in, or predefined, functions in your programs. All of these functions are part of the various header files included with C++. Now it is time to develop your own functions and employ them to create modular, well-structured, C++ programs. Functions that you create for your own use in a program are called *user-defined* functions. In this sense, the "user" is you, the programmer.

A *user-defined function* is a block of statements, or subprogram, that are written to perform a specific task required by you, the programmer.

The function is given a name and *called*, or *invoked*, using its name each time the task is to be performed within the program. The program that calls, or invokes, a function is often referred to as the *calling program.*

Functions eliminate the need for duplicate statements within a program. Given a task to be performed more than once, the statements are written just once for the function. Then, the function is called each time the task must be performed. In addition, the use of functions enhances the program listing clarity and readability. And most important, the use of functions within a structured language such as C++ allows you to solve very large complex problems using a top/down program design approach. The meaning of a top/down program design should become clear by the end of this chapter.

If you are familiar with the Pascal language, you are aware that subprograms can take the form of either a function or a procedure. In C++, the function serves both roles: A function can be made to return a single value to the calling program, or functions can be written to perform specific tasks or return a set of values to the calling program.

7-1 FUNCTIONS THAT RETURN A SINGLE VALUE

You have already had some experience with functions that return a single value in C++. Recall the standard functions that you learned about in Chapter 4 such as *sqrt(), sin(), cos()*, and *getchar()*, just to mention a few. You found that C++ included several predefined mathematical, string, I/O, and graphics functions. However, suppose you wish to perform some operation that is not a predefined function in C++, such as cube. Since C++ does not include any standard function for the cube operation, you could code the operation as a statement in your program like this:

$$cube = x * x * x;$$

Then, you insert this statement into your program each time the value of *x* must be cubed. However, wouldn't it be a lot easier simply to insert the command *cube(x)* each time *x* is to be cubed, where C++ knows what to do just as it knows how to execute *sqrt(x)*? You can do this by defining your own *cube()* function. Such a function is called a ***user-defined function***, for obvious reasons.

A user-defined function is a subprogram that, when invoked, performs some task or returns a single value that replaces the function name wherever the name is used in the calling program. Thus, if *cube()* is a user-defined function that will cube a value, say *x*, the statement *cout << cube(x);* will invoke the function and cause the cube of *x* to be displayed. Now you need to learn how you can create such user-defined functions.

Here is the format that you must use when defining your own functions:

USER-DEFINED FUNCTION FORMAT

```
// FUNCTION HEADER
    <return data type> <function name> (<parameter list>)
{
// LOCAL VARS AND CONSTS
    <local constant and variable should go here>

// FUNCTION STATEMENTS or BODY
    function statement #1;
    function statement #2;
            •

            •

    function statement #n;
    return(<return value>);
}
```

The function definition format consists of three main sections: a *function header* line, any *local variables or constants* required by the function, and a *statement* section.

The Function Header

The *function header* provides the data *interface* for the function.

A *function interface*, or *header*, is a statement that forms a common boundary between the function and its calling program.

This idea is illustrated by Figure 7-1. Thus, the header dictates what types of data the function will accept from the calling program, and what type of data the function will return to the calling program.

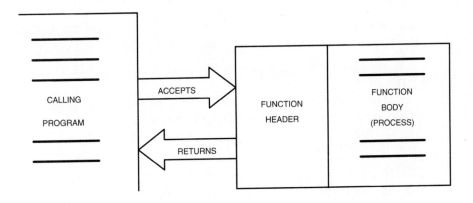

Figure 7-1 The function header forms the interface between the calling program and the function.

In general, the function header consists of the following three parts:

- The data type of the value to be returned by the function, if any.

- The name of the function.

- A parameter listing.

The Return Data Type

The first thing that appears in the function header is the data type of the return value. Recall that a function can be made to return a single value which replaces the function name wherever the name appears in a calling program. The value that replaces the function name in the calling program is referred to as the **return value**. When a function is used for this purpose, the data type of the return value must be specified in the function heading. For example, suppose that our *cube()* function returns the cube of an integer. Since the cube of an integer is an integer, the function will return an integer value. As a result, the return value data type must be *int* and specified in the function header like this:

int cube(<parameter listing>)

On the other hand, if our *cube()* function were to cube a floating point value, the return data type would have to be *float* and the header would look like this:

float cube(<parameter listing>)

When a function does not return any value to the calling program you must use the keyword **void** as the return data type like this:

void Sample_Function(<parameter listing>)

Functions that do not return a value to the calling program are used to perform specific tasks, such as I/O. More about these types of functions later.

The Function Name

The function name can be any legal identifier in C++. However, the function name *should not* begin with an underscore symbol for debugging purposes. This is because some debuggers always place an underscore symbol in front of the function name if an error is found in the function. The function name should be descriptive of the operation that the function performs, such as *cube* describes the cubing of a value. When you invoke the function within your calling program, you will use this name.

Two things to remember:

1. The function name can never be used *inside of the function*. In other words, the following statement inside the *cube()* function will generate an error:

cube = x * x * x;

There is one exception to this rule called ***recursion***, which will be discussed later.

2. The function identifier can never be used on the left side of the assignment symbol *outside of the function*. Therefore, the following statement will cause an error in the calling program:

cube = x * x * x;

The Parameter Listing

The function parameter listing includes variables, called ***parameters***, that will be passed from the calling program and evaluated by the function. Think of a parameter as a function variable, waiting to receive a value from the calling program when the function is invoked. To determine the function parameters, ask yourself: What types of data must the function accept to perform its designated task? Suppose that our *cube()* function will cube integer values. Then, the function must accept an integer value from the calling program and return an integer value to the calling program. Thus, our function interface can be described as follows:

Function *cube()*: Cubes an integer.

Accepts: An integer value.

Returns: An integer value.

Let's designate x as the integer variable that the function will accept. In C++, a given parameter must be specified in the function header by indicating its data type followed by its identifier. As a result, the appropriate parameter listing for the *cube()* function would be *(int x)*. Putting everything together, the complete header would be:

int cube(int x)

If the *cube()* function were to cube floating point values, the appropriate header would be:

float cube(float x)

Example 7-1:

Suppose you wish to write a user-defined function to calculate the voltage in a dc circuit using Ohm's law. Write an appropriate function heading.

Solution:

Let's call the function *Voltage*, since this is what the function must return to the calling program each time the function is called.

To develop the function header, we will treat the function like a black box and ask ourselves the following two questions: (1) What types of data must the function accept from the calling program in order to perform the application task? (2) What type of data must it return to the calling program? The answers to these questions will dictate the function header. To answer the first question, think about what the function must evaluate. In order to calculate voltage using Ohm's law, the function must evaluate two things: current and resistance. So let's use the words *Current* and *Resistance* as our parameters. Of what data type should the parameters be? The obvious choice is floating point, since you want to allow the function to evaluate decimal values of current and resistance. Thus, the function must accept a floating point value of *Current* and a floating point value of *Resistance*.

Next, you must decide what type of data the function must return to the calling program. Since the function is evaluating floating point values, it makes mathematical sense that the returned value should also be a floating point value.

Now, the function interface can be described as follows:

Function *Voltage()*: Calculates voltage using Ohm's law.

Accepts: A floating point value for *Current* and a floating point
                    value for *Resistance*.

Returns: A floating point value for *Voltage*.

Once you have decided what the function accepts and returns, the function header is easily constructed in C++ syntax as follows:

float Voltage (float Current, float Resistance)

The Statement Section

The statement section of the function includes those operations that the function must perform to return a value to the calling program or perform some given task. Look at the general format for a user-defined function again. As you can see, the entire statement section is framed with curly braces. After the opening curly brace, you should begin the statement section by declaring any constants and defining variables that will be used within the function. Any constants or variables listed here are called **local**, since they are defined only for local use within the function itself. Local variables have no meaning outside of the function in which they are defined. You do not duplicate any of your function parameters here. You only list any additional constants or variables that the function might require during its execution. A common example of a local variable is a loop counter that is employed as part of a **while**, **do/while**, or **for** loop within the function. Actually, you can declare local constants and define local variables anyplace within the function as long as they are listed prior to their use. However, good style dictates that they be declared/defined at the beginning of the statement section of the function.

The executable statements of the function follow any local definitions. The last statement in the function is the **return** statement. The **return** statement is used when a single value must be returned to the calling program. So, if our *cube()* function must return the cube of *x*, an appropriate return statement would be:

```
return(x * x * x);
```

Combining the function header and statement section for the cube function will give us the complete function as follows:

```
int cube(int x)
{
   return(x * x * x);
}
```

Obviously, this is a relatively simple function that doesn't require any local definitions or executable statements other than the **return** statement.

Example 7-2:

Complete the *Voltage()* function whose header was developed in Example 7-1.

Solution:

Ohm's law requires the function to multiply *Current* by *Resistance* to get *Voltage*. Thus, the only statement required in the function is a **return** statement that will return the product of *Current* and *Resistance*. Putting it all together, the complete function becomes:

```
float Voltage(float Current, float Resistance)
{
   return(Current * Voltage);
}
```

Example 7-3:

Write a function to return the sum of all integers from 1 to some maximum integer value, called *Max*. The function must obtain the value of *Max* from the calling program.

Solution:

Let's call this function *Sum()*. Now, the function must receive an integer value, called *Max*, from the calling program. Since the function is to sum all the integers from 1 to *Max* it must return an integer value. Thus, our function interface can be described as follows:

Function *Sum()*:   Sums all integers from 1 to *Max*.

Accepts: An integer value, *Max*.

Returns: An integer value.

Using this information, the function header becomes:

int Sum(int Max)

The next step is to determine if there are any local variables required by the function statements. You can use a **for** loop to calculate the sum of integers from 1 to *Max*. However, the **for** statement requires a counter variable. This is a classic application for a local variable. Let's call this local counter variable *Count*. Next, you also need a temporary variable within the **for** loop to keep a running subtotal of the sum each time the loop executes. Let's call this local variable *SubTotal*. Using these ideas, the complete function is:

```
int Sum(int Max)
{
  int Count;
  int SubTotal = 0;

  for (Count = Max; Count; --Count)
    SubTotal += Count;
  return(SubTotal);
}
```

Why can't you use *Sum* instead of *SubTotal* within the function **for** loop? This would cause an error during compilation. The reason? *Sum* is the function identifier and cannot appear within the body of the function except when used as part of a recursive operation (to be discussed later).

Calling Functions That Return a Single Value

You call, or invoke, a user-defined function just about anywhere in your program just as you call many of the standard functions in C++. For example, you can call a function by using an assignment operator or an *cout* statement like this:

y = cube(2);

or

cout << cube(2);

In both cases, the value 2 is passed to the function to be cubed. Thus, in our *cube()* function, the parameter *x* takes on the value 2. The function will return the cube of 2, which is 8. With the assignment statement, the variable *y* will be assigned the value 8, while the *cout* statement causes the value 8 to be displayed on the monitor.

Here are two other ways that our *cube()* function can be invoked:

int A = 2;
y = cube(A);

or

cout << cube(A);

In these cases, the function is cubing the variable *A*, where *A* has been previously assigned the value 2. Thus, the value of *A*, or 2, is passed to the function to be cubed. In our *cube()* function, the parameter *x* takes on the value of *A*.

Functions can also be invoked as part of arithmetic expressions or relational statements. For instance, our *cube()* function can be invoked as part of an arithmetic expression like this:

int A = 2;
y = 1 + cube(A) * 2;

What will be assigned to *y* ? Well, C++ evaluates the *cube()* function first to get 8, then performs the multiplication operation to get 16, and finally adds 1 to 16 to get 17.

You also can use functions as part of relational operations like this:

if (cube(A) >= 27)

When will the relationship be TRUE? When *A* is greater than or equal to 3, right? When *A* is greater than or equal to 3, *cube(A)* is greater than or equal to 27. Just remember that when a function is designed to return a single value to the calling program, the *value returned replaces the function name wherever the name is used in the calling program.*

Actual Arguments versus Formal Parameters

Some terminology is appropriate at this time. In the foregoing *cube()* example, the variable *A* used in the calling program is called an ***actual argument.*** On the other hand, the corresponding variable *x* used in the function header is called a ***formal parameter***.

Actual arguments are values/variables used within the function call, while ***formal parameters*** are variables used within the function header.

Thus, the formal parameter in our *cube()* function, *x*, takes on the value of the actual argument, *A*, used in the function call. Here are some things that you will want to remember about actual arguments and formal parameters:

- Actual argument variables must be defined in the calling program. This will be the main function, unless functions are calling other functions.

- The data type of the corresponding actual arguments and formal parameters should be the same.

- Formal parameters are place holders for the actual argument values during the execution of the function. Formal parameters are always listed in the parameter section of the function heading.

- The number of actual arguments used during the function call must be the same as the number of formal parameters listed in the function heading.

- The correspondence between actual arguments and formal parameters is established on a one-to-one basis according to the respective listing orders.

- Although the actual argument and formal parameter variables often have different variable names, they can be the same. When this is the case, the respective variables must still be defined in the calling program as well as appear in the parameter listing of the function.

Quick Check

1. What is the role of a function in a C++ program?
2. The three main sections of a function are the _____,
   _____, and _____ sections.
3. What is the purpose of the function header in a C++ program?
4. List the three parts of a function header.
5. A function variable, waiting to receive a value from the calling program is
   called a _____.
6. What is the purpose of a **return** statement in a function?
7. Explain the difference between an actual argument in a calling program and a
   formal parameter in a function header.

7-2 FUNCTIONS THAT DO NOT RETURN A SINGLE VALUE

Functions that do not return a single value to the calling program are often written
to return a set of values or perform some specific task. When a function is not
returning a single value to the calling program, you must use the keyword **void** as
the return data type. In addition, these functions may or may not require
parameters. When no parameters are required you simply leave the parameter
listing blank to indicate to the compiler that the function does not need to receive
any values from the calling program. Functions that do not return a value or do
not require any parameters are the simplest type of functions in C++. For
example, suppose that you wish to write a function that will display the following
header on the monitor each time it is called:

NAME   STREET ADDRESS   STATE   CITY   ZIP
_____   _____ _____   _____   ____   ___

Let's call this function *Display_Header()*. To develop the function header,
ask yourself what the function must accept to perform its designated task, and
what it must return. In this case, the function is simply displaying constant header

information and does not need to accept any data or return any data. Thus, our function interface can be described as follows:

Function *Display_Header()*:   Displays fixed header information.

Accepts: Nothing.

Returns: Nothing.

Using this information, the header becomes:

void Display_Header()

Look at the function header and you will see the keyword **void** used as the function return data type. The keyword **void** used here indicates to the compiler that there is no return value. Furthermore, notice that there are no parameters required by this function, since the parameter listing is left blank. In other words, the function does not return a value and does not require any arguments to evaluate: it simply performs a given task, in this case displaying a header. To display the header, all you need is a *cout* statement in the body of the function. Putting everything together, the function becomes:

```
void Display_Header()
{
 cout << "\tNAME\tSTREET ADDRESS\tCITY\tSTATE\tZIP"
          "\n\t____\t_____\t____\t____\t____\t___";
}
```

Finally, you do not see a **return** statement at the end of the function, since no value is being returned by the function.

How would you call this function in your program? Simple, just use the function name as a statement within the calling program each time the header must be displayed like this:

Display_Header();

No actual arguments are listed in the function call, since no arguments need to be evaluated by the function.

Value versus Reference Parameters

The above *Display_Header()* function did not require any formal parameter listing, since it did not need to receive any arguments from the calling program to evaluate. When formal parameters are required for evaluation by the function, they must be listed in the function header in one of two ways: as *value parameters* or as *reference parameters*.

Value Parameters

You have been using value parameters up to this point in this chapter. Value parameters allow for *one-way communication* of data from the calling program to the function. This concept is illustrated in Figure 7-2a.

> A *value parameter* provides for one-way communication of data from the calling program to the function.

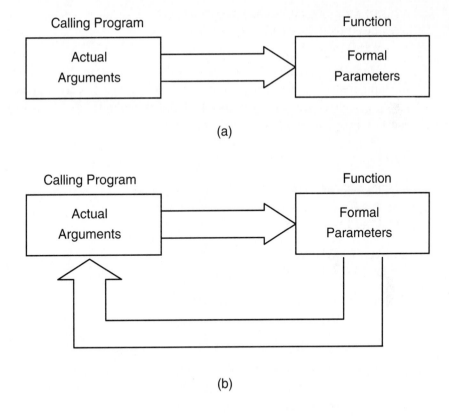

(a)

(b)

Figure 7-2 (a) Passing parameters by value and (b) by reference.

Observe that the actual argument values in the calling program are passed (by value) to the formal parameters in the function. Another way to think of it is that the formal parameter receives a *copy* of the actual argument value. Thus, the actual argument value in the calling program is protected from being accidentally changed by the function. The important thing to remember is that any manipulation of the formal parameters within the function does not affect the actual argument values used for the function call. For instance, consider the following function:

```
void Pass_By_Value(int x,int y)
{
// INCREMENT AND DECREMENT FORMAL PARAMETERS
 ++x;
 --y;

// DISPLAY FORMAL PARAMETER VALUES
  cout << "\nx = " << x << "\ny = " << y;
}
```

Here, the parameters *x* and *y* are value parameters. Notice that, within the function, the value of *x* is incremented and the value of *y* is decremented. Then, the resulting values are displayed using a *cout* statement. Now, suppose the above function is called by the following program:

```
void main()
{
// DECLARE ACTUAL AGUMENT VARIABLES
  int A = 0;
  int B = 0;

// CALL FUNCTION
  Pass_By_Value(A,B);

// DISPLAY ACTUAL ARGUMENT VALUES
  cout << "\nA = " << A << "\nB = " << B;
}
```

First, notice how the function is called. It is simply a statement in the calling program. The function name is listed, followed by the required actual arguments within parentheses. The actual arguments are *A* and *B*, since they are listed in the function call. When the function call is executed, the value of *A* is passed to the formal parameter *x* and the value of *B* is passed to the formal parameter *y*. Notice that, before the function call, the calling program initializes both *A* and *B* to the value 0. As a result, both *x* and *y* receive the value 0 from the calling program. The function then increments the value of *x*, decrements the value of *y*, and displays the new values of *x* and *y*. However, the operations on *x* and *y* have no effect on the actual arguments (*A* and *B*) in the calling program. The values of *A* and *B* remain 0. Notice that after the function call, the calling program displays the values of *A* and *B*. What would you see on the display by executing the program? Well, the *Pass_By_Value()* function displays *x* and *y*, then *main()* displays *A* and *B*. Therefore, the resulting display is:

$$x = 1$$
$$y = -1$$
$$A = 0$$
$$B = 0$$

Reference Parameters

Reference parameters, sometimes called ***variable parameters***, differ from value parameters in that they provide two-way communication between the calling program and the function as illustrated in Figure 7-2b.

A ***reference parameter*** provides two-way communication of data between the calling program and function.

Observe the two-way communication path: the actual argument values are passed to the formal parameters in the function, then the formal parameter values are passed back to the actual arguments. This allows the function to change the actual argument values in the calling program. Recall that a value parameter is simply a copy of the actual argument value and, therefore, any operations on the parameter within the function have no effect on its original argument value. On the other hand, a reference parameter represents the address in memory of the actual argument value. As a result, any changes made to the reference parameter within the function will change what's stored at that address. This obviously changes the original value of the actual argument in the calling program. To create a reference parameter, you simply insert the ampersand symbol, &, prior to the appropriate parameter identifiers in the function heading. Let's change our preceding example to use reference parameters as follows:

```
void Pass_By_Reference(int &x,int &y)
{
// INCREMENT AND DECREMENT FORMAL PARAMETERS
 ++x;
 --y;

// DISPLAY FORMAL PARAMETER VALUES
  cout << "\nx = " << x << "\ny = " << y;
}
```

The major change here is to insert the $\&$ symbol prior to x and y in the function heading. Of course, the function name has also been changed to reflect the new application. What would you see on the display as a result of executing the following program?

```
void main()
{
// DECLARE ACTUAL ARGUMENT VARIABLES
  int A = 0;
  int B = 0;

// CALL FUNCTION
  Pass_By_Reference(A,B);

// DISPLAY ACTUAL ARGUMENT VALUES
  cout << "\nA = " << A << "\nB = " << B;
}
```

Since x and y are now reference parameters and not value parameters, any operations that affect x and y within the function will also affect the values of the actual arguments, A and B, used in the function call. Here are the values displayed by the program:

$$x = 1$$
$$y = -1$$
$$A = 1$$
$$B = -1$$

As you can see, the new values of x and y are passed back to A and B, respectively.

Example 7-4:

What will be displayed as a result of the following program?

```
#include <iostream.h>

// FUNCTION PROTOTYPE
  void Display_Parameters(int&, int);

void main()
{
// DECLARE ACTUAL ARGUMENT VARIABLES
  int A = 0;
  int B = 0;

// CALL FUNCTION
  Display_Parameters(A,B);

// DISPLAY ACTUAL ARGUMENT VALUES
  cout << "\nA = " << A << "\nB = " << B;
}           // END main()

//*****************************************************************************
//
// THIS FUNCTION DEMONSTRATES THE USE OF VALUE VERSUS
// REFERENCE PARAMETERS
//
// *****************************************************************************
void Display_Parameters(int &x, int y)
// INCREMENT AND DECREMENT FORMAL PARAMETERS
  ++x;
  --y;

// DISPLAY FORMAL PARAMETER VALUES
  cout << "\nx = " << x << "\ny = " << y;
}
```

Solution:

Here you see an entire program that incorporates a function. The function is located immediately following the closing brace of function *main()*. The function is then called within the statement section of *main()* by simply listing its name followed by a listing of the required actual arguments. Notice that the actual arguments (*A* and *B*) are declared as integer variables in *main()*. Now look at the function heading. The formal parameters are *x* and *y*. Both are integers; however, *x* is a reference parameter while *y* is a value parameter. Observe the use of the & symbol prior to *x*. This defines *x* as a reference parameter. However, a comma follows *x*, ending this definition. Then, *y* is defined separately as a value parameter. As a result, the value of *x* is passed back to *main()*, but the value of *y* is not. Here's what you would see on the display:

$$x = 1$$
$$y = -1$$
$$A = 1$$
$$B = 0$$

Example 7-5:

Write a function called *Exchange()* that will accept two integer variables from the calling program and return the variables with their values exchanged.

Solution:

This is an ideal application for reference parameters since, to exchange the variable values, the exchange process within the function must have an effect on the original variable values in the calling program. So, the function must accept two integer variables and return the same two variables with the values exchanged. Here's a description of the function interface:

Function *Exchange()*:   Exchanges the values of two integer variables.

Accepts: Two integer variables.

Returns: The same two integer variables.

Since the function must return the same two integer variables that it accepts, both will be reference parameters. Let's label the parameters *Variable1* and *Variable2*. The function header then becomes:

void Exchange(int &Variable1, int &Variable2)

Notice the use of the ampersand symbol to indicate that the parameters are reference parameters. Because *Variable1* and *Variable2* are reference parameters, the values of the actual argument variables used in the function call will be exchanged. Now, to exchange the two variable values within the function, you must create a temporary local variable so that one of the values is not lost. Using this idea, the complete function is:

```
void Exchange(int &Variable1, int &Variable2)
{
  int Temp = Variable1;
  Variable1 = Variable2;
  Variable2 = Temp;
}
```

Locating Functions Within Your Program

As you can see from Example 7-4, user-defined functions are located just after the closing brace of function *main()*. There is no limit on the number of user-defined functions that can be used in a program. To call a function that returns a single value you must insert the function name where you want the value to be returned. To call a user-defined function that doesn't return a single value, you simply list its name as a statement within the calling program. Of course, in both cases any actual arguments required by the function must be listed within parentheses after the function name when it is called. In addition, the number of actual arguments used in the function call must be the same as the number of formal parameters defined in the respective function header.

The placement of functions in a C++ program is summarized in Figure 7-3. Notice the block structure of the overall program. Function *main()* forms the overall outer program block, while the user-defined functions form the inner blocks which are nested within function *main()* via the function calls. This is why C++ is called a **block-structured language**. From now on when we develop C++ programs we will attempt to divide the overall programming problem down into a group of simpler subproblems whose combined solution solves the original problem. How will these subproblems be coded? You got it—as functions! This is the essence of structured programming and top/down software design.

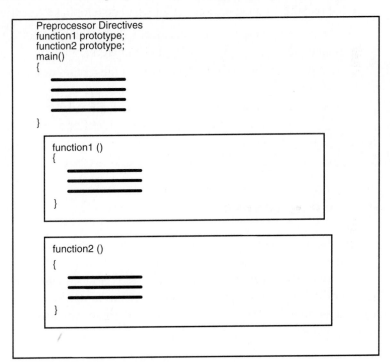

Figure 7-3 Functions are usually placed after *main()* in a C++ program.

PROGRAMMING NOTE

Although functions that employ reference parameters might have a **void** return type, they are in fact returning values to the calling program via the reference parameters. Do not get the idea of the function return data type confused with the idea of returning values via reference parameters. They are two different things.

 Quick Check

1. What must be used as the return data type when a function does not return a single value to the calling program?

2. What two things must be considered when developing a function header?

3. One-way communication of data from the calling program to a function is provided via _____ parameters.

4. Two-way communication of data between the calling program and a function is provided via _____ parameters.

5. To specify a reference parameter in a function header you must use the _____ symbol prior to the parameter identifier.

6. Where is the body of a function normally located in a C++ program?

7-3 FUNCTION PROTOTYPES

You undoubtedly noticed the presence of a *function prototype* in the program of Example 7-4 and the illustration in Figure 7-3.

A *function prototype*, sometimes referred to as a *function declaration*, is a model of the *interface* to the function that can be used by the compiler to check calls to the function for the proper number of arguments and the correct data types of the arguments.

A *function prototype* is a model of the interface to the function.

Prototyping forces the compiler to perform additional data type checking of your function calls, thus aiding in the detection of programming errors associated with function calls. For example, if a function expects to receive an integer value and the programmer tries to pass it a character string, the compiler can detect the error because C++ requires that the function prototype be specified prior to the function call. Because prototyping forces the compiler to check for errors during compile time, it does not affect the size or speed of the run-time program. Although it takes the compiler slightly longer to perform this error checking task, any errors detected via prototyping can save hours of debugging time had prototyping not been employed. For these reasons, function prototypes are required by the C++ language. You should be aware, however, that function prototyping is optional in the C language. As a result, the C++ language is considered more strongly typed than the C language.

In the foregoing definition of a prototype you see it provides a model of the interface to the function. Well, the function interface is the function header; therefore the function prototype is simply a copy of the function header used by the compiler to verify the calls to the function. Thus, the prototype dictates what types of data the function will accept from the calling program, and what type of data the function will return to the calling program.

You see from Figure 7-3 that the function prototypes are located just after the preprocessor directives and just prior to function *main()*. The function prototype can be nothing more than a copy of the function header followed by a semicolon like this:

void Student(int Number, float Average, char Grade);

Here, the prototype tells the compiler that the function *Student()* will not be returning a value to the calling program. In addition, *Student()* expects to receive three parameters when it is called. The first parameter will be interpreted as an integer, the second as a floating point value, and the third as a character. If the function is called with more than or fewer than the number of parameters listed in the prototype, the compiler will generate an error. If the function is called with parameters that have different data types than those listed in the prototype, the parameters will be treated as if they were the respective data types listed. Here is a program that uses the *Student()* function whose prototype is shown above:

```
#include <iostream.h>
#include <iomanip.h>

// FUNCTION PROTOTYPE
   void Student(int Number, float Average, char Grade);
```

```
void main()
{
  Student(5, 85.6, 'B');
}

//****************************************************************************
// THIS FUNCTION WILL DISPLAY A STUDENT'S AVERAGE AND
// GRADE
//****************************************************************************
void Student(int Number, float Average, char Grade)
{
  cout << setprecision(1);
  cout << "\n\nThere are " << Number << " tests, resulting "
       << "in an average of " << Average << " and a grade of "
       << Grade << '.';
}
```

The output generated by this program is:

There are 5 tests, resulting in an average of 85.6 and a grade of B.

As you can see, the actual arguments in the function call were passed to *Student()* and used to construct the *cout* statement. If more or less parameters would have been used in the function call, a compiler error would result. But what would happen if the parameter data types were not the same as those listed in the prototype? Consider this function call:

Student('B', 'A', 67);

This call would not produce a compiler error, since the number of parameters is correct. However, the compiler would interpret the first parameter as an integer, the second as a floating point value, and the third as a character value. As a result, the output generated by the function call would be:

There are 66 tests resulting in an average of 65.0 and a grade of C.

Do you see what happened? The function used the integer equivalent of the character 'B' for the first parameter, the floating point equivalent of the character 'A' for the second parameter, and the character equivalent of the integer 67 for the third parameter. Of course, these equivalencies are derived from the ASCII character code. So, the lesson here is to make sure that the argument data types match the formal parameter data types or you may get unpredictable results.

Look at the *Student()* function prototype again and you will see that it is just a copy of the function header. Because of this, prototypes are easily coded into your program by using the block copy feature of the program editor. Once you code your function, simply mark the function header and copy it to the prototype area just prior to function *main()*. Don't forget to add a semicolon at the end of the prototype, since the copied function header will not have one.

You may also list your function prototypes without any parameter identifiers like this:

void Student(int, float, char);

After all, the compiler is not interested in the parameter names, it is only interested in the number of parameters and their data types. One final point: If you forget to include a prototype for a function you will get the familiar "prototype expected" error when you compile your program. You will also get this error if you forget to include a header file for a standard function in your program. The reason for this is that the prototypes for the standard functions in C++ are included in the respective function header files.

Default Parameters

When a parameter has a default value, the parameter assumes its default value when no argument is supplied for that parameter in the function call.

A *default parameter* is a function parameter that is assigned a default value in the function prototype or the function header, but not both.

Consider the following program:

```
// PREPROCESSOR DIRECTIVES
#include <iostream.h>

// FUNCTION PROTOTYPE
int Volume(int Length, int Width = 5, int Height = 2);

void main()
{

// ACTUAL ARGUMENT DEFINITIONS
  int  L = 10;                      // LENGTH
```

```
    int W = 15;                    // WIDTH
    int H = 12;                    // HEIGHT

// FUNCTION CALLS
    cout << "\nThe volume for this function call is:  " << Volume(L,W,H)
        << "\n\n";
    cout << "\nThe volume for this function call is:  " << Volume(L,W)
        << "\n\n";
    cout << "\nThe volume for this function call is:  " << Volume(L)
        << "\n\n";
    cout << "\nThe volume for this function call is:  " << Volume(3,3,3)
        << "\n\n";
} // END MAIN

// FUNCTION DEFINITION
int Volume(int Length, int Width, int Height)
{
    cout << "\nThe formal parameters for this function call are: " << Length << ', '
        << Width << ', ' << Height;
    return (Length * Width * Height);
}
```

Here you see a prototype for function *Volume()* where the *Width* and *Height* parameters are assigned default values of 5 and 2, respectively. Looking at the function definition, you see that the function simply writes its formal parameter values and returns the product of these values. Now, look at the function calls in the body of *main()*. Notice how the function is called several times, each time with a different set of actual arguments. Here is what you would see on your monitor after executing this program:

```
            The formal parameters for this function are:  10, 15, 12
            The volume for this function is:  1800

            The formal parameters for this function are:  10, 15, 2
            The volume for this function is:  300

            The formal parameters for this function are:  10, 5, 2
            The volume for this function is:  100

            The formal parameters for this function are:  3, 3, 3
            The volume for this function is:  27
```

The first time the function is called, all three arguments are supplied by the way of the three variables *L, W,* and *H,* which are initialized to 10, 15, and 12, respectively, in *main( ).* The second time the function is called, only *L* and *W* are supplied as function arguments. Since the *Height* argument is not supplied, the compiler inserts the default *Height* value of 2 for this argument. Thus, the returned volume is 10 * 15 * 2, or 300. In the third call, only the value of *L* is supplied as a function argument and the compiler inserts the default values of 5 and 2 for the *Width* and *Height* arguments, respectively. This results in a volume value of 10 * 5 * 2, or 100. Finally, in the last function call, all three arguments are hard-coded into the call and the resulting volume is 3 * 3 * 3, or 27.

Here are some things that you will want to remember when using default parameters:

- Default parameter values are supplied by the compiler in a function call when an argument is not provided in the call for a given parameter.

- Default values can be provided in either the function prototype or function header, but not both.

- Once you assign a default value to a parameter in either a function prototype or header, all the remaining parameters must have default values. So, if a default value is specified for parameter *n* then default parameters must also be specified for parameters *n + 1, n + 2,* and so on.

- The default values for a given parameter must be the correct data type for that parameter.

Function Overloading

The idea of function overloading is important to modular programming in C++. When a function is overloaded it is designed to perform differently when it is supplied with a different number of arguments or argument data types. Thus, a given function might perform one way when supplied one argument and an entirely different way when supplied two arguments. For example, consider the following program:

```
#include <iostream.h>

// FUNCTION PROTOTYPES
int Sample(int);
int Sample(int, int);
float Sample(float, float);
```

```
void main()
{
// DEFINE VARIABLES
   int index = 3;
   int x = 4;
   int y = 5;
   float a = 6.0;
   float b = 7.0;

// FUNCTION CALLS
   cout << "\n\nThe square of " << index << " is:  " << Sample(index);
   cout << "\n\nThe product of " << x << " and " << y << " is:  "
        << Sample(x,y);
   cout << "\n\nThe average of " << a << " and " << b << " is:  "
        << Sample(a,b);
}

// THIS FUNCTION SQUARES AN INTEGER VALUE
int Sample(int value)
{
   return (value * value);
}

// THIS FUNCTION MULTIPLIES TWO INTEGER VALUES
int Sample(int value1, int value2)
{
   return (value1 * value2);
}

// THIS FUNCTION AVERAGES TWO FLOAT VALUES
float Sample(float value1, float value2)
{
   return ((value1 + value2)/2);
}
```

Look at the function prototyping section. The first thing you see is three different prototypes for *Sample()*. In the first prototype, *Sample()* requires a single integer argument and returns an integer value. In the second prototype, *Sample()* requires two integer arguments and returns an integer value. In the third prototype, *Sample()* requires two floating point arguments and returns a floating point value. Looking at the function definitions at the bottom of the program you find that the single function *Sample()* is defined three different times to do three different things. The way *Sample()* will perform is determined by the number and data types of the arguments supplied when it is called. If a single integer argument is provided when *Sample()* is called, it will return the square of the argument. If two integer arguments are supplied in the call, *Sample()* will return the product of the two arguments. However, if two floating point arguments are supplied in the call, *Sample()* will return the average of the two arguments. Here is the result of the program execution:

> The square of 3 is: 9
>
> The product of 4 and 5 is: 20
>
> The average of 6 and 7 is: 6.5

Obviously, you could say that *Sample()* is *overloaded* with work, since it is performing three different tasks, depending on the number and data types of the arguments used in its call. You are probably wondering: Why not just write three separate functions rather than overloading a single function? Well in this case you normally would write separate functions, since the three tasks shown are totally unrelated. However, overloading is used where the tasks are very similar, only differing in the number of arguments required by the function, or the data types of the arguments. Without overloading you would have to invent different names for each similar task instead of just one, thus requiring you and your program users to remember all of them.

Function overloading is related to the concept of **polymorphism**, which is one of the cornerstones of object-oriented programming as you will find out later. I am introducing it here so that you understand the concept. You will see how it is applied when you learn about OOP in a later chapter. By the way, function overloading is not possible in the C language.

 Quick Check

1. What is the primary purpose of a function prototype?
2. Where is a function prototype normally located in a C++ program?
3. True or False: Parameters listed in a function prototype can be listed only by data type, without any corresponding identifiers.
4. True of False: Default parameters can appear on either the function prototype or function header, but not both.

5. True or False: Once a default parameter is specified in a function prototype, the remaining parameters in the parameter listing must be default parameters.
6. When overloading a function, what determines how the function will perform?

7-4 SCOPING-OUT VARIABLES AND CONSTANTS ⇒ BLOCK STRUCTURE

In the last two sections, you observed the use of local variables.

> A *local variable* is a variable that is defined within a function.

Don't get local variables confused with the function parameters listed in the function heading. Local function variables are defined after the opening brace of a function, while parameters are defined in the function heading.

A local variable is only defined for use within the function block and has no meaning outside of the respective function.

> A *global variable* is a variable that can be used by all functions of a given program, including *main( )*.

To make variables global in C++, you must define them outside of function *main( )*. This makes them global to function *main( )* as well as any functions called by *main( )*. Of course, this would be all the functions defined in a given program. This is why global variables are sometimes called *file variables* in C and C++.

To illustrate the use of local and global variables, look at the block structure in Figure 7-4. Here, the global variable is *X0 and* the local variable is *X1*. The function can perform operations on both *X0* and *X1*. However, *main( )* can only operate with *X0*, since *X1* is not defined outside of the *Function1( )* block. Any attempt to use *X1* outside of *Function1( )* will result in an error. In addition, any value assigned to *X1* during the *Function1( )* execution is destroyed and cannot be retrieved for subsequent executions of the function.

Now look at Figure 7-5. This time, there are two functions, both of which define *X1* as a local variable. Again, the global variable is *X0* and can be used within *main( )* as well as any other functions defined in the program. The variable *X1* can only be used within the two functions. However, any operations on *X1* within *Function1( )* do not affect the value of *X1* in *Function2( )*, and vice versa. In other words, the *X1* in *Function1( )* is considered a separate variable from the *X1* in *Function2()*. It's as if they are two completely different variables! This provides a very important feature of structured programming, called ***modularity***.

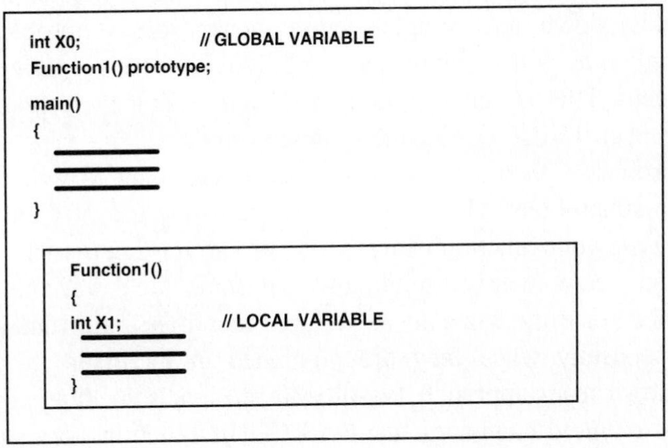

```
int X0;              // GLOBAL VARIABLE
Function1() prototype;

main()
{
    ≡≡≡
    ≡≡≡
}

    Function1()
    {
    int X1;          // LOCAL VARIABLE
    ≡≡≡
    }
```

Figure 7-4 *X0* is global to entire program while *X1* is local to *Function1()*.

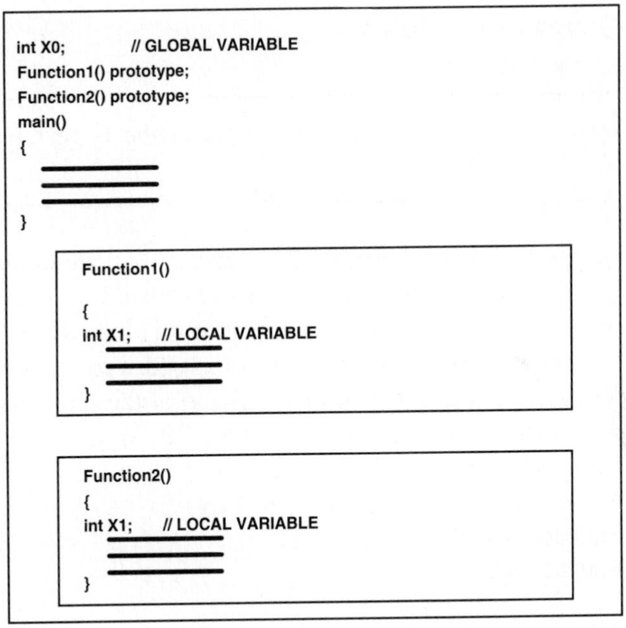

```
int X0;              // GLOBAL VARIABLE
Function1() prototype;
Function2() prototype;
main()
{
    ≡≡≡
    ≡≡≡
}

    Function1()

    {
    int X1;     // LOCAL VARIABLE
    ≡≡≡
    }

    Function2()
    {
    int X1;     // LOCAL VARIABLE
    ≡≡≡
    }
```

Figure 7-5 *X0* is global to the entire program, *X1* is local to both *Function1()* and *Function2()*, but treated as two unique variables.

To realize the importance of modularity, suppose that you are a member of a programming team that must develop the software to solve a very complex industrial problem. The easiest way to solve any complex problem is to break the problem down into simpler, more manageable subproblems. Then, solve the subproblems and combine their solutions in order to solve the overall complex problem. This is called *top/down design*. Using the top/down design approach, your team leader breaks the complex programming problem down into simpler subproblems, then asks each member of the team to write a function to solve a given subproblem. How does this relate to the use of local variables? Well, you can write your function using any local variables you wish, without worrying that another team member might use the same local variables. Even if two team members use the same local variable identifiers, the functions will still execute independently when they are combined in the main program. This allows a top/down team approach to software design, something that is not available in non-structured languages like BASIC. The functions in a structured language act as modular building blocks to form the overall program. This is why a structured language, like C++, is often referred to as a modular, block-structured language.

The Scope of Variables

> The *scope* of a variable identifier refers to the largest block in which a given variable is accessible.

A global variable defined prior to *main()* has *file scope*, since it is accessible to any block in the same file. On the other hand, a local variable defined in a function is said to have *block scope*, since it is only available within the function block that it is defined. A term often associated with scope is *visibility*. You could say that the visibility of a global variable is the entire program file, while the visibility of a local variable is the block in which it is defined. Look at the following code to get the idea.

```
void Function1();
void Function2();

int X0;          // GLOBAL TO ENTIRE PROGRAM
```

```
void main()
{
  int X1;        // LOCAL TO main();
}

int X2;          // GLOBAL TO Function1() AND Function2()

void Function1()
{
  int X3;        // LOCAL TO Function1()
}

void Function2()
{
  int X0;        // LOCAL TO Function2()
}
```

Here, *X0* has file scope, since it is visible, or global, to all blocks in the program. However, *X1* has block scope, since it is defined local to *main()* and therefore is only visible in *main()* and cannot be accessed by *Function1()* or *Function2()*. Next, *X2* is defined after *main()* but prior to any functions. Thus, the scope of *X2* extends to any functions defined after *X2* making it visible to *Function1()* and *Function2()*, but not to *main()*. How about *X3*? Here, *X3* is defined inside of *Function1()* and, therefore, is local to this function and cannot be used by any other function, including *main()*. Finally, notice that the variable *X0* is also defined in *Function2()* as a local variable. Is there a problem here, since *X0* is also global to the entire program? No! The local variable *X0* in *Function2()* is independent of the global variable *X0* defined prior to *main()*. Since *X0* is defined locally in *Function2()*, any operations on *X0* within this function will not affect the global variable *X0*. It's as if they are two separate variables.

In summary, we could make the following statements concerning the scope of the variables in the foregoing program.

- *X0* is visible to the entire program. However, the *X0* in *Function2()* is different from the global *X0*.

- *X1* is visible to *main()* but not visible to *Function1()* or *Function2()*.

- *X2* has a scope that extends to *Function1()* and *Function2()*, but not *main()*.

- *X3* has a block scope of *Function1()*.

All of the functions except *Function2()* have access to the global variable *X0*. As a result, the value of *X0* can be altered by any of these functions. The altering of a global variable by a function is referred to as a **side effect**. In most cases, side effects are undesirable. It is not good practice to alter global variables within a function, since it defeats the modularity characteristic of a structured language. Therefore, always *define your variables as locally as possible* within a given function block. One exception to this rule is when several functions need to share a common variable or data structure. You will observe this application when you learn about arrays in the next chapter.

The Scope of Constants

Constants, like variables, can also be termed global or local. In other words, you can declare constants globally prior to *main()*, or locally within a function. The scope of a constant works just like that of a variable. Its scope is the largest block in which it is available. However, the general rule for declaring constants is just the opposite of defining variables—You should *declare constants as globally as possible*. In other words, all constants should be declared prior to *main()* if possible.

Declaring constants globally allows all functions access to a given constant. No side effects are possible, since a constant cannot be changed by the program. Moreover, constants are not always constant. Remember the *Postage* and *SalesTax* constants we used in Chapter 2? These constants are subject to change over a period of time. When they must be changed, you only need to make a change in one place in the program if they are declared globally. However, if they are declared locally, a change must be made in each function in which they are declared.

Static Variables

Earlier I stated that any value assigned to a local variable within a function block is destroyed and cannot be retrieved for subsequent executions of the function. This is true unless you use the keyword **static** in front of the variable definition. By making a local variable static, its value is retained from one call to the next of the function in which it is defined. Here's a program that should illustrate this idea:

```
#include <iostream.h>
// FUNCTION PROTOTYPE
void Static_Example(int);
```

```
void main()
{
  Static_Example(1);
  Static_Example(2);
  Static_Example(3);
}

// THIS FUNCTION ILLUSTRATES THE USE OF A STATIC VARIABLE
void Static_Example(int Call)
{
  static int Count;
  if (Call == 1)
    Count = 1;
  cout << "\n\nThe value of Count in call #" << Call << " is:  " << Count;
  ++Count;
}
```

From the function prototype you see that *Static_Example()* expects to receive an integer and doesn't return any value to the calling program. Looking at the function definition, you find that a variable called *Count* is defined as a local *static* variable within the function. The value of this variable is displayed on the monitor each time the function is called. After *Count* is displayed, its value is incremented in the last statement of the function. On the first call, *Count* will be initialized to the value 1 by the **if** statement within the function. On all subsequent calls, the value of *Count* is not initialized. Thus, its value has to be the value it had when leaving the previous function call. Notice that in the main program, *Static_Example()* is called three times. Here is what you would see on the display:

The value of Count in call #1 is: 1

The value of Count in call #2 is: 2

The value of Count in call #3 is: 3

In order for this output to occur, the value of the static variable *Count* had to be retained from one function call to the next. What happens if you remove the keyword **static** from in front of the variable definition? Here are the results that I obtained on my display:

The value of Count in call #1 is: 1

The value of Count in call #2 is: 1046

The value of Count in call #3 is: 1046

As you can see, *Count* was initialized to the value 1 in the first call. However, its value was not retained for subsequent calls. In fact, you cannot predict its value on subsequent calls, since it might be any arbitrary memory value. So, the lesson to be learned here is that if you want a local variable to retain its value from one call of a function to the next, define the variable as a static variable using the keyword **static** in front of the local variable definition.

Quick Check

1. Where must a global variable that has file scope be placed in a C++ program?
2. A local variable has _____ scope.
3. The altering of a global variable by a function is referred to as a _____.
4. How can you retain the value of a local function variable from one call of the function to the next?

7-5 RECURSION

C++ supports a very powerful process called *recursion*.

> *Recursion* is a process whereby an operation calls itself until a primitive state is reached.

A recursive function is a function that calls itself. That's right, with the power of recursion a given function can actually contain a statement that calls, or invokes, the same function, thereby calling itself.

To get the idea of recursion, consider a typical compound interest problem. Suppose you deposit $1,000 in the bank at a 12 percent annual interest rate, but it is compounded monthly. What this means is that the interest is calculated and added to the principle on a monthly basis. Thus, each time the interest is calculated, you get interest on the previous months interest. Let's analyze the problem a bit closer.

Your initial deposit is $1,000. Now, the annual interest rate is 12 percent, which translates to a 1 percent monthly rate. Since interest is compounded monthly, the balance at the end of the first month will be:

$$\text{Month 1 balance} = \$1,000 + (0.01 \times \$1,000) = \$1,010.00$$

As you can see, the interest for month 1 is $0.01 \times \$1,000$, or $10.00. This interest amount is then added to the principle ($1,000) to get a new balance of $1,010.00. Using a little algebra, the same calculation can be made like this:

$$\text{Month 1 balance} = 1.01 \times \$1,000 = \$1,010.00$$

Now, how would you calculate the interest for the second month? You would use the balance at the end of the first month as the principle for the second month calculation, right? So, the calculation for month 2 would be:

$$\text{Month 2 balance} = 1.01 \times \$1,010.00 = \$1,020.10$$

For month 3 the calculation would be:

$$\text{Month 3 balance} = 1.01 \times \$1,020.10 = \$1,030.30$$

Do you see a pattern? Notice that to calculate the balance for any given month, you must use the balance from the previous month. In general, the calculation for any month becomes:

$$Balance = 1.01 \times Previous\ Balance$$

Let's let B_i represent the balance of any given month and B_{i-1} the previous month's balance. Using this notation, the balance for any month, B_i is:

$$B_i = 1.01 \times B_{i-1}$$

Let's use this relationship to calculate what your balance would be after four months. Here's how you must perform the calculation:

First, the balance for month 4 is:

$$B_4 = 1.01 \times B_3$$

However, to find B_4 you must find B_3 like this:

$$B_3 = 1.01 \times B_2$$

Then B_2 must be found like this:

$$B_2 = 1.01 \times B_1$$

Finally, B_1 must be found like this:

$$B_1 = 1.01 \times B_0$$

Now, you know that B_0 is the original deposit of \$1,000. This is really the only thing known, aside from the interest rate. Therefore, working backwards you get:

$$B_1 = 1.01 \times \$1,000.00 = \$1,010.00$$

$$B_2 = 1.01 \times \$1,010.00 = \$1,020.10$$

$$B_3 = 1.01 \times \$1,020.10 = \$1,030.30$$

$$B_4 = 1.01 \times \$1,030.30 = \$1,040.60$$

This is a classic example of recursion, since in order to solve the problem, you must solve the previous problem condition using the same process, and so on, until you encounter a known condition (in our case the initial \$1,000 deposit). This known condition, or state, is called a ***primitive state***. Thus, a recursive operation is an operation that calls itself until a primitive state is reached. Likewise, a recursive function is one that calls, or invokes, itself until a primitive state is reached.

Now, suppose we wish to express the above compound interest calculation as a recursive function. The mathematical function would be:

$$B_0 = 1000 \text{ and } B_i = 1.01 \times B_{i-1} \text{ (for } i > 0)$$

This mathematical function can be expressed in pseudocode form like this:

If $i == 0$ Then
 B_i = *1000*
Else
 B_i = *1.01* $\times B_{i-1}$

Next, let's assume the we use a variable called *Deposit* to represent the initial deposit and a variable called *Rate* to represent the annual interest rate. Then, our balance could be calculated using recursion as follows:

If $i == 0$ Then
 B_i = *Deposit*
Else
 B_i = *(1 + Rate / 12 / 100)* $\times B_{i-1}$

If a programming language supports recursive operations, a software function can be coded directly from the above algorithm. Since C++ employs the power of recursion, the C++ function is:

```
float Balance(int i)
{
  if (i==0)
    return (Deposit);
  else
    return ((1 + Rate / 12 / 100) * Balance(i - 1));
}
```

That's all there is to it! This function will calculate the balance at the end of any month, *i*, passed to the function. Notice how the function calls itself in the **else** clause. Here's how it works. When the computer encounters the recursive call in the **else** clause, it must temporarily delay the calculation to evaluate the recursive function call just like we did as part of the compounded interest calculation. When it encounters the **else** clause a second time, the function calls itself again, and keeps calling itself each time the **else** clause is executed until the primitive state is reached. When this happens, the **if** clause is executed, since $i = 0$ and the recursive calling ceases.

Now, let's insert this function into a program to calculate compounded interest as follows:

```
#include <iostream.h>
#include <iomanip.h>

// FUNCTION PROTOTYPES AND GLOBAL VARIABLES
float Balance(int);        // RETURN NEW BALANCE
float Deposit;             // INITIAL DEPOSIT
float Rate;                // ANNUAL INTEREST RATE
void main()
{

// VARIABLES LOCAL TO MAIN
   int Months;             // NUMBER OF MONTHS AFTER INITIAL
                           // DEPOSIT TO DETERMINE BALANCE
  cout << "\nEnter the initial balance:  $";
  cin >> Deposit;
  cout << "\nEnter the number of months to compound:  ";
  cin >> Months;
  cout << "\nEnter the annual interest rate:  ";
  cin >> Rate;
  cout << setprecision(2);
  cout << "\n\nWith an initial deposit of $" << Deposit
       << " and an interest rate of " << Rate
       << "% \nthe balance at the end of " << Months
       << " months would be $" << Balance(Months) ;
}


//******************************************************************************
//
// THIS RECURSIVE FUNCTION WILL CALCULATE A BANK BALANCE
// BASED ON A MONTHLY COMPOUNDED INTEREST RATE
//
//******************************************************************************
float Balance(int i)
{
  if (i==0)
    return (Deposit);
  else
    return ((1 + Rate / 12 / 100) * Balance(i - 1));
}
```

This program prompts the user to enter the deposit, number of months to compound, and the current annual interest rate. The *Deposit* and *Rate* variables are defined globally, since they must be used by *main()* and the *Balance()*

function. The number of months to compound is passed to the function as a value parameter. Actually the deposit and rate variables could be defined locally to *main()* and passed to the function as value parameters. This will be left as an exercise at the end of the chapter. Once the user enters the required values, the recursive calls are made and the program will write the ending balance. Here is a sample of the program output:

Enter the initial deposit: **$1000.**↵

Enter the number of months to compound: **4.**↵

Enter the annual interest rate: **12.**↵

With an initial deposit of $1000 and an interest rate of 12%
the balance at the end of 4 months would be $1040.60

During any recursive call, all information required to complete the calculation after the recursive call is saved by the computer in a memory area called a *stack*. As the recursive calls continue, information is saved on the memory stack until the primitive state is reached. Then the computer works backward from the primitive state, retrieving the stack information to determine the final result. The process that the computer goes through is identical to what we did when working the compound interest problem.

One word of caution: There must always be a primitive state for the recursive function. If not, the function will keep calling itself forever, resulting in a run-time error.

Example 7-6:

Write a recursive C++ function to find the sum of all integers from 1 to some number, *N*.

Solution:

Think about this operation for a minute. Isn't it a classic recursive operation? To find the sum of integers 1 to, say 5, couldn't you add 5 to the sum of integers from 1 to 4? Then, to find the sum of integers from 1 to 4, you add 4 to the sum of integers from 1 to 3, and so on, right? Expressed in symbols:

Sum 5 = 5 + Sum 4
Sum 4 = 4 + Sum 3
Sum 3 = 3 + Sum 2
Sum 2 = 2 + Sum 1
Sum 1 = 1

Notice that *Sum 1* is the primitive state, since its value is known. Now, translating this process to a recursive function you get:

$$Sum\ 1 = 1 \text{ and } Sum\ N = N + Sum\ (N-1) \quad (\text{for } N > 1)$$

This function can be expressed in pseudocode like this:

> If *N* == 1 Then
>   *Sum = 1*
> Else
>   *Sum = N + Sum (N – 1)*

The C++ function is then coded directly from the algorithm as:

```
//*****************************************************************
//
// THIS RECURSIVE FUNCTION WILL CALCULATE SUM OF
// INTEGERS 1 THRU N
//
//*****************************************************************
int Sum(int N)
{
  if (N == 1)
    return (1);
  else
    return (N + Sum(N - 1));
}
```

Although recursion is a very powerful feature of any language, you should be aware that it is not always the most efficient method of solving a problem. Whenever we talk about computer efficiency, we must consider two things: *execution speed* and *memory usage*. When using recursion, the computer must keep track of each recursive call so that it can work backwards to obtain a solution. This requires large amounts of both memory and time. As a result, a recursive solution to a problem may not always be the most efficient solution. All recursive problems can also be solved non-recursively using iteration. For instance, consider the sum of integers from 1 to *N* done recursively in Example 7-6. This problem can be solved using an iterative function like this:

```
//*****************************************************************
//
// THIS ITERATIVE FUNCTION WILL CALCULATE SUM OF
// INTEGERS 1 THRU N
//
//*****************************************************************
```

```
int Sum(int N)
{
  int Count;
  int Temp = 0;
  for (Count = N; Count; --Count)
    Temp += Count;
  return (Temp);
}
```

So, why use recursion? Probably the main reason to use recursion is that many recursive solutions are much simpler than iterative solutions. In addition, there are some problems in data structures, such as linked lists and binary trees, where recursion isn't a mere convenience, it is essential to keep the code manageable. Here are two guidelines that should help you decide when to use recursion:

1. Consider a recursive solution only when a simple iterative solution is not possible.

2. Use a recursive solution only when the execution and memory efficiency of the solution is within acceptable limits, considering the system limitations.

By the way, notice how the two variables *Count* and *Temp* are used as local variables in the above function. This is an ideal application for non-static local variables, since they only need to be used within this function block and do not need to be saved from one function call to the next.

 Quick Check

1. True or False: There is no way that a C++ function can call itself.
2. Explain why we can describe recursion as a "winding" and "un-winding" process.
3. What terminates a recursive function call?
4. A factorial operation (*N!*) finds the product of all integers from 0 to some positive integer *N*. Thus, 5! = 5 * 4 * 3 * 2 * 1. Write the pseudocode required to find *N!*, where *N* is any integer. Note: By definition, 0! = 1.
5. True or False: An advantage of recursion is that it does not require a lot of memory to execute.

6. True or False: All recursive problems can also be solved using iteration.

CHAPTER SUMMARY

In this chapter, you learned how to write and use functions in C++. All user defined functions to be used in *main()* are defined after the closing brace of *main()*. The function is defined by writing a function header which includes the function return type, the function name, and a parameter listing. The body, or statement section, of the function then follows the function header. Unlike the C language, the C++ language requires that each function have a prototype. The function prototypes must be listed prior to *main()* and must include the return data type of the function, the function name, and a listing of the parameter data types. Prototypes are used by the compiler to check for the proper number of arguments when the function is called.

Functions in C++ can be made to return a single value to the calling program or perform some specific task. When a function is designed to return a single value to the calling program, the value returned replaces the function name wherever the name is used in the calling program. Thus, the function name can appear as part of an assignment operator, a *cout* statement, an arithmetic operator, or a test statement. When a function is designed to perform a specific task, the function is called by using the function name (followed by a list of actual arguments) as a statement in the program.

Actual arguments are data passed to the function when the function is called. Formal parameters are defined within the function header and take on the value(s) of the actual arguments when the function is called. Furthermore, parameters can be passed between the calling program and function by value or reference. When passing parameters by value, the actual arguments in the calling program are not affected by operations on the formal parameters within the function. When passing parameters by reference, the actual arguments in the calling program will reflect any changes to the formal parameters within the function. Thus, passing parameters by value is one-way communication of data from the calling program to the function. Passing parameters by reference is two-way communication of data from the calling program to the function and back to the calling program. In C++, reference parameters are defined using the ampersand (&) symbol prior to the parameter name in the function heading.

In addition to parameters, functions can operate with local variables that are defined within the function body. Such local variables are only available for use within the function in which they are defined. Local variables are destroyed once the function execution is terminated, unless they are defined as static local variables. A static variable retains its value from one call of a function to the next. Global, or file, variables are available for use by any functions defined in a given program and must be defined prior to *main( )*. The scope of a variable refers to the largest block in which a variable is accessible. A side effect occurs when a function changes the value of a global variable. Variables should always be defined as locally as possible, while constants should be declared as globally as possible.

A recursive function is a function that calls itself until a primitive state is reached. There must always be a primitive state to terminate a recursive function call. Otherwise, a run-time error will occur. Recursive operations can be performed as part of an **if/else** statement. The primitive state forms the **if** clause, while the recursive call is part of the **else** clause of the statement. All recursive operations can also be performed using iteration. Since recursion eats up time and memory as compared to iteration, you should only consider recursion when a simple iterative solution is not possible, and when the execution and memory efficiency of the solution is within acceptable limits.

QUESTIONS AND PROBLEMS

Questions

1. What three things must be specified in a function header?
2. Explain the difference between an actual argument and a formal parameter.
3. Which of the following are invalid function headings? Explain why they are invalid.
   a.   float Average (Num1, Num2)
   b.   int Largest (X,Y : int)
   c.   float Smallest (float a,b)
   d.   string Result (char Character)
4. Write the appropriate headings for the following functions:
   a.   Inverse of *x: 1/x*
   b.   *Tan (x)*
   c.   Convert a decimal test score value to a letter grade.
   d.   Convert degrees Fahrenheit to degrees Celsius.
   e.   Compute the factorial of any integer *N* (*N!*)
   f.   Compute the average of 3 integer test scores.

5. True or False: When a function does not have a return type, you must indicate this with the keyword **null.**.

6. Explain the difference between a value parameter and a reference parameter.

7. When passing a parameter to a function by reference:

   a.   The actual argument takes on the formal parameter value.

   b.   The formal parameter takes on the actual argument value.

   c.   The actual argument reflects any changes to the formal parameter after the function execution.

   d.   a and b

   e.   b and c

   f.   a and c

8. When using an assignment operator to call a function, the function must include a _____ statement.

9. Which of the following are invalid function prototypes? Explain why they are invalid.

   a.   void PrintHeader ();

   b.   int Error(float Num1, char Num2);

   c.   void GetData (&int Amount, char Date);

   d.   float Average (int Number, float Total)

   e.   char Sample (int, char, float);

10. True or False: A variable defined in *main()* has visibility in all functions called by *main()*.

11. Which of the following are value parameters and which are reference parameters?

   a.   char Prob_a (char &A, char &B, float X, int Y);

   b.   int Prob_b (int Num1, int Num2, int Num3, float &Avg);

   c.   float Prob_c (int, float, char &);

12. Write the appropriate headers for the following functions:

   a.   A function called *Sample()* that must return a floating point value and receive an integer, a floating point value, and a character (in that order) when it is called.

   b.   A function called *Skip()* that will cause the printer to skip a given number of lines where the number of lines to skip is obtained from the calling program.

c. A function called *Swap()* that will swap the values of two integer variables obtained from the calling program and return the swapped values to the calling program.

d. A function called *Hypot()* that will return the hypotenuse of a right triangle, given the values of the two sides from the calling program.

13. Write prototypes for the functions in question 12.

14. Write C++ statements that will call the four functions in question 12.

15. Given the following function:

```
void Swap(int &X, int &Y)
{
  int Temp;
  Temp = X;
  X = Y;
  Y = Temp;
}
```

determine the output for each of the following segments of code that call function *Swap()*.

a.
```
A = 2;
B = 10;
cout << "\nA = " << A << " B = " << B;
Swap(A,B);
cout << "\nA = " << A << " B = " << B;
```

b.
```
A = 20;
B = -5;
cout << "\nA = " << A << " B = " << B;
if (A < B)
  Swap(A,B);
else
  Swap(B,A);
cout << "\nA = " << A << " B = " << B;
```

c.
```
Num1 = 1;
Num2 = 5;
for (int Count = 5; Count; --Count)
{
  Swap(Num1,Num2);
  cout << "\nNum1 = " << Num1 << " Num2 = " << Num2;
```

```
                ++Num1;
                --Num2;
             }
```

16. Explain the difference between a local and global variable.

17. What is meant by the scope of a variable?

18. What is a side effect?

19. True or False: Variables should be defined as locally as possible and constants as globally as possible.

20. A local variable has _____ scope.

21. Suppose that a local integer variable called *SubTotal* must retain its value from one call of a function to the next. Write a definition for this variable.

22. Suppose that a function must have access to a variable defined in *main()*. How must this be accomplished?

23. Explain recursion.

24. When should you consider a recursive solution to a problem?

Problems

Least Difficult

Write functions to perform the following tasks:

1. Convert a temperature in $°F$ to $°C$.

2. Find x^y, where x is a real value and y is an integer value.

3. Calculate $Tan(\theta)$, for some angle θ in degrees.

4. Find the inverse $(1/x)$ of any real value x.

5. Find the maximum of two integer values.

6. Find the minimum of two integer values.

7. Find $N!$ using iteration.

8. Find $N!$ using recursion.

9. Place the functions that you developed in problems 7 and 8 in a menu-driven program that will allow the user to select either an iterative or recursive solution to $N!$. Execute each option for the same value of N and determine the amount of time it takes to execute each option with the

given value of *N*. Repeat this process for increasing values of *N*. What conclusions can you draw about iterative versus recursive solutions?

10. Examine a range of values and return the Boolean value TRUE if a value is within the range and FALSE if the value is outside of the range.

11. Find your bank balance at the end of any given month for some initial deposit value and interest rate. Define the number of months, deposit, and interest rate variables in *main()* and pass them to your function.

12. Print your name, class, instructor, and hour.

13. Cause the printer to skip a given number of lines, where the number of lines to be skipped is passed to the function.

14. Swap, or exchange, any two floating point values.

15. Compare some new floating point value to a maximum value obtained from the calling program. Replace the maximum value with the new value if the new value is greater than the maximum value. Use the function that you developed in problem 14 for the exchange operation.

More Difficult

In problems 16–20, write three independent functions for each problem as follows:

- *One function to read the required input values.*
- *A second function to perform the required calculations using the input values from the first function.*
- *A third function to display the results of the second function.*

16. Revise the payroll program you developed for Ma and Pa in problem 11 of Chapter 4 to employ functions. Recall that the payroll program will calculate Herb's net pay given the following information:

> Employee's Name
> Number of weekly hours worked
> Hourly rate of pay
> FICA (7.15%)
> Federal Withholding (16%)
> State Withholding (4.75%)

Ma or Pa will only be required to enter the first three items when running the program. The program must generate a printed report using the following:

```
Employee Name: XXXXXXXXXXXXXXXXXXXXX

Rate of Pay:                                $XXXXX
Hours Worked:                               $XXXXX
Gross Pay:                                  $XXXXX
Deductions:
    FICA                                    $XXXXX
    Federal withholding                     $XXXXX
    State withholding                       $XXXXX
                                            -----------
    Total Deductions                        $XXXXX
Net Pay:                                    $XXXXX
```

17. Find the height at which the ladder in Figure 7-6 makes contact with the wall, given the length of the ladder and the distance the base of the ladder is from the wall.

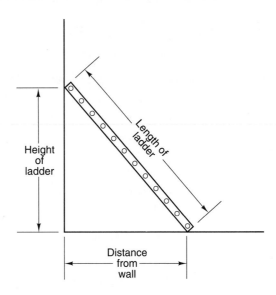

Figure 7-6 A ladder for problem 17.

Most Difficult

18. A Fibonacci sequence of numbers is defined as follows:

$$F_0 = 0$$
$$F_1 = 1$$

$$F_n = F_{n-1} + F_{n-2}, \text{ for } n > 1$$

This says that the first two numbers in the sequence are 0 and 1. Then, each additional Fibonacci number is the sum of the two previous numbers in the sequence. Thus, the first ten Fibonacci numbers are:

$$0, 1, 1, 2, 3, 5, 8, 13, 21, 34$$

Here, we say that the first number occupies position 0 in the sequence, the second number position 1 in the sequence, and so on. Thus, the last position in a ten number sequence is position 9.

Develop a program that employs a recursive function to generate a Fibonacci sequence of all numbers up to some position, n, entered by the user.

19. Develop a program that employs an iterative function to generate a Fibonacci sequence of all numbers up to some position, n, entered by the user.

20. Measure the amount of time it takes each of the programs in problems 18 and 19 to generate a Fibonacci sequence of 100 elements. What do you conclude about the efficiency of recursion versus iteration? Why does the recursive program take so long?

ARRAYS

INTRODUCTION

This chapter will introduce you to a very important topic in any programming language: *arrays*. The importance of arrays cannot be overemphasized, since they lend themselves to so many applications.

An *array* is an indexed data structure which is used to store data elements of the same data type.

Arrays simply provide an organized means for locating and storing data, just as the post office boxes in your local post office lobby provide an organized means of locating and storing mail. This is why an array is referred to as a *data structure*. The array data structure can be used to store just about any type of data including integers, floats, characters, arrays, pointers, and records (structs). In addition, arrays are so versatile that they can be used to implement other data structures such as stacks, queues, linked lists, and binary trees. In fact, in some languages, like FORTRAN, the array is the only data structure available to the programmer, since most other structures can be implemented using arrays.

8-1 THE STRUCTURE OF AN ARRAY

An array is a data structure. In other words, an array consists of data that are organized, or structured, in a particular way. This array data structure provides a convenient means of storing large amounts of data in primary, or user, memory. There are both one-dimensional and multidimensional arrays. In this section you will learn about one-dimensional arrays. Then, in the next section you will literally expand this knowledge into multidimensional arrays.

To get the idea of an array, look at the illustration in Figure 8-1. Here you see a single row of post office boxes as you might find in any common post office lobby. As you know, each box has a post office (P.O.) box number. In Figure 8-1, our P.O. box numbers begin with 0 and go up to some finite number N. How do you locate a given box? By using its P.O. box number, right? However, the P.O. box number has nothing to do with what's inside the box. It is simply used to locate a given box. Of course, the contents of a given box is the mail delivered to that box. The reason the postal service uses the P.O. box method is that it provides a convenient, well-organized method of storing and accessing the mail for its postal customers. An array does the same thing in a computer program; it provides a convenient, well-organized method of storing and accessing data for you, the programmer. By the way, how many post office boxes are there in Figure 8-1? Since the first box number is 0 and the last is *N*, there must be *N + 1* boxes.

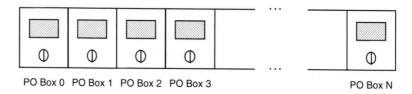

PO Box 0   PO Box 1   PO Box 2   PO Box 3   PO Box N

Figure 8-1 A one-dimensional array is like a row of post office boxes.

You can think of a one-dimensional array, like the one shown in Figure 8-2, as a row of post office boxes. The one-dimensional array consists of a single row of storage locations, each labeled with a number called an ***index***. Each index location is used to store a *given type of data*. The data stored at a given index location is referred to as an array ***element***. Thus, a one-dimensional array is a sequential list of storage locations that contain individual data elements which are located, or accessed, via indices.

Element 0	Element 1	Element 2	Element 3			Element N
[0]	[1]	[2]	[3]			[N]

INDICES

Figure 8-2 A one-dimensional array, or list, is a sequential list of storage locations that contain data elements which are located via indices.

The two major components of any array are the elements stored in the array and the indices which locate the stored elements. Don't get these two array components confused! Although array elements and indices are related, they are completely separate quantities, just like the contents of a post office box is something different from its P.O. box number. With this in mind, let's explore array elements and indices a bit further.

The Array Elements

The elements of an array are the data stored in the array. These elements can be any type of data that you have seen so far. Thus, a given array can store integer elements, floating point elements, and character elements. In addition to these standard data type elements, an array can also be used to store enumerated data elements. In fact, the elements in an array can even be other arrays. However, there is one major restriction that applies to the array elements: *The elements in a given array must all be of the same data type.*

As you will see shortly, you must define arrays in a C++ program. Part of the definition is to specify the data type of the elements that the array will store. Once a given array is defined for a certain data type, only elements of that data type should be stored in that array.

The Array Indices

The array indices locate the array elements. In C and C++, the compiler automatically assigns integer indices to the array element list beginning with index 0. So, the first element of the array in Figure 8-2 is located at index 0, while the last element is located at index N. Since the indices begin with 0 and go to N, there must be $N + 1$ elements in the array. Also, since this is a one-dimensional array, or **list**, we say that it has a **dimension** of $1 \times (N + 1)$, meaning that there is one row of $N + 1$ elements. The dimension of an array indicates the size of the array, just like the dimension of a piece of lumber indicates its size.

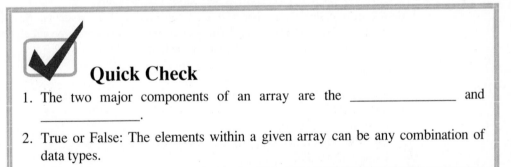

Quick Check

1. The two major components of an array are the _____ and _____.

2. True or False: The elements within a given array can be any combination of data types.

8-2 DEFINING ONE-DIMENSIONAL ARRAYS IN C++

All arrays in C++ must be defined. In order to define an array, you must specify three things:

1. The data type of the array elements

2. The name of the array.

3. The size of the array.

Here's the general format:

> **ONE-DIMENSIONAL ARRAY FORMAT**
>
> <element data type> <array name> [<number of array elements>];

The first thing you see in the definition is the data type of the array elements. The array data type is followed by the array identifier, or name, which is followed by the number of elements that the array will store enclosed within square brackets, [ ]. A semicolon terminates the definition. For instance, the following defines an array of ten characters whose name is *Characters*.

char Characters [10];

Example 8-1

Write definitions for the following arrays:
a. An array called *Integers* that will store ten integers.
b. An array called *Reals* that will store five floating point values.
c. An array called *Characters* that will store 11 characters.
d. An array called *Class* that will store the grades of 25 students. Assume the grades A, B, C, D, and F are defined in an enumerated data type called *Grades*.
e. What index locates the last element in each of the above arrays?

Solution:

a. int Integers[10];
b. float Reals[5];
c. char Characters[11];
d. enum Grades {F, D, C, B, A};
   Grades Class[25];
e. The index that locates the last element in each of the above arrays is one less than the defined size of the array.

In each of the above definitions, the element data type is listed first, followed by the array identifier, followed by the size of the array enclosed in square brackets. Each definition should be fairly obvious, except perhaps the *Class* array definition. In this definition, the data type of the array is the enumerated data type called *Grades*, which must be defined prior to the array definition. So, we would say that the *Class* array can store elements whose data type is *Grades*. Thus, the elements that can be stored in the *Class* array are limited to the enumerated data type elements of F, D, C, B, A. Take note that these are not considered characters by the compiler, but rather elements of an enumerated data type called *Grades*.

Initializing Arrays

Arrays, like variables, can be initialized when they are created. The initializing values can be supplied for any array wherever the array is defined in the program. Let's consider some example array definitions to illustrate how arrays can be initialized.

int Integers[3] = {10,20,30};

In this definition, an integer array of three elements has been defined. The three integer elements have been initialized to the values 10, 20, and 30, respectively. Notice the syntax. The array definition is followed by an equals symbol, which is followed by the initialization values enclosed within curly braces. Here is what you would see if you inspected the array using a debugger:

Inspecting Integers

[0]   10
[1]   20
[2]   30

As you can see, the first initialization value, 10, is placed at index 0 of the array, the value 20 is placed at index 1, and the value 30 is placed at the last index position which is 2. Now, what do you suppose happens if you were to provide fewer initialization values than there are positions in the array? Well, suppose you define the array like this:

int Integers[3] = {10,20};

Here is what you would find when inspecting the array using a debugger:

Inspecting Integers

[0]   10
[1]   20
[2]   00

As you can see, the compiler has initialized the last position of the array with zero. Zero is the default initialization value for integer arrays when not enough values are supplied to fill the array.

The next obvious question is: What happens if you supply too many initialization values? For instance, suppose you define the array like this:

int Integers[3] = {10,20,30,40};

In this case, you will get a compiler error stating "Too many initializers." One way to solve this problem is to increase the size of the array. Another, more preferred, way is to define the array without any specified size as follows:

int Integers[] = {10,20,30,40};

With this definition, the compiler will set aside enough storage to hold all the initialization values. Here is what you would see if you inspected this array definition using a debugger:

Inspecting *Integers*

[0]   10
[1]   20
[2]   30
[3]   40

Next, let's consider character arrays. Suppose that you define a character array of size 5 like this:

char Characters[5] = {'H','E','L','L','O'};

Again you see that the initialization values are enclosed in curly braces after an equals symbol. Here is what a debugger would reveal:

Inspecting *Characters*

[0]   'H'
[1]   'E'
[2]   'L'
[3]   'L'
[4]   'O'

You see here that the five initialization characters are placed in the array starting at index zero and ending at the last index position, 4. What happens if you supply fewer initialization characters than are required to fill the array? Well, suppose that you define the array this way:

char Characters[5] = {'H','E'};

The contents of the array would now be:

Inspecting *Characters*

[0]   'H'
[1]   'E'
[2]   '\0'
[3]   '\0'
[4]   '\0'

This time, the compiler has inserted a null terminator character as the default character to fill the array. On the other hand, if you supply too many characters, the compiler will generate a "Too many initializers" error message. Again, the safe way to handle this problem is to let the compiler determine the array size to fit the number of initialization values.

Finally, let's consider how to initialize character arrays with string values. Remember, a string is nothing more than an array of characters, terminated with a null terminator. Here is how a character array can be initialized with a string value:

char Characters[6] = "HELLO";

Notice that the syntax is different. The initialization string must be enclosed in double quotation marks rather than curly braces. Another thing you see is that the size of the array is one larger than the number of characters in the string. The reason for this becomes obvious when you inspect the array using a debugger. Here is what you would see:

Inspecting *Characters*

[0]   'H'
[1]   'E'
[2]   'L'
[3]   'L'
[4]   'O'
[5]   '\0'

Recall that a string must be terminated with a null terminator. Making the size of the array one larger than the number of string characters allows room for the compiler to insert the null terminator. If you don't leave room for the null terminator, it will be truncated (dropped) from the array and you *will not* get an error message. Again, the best way to avoid this problem is to let the compiler determine the size of the array like this:

char Characters[] = "HELLO";

With this definition, the compiler will create enough array positions to hold all the string characters with the null terminator inserted as the last character in the array.

Default Initialization of Global and Static Arrays

Arrays can be defined and initialized anywhere in your C++ program. The scope of an array works just like the scope of a variable or constant. An array defined prior to *main()* is visible in the entire source file in which it is defined. An array defined within a block has block scope, and therefore is only visible within the block that it is defined.

If you define an array globally or as a static array and don't provide any initialization values, the compiler will initialize the array with the respective default value (zeros for integer and floating point arrays, null terminators for character arrays). Here's an example:

```
int Integers[5];
void main()
{
static char Characters[5];
}
```

The integer array has been defined globally and the character array has been defined as a local static array within *main()*. Inspecting these arrays with a debugger would reveal the following:

Inspecting *Integers*		Inspecting *Characters*	
[0]	0	[0]	'\0'
[1]	0	[1]	'\0'
[2]	0	[2]	'\0'
[3]	0	[3]	'\0'
[4]	0	[4]	'\0'

The debugger shows that the global integer array has been initialized with zeros, while the static character array has been initialized with null terminator characters. If you define an array of local block scope that is not static and do not initialize it, no default initialization values will be supplied by the compiler. The array will contain garbage! Thus, if we were to remove the keyword **static** from the above *Characters* array definition, the debugger would reveal arbitrary memory values in the array.

Here is a summary of the foregoing discussion:

- Integer, floating point, and character arrays are initialized by using an equals symbol after the array definition, followed by a listing of the individual initializing values within curly braces.

- Too few initializing values will result in default values (zeros for integer and floating point arrays, null terminators for character arrays) being inserted in the extra array positions.

- Too many initializing values will result in a compiler error.

- Character arrays can be initialized with a string by enclosing the string within double quotes.

- The size of a string array must be one greater than the number of characters within the string to leave room for the null terminator character.

- If no size is specified in the array definition, the compiler will create just enough storage to hold the initialization values.

- Global arrays and static arrays are always initialized with the respective default values when no initialization values are supplied in the array definition.

- Local arrays that are not static will not be initialized with any specific values, unless they are supplied in the array definition.

 Quick Check

1. Define an array and initialize it with the integer values –3 through +3.

2. What is the dimension of the array that you defined in question 1?

3. Show the contents of the following array:

```
char Language[5] = {'C','+','+'};
```

4. Show the contents of the following array:

   char Language[] = "C++";

5. Suppose that you define a character array globally without any initializing values. What does the compiler store in the array?

8-3 ACCESSING ARRAYS

Accessing the array means to insert elements into the array for storage or to get stored elements from the array.

Inserting Elements into One-Dimensional Arrays

There are basically three major ways to insert elements into an array: by using a *direct assignment* statement, by *reading*, or by using *loops*.

Direct Assignment

Here's the general format for inserting an element into an array using a direct assignment:

> *DIRECT ASSIGNMENT FORMAT (INSERTING ARRAY ELEMENTS)*
>
> <array name> [array index] = element value;

Using the following array definitions:

```
char Characters[6];
int Integers[3];
```

direct assignments might go something like this:

```
Characters[0] = 'H';
Characters[5] = '\0';
Integers[0] = 16;
Integers[2] = -22;
```

In each of these instances, an element is placed in the first and last storage positions of the respective array. The character 'H' is placed in the first position of the *Characters* array and the null terminator is placed in the last position of this array. Recall that the first position of an array is always [0], while the last array position is always one less than the array size. The integer 16 is placed in the first position of the *Integers* array and the integer –22 placed in the last position of this array.

Observe that the respective array name is listed, followed by the array index within brackets. An assignment operator (=) is then used and followed by the element to be inserted. The data type of the element being inserted should be the same as the data type defined for the array elements; otherwise, you could get unpredictable results when working with the array elements.

Reading Elements Into the Array

You can also use any of the C/C++ input functions or objects to insert array elements from a keyboard entry like this:

```
cin >> Characters[1];
cin >> Integers[0];
Characters[5] = getchar();
Characters[1] = getche();
```

Here, the user must type the respective array element value on the keyboard and press the ENTER key to execute each statement, with the exception of the last statement which does not require the ENTER key to be pressed. A character should be entered for the first *cin* statement and an integer for the second *cin* statement. (Why?) The character entered from the keyboard will be stored in the second position (index [1]) of the *Characters* array, while the integer entered from the keyboard will be stored in the first position (index [0]) of the *Integers* array. Notice that the last two statements employ standard character functions to obtain a keyboard character. Here, the keyboard entry returned by *getchar()* is assigned to index [5] of the *Characters* array and the keyboard entry returned by *getche()* is assigned to index [1] of the *Characters* array. The difference between the two character functions is that *getchar()* is buffered, while *getche()* is unbuffered input.

Inserting Array Elements Using Loops

The obvious disadvantage to using direct assignments to insert array elements is that a separate assignment statement is required to fill each array position. You can automate the insertion process by using a loop structure. Although any of the three loop structures (**while, do/while, for**) can be employed, the **for** structure is the most common. Here's the general format for using a **for** loop:

**INSERTING INTO A ONE-DIMENSIONAL ARRAY USING A *for*
LOOP**

```
for (int Index = 0; Index < Array Size;  ++Index)
    <assign or read to Array[Index]>
```

Consider the following program:

```
// FILLING AN ARRAY USING A FOR LOOP

#include <iostream.h>

// GLOBAL CONSTANTS AND VARIABLES
const int MAX = 10;
int Sample[MAX];

void main()
{
  cout << "Enter a list of " << MAX << " elements and press"
          "the ENTER key after each entry.\n\n";
  for (int i = 0; i < MAX; ++i)
    cin >> Sample[i];
}
```

First, you see a global constant called *MAX* declared. Notice where *MAX* is
used in the program. It is the array size value and the final counter value in the **for**
loop. Using a constant like this allows you to easily change the size of the array.
Here, the array size is ten elements. To change the size of the array, you only need
to make a change one place in the program under the constant definition.

Next, look at the array definition. The array *Sample* is defined globally as an
array of integer elements. Thus, the compiler will automatically initialize all the
array elements to zero.

Now, look at the statement section of *main()*. The user is told to "Enter a list
of *MAX* (where *MAX* is 10) values and press the ENTER key after each entry."
Once this prompt is displayed, the program enters a **for** loop. The loop counter
variable is *i*, which ranges from 0 to *MAX*. When the loop counter reaches the
value of *MAX*, the loop is broken, since the loop test is $i < MAX$. It is important to
use the "less than" ($<$) test here rather than the "less than or equal to" ($<=$) test;
otherwise the loop will execute one too many times. (Why?) The loop counter is

employed as the index value for the array. With each loop iteration, a single *cin* statement is executed to insert an element into the array at the respective position specified by the loop counter, *i*.

Let's analyze the *cin* statement. First, the identifier, *Sample*, is listed with the loop counter variable, *i*, as the array index in brackets. What does *i* do with each loop iteration? It increments from 0 to *MAX*, right? As a result, the first loop iteration reads a value into *Sample*[0], the second iteration reads a value into *Sample[1]*, and so on, until the last loop iteration reads a value into the last array position *Sample[MAX − 1]*. When the loop counter increments to the value of *MAX* at the end of the last loop iteration, the loop is broken and no more elements are inserted into the array. That's all there is to it! The array is filled!

You can also use loops for assigning values to array elements. For instance, using the foregoing definitions, consider this loop:

```
for (i = 0; i < MAX; ++i)
    Sample[i] = 2 * i;
```

This time, the array elements are assigned to twice the loop counter value with each loop iteration. What values are actually inserted into the array? How about the ten even integers from 0 through 18?

Extracting Elements from One-Dimensional Arrays

First, let me caution you that the word *extract* is not a good term here. Why? Because, in general, the word *extract* means to remove something. When we extract an element from an array, we don't actually remove it! We simply copy its value. The element remains stored in the array until it is replaced by another value using an insertion operation.

As with insertion, you can extract array elements using one of three general methods: *direct assignment*, *writing*, or *looping*.

Direct Assignment

Extracting array elements using assignment statements is just the reverse of inserting elements using an assignment statement. Here's the general format:

DIRECT ASSIGNMENT FORMAT (EXTRACTING ARRAY ELEMENTS)

<variable identifier> = <array name> [array index];

As an example, suppose we make the following definitions:

```
const int MAX = 10;
int Sample[MAX];
int x;
```

As you can see, the array *Sample[]* consists of ten integer elements. Now, assuming the array has been filled, what do you suppose the following statements do?

```
x = Sample[0];
x = Sample[MAX - 1];
x = Sample[3] * Sample[5];
x = 2 * Sample[2] - 3 * Sample[7];
```

The first statement assigns the element stored in the first array position to the variable *x*. The second statement assigns the element stored in the last array position to the variable *x*. The third statement assigns the product of the elements located at indices [3] and [5] to *x*. Finally, the fourth statement assigns two times the element at index [2] minus three times the element at index [7] to *x*. The last two statements illustrate how arithmetic operations can be performed on array elements.

In all of the foregoing cases, the array element values are not affected by the assignment operations. The major requirement is that *x* should be defined as the same data type as the array elements so that you don't get unexpected results.

As a final example, consider these assignment statements:

```
Sample[0] = Sample[MAX - 1];
Sample[1] = Sample[2] + Sample[3];
```

Can you determine what will happen here? In the first statement, the first array element is replaced by the last array element. Is the last array element affected? No, since it appears on the right side of the assignment operator. In the second case, the second array element at index [1] is replaced by the sum of the third and fourth array elements at indices [2] and [3]. Again, the third and fourth array elements are not affected by this operation, since they appear on the right side of the assignment operator.

Writing Array Elements

cout objects can be used to display array elements. Let's use the same array to demonstrate how to write array elements. Here's the array definition again:

```
const int MAX = 10;
int Sample[MAX];
```

Now what do you suppose the following statements will do?

```
cout << Sample[0];
cout << Sample[MAX - 1];
cout << Sample[1] / Sample[2];
cout << sqrt(Sample[6]);
```

The first statement will display the element contained at index [0] of the array. The second statement will display the last element of the array, located at index [*MAX – 1*]. The third statement will divide the element located at index [1] by the element located at index [2] and display the integer quotient. Finally, the fourth statement will display the square root of the element located at index [6]. None of the array element values are affected by these operations.

Extracting Array Elements Using Loops

As with inserting elements into an array, extracting array elements using loops requires less coding, especially when extracting multiple elements. Again, any of the loop structures can be used for this purpose, but **for** loops are the most common.

Consider the following program:

```
// DISPLAYING AN ARRAY USING A FOR LOOP
#include <iostream.h>

// GLOBAL CONSTANTS AND VARIABLES
const int MAX = 10;
int Sample[MAX];

void main()
{
  for (int i = 0; i < MAX; ++i)
    Sample[i] = i * i;
  for (i = 0; i < MAX; ++i)
    cout << Sample[i] << '\t';
}
```

Here again, the array is defined globally as an array of *MAX* (10) integer values. The array name is *Sample*. Notice that the loop counter variable, *i,* is used as the array index in both **for** loops. The first loop will fill the array locations with the square of the loop counter. Then, the second loop will display each of the array elements located from index [0] to index [*MAX − 1*]. A *cout* statement is used to display the array elements horizontally across the face of the display. Notice also that each time an element is displayed, a tab is written after the element to separate it from the next sequential element. Here is what you would see on the display:

0   1   4   9   16   25   36   49   64   81

Quick Check

1. Write a **for** loop that will fill the following array from user entries:

    char Characters[15];

2. Write a **for** loop that will display the contents of the array in question 1.

8-4 PASSING ARRAYS AND ARRAY ELEMENTS TO FUNCTIONS

You can pass an entire array to a function, or pass single array elements to a function. The important thing to remember is that to pass the entire array, you must pass the address of the array. In C and C++, *the array name is the address of the first element (index [0]) of the array.* Let's begin by looking at the required function header. Here is typical prototype for passing a one-dimensional array to a function:

void Weird (char Array[MAX]);

Looking at the prototype, you see that the function does not return a value. There is one character parameter called *Array[MAX]*. The single set of square brackets after the parameter identifier indicate that the parameter is a one-dimensional array with a size of *MAX*. When passing arrays to a function, the function must know how big of an array to accept. Now, since the array identifier references the address of the array, the array is passed by reference to the function. Thus, any operations on the array within the function will affect the original array contents in the calling program. Also, since the parameter is the address of the array, no ampersand symbol, &, is required to pass the array by reference. In fact, the use of an ampersand prior to the array parameter will cause a compile error.

Next, to call this function and pass the array, you simply use the following statement:

Weird(Name);

Of course, this call assumes that *Name* is the array name in the calling program. (Remember that the actual argument identifier and the formal parameter identifier *can be* different.) Since the call to *Name* references the address of the array, the array address is passed to the function rather than a copy of the array. Thus, any operations on the array within the function will affect the original array elements. Here's a complete program:

```
// PASSING AN ARRAY TO A FUNCTION

#include <iostream.h>

// GLOBAL CONSTANTS AND VARIABLES
const int MAX = 4;

// FUNCTION PROTOTYPE
void Weird(char Array[MAX]);

void main()
{
  char Name[MAX] = "IBM";

  cout << "\n\nThe string in Name[] before Weird() is:  " << Name;
  Weird(Name);
  cout << "\n\nThe string in Name[] after Weird() is:  " << Name;
}

// THIS FUNCTION DECREMENTS EACH OF THE ARRAY ELEMENTS
void Weird(char Array[MAX])
{
  for (int i = 0; i < MAX - 1; ++i)
    --Array[i];
}
```

The array *Name[]* is defined as an array of characters and initialized with the string "IBM" in *main()*. The string stored in the array is displayed on the monitor. Then, the function *Weird()* is called using the array name, *Name*, as its argument. This passes the address of the array to function *Weird()* where each of the elements in the array are decremented. What do you suppose the user will see on the monitor after executing the program? Well, this is why things are "weird."

The string in Name[] before Weird() is: IBM

The string in Name[] after Weird() is: HAL

The point here is that the decrement operation within the function affected the original array elements. Thus, the string "IBM" was converted to the string "HAL." Is there anything weird here? Recall that HAL was the artificially intelligent computer in the book and movie *2001 A Space Odyssey*. Is there a message here or is this just a coincidence? You will have to ask the author, Arthur Clarke, to find out.

One final point: You cannot pass the entire array by value to a function. If you do not want operations within the function to affect the array elements, you should pass the array to the function, make a temporary local copy of the array within the function, then operate on this temporary array.

On the other hand, you can pass individual array elements by value to a function. Look at the following function prototype:

void Pass_By_Value(int array_element);

The header says that the function does not return any value and expects to receive an integer value from the calling program. Suppose the function were called as follows:

Pass_By_Value(Scores[0]);

Notice that the actual argument in the function call is *Scores[0]*. This will cause a copy of the element stored at index [0] in the *Scores[]* array to be passed to the function by value. As a result, any operations on this element within the function will not affect the element value in the original *Scores[]* array. If you want the element to reflect any operations within the function, you must pass it by reference using the ampersand symbol in the function prototype like this:

void Pass_By_Reference(int &array_element);

Now, any call to the function will pass the address of the element to the function; thereby passing the element by reference. The following program illustrates how array elements can be passed by value or reference.

```
// PASSING ARRAY ELEMENTS BY VALUE AND REFERENCE

#include <iostream.h>

// GLOBAL CONSTANTS AND VARIABLES
const int MAX = 3;

// FUNCTION PROTOTYPES
void Pass_By_Value(int array_element);
void Pass_By_Reference(int &array_element);

void main()
{
  int Scores[MAX] = {10,20,30};
  cout << "\nElement at Scores[0] before Pass_By_Value is:  "
       << Scores[0];
  Pass_By_Value(Scores[0]);
  cout << "\n\nElement at Scores[0] after Pass_By_Value is:  "
       << Scores[0];

  cout << "\n\nElement at Scores[0] before Pass_By_Reference is:  "
       << Scores[0];
  Pass_By_Reference(Scores[0]);
  cout << "\n\nElement at Scores[0] after Pass_By_Reference is:  "
       << Scores[0];
}

void Pass_By_Value(int array_element)
{
  ++array_element;
}

void Pass_By_Reference(int &array_element)
{
  ++array_element;
}
```

The output produced by the program reflects the effect of the two functions on the array element.

Element at Scores[0] before Pass_By_Value is: 10
Element at Scores[0] after Pass_By_Value is: 10

Element at Scores[0] before Pass_By_Reference is: 10
Element at Scores[0] after Pass_By_Reference is: 11

Study the two programs provided above to make sure that you understand how entire arrays and individual array elements are passed to functions.

Example 8-2

Write a program that uses an array to store a maximum of twenty-five test scores and calculate their average. Use one function to fill the array with the scores, a second function to calculate the average, and a third function to display all the scores along with the calculated average.

Solution:

We will begin in true structuring style and develop the interfaces for the required functions. Let's call the three functions *Get_Scores()*, *Average()*, and *Display_Results()*. Now, the *Get_Scores()* function must obtain the test scores from the user and place them in an array. Thus, the function must accept the array structure and return the array containing the test scores. This leads to the following function interface description:

Function *Get_Scores()*:	Obtain test scores from user and place them in an array.
Accepts:	Test scores array structure of size *MAX*.
Returns:	Test scores array filled with scores entered by the user.

The function interface requires that it must accept and return the array structure. Let's assume that the test scores will be decimal values and, therefore, require a floating point array. Using these ideas, the function prototype becomes:

```
void Get_Scores (float Scores[MAX]);
```

From here, writing the function is easy. We will employ a *cin* statement within a **for** loop in the function body to fill the array with the test scores. Here's the entire function:

```
void Get_Scores (float Scores[MAX])
{
  cout << "How many scores do you want to average?  ";
  cin >> Number;
```

```
cout << "\n\nEnter each score, and press ENTER after each entry.\n";
for (int i = 0; i < Number; ++i)
{
  cout << "\nEnter score #" << i + 1 << ":  ";
  cin >> Scores[i];
}  // END FOR
}  // END FUNCTION
```

Within the function body you see that the user is prompted to enter the number of test scores and each individual score. The scores are entered and placed in the array via a *cin* statement within a **for** loop. Notice that the value the user enters for *Number* is employed to terminate the **for** loop. We will define *Number* as a global variable, since all the functions in this program must have access to it.

Next, a function called *Average()* must be written to average the test scores in the array. This function must accept the array to obtain the test scores and return a single floating point value which is the average of the scores. So, the function interface description is:

Function *Average()*: Computes the average of the test scores.

Accepts: The array of test scores of size *MAX*.

Returns: A single value which is the average of the test scores.

This time, the array must be passed to the function and the function must return a single value. Therefore, the function prototype becomes:

float Average(float Scores[MAX]);

The body of the function simply adds up all the test scores in the array and divides by their number. Here is the complete function:

```
float Average(float Scores[MAX])
{
  float Total = 0;
  for (int i = 0; i < Number; ++i)
    Total += Scores[i];
  return (Total/Number);
}
```

There are two local function variables defined: *Total* and *i*. *Total* will act as a temporary variable to accumulate the sum of the scores and the variable *i* is the loop counter variable. The variable *Total* is first initialized to 0. Then the loop is used to obtain the array elements, one at a time, and add them to *Total*. Observe that the loop counter (*i*) acts as the array index within the loop. Thus, the array elements, from index 0 to *Number – 1* are sequentially extracted with each loop iteration and added to *Total*. The last test score is located at index *[Number – 1]*. Since *Number* will be made a global variable it will be accessible to this function. Once the loop calculates the sum total of all the test scores, a **return** statement is used to calculate the average.

Finally, the *Display_Results()* function must display the individual test scores obtained from the user along with their average. To do this we must pass the array to the function to obtain the test scores. Here's the function description:

Function *Display_Results()*:   Displays the individual test scores and their average.

Accepts: The array of test scores of size *MAX*.

Returns: Nothing.

To display the average, we will simply call the *Average()* function within this function as part of a *cout* statement. The entire function then becomes:

```
void Display_Results(float Scores[MAX])
{
  cout << "Test Scores";
  cout << "\n____ _____\n";
  cout << setprecision(2);
  for (int i = 0; i < Number; ++i)
    cout << "\n\t" << Scores[i];
  cout << "\n\n\nThe average of the above scores is:  "
       << Average(Scores);
}
```

Again, a **for** loop is employed to display the individual test scores. Notice how the *Average()* function is called in the final *cout* statement to calculate the test average.

Now, putting everything together we get the following program:

```
//********************************************************************
//
// THIS PROGRAM WILL CALCULATE A TEST AVERAGE
// FROM SCORES ENTERED BY THE USER INTO AN ARRAY
//
//********************************************************************

#include <iostream.h>
#include <iomanip.h>
```

```
// GLOBAL CONSTANTS AND VARIABLES
const int MAX = 25;          // MAXIMUM NUMBER OF SCORES
int Number;                  // ACTUAL NUMBER OF SCORES

// FUNCTION PROTOTYPES
void Get_Scores (float Scores[MAX] );
float Average(float Scores[MAX]);
void Display_Results(float Scores[MAX]);

void main()
{
  float Scores[MAX];

  Get_Scores(Scores);
  Display_Results(Scores);
}

//********************************************************************
//
// THIS FUNCTION WILL GET THE SCORES FROM THE USER
// AND PLACE THEM INTO THE SCORES ARRAY
//
//********************************************************************
void Get_Scores (float Scores[MAX])
{
  cout << "How many scores do you want to average?   ";
  cin >> Number;
  cout << "\n\nEnter each score, and press ENTER after each entry.\n";
  for (int i = 0; i < Number; ++i)
  {
    cout << "\nEnter score #" << i + 1 << ": ";
    cin >> Scores[i];
  }
}

//********************************************************************
//
// THIS FUNCTION DISPLAYS THE ARRAY SCORES AND THE
// FINAL SCORE AVERAGE
//
//********************************************************************
void Display_Results(float Scores[MAX])
{
  cout << "Test Scores";
  cout << "\n____ _____\n";
```

```
        cout << setprecision(2);
        for (int i = 0; i < Number; ++i)
          cout << "\n\t" << Scores[i];
        cout << "\n\n\nThe average of the above scores is:  "
              << Average(Scores);
      }


//**********************************************************************
//
// THIS FUNCTION WILL CALCULATE THE AVERAGE OF THE
// SCORES IN THE ARRAY
//
//**********************************************************************
      float Average(float Scores[MAX])
      {
        float Total = 0;
        for (int i = 0; i < Number; ++i)
          Total += Scores[i];
        return (Total/Number);
      }
```

As you can see, a global constant (*MAX*) is first defined. This will be the maximum number of elements in the array. In addition to this constant, there is a global variable called *Number*. *Number* will be the number of test scores that the user wishes to average. It has been defined globally, since each function must have access to it. After the global values are defined, the three function prototypes are listed. Now, look at the statement section of *main()*. Are you surprised at its simplicity? Function *main()* is relatively short, since all the work is done in the other functions. This is the "beauty" of structured programming! All *main()* does is simply call the two other functions in the order that they are needed. You see that at the beginning of *main()* the array, called *Scores[]*, is first defined to be an array of *MAX*, or 25, floating point elements. Since the array name is *Scores,* this identifier must be used when accessing the array. After the array is defined, the *Get_Scores()* function is called followed by the *Display_Results()* function. Observe that in both cases, the array is passed to the function by listing its name as the function argument. The function *Get_Scores()* is first called to obtain the scores from the user and insert them into the array. Next, the function *Display_Results()* is called. Again, the array name (*Scores*) is used to pass the array to the function. This function displays the test scores from the array and calls the *Average()* function to calculate the test average.

Quick Check

1. True or False: An array name is the address of index [1] of the array.

2. Write a prototype for a function called *Sample()* that must alter the following array:

   char Characters[15];

   Assume that the function does not return any values except the altered array.

3. Write a prototype for a function called *Test()* that will alter a single array element in the array defined in question 2.

4. Write a statement that will call the function declared in question 3 to alter the element stored at index [5] of the array defined in question 2.

CASE STUDY: SEARCHING AN ARRAY USING ITERATION (SEQUENTIAL SEARCH)

Many applications require a program to search for a given element in an array. Two common algorithms used to perform this task are *sequential*, or *serial*, *search* and *binary search*. Sequential search is commonly used for unsorted arrays, while binary search is used on arrays that are already sorted. In this case study you will learn about sequential search, then in a later case study you will learn about binary search.

Problem:

Develop a function that can be called to sequentially search an array of integers for a given element value and return the index of the element if it is found in the array.

Problem Definition

Since we are dealing with a function, the problem definition will focus on the function interface, or prototype. As a result, we must consider what the function will accept and what the function will return. Let's call the function *SeqSearch( )*. Now, from the problem statement you find that the function must search an array of integers for a given element value. Thus, the function needs two things to do its job: (1) the array to be searched and (2) the element to search for. These will be our function parameters. Do these need to be value or reference parameters? Well, the function will not be changing the array or the element being searched for, right? Therefore, the parameters will be value parameters.

   Next we need to determine what the function is to return to the calling program. From the problem statement you see that the function needs to return the index of the element being searched for if it is found in the array. Since all array indices in C++ are integers, the function will return an integer value. But, what if the element being search for is not found in the array? We need to return some integer value that will indicate this situation. Since array indices in C++ range from 0 to some finite positive integer, let's return the integer −1 if the element is not found in the array. Thus, we will use −1 to indicate the "not-found" condition, since no array index in C++ can have this value. Here is the function interface description:

Function *SeqSearch( )*:   Searches an integer array for a given element value.

Accepts: An array of integers and the element to search for.

Returns: The array index of the element if found, or the value −1 if the element is not found.

   The above function interface description provides all the information required to write the function prototype. Here it is:

                        int SeqSearch(int A[MAX], int Element);

   The prototype dictates that the function will accept two things: (1) an array of *MAX* integer elements, and (2) an integer value, called *Element*, that will be the value to search for.
   The next task is to develop the sequential search algorithm.

The Algorithm

   Sequential search does exactly what it says: it *sequentially* searches the array, from one element to the next, starting at the first array position and stopping when either the element is found or it reaches the end of the array. Thus, the algorithm must test the element stored in the first array position, then the second array position, then the third, and so on until the element is found or it runs out of array elements. This is obviously a repetitive task of testing an array element, then moving to the next element and testing again, and so on. Consider the following algorithm that employs a **while** loop to perform the repetitive testing operation:

SeqSearch() **Algorithm**

SeqSearch()
BEGIN
   Set *Found* = FALSE.
   Set *Index* = first array index.
   While (*Element* is not *Found*) AND (*Index* <= last array index) Do
     If (*A[Index]* == *Element*) Then
       Set *Found* = TRUE.
     Else
       Increment *Index*.
   If (*Found* == TRUE) Then
     Return (*Index*).
   Else
     Return (–1).
END.

The idea here is to employ a Boolean variable, called *Found*, to indicate if the element was found during the search. The variable *Found* is initialized to FALSE and a variable called *Index* is initialized to the index of the first element in the array. Notice the **while** loop test. Due to the use of the AND operator, the loop will continue as long as the element is not found *and* the value of *Index* is less than or equal to the last index value of the array. Another way to say this is that the loop will repeat until the element is found *or* the value of *Index* exceeds the last index value of the array. Think about it!

    Inside the loop, the value stored at location [*Index*] is compared to the value of *Element*, received by the function. If the two are equal, the Boolean variable *Found* is set to TRUE. Otherwise, the value of *Index* is incremented to move to the next array position.

    When the loop terminates, either the element was found or not found. If the element was found, the value of *Found* will be TRUE and the value of *Index* will be the array position, or index, at which the element was found. Thus, if *Found* is

TRUE, the value of *Index* is returned to the calling program. If the element was not found, the value of *Found* will still be FALSE from its initialized state and the value –1 is returned to the calling program. That's all there is to it!

The Program

Here is the C++ code that reflects the foregoing algorithm:

```
int SeqSearch(int A[MAX], int Element)
{
  enum {FALSE, TRUE};        // DEFINE FALSE = 0 AND TRUE = 1
  int Found = FALSE;         // INITIALIZE Found TO FALSE
  int i = 0;                 // ARRAY INDEX VARIABLE

// SEARCH ARRAY UNTIL FOUND OR REACH END OF ARRAY
  while ((!Found) && (i <= MAX-1))
  {
    if (A[i] == Element)     // TEST ARRAY ELEMENT
      Found = TRUE;          // IF EQUAL, SET Found TO TRUE
    else                     // ELSE INCREMENT ARRAY INDEX
      ++i;
  }

// IF ELEMENT FOUND, RETURN ELEMENT POSITION IN ARRAY
// ELSE RETURN -1.
  if (Found)
    return (i);
  else
    return (-1);
}
```

There should be no surprises in this code. At the top of the function, you see the header that is identical to the function prototype developed earlier. Then you see an enumerated data type created to define FALSE and TRUE. Recall that the default values for enumerated data elements are the integers, beginning with 0. Thus, FALSE is defined to be the value 0 and TRUE is defined to be the value 1. This allows us to use the identifiers FALSE and TRUE within our program to represent the integer values 0 and 1, respectively. In addition, Boolean tests can be made against these values, since C++ interprets a 0 as a logical FALSE and a 1 as a logical TRUE.

Since there is no Boolean data type in C++, we define the variable *Found* as an integer and set it to FALSE, or 0. We will use the variable *i* as our array index variable. This variable is declared as an integer and set to the first array index, 0. Remember that arrays in C++ always begin with index 0. The **while** loop employs the AND (&&) operator to test the values of *Found* and *i*. The loop will repeat as long as the element is not found (!*Found*) and the value of *i* is less than or equal to the maximum array index, *MAX* – *1*. Remember that when the size of the array is *MAX*, the last array index is *MAX* – *1*. When the loop is broken, the value of *Found* is tested. If *Found* is TRUE, or 1, the value of *i* is returned, otherwise if *Found* is FALSE, or 0, the value –1 is returned to indicate that the element was not found in the array.

CASE STUDY: SORTING AN ARRAY USING ITERATION (INSERTION SORT)

To sort an array means to place the array elements in either ascending or descending order from the beginning to the end of the array. There are many common algorithms used for sorting. There is *insertion sort*, *bubble sort*, *selection sort*, *quick sort*, *merge sort*, and *heap sort*, just to mention a few. In a Data Structures course you will most likely learn about and analyze all of these sorting algorithms. In this case study we will develop the *insertion sort* algorithm and code it as a function in C++.

Problem:

Develop a function that can be called to sort an array of characters in ascending order using the *insertion sort* algorithm.

Problem Definition

Again, since we will code the algorithm as a C++ function, the problem definition will focus on the function interface, leading us to the function prototype. Let's call our function *InsertSort()*. Think about what *InsertSort()* needs to do its job. Well, it must receive an unsorted array of characters and return the same array as a sorted array, right? Does it need anything else? No, additional data are not required by the function, since the only thing being operated upon is the array itself.

What about return values? Does the function need to return a single value or a set of values? The function does not return any single value, but must return the sorted array. Therefore, the return type of the function must be **void**, and the array must be a reference parameter, right? Remember that when arrays are passed to C++ functions, they are always treated as reference parameters because the array name represents an address in memory. So, here's our *InsertSort()* function interface description:

Function *InsertSort()*:   Sorts an array of characters.

Accepts: An array of characters.

Returns: A sorted array of characters.

From the above interface description, the function prototype is easily coded as:

void InsertSort(char Array[MAX]);

The prototype says that *InsertSort()* will receive a character array of size *MAX*. The return type is **void**, since no single value is returned. However, since the entire array is being passed to the function, any sorting operations on the array within the function will be reflected back in the calling program. Now for the insertion sort algorithm.

The Algorithm

Before we set up the algorithm, let's see how insertion sort works. Look at Figure 8-3. We will assume that we are going to sort a five character array in ascending order. Before getting into the details look at the figure from top-to-bottom and from left-to-right. The unsorted array is shown at the top of the figure and the sorted array is shown at the bottom of the figure. Notice that shading is employed in the figure to show the sorting process from top-to-bottom. As we proceed from the unsorted array at the top, the shading increases showing the portion of the array that is sorted, until the entire array is shaded at the bottom of the figure.

The top-to-bottom sequence shows that we will make four passes through the array to achieve the sorted array shown at the bottom of the figure. With each pass an element is placed into its sorted position *relative to the elements that occur before it* in the array. The first pass begins with the first element, 'E', sorted as indicated by the shading. The single character 'E' is considered to be sorted by itself, since it does not have any elements preceding it. Thus, the task in this first pass is to sort the second element, 'D', relative to the character 'E' that precedes it.

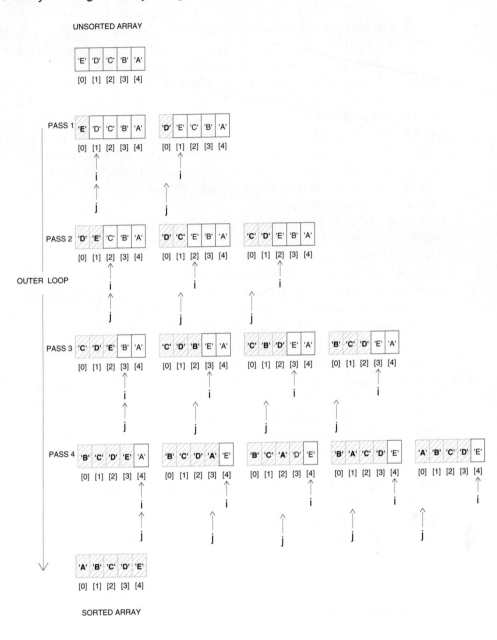

Figure 8-3 Insertion sort is a nested repetition process.

The second pass begins with the characters 'D' and 'E' sorted, as indicated by the shading. The task in this pass is to sort the third character, 'C', relative to these two characters. In the third pass, the elements 'C', 'D', and 'E' are sorted, and the task is to sort the character 'B' relative to these characters. Remember, in each pass the task is to sort the first character of the unsorted portion of the array relative to the characters that precede it in the sorted portion of the array. The process continues until all the characters are sorted as shown at the bottom of the figure. With each pass, you are essentially repeating what was done in the previous pass. As a result, you can identify a repetitive process, from pass to pass, from the top to the bottom of the figure. This repetition will result in a loop structure in our algorithm.

Now, the question is: What happens during each pass to eventually sort the entire array? Well, during each pass the first element in the unsorted (unshaded) portion of the array is examined by comparing it to the sorted sequence of elements that precede it. If this element is less than the element preceding it, the two elements are exchanged. Once the element is exchanged with its predecessor, it is compared with its new predecessor element. Again, if it is less than its predecessor, the two elements are exchanged. This process is repeated until one of two things happen: 1) the element is greater than or equal to its predecessor, or 2) the element is in the first position of the array (index [0]). In other words, the left-to-right compare/exchange process shown in Figure 8-3 ceases when the element under examination has been "inserted" into is proper position in the sorted portion of the array. This compare/exchange process represents repetition from left-to-right in the figure and will result in another loop structure in our algorithm.

So, we can identify two repetitive processes in the figure: one from top-to-bottom and one from left-to-right. How are the two repetitive processes related? Well, it looks like for each top-to-bottom pass through the array, the compare/exchange process is executed from left-to-right. Thus, the left-to-right process must be nested within the top-to-bottom process. This will be reflected in our algorithm by two loop structures: one controlling the left-to-right compare/exchange process that must be nested inside a second loop controlling the top-to-bottom process. Look at the figure again to make sure that you see this nested repetition. Now that you have an idea of how insertion sort works, here is the formal algorithm:

InsertSort() Algorithm

InsertSort()
BEGIN
  Set i = second array index.
  While (i <= last array index) Do
    Set $j = i$.
    While ((j > first array index) AND ($A[j] < A[j–1]$)) Do
      Exchange $A[j]$ and $A[j–1]$.
      Decrement j.
    Increment i.
END.

The variables i and j in the algorithm correspond to the i and j shown in Figure 8-3. The variable i controls the outer loop, while j controls the inner loop. Notice that i begins at the second array index, [1]. Why not the first array index, [0]? Because the first element in the array is always sorted relative to any preceding elements, right? So, the first pass begins with the second array element. The first statement in the outer loop sets j equal to i. Thus, both i and j locate the first element in the unsorted portion of the array at the beginning of each pass. Now, the inner loop will exchange the element located by j, which is $A[j]$, with its predecessor element, which is $A[j–1]$, as long as j is greater than the first array index [0] *and* element $A[j]$ is less than element $A[j–1]$. Once the exchange is made, j is decremented. This forces j to follow the element being inserted into the sorted portion of the array. The exchanges continue until either there are no elements preceding element $A[j]$ that are less than element $A[j]$ or the element is inserted into the first element position.

Once the inner loop is broken, element $A[j]$ is inserted into its correct position relative to the elements that precede it. Then, another pass is made by incrementing the outer loop control variable, i, setting j to i, and executing the inner loop again. This nested looping process continues until i is incremented past the last array position.

Study the above algorithm and compare it to Figure 8-3 until you are sure that you understand *InsertSort()*. Now for the C++ code.

The Program

We have already developed the *InsertSort()* function interface. The algorithm is easily coded as a function in C++ like this:

```
// EXCHANGE FUNCTION
void Exchange(char &x, char &y)
{
  char Temp;                    // CREATE TEMPORARY VARIABLE
  Temp = x;                     // SET Temp TO x
  x = y;                        // SET x TO y
  y = Temp;                     // SET y TO Temp
}


// INSERTION SORT FUNCTION
void InsertSort(char A[MAX])
{
  int i;                        // OUTER LOOP CONTROL VARIABLE
  int j;                        // INNER LOOP CONTROL VARIABLE
  i = 1;                        // SET i TO SECOND ARRAY INDEX
  while (i <= MAX-1)            // MAKE MAX-1 PASSES THRU ARRAY
  {
    j = i;                      // j LOCATES FIRST ELEMENT
                               // OF UNSORTED PORTION
    while ((j > 0) && (A[j] < A[j-1]))  // COMPARE/EXCHANGE A[j] AND A[j-1]
      {
        Exchange(A[j], A[j-1]);
        --j;                   // MAKE j FOLLOW INSERT ELEMENT
      } // END INNER WHILE
    ++i;                       // MAKE i LOCATE FIRST ELEMENT OF
                               // UNSORTED PORTION
  } // END OUTER WHILE
} // END INSERTION SORT
```

Here you see two functions coded in C++. Recall that the *InsertSort()* algorithm requires an exchange operation. A function called *Exchange()* has been coded to accomplish this task. Notice that this function has two reference parameters that are characters. Thus, the function receives two characters which are exchanged by using a temporary local variable (*Temp*) within the function. The exchanged characters are sent back to the calling program via the reference parameters. Of course, the calling program will be our *InsertSort()* function.

The *InsertSort()* code should be straightforward from the algorithm that we just analyzed. Study the code and compare it to the algorithm. You will find that they are identical from a logical and structural point of view. You might notice how the *Exchange()* function is called within *InsertSort()*. The array elements *A[j]* and *A[j–1]* are passed to the function. These elements are simply characters, right? So, the function receives two characters and exchanges them. The respective characters in the array reflect the exchange operations, since *Exchange()* employs reference parameters.

CASE STUDY: SEARCHING AN ARRAY USING RECURSION (BINARY SEARCH)

In this case study we will develop another popular searching algorithm, called **binary search**. The binary search algorithm that we will develop will employ recursion, although it can also be done using iteration. One of the major differences between binary search and sequential search is that binary search requires that the array be sorted prior to the search, while sequential search does not have this requirement. If, however, you have a sorted array to begin with, binary search is much faster than sequential search, especially for large arrays. For example, if you were to apply sequential search to an array of 1000 integers, the sequential search algorithm will make an *average* of 500 comparisons to find the desired element. Even worse, if the desired element is in the last array position, sequential search will make 1000 comparisons to find the element. On the other hand, a binary search would only require a maximum of 10 comparisons to find the element, even if it is in the last array position! Of course, you must pay a price for this increased efficiency. The price you must pay is that of a more complex algorithm. So, when searching a sorted array, the advantage of sequential search is simplicity, while the advantage of binary search is efficiency.

Problem:

Develop a C++ function that can be called to search a sorted array of integers for a given element value and return the index of the element if it is found in the array. Employ a recursive binary search to accomplish this task.

Since we will be developing a C++ function, our problem definition will focus on the function interface, or prototype. However, before we can consider the function interface we must see how a recursive binary search works, since the search algorithm will dictate our function parameters. So, let's first deal with the algorithm, then develop the function interface.

The Algorithm

Binary search represents a natural recursive operation. Remember that the idea behind recursion is to divide and conquer. You keep breaking a problem down into simpler subproblems of exactly the same type until a primitive condition occurs. This is not the same as top/down software design which breaks problems down into simpler subproblems. The difference with recursion is that the subproblems are exactly the same type of problem as the original problem. For example, suppose that you are searching for a name in a telephone book. Imagine starting at the beginning of the telephone book and looking at every name until you found the right one. This is exactly what sequential search does. Wouldn't it be much faster, on the average, to open up the book in the middle? Then, determine which half of the book contains the name that you are looking for, divide this section of the book in half, and so on, until you obtain the page on which the desired name appears. Here is an algorithm that describes the telephone book search just described:

A Recursive Telephone Book Search Algorithm

TeleSearch( )
BEGIN
   If (the telephone book only contains one page) Then
      Look for the name on the page.
   Else
      Open the book to the middle.
      If (the name is in the first half) Then
         TeleSearch(first half of the book for the name).
      Else
         TeleSearch(second half of the book for the name).
END.

Do you see how this search is recursive? You keep performing the same basic operations until you come to the page that contains the name for which you are looking. In other words, the *TeleSearch( )* function keeps calling itself in the nested **if/else** statement until the correct page is found. The reason that this is called a *binary* search process is that you must divide the book by 2 (*bi*) each time the algorithm calls itself.

Now, let's see how this process can be applied to searching an array of integers. We will call our recursive binary search function *BinSearch( )* and will develop our algorithm in several steps. Here is the first-level algorithm.

BinSearch() **Algorithm: First Level**

```
BinSearch()
BEGIN
   If (the array has only one element) Then
      Determine if this element is the element being searched for.
   Else
      Find the midpoint of the array.
      If (the element is in the first half) Then
         BinSearch(first half).
      Else
         BinSearch(second half).
END.
```

Notice how this algorithm is almost identical to the *TeleSearch()* algorithm. Here, the divide-and-conquer searching process continues until the array is reduced to one element which is tested against the element that we are searching for. Do you see how the search keeps calling itself until the primitive condition occurs? Although this algorithm provides the general binary search idea, we need to get more specific in order to code the algorithm. To do this, we must ask ourselves what data *BinSearch()* needs to accomplish its task. Well, like sequential search, it needs an array to search and the element to search for, right? However, sequential search dealt with one array of a given size, while binary search needs to deal with arrays of different sizes as it keeps dividing the original array in half. Not only are these arrays of different sizes, but the first and last indices of each half are different. As a result, we must provide *BinSearch()* with the boundaries of the array that it is dealing with at any given time. This can be done by passing the first and last indices of the given array to the function. Let's call these indices *First* and *Last*.

We are now ready to write the function interface description:

Function *BinSearch()*:　Searches an array of integers for a given value.

Accepts:　An array of integers, an element to search for, the first index of the array being searched, and the last index of the array being searched.

Returns:　The array index of the element if found, or the value −1 if the element is not found.

The function interface description gives us enough information to write the C++ function prototype as follows:

int BinSearch(int Array[], int Element, int First, int Last);

Here, *BinSearch()* will return an integer value that represents the index of the element being searched for. Again, you will see that the value −1 will be returned if the element is not found in the array. The function receives the integer array being searched (*A[]*), the element being searched for (*Element*), the first index of the array being searched (*First*), and the last index of the array being searched (*Last*). Notice that no size is provided for the array being searched because the function will recursively search arrays of different sizes.

The next problem is to determine what the value of *First* and *Last* will be for any given array during the search. Well, remember that we must divide any given array in half to produce two new arrays each time a recursive call to *BinSearch()* is made. Given any array where the first index is *First* and the last index is *Last*, we can determine the middle index like this:

$$Mid = (First + Last) / 2$$

Using this calculation, the first half of the array begins at *First* and ends at *Mid − 1*, while the second half of the array begins at *Mid + 1* and ends at *Last*. This idea is illustrated in Figure 8-4.

But, notice that neither half of the array contains the middle element. Using this technique the two halves do not make a whole, right? So, before the split is made suppose that we test the middle element to see if it is the element that we are looking for. The following test will do the job.

If (*A[Mid]* == *Element*) Then
    Return (*Mid*).

If this test is TRUE prior to the split we have found the element that we are looking for and we can cease the recursive calls. Otherwise, the element stored in *A[Mid]* is not the element that we are looking for and this array position can be ignored during the rest of the search. If this is the case, we will split the array and continue the recursive process. However, we have just added a second primitive condition to our recursive algorithm. Here are the two primitive conditions that we now have:

1. The array being searched has only one element.

2. *A[Mid] == Element.*

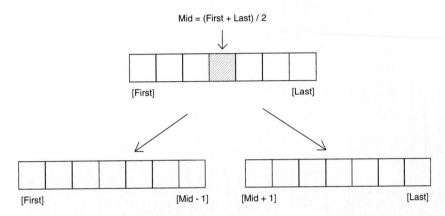

Figure 8-4: Recursive binary search requires that an array be divided in half with each recursive call.

Either of these primitive conditions will cause the recursive calls to cease. Now, let's consider the first primitive condition more closely. How do we know if the array being searched has only one element? Well, as the recursive calls continue without finding the element, the array will eventually be reduced to a single element. If this is the element that we are looking for, the test *If A[Mid] == Element* will be TRUE and the recursive calls will stop. If this is not the elment that we are looking for, the value of *First* will become greater than the value of *Last* on the next split. Why? Because if you think about the splitting action of the algorithm, you will realize that each recursive call causes *First* to increase and *Last* to decrease. Thus, if the element is not in the array, the value of *First* will eventually become larger than the value of *Last*. So we can use this idea to test for the element not being in the array, as well as use it for a primitive condition. Thus, we will replace the original primitive condition with the following statement:

If (*First > Last*) Then
        Return (–1)

If this condition occurs, the value –1 is returned, indicating that element was not found, and the recursive calls cease.

Now, let's apply this knowledge to a second level algorithm. Here it is:

BinSearch( ) **Algorithm: Second Level**

BinSearch(A, Element, First, Last)
BEGIN
  If (*First > Last*) Then
    Return (–1).
  Else
    Set *Mid = (First + Last) / 2.*
    If (*A[Mid] == Element)* Then
      Return (*Mid*).
    Else
      If (the element is in the first half) Then
          BinSearch(A, Element, First, Mid – 1).
      Else
          BinSearch(A, Element, Mid + 1, Last).
END.

It is much clearer now that our algorithm is performing recursion, since you see the function calling itself in either one of two places, depending on which half of the split array the element is likely to be found. Also, observe where the two delimiting cases are tested. If at the beginning of any recursive call *First > Last*, the element is not in the array and the recursive calls cease. In addition, if after calculating *Mid* we find the element at *A[Mid]* the recursive calls cease. In both cases the function is done executing and a value is returned to the calling program. The last thing our algorithm needs is a way to determine if the element being searched for is likely to be in the first half or the second half of the split array. Here is where the requirement for a sorted array comes in. If the array is sorted, the element will likely be in the first half of the array when *Element < A[Mid]*, otherwise the element is likely to be in the second half of the array. Notice that we are using the term "likely." We can not guarantee that the element is in either half, since it might not be in the array at all! All we can do is to direct the search to that half where the element is likely to be, depending on the sorted ordering of elements. So, we can now complete our algorithm using this idea. Here is the final algorithm:

BinSearch( ) **Algorithm**

BinSearch(A, Element, First, Last)
BEGIN
  If (*First > Last*) Then
    Return (–1).

Else
  Set *Mid = (First + Last) / 2.*
  If *(A[Mid] == Element)* Then
    Return *(Mid).*
  Else
    If *(Element < A[Mid])* Then
      BinSearch(A, Element, First, Mid – 1).
    Else
      BinSearch(A, Element, Mid + 1, Last).
END.

Notice how ***elegant*** the algorithm is. By elegance, we mean that the rather complicated binary search process is reduced to just a few statements. You *know* there is a lot going on here, but recursion allows us to express all of this processing in just a few statements. As you can see, recursive algorithms often provide simple solutions to problems of great complexity, where an equivalent iterative solution might be rather complex. This is not always the case, since some recursive solutions are impractical relative to speed and memory efficiency. Remember the general rule of thumb when considering recursion: Only consider a recursive solution to a problem when a simple iterative solution is not possible. You should be aware that binary search has a relatively simple iterative solution. You will code this solution for one of the problems at the end of the chapter.

The Program

The required C++ function can now be easily coded from the final algorithm. Here it is:

```cpp
int BinSearch(int A[ ], int Element, int First, int Last)
{
  int Mid;                       // ARRAY MIDPOINT
  if (First > Last)              // IF ELEMENT NOT IN ARRAY
    return (-1);                 // RETURN -1, ELSE CONTINUE SEARCH
  else
  {
    Mid = (First + Last) / 2;    // FIND MID POINT OF ARRAY
    if (Element == A[Mid])       // IF ELEMENT IS IN A[MID]
      return (Mid);              // RETURN MID
    else                         // ELSE SEARCH APPROPRIATE HALF
      if (Element < A[Mid])
        return (BinSearch(A, Element, First, Mid - 1));
      else
```

```
            return (BinSearch(A, Element, Mid + 1, Last));
      }                                  // END OUTER ELSE
}                                        // END FUNCTION
```

You should not have any trouble understanding this code, since it reflects the function interface and algorithm developed above.

CHAPTER SUMMARY

An array is an important structured data type used to locate and store elements of a given data type. The two components of any array are the elements that are stored in the array and the indices that locate the stored elements. Array elements can be any given data type, while array indices are always integers ranging from [0] to [*MAX – 1*], where *MAX* is the size of the array.

There are both one-dimensional arrays and multidimensional arrays. A one-dimensional array, or list, is a single row of elements. It has dimensions of $1 \times n$, where n is the number of elements in the list. In C++, the maximum index in any dimension is the size of the dimension (n) minus 1.

Arrays are defined in C++ by specifying the element data type, the array name, and the size of each dimension in the array. To access the array elements, you must use direct assignment statements, read/write statements, or loops. The **for** loop structure is the most common way of accessing multiple array elements.

Searching and sorting are common operations performed on arrays. *Sequential search* is an iterative search that looks for a given value in an array by sequentially comparing the value to the array elements, beginning with the first array element until the value is found in the array or until the end of the array is reached. *Binary search* can be iterative or recursive. Binary search keeps dividing the array in half, directing itself to the half where the value is likely to be found. Binary search requires the array be sorted, while sequential search does not have this requirement. On the other hand, binary search is much faster than sequential search, especially on large sorted arrays.

Many real-world applications require that information be sorted. There are several common sorting algorithms including *insertion sort*, *bubble sort*, *selection sort*, and *quick sort*. All of these algorithms operate on arrays. The insertion sort algorithm is an iterative process that inserts a given element in the array in its correct place relative to the elements that precede it in the array. You will be acquainted with bubble sort and selection sort in the chapter problems.

QUESTIONS AND PROBLEMS

Questions

1. What three things must be specified in order to define an array?

Use the following array definition to answer questions 2–7.

```
char Characters[15];
```

2. What is the index of the first array element?

3. What is the index of the last array element?

4. Write a statement that will place the character 'Z' in the third cell of the array.

5. Write a statement that will display the last array element.

6. Write the code necessary to fill the array from keyboard entries. Make sure to prompt the user before each character entry.

7. Write a loop that will display all the array elements vertically on the screen.

8. Show the contents of the following array:

```
int Integers[5] = {1,2,3};
```

9. Show the contents of the following array:

```
char Characters[5] = {'C','+','+'};
```

10. What is wrong with the following array definition?

```
char OOP[3] = "C++";
```

How would you correct the problem in this definition?

11. Write a statement to define a floating point array that will be initialized with all zeros and is local to *main()*.

12. What is wrong with the following array definition?

```
int Numbers[4] = {0,1,2,3,4};
```

13. Given the following array definition:

```
int Values[10];
```

Write a statement to place the product of the first and second array elements in the last element position.

Use the following array definition to answer questions 14–18:

```
const int MAX = 4;
char String[MAX] = "C++";
```

14. Write the prototype for a function called *StringLength()* that will receive the entire array, and return the length of the string.

15. Write a prototype for a function called *StringElement()* that will receive a single element of the string such that any operation on that element within the function will not affect the element value within the array.

16. Write a statement to call the function in question 15 and pass the first element of the array to the function.

17. Write a prototype for a function called *ChangeElement()* that will receive a single element of the string such that any change to that element within the function will change the element value in the array.

18. Write a statement to call the function in question 17 and pass the last element of the array to the function.

19. In general, what element position will be returned by the sequential and binary search functions developed in this chapter if there are multiple occurrences of the element in the array?

20. Why is binary search faster, on the average, than sequential search?

21. When would sequential search be faster than binary search?

22. Revise the *InsertSort()* algorithm to sort the array in descending order.

Problems

Least Difficult

1. Write a program to fill an array with all the odd integers from 1 to 99. Write one function to fill the array and another function to display the array, showing the odd integers across the screen separated by commas.

2. Write a function to read the user's name from a keyboard entry and place it in a character array. Write another function to display the user's name stored in the array. Test your functions via an application program.

3. Write a program to read a list of 25 character elements from a keyboard entry and display them in reverse order. Use one function to fill the list with the entered elements and another function to display the list.

4. Write program that uses six character arrays to store the user's name, street address, city, state, zip code, and telephone number. Provide one function to fill the arrays and another to display the array contents using proper addressing format.

More Difficult

5. Write a program to test the *SeqSearch()* function developed in this chapter. Use the *random()* function available in *stdlib.h* to fill an array

with random integer values prior to applying *SeqSearch()*. Consult your C++ reference manual for the details on how to use *random()*.

6. Write a program to test the *BinSearch()* function developed in this chapter. Use the standard *random()* function available in *stdlib.h* to fill an array with random integer values. Then, apply *InsertSort()* to sort the array prior to using *BinSearch()*. Note: If you use the *InsertSort()* code developed in this chapter, you must change the code to sort an integer array rather than a character array.

Most Difficult

7. Here is the iterative solution for binary search in pseudocode form:

```
BinarySearch()
BEGIN
     Set Found = FALSE.
     While ( !Found AND First <= Last ) Do
          Set Mid = (First + Last) / 2.
          If (Element == A[Mid]) Then
             Set Found = TRUE.
          Else
             If (Element < A[Mid]) Then
                 Set Last = Mid – 1.
             Else
                 Set First = Mid + 1.
     If (Found) Then
          Return (Mid).
     Else
          Return (–1).
END.
```

Code this algorithm as a C++ function to search for a given element in an integer array. Write an application program to test the function. Remember to sort the array using a sorting function prior to calling the binary search function.

8. Another common iterative sorting algorithm is **bubble sort**. Here's the algorithm:

```
BubbleSort()
BEGIN
     Set Passes = 1.
     Set Exchange = TRUE.
```

While (Passes < Number of Array Elements) AND (Exchange == TRUE)
    Set Exchange = FALSE.
    For Index = (First Array Index) To (Last Array Index – Passes)
      If A[Index] > A[Index + 1]
        Swap(A[index], A[Index + 1]).
        Set Exchange = TRUE.
    Set Passes = Passes + 1.
END.

The bubble sort algorithm makes several passes through the array, comparing adjacent values during each pass. The adjacent values are exchanged if the first value is larger than the second value. The process terminates when $N – 1$ passes have been made (where N is the number of elements in the array) or when no more exchanges are possible.

Your job is to code the above algorithm as a C++ function called *BubbleSort()*. In addition, you will have to code a *Swap()* function that can be called by the *BubbleSort()* function to exchange two array elements as shown in the algorithm. Write your functions to sort a character array. Incorporate them into a program that will test the sorting procedure. Why is bubble sort less efficient that insertion sort?

9. Another common iterative sorting algorithm is **selection sort.** The algorithm goes like this:

SelectSort()
BEGIN
    For Index1 = (First Array Index) To (Last Array Index) Do
      Set Position = Index1.
      Set Smallest = A[Position].
      For Index2 = (Index1+1) To (Last Array Index) Do
        If A[Index2] < Smallest
          Set Position = Index2.
          Set Smallest = A[Position].
      Set A[Position] = A[Index1].
      Set A[Index1] = Smallest.
END.

As with bubble sort, selection sort makes several passes through the array. The first pass examines the entire array and places the smallest element in the first array position. The second pass examines the array beginning at the second element. The smallest element in this array segment is found and placed in the second array position. The third pass examines the array beginning at the third element, finds the smallest element in this array segment, and places it in the third element position. The process continues until there are no more array segments left.

Your job is to code the above algorithm as a C++ function called *SelectionSort()*. Write your function to sort a character array. Then use it in a program that will test the sorting procedure.

Why is selection sort less efficient than insertion sort?

10. Write a program that will take an *unsorted* integer array and find the location of the maximum value in the array. (*Hint:* Copy the array into another array and sort this second array to determine its maximum value. Then search the original array for this value.)

9

MULTIDIMENSIONAL ARRAYS

INTRODUCTION

A multidimensional array is simply an extension of a one-dimensional array. Rather than storing a single list of elements, you can think of a multidimensional array as storing multiple lists of elements. For instance, a two-dimensional array stores lists in a two-dimensional table format of rows and columns, where each row is a list. The rows provide the vertical dimension of the array and the columns provide the horizontal array dimension. A three-dimensional array stores lists in a three-dimensional format of rows, columns, and planes, where each plane is a two-dimensional array. The rows provide the vertical dimension, the columns provide the horizontal dimension, and the planes provide the depth dimension of the array.

In this chapter, you will learn about two- and three-dimensional arrays, since arrays larger than this are seldom needed in programming. The chapter will conclude with a comprehensive case study employing two-dimensional arrays to solve sets of simultaneous equations using Cramer's rule.

9-1 TWO-DIMENSIONAL ARRAYS

The most common multidimensional array is the ***two-dimensional*** array shown in Figure 9-1. Here, you see that a two-dimensional array contains multiple rows. It's as if several one-dimensional arrays are combined to form a single rectangular structure of data. As a result, you can think of this rectangular data structure as a ***table*** of elements.

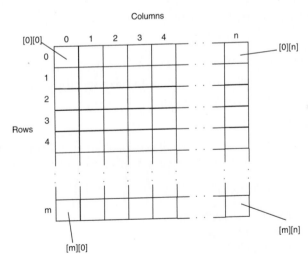

Figure 9-1 The structure of a two-dimensional array.

Observe that the two-dimensional array in Figure 9-1 is composed of elements that are located by rows and columns. The rows are labeled on the vertical axis and they range from 0 to *m*. The columns are labeled on the horizontal axis and range from 0 to *n*. How many rows and columns are there? Since each dimension starts with index [0], there must be *m* + 1 rows and *n* + 1 columns, right? As a result, we say that this two-dimensional array has a dimension, or size, of *m* + 1 rows by *n* + 1 columns, written as *(m + 1) × (n + 1)*.

How many elements are in the array? You're right, *(m + 1)* times *(n + 1)* elements! How do you suppose a given element is located? You're right again: by specifying its row and column index values. For instance, the element in the upper left-hand corner is located at the intersection of row 0 and column 0, or index [0][0]. Likewise, the element in the lower right-hand corner is located where row *m* meets column *n*, or index [*m*][*n*]. We say that two-dimensional arrays in C/C++ are **row major ordered**. This means that the row index is listed first, followed by the column index.

Defining Two-Dimensional Arrays in C++

You define a two-dimensional array in C++ almost the same as you define a one-dimensional array. Here's the general format:

TWO-DIMENSIONAL ARRAY FORMAT

<element data type> <array name> [<number of rows>][<number of columns>];

The only difference between this definition and that required for a one-dimensional array is found within the size specification. You must specify both the row and column sizes as shown.

Example 9-1

Given the following two-dimensional array definitions, sketch a diagram of the array structures showing the respective row/column indices.

a. float Table[5][7];

b. const int ROWS = 5;
   const int COLS = 7;
   float Table[ROWS][COLS];

c. const int CURRENT = 26;
    const int RESISTANCE = 1001;
    int Voltage[CURRENT][RESISTANCE];

d. const int WEEKS = 6;
    const int DAYS = 7;
    int May[WEEKS][DAYS];

e. const int ROW = 57;
    const int SEAT = 10;
    int SeatOccupied[ROW][SEAT];

Solution:

a. See Figure 9-2(a). This is a rectangular array, or table, whose rows range from 0 to 4 and columns range from 0 to 6. Remember that, since array indices start with [0], the last index in a given array dimension is one less than its size. The array name is *Table* and it will store floating point values.

b. See Figure 9-2(a) again. This array is identical to the first array. The only difference here is in the way the array is defined. Notice that the row and column indices are defined as simply *[ROWS][COLS]* where *ROWS* and *COLS* are defined as constants.

c. See Figure 9-2(b). Here, the rows are called *CURRENT* and range from 0 to 25. The array columns are labeled *RESISTANCE* and range from 0 to 1000. The array name is *Voltage* and it will store integer elements. Obviously, the array will store the *Voltage* values corresponding to *CURRENT* values from 0 to 25 and *RESISTANCE* values from 0 to 1000, using Ohm's law.

d. See Figure 9-2(c). This array is constructed to store the dates for the month of *May* just like a calendar. Look at a common calendar if you have one handy. Isn't a given month simply a table of integers whose values are located by a given week and a given day within that week? As you can see from Figure 9-2(c), the array structure duplicates a monthly calendar. The rows are labeled 0 through 5, representing the six possible weeks in any given month. The columns of the array are labeled 0 through 6, representing the seven days of the week.

e. See Figure 9-2(d). This last array also has a practical application. Can you determine what it is from the definition? Notice that it is an array of integer elements. The rows range from 0 to 56 and the columns range from 0 to 9 as shown. The array name is *SeatOccupied*. Suppose that you use this array to store integer values of 0 and 1, where a 0 represents the Boolean value of FALSE and 1 represents the Boolean value of TRUE. Then, this array could be used in a reservation program for a theater or airline flight to indicate whether or not a given seat is occupied or not occupied.

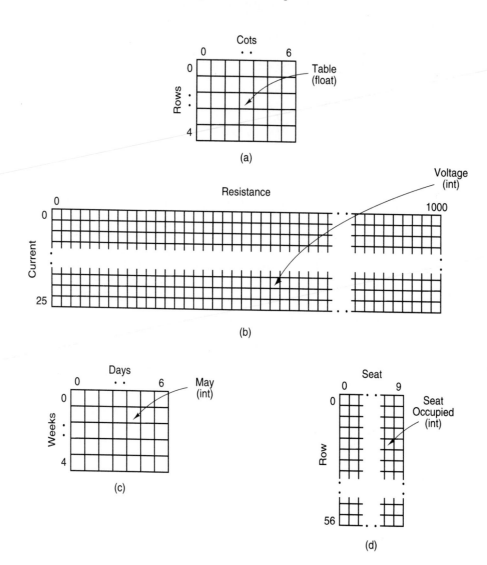

Figure 9-2 Four two-dimensional arrays for Example 9-1.

Example 9-2

How many elements will each of the arrays in Example 9-1 store and what type of elements will they store?

Solution:

a. The array in Figure 9-2(a) will store 5 × 7, or 35 elements. The elements will be floating point values.
b. The array in Figure 9-2(b) has 26 rows, from 0 to 25, and 1001 columns, from 0 to 1000. Thus, the array will store 26 × 1001 = 26,026 integer elements.
c. The array in Figure 9-2(c) has 6 rows and 7 columns and, therefore, will store 6 × 7 = 42 integer elements.
d. The array in Figure 9-2(d) has 57 rows and 10 columns and will store 57 × 10 = 570 integer elements that will be treated as Boolean values.

The above figures can be verified by using the *sizeof()* function. Recall that *sizeof()* returns the *number of bytes* required to store an expression or a data type. So, coding the following statements will display the number of elements in each array:

```
cout << sizeof(Table)/sizeof(float) << "\n\n"
     << sizeof(Voltage)/sizeof(int) << "\n\n"
     << sizeof(May)/sizeof(int) << "\n\n"
     << sizeof(SeatOccupied)/sizeof(int) << "\n\n";
```

Here, the *sizeof()* function is called twice to calculate the number of elements in each array. Notice that the size of the array in bytes is divided by the size of the data type of the array in bytes. The quotient should therefore be the number of elements that the array can store, right? You should be aware that the above code is totally portable between systems that might represent data types using a different number of bytes. This calculation will always determine the *number of elements* in the respective array regardless of how many bytes are employed to store a given data type.

Accessing Two-Dimensional Array Elements

You access two-dimensional array elements in very much the same way as one-dimensional array elements. The difference is that to locate the elements in a two-dimensional array you must specify a row index and a column index.

You can access the array elements using direct assignment, reading/writing, or looping.

Direct Assignment of Two-Dimensional Array Elements

The general format for direct assignment of element values is:

TWO-DIMENSIONAL ARRAY DIRECT ASSIGNMENT FORMAT
(inserting elements)

<array name> [row index][column index] = element value;

TWO-DIMENSIONAL ARRAY DIRECT ASSIGNMENT FORMAT
(extracting elements)

<variable identifier> = <array name> [row index][column index];

First, you see the format for inserting elements into a two-dimensional array, followed by the format for obtaining elements from the array. Notice that in both instances you must specify a row and column index to access the desired element position. The row index is specified first, followed by the column index. Using the arrays defined in Example 9-1, possible direct assignments for insertion might be:

Table[2][3] = 0.5;
Voltage[2][10] = 20;
May[1][3] = 8;
SeatOccupied[5][0] = 1;

In the first case, the floating point value 0.5 is placed in row [2], column [3] of the *Table* array. In the second case, a value of 20 is inserted into row [2], column [10] of the *Voltage* array. Notice that this voltage value corresponds to a current value of 2 and a resistance value of 10 when using Ohm's Law. In the third case, a value of 8 is placed in row [1] column [3] of the *May* array. Finally, the last case assigns the integer value 1 to row [5] column [0] of the *SeatOccupied* array. If interpreted as a Boolean value, this would indicate that the seat is occupied.

Using the same arrays, direct assignment statements to extract elements might be:

Sales = Table[0][0];
Volts = Voltage[5][100];
Today = May[2][4];
Tomorrow = May[2][5];
SeatTaken = SeatOccupied[3][3];

In each of the above statements, the element value stored at the row/column position within the respective array is assigned to a variable identifier. Of course, the variable identifier should be defined as the same data type as the array element being assigned to it.

Remember that extraction operations have no effect on the array elements. In other words, the elements are not actually removed from the array, their values are simply "copied" to the assignment variable.

Reading and Writing Two-Dimensional Array Elements

cin statements can be used to insert two-dimensional array elements, while *cout* statements can be used to extract array elements like this:

```
cin >> Table[1][1];
cout << Table[1][1];
cin >> Voltage[5][20];
cout << Voltage[5][20];
cin >> May[1][3];
cout << May[1][3];
if (SeatOccupied[3][1])
   cout << "TRUE";
else
   cout << "FALSE";
```

Again you can see that both a row and column index must be specified. The *cin* statements will insert elements obtained from a keyboard entry. The *cout* statements will then extract the array element just inserted and simply "echo" the user entry back to the display. Notice that the last *cout* statement is contained within an **if/else** statement to determine if the element is a Boolean TRUE or FALSE value. This statement will produce a TRUE or FALSE on the display, depending on the contents of location [3][1] of the *SeatOccupied* array.

Using Loops To Access Two-Dimensional Arrays

As you know, loops provide a more efficient way to access arrays, especially when working with large multidimensional arrays. The thing to remember with multidimensional arrays is that *a separate loop is required for each dimension of the array*. In addition, the loops must be nested. Thus, a two-dimensional array requires two nested loops.

Look at the calendar pictured in Figure 9-3. As you have seen, this calendar can be stored in memory using a two-dimensional array. How do you suppose you might go about filling the calendar with the dates required for a given month? A logical approach would be to fill in all of the dates of week 0, from *Sun* to *Sat*, then go to week 1 and fill in its dates, then fill in the week 2 dates, and so on.

Think about what the array indices must do to perform this filling operation. The week index would start at [0], then the days index would begin at [0] and increment through the days of the week to [6]. This will fill the first week. To fill the second week, the week index must be incremented to 1 with the days index starting at [0] and incrementing to [6] all over again. To fill the third week, the week index is incremented to 2 and the days index incremented from [0] to [6] again. In other words, you are filling in the dates week by week, one week at a time. Each time the week index is incremented, the days index starts at [0] and increments to [6], before the week index is incremented to the next week.

May

	Sun [0]	Sat [1]	Mon [2]	Tue [3]	Wed [4]	Thu [5]	Fri [6]
Week [0]							1
Week [1]	2	3	4	5	6	7	8
Week [2]	9	10	11	12	13	14	15
Week [3]	16	17	18	19	20	21	22
Week [4]	23	24	25	26	27	28	29
Week [5]	30	31					

Figure 9-3 May calendar.

Does this suggest two loops, one to increment the week index and a second to increment the days index? Moreover, doesn't this process suggest that the days loop must be nested within the week loop, since the days must run through its entire range for each week?

Here's the general loop structure for accessing elements in a two-dimensional array.

LOOPING FORMAT FOR ACCESSING TWO-IMENSIONAL ARRAY ELEMENTS

```
for (int Row Index = 0; Row Index < Row Size; ++Row Index)
    for (int Col Index = 0; Col Index < Col Size; ++Col Index)
        <Process Array[Row Index][Col Index]>
```

You see that the column index loop is nested within the row index loop. Thus, the column loop runs through all of its iterations for each iteration of the row loop. The actual insertion takes place within the column loop. Let's look at an example to get the idea.

Example 9-3:

Write a function using loops to fill a calendar array for the month of *May*. Write another function to display the *May* calendar.

Solution:

We will begin by defining the month array as before.

```
const int WEEKS = 6, DAYS = 7;
int May[WEEKS][DAYS];
enum DaysOfWeek {Sun,Mon,Tue,Wed,Thur,Fri,Sat};
```

In addition, you see that an enumerated data type called *DaysOfWeek* has been defined. This enumerated data type will be used to access the days of the week within the array as you will see shortly.

Next, we must write a function to fill the array with the dates for May. But first, we must consider the function interface. The function must receive the array, get the dates from the user, and return the filled array to the calling program. Thus, the function interface description becomes:

Function *Fill_Month()*:	Obtains dates of the month from the user and fills a two-dimensional integer array.
Accepts:	A two-dimensional integer array of size *WEEKS* × *DAYS*.
Returns:	A two-dimensional integer array of size *WEEKS* × *DAYS*.

Now, here's a function that will do the job:

```
// THIS FUNCTION WILL FILL A 2-DIM ARRAY FOR A
// CALENDAR MONTH
void Fill_Month(int Month[WEEKS][DAYS])
{
 cout << "What month do you want to fill and display?  "
 cin >> ThisMonth;
 cout << "\n\nEnter the dates of the month, beginning Sunday of the first\n"
         "week in the month.  If there is no date for a given day\n"
         "enter a 0.  Press the ENTER key after each entry.\n\n";
```

```
for (int Week = 0; Week < WEEKS; ++Week)
  for (int Day = Sun; Day < Sat + 1; ++Day)
  {
    cout << "\nEnter the date for Week " << Week
         << " day " << Day << ": ";
    cin >> Month[Week][Day];
  }
}
```

The first few lines of the function provide a few simple directions to the user and obtain the month to be filled and displayed. The array filling operation takes place within the two **for** loops. Notice that the *Week* loop is the outer loop, while the *Day* loop is the inner loop. Here's how it works: The *Week* counter begins with 0 and the *Day* counter begins with *Sun*. As a result, the first date is inserted into *Month[0][Sun]* corresponding to Sunday of week 0 in the month. Notice that the array name is *Month*. How can this be, since we defined *May* as the array name? Well, the array *May* will be the actual argument used in the function call. However, *Month* is the formal parameter listed in the function header. Thus, the function will receive the *May* array from the calling program, fill it, and return it to the calling program. The reason I used a different array name (*Month*) in the function is to make it more general. For example, additional arrays, such as *June, July, August* and the like, could be defined to create arrays for these months. Again, these would act as actual arguments when calling the function. The respective month arrays (*June, July, August,* etc.) could then be filled separately using separate calls to this same function. In each case, the function parameter *Month* would take on the actual array argument used in the function call. Now, back to the loops. After an element is read into *Month [0][Sun]*, the inner **for** loop increments the *Day* counter to *Mon* and an element is read into *Month [0][Mon]*. Notice that the *Week* counter remains the same. What is the next array position to be filled? You're right: *Month [0][Tue]*. In summary, the inner *Day* loop will increment from *Sun* to *Sat* for each iteration of the outer *Week* loop. Thus, the first iteration of the outer *Week* loop will fill:

Month [0][Sun]
Month [0][Mon]
Month [0][Tue]
Month [0][Wed]
Month [0][Thur]
Month [0][Fri]
Month [0][Sat]

The second iteration of the outer *Row* loop will fill the second week like this:

Month [1][Sun]

Month [1][Mon]
Month [1][Tue]
Month [1][Wed]
Month [1][Thur]
Month [1][Fri]
Month [1][Sat]

This filling process will continue for week 2, 3, 4, and 5. The looping is terminated when a value is read into the last array position, *Month [5][Sat]*.

Now, let's look at a similar function to display our *May* calendar once it has been filled. Again, consider the following function interface description:

Function *Display_Month()*:   Displays the two-dimensional calendar month array.

Accepts: A two-dimensional integer array of size *WEEKS* × *DAYS*.

Returns: Nothing

Here is the completed function:

```
// THIS FUNCTION WILL DISPLAY THE CALENDAR MONTH ARRAY
void Display_Month(int Month[WEEKS][DAYS])
{
  cout << "\n\n\t\tCALENDAR FOR THE MONTH OF " << ThisMonth
       << "\n\n\tSun\tMon\tTue\tWed\tThur\tFri\tSat\n\n";
  for (int Week = 0; Week < WEEKS; ++Week)
  {
    cout << '\n';
    for (int Day = Sun; Day < Sat + 1; ++Day)
      cout << '\t' << Month[Week][Day];
  }
}
```

Again, *Month* is the formal parameter defined in the function header. The first part of the function statement section simply writes the header information required for the calendar. Then, the nested **for** loops are executed to display the array contents. The basic loop structures are the same as those we discussed for the filling operation: the *Day* counter is incremented from *Sun* through *Sat* for every iteration of the *Week* loop. Thus, the array contents are displayed in a row-by-row, or week-by-week, fashion. Notice that a *cout* statement is used to display the element values. The *cout* statement is the only statement within the inner **for** loop.

Now putting everything together here is the entire program:

```
//*********************************************************
//
// THIS PROGRAM WILL FILL AND DISPLAY
// A 2-DIM ARRAY FOR A CALENDAR MONTH
//
//*********************************************************
#include <iostream.h>
// GLOBAL CONSTANTS, VARIABLES AND ENUMERATED DATA
const int WEEKS = 6;
const int DAYS = 7;
char ThisMonth[10];
enum DaysOfWeek {Sun,Mon,Tue,Wed,Thur,Fri,Sat};

// FUNCTION PROTOTYPES
void Fill_Month(int May[WEEKS][DAYS]);
void Display_Month(int May[WEEKS][DAYS]);

void main()
{
// ARRAY DEFINITION
   int May[WEEKS][DAYS];

// FUNCTION CALLS
   Fill_Month(May);
   Display_Month(May);
}  // END MAIN

// THIS FUNCTION WILL FILL A 2-DIM ARRAY FOR A
// CALENDAR MONTH
void Fill_Month(int Month[WEEKS][DAYS])
{
  cout << "What month do you want to fill and display?";
  cin >> ThisMonth;
  cout << "\n\nEnter the dates of the month, beginning Sunday of the first\n"
          "week in the month.  If there is no date for a given day\n"
          "enter a 0.  Press the ENTER key after each entry.\n\n";
  for (int Week = 0; Week < WEEKS; ++Week)
   for (int Day = Sun; Day < Sat + 1; ++Day)
   {
     cout << "\nEnter the date for Week " << Week
        << " day " << Day << ":  ";
     cin >> Month[Week][Day];
   }
}
```

```
// THIS FUNCTION WILL DISPLAY THE CALENDAR MONTH ARRAY
void Display_Month(int Month[WEEKS][DAYS])
{
  cout << "\n\n\t\tCALENDAR FOR THE MONTH OF " << ThisMonth
       << "\n\n\tSun\tMon\tTue\tWed\tThur\tFri\tSat\n\n";
  for (int Week = 0; Week < WEEKS; ++Week)
  {
    cout << '\n';
    for (int Day = Sun; Day < Sat + 1; ++Day)
      cout << '\t' << Month[Week][Day];
  }
}
```

First you see that *WEEKS, DAYS, ThisMonth,* and *DaysOfWeek* have been defined globally so that all functions have access to them. Notice that the statement section of *main()* is short. Function *main()* simply defines the array and calls the two other functions. In each function call, the actual array argument, *May*, is employed. As stated earlier, other monthly arrays could also be defined to create additional monthly calendars. In fact, all twelve months could be defined to create a yearly calendar. To fill or display a given month, you simply use that array name in the respective function call.

Assuming that the user executes this program and keys in the proper dates for May, the program will generate the following calendar display:

CALENDAR FOR THE MONTH OF MAY

Sun	Mon	Tue	Wed	Thur	Fri	Sat
0	0	0	0	0	0	1
2	3	4	5	6	7	8
9	10	11	12	13	14	15
16	17	18	19	20	21	22
23	24	25	26	27	28	29
30	31	0	0	0	0	0

Of course, this calendar could also be printed by defining a print object and using it to write the array.

Example 9-4:

Write a program that uses an array to store the names of all the students in your C++ class. Use one function to insert the student names into the array and a second function to display the contents of the array once it is filled. Assume that there are no more than 25 characters in any student name and the maximum class size is 20 students.

Solution:

First, an array must be defined to hold the student names in your C++ class. Since the student names are strings, we must define a two-dimensional array of characters such that each name string will occupy a row in the array. Consider the following:

```
const int MAX_STUDENTS = 20;
const int MAX_CHARACTERS = 26;
char CPP[MAX_STUDENTS][MAX_CHARACTERS];
```

Here, the array name is *CPP* and it is defined as a character array with 20 rows and 26 columns. This will allow for 20 name strings with a maximum of 25 characters per string (an extra column must be provided for the null terminator character).

Next, we will work on the function that gets the student names from the user. We will call this function *Get_Students()*. Here is the function interface description:

Function *Get_Students()*:	Obtains student names from the user and fills a two-dimensional character array.
Accepts:	A two-dimensional character array of size *MAX_STUDENTS × MAX_CHARACTERS*.
Returns:	A two-dimensional character array of size *MAX_STUDENTS × MAX_CHARACTERS*.

This interface requires that the two-dimensional *CPP* array be passed to the function, then returned filled with the student names. Of course, passing an array to a function is easy regardless of its size, since you simply use the array name as the actual function argument. Here is the complete function:

```
//*************************************************************************
//
// THIS FUNCTION GETS THE STUDENT NAMES FROM THE
// USER AND ENTERS THEM INTO THE ARRAY
//
//*************************************************************************
void Get_Students(char Students[MAX_STUDENTS][MAX_CHARACTERS])
{
 cout << "Enter number of students:  ";
 cin >> Number;
 for (int Row = 0; Row < Number; ++Row)
 {
   cout << "\nEnter student number " << Row + 1 << ":  ";
```

```
    gets(&Students[Row][0]);
  }
}
```

Again, you see a different name employed for the array in the function header. This makes the function more generic, since you might want to use this same function to fill other arrays from other classes. The function begins by prompting the user to enter the number of students in the class, then reading this number and assigning it to a global variable called *Number*. The value entered will provide a maximum value for the row counter in the **for** loop. Next you see a single **for** loop. Is there a problem here, since we are filling a two-dimensional array? No, this single loop is all that is required, since we are filling the array with strings, not individual characters. Notice that the loop counter only increments the row index. The column index is fixed at [0]. This will place the first string in the array beginning at [0][0], the second string at [1][0], the third string at [2][0], and so on. The standard *gets()* function is used to read the strings rather than *cin*. Recall that *cin* will terminate when a whitespace character is encountered, thereby interpreting a first and last name as two separate strings. Look at the argument used in the *gets()* function call. An ampersand symbol is used to tell *gets()* to place the string beginning at the *address* associated with *Students [Row][0]*. When reading string data we must tell the compiler to insert the string beginning at a specified address. So, the first string is inserted into the array beginning at the memory address associated with index [0][0], the second string begins at the memory address associated with index [1][0], and so on. Remember, when working with string data, you must specify the beginning *address* of the string.

Next, we will write a function called *Display_Students()* to display the array of student names. Here is the interface description for this function:

Function *Display_Students()*: Displays the strings of a two-dimensional array.

Accepts:	A two-dimensional character array of size $MAX\_STUDENTS \times MAX\_CHARACTERS$.
Returns:	Nothing.

The parameter listing for this function will be identical to the previous function, since it accepts the same array structure. Here is the entire function:

```
//******************************************************************************
//
// THIS FUNCTION DISPLAYS THE CONTENTS OF THE ARRAY
//
//******************************************************************************
void Display_Students(char Students[MAX_STUDENTS][MAX_CHARACTERS])
```

```
{
  cout << "The students entered in the array are:\n\n";
  for (int Row = 0; Row < Number; ++Row)
    cout << "\nArray position [" << Row << "] [0]  " << &Students[Row][0];
}
```

Again, you see a single **for** loop employed, since we only need to reference the beginning address of each string. The ampersand symbol is required in front of the array name in the *cout* statement to specify the string address. Without the ampersand, you would only see the first character of each string. (Why?)

In addition to displaying the student names, the *cout* statement is formatted to display the array position of each name string. Here is a sample of what you would see on the monitor:

    Array position [0][0] Brenda Snider
    Array position [1][0] Anna Simon
    Array position [2][0] Doug Hahn
    Array position [3][0] Steve Weston

Finally, the entire program is given below:

```
//*****************************************************************************
//
// THIS PROGRAM WILL FILL A 2-DIM CHARACTER ARRAY WITH
// STRINGS ENTERED BY THE USER, THEN DISPLAY THE
// FILLED ARRAY
//
//*****************************************************************************
#include <iostream.h>
#include <stdio.h>
// GLOBAL CONSTANTS AND VARIABLES
const int MAX_STUDENTS = 20;
const int MAX_CHARACTERS = 26;
int Number                            // ACTUAL NUMBER OF STUDENTS;

// FUNCTION PROTOTYPES
void Get_Students(char Students[MAX_STUDENTS][MAX_CHARACTERS]);
voidDisplay_Students(char Students[MAX_STUDENTS][MAX_CHARACTERS]);

void main()
{
  char CPP[MAX_STUDENTS][MAX_CHARACTERS];
  Get_Students(CPP);
  Display_Students(CPP);
}
```

```
//******************************************************************
//
// THIS FUNCTION GETS THE STUDENT NAMES FROM THE
// USER AND ENTERS THEM INTO THE ARRAY
//
//******************************************************************
void Get_Students(char Students[MAX_STUDENTS][MAX_CHARACTERS])
{
  cout << "Enter number of students:  ";
  cin >> Number;
  for (int Row = 0; Row < Number; ++Row)
  {
    cout << "\nEnter student number " << Row + 1 << ":  ";
    gets(&Students[Row][0]);
  }
}


//******************************************************************
//
// THIS FUNCTION DISPLAYS THE CONTENTS OF THE ARRAY
//
//******************************************************************
void Display_Students(char Students[MAX_STUDENTS][MAX_CHARACTERS])
{
  cout << "The students entered in the array are:\n\n";
  for (int Row = 0; Row < Number; ++Row)
    cout << "\nArray position [" << Row << "] [0]  " << &Students[Row][0];
}
```

 Quick Check

1. Given the following two-dimensional array definition:

   float Sample[10][15];

   What is the maximum row index?   What is the maximum column index?

2. What will the following statement display when applied to the array defined in question 1?

   cout << sizeof(Sample)/sizeof(float);

3. Write a statement that will read a value from the keyboard and place it in the first row and last column of the array defined in question 1.

4. Write a statement that will display the value stored in the second row and third column of the array defined in question 1.

5. Write the code, using **for** loops, that will display the elements of the array defined in question 1 in row/column format.

6. Write a prototype for a function called *Display()* that will display the contents of the array defined in question 1.

7. Write a statement to call the function in question 6.

8. A two-dimensional array in C++ is _____ major order.

9-2 ARRAYS OF MORE THAN TWO DIMENSIONS

Arrays of more than two dimensions are required for some applications. In this text, we will only consider three-dimensional arrays, since few common applications require larger arrays. The easiest way to picture a three-dimensional array is to imagine a cube such as that shown in Figure 9-4.

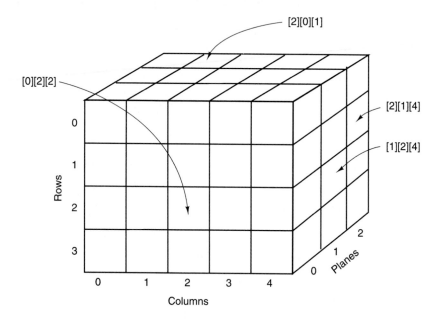

Figure 9-4 A $3 \times 4 \times 5$ three-dimensional array.

Think of a three-dimensional array as several two-dimensional arrays combined together to form a third dimension, depth. The cube is made up of rows (vertical dimension), columns (horizontal dimension), and planes (depth dimension). Thus, a given element within the cube array is located by specifying its plane, row, and column. See if you can verify for yourself the element positions indicated in Figure 9-4.

Now, let's look at a practical example of a three-dimensional array so you can see how one is defined and accessed in C++. Think of this excellent textbook as a three-dimensional array where each page of the book is a two-dimensional array made up of rows and columns. The combined pages then form the planes within a three-dimensional array that make up the book. Let's suppose there are 45 lines on each page that form the rows for the array and 80 characters per line that form the columns of the array. If there are 750 pages in the book, there are 750 planes in the array. Thus, this book array is a $45 \times 80 \times 750$ array. What are the array elements, and how many are there? Well, the array elements must be characters, since characters form the words within a page. In addition, there must be $45 \times 80 \times 750 = 2,700,000$ of them, including blanks, since this is the size of the book in terms of rows, columns, and pages.

CAUTION

When you define an array, C++ actually sets aside enough primary memory to store the array. This memory is reserved exclusively for the defined array and cannot be used for other programming or system chores. In other words, a large array "eats up" a lot of memory. For instance, the foregoing book array contains 2,700,000 character elements. Since each character requires one byte of memory to store, C++ will allocate about 2637K bytes of user memory for the book array. This is much more than is available in most PC systems, and would create an "Array size too big" error during compilation. So be careful that your arrays don't get too big for your system to store. There are other, more memory efficient, ways to store large amounts of data. One such structure is a linked list, which will be covered later in the text.

How might our book array be defined in C++? How about this:

```
const int PAGES = 750;
const int LINES = 45;
const int COLUMNS = 80;
char Text_Book[PAGES][LINES][COLUMNS];
```

You should be able to understand this definition from your work with one- and two-dimensional arrays. There are three dimensions *[PAGES]*, *[LINES]*, and *[COLUMNS]* that define the size of the *Text_Book* array. A three-dimensional array in C/C++ is **plane major order.** This is why the plane size is specified first, followed by the row size, followed by the column size. The array data type is *char*, since the elements are characters. Of course, additional arrays could be used to create arrays for other books of the same general dimensions, right? Well, theoretically yes, but just one of these book arrays would be too large for most PC systems. In most systems, the definition would result in a "Array size too big" error when the program is compiled.

Next, how do you suppose you might access the book information? The easiest way is to use nested loops. How should the loops be nested? Because the array is plane major ordered, the page loop must be the outermost loop, and the column loop the innermost loop. This leaves the row loop to be inserted between the page and column loops. Translating this to our book array, you get:

```
for (int Page = 0; Page < PAGES; ++Page)
      for (int Line = 0; Line < LINES; ++Line)
            for (int Column = 0; Column < COLUMNS; ++Column)
                  <process Text_Book[Page][Line][Column]>
```

Using this nesting approach, the *Column* loop is executed 80 times for each iteration of the *Line* loop, which is executed 45 times for each iteration of the *Page* loop. Of course, the *Page* loop is executed 750 times. This **for** structure would process elements one line at a time for a given page. Notice the use of the variables *Page, Line,* and *Column* as the loop counters. These variables must be different from the constants (*PAGES, LINES, COLUMNS*) used to define the array, since they are local to the **for** loops.

Example 9-5:

Given the foregoing *Text_Book* array definition:
a. Write a program segment that could be used to fill the book.
b. Write a program segment that could be used to print the entire book.
c. Write a program segment that could be used to print page 2 of the book.

Solution:

a. Using the three foregoing nested loops, you could fill the book like this:

```
for (int Page = 0; Page < PAGES; ++Page)
      for (int Line = 0; Line < LINES; ++Line)
            for (int Column = 0; Column < COLUMNS; ++Column)
                  Text_Book[Page][Line][Column] = getche();
```

The innermost loop employs a *getche()* function to read one character at a time and place it in the indexed position. A *cin* statement will not work here, since *cin* ignores white space which would obviously be part of the text material.

b. A *print* object is employed in the innermost loop to print the book:

```
for (int Page = 0; Page < PAGES; ++Page)
        for (int Line = 0; Line < LINES; ++Line)
        {
            print << '\n';
            for (int Column = 0; Column < COLUMNS; ++Column)
                print << Text_Book[Page][Line][Column];
        }
```

Notice the single *cout* statement used in the middle loop to provide a CRLF after a given line has been printed. Of course, the *print* object must be defined as discussed in Chapter 3 for these statements to compile.

c. You only need two loops to print a given page number as follows:

```
for (int Line = 0; Line < LINES; ++Line)
{
    print << '\n';
    for (int Column = 0; Column < COLUMNS; ++Column)
            print << Text_Book[1][Line][Column];
}
```

Observe that the *Page* index is fixed at [1] within the *cout* statement in order to print page 2 of the book (remember that the first page of the book is actually at page index [0]). How could this segment be modified to print any page desired by the user? Think about it! This will be left as an exercise at the end of the chapter.

 Quick Check

1. What problem might be encountered when defining large multidimensional arrays?
2. A three-dimensional array in C++ is _____ major order.
3. Define a three-dimensional array of integers that has 10 planes, 15 rows, and 3 columns.

4. How many bytes of storage is occupied by the array that you defined in question 3?

5. Write the code necessary to display the contents of the array that you defined in question 3, one plane at a time.

CASE STUDY: SIMULTANEOUS EQUATION SOLUTION

Problem

Recall from your algebra class that a set of simultaneous equations exist when you have two or more equations with two or more common unknowns. For instance, consider the following:

$$7x - 5y = 20$$
$$-5x + 8y = -10$$

Here you have two equations and two unknowns. To solve the equations, you must find both x and y. This is impossible using just one of the equations alone, but does not present a problem when both equations are solved "simultaneously," or together. One thing you might remember from algebra class is that in order to solve simultaneous equations, there must be at least as many equations as there are unknowns. This is why you cannot solve for two unknowns using a single equation. However, two unknowns can be solved using two or more equations.

Determinants

A common way to solve simultaneous equations is by using determinants. You might recall from algebra that a ***determinant*** is simply a *square array*. By a square array, we mean an array that has the same number of rows and columns. Here is a simple 2×2, called an ***order*** 2, determinant:

$$\begin{vmatrix} A_1 & B_1 \\ A_2 & B_2 \end{vmatrix}$$

The elements are A_1, B_1, A_2 and B_2. (Note: These elements will be numeric values when we actually use determinants to solve simultaneous equations.)

Notice the vertical "bars" on the left and right sides of the array. These bars are used to indicate that the array is a determinant. This determinant is called an order 2 determinant, since it has two rows and two columns. There are also order 3, order 4, order 5, etc., determinants. In each case, the determinant is a square array. Here is an order 3 determinant:

$$\begin{vmatrix} A_1 & B_1 & C_1 \\ A_2 & B_2 & C_2 \\ A_3 & B_3 & C_3 \end{vmatrix}$$

Expansion of a Determinant

A determinant is said to be expanded when you replace the array with a single value. An order 2 determinant expansion is the simplest. To get the idea, look at the diagram below:

$$\begin{vmatrix} A_1 & B_1 \\ A_2 & B_2 \end{vmatrix} = A_1B_2 - A_2B_1$$

Imagine the two diagonals in the determinant. There is one diagonal running from top-left to bottom-right. We will call this the *down diagonal* which forms the product A_1B_2. The second diagonal runs from bottom-left to top-right. We will call this the *up diagonal* which forms the product A_2B_1. In the expansion on the right side of the equals sign, you see that the up diagonal product is subtracted from the down diagonal product.

Example 9-6:

Expand the following determinants:

a. $\begin{vmatrix} 20 & -5 \\ -10 & 8 \end{vmatrix}$

b. $\begin{vmatrix} 7 & 20 \\ -5 & -10 \end{vmatrix}$

c. $\begin{vmatrix} 7 & 5 \\ -5 & 8 \end{vmatrix}$

Solution:

a. $\begin{vmatrix} 20 & -5 \\ -10 & 8 \end{vmatrix} = (20)(8) - (-10)(-5) = 160 - 50 = 110$

b. $\begin{vmatrix} 7 & 20 \\ -5 & -10 \end{vmatrix} = (7)(-10) - (-5)(20) = -70 - (-100) = -70 + 100 = 30$

c. $\begin{vmatrix} 7 & 5 \\ -5 & 8 \end{vmatrix} = (7)(8) - (-5)(5) = 56 - (-25) = 56 + 25 = 81$

Expansion of an order 3 determinant is a bit more challenging. Here is a general order 3 determinant again:

$$\begin{vmatrix} A_1 & B_1 & C_1 \\ A_2 & B_2 & C_2 \\ A_3 & B_3 & C_3 \end{vmatrix}$$

To manually expand this determinant, you must rewrite the first two columns to the right of the determinant and then use the diagonal method as follows:

$$\begin{array}{ccccc} A_1 & B_1 & C_1 & A_1 & B_1 \\ A_2 & B_2 & C_2 & A_2 & B_2 \\ A_3 & B_3 & C_3 & A_3 & B_3 \end{array} = A_1B_2C_3 + B_1C_2A_3 + C_1A_2B_3 - A_3B_2C_1 - B_3C_2A_1 - C_3A_2B_1$$

Here, you create three down diagonals that form the products $A_1B_2C_3$, $B_1C_2A_3$, and $C_1A_2B_3$ and three up diagonals that form the product $A_3B_2C_1$, $B_3C_2A_1$, and $C_3A_2B_1$. The three up diagonal products are subtracted from the sum of the three down diagonal products. This is called the "method of diagonals" for expanding order 3 determinants. I should caution you, however, that the method of diagonals does not work for determinants larger than order 3. To expand determinants larger than order 3, you must use the method of *cofactors*. The cofactor method is a recursive process and will be left as an exercise at the end of the chapter.

Example 9-7:

Expand the following order 3 determinant:

$$\begin{vmatrix} 6 & -2 & -4 \\ 15 & -2 & -5 \\ -4 & -5 & 12 \end{vmatrix}$$

Solution:

Rewriting the first two columns to the right of the determinant you get:

6	−2	−4	6	−2
15	−2	−5	15	−2
−4	−5	12	−4	−5

Now, multiplying the diagonal elements and adding/subtracting the diagonal products you get:

$+ (6)(-2)(12) + (-2)(-5)(-4) + (-4)(15)(-5)$
$- (-4)(-2)(-4) - (-5)(-5)(6) - (12)(15)(-2)$

Finally, performing the required arithmetic gives you:

$+ (-144) + (-40) + (300)$
$- (-32) - (150) - (-360)$

$= -144 - 40 + 300 + 32 - 150 + 360$

$= 358$

As you can see from the above example, expanding an order 3 determinant can get a bit tricky! You have to pay particular attention to the signs. One simple sign error during your arithmetic will result in an incorrect expansion. Wouldn't it be nice if a computer program could be written to perform the expansion? This is an ideal application for a C++ function, since the expansion operation returns a single value.

An Order 2 Determinant Expansion Function

Let's write a C++ function to expand an order 2 determinant. We will assume that the elements in the determinant are stored in a 2 × 2 array. This array must be passed to the function, then the function must evaluate the array and return a single expansion value. Here is the function interface description:

Function *Expand( )*:   Expands an order 2 determinant.

Accepts: A 2 × 2 array.

Returns: The expansion value.

Using this interface description, the function prototype becomes:

float Expand(float Determinant[2][2]);

The function name is *Expand( )*. The formal parameter is *Determinant[2][2]*, since this is the size of the array that will be expanded. The data type of the returned expansion value is *float*. Now, the *Determinant* array has row indices which range from [0] to [1], and column indices which range from [0] to [1]. Here is the array showing the row/column index layout:

[0] [0]   [0] [1]

[1] [0]   [1] [1]

Remember that these are only the array indices and not the elements stored in the array. Recall that to expand the determinant, the up diagonal must be subtracted from the down diagonal. Thus, the product of indices [1] [0] and [0] [1] must be subtracted from the product of [0] [0] and [1] [1]. Using this idea in our function, we get a single **return** statement as follows:

return (Determinant[0][0] * Determinant[1][1]
            - Determinant[1][0] * Determinant[0][1]);

That's all there is to it! Here is the complete function:

```
// THIS FUNCTION WILL EXPAND A 2 x 2 DETERMINANT
float Expand(float Determinant[2][2])
{
 return  (Determinant[0][0] * Determinant[1][1]
        - Determinant[1][0] * Determinant[0][1]);
}
```

Writing a function to expand an order 3 determinant will be left as an exercise at the end of the chapter.

Cramer's Rule

Cramer's rule allows you to solve simultaneous equations using determinants. Let's begin with two equations and two unknowns.

An equation is said to be in ***standard form*** when all the variables are on the left-hand side of the equals sign and the constant term is on the right-hand side of the equals sign. Here is a general equation containing two variables in standard form:

$$Ax + By = C$$

This equation has two variables, x and y. The x-coefficient is A and the y-coefficient is B. The constant term is C.

Here is a set of two general simultaneous equations in standard form:

$$A_1x + B_1y = C_1$$
$$A_2x + B_2y = C_2$$

The common variables between the two equations are x and y. The subscripts, 1 and 2, denote the coefficients and constants of equations 1 and 2, respectively. Cramer's rule allows you to solve for x and y using determinants like this:

$$x = \frac{\begin{vmatrix} C_1 & B_1 \\ C_2 & B_2 \end{vmatrix}}{\begin{vmatrix} A_1 & B_1 \\ A_2 & B_2 \end{vmatrix}} \qquad y = \frac{\begin{vmatrix} A_1 & C_1 \\ A_2 & C_2 \end{vmatrix}}{\begin{vmatrix} A_1 & B_1 \\ A_2 & B_2 \end{vmatrix}}$$

As you can see, the determinants are formed using the coefficients and constants from the two equations. Do you see a pattern? First, look at the denominator determinants. They are identical, and are formed using the x and y coefficients directly from the two equations. However, the numerator determinants are different. When solving for x, the numerator determinant is formed by replacing the x-coefficients with the constant terms. When solving for y, the numerator determinant is formed by replacing the y-coefficients with the constant terms. Here's an example.

Example 9-8:

Solve the following set of simultaneous equations using Cramer's rule:

$$x + 2y = 3$$
$$3x + 4y = 5$$

Solution:

Forming the required determinants you get:

$$x = \frac{\begin{vmatrix} 3 & 2 \\ 5 & 4 \end{vmatrix}}{\begin{vmatrix} 1 & 2 \\ 3 & 4 \end{vmatrix}} \qquad\qquad y = \frac{\begin{vmatrix} 1 & 3 \\ 3 & 5 \end{vmatrix}}{\begin{vmatrix} 1 & 2 \\ 3 & 4 \end{vmatrix}}$$

Expanding the determinants and dividing gives you x and y:

$$x = \frac{(3)(4)-(5)(2)}{(1)(4)-(3)(2)} = \frac{2}{-2} = -1 \qquad\qquad y = \frac{(1)(5)-(3)(3)}{(1)(4)-(3)(2)} = \frac{-4}{-2} = 2$$

Implementing Cramer's Rule in C++

Think about the "functions" you just went through using Cramer's rule to solve the previous set of simultaneous equations. There are three major tasks to be performed:

- Task 1: Obtain the equation coefficients and constants.
- Task 2: Form the determinants: both numerator and denominator.
- Task 3: Expand the determinants.

We have already developed a function to perform the third task. We must now develop C++ functions to accomplish the first two tasks.

To perform Task 1, we must write a function that will obtain the coefficients and constants of the equations to be solved. There are two equations and three items (two coefficients and a constant) that must be obtained from each equation. Does this suggest any particular data structure? Of course, a 2 × 3 array! So, let's write a function to fill a 2 × 3 array from coefficient and constant terms of the two equations that will be entered by the user. Here it is:

```
// THIS FUNCTION WILL FILL AN ARRAY WITH THE
// EQUATION COEFFICIENTS
void Fill(float Equations[2][3])
{
```

```
for(int Row = 0; Row < 2; ++Row)
{
  cout << "\nEnter the variable coefficients and constant for equation "
      << Row + 1 << "\nNote the equation must be in standard form.\n\n";
  for(int Col = 0; Col < 3; ++Col)
   {
      if (Col == 2)
        cout << "Enter the constant term:  ";
      else
        cout << "Enter the coefficient for variable " << Col + 1 << ": ";
      cin >> Equations[Row][Col];
   } // END COLUMN FOR
} // END ROW FOR
} // END FUNCTION FILL
```

Such a function should be nothing new to you, since it simply employs nested **for** loops to fill an array. The function name is *Fill()*. It fills an array called *Equations* that must be defined as a 2×3 array in the calling program. The array will be passed to the function by reference using the array name in the function call. Thus, once the function fills the array, it is passed back to the calling program.

Given the following two general equations in standard form:

$$A_1x + B_1y = C_1$$
$$A_2x + B_2y = C_2$$

The *Fill()* function will fill the 2×3 array like this:

$$A_1 \quad B_1 \quad C_1$$
$$A_2 \quad B_2 \quad C_2$$

As you can see, the first equation coefficients and constant term are inserted into the first row of the array. The second row of the array stores the coefficients and constant term of the second equation. Of course, the function assumes that the user will enter the coefficients and constants in their proper order.

To accomplish Task 2, we will develop a function to form the determinants from the equation coefficients and constants. How can we obtain the coefficients and constants? You're right, from the 2×3 array that was just filled! Now, how many unique determinants does Cramer's rule require to solve two equations and two unknowns? Three: A numerator determinant for the *x* unknown, a numerator determinant for the *y* unknown, and a denominator determinant that is the same for both the *x* and *y* unknowns. All of the determinants must be order 2, right?

So, our function must obtain the single 2 × 3 array that was filled with coefficients and constants in the *Fill()* function; and generate three 2 × 2 arrays that will form the two numerator and one denominator determinant required by Cramer's rule. Here's the function:

```
// THIS FUNCTION WILL FORM THE DETERMINANTS
void Form_Det(float Equations[2][3], float x[2][2],  float y[2][2], float D[2][2])
{
  for(int Row = 0; Row < 2; ++Row)
    for(int Col = 0; Col < 2; ++Col)
      {
          x[Row][Col] = Equations[Row][Col];
          y[Row][Col] = Equations[Row][Col];
          D[Row][Col] = Equations[Row][Col];
      }
   x[0][0] = Equations[0][2];
   x[1][0] = Equations[1][2];
   y[0][1] = Equations[0][2];
   y[1][1] = Equations[1][2];
}
```

First, look at the function header. The function name is *Form_Det()*. There are four parameters: *Equations[2][3]*, *x[2][2]*, *y[2][2]*, and *D[2][2]*. *Equations[2][3]*, is the 2 × 3 array containing the coefficients and constants from the *Fill()* function. The *x[2][2]* parameter represents the numerator determinant for the *x* unknown. The *y[2][2]* parameter represents the numerator determinant for the *y* unknown. The *D[2][2]* parameter represents the denominator determinant for both the *x* and *y* unknowns.

Next, look at the statement section of the function. The first two columns of the equation array are copied into each of the determinant arrays using **for** loops. Then, the constant terms are inserted into the *x* and *y* determinant arrays at the required positions using direct assignment. The formation pattern results from Cramer's rule. Notice that in all instances the determinants are formed using the elements from the 2 × 3 *Equations* array of coefficients and constants generated by the *Fill()* function.

Now we have all the ingredients for a C++ program that will solve two equations and two unknowns using Cramer's rule. Combining our *Fill()* function, our *Form_Det()* function, and our *Expand()* function into a single program, we get the following:

```
//**************************************************************************
//
// THIS PROGRAM WILL SOLVE TWO EQUATIONS AND TWO
// UNKNOWNS USING CRAMER'S RULE (CASE9-1.CPP)
//
//**************************************************************************

#include <iostream.h>

// FUNCTION PROTOTYPES
void Fill(float Equations[2][3]);
void Form_Det(float Equations[2][3], float x[2][2], float y[2][2], float D[2][2]);
float Expand(float Determinant[2][2]);

void main()
{

// ARRAY DEFINITIONS
   float Equations[2][3];
   float x[2][2];
   float y[2][2];
   float D[2][2];

// CALL FUNCTIONS TO FILL EQUATION ARRAY
// AND FORM DETERMINANTS
   Fill(Equations);
   Form_Det(Equations, x, y, D);

// IF DENOMINATOR = 0 WRITE ERROR MESSAGE,
// ELSE CALCULATE x AND y
   if(!Expand(D))
     cout << "\n\n\nDenominator = 0.  Equations are unsolvable.";
   else
     cout << "\n\n\nThe value of the first variable is: "
          << Expand(x)/Expand(D)
          << "\n\nThe value of the second variable is: "
          << Expand(y)/Expand(D);

} // END MAIN
```

```
//*******************************************************************************
//
// THIS FUNCTION WILL FILL AN ARRAY WITH THE EQUATION
// COEFFICIENTS
//
//*******************************************************************************
void Fill(float Equations[2][3])
{
  for(int Row = 0; Row < 2; ++Row)
  {
    cout << "\nEnter the variable coefficients and constant for equation "
         << Row + 1 << "\nNote the equation must be in standard form.\n\n";
    for(int Col = 0; Col < 3; ++Col)
      {
        if (Col == 2)
          cout << "Enter the constant term:  ";
        else
          cout << "Enter the coefficient for variable " << Col + 1 << ":  ";
        cin >> Equations[Row][Col];
      } // END COLUMN FOR
  } // END ROW FOR
} // END FUNCTION FILL


// *****************************************************************
//
// THIS FUNCTION WILL FORM THE DETERMINANTS
//
// *****************************************************************
void Form_Det(float Equations[2][3], float x[2][2], float y[2][2], float D[2][2])
{
  for(int Row = 0; Row < 2; ++Row)
    for(int Col = 0; Col < 2; ++Col)
      {
        x[Row][Col] = Equations[Row][Col];
        y[Row][Col] = Equations[Row][Col];
        D[Row][Col] = Equations[Row][Col];
      }
  x[0][0] = Equations[0][2];
  x[1][0] = Equations[1][2];
  y[0][1] = Equations[0][2];
  y[1][1] = Equations[1][2];
}
```

```
// ***********************************************************************
//
// THIS FUNCTION WILL EXPAND A 2 x 2 DETERMINANT
//
// ***********************************************************************
float Expand(float Determinant[2][2])
{
  return  (Determinant[0][0] * Determinant[1][1]
          - Determinant[1][0] * Determinant[0][1]);
}
```

Observe that all the arrays are defined local to *main()*. *Equations* is a 2×3 array that will store the coefficients and constants of the two equations. This is followed by definitions for the three 2×2 determinant arrays. The prototypes for our three functions are given prior to *main()* and the functions themselves are listed after *main()*.

Now, look at the statement section of the *main()*. The *Fill()* function is called first to obtain the coefficient and constant terms of the two equations. The actual parameter used for the function call is the name of the equations array, *Equations*. Next, the *Form_Det()* function is called to form the required determinants. The actual parameters used in this function call are *Equations*, *x*, *y*, and *D*. The *Equations* parameter is required to pass the 2×3 array to the function. The *x*, *y*, and *D* parameters are required to pass the three determinant arrays to the function and back.

Finally, look at how the *Expand()* function is invoked. It is first invoked as part of an **if/else** statement to see if the denominator determinant value is zero. If it is, the equations cannot be solved using Cramer's rule because division by zero is undefined. If the denominator determinant is not zero, the *Expand()* function is invoked twice to calculate the first unknown (*x*) within a *cout* statement like this: *Expand(x) / Expand(D)*. This expands the *x* determinant, expands the common denominator determinant, and divides the two to obtain the value of the first unknown (*x*). The function is called twice again to find the second unknown (*y*).

Given the following two equations,

$$x + 2y = 3$$
$$3x + 4y = 5$$

here is what you would see when the program is executed:

Enter the variable coefficients and constant for equation 1
Note the equation must be in standard form.

Enter the coefficient for variable 1: **1**↵
Enter the coefficient for variable 2: **2**↵
Enter the constant term: **3**↵

Enter the variable coefficients and constant for equation 2
Note the equation must be in standard form.

Enter the coefficient for variable 1: **3**↵
Enter the coefficient for variable 2: **4**↵
Enter the constant term: **5**↵

The value for the first variable is: −1

The value for the second variable is: 2

Do you think that you could develop a similar program to solve a set of three simultaneous equations? You now have all the required knowledge! Guess what you will be doing in the programming exercises at the end of the chapter.

CHAPTER SUMMARY

A two-dimensional array, or table, is a combination of two or more element rows, or lists. It has dimensions of $m \times n$, where m is the number of rows in the array and n is the number of array columns. A three-dimensional array is the combination of two or more two-dimensional arrays. It is comprised of rows, columns, and planes. Thus, a three-dimensional array has dimensions of $p \times m \times n$ where p is the number of planes in the array, m is the number of array rows, and n is the number of columns. In C++, two-dimensional arrays are row major ordered, and three-dimensional arrays are plane major ordered.

A separate **for** loop is required to access each array dimension. In addition, the loops must be nested when accessing multidimensional arrays. Thus, to access a three-dimensional array, the column loop is nested in the row loop, which is nested in the plane loop.

There are many technical applications for arrays. A common use of an array is to store determinants that are used to solve systems of simultaneous equations using Cramer's rule.

QUESTIONS AND PROBLEMS

Questions

Use the following array definitions to answer questions 1–11.

```
float Semester_Scores[10];

const int MULTIPLIER = 12;
const int MULTIPLICAND = 20;
int Product[MULTIPLIER][MULTIPLICAND];

int Cube[3][7][4];

enum Colors {Brown, Black, Red, Orange, Yellow, Green, Blue, Violet,
             Gray, White};

float Color_Code[10][10][10];
```

1. Sketch a diagram showing each array structure and its indices.

2. List the identifiers that must be used to access each array.

3. What are the dimensions of each array?

4. How many elements will each array store?

5. List all of the possible element values for the *Cube* array, assuming that it will be used to store Boolean data.

6. Write a C++ statement that will display the element in the fourth row and second column of the *Product* array.

7. Write a C++ statement that will assign any legal element to the second row and last column of the *Product* array.

8. Write a C++ statement that will display the element values in the third row, second column, and third plane of the *Cube* and *Color_Code* arrays. Assume that the enumerated data type elements will be used as indices to access the *Color_Code* array.

9. Write C++ statements that will insert values into the *Color_Code* array using the following color code combinations and associated values:

   a. Brown, Black, Red = 1000

   b. Brown, Black, Green = 1000000

   c. Yellow, Violet, Red = 4700

   d. Red, Red, Red = 2200

10. Write the C++ code required to fill each array from keyboard entries.

11. Write the C++ code required to display each array and include appropriate table headings.

Problems

Least Difficult

1. Write a program to read 15 integer elements from the keyboard and store them in a 3×5 array. Once the elements have been read, display them as a 5×3 array. (Hint: Reverse the rows and columns.)

2. Write a function that will display any given page of the book array used in Example 9-5. Assume that the user will enter the page number to be displayed.

3. Write a program that will store the state table for a 4-bit decade (BCD) counter. Write functions to fill and display the state table. Here is what its state table looks like:

State	Count
0	0000
1	0001
2	0010
3	0011
4	0100
5	0101
6	0110
7	0111
8	1000
9	1111

4. Write a program that employs two functions to fill and print a calendar for the current month.

More Difficult

Employ the program developed in the chapter Case Study to solve problems 5–7. Modify the program to meet the given application.

5. The circuit diagram in Figure 9-5 shows two unknown currents, I_1 and I_2. An engineer writes two equations that describe the circuit as follows:

$$300I_1 + 500(I_1 - I_2) - 20 = 0$$
$$200I_2 + 500(I_2 - I_1) + 10 = 0$$

Put these equations in standard form and solve for the two currents using the software developed in the chapter Case Study.

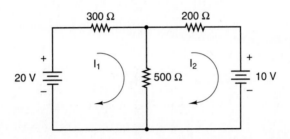

Figure 9-5 A two-loop circuit for problem 5.

6. Look at the lever in Figure 9-6. If you know one of the weights and all the distances of the weights from the fulcrum, you can calculate the other two weights using two simultaneous equations. The two equations have the following general form:

$$w_1 d_1 + w_2 d_2 = w_3 d_3$$

where: w_1, w_2, and w_3 are the three weights.

d_1, d_2, and d_3 are the distances the three weights are located from the fulcrum, respectively.

Using this general equation format, you get two equations by knowing two balance points. Suppose weight w_3 is 5 pounds and you obtain a balance condition for the following distance values:

Balance point 1:

$d_1 = 3$ in.

$d_2 = 6$ in.

$d_3 = 36$ in.

Balance point 2:

$d_1 = 5$ in.

$d_2 = 4$ in.

$d_3 = 30$ in.

Find the two unknown weights, w_1 and w_2.

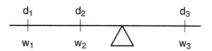

Figure 9-6 A lever/fulcrum arrangement for problem 6.

7. The following equations describe the tension, in pounds, of two cables supporting an object. Find the amount of tension on each cable (T_1 and T_2).

$$0.5T_2 + 0.93T_1 - 120 = 0$$
$$0.42T_1 - 0.54T_2 = 0$$

Most Difficult

8. Write a function to fill a 3×4 array with the coefficients and constant terms from three simultaneous equations expressed in standard form. Assume that the user will enter the array elements in the required order.

9. Write a function to display the equation array in problem 8.

10. Using Cramer's rule, write a function to form 3×3 determinants from the 3×4 equation array you filled in problem 8.

11. Write a function to expand an order 3 determinant.

12. Employ the functions you developed in problems 8 through 11 to write a program that will solve a set of three simultaneous equations.

13. Use the program in problem 12 to solve the three currents (I_1, I_2, I_3) in the Wheatstone bridge circuit shown in Figure 9-7. Here are the equations that an engineer writes to describe the circuit:

$$2000(I_1 - I_2) + 4000(I_1 - I_3) - 10 = 0$$
$$2000(I_2 - I_1) + 8000I_2 + 5000(I_2 - I_3) = 0$$
$$5000(I_3 - I_2) + 3000I_3 + 4000(I_3 - I_1) = 0$$

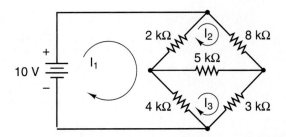

Figure 9-7 The three-loop Wheatstone Bridge circuit for problem 13.

14. Suppose the perimeter of a triangle is 14 inhes. The shortest side is half as long as the longest side and 2 inches more than the difference of the two longer sides. Find the length of each side using the program you developed in problem 12.

15. Assume the following table represents the monthly rental price of six resort cabins over a five-year period.

		YEAR				
		FIRST	SECOND	THIRD	FOURTH	FIFTH
	1	200	210	225	300	235
	2	250	275	300	350	400
CABIN	3	300	325	375	400	450
	4	215	225	250	250	275
	5	355	380	400	404	415
	6	375	400	425	440	500

Write a program that employs functions to perform the following tasks:

- Fill a two-dimensional array with the above table.

- Compute the total rental income for each cabin by year and store the yearly totals in a second array.

- Compute the percentage increase/decrease in price between adjacent years for each cabin and store the percentages in a third array.

- Print a report showing all three arrays in table form with appropriate row/column headings.

16. The method of *cofactors* used to find a value of a determinant is a recursive process. Write a function that will find the value of an order n determinant, where the order of the determinant, n, is entered by the user. Incorporate this function into a program that will find the solution to n equations of n unknowns. (You might need to consult a good linear algebra textbook for information on using the method of cofactors to solve a determinant.)

10

POINTERS

INTRODUCTION

Pointers are fundamental to programming in either the C or C++ language. A pointer is nothing more than an actual address in memory.

A ***pointer*** represents a physical memory address.

Although you may not have realized it, you have been working with pointers already. For instance, recall that an array name actually represents the memory address of the first element of an array. Furthermore, by preceding a variable identifier with an ampersand, &, you are representing the memory address of the variable. Therefore, an array name and a variable preceded with an ampersand are actually pointers. However, these pointers are ***constant pointers***, since the address to which they point can never be changed by the program. On the other hand, a ***variable pointer*** is a pointer whereby the address to which it points can be changed by the program. In this chapter, you will learn how to use variable pointers in preparation for their use in the chapters that follow. Pointers provide a powerful and efficient means of accessing data, especially when that data is part of a data structure, such as an array. This is an important topic, so stay with me.

10-1 THE IDEA OF POINTERS

Let's begin by comparing a pointer to a variable. Assume for a moment that *Value1* and *Value2* are defined as an integer variables and initialized to the values of 10 and 20, respectively. Also, assume that *p1* and *p2* are defined as pointers. The boxes in Figure 10-1 illustrate these assumptions. Here, you see the boxes labeled *Value1* and *Value2* storing the integers 10 and 20, respectively. Now, you already know that *&Value1* and *&Value2* represent the memory addresses of the variables. Thus, *&Value1* points to the box containing the integer 10 and *&Value2* points to the box containing the 20. The boxes labeled *p1* and *p2* contain a dot, •, indicating that they do not point to anything at this time.

Since *p1* and *p2* are pointer variables, we can reassign them at any time to point to data in memory. For instance, we can assign the address of *Value1* to *p1* and the address of *Value2* to *p2* like this:

```
p1 = &Value1;
p2 = &Value2;
```

There is no problem with these assignments because *p1, p2, &Value1,* and *&Value2* all represent memory addresses. What you get is illustrated by Figure 10-2(a). After these assignments, *p1* and *&Value1* point to the value 10, while *p2* and *&Value2* point to the value 20.

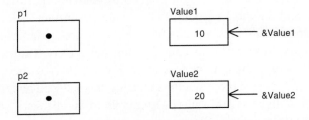

Figure 10-1 *p1* and *p2* are pointers while *Value1* and *Value2* are integer variables.

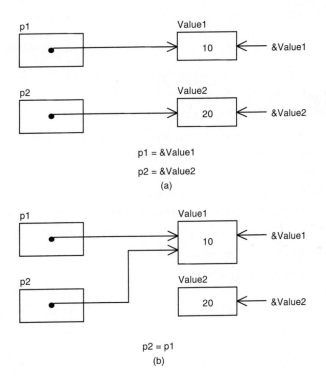

Figure 10-2 The effect of (a) assigning the address of a variable to a pointer, and (b) assigning a pointer to a pointer.

Likewise, since both *p1* and *p2* are pointers, we can assign *p1* to *p2* like this:

p2 = p1;

The result of this assignment is illustrated in Figure 10-2(b). Notice now that *p1*, *p2* and *&Value1* all point to the value 10. In fact, we can alter *p1* and *p2* to point to any address in memory, since they are variable pointers. However, we cannot alter *&Value1* or *&Value2*, since they are constant pointers.

It is important to note that in Figure 10-2(b) there is only one *Value1*; however, we have three pointers locating this value. Thus, if we change the value of *Value1* there is still only one variable to be changed, not three. For instance, suppose we make the following assignment:

Value1 = 30;

After this assignment, *p1*, *p2* and *&Value1* will all locate the new value, 30.

 Quick Check

1. Suppose that *pchar* is a pointer to a character and *Character* is a character variable. Write a statement to make *pchar* point to the character stored in *Character*.

2. Write a statement that will make an integer pointer called *p1int* point to the same integer to which an integer pointer called *p2int* is pointing.

3. True or False: If *Character* is defined as a character variable, then *&Character* can be altered at any time.

4. True or False: If *pchar* is defined as a character pointer, then *pchar* can be altered at any time.

10-2 DEFINING POINTERS AND INITIALIZING POINTER DATA

To define a pointer you must tell the compiler what type of data the pointer is pointing to, just like you do when defining a variable. Here's the general format:

POINTER DEFINITION FORMAT

<data type being pointed to> * <pointer identifier>;

Here are some sample pointer definitions:

```
int *Integer_Pointer;
char *Character_Pointer;
float *Float_Pointer;
```

The first definition says that *Integer_Pointer* is a pointer to an integer value, the second says that *Character_Pointer* points to a character, and finally *Float_Pointer* points to a floating point value. Note the use of the asterisk, or star, in all the definitions. The star must immediately precede the pointer identifier. This is what tells the compiler that you are defining a pointer variable rather than a common variable. From now on, I will refer to a pointer variable as simply a pointer.

The *star*, *, in front of a pointer variable denotes "the contents of." In other words *p1* is read as "the contents of the memory location where *p1* is pointing."

There are two ways to initialize a pointer to point to a value.

1. Allocating memory **statically** by defining a variable and then making the pointer point to the variable value.
2. Allocating memory **dynamically** and initializing the pointer to point to a value.

Let's define a pointer to an integer and an integer variable, as follows, to illustrate these methods:

```
int *p1;
int Value;
```

Using these definitions, we can then make the following assignments:

```
p1 = &Value;
*p1 = 25;
```

The first assignment makes *p1* point to the variable called *Value*. The second assignment stores the value 25 in memory where *p1* is pointing. Notice the use of the star, *, symbol again. A star in front of a pointer variable means "the contents of." Therefore, the second assignment reads "store the value 25 in the contents of memory to where *p1* is pointing." Of course, this is the same memory location as *&Value*. We can say that **p1* is an ***alias*** for the variable *Value*, since the integer value stored in *Value* can also be accessed via **p1*.

There is no ambiguity in the use of the star to define a pointer and to initialize a pointer to point to a value. Both reference "the contents of." When defining a pointer, the * indicates that "the contents of" memory pointed to by the pointer will be a given a data type. When initializing a pointer to point to a value, the * indicates "the contents of" memory pointed to by the pointer will be a given value.

We say that this type of initialization is ***static*** because the allocation of memory used to store the value is fixed and cannot go away. Once the variable is defined, the compiler sets aside enough memory to store a value of the given data type. This memory remains reserved for this variable and cannot be used for anything else during the program execution. In other words, you cannot ***deallocate*** the memory set aside for a variable. The pointer to that variable can be changed, but the amount of memory set aside for the variable remains.

The second way to initialize a pointer to point to a value is by allocating memory ***dynamically***. By allocating memory dynamically, we mean to set aside memory when it is needed to store a value of a given data type. Then, once the value is no longer needed, we can deallocate the memory and make it available for other use by the system. Using the same definition for pointer *p1* as above, we can initialize *p1* dynamically to point to a value like this:

```
p1 = new int;
*p1 = 25;
```

This time, we did not need to first initialize *p1* to the address of a static variable. Rather, the **new** operator creates enough memory to hold an integer value pointed to by *p1*. Then, we stored the value 25 in that memory area. Once memory is allocated dynamically like this, we can deallocate the same memory area by using the **delete** operator as follows:

```
delete p1;
```

This operation will free up the memory pointed to by *p1* for other use by the program and/or system. It is important to note that the **delete** operator does not delete the pointer, it simply destroys the data to which the pointer points.

Therefore, after the above statement is executed, *p1* still exists as a pointer that does not point to anything, but can be again initialized to point to another data by using the **new** operator.

The **new** operator is used to dynamically allocate memory for pointer data, while the **delete** operator is used to deallocate memory pointed to by a pointer.

DEBUGGING TIP

It is very easy to make incorrect assignments when working with pointers. For example, using the foregoing pointer definitions, the following three assignments will create an error:

```
*p1 = &Value;
p1 = Value;
p1 = 25;
```

In all cases, an attempt is made to "mix apples and oranges." In the first case, an attempt is made to assign an address (*&Value*) to a value, since **p1* locates a value. In the second case, an attempt is made to assign a value (*Value*) to an address, since *p1* is an address. Likewise in the third case, an attempt is made to assign a value to an address. The correct assignments would be:

```
*p1 = Value;
p1 = &Value;
*p1 = 25;
```

Example 10-1:

Determine the output generated by the following program:

```
// EXAMPLE 10-1:  INITIALIZING POINTER DATA (E10-1.CPP)

#include <iostream.h>

void main()
{
```

```
// DEFINE TWO POINTERS AND A VARIABLE
    int *p1;
    int *p2;
    int Index;

// INITIALIZE POINTER DATA STATICALLY
    p1 = &Index;
    Index = 10;

// INITIALIZE POINTER DATA DYNAMICALLY
    p2 = new int;
    *p2 = 20;

// DISPLAY POINTER DATA
    cout << "\n\nThe contents of memory pointed to by p1 is:  " << *p1;
    cout << "\n\nThe contents of memory pointed to by p2 is:  " << *p2;

// DEALLOCATE MEMORY POINTED TO BY p2
    delete p2;
}
```

Solution:

The output generated by the program is:

> The contents of memory pointed to by p1 is 10

> The contents of memory pointed to by p2 is 20

Notice that the program initializes the *p1* pointer data statically and the *p2* pointer data dynamically. Both produce the same results; however, the memory pointed to by *p1* is set aside until the program terminates, while the memory pointed to by *p2* is deallocated immediately after the *cout* statement. Notice also how the pointer data is accessed in the *cout* statement. The * is employed to indicate that "the contents of" memory pointed to by the pointer is to be displayed. What do you suppose would happen if the * were omitted? Well, since a pointer is a memory address, you would see the actual memory address, in hex, assigned to the pointer. This leads us to our next topic.

Quick Check

1. Define a static character pointer called *pchar* and a character variable called *Character*.

2. Write a statement to make *pchar* point to the variable *Character* defined in question 1.

3. Write a statement to initialize *pchar* defined in question 1 to the character 'A'.

4. True or False: The assignment *pchar* = 'Z' is legal, as long as *pchar* is defined as a character pointer.

5. When a pointer is initialized dynamically, the _____ operator must be used in the pointer definition.

6. Write the statements to initialize a dynamic character pointer called *pchar* to the value 'B'.

7. Write a statement that will deallocate the memory allocated in question 6.

8. True or False: When you deallocate pointer memory using the **delete** operator, the respective pointer is deleted.

10-3 ACCESSING POINTER DATA AND POINTER ARITHMETIC

You have already seen how to access the data pointed to by a pointer through the use of the star, *, operator. Remember, *p means "the contents of memory pointed to by *p*." Let's see how we can expand on this knowledge by using a pointer to a string. Consider the following pointer definition:

```
char  *sptr = "HAL";
```

The foregoing definition creates a character pointer called *sptr*. In addition, the pointer data is initialized to the string "HAL". If you were to view the data stored to where *sptr* is pointing via a debugger you would observe the following:

Inspecting *sptr*

[0]	'H'
[1]	'A'
[2]	'L'
[3]	'\0'

As you can see, *sptr* locates the entire string in memory just like an array name locates an array in memory. In fact, you see that the compiler has placed the string in an array located by the variable pointer *sptr*. Now, what do you suppose you would see on the display after the following *cout* statements were executed?

```
cout << *sptr;
cout << sptr[0];
```

Even though the pointer data is initialized to a string, *sptr* is still only a character pointer. Therefore, the first *cout* statement will display the single character 'H'. Likewise, since the compiler has placed the string into an array pointed to by *sptr*, the second statement will also produce the single character stored at index [0] in the array, which is the single character 'H'.

Next, what do you suppose will be displayed by the following?

```
cout << sptr;
```

With this definition, *sptr* is simply a pointer to an array of characters. In other words, the compiler will treat it just like an array name when used like this. As a result, the foregoing statement will display the entire string "HAL". Remember, although *sptr* is treated just like an array name in this operation, it is different! When *sptr* is defined as a pointer to an array, it is a variable pointer and therefore could be altered to point to another location in memory. On the other hand, if *sptr* were an array name, it would be a constant pointer and could not be altered to point to a different location.

Next, consider the following two statements:

```
cout << *(sptr + 1);
cout << (sptr + 1)[0];
```

The first statement is read "display the contents of *sptr + 1.*" Since *sptr* locates the first character in the array, *(sptr + 1)* must locate the second array character, right? Therefore, the contents of *(sptr + 1)* must be the character 'A'. This statement doesn't change the pointer location, it simply *offsets* the pointer for the purpose of the *cout* operation. The second statement will produce the same character 'A'. This statement would be read as "display the character stored at index [0] of location *(sptr + 1).*" This time, the pointer is being treated just like an array name; however it might be a bit confusing, since the character 'A' is located at index [1] in the array. This is true relative to *sptr*, but relative to *(sptr + 1)*, index [0] locates the second character in the array which is the character 'A'. What character do you suppose is stored at *(sptr + 1)[1]* ? You're right if you thought the character 'L'. How about position *(sptr + 2)[0]* ? Again, you would be accessing the character 'L'. Think about it! These concepts are illustrated in Figure 10-3.

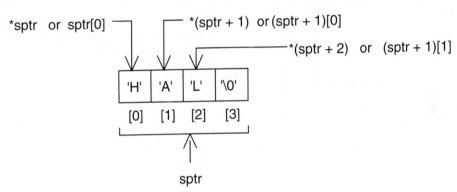

Figure 10-3 Accessing string pointer data.

Pointer Arithmetic

Unlike an array name which is a constant pointer and cannot be altered, a pointer is a variable pointer which can be altered. As a result, you can perform certain arithmetic operations on pointers.

Keep in mind that a pointer is an address. As a result, only those arithmetic operations that "make sense" are legal. You can add or subtract an integer constant to or from a pointer. Adding or subtracting an integer, say *x*, to or from a pointer will produce a new pointer which is *x* elements away from the original pointer.

Adding or subtracting a floating point constant to or from a pointer would not make sense, considering that an address must result from the operation.

Likewise, it wouldn't make sense to multiply or divide a pointer by a constant, considering that a pointer is an address.

Here is what you *should not* do:

- You should not add two pointers.

- You should not multiply two pointers.

- You should not divide two pointers.

CAUTION

Performing arithmetic operations on pointers may be hazardous to your system! Since pointers can be altered to point anywhere in the system memory, you could accidentally make a pointer operate in a area of memory being used by the operating system for other system chores. The result of such an accident is usually a system crash which can only be corrected by re-booting the system.

The only thing you *can* do is subtract two pointers when both pointers are pointing to the same array. When you subtract two pointers that point to the same array, you get a constant value which is the number of array positions, or elements, between the two pointers. So, if *p1* is a pointer which points to index [0] in an array, and *p2* is a pointer which points to index [5] in the same array, then *p2 – p1* will yield the value 5.

Legal arithmetic operations on pointers are **scaled**. This means that when you perform pointer arithmetic, the compiler scales the result relative to the data type being pointed to, rather than bytes of memory. For instance, you know that an integer requires two bytes of storage, therefore requiring two memory addresses to store an integer value. So, if *iptr* is a pointer to an integer, then adding 1 to *iptr* yields a pointer that will point two bytes, or addresses, away from where *iptr* was originally pointing. Likewise, if *iptr1* points to index [1] in an integer array, and *iptr2* points to index [2] of the same integer array, then *iptr2 – iptr1* will yield the constant value 1, even though the two addresses being pointed to are two bytes from each other.

Example 10-2:

Determine the output generated by the following program:

```
// EXAMPLE 10-2 (E10-2.CPP)

#include <iostream.h>

void main()
{
// DEFINE THREE CHARACTER POINTERS AND
// INITIALIZE ONE TO A STRING
   char *sptr1;
   char *sptr2;
   *sptr= "HAL";

// DISPLAY POINTER DATA
   cout << "\n*sptr --> " << *sptr;
   cout << "\nsptr[0] --> "<< sptr[0];
   cout << "\n*(sptr + 1) --> " << *(sptr + 1);
   cout << "\n(sptr + 1)[0] --> " << (sptr + 1)[0];
   cout << "\n*(sptr + 2) --> " << *(sptr + 2);

// ADD ONE TO sptr AND OUTPUT STRING
   ++sptr;
   cout << "\nsptr --> " << sptr;

// SUBTRACT ONE FROM sptr AND OUTPUT STRING
   --sptr;
   cout << "\nsptr --> " << sptr;

// WEIRD
   for (int i = 0; i < 3; ++i)
     *(sptr + i) = *(sptr + i) + 1;
   cout << "\nsptr --> " << sptr;

// INITIALIZE sptr1, sptr2 AND OUTPUT DIFFERENCE
   sptr1 = sptr;
   sptr2 = sptr + 2;

// OUTPUT sptr2 - sptr1
   cout << "\nsptr2 - sptt1 = " << sptr2 - sptr1;
}
```

Solution:

Here is what you would see on the display:

$$*sptr --> H$$
$$sptr[0] --> H$$

```
*(sptr + 1) --> A
(sptr + 1)[0] --> A
*(sptr + 2) --> L
sptr --> AL
sptr --> HAL
sptr --> IBM
sptr2 - sptr1 = 2
```

The first five single character outputs demonstrate the operations discussed earlier. See if you can verify the output characters knowing that *sptr* is initialized to the string "HAL". The sixth output, "AL" results from adding 1 to *sptr* and then displaying the string located by *sptr*. Adding 1 to *sptr* yields a new pointer that points to the second character in the string. The seventh output, "HAL", is produced by subtracting 1 from *sptr* to make it point to its original location at the beginning of the string. The eighth output, "IBM", results from a **for** loop that adds 1 to each character in the string pointed to by *sptr*. The body of the **for** loop is the single statement **(sptr + i) = *(sptr + i) + 1* . Think about what this statement does. When *i* is 0, the statement becomes **(sptr) =   *(sptr) + 1*. Doesn't this add one to the value pointed to by *sptr* and assign this sum back to the contents of *sptr*? Well, **sptr* is the character 'H'. If you add one to this character value you get the character 'I'. As a result, the first loop iteration replaces the character 'H' in **stpr* with the character 'I'. Likewise, the second iteration replaces 'A' with 'B' and the third iteration replaces 'L' with 'M'. After the loop terminates, the string pointed to by *sptr* is "IBM" which can be verified by observing the output generated by the respective *cout* statement.

Finally, the last output is produced by initializing *sptr1* to point to the beginning of the string and *sptr2* to point to the end of the string. The output is the value 2 which is the number of elements between *sptr1* and *sptr2*.

Quick Check

1. Define a string pointer called *pstring* and initialize it to the string "C++".

2. Write a statement to display the entire string in question 1.

3. Write a statement to display just the first character of the string in question 1.

4. Write a statement to display just the last character of the string in question 1.

5. Write a statement to display the last two characters of the string in question 1.

6. Suppose that *p1* is a pointer which points to index [5] of an array of double floating point values, and *p2* is a pointer pointing to index [15] of the same array. Then *p2 – p1* will yield the value _____.

10-4 CONSTANT POINTERS VERSUS POINTERS TO CONSTANTS

You are already familiar with constant pointers as in the case of an array name. A constant pointer is a pointer that cannot be changed, but the data pointed to by the pointer can be changed. On the other hand, a pointer to a constant can be altered to point to a different constant, but the data pointed to by the pointer cannot be changed.

Constant Pointers

To create a constant pointer other than an array name, you use the following format:

CONSTANT POINTER DEFINITION

<element data type> **const** <pointer name> = <address of variable or
                                            actual string value>;

As an example of a constant pointer definition, consider the following:

```
int x;
int y;
int *const P1 = &x;
```

Here, *x* and *y* are defined as integer variables and *P1* is defined as a constant pointer which points to *x*. This makes *P1* a constant, but **P1* is a variable. Therefore, you can change the value at **P1*, but not *P1* itself. For instance, the following assignment is legal, since the contents of memory to where *P1* is pointing is changed, but not the pointer itself.

```
*P1 = y;
```

On the other hand, this next assignment is not legal, since it attempts to change the value of the pointer.

$$P1 = \&y;$$

Here is how you can create a constant pointer to a string:

$$\text{char *const FIRST\_NAME = "Andy";}$$

Again, the string value can be modified, but the pointer, *FIRST_NAME*, cannot be modified to point to a different string in memory. Thus,

$$\text{*FIRST\_NAME = 'B';}$$

is legal, since the data pointed to by *FIRST_NAME* is being modified. However,

$$\text{FIRST\_NAME = \&Another\_String;}$$

is *not* legal, since it is attempting to modify the pointer itself.

Pointers to Constants

Here is the format for defining a pointer to a constant:

> **POINTER TO A CONSTANT DEFINITION**
>
> **const** <element data type> * <pointer name> = <address of const or
> actual string value>;

To illustrate this idea, consider the following definitions:

```
const int X = 5;
const int Y = 6;
const int *P1 = &X;
```

Here, *P1* is defined as a pointer to the constant *X*. Since only the data is constant and not the pointer, we can make *P1* point to another constant like this:

$$P1 = \&Y;$$

However, any attempt to change what is stored at the memory location where *P1* is pointing will create a compile error. So, the following assignment will not compile:

$$*P1 = 7;$$

Creating a pointer to a string constant can be done as follows:

```
const char *FIRST_NAME = "Andy";
```

With this definition, the pointer *FIRST_NAME* can be reassigned to point to another string in memory; however, any string pointed to by *FIRST_NAME* cannot be altered. Look again at the constant pointer definition format and the pointer to a constant definition format given above. Notice that a constant pointer definition has the keyword **const** listed prior to the pointer name whereas the pointer to a constant definition requires that the keyword **const** be placed prior to the data type. So, in the first case, the definition can be read as "constant pointer," while in the second case the definition is read as "constant data type."

Constant Pointers to Constants

Finally, you can create constant pointers to constants using the following format:

CONSTANT POINTER TO A CONSTANT DEFINITION

const <element data type> * **const** <pointer name> = <address of const
or actual string>;

Here you find the keyword **const** in two places, just prior to the data type and just prior to the pointer name. Thus, the definition is read as "constant data type and constant pointer." If you use this type of definition, you cannot alter either the pointer or the data to which the pointer is pointing. Consider the following definition as an example:

```
const int X = 5;
const int *const P1 = &X;
```

The above definition is read "*P1* is a constant pointer pointing to the constant integer *X*." Any attempt to alter either the pointer *P1* or **P1* will produce a compile error.

The bottom line is this:

- If you know that a pointer will always point to the same place and never need to be relocated, define it as a constant pointer.

- If you know that the data pointed to by a pointer will never need to change, define the pointer as a pointer to a constant.

By defining items as constants when they are constant due to their nature, you will be producing better quality code by providing additional compile time checking. Any attempt to accidentally change a constant within the code will be caught by the compiler.

 Quick Check

1. True or False: An array name is always a constant pointer.
2. Define a constant pointer called *pstring* to point to the string "Zane".
3. Rewrite the definition in question 2 so that the pointer will be variable and the string will be constant.
4. Rewrite the definition in question 3 so that both the pointer and string will be constant.

10-5 ARRAYS OF POINTERS ⇒ INDIRECTION

We can easily define an array that stores pointers, thus creating an *array of pointers*. Here is how it's done:

```
char *Ptr_Array[2];
Ptr_Array[0] = "Dog";
Ptr_Array[1] = "Cat";
```

The first line of code defines an array of pointers to character data. The star in front of the array name is used to specify an array of pointers. Since the array size is 2, this array holds two pointers, or addresses. This definition represents two levels of *indirection*, since an array name is always a pointer and this pointer points to the pointers contained in the array.

Indirection has to do with the levels of addressing it takes to access data.

The two lines of code following the array definition are used to initialize the array. The pointer at position [0] of this array is initialized to point to the string "Dog", while the pointer (address) contained at position [1] of the array is initialized to point to the string "Cat". Notice that the "pointer" is initialized to point to a given string.

Although the array is easily defined and initialized, interpreting the indirection gets a bit tricky. Study Figure 10-4 to get an idea of how the array data is accessed using pointers. First, you see that each position in the array is a pointer which locates an entire string. Thus, *Ptr_Array[0]* locates the string "Dog" and *Ptr_Array[1]* locates the string "Cat". You also see that **Ptr_Array* and **(Ptr_Array + 1)* locate the same two strings, "Dog" and "Cat", respectively. The reason for this is that the *contents of Ptr_Array* is the address of the first string and the *contents of (Ptr_Array + 1)* is the address of the second string.

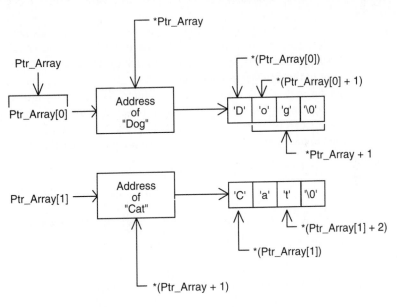

Figure 10-4 An array of pointers pointing to strings.

What do you suppose is pointed to by *Ptr_Array + 1*? This statement offsets the contents of the first pointer by 1, resulting in a string pointer that points one character away from the original pointer. Thus, *Ptr_Array + 1* points to the string "og".

Next, since *Ptr_Array* locates the entire string "Dog", what do you suppose is located by *(Ptr_Array[0])*? You're right if you thought the first character, 'D', of the first string, "Dog". Likewise, *(Ptr_Array[0] + 1)* locates the second character, 'o', of this same string. How would you access the character 'C' in the second string? How about *(Ptr_Array[1])*? Extending this idea, *(Ptr_Array[1] + 2)* will locate the character 't' of the second string.

Let's look at a practical application for an array of pointers.

Example 10-3:

Write a program to define an array of pointers, called *Names*, to strings. Initialize the array pointers to point to the strings "Andy", "Brenda", "Neil", "Lori", and "Doug" and display the strings using the array of pointers.

Solution:

First, we must define an array of pointers and initialize the pointers to point to the given strings. This can be accomplished in one line as follows:

```
char *Names[] = {"Andy", "Brenda", "Neil", "Lori", "Doug", NULL};
```

This defines an array of pointers called *Names*. The pointers point to character strings. Since there is no array size specified, the number of pointers in the array depends on the number of initializing string values. The pointers are initialized to point to the five string values given in the problem statement. In addition, the last pointer in the array is initialized to point to **NULL**. The word **NULL** is predefined in the standard C++ library header files, such as *iostream.h* and *stdio.h*. Any pointer can be tested for equality or inequality to **NULL**. As a result, it can be used to terminate a loop which will display the string values. Here's such a loop:

```
int i = 0;
while (*(Names + i) != NULL)
{
    cout << '\n' << *(Names + i);
    ++i;
}
```

The **while** statement displays the strings pointed to by *(Names + i)*. Thus, the first loop iteration will display the string pointed to by *(Names + 0)* which is the string "Andy". The second iteration will display the string pointed to by *(Names + 1)*, which is the string "Brenda", and so on. The loop terminates when *(Names + i)* points to **NULL**. In our example, this happens when *i* equals the value 5, since *Names + 5* was initialized as a pointer to NULL. Notice that the loop test is *(*(Names + i) != NULL)*. This might seem very logical, but you can save some typing and simply code this test as follows:

while (*(Names + i))

This test will work because **NULL** is interpreted as FALSE by the compiler. Here is the complete program:

```
//*****************************************************************************
//
// THIS PROGRAM WILL DEFINE AN ARRAY OF POINTERS TO POINT
// TO STRINGS THEN DISPLAY THE STRINGS USING POINTERS
//
//*****************************************************************************

#include <iostream.h>

// DEFINE AND INITIALIZE ARRAY OF POINTERS TO STRINGS
char *Names[] = {"Andy", "Brenda", "Neil", "Lori", "Doug", NULL};

void main()
{
  int i = 0;

// DISPLAY NAMES IN ARRAY UNTIL NULL POINTER IS ENCOUNTERED
  while (*(Names + i))
  {
    cout << '\n' << *(Names + i);
    ++i;
  }
}
```

The output produced by the program is:

Andy
Brenda
Neil
Lori
Doug

Quick Check

1. Define an array of pointers called *Courses* to point to the strings "Calc", "Assembler", and "C++".
2. What is located at **Courses* using the array in question 1?
3. What is located at *Courses[2]* using the array in question 1?
4. What is located at **Courses + 2* using the array in question 1?
5. What is located at **(Courses[1] + 3)*?
6. The concept of using several levels of addressing to access data is known as _____.

10-6 USING POINTERS AS FUNCTION ARGUMENTS AND PARAMETERS

When you use a pointer as an argument in a function call, you are passing the address that the pointer contains to the function. Recall, that when you pass an address to a function, you are passing by reference rather than by value. When passing by reference, any operations on the parameter variables within the function will alter the corresponding actual argument variables listed in the function call. Up to this point, you have only had two way to pass variables to a function by reference: (1) By using the ampersand symbol, &, prior to the parameter in the function header, or (2) by passing an array using an array name. Well, think about what you are doing in both cases. You are passing an address to the function, right? Since a pointer is an address we can also pass by reference using a pointer variable. Consider the following program:

```
#include <iostream.h>

// FUNCTION PROTOTYPE
void Swap(int *, int *);

void main()
{
  int Value1 = 10;
  int Value2 = 20;
```

```
    int *Pointer2 = &Value2;
    cout << "\nThe values before the function call are " << Value1
        << " " << Value2;
    Swap(&Value1,Pointer2);
    cout << "\nThe values after the function call are " << Value1
        << " " << Value2;
}


// FUNCTION WILL EXCHANGE THE TWO PARAMETER VALUES
void Swap(int *p1, int *p2)
{
  int Temp;
  Temp = *p1;
  *p1 = *p2;
  *p2 = Temp;
}
```

At the beginning of this program, a function called *Swap()* is prototyped to accept two integer pointers. Looking at the function definition at the end of the program you see that the function simply exchanges the two integer values that it receives from the calling program. In function *main()* you find that two integer variables are defined and initialized to the values of 10 and 20, respectively. Then, a pointer variable called *Pointer2* is defined to point to the value of *Value2*. In the function call, the address of *Value1* is passed using the ampersand, &, symbol as we did earlier in the text. In addition, the address of *Value2* is also passed as the second argument via pointer *Pointer2*. Therefore both variables are passed by reference to the function. The function expects to "see" two addresses, since its prototype dictates that it will accept two pointers. Since the variables are passed by reference, their values will be swapped by the function. Here is the output generated by the program:

The values before the function call are 10 20
The values after the function call are 20 10

Look at the actual arguments and the prototype parameters again. You probably don't have any question about the second argument versus the second parameter, since both are pointers. But, what about the first argument versus the first parameter. Is there a problem here, since an & symbol is used for the argument and a * symbol is used for the corresponding parameter? No! Both are addresses of integers and therefore there is no mismatch between the type of data being passed to the function and the type of data being received by the function.

Next, let's see how strings can be passed to functions using pointers. Look at the following program:

```
#include <iostream.h>
// DEFINE AND INITIALIZE A POINTER TO A STRING
char *String = "Hello";

// FUNCTION PROTOTYPE
void Display_String(char *);

void main()
{
  Display_String(String);
}


//*****************************************************************************
//
// THIS FUNCTION DISPLAYS THE STRING POINTED TO BY *String
//
//*****************************************************************************
void Display_String(char *String)
{
  cout << "The string value is:  " << String;
}
```

First, you see a pointer defined to point to a string of characters and initialized to the string value "Hello". Nothing is new here. Next, you see the function prototype. The prototype dictates that the function will accept a character pointer and not be returning any single value. Looking at the function definition, you see that the function simply displays the string value whose address is pointed to by *String*. The function call in *main()* passes the pointer to the function by listing the pointer identifier as the function argument. Since the pointer already represents an address, you must never use the ampersand symbol, &, prior to a pointer name in a function call. So, in summary, the address of the string is passed to the function where it is used to display the string value. That's all there is to it!

The foregoing program represents one level of indirection using a pointer which points to a character string. Next, let's consider two levels of indirection by defining an array of pointers to strings and see how such a structure is passed to and operated upon by a function. We will use the same array of pointers employed in Example 10-3. Here is the definition/initialization again:

```
char *Names[] = {"Andy", "Brenda", "Neil", "Lori", "Doug", NULL};
```

Remember, that *Names* is a pointer to an array of pointers thereby creating two levels of indirection. Now, we will develop a prototype for a function that will display the string values pointed to by the array pointers. Consider this:

```
void Display_Names(char **);
```

Notice that the function parameter is *char ***. The reason that two stars are required is that it requires two levels of indirection to get to the fundamental character elements. Using this prototype we will write a function to display the string values as follows:

```
void Display_Names(char **Names)
{
  cout << "The names in the array are:\n";
  while (*Names)
  {
   cout << '\n' << *Names;
   ++Names;
  }
```

First you see that the function header reflects the prototype. Next, you see that a **while** loop is employed to display the string values. Since the last pointer in the array is initialized to **NULL**, we can test for the null condition in the **while** statement as we did in Example 10-3. The *cout* statement within the loop displays the strings pointed to by the pointers in the *Names* array. Observe how the two levels of indirection are working here. To access the individual characters you must use ***Names* and to access the entire string at a given pointer address you use **Names*. Thus, ***Names* points to the character 'A', while **Names* points to the string "Andy".

The real power of pointers is demonstrated where the loop is incrementing from one string to the next to provide the sequential string display. To do this, you simply increment from one string pointer to the next by incrementing the array pointer, *Names* using a *++Names* statement. That's all there is to it!

Finally, the function call is:

```
Display_Names(Names);
```

Again you see that you only need to list the pointer array name as the argument in the function call. Putting everything together you get the following program:

```
//******************************************************************************
//
// THIS PROGRAM WILL DEFINE AN ARRAY OF POINTERS TO
// POINT TO STRINGS THEN DISPLAY THE STRINGS BY PASSING
// THE POINTER ARRAY TO A FUNCTION
//
//******************************************************************************

#include <iostream.h>

// FUNCTION PROTOTYPE
void Display_Names(char **);

// DEFINE AND INITIALIZE ARRAY OF POINTERS TO STRINGS
char *Names[] = {"Andy", "Brenda", "Neil", "Lori", "Doug", NULL};

void main()
{
  Display_Names(Names);
}

//******************************************************************************
//
// THIS FUNCTION DISPLAYS THE STRINGS POINTED TO
// BY THE ARRAY
//
//******************************************************************************
void Display_Names(char **Names)
{
  cout << "The names in the array are:\n";
  while (*Names)
  {
    cout << '\n' << *Names;
    ++Names;
  }
}
```

 Quick Check

1. True or False: When a pointer is used in a function call, any operations on the pointer data in the function will affect the pointer data in the calling program.

2. True or False: A pointer argument in a function call must have a corresponding pointer parameter in the function prototype.
3. Write a prototype for a function called *MyFunc()* that will receive a pointer to a string.
4. Write a prototype for a function called *MyFunc()* that will receive an array of pointers to strings.
5. Assuming that *MyNames* is defined as an array of pointers to strings, write a statement that will call the function in question 4.

10-7 POINTERS TO FUNCTIONS

In this last section we will use pointers to point to functions. The idea is similar to using pointers to point to arrays. Recall that an array name is actually a constant pointer which locates the array in memory. Likewise, a function name is actually a constant pointer which locates the function code in memory. In both cases, these pointers are fixed and cannot be made to point to different arrays or functions, respectively. However, a pointer variable does not have this limitation. An array pointer variable can be altered to point to different arrays of the same type. Likewise, we can create a function pointer variable that can be altered to point to different functions of the same type. Consider the following:

```
#include <iostream.h>

// FUNCTION PROTOTYPES
void Display_Header(char *);
void Display_Name(char *);
void Display_Address(char *);
void (*Function_Ptr)(char *);

void main()
{
  char *Garbage = "  ";
  char *Name = "Jane Doe";
  char *Address = "C++ City, USA";
  Function_Ptr = Display_Header;
  Function_Ptr(Garbage);
  Function_Ptr = Display_Name;
  Function_Ptr(Name);
  Function_Ptr = Display_Address;
```

```
    Function_Ptr(Address);
}

void Display_Header(char *Garbage)
{
  cout << "\n\tNAME\t\tADDRESS"
       << "\n\t----\t\t-------";
}

void Display_Name(char *Nam)
{
  cout << "\n\t" << Nam;
}

void Display_Address(char *Addr)
{
  cout << '\t' << Addr;
}
```

When analyzing a program, always look at the prototypes first. Here we see four void functions that each accept a character pointer. The first three function prototypes should be self-explanatory by now. However, notice that the last function prototype employs a * symbol prior to the function name. In addition, the * and function name are enclosed together within parentheses. This is a prototype for a variable function pointer. Since *Function_Ptr()* is a variable function pointer, it can be made to point to any function of the same type. By the same type we mean a function that accepts and returns the same type of data. Notice that all the function prototypes indicate that they are the same function type. At the beginning of *main()* you see three character pointers defined and initialized to string values. Next you see that the *Display_Header()* function is assigned to the *Function_Ptr()* function. This makes *Function_Ptr()* point to the *Display_Header()* function. Thus, we can use *Function_Ptr()* to display the header information instead of *Display_Header()*, since they both locate the same code. Notice that *Garbage* is passed to the function as an actual argument in the function call. Actually, *Display_Header()* does not need to accept any data, since it simply displays fixed header information contained in the function definition. However, to permit the assignment of *Display_Header()* to *Function_Ptr()*, they must have the same parameter types. So, garbage string data is passed, but not utilized.

Next, you see that the *Display_Name()* function is assigned to our variable function pointer. *Function_Ptr()* is then called using the *Name* argument to display the name string just as if you had called *Display_Name()*. Finally, *Display_Address()* is assigned to *Function_Ptr()* and called using *Address* as an argument. As a result, the address string is displayed. Here is what you would see on your monitor after executing the program:

<u>Name</u>   <u>Address</u>

Jane Doe   C++ City, USA

The diagram in Figure 10-5 illustrates how the function pointer in the above program can be made to point to different functions using an assignment statement.

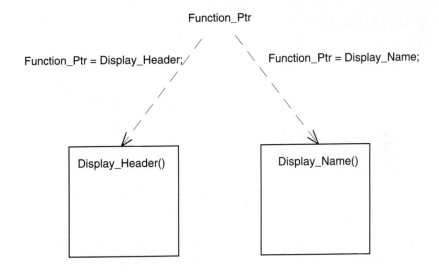

Figure 10-5 A function pointer can be made to point to different functions.

 Quick Check

1. True of False: A function name is a constant pointer.
2. Write a prototype for a variable function pointer called *My_Func_Ptr* that can be used to point to functions that receive a single integer value and return a single integer value.

3. Given the following function prototypes:

    int Square(int);
    int Cube(int);

Write a statement to make the function pointer defined in question 2 point to the *Square()* function.

Write a statement to make the function pointer defined in question 2 point to the *Cube()* function.

4. True or False: When a function pointer is created, the parameter data types and return data type must match those of any function to which it must point.

CHAPTER SUMMARY

A pointer represents a physical memory address. Pointers can be used to point to anything in memory, including other pointers. You can initialize a pointer by allocating memory statically or dynamically. To initialize a pointer statically, you must define a variable first, then make the pointer point to the address of the variable. To initialize a pointer dynamically, you must use the **new** operator. Dynamic memory allocation is most efficient, since memory can be allocated and deallocated as needed in the program.

You can add and subtract integer values to or from a pointer. The result will be a pointer which is displaced from the original pointer value by the number added or subtracted. The displacement is relative to the size of the data pointed to by the pointer. We therefore say that pointer arithmetic is scaled. If you subtract two pointers pointing to the same array, you get the number of elements between the two pointer locations, regardless of the data type size. You cannot add, multiply, or divide pointers.

Variable pointers can be altered to point to any data of the same type. A constant pointer, like an array or function name, cannot be changed to point to anything other than where it has been originally defined to point. When a variable pointer points to a constant, the pointer can be changed but the constant pointed to cannot be changed. Constant pointers can be defined to point to constants. In this case, neither the pointer or the value pointed to can be changed.

Pointers can be used as function arguments and parameters. Since a pointer is an address, a pointer parameter is a reference parameter. Therefore, any operations on the pointer parameter within the function affect the pointer data in the calling program.

Like array names, function names are actually constant pointers. A function name points to the function code in memory. You can create variable function pointers that can be made to point to any other function of the same type. This means that the interface, or prototype, of the variable function pointer must match the interface, or prototype, of any function to which it will point.

QUESTIONS AND PROBLEMS

Questions

1. What is a pointer?

2. Explain the difference between static memory allocation and dynamic memory allocation.

3. Define a static pointer to point to the character 'Z'.

4. Define a dynamic pointer to point to the character 'Z'.

5. Write a statement that will deallocate the memory pointed to by the pointer in question 4.

6. If *p* is defined as a pointer, what is the meaning of *p?

7. Define a pointer to point to the string "This text is great!"

8. What would you see when you view the data pointed to by the pointer in question 7 using your C++ debugger?

9. Given the following pointer definition:

   char *String = "Computer Science";

   What output will be generated by the following statements?

   a. cout << String;

   b. cout << *String;

   c. cout << String[0];

   d. cout << *(String + 1);

   e. cout << (String + 1)[1];

   f. cout << *String +5;

10. List the arithmetic operations that can and can't be performed with pointers.

11. Suppose *p1* is pointing to index [2] in a given array and *p2* is pointing to index [7] of the same array. What is the result of subtracting *p1* from *p2*?

12. Define a variable pointer which will point to a constant called *PI* which has a value of 3.14159.

13. Define a constant pointer which will point to a variable called *Number*, where the initial value of *Number* is 0.

14. Define a constant pointer which will point to a constant called *PI* which has the value of 3.14159.

15. Define an array of pointers called *Courses* that point to the following strings:

    "Assembler"

    "C++"

    "Data Structures"

    "Data Communications"

16. Write a function that contains a loop that will display each of the strings in question 15 using pointers.

17. Explain why using pointer parameters in a function facilitates passing data by reference.

18. Three functions meet the following interface criteria:

    Accepts: A character, a float, and an integer pointer.

    Returns: An integer.

    Write the prototype for a variable function pointer called *Function_Ptr()* that can be made to point to any of the three functions.

Problems

Least Difficult

1. Write a program that will fill a character array with a string of up to 25 characters using pointers and display the string in reverse order using pointers.

2. Write a program that will determine whether or not a word is a palindrome. Place a word entered by the program user into an array and use pointers to compare the character elements for the palindrome determination.

   Note: A palindrome is a word that is spelled the same way both forward and backward. Example: "MOM."

More Difficult

3. Write a pointer version of the program in Chapter 9 that uses Cramer's rule to solve two equations and two unknowns.

4. Suppose that you have the following strings in an array:

"BOB"

"ANDY"

"JANET"

"BRENDA"

"LARRY"

"ZANE"

"ANDREW"

"DAVID"

"RON"

Write a program using pointers to initialize an array with the above names in the order given. Employ a function in the program to sort the names within the array using the following sort algorithm:

For i = 0 to Array Size

   For j = i + 1 to Array Size

            If Array[i] > Array[j]

                     Swap Array[i] and Array[j]

Employ another function that employs pointers to display the array names to verify the sorting operation.

5. Write a program that employs pointers to find the maximum and minimum elements in a two-dimensional integer array. Initialize the array from the keyboard via user entries.

Most Difficult

6. In Section 10-5 we created an array of pointers to strings. Since each pointer locates a separate string, the individual strings can be of different lengths. If you view the strings as a two-dimensional array of characters, the right side of the array has a ragged edge, since the strings have different lengths. For this reason, such an array is called a ***ragged edge array***. Write a program that uses an array of pointers to point to a ragged edge array of characters that contains the names of the students in your class. Write functions to enter the names into the array and display the names.

7. Write a program that employs pointers to reverse the rows and columns of a two-dimensional array. Write functions to allow the user to fill the array, reverse the rows and columns, then display the reversed array, all using pointers.

8. A ***stack*** is a sequential data structure whereby the last element placed into the stack is the first element to be removed from the stack. This idea is referred to as *last-in, first-out (LIFO)*. The last element placed into the stack is located by a pointer called *Top*. Suppose that you use an array to implement a stack and a pointer called *Top*. As you add elements to the stack, *Top* increments through the array and as you remove elements from the stack, *Top* decrements through the array. Adding elements to a stack is called a ***Push*** operation and removing elements from a stack is called a ***Pop*** operation.

Write two functions, called *Push()* and *Pop()*, that employ a pointer called *Top* to push and pop character elements to and from a stack contained in an array. Remember, the only legal way to access the stack is through the single pointer *Top*. Place your functions in a program that will allow you to test the functions. Here are the function descriptions to help get you started:

Function *Push()*:	Places an element onto the stack.
Accepts:	An element to be pushed and a pointer called *Top* which locates the position in the array where the element is to be placed.
Returns:	Nothing
Function *Pop()*:	Removes an element from the stack.
Accepts:	A pointer called *Top* which locates the position in the array from where the element is to be obtained.
Returns:	The popped element.

9. When pushing and popping elements to and from a stack that is being held in an array, you must have a way of determining when the stack is empty or full. You know the stack is empty when the *Top* pointer points to array position [0]. You know the stack is full when *Top* points to the maximum array index. Write two functions called *Empty_Stack()* and *Full_Stack()* that will return a non-zero (TRUE) value if the stack is empty or full, respectively; and a zero (FALSE) value if the stack is not empty or full, respectively.

10. You can use stacks to test a word to see if it's a palindrome. Here's the idea: Enter the word to be tested into two separate stacks. Pop the elements from one stack of the two stacks and place them in a third stack. Pop the two remaining stacks and compare the popped elements character by character as they are popped. Continue popping until two elements do not match or until the stacks are empty. As soon as you find two elements

that are not the same, you don't have a palindrome. On the other hand, if no mismatches have been detected after all the elements are popped, you have a palindrome. Why does this work?

Write a program that uses this idea to test a word to see if it is a palindrome. Employ the functions that you developed in problems 8 and 9.

11

STRUCTURES

INTRODUCTION

The second important data structure that you need to learn about is the ***structure***. Like an array, a structure is a structured data type, meaning that it provides a well-organized, convenient means of storing data. In many programming languages, such as BASIC and FORTRAN, the only structured data type available is the array. Recall that when you define an array, you must specify the number of elements it contains (its size) and the data type of the elements. The idea that all the elements must be the same data type is a serious limitation of an array. For instance, suppose an academic application requires a data structure for storing student information. Such information might include the student's name, student number, GPA, year enrolled, and whether or not the student has graduated. This information is composed of a variety of unique data types. As a result, an array would not be a suitable data structure for this application. Fortunately, C++ provides the structure data type which permits information of different data types to be conveniently stored, accessed, and manipulated. You should be aware that structures are also called records in some other programming languages, such as Pascal.

In this chapter, you will learn how to define and access C++ structures. In addition, you will learn how to create very powerful complex data structures by building structures of structures, called ***nested structures***.

11-1 STRUCTURE FORMAT AND DECLARATION

> A ***structure*** is a collection of ***members***.

A ***structure member*** is simply an item of meaningful data or it can also be a function. For example, the string of characters that form your name can be classified as a member, the collection of numbers that form your student number can be a member, and the collection of numbers and the decimal point that form your GPA can form a member. Thus, a student structure might consist of a collection of student-related members as shown in Figure 11-1. Notice that each member within the structure is a unique data type, while the collection of all the members (the structure) represents different data types.

A structure can contain any number of members, with each member having a unique name, called the ***member name***. Thus, the member names in the student structure are *Name*, *Student_Number*, *GPA*, *Year_Enrolled*, and *Graduated*.

Now that you have an idea of the format of a simple structure, you are ready to learn how to declare structures in C++.

Student Structure

Member Name	Member Data Type
Name	A string
Student_Number	An integer value
GPA	A floating point value
Year_Enrolled	An integer value
Graduated	A Boolean value

Figure 11-1 A student structure consists of a collection of student-related members

Declaring Structures

Like enumerated data, a structure is a user-defined data structure that must be declared before it can be used. Here's the declaration format:

STRUCTURE DECLARATION FORMAT

```
struct <structure name>
{
    <member 1 data type>  <member 1 name>;
    <member 2 data type>  <member 2 name>;
                    •
                    •
    <member n data type>  <member n name>;
};
```

As you can see, the structure declaration in C++ literally shows that the structure is a collection of individual members, each identified by its data type and member name. After the keyword **struct**, you must first list the structure identifier, or name. The name can be any valid identifier, but should be descriptive of the structure meaning. The structure name is followed by a left curly brace, {, which is followed by a list of the individual members that make up the structure. The structure declaration is concluded with a right curly brace, }.

The individual members are declared using an indentation scheme below the keyword **struct**. Here are some things you will want to remember about the member declarations:

- Each member within the structure must have a unique name. However, a given member name may be used again in another structure declaration.

- A data type must be specified for each member. All the data types discussed so far are legal. Thus, a member can be an integer, float, character, or enumerated data type. Of course, if a member is an enumerated data type, the enumerated data type must be declared prior to the structure declaration.

Defining Structure Variables

Like the enumerated data type, a structure is accessed using a variable or variables that must be defined after the structure declaration. Here we go again with the two words, *declaration* and *definition*. Remember the technical difference? A declaration simply specifies the name and format of the data structure, but does not reserve storage. On the other hand, a definition reserves storage. Thus, each variable definition for a given structure creates an area in memory where data will be stored according to the declared structure format. Structure variables can be defined in two ways: (1) By listing them immediately after the closing brace of the structure declaration, or (2) By listing the structure name followed by the corresponding variables anyplace in the program prior to their use. Clearly, the variable name must be different from the structure name. Now, let's declare some structures and define their associated variables.

Example 11-1:

Declare the following structures:

a. A *Student* structure, consisting of the student's name, student number, year enrolled, GPA, and whether or not the student has graduated. Define a variable called *Fred* to access the *Student* structure.

b. An *Automobile* structure, consisting of the automobile year, color (blue, black, yellow, red, or green), and price. Make provision to use this same structure for a *Ford, Chevy,* or *Dodge.*

c. A *Weather* structure, consisting of the date, temperature, barometric pressure, and conditions. Assume that there are three reportable conditions: clear, cloudy, and rain. Make provision to use this structure for storing morning, afternoon, evening, and night weather information.

Solution:

a.   struct Student
     {
      char Name[30];
      int Student_Number;
      int Year_Enrolled;
      float GPA;
      int Graduated;
     } Fred;

This structure declaration is straightforward. The structure name is *Student*, which contains five members: *Name, Student_Number, Year_Enrolled, GPA,* and *Graduated.* Observe that the *Student_Number* and *Year_Enrolled* members are both integer data types, but declared on separate lines. They could be listed on the same line, but many software engineers prefer to use separate line declarations for clarity and program readability. The *Name* member is declared as a character array member so that we can easily store a character string in this member. Why is the *Graduated* member an integer member?

Finally, notice that the structure variable is *Fred,* which is different from the structure name *Student,* and is defined just after the closing brace of the structure declaration.

b.   enum Colors {Blue, Black, Yellow, Red, Green};
    struct Automobile
     {
      int Year;
      Colors Color;
      float Price;
     } Ford, Chevy, Dodge;

You see two different twists in this structure definition. First, the enumerated data type *Colors* is used as the data type of the *Color* member. Thus, the automobile color can be Blue, Black, Yellow, Red, or Green. Of course, the enumerated data type *Colors* must be defined prior to the structure definition.

Second, you see that the structure has three variables: *Ford, Chevy,* and *Dodge.* This creates three separate structures of the same format in memory, one for each structure variable.

c.   enum Conditions {Clear, Cloudy, Rain};
    struct Weather
     {
      char Date[10];

```
     float Temperature;
     float Pressure;
     Conditions Condition;
   } Morning, Afternoon, Evening, Night;
```

Here again, an enumerated data type is employed for the weather *Condition* member. In addition, four structure variables are defined so that a separate weather structure can be stored for morning, afternoon, evening, and night.

Example 11-2:

In Example 11-1, the structure variables were defined immediately after the respective structure declarations. Assuming that this was not done, define the same variables for these structures that could be inserted anyplace in the program prior to their use to access the respective structure.

Solution:

a. Student Fred;

b. Automobile Ford;
   Automobile Chevy;
   Automobile Dodge;

c. Weather Morning;
   Weather Afternoon;
   Weather Evening;
   Weather Night;

In each of the above cases, the respective structure name is listed, followed by the variable that will be used to access the structure. Thus, a structure variable can be created immediately after the structure declaration or anyplace in the program code prior to its use.

Initializing Structures When They Are Defined

Structure variables can be initialized when they are defined just like any other variable. This means that they can be initialized if they are defined as part of the structure declaration or anywhere where they are defined after the structure declaration.

To initialize a structure variable you must use an assignment operator, =, after the variable and place the initializing values within curly braces. Here's the general format:

INITIALIZING STRUCTURE VARIABLES

```
<structure name> <structure variable name> = {member 1 value,
                                              member 2 value,
                                                     •
                                                     •
                                              member n value};
```

As an example, let's consider the *Student* structure that was declared in Example 11-1. Here's the declaration again:

```
struct Student
{
  char Name[30];
  int Student_Number;
  int Year_Enrolled;
  float GPA;
  int Graduated;
};
```

Applying this format we can initialize the variable *Fred* as follows:

```
Student Fred = {"Fred Smith",
               12345,
               1990,
               3.15,
               0};
```

Here, you will find a value for each of the members declared in the *Student* structure. As you can see, an assignment operator is used with the individual initializing values separated by commas and enclosed within curly braces following the assignment operator. The order of the initializing values must be the same as that of their respective members in the structure declaration. The initializing values could have been listed on the same line as the variable, but good style dictates that each initializing value appear on a separate line just like its respective member declaration. This allows anyone looking at the code to immediately associate an initializing value with a member name in the structure.

Example 11-3:

In Example 11-1 we declared a *Weather* structure. Then, in Example 11-2 we defined four variables for this structure. Repeat the structure declaration and variable definitions; however, this time initialize the *Afternoon* variable to the following values:

Date:	12/28/94
Temperature:	41
Pressure:	30.15
Condition:	Cloudy

Solution:

Here is the *Weather* structure declaration from Example 11-1:

```
enum Conditions {Clear, Cloudy, Rain};
struct Weather
{
  char Date[10];
  float Temperature;
  float Pressure;
  Conditions Condition;
};
```

To define the four variables, you must list the structure name followed by the variable names. To initialize any of the variables you must use an assignment operator followed by the initializing values enclosed within curly braces. Using this idea, the *Weather* variables are defined as follows.

```
Weather Morning;
Weather Evening;
Weather Night;
Weather Afternoon = {"12/28/94",
              41,
              30.15,
              Cloudy
            };
```

You see that the *Afternoon* variable is initialized, while the others are not. If any of the other variables must be initialized you use the same format. The variable *Afternoon* was placed last in the variable listing for clarity. Actually, this variable, along with its initializing values, could be placed anywhere in the variable listing as long as the correct syntax is applied.

Quick Check

1. True or False: All the members of a given structure must have the same data type.
2. Declare a structure called *Account* that has four floating point members named *Deposits*, *Withdrawals*, *Interest_Rate*, and *Balance*.
3. Define an unitialized variable called *Checkbook* for the structure you declared in question 2.
4. Define a variable called *Passbook* for the structure you declared in question 2 and initialize it to the following values:

> Deposits of $1500.00
> Withdrawals of $500
> Interest Rate of 10%
> Balance of $2345.49

11-2 STRUCTURE ACCESS

When accessing a structure, you will either store information into the structure or retrieve information from the structure. Of course, you are actually accessing the members that make up the structure when storing or retrieving structure data. You can access the structure members in one of two ways: (1) By using the dot, •, operator, or (2) By using the pointer, →, operator.

Storing Information into Structures

You can get information into a structure through initialization, direct assignment, or reading from the keyboard. The initialization process has already been discussed, so let's see how direct assignment and reading from the keyboard works.

Direct Assignment

When assigning information to a structure, you must assign the information directly to the respective member within the structure. How can you access a given member? Well, think about the structure declaration and variable definition. How do you access the structure itself? By using the structure variable, right?

Next, how do you suppose you would access a given member within the structure? Of course, by using its member name! So, the ***path*** to a given member within the structure is via the structure variable and the respective member name.

Consider the *Student* structure in Example 11-1. Suppose you wish to store a name in the *Name* member. Ask yourself: "Self, what *path* must I take to get to the name member?" Well, you must use the structure variable, *Fred*, to get you to the structure and the member name, *Name*, to get you to the required member within the structure. You must provide the path to a given member using the dot operator or the pointer operator.

Using the Dot Operator to Access Structure Data

Here's the C++ syntax required when using the dot operator:

> ### *ASSIGNING DATA TO STRUCTURES USING THE DOT OPERATOR*
>
> <structure variable name> • <member name> = data;

Notice that the structure variable name is listed first, followed by the dot operator, •, followed by the required member name, an assignment operator, =, and the data to be stored. Here are just a few examples of how you might store information into the structures and variables declared/defined in Example 11-1.

```
Fred . Name = "Fred Smith";
Fred . Student_Number = 0001;
Fred . Year_Enrolled = 1990;
Fred . GPA = 4.0;
Fred . Graduated = 1;
```

As you can see, the "dot"" notation provides a path directly to the member in which the information is to be stored. One final point: The data being stored in a given member should be the same data type that has been declared for that member.

Using The Pointer Operator to Access Structure Data

The structure pointer operator, →, is specifically designed for accessing structure data. To use this operator you must first define a pointer variable to point to the structure. Then, simply use the pointer operator to point to a given member. Recall our *Student* structure declared earlier. We can define a pointer to this structure as follows:

```
Student  Stu, *Fred;
Fred = &Stu;
```

Now, this defines *Fred* as a pointer variable which points to the entire *Student* structure. To get to the individual members within the structure you must use the pointer, →, operator. Here is the general format for the pointer operator:

ASSIGNING DATA TO STRUCTURES USING THE POINTER OPERATOR

<structure pointer> → <member name> = data;

Using this format, the members within the Student structure can be assigned data as follows:

```
Fred -> Name = "Fred Smith";
Fred -> Student_Number = 0001;
Fred -> Year_Enrolled = 1990;
Fred -> GPA = 4.0;
Fred -> Graduated = 1;
```

Of course, the variable *Fred* must be defined as a pointer variable to use the pointer operator. Notice also that the pointer operator is coded by using a dash, –, followed by a right angle bracket, >. No space is allowed between the two symbols.

Reading Information into a Structure

Now suppose you want the user to enter the information into the structure via the system keyboard. When this is desired, you simply employ an input statement, while accessing the members using either the dot or pointer operators. As an example, suppose the user must enter information into the *Student* structure declared in Example 11-1. If *Fred* is defined as an ordinary structure variable, you use the dot operator like this:

```
cout << "\n\nEnter the student name:  ";
gets (Fred . Name);
```

```
cout << "\n\nEnter the student number:  ";
cin >> Fred . Student_Number;
cout << "\n\nEnter the year the student enrolled:  ";
cin >> Fred . Year_Enrolled;
cout << "\n\nEnter the student GPA:  ";
cin >> Fred . GPA;
cout << "\n\nHas the student graduated? (Y/N):  ";
cin >> Answer;
if (Answer == 'y' || Answer == 'Y')
  Fred . Graduated = 1;
else
  Fred . Graduated = 0;
```

As you can see, the appropriate user prompts have been inserted via *cout* statements. The respective data is then read from the keyboard using a *gets()* function or *cin* statement. Notice that a *gets()* function is employed to obtain the string data. In addition, an **if/else** statement is used to make the correct Boolean assignment on the *Graduated* member.

Now, if *Fred* is defined as a pointer variable to the structure, you use the pointer operator like this:

```
cout << "\n\nEnter the student name:  ";
gets (Fred -> Name);
cout << "\n\nEnter the student number:  ";
cin >> Fred -> Student_Number;
cout << "\n\nEnter the year the student enrolled:  ";
cin >> Fred -> Year_Enrolled;
cout << "\n\nEnter the student GPA:  ";
cin >> Fred -> GPA;
cout << "\n\nHas the student graduated? (Y/N):  ";
char Answer;
cin >> Answer;
if (Answer == 'y' || Answer == 'Y')
  Fred -> Graduated = 1;
else
  Fred -> Graduated = 0;
```

Retrieving Information from Structures

You retrieve structure information using the assignment operator or a *cout* statement. Again, either the dot or structure pointer operator can be employed to access the members. Here's the general format:

RETRIEVING STRUCTURE INFORMATION USING ASSIGNMENT

<variable name> = <structure variable name> • <member name>;

or

<variable name> = <structure pointer> → <member name>;

RETRIEVING STRUCTURE INFORMATION USING cout

cout << <structure variable name> • <member name>;

or

cout << <structure pointer> → <member name>;

Here are some examples using the *Student* structure defined in Example 11-1:

```
Number = Fred . Student_Number;
Grad = Fred -> Graduated;
cout << Fred . Name;
cout << Fred -> GPA;
```

The first two statements show how the assignment operator is used to copy the structure information to another variable within the program. The first statement employs the dot operator and the second statement employs the structure pointer operator to access the member. Remember, however, that the variable *Fred* must be defined as an ordinary structure variable to use the dot operator. To use the structure pointer operator, *Fred* must be defined as a pointer variable to the structure. Clearly, the variable receiving the assignment must be defined as the same data type as the respective member information. Consequently, *Number* and *Grad* must be defined as integers for this application.

The second two statements show how *cout* is employed to retrieve structure information. Again, either the dot operator or the structure pointer operator can be used to get to the required structure member, depending on how the structure variable is defined.

Example 11-4:

Your instructor needs a student structure consisting of the following items:

- Student name
- Student number
- Major
- Semester test scores
- Semester test average
- Equivalent letter grade of the test average

a. Declare an appropriate structure.
b. Write a function that will allow the instructor to fill the structure from the keyboard.
c. Write a function that will display the contents of the structure.

Solution:

a. The structure is a student structure for a given class. Consequently, let's give the structure an appropriate name, such as *Student*. Then, we can use the class name, such as *CS1*, as the structure variable to access the grades of a given class.

Next, there are six members that need to be declared as part of the structure. Let's call them *Name*, *Student_Number*, *Major*, *Test_Scores*, *Test_Average*, and *Test_Grade*. The *Name*, *Student_Number*, and *Major* members will be declared as character array members because they will store string values.

Since several individual test scores must be stored, we will declare the *Test_Scores* member as an array of floating point elements. That's right, a member within a structure can be an array!

Next, we will declare the *Test_Average* member an integer member, since we will use a rounded-off average of the test scores.

Finally, the *Grade* member must be a character member to represent a letter grade. Here's a structure declaration that will work:

```
struct Student
  {
    char Name[30];
    char Student_Number[15];
    char Major[20];
    float Test_Scores[15];
    float Test_Average;
    char Test_Grade;
  } Stu, *CS1;

CS1 = &Stu;
```

Notice in particular that the *Test_Scores* member is declared as an array of fifteen floating point elements. The value 15 was used to allow for a maximum of fifteen test scores. The structure variable is a pointer variable called *CS1*.

b. Here's a function that will fill the structure:

```
void Fill_Structure(Student *S)
{
  int Test_Total = 0;
  cout << "\nEnter the student name:  ";
  gets(S -> Name);
  cout << "Enter the student number:  ";
  gets(S -> Student_Number);
  cout << "Enter the student major:  ";
  gets(S -> Major);
  cout << "How many test scores are there?  ";
  cin >> Number;
  for (int i = 0; i < Number; ++i)
  {
    cout << "Enter test score " << i + 1 << ": ";
    cin >> S -> Test_Scores[i];
    Test_Total += S -> Test_Scores[i];
  }
  S -> Test_Average = Test_Total/Number;
  if (S -> Test_Average < 60)
    S -> Test_Grade = 'F';
  if (S -> Test_Average >= 60 && S -> Test_Average < 70)
    S -> Test_Grade = 'D';
  if (S -> Test_Average >= 70 && S -> Test_Average < 80)
    S -> Test_Grade = 'C';
  if (S -> Test_Average >= 80 && S -> Test_Average < 90)
    S -> Test_Grade = 'B';
  if (S -> Test_Average >= 90 && S -> Test_Average <= 100)
    S -> Test_Grade = 'A';
}
```

First, observe the function header. The function name is *Fill_Structure*. There is a single reference parameter, *S*. It is important to note that *S* is a pointer variable which has a data type of *Student*, which is the structure we declared in part a. This allows a pointer to the *Student* structure to be passed by reference to the function. The structure variable in the calling program will be the structure pointer variable, *CS1*, while the structure variable within the function is the structure pointer variable *S*. Consequently, any operations on the structure within this function employ the pointer variable, *S*.

Next you see that a local function variable called *Test_Total* is defined. You will observe its use shortly.

Now look at how the structure is being filled. The structure pointer, *S*, must be referenced here, since it will take on the values of the structure pointer, *CS1*, in the calling program. Notice that in all cases the structure pointer operator, →, is employed to fill the respective members. The first member to be filled is the *Name* member. This is accomplished by prompting the user and reading the member name, *Name,* using the *gets()* function. After the student name is read, the user is prompted to enter the student number and major. This information is read into the structure and stored using the member names *Student_Number* and *Major*, respectively.

Next, the user is prompted for the number of test scores that will be entered into the structure. A global variable, *Number*, receives this value. This value is needed to control the number of times that the subsequent **for** loop will be executed.

A **for** loop is used to fill the *Test_Scores* array. A local variable, *i*, is incremented from 0 to the number (*Number*) of test scores. With each loop iteration, the user is prompted for the respective score value and the corresponding entry is read into the *Test_Scores* array. In addition to filling the array member, the **for** loop calculates a running total (*Test_Total*) of the test scores as they are entered.

The next member to be filled is the *Test_Average* member. Observe that this member is filled using an assignment statement. The total sum of the test scores (*Test_Total*) is divided by the number of scores (*Number*) and assigned to the *Test_Average* member.

Finally, the *Test_Grade* member is filled using a series of **if** statements. As you can see, the **if** statements translate the numerical average to a letter grade. A given **if** simply assigns the appropriate letter grade to the *Test_Grade* member. Here is a sample of what the user will see when this function is executed:

```
Enter the student name:  Bjarne Stroustrup↵
Enter the student number:  1↵
Enter the student major:  Computer Science↵
How many test scores are there?  3↵
Enter test score 1:  98.7↵
Enter test score 2:  97↵
Enter test score 3:  95.2↵
```

c. A function to display the student structure is given below:

```
void Display_Structure(Student *S)
{
```

```
    cout << "\nStudent Name:  " << S -> Name
        << "\n\n\tStudent Number: " << S -> Student_Number
        << "\n\tMajor:  " << S -> Major
        << "\n\tTest Scores:  ";
  for (int i = 0; i < Number; ++i)
    cout  << S -> Test_Scores[i] << ", ";
  cout << "\n\tTest Average:  " << S -> Test_Average
        << "\n\tTest Grade:  " << S -> Test_Grade;
}
```

Again, the function employs a pointer parameter, *S, that will receive the structure pointer from the calling program. This becomes the structure pointer variable within the function. The student's name, number, and major are displayed first along with appropriate headings. Then the individual test scores are displayed using a **for** loop. Notice the use of the global variable *Number*. *Number* represents the number of test scores that have been entered. How is this value obtained by the *Display_Structure* function? Well, *Number* will be defined as a global variable. As a result, both functions have access to its value. This is a classic use of a global variable.

After the individual test scores are displayed, the *Test_Average* and *Test_Grade* members are displayed, respectively.

Here is the display generated by the *Display_Structure()* function with the values obtained by the *Fill_Structure()* function:

Student Name: Bjarne Stroustrup

       Student Number: 1
       Major: Computer Science
       Test Scores: 98.7, 97, 95.2,
       Test Average: 96
       Test Grade: A

Finally, you might be wondering what the entire program looks like. Here it is:

```
#include <iostream.h>
#include <stdio.h>

// STUDENT STRUCTURE DECLARATION
struct Student
  {
    char Name[30];
    char Student_Number[15];
    char Major[20];
    float Test_Scores[25];
```

```
   float Test_Average;
    char Test_Grade;
 } Stu, *CS1;

// FUNCTION PROTOTYPES
void Fill_Structure(Student *);
void Display_Structure(Student *);

// GLOBAL VARIABLES
int Number;

void main()
{
  CS1 = &Stu;
  Fill_Structure(CS1);
  Display_Structure(CS1);
}

// THIS FUNCTION WILL FILL THE STUDENT STRUCTURE WITH
// VALUES ENTERED FROM THE KEYBOARD
void Fill_Structure(Student *S)
{
  int Test_Total = 0;
  cout << "\nEnter the student name:  ";
  gets(S -> Name);
  cout << "Enter the student number:  ";
  gets(S -> Student_Number);
  cout << "Enter the student major:  ";
  gets(S -> Major);
  cout << "How many test scores are there?:  ";
  cin >> Number;
  for (int i = 0; i < Number; ++i)
  {
    cout << "Enter test score " << i + 1 << ":  ";
    cin >> S -> Test_Scores[i];
    Test_Total += S -> Test_Scores[i];
  }
  S -> Test_Average = Test_Total/Number;
  if (S -> Test_Average < 60)
    S -> Test_Grade = 'F';
  if (S -> Test_Average >= 60 && S -> Test_Average < 70)
    S -> Test_Grade = 'D';
  if (S -> Test_Average >= 70 && S -> Test_Average < 80)
    S -> Test_Grade = 'C';
  if (S -> Test_Average >= 80 && S -> Test_Average < 90)
```

```
        S -> Test_Grade = 'B';
    if (S -> Test_Average >= 90 && S -> Test_Average <= 100)
        S -> Test_Grade = 'A';
}

// THIS FUNCTION WILL FILL DISPLAY THE STUDENT STRUCTURE
void Display_Structure(Student *S)
{
  cout << "\nStudent Name:  " << S -> Name
       << "\n\n\tStudent Number: " << S -> Student_Number
       << "\n\tMajor:  " << S -> Major
       << "\n\tTest Scores:  ";
  for (int i = 0; i < Number; ++i)
      cout << S -> Test_Scores[i] << ", ";
  cout << "\n\tTest Average:  " << S -> Test_Average
       << "\n\tTest Grade:  " << S -> Test_Grade;
}
```

It is important to note that the structure is declared prior to *main()* so that the function prototypes can employ this structure as a data type. Observe that the function prototypes list a pointer to the structure name, *Student*, as the parameter in each case. Thus, each function expects to receive a pointer to the *Student* structure. The actual structure pointer variable, *CS1*, is defined at the beginning of *main()* and passed to the functions when they are called. That's all there is to it!

 Quick Check

Use the following structure definition to answer questions 1–9:

```
            struct Account
            {
              float Deposits;
              float Withdrawals;
              float Interest_Rate;
              float Balance;
            } Checkbook, Pass, *Passbook;
            Passbook = &Pass;
```

1. The structure variables are _____.
2. Write a statement to assign a value of $250.00 to the *Deposits* member of the *Checkbook* structure.

3. Write a statement to assign a value of 12% to the *Interest_Rate* member of the *Passbook* structure.

4. Write a statement to allow the user to input a value for the *Withdrawals* member of the *Checkbook* structure.

5. Write a statement to allow the user to input a value for the *Deposits* member of the *Passbook* structure.

6. Write a statement to display the account balance in the *Checkbook* structure.

7. Write a statement to display the account balance in the *Passbook* structure.

8. Write the header for a function called *Input()* that would obtain user entries for the *Checkbook* structure.

9. Write a header for a function called *Output()* that would display the contents of the *Passbook* structure.

11-3 STRUCTURES OF STRUCTURES ⇒ NESTED STRUCTURES

Now that you know how to work with single structures, it is time to literally build on this knowledge and create structures of structures. That's right, we can create a structure that contains other structures, called *nested structures.*

A *nested structure* is a structure within a structure. In other words, a nested structure is a member of another structure.

In the last section, we worked with a student structure that contained the student's name, number, major, and test results. From an organizational perspective, it might make more sense to create a separate structure to hold the test results and include, or nest, this structure inside of the student structure. This way those test members that relate closely to each other are stored in a separate structure. Thus, our new nested student structure will contain the following members:

- A student name member

- A student number member

- A major member

- A nested structure member that contains test results

Here are the required C++ declarations:

```
struct Tests
{
  float Test_Scores[15];
  float Test_Average;
  char Test_Grade;
};

struct Student
{
    char Name[30];
    char Student_Number[15];
    char Major[20];
    Tests Test;
} Stu, *CS1;
```

Next, we will define a pointer variable to point to the *Student* structure as follows:

```
CS1 = &Stu;
```

As you can see, the nested *Tests* structure is declared first, then included as a member within the main *Student* structure. The declaration for a nested structure uses the same format as that of any structure declaration. In the main *Student* structure, the nested *Tests* structure becomes the data type for the *Test* member. Thus, each member within the nested structure actually forms a sub-member of the main structure member. You can actually have multiple levels of nesting. In other words, you can have a structure within a structure within a structure, and so on.

Now you are probably wondering how you can gain access to the nested structure members. For instance, how can you get to the *Test_Scores* member within the nested *Tests* structure? Well, the structure pointer variable, *CS1*, will get you into the main *Student* structure, then the nested member *Test* will get you into the nested structure, *Tests,* and finally the member name, *Test_Scores*, will get you into the required member. Thus assignment statements such as:

```
CS1 -> Test . Test_Scores[0] = 95;
CS1 -> Test . Test_Scores[1] = 87;
CS1 -> Test . Test_Scores[2] = 93;
```

would allow you to place three test scores into the *Test_Scores* member. Here, both the structure pointer variable (*CS1*) and the nested structure member name

(*Test*) must be referenced within the statement followed by the desired sub-member name. Listing the structure pointer followed by the nested structure member name "opens up'" any sub-members within the nested structure. In this case we have opened up the *Test_Scores[]* sub-member. Notice that the structure pointer operator is used to access the member in the main *Student* structure and the dot operator is employed to access the sub-member in the nested *Tests* structure. Now, using this idea, let's construct a function to fill this new student structure. Here it is:

```
void Fill_Structure(Student *S)
{
  int Test_Total = 0;
  cout << "\nEnter the student name:  ";
  gets(S -> Name);
  cout << "Enter the student number:  ";
  gets(S -> Student_Number);
  cout << "Enter the student major:  ";
  gets(S -> Major);
  cout << "How many test scores are there?:  ";
  cin >> Test_Number;
  for (int i = 0; i < Test_Number; ++i)
  {
     cout << "Enter test score " << i + 1 << ": ";
     cin >> S -> Test . Test_Scores[i];
     Test_Total += S -> Test . Test_Scores[i];
  }
  S -> Test . Test_Average = Test_Total/Test_Number;
  if (S -> Test . Test_Average < 60)
     S -> Test . Test_Grade = 'F';
  if (S -> Test . Test_Average >= 60 && S -> Test . Test_Average < 70)
     S -> Test . Test_Grade = 'D';
  if (S -> Test . Test_Average >= 70 && S -> Test . Test_Average < 80)
     S -> Test . Test_Grade = 'C';
  if (S -> Test . Test_Average >= 80 && S -> Test . Test_Average < 90)
     S -> Test . Test_Grade = 'B';
  if (S -> Test.Test_Average >= 90 && S -> Test.Test_Average <= 100)
     S -> Test . Test_Grade = 'A';
}
```

Look at the function header and you will see that the function expects to receive a pointer to the main structure, *Student*. Even though the *Student* structure contains a nested structure, all we need to pass to the function is a pointer to the main structure. Within the function, you will find that the nested structure members are simply accessed using the pointer to the main structure member, followed by a dot to the nested structure sub-member as described above. Once the nested structures are "opened up'" using their respective names, the sub-members are filled directly using the respective sub-member names. Study the above function! You should now have all the prerequisite knowledge to understand its operation.

How about a function to display the contents of the foregoing structure? Here's one that will do the job:

```
void Display_Structure(Student *S)
{
  cout << "\nStudent Name:  " << S -> Name
       << "\n\n\tStudent Number: " << S -> Student_Number
       << "\n\tMajor:  " << S -> Major
       << "\n\tTest Scores:  ";
  for (int i = 0; i < Test_Number; ++i)
     cout  << S -> Test.Test_Scores[i] << ", ";
  cout << "\n\tTest Average:  " << S -> Test.Test_Average
       << "\n\tTest Grade:  " << S -> Test.Test_Grade;
}
```

Now, let's place these two functions in a program that will allow the user to fill and display the structure. Here's the program:

```
#include <iostream.h>
#include <stdio.h>

// TESTS STRUCTURE DECLARATION
struct Tests
{
  float Test_Scores[15];
  float Test_Average;
  char Test_Grade;
};

// STUDENT STRUCTURE DECLARATION
struct Student
{
  char Name[30];
  char Student_Number[15];
  char Major[20];
  Tests Test;
} Stu, *CS1;
```

```
// FUNCTION PROTOTYPES
void Fill_Structure(Student *);
void Display_Structure(Student *);

// GLOBAL VARIABLES
int Test_Number;

void main()
{
  CS1 = &Stu;
  Fill_Structure(CS1);
  Display_Structure(CS1);
}

// THIS FUNCTION WILL FILL THE STUDENT STRUCTURE WITH
// VALUES ENTERED FROM THE KEYBOARD
void Fill_Structure(Student *S)
{
  int Test_Total = 0;
  cout << "\nEnter the student name:  ";
  gets(S -> Name);
  cout << "Enter the student number:  ";
  gets(S -> Student_Number);
  cout << "Enter the student major:  ";
  gets(S -> Major);
  cout << "How many test scores are there?  ";
  cin >> Test_Number;
  for (int i = 0; i < Test_Number; ++i)
  {
    cout << "Enter test score " << i + 1 << ":  ";
    cin >> S -> Test.Test_Scores[i];
    Test_Total += S -> Test.Test_Scores[i];
  }
  S -> Test.Test_Average = Test_Total/Test_Number;
  if (S -> Test.Test_Average < 60)
    S -> Test.Test_Grade = 'F';
  if (S -> Test.Test_Average >= 60 && S -> Test.Test_Average < 70)
    S -> Test.Test_Grade = 'D';
  if (S -> Test.Test_Average >= 70 && S -> Test.Test_Average < 80)
    S -> Test.Test_Grade = 'C';
  if (S -> Test.Test_Average >= 80 && S -> Test.Test_Average < 90)
    S -> Test.Test_Grade = 'B';
  if (S -> Test.Test_Average >= 90 && S -> Test.Test_Average <= 100)
    S -> Test.Test_Grade = 'A';
}
```

```
// THIS FUNCTION WILL DISPLAY THE STUDENT STRUCTURE
void Display_Structure(Student *S)
{
  cout << "\nStudent Name:  " << S -> Name
       << "\n\n\tStudent Number: " << S -> Student_Number
       << "\n\tMajor:  " << S -> Major
       << "\n\tTest Scores:  ";
  for (int i = 0; i < Test_Number; ++i)
    cout  << S -> Test.Test_Scores[i] << ", ";
  cout << "\n\tTest Average:  " << S -> Test.Test_Average
       << "\n\tTest Grade:  " << S -> Test.Test_Grade;
}
```

You should now have all the knowledge you need to completely understand this program.

Quick Check

Use the following structure definitions to answer questions 1–6.

```
struct Address
{
  char *Street;
  char *City;
  char *State;
  char *Zip;
};
struct Employee
{
  char *Name;
  int ID;
  Address Addr;
  float Salary;
};
Employee  JD;
```

1. How are the structures nested?

2. Write a statement to assign "John Doe" for the employee name.

3. Write the statements to allow the user to enter the employee's state of residence.

4. Write the statements to allow the user to enter the employee's salary.
5. Write a header for a function called *Display_Employee()* that will display the data stored in the *Employee* structure.
6. Write the statements required for the function in question 5 to display the employee data.

CHAPTER SUMMARY

A structure is a collection of member data. Unlike an array, the elements that make up a structure, the members, can be different data types. Structures are declared in C++ using the keyword **struct**. In addition, a structure variable must be defined to access the structure information. Storage for a structure is not allocated until a variable is defined for that structure.

There are basically two ways to access structure information: By using the dot operator or by using the structure pointer operator. The dot operator is used when the structure variable is not a pointer variable, while the structure pointer operator is employed when the structure variable is defined as a pointer variable. To gain access to a member using dot notation, the structure variable is listed first, followed by a dot, followed by the member name. To gain access to a member using the pointer notation, the structure pointer variable is listed first, followed by a dash and right angle brace, ->, followed by the member name.

Nested structures are structures within structures. Thus, a nested structure is actually a member of another structure. A given nested structure is declared using the standard structure declaration format. The nested structure must be declared first, followed by the main structure. The main structure then includes the nested structure as the data type of a member within its declaration. When accessing nested structures, the nested structure member name must be listed in the dot and/or pointer notation path.

QUESTIONS AND PROBLEMS

Questions

1. What is a structure?
2. How do the contents of a structure differ from that of an array?
3. Why is a variable definition required to access a structure?
4. What two operators can be employed for accessing structure members?

5. True or False: Structures cannot be part of other structures.

6. True or False: Structure members can be initialized when the structure is declared.

7. True or False: A given structure can contain members of any legal data type.

Use the following structure declarations to answers questions 6–11 and problems 1–3.

```
// PITCHING STATS STRUCTURE DECLARATION
struct Pitching
{
  int Wins;
  int Losses;
  float ERA;
};

// HITTING STATS STRUCTURE DECLARATION
struct Batting
{
  int At_Bat;
  int Home_Runs;
  int RBIs;
  float Average;
};

// NL BASEBALL PITCHER STRUCTURE DECLARATION
struct Baseball_Pitcher
{
   char Name[30];
   char Team[30];
   int Year;
   Pitching Pitch;
   Batting Bat;
};

void main()
{
  Baseball_Pitcher Pitcher;
```

8. Explain the structure nesting.

9. Write statements to assign the structure members with the following data:

Name:	John Smoltz
Team:	Atlanta Braves
Year:	1989
Wins:	12
Losses:	11
ERA:	2.94
At Bats:	20
Home Runs:	0
RBIs:	11
Average:	.190

10. Write statements to display the structure data that was assigned in question 9.

11. Suppose that you define a pointer variable to the above *Baseball_Pitcher* structure as follows:

```
Baseball_Pitcher   Pitch, *Pitcher;
Pitcher = &Pitch;
```

Write a prototype for a function that would fill the structure members from keyboard entries.

Problems

Least Difficult

1. Write a function that uses a structure pointer variable to fill the structure members of the foregoing *Baseball_Pitcher* structure from the keyboard.

2. Write a function that uses a structure pointer variable to display the structure members of the foregoing *Baseball_Pitcher* structure.

3. Write a program that incorporates the functions you developed in problems 1 and 2 to fill and display a baseball pitcher's stats.

4. Declare a *Name* structure consisting of a person's last name, first name, and middle initial.

5. Define a variable for the structure in question 4 and write the code to initialize it with your name.

6. Declare an *Address* structure consisting of a street number, street name, city, state, and zip code.

7. Define a variable for the structure in question 6 and write the code to initialize it with your address.

8. Declare a *Person* structure consisting of the *Name* and *Address* structures declared in problems 4 and 6.

9. Write a function to fill the structure in question 8 from keyboard entries.

10. Write a function to display the contents of the structure declared in question 8.

11. Write a program that incorporates the functions developed in questions 9 and 10 to fill and display a person's name and address.

More Difficult

12. Modify the program given in Section 11-3 to include a nested structure for laboratory grades similar to the one given for test grades. Compile and execute your program to verify its operation.

INTRODUCTION TO OBJECT-ORIENTED PROGRAMMING (OOP)

INTRODUCTION

This chapter will introduce you to the important topic of object-oriented programming (OOP) and is intended to prepare you for further study of the topic. This means that you will need to study OOP further to become a competent object-oriented programmer.

Recall that C++ was first created to add object-oriented programming ability to the C language. With object-oriented programming, you construct complex programs from simpler program entities called *objects*, which are real instances, or specimens, of abstract *classes*. Object-oriented programs are organized as a collection of objects which cooperate with each other. Thus, object-oriented programming employs objects, rather than algorithms, as the fundamental building blocks for program development.

Object-oriented programming facilitates the extension and reuse of general purpose classes in other applications with minimal modification to the original code. Although this can be accomplished with ordinary functions in procedural programming, OOP provides an important feature called *inheritance* which is a mechanism of deriving new classes from existing ones. As a result, classes are related to each other to create a hierarchy of classes through inheritance. This inheritance feature also allows new applications to "inherit" code from existing applications, thereby making the programming chore much more productive.

In summary, the goals of OOP are to improve programmer productivity by managing software complexity via the use of classes and their associated objects which provide for reusable code via the class inheritance feature.

Up to this point you have been learning how to construct programs using a structured top/down approach. Although the overall design of any software is a top/down process, writing object-oriented programs requires a different approach. You create object-oriented programs from the inside out by expanding on classes. For example, you might approach a banking problem by creating a bank account class which defines the basic data that all accounts must contain (account number, balance, etc.) as well as the fundamental operations that are performed on bank accounts (deposit, withdrawal, etc.). This basic bank account class can then be expanded into classes that define specific types of bank accounts such as checking accounts, super-now accounts, savings accounts, and so on.

There are four concepts central to OOP: *encapsulation with information hiding*, *inheritance*, *polymorphism*, and *dynamic binding*. In this chapter you will be exposed to the idea of encapsulation and information hiding. The next chapter is devoted entirely to inheritance. The concepts of polymorphism and dynamic binding are beyond the scope of this text and, as a result, will only be covered lightly in the next chapter.

Object-oriented programming has its own unique terminology. Be sure to grasp the terminology as you progress through the chapter. A glossary of OOP terms is provided at the end of this text for quick reference.

12-1 CLASSES AND OBJECTS

A thorough understanding of classes and objects is essential to developing efficient object-oriented code. Before we get into a technical definition of classes and objects, let's try to develop a more intuitive idea of what they are.

The Idea of Classes and Objects

For now, you can think of a class as a template, or pattern, for its objects. If you have used a word processor you are aware that most word processing programs include templates for business letters, personal letters, interoffice memos, press releases, etc. (Note: Be aware that OOP uses the term *template* in a different sense than it is used here in word processing.) The idea is to first open one of the built-in general purpose template files when you want to generate, let's say, an interoffice memo. An example of such a template from Microsoft's Word for Windows® is provided in Figure 12-1.

InterOffice Memo

To:	Recipient
From:	Sender
Date:	January 23, 1994
Subject:	The Subject of the Memo

CC:

Figure 12-1 A *class* can be thought of as a template, or pattern, like this memo template from Microsoft's Word for Windows®.

As you can see, the template provides the accepted interoffice memo formatting, the memo type style, and any fixed information such as headings, and the date. Using this template you fill in all the variable information required for the memo, including the text of the memo as shown in Figure 12-2.

InterOffice Memo

To:	All C++ Students
From:	Prof. Andrew C. Staugaard, Jr.
Date:	October 14, 1993
Subject:	Classes and Objects

This memo represents an object of the class template shown in Figure 12-1. The class provides a general framework from which objects are created. It is important that you understand this concept.

CC:

Your Instructor

Figure 12-2 An *object* is a particular instance, or specimen, of a class like this memo is an instance of the memo template in Figure 12-1.

In other words, you provide the details that might make one memo different from another. You can think of a class as the memo template and the actual memo that you generate as an object of that template. Different memos made from the same memo template would represent unique objects of the same class. The class template provides the framework for each of its object memos. All the object memos would have the same general format and type style defined by the class template, but would have different text information defined by a given object memo. You could load in another template file, let's say for a business letter, that would represent a different class. Then using this template you could construct different object business letters from the business letter template.

The word *class* in OOP is used to impart the notion of classification. Objects defined for a class share the fundamental framework of the class. Thus, the class is common to the set of objects defined for it. In the above example the interoffice memo template defines the characteristics that are common to all interoffice memos created by Word for Windows®. In fact, many current word processing programs, like Word for Windows®, employ classes and objects for this purpose. A given class provides the foundation for creating specific objects, each of which share the general characteristics and *behavior* of the class.

As you can see from this example, classes and objects are closely related. In fact, it is difficult to discuss one without the other. The important difference is that a class is only an **abstraction**, or pattern, while an object is a real entity. The interoffice memo class is only an abstraction for the real memo object that can be physically created, printed, and mailed. As another example, think of a class of fish. The fish class describes the general characteristics and behavior of all fish. However, the notion of a fish only provides an abstraction of the real thing. To deal with the real thing, you must consider specific fish objects such as a bass, trout, marlin, and so on. A fish, in general, behaves as you would expect a fish to behave, but a particular kind of fish has its own unique behavior.

Classes

In order to completely understand the nature of a class, we must consider two levels of definition: the **abstract** level and the **implementation** level.

The Abstract Level

The abstract level of a class provides the *essence* of the class. Here's how we define a class at the abstract level.

At the abstract level, a **class** can be described as an *interface* that defines the behavior of its objects.

A class can be described as an interface, since its main purpose is to describe the operations, or functions, that can be performed by its objects. In this way, it defines the behavior common to all of its objects. By behavior, we mean how an object of a given class acts and reacts when it is accessed.

The abstract view of a class as an interface provides its *outside* view while hiding its internal structure and behavioral details. Thus, an object of a given class can be viewed as a black box as shown in Figure 12-3.

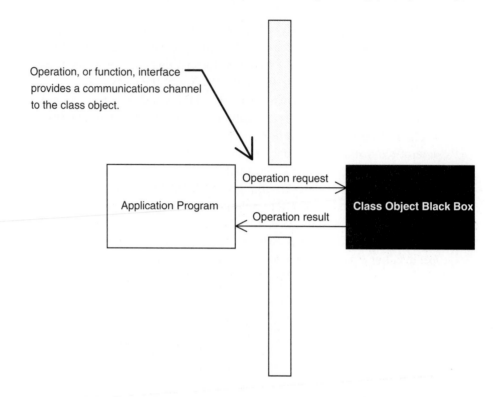

Operation, or function, interface
provides a communications channel
to the class object.

Application Program

Operation request

Operation result

Class Object Black Box

Figure 12-3 At the abstract level, a class is an interface that defines the behavior of its objects.

As you can see, the operation, or function, interface provides a communications channel to and from the class object. The application program generates an operation request to the object and the object responds with the desired result. The interface dictates *what* must be supplied to the object and *how* the object will respond. As a result, a class, through its operation interfaces, defines how its objects will behave. At the client application level, you treat the class object as a black box because you do not care about what goes on inside the object. All you care about is how to work with the object.

As a real example, suppose that we create a class of integers as illustrated in Figure 12-4. Arithmetic operations defined by this class would include addition, subtraction, multiplication, and division. These operations dictate how any objects defined for this class will behave. Let's take the addition operation as an example. The *Add()* function represents an interface to the class. In other words, *Add()* by its definition dictates that you must supply two integer arguments to be added and it will return the integer sum of the two. Do you care about the details of how the compiler implements addition or how the compiler represents integers in memory? Of course not! All you care about is what information needs to be supplied to the addition operation to perform its job, and what information is returned by the operation. In other words, all you care about is *what* must be supplied to the addition operation and *how* the operation will respond. This is behavior—how the object will act and react for a given operation.

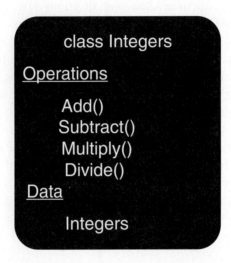

Figure 12-4 The integers can be implemented as a class where the arithmetic operations on integers define the behavior of the class objects.

The Implementation Level

The class implementation provides its *inside* view, showing the secrets of its data organization and function implementation. As a result, the class implementation reveals the secrets of its behavior, since it is primarily concerned with the operations that define the abstract level, or interface.

> At the implementation level, a ***class*** is a syntactical unit that describes a set of data and related operations that are common to its objects.

The implementation of a class consists of two major sections: (1) A public section, and (2) A private section. Any item declared in a class is called a class ***member***. Consequently, to implement a class we create public members and private members.

The Public Section

The public section of the class can consist of both ***member data*** and ***member functions***. The member data and functions are "public" because they can be accessed anywhere within the scope of a given class. In other words, member data can be changed and member functions can be called from outside the class, as long as the class is visible at the time of access. As you might suspect, it is the public member functions that form the interface to the class objects.

There is nothing special about public member functions, except that they are used to operate on the private members of the class. The important thing to remember is that *no functions outside of a given class can access the private members of the class*, unless they are special ***friend functions*** defined for a given class. Since friend functions are beyond the scope of this text, we will assume that *only* the member functions defined for a given class can access the private members of that class.

You should be aware that member functions are sometimes called ***methods*** in object-oriented programming.

The Private Section

The private section of a class can consist of both ***member data*** and ***member functions***. The private member data can be variables of any legal data type in C++ including *int*, *char*, *float*, *enum*, as well as arrays and pointers. In addition, private members can be functions. We say that these members are "private" because they are *only accessible by the public member functions defined for the class*. This means that the private member data can only be changed by the public member functions in the class or that private member functions can only be called by the public member functions.

The Class Declaration

The implementation level of a class can be clearly seen by its declaration format as follows:

CLASS DECLARATION FORMAT

```
class <class name>
{
public:
<return type> <function 1 name> (<function 1 parameter listing>);
<return type> <function 2 name> (<function 2 parameter listing>);
                    •
                    •
<return type> <function n name> (<function n parameter listing>);
<data type>  <variable name 1>;
<data type>  <variable name 2>;
                    •
                    •
<data type>  <variable name n>;

private:
<data type>  <variable name 1>;
<data type>  <variable name 2>;
                    •
                    •
<data type>  <variable name n>;
<return type> <function 1 name> (<function 1 parameter listing>);
<return type> <function 2 name> (<function 2 parameter listing>);
                    •
                    •
<return type> <function n name> (<function n parameter listing>);
};
```

The declaration begins with the keyword **class**, followed by the class name. The entire class declaration is enclosed in a set of curly braces. Normally, the public section of the class is declared first using the keyword **public** followed by a colon and a listing of the public members. The private section of the class is declared second using the keyword **private** followed by a colon and a listing of the private members of the class. You might see the public and private sections reversed in some texts; however, I will always declare the public section first, to emphasize the fact that the public member functions are the important aspect of the class, since they define the class behavior through its interface.

To declare a function as a member of a class, you simply list the function prototype, or interface. The entire member function definition, often called an ***implementation***, is provided after the class declaration.

Encapsulation

Encapsulation is simply the idea of packaging things together in a well-defined programming unit. If you are familiar with Pascal, a record is encapsulated, since it is a collection of data fields that are combined into a well-defined record unit. Likewise, in C and C++, a structure (struct) is encapsulated, since data fields are combined into a single structure unit. The class structure in C++ obviously provides for encapsulation by packaging both data and function members into a single class unit.

Encapsulation means to package data and/or operations into a single well-defined programming unit.

Information Hiding

The idea of encapsulation can be enhanced with ***information hiding***.

Information hiding means that there is a binding relationship between the information, or data, and its related operations such that operations outside of an encapsulated unit can not affect the information inside the unit.

With information hiding, there is a *binding* relationship between the information and the operations that are performed on that information. The class provides for information hiding in OOP. The public section provides the interface that is accessible outside the class and the private section provides the information that is only accessible from within the class itself. Only the member functions declared for the class can operate on the private class members. Thus, the private section of a class provides the information hiding. Without encapsulation and information hiding, there is no such binding relationship. In programming languages that do not support information hiding, you define data structures and the code that operates on those data structures separately. Then, you place both in a single source code file while attempting to treat the data and code as separate modules within the file. After all, isn't this the idea behind structured programming that has worked for you until now? Although such an approach seems reasonable, it can create problems. Since there is no defined, or explicit, binding relationship between the data and the code, another programmer could write functions to access and inadvertently change the data.

For instance, suppose that you are writing a program for a bank that calculates bank account interest. To write such a program you would define an account balance variable, among others, and write functions to change the balance based on deposits, withdrawals, interest rate, etc. These functions would be written according to the policies dictated by the bank, and the government for that matter. Would you want another programmer to be able to write functions that would affect the account balances differently than yours? Even worse, would you want the transactions of one account to affect the balance of another account? Of course not!

With information hiding you can truly separate the account data and the functions operating on those data into two separate sections, a private section and a public section, but bind them tightly together in an encapsulated class unit. Only those member functions in the public section can operate on the private account data. This means that outside functions written by another programmer cannot corrupt the data. Thus, only the operations that you have defined for a given type of account can be applied to that type of account and no others. In addition, these same operations applied to one account cannot affect another account of the same type. The class dictates the data format and legal operations for all accounts of a given type. Then, individual accounts of the same type are created as objects of the account class. Let's illustrate this idea with an example.

Encapsulation Without Information Hiding

Here is how a banking program might be coded using C, without the information hiding ability of C++.

```
#include <iostream.h>

//DECLARE Account STRUCTURE
struct Account
{
  float Balance;              // ACCOUNT BALANCE
  float Interest_Rate;        // MONTHLY INTEREST RATE

};
```

```
//FUNCTION PROTOTYPES
void Initialize(Account Acct, float Bal, float Rate);// INITIALIZE DATA
void Add_Interest(Account Acct);                 // ADD MONTHLY INTEREST
void Deposit(Account Acct, float Amount);        // ADD DEPOSIT
void Withdraw(Account Acct, float Amount);       // SUBTRACT WITHDRAWAL
float Current_Balance(Account Acct);             // RETURN BALANCE

void main()
{
//DEFINE STRUCTURE VARIABLES
   Account Acct1, Acct2;

//INITIALIZE STRUCTURE DATA AND ADD INTEREST
   Initialize(Acct1, 1000, 10);
   Current_Balance(Acct1);

//ATTEMPT TO CORRUPT ACCOUNT DATA
   Acct1.Balance = 1000000;             // THIS OPERATION IS LEGAL
                                        // USING A STRUCT
   Acct2.Balance = Acct1.Balance;       // THIS OPERATION IS LEGAL
                                        // USING A STRUCT

//OUTPUT ACCOUNT BALANCES
   cout << "\nYour new Account 1 balance is:  $" << Current_Balance(Acct1);
   cout << "\nYour new Account 2 balance is:  $" << Current_Balance(Acct2);
}

// INITIALIZE STRUCTURE DATA
void Initialize(Account Acct, float Bal, float Rate)
{
   Acct.Balance = Bal;
   Acct.Interest_Rate = Rate;
}

// CALCULATE MONTHLY BALANCE
void Add_Interest(Account Acct)
{
   Acct.Balance += Acct.Balance * Acct.Interest_Rate/12/100;
}

// ADD DEPOSIT
void Deposit(Account Acct, float Amount)
{
   Acct.Balance += Amount;
}
```

```
// SUBTRACT DEPOSIT
void Withdraw(Account Acct, float Amount)
{
  Acct.Balance -= Amount;
}


// RETURN MONTHLY BALANCE
float Current_Balance(Account Acct)
{
  return(Acct.Balance);
}
```

This program starts off by declaring a bank account structure called *Account*. The structure defines the account variables and is encapsulated, since the account variables are packaged within a single structure (struct). Five functions, called *Initialize()*, *Add_Interest()*, *Deposit()*, *Withdraw()*, and *Current_Balance()* are prototyped and defined to initialize the structure variables, add monthly interest to the balance, make a deposit, make a withdrawal, and return the account balance, respectively. Two structure variables, called *Acct1* and *Acct2*, are defined at the beginning of *main()*. Notice that function *Initialize()* is called to initialize the *Acct1* structure. The account balance is set to $1000 and the interest rate is set to 10%. A call to function *Add_Interest()* is then made to calculate a new monthly balance. Next, a successful attempt is made to alter the balance in both accounts, resulting in the following balances:

> Your new Account 1 balance is: $1000000
> Your new Account 2 balance is: $1000000

Wow! Both accounts have been corrupted, most likely illegally, by the insertion of two lines of code. Not only has the *Acct1* balance been corrupted, but the corrupted *Acct1* balance has been transferred to *Acct2*. This can only happen if the data and related functions are not tightly bound, as is the case with this structure and its related functions. This points out a definite weakness in the traditional algorithmic approach to programming.

Encapsulation With Information Hiding

Now let's see how to protect the bank account data using a class. Look closely at the following program:

```
#include <iostream.h>

//DECLARE Account CLASS
class Account
{
public:
  void Initialize(float Bal, float Rate);     // INITIALIZE PRIVATE DATA
  void Add_Interest();                        // ADD MONTHLY INTEREST
  void Deposit(float Amount);                 // ADD DEPOSIT
  void Withdraw(float Amount);                // SUBTRACT WITHDRAWAL
  float Current_Balance();                    // RETURN BALANCE

private:
  float Balance;                              // ACCOUNT BALANCE
  float Interest_Rate;                        // MONTHLY INTEREST RATE
};

void main()
{
//DEFINE ACCOUNT OBJECTS
  Account Acct1, Acct2;

//INITIALIZE OBJECT DATA AND ADD INTEREST
  Acct1.Initialize(1000, 10);
  Acct1.Add_Interest();

//ATTEMPT TO CORRUPT ACCOUNT DATA
// Acct1.Balance = 1000000;          // THIS OPERATION IS ILLEGAL
                                     // USING A CLASS
// Acct2.Balance = Acct1.Balance;    // THIS OPERATION IS ILLEGAL
                                     // USING A CLASS

//OUTPUT ACCOUNT BALANCES
  cout << "\nYour new Account 1 balance is:  $" << Acct1.Current_Balance();
  cout << "\nYour new Account 2 balance is:  $" << Acct2.Current_Balance();
}

// INITIALIZE ACCOUNT OBJECT DATA
void Account :: Initialize(float Bal, float Rate)
{
  Balance = Bal;
  Interest_Rate = Rate;
}
```

```
// CALCULATE MONTHLY BALANCE
void Account :: Add_Interest()
{
  Balance += Balance * Interest_Rate/12/100;
}


// ADD DEPOSIT
void Account :: Deposit(float Amount)
{
  Balance += Amount;
}


// SUBTRACT DEPOSIT
void Account :: Withdraw(float Amount)
{
  Balance -= Amount;
}


// RETURN MONTHLY BALANCE
float Account :: Current_Balance()
{
  return(Balance);
}
```

This program does basically the same thing as the previous program. Don't worry about the coding details for now, as they will be covered shortly. This time the bank account is declared as a class. The class consists of the same account variables as the earlier struct; however, they are now private members of the class and can only be accessed by the public member functions of the class. There are five public member functions: *Initialize(), Add_Interest(), Deposit(), Withdraw()* and *Current_Balance()*. These functions accomplish the same tasks as the functions defined in the previous program. At the beginning of *main()* you see two objects, *Acct1* and *Acct2*, defined for the *Account* class. The *Acct1* object data are then initialized by a call to the *Initialize()* function and a new monthly balance is calculated for this account by calling the *Add_Interest()* function. Next, an attempt is made to corrupt the balances of both the *Acct1* and *Acct2* objects. However, in this program the attempt is unsuccessful as verified by the following account balance values:

Your new Account 1 balance is: $1008.75
You new Account 2 balance is: $0

Notice that the *Acct1* balance reflects the interest calculation and would not be corrupted by the illegal assignment to $1000000. Likewise, the *Acct2* balance remains $0, indicating that it would not be corrupted by the assignment of the *Acct1* balance. In fact, these two assignment statements have been commented out of the program because they are illegal operations and will cause a compile error. This means that the compiler will enforce information hiding when using a class.

The effect of this program is to bind the data and the code operating on that data so tightly that the data cannot be corrupted by any outside code. This is encapsulation with information hiding! The private section of a class hides the data from any operations that are not defined for the class. It is difficult to provide information hiding in some programming languages, like C, since the overhead is too great. On the other hand, a class in C++ inherently enforces information hiding.

There is a cost, however. You must use a function call to access private data. This reduces the efficiency of the code slightly. On the other hand, using the compiler to enforce the rules that relate data to code can pay off in a big way when it comes time to debug a large program. In addition, object-oriented code is much easier to maintain, since the classes and their objects closely match the application. Finally, once object-oriented code is developed for a given application program, it can be easily re-used in another program that has a similar application. Consider a windows program. All windowing programs employ the same window classes. To create a new windows application program you simply "inherit" the general window classes and customize them to the new application.

The ideas of encapsulation and information hiding are not new. Only languages like Ada, Module II, and C++ that easily and efficiently provide for encapsulation and information hiding are new. These concepts have been around as long as computers. Common examples of information hiding include those data and routines that are part of BIOS to control your PC keyboard, monitor, and file access. Also, the file handling routines built into most compilers employ information hiding. Imagine what would happen if you could inadvertently corrupt these data and routines (system crash, lost unrecoverable files, etc.). You can use these built-in routines just by knowing how to operate them, but you cannot get at the inner workings of the routines. Likewise, you can operate your CD player via its controls without worrying about the inner workings of the player. Imagine what might happen if a non-technical user could get to the inner workings of your CD player. This is why it is so important to think of a class in the abstract sense of an interface.

You should be aware that some texts equate encapsulation with information hiding. However, remember that encapsulation does not necessarily relate to information hiding. Each language permits various parts of a programming entity to be accessible to the outside world. Those parts that are not visible to the outside world represent the information hiding aspect of encapsulation. Pascal records, for example, are encapsulated and permit all record data to be visible and manipulated by outside operations and, therefore, do not provide any information hiding. C++ classes are encapsulated, but in addition provide information hiding through the private declaration section of the class.

Now, let's take a closer look at the foregoing *Account* class declaration. Here is the declaration again, without the rest of the program:

```
class Account
{
public:
    void Initialize(float Bal, float Rate);     // INITIALIZE PRIVATE DATA
    void Add_Interest();                        // ADD MONTHLY INTEREST
    void Deposit(float Amount);                 // ADD DEPOSIT
    void Withdraw(float Amount);                // SUBTRACT WITHDRAWAL
    float Current_Balance();                    // RETURN BALANCE

private:
    float Balance;                              // ACCOUNT BALANCE
    float Interest_Rate;                        // MONTHLY INTEREST RATE
};
```

The declaration begins by describing the class interface via its public function prototypes. The public section begins with the keyword **public.** This class contains five public member functions. All the functions operate on the private data members. The *Initialize()* function initializes the private members to beginning values received from the calling program, but does not return any data to the calling program. The *Add_Interest()* function calculates a new balance from the current private member values. The *Deposit()* function adds an amount received from the calling program to the account balance. The *Withdraw()* function subtracts an amount received from the calling program from the account balance. Finally, the *Current_Balance()* function returns the value of the account balance to the calling program. You see that only the function prototypes are listed in the class declaration. The entire function definition, or ***implementation***, is separate from the class declaration.

After the public section you find a listing of the private members which make up the private section of the declaration. There are two private floating point members, *Balance* and *Interest_Rate,* which are listed after the keyword **private** in the class declaration.

Example 12-1:

Write class declarations for the following:

a. A rectangle class that consists of the rectangle length and width with functions to initialize the private members, calculate the perimeter of the rectangle, and calculate the area of the rectangle.

b. A circle class that consists of the circle radius with functions to initialize the private member, calculate the circumference of the circle, and calculate the area of the circle.

Solution:

a. The rectangle class requires three public functions: *Initialize()*, *Perimeter()*, and *Area()* and two private members, *Length* and *Width*. Here's the declaration:

```
class Rectangle
{
public:
    void Initialize(float L, float W);    // INITIALIZE PRIVATE DATA
    float Perimeter();                     // RETURN PERIMETER
    float Area();                          // RETURN AREA

private:
    float Length;                          // RECTANGLE LENGTH
    float Width;                           // RECTANGLE WIDTH
};
```

The *Initialize()* function receives length and width values from the calling program. This function does not require any return data type, since it is operating directly on the private members of the class. The *Perimeter()* and *Area()* do not receive any data from the calling program, but will both return floating point values to the calling program.

b. The circle class requires three public member functions: one to initialize the radius, one to calculate the circumference, and one to calculate the area. The only private member required is the circle radius. Here's the declaration:

```
class circle
{
public:
    void Initialize(float R);      // INITIALIZE PRIVATE DATA
    float Circumference();          // RETURN CIRCUMFERENCE
    float Area();                   // RETURN AREA

private:
    float Radius;                   // CIRCLE RADIUS
};
```

The *Initialize()* function receives an initializing radius value from the calling program and doesn't return any values, since it is operating directly on the private data member. The *Circumference()* and *Area()* functions do not receive any parameters from the calling program, but return the circumference and area of the circle, respectively. The single private member is the circle radius which is declared as a floating point variable.

Objects

You should now have a pretty good handle on what an object is. Here is a technical definition for your reference.

An *object* is an instance, or specimen, of a given class. An object of a given class has the structure and behavior defined by the class which is common to all objects of the same class.

An object is a real thing that can be manipulated in a program. An object must be defined for a given class to use the class, just like a variable must be defined for an integer to use the **int** data type. An object defined for a class has the structure and behavior dictated by the class, which are common to all objects defined for the class.

You see from the foregoing definition that an object is an "instance" of a class. The word *instance* means an example or specimen of something. In this case you could say that an object is an example or specimen of a class. If you have a class of dogs, then a Brittany Spaniel is an example or specimen of a dog. The same idea applies between objects and classes.

Defining Objects

You define an object for a class just like you define a variable for a structure. When the object is defined, memory is allocated to store the class for which the object is defined. Many different objects can be defined for a given class with each object made up of the data described by the class and responding to functions defined by the class. However, the private member data is hidden from one object to the next, even when multiple objects are defined for the same class.

Objects are usually nouns. This means that they are persons, places, or things like a *Square* object for a *Rectangle* class, a *Checkbook* object for a *Bank Account* class, a *File_Window* object for a *Window* class, and so on.

You can create objects either statically or dynamically. Here are the required definition formats:

FORMAT FOR DEFINING STATIC OBJECTS

`<class name> <object name>;`

or

`<class name> <object name>;`
`<class name> *<pointer name> = &<object name>;`

FORMAT FOR DEFINING DYNAMIC OBJECTS

`<class name> *<pointer name> = new <class name>;`

When defining static objects, you simply list the object name after the class name. The object can be a variable name or a pointer name. If you are defining a pointer to a static object, you should define the object first, then define a pointer to the address of the object. When defining dynamic objects, the object name must be a pointer and the keyword **new** must be employed to create the dynamic object. Notice that the class name must appear again after the keyword **new**. Of course, if you create a dynamic object you should delete it using the keyword **delete** when you are finished with it.

One final point: You will normally define objects separate from the class declaration. The reason for this is that the object definition will appear in the application program, while the class declaration will appear in a header file. More about this later.

Example 12-2:

Create a *Square* object for a class called *Rectangle* and a *Checkbook* object for a class called *Bank_Account*. Define these objects both statically and dynamically.

Solution:

The *Square* object definition is:

Rectangle Square;   // STATIC OBJECT

   or

Rectangle Sqr;
Rectangle *Square = &Sqr;   // STATIC OBJECT WITH POINTER

   or

Rectangle *Square = new Rectangle;   // DYNAMIC OBJECT

The *Checkbook* object definition is:

Bank_Account Checkbook;   // STATIC OBJECT

   or

Bank_Account Check;
Bank_Account *Checkbook = &Check;   // STATIC OBJECT WITH POINTER

   or

Bank_Account *Checkbook = new Bank_Account;   // DYNAMIC OBJECT

Notice that each of the objects can be defined one of three ways: as a static variable, as a static pointer variable, or as a dynamic pointer variable.

Quick Check

1. What do we mean when we say that a class defines the behavior of its objects?

2. True or False: Encapsulation ensures information hiding.

3. True or False: Private class members can only be accessed via public member functions.

4. Combining data with the functions that are dedicated to manipulating the data such that outside operations cannot affect the data is known as

      _____.

5. True or False: A struct is an encapsulated unit.
6. Information hiding is provided by the _____ section of a class.
7. The behavioral secrets of a class are revealed at the _____ level.
8. Define a static object called *Pick_Up* for a class called *Truck*.
9. Define a dynamic object called *Station_Wagon* for a class called *Automobile*.

12-2 MEMBER FUNCTIONS

One thing that makes C++ different from C is the ability to include functions as part of class declarations. The member functions in a class provide the interface to the class objects. Recall that to include a function as part of a class declaration, you simply list the function prototype in the public section of the class. The body of the function, or ***implementation***, is given separate from the class declaration.

A function ***implementation*** is the definition of the function that includes the function header and the body of the function.

In object-oriented programming, a function implementation is the same as a function definition. Here is the general format required to implement a function:

FORMAT FOR FUNCTION IMPLEMENTATION

```
<return type> <class name> :: <function name> (<function parameter
                                                            listing>)
{

// BODY OF FUNCTION GOES HERE

}
```

As an example, remember earlier that we declared a class called *Account* which included a function called *Initialize()*. The *Initialize()* function was used to set the private members of the class to initial values. Here is the class declaration again:

```
class Account
{
public:
  void Initialize(float Bal, float Rate);      // INITIALIZE PRIVATE DATA
  void Add_Interest();                         // ADD MONTHLY INTEREST
  void Deposit(float Amount);                  // ADD DEPOSIT
  void Withdraw(float Amount);                 // SUBTRACT WITHDRAWAL
  float Current_Balance();                     // RETURN BALANCE

private:
  float Balance;                               // ACCOUNT BALANCE
  float Interest_Rate;                         // MONTHLY INTEREST RATE
};
```

The important thing to remember is that the class declaration only shows the function prototypes which define the class interface. The details of how a given function works are provided in the function implementation. Here is the implementation for the *Initialize( )* function:

```
void Account :: Initialize(float Bal, float Rate)
{
  Balance = Bal;
  Interest_Rate = Rate;
}
```

Look closely at the function header and you will see a double colon, ::, separating the class name and the function name. The double colon is called the **scoping operator**. To implement a function as part of a class you *must* include the scoping operator in the function header to tell the compiler that the function is part of a class. In words, the foregoing function header tells the compiler that "the *Initialize( )* function has scope within the *Account* class."

Once the function header is properly coded using the scoping operator, the body of the function is coded within curly braces just like any other function body.

Example 12-3:

Write function implementations for the following *Rectangle* class:

```
class Rectangle
{
public:
  void Initialize(float L, float W);      // INITIALIZE PRIVATE DATA
  float Perimeter();                      // RETURN PERIMETER
```

```
float Area();                              // RETURN AREA

    private:
      float Length;                        // RECTANGLE LENGTH
      float Width;                         // RECTANGLE WIDTH
    };
```

Solution:

The *Initialize()* function is used to set the private class members to initial values received from the calling program. As a result, the function implementation is:

```
void Rectangle :: Initialize(float L, float W)
{
  Length = L;
  Width = W;
}
```

The *Perimeter()* function needs to calculate and return the perimeter of the rectangle. Here is the appropriate implementation:

```
float Rectangle :: Perimeter()
{
  return(2 *(Length + Width));
}
```

The *Area()* function must calculate and return the area of the rectangle, resulting in an implementation of:

```
float Rectangle :: Area()
{
  return(Length * Width);
}
```

In all of the above member function implementations you see the scoping operator employed to tell the compiler the class scope of the function. In addition, notice that each function operates on or with the private members of the class.

Constructors

A *constructor* is a special class function that is used to initialize an object automatically when the object is defined.

Although a constructor is a function used to initialize an object, it is often used to allocate dynamic memory, open files, and generally get an object ready for processing. In several previous examples you have seen the *Initialize()* function used to set the private class members to initial values. However, to set the values of a given object using this function, you would have to call the *Initialize()* function someplace in the program code. The advantage of using a constructor is that the constructor function is called automatically when an object is defined.

Here are the rules governing the creation and use of constructors:

- The name of the constructor is the same as the name of the class.

- The constructor cannot have a return type, not even **void**.

- The constructor can have default parameters.

- A class cannot have more than one constructor; however the constructor can be overloaded.

- Overloaded constructors with default parameters can cause ambiguity problems for the compiler.

- Constructors should not be developed for tasks other than to initialize an object for processing.

To illustrate how to set-up a constructor, consider the following *Rectangle* class declaration:

```
class Rectangle
{
public:
  Rectangle(float L, float W);    // CONSTRUCTOR
  float Perimeter();              // RETURN PERIMETER
  float Area();                   // RETURN AREA

private:
  float Length;                   // RECTANGLE LENGTH
  float Width;                    // RECTANGLE WIDTH
};
```

This is the declaration for the *Rectangle* class that you saw earlier, with one big difference: it includes a constructor. Here, the constructor is *Rectangle()* which takes the place of the *Initialize()* function that you observed earlier. Aside from the comment, you can recognize the constructor because it has the same name as the class and does not have any return type, not even **void**. The format of the *Rectangle()* constructor header is illustrated in Figure 12-5.

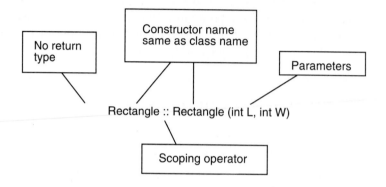

Figure 12-5 The format of a constructor header.

Once the constructor is declared in the class declaration, it must be defined, or implemented. Here is how the *Rectangle()* constructor might be implemented:

```
Rectangle :: Rectangle(float L, float W)
{
  Length = L;
  Width = W;
}
```

The implementation shows that the two private class members, *Length* and *Width*, are being initialized to the values received by the constructor parameters, *L* and *W*, respectively, just like our former *Initialize()* function.

Now, the next question is: How is the constructor called? Well, the reason for using a constructor over a regular function to initialize an object is that the constructor is called automatically when an object is defined. So, let's define two objects for the *Rectangle* class and therefore automatically call the constructor.

```
Rectangle  Small_Box(2,3);
Rectangle  Large_Box(10,20);
```

Here, *Small_Box* and *Large_Box* are defined to be objects of the *Rectangle* class. Notice that two argument values are passed to each object. The *Small_Box* object receives the argument values (2,3) and the *Large_Box* receives the argument values (10,20). What do you suppose happens with these arguments? You're right, the argument values are passed to the constructor which is automatically called to set the *Length* and *Width* of the *Small_Box* object to 2 and 3, respectively. Likewise, the *Length* and *Width* of the *Large_Box* object are initialized to the values 10 and 20, respectively. So, the idea is to list the constructor arguments in parentheses after the object name when the object is defined. This passes the arguments to the constructor, which is automatically called to perform its initializing task.

Default Parameters for Constructors

Like any other function, a constructor can have default parameters. Recall that a default parameter is used when no arguments are supplied for that parameter. The default parameter values must be supplied in the function prototype. This means that the default parameter values must be present in the class declaration. Here is our *Rectangle* class again with default parameters inserted into the constructor prototype:

```
class Rectangle
{
public:
  Rectangle(float L = 0, float W = 0);     // CONSTRUCTOR
  float Perimeter();                        // RETURN PERIMETER
  float Area();                             // RETURN AREA

private:
  float Length;                             // RECTANGLE LENGTH
  float Width;                              // RECTANGLE WIDTH
};
```

Now, when we define our objects like this:

```
Rectangle  Small_Box;
Rectangle  Large_Box(4,5);
```

the *Small_Box* object will have its *Length* and *Width* initialized to the default parameter values (0,0) and the *Large_Box* object will have its *Length* set to 4 and its *Width* set to 5. Notice that no argument values are present in the *Small_Box* object definition. When this is the case, the compiler will substitute the default values for any missing parameters.

Overloaded Constructors

Any function, even a constructor, can be overloaded. Recall from Chapter 7 that an overloaded function is one that performs different tasks depending on the number and/or type of arguments that it receives. Let's overload our *Rectangle()* constructor as follows:

```
class Rectangle
{
public:
  Rectangle(float S);              // CONSTRUCTOR FOR
                                   // A SQUARE  RECTANGLE

  Rectangle(float L, float W);     // CONSTRUCTOR FOR
                                   // A NON-SQUARE RECTANGLE

  float Perimeter();               // RETURN PERIMETER
  float Area();                    // RETURN AREA
};

private:
  float Length;                    // RECTANGLE LENGTH
  float Width;                     // RECTANGLE WIDTH
```

You are probably thinking that there are two constructors in the above declaration. No, there is a single constructor called *Rectangle()* which is overloaded. You can tell that the *Rectangle()* constructor is overloaded, since it has two different sets of parameters.

Now, let's look at the constructor implementations. Here they are:

```
// IMPLEMENTATION OF SQUARE CONSTRUCTOR
Rectangle :: Rectangle(float S)
{
  Length = Width = S;
}

// IMPLEMENTATION OF NON-SQUARE CONSTRUCTOR
Rectangle :: Rectangle(float L, float W)
{
  Length = L;
  Width = W;
}
```

There are two implementations of this constructor, since it is overloaded. The first implementation is for a square and the second for a non-square rectangle. The square implementation sets the *Length* and *Width* members of the rectangle equal to the same value, *S,* that is received when the constructor is called. The non-square implementation sets the *Length* and *Width* to two different values, *L* and *W,* when the constructor is called. What determines which implementation is used? Well, if the constructor is called with a single argument, the square implementation is executed. If the constructor is called with two arguments, the non-square implementation is executed. How is the constructor called? Of course, by defining objects for the class. Here is a sample object definition:

```
Rectangle  Square(1);
Rectangle  Box(2,3);
```

Here, two objects, *Square* and *Box,* are defined. In addition, a single argument of (1) is passed to the *Square* object and a double argument of (2,3) is passed to the *Box* object. What do you suppose happens? When the *Square* object is defined, the first constructor implementation is executed, setting the *Length* and *Width* of the *Square* object to the same value, 1. When the *Box* object is defined, the second constructor implementation is executed, setting the *Length* to 2 and the *Width* to 3. That's all there is to it!

CAUTION

When overloading a constructor and using default values you can easily create *ambiguity* as to which constructor implementation should be executed. Such ambiguity always results in a compiler error.

Be careful to prevent ambiguity when using default values with overloaded constructors. For example, suppose we would have declared the *Rectangle* class as follows:

```
class Rectangle // THIS CLASS DECLARATION CREATES AMBIGUITY
{
public:
  Rectangle(float Side = 0);            // CONSTRUCTOR FOR
                                        // A SQUARE
  Rectangle(float L = 0, float W = 0);  // CONSTRUCTOR FOR
```

```
                                    // A NON- SQUARE
float Perimeter()                   // RETURN PERIMETER;
float Area();                       // RETURN AREA

private:
  float Length;                     // RECTANGLE LENGTH
  float Width;                      // RECTANGLE WIDTH
};
```

Then we define our objects like this:

```
        Rectangle  Square;
        Rectangle  Box;
```

When this code is compiled the compiler will generate an "... ambiguity ..." error message. Why? The reason is that the compiler doesn't know which constructor implementation to execute. Does it execute the implementation containing one parameter, or the implementation containing two parameters? For this reason, it is wise not to use default parameters with an overloaded constructor. Obviously, there can never be an ambiguity problem with non-overloaded constructors, since there is only one implementation for the constructor.

Destructors

The primary use for a destructor is to deallocate memory allocated dynamically by a constructor. Like a constructor, a destructor is called automatically. However, rather than being called when the object is defined, a destructor is called *when program execution leaves the block of code in which the object is defined*. Here are some rules governing the use of destructors:

- The name of the destructor is the same as the name of the class.

- The destructor cannot have a return type, not even **void**.

- The destructor cannot have any parameters.

- A class cannot have more than one destructor.

- The destructor cannot be overloaded.

A *destructor* is the counterpart of an constructor and is used to "clean-up" an object after it is no longer needed.

Here is another declaration for our *Rectangle* class that includes a destructor:

```
class Rectangle
{
public:
    Rectangle(float L, float W);        // CONSTRUCTOR
    float Perimeter();                  // RETURN PERIMETER
    float Area();                       // RETURN AREA
    ~Rectangle();                       // DESTRUCTOR

private:
  float *Length;                        // RECTANGLE LENGTH
  float *Width;                         // RECTANGLE WIDTH
  };
```

First look at the private member declarations and you will see that they are defined as pointer variables. This has been done to facilitate the use of a destructor, since we will use the constructor to allocate memory dynamically for these members. Next, you see that the constructor prototype has not changed from the one you observed earlier. The constructor receives two floating point values that will be used to initialize the private members of the class. Now look at the destructor prototype. The format for the header of this typical destructor is illustrated in Figure 12-6.

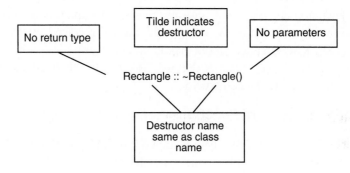

Figure 12-6 Header format for a destructor.

Like the constructor, the destructor has the same name as the class, but its name is preceded with a tilde, ~, symbol. In addition, there is no return type and there are no parameters. Destructors cannot have a return type and generally no parameters are needed. Now, here are implementations for both the constructor and destructor:

```
// IMPLEMENTATION OF CONSTRUCTOR
Rectangle :: Rectangle(float L, float W)
{
  Length = new float;
  *Length = L;
  Width = new float;
  *Width = W;
}
// IMPLEMENTATION OF DESTRUCTOR
Rectangle :: ~Rectangle()
{
  delete Length;
  delete Width;
}
```

In the constructor implementation you find that the private class members, *Length* and *Width* are being allocated dynamically using the **new** operator. Once allocated, each is set with an initializing value received by the constructor. In the destructor implementation, you see that the memory allocated to *Length* and *Width* is deallocated using the **delete** operator.

So, when an object is defined for the *Rectangle* class, the constructor is called automatically which allocates memory for the private members of the object and initializes them to the values of *L* and *W* received by the constructor. Then, the destructor is called automatically when program execution leaves the block of code in which the object is defined. The destructor deallocates the memory that was allocated by the constructor.

Scoping Inside of Functions

There can be a problem using a constructor, or any class function for that matter, when the private member names are the same as the function parameter names. For instance, suppose that we declare a simple *Circle* class that contains a private member called *Radius*. You then decide to use the *Radius* name as a parameter for the constructor. Here is the appropriate class declaration:

```
class Circle
{
public:
  Circle(float Radius = 0);        //CONSTRUCTOR
```

```
private:
  float Radius;                          // CIRCLE RADIUS
};
```

There is nothing wrong with this declaration. The problem arises in the constructor implementation. Consider the following implementation:

```
// CONSTRUCTOR IMPLEMENTATION
Circle :: Circle(float Radius)
{
Radius = Radius;
}
```

The implementation will compile; however, it will initialize *Radius* to garbage! Look at the statement within the implementation and you will see ambiguity in the use of the *Radius* name. It appears that *Radius* is being assigned to itself. How does the compiler know what *Radius* to use? Is *Radius* the variable declared as the private class member, or is *Radius* the value received by the constructor, or both? We must tell the compiler that the *Radius* on the left side of the assignment operator is the private class member and the *Radius* on the right side of the assignment operator is the value received by the constructor. There are two ways to solve this problem: 1) By using the scoping operator, or 2) By using the **this** pointer.

The Scoping Operator Revisited

You were introduced to the double colon scoping operator, ::, when you learned how to code the header of a member function implementation. The scoping operator simply defines the scope of something. In the case of a function header, it is used to tell the compiler that the function belongs to a certain class, and therefore has class scope. The scoping operator can also be used inside of a function to define the scope of a variable. Using the scoping operator, we can fix the above ambiguity problem by coding the *Circle()* constructor implementation as follows:

```
// CONSTRUCTOR IMPLEMENTATION
Circle :: Circle(float Radius)
{
Circle :: Radius = Radius;
}
```

The addition of the scoping operator in the constructor statement tells the compiler that the *Radius* on the left side of the assignment operator belongs to the

Circle class. Therefore, the *Radius* on the right side of the assignment operator must be the function parameter. Now there is no ambiguity between the two *Radius* names.

The "this" Pointer

All the member functions of a class carry with them an invisible pointer, called **this,** that points to the object that called the function. Although the pointer is invisible, it can be used to prevent ambiguity problems like the one in the above *Circle()* constructor. Here is how the **this** pointer can be employed in the constructor implementation to solve an ambiguity problem:

```
// CONSTRUCTOR IMPLEMENTATION
Circle :: Circle(float Radius)
{
this -> Radius = Radius;
}
```

The compiler knows that **this** points to the object that called the constructor, and it knows what class the object belongs to. As a result, this -> Radius references the private member *Radius* of the *Circle* class. Now there is no ambiguity between the two *Radius* names.

PROGRAMMING NOTE

A simple solution to the use of duplicate names in a program is to make sure that you employ different names to avoid any ambiguity. For instance, the radius of a circle could be named *Radius*, *Rad*, or *R* depending on where it is used in the program. Thus, the *Circle()* constructor could be coded like this:

```
// CONSTRUCTOR IMPLEMENTATION
Circle :: Circle(float Rad)
{
Radius = Rad;
}
```

This represents much better overall programming style and is less confusing to anyone looking at the code.

Example 12-4:

Declare a *Point* class that defines an *(x,y)* coordinate for a cursor position on the monitor. Provide a constructor to initialize the coordinate when an object is defined for *Point*. The default coordinate should be (0,0). Include a function, called *Plot*, as part of the class that will display the string "C++" at the *(x,y)* coordinate location. Finally, code a statement required to define an object, *P*, of the *Point* class and initialize this object to point to the middle of the monitor screen. Also, write a statement to call the *Plot* function.

Solution:

First, the class declaration:

```
// Point CLASS DECLARATION
class Point
{
public:
  Point(int x = 0, int y =0); // CONSTRUCTOR
  void Plot ();               // PLOT POINT(X,Y)

private:
  int x;                      // X-COORDINATE
  int y;                      // Y-COORDINATE
};
```

This declaration should be straightforward. The *Point* class consists of two private integer members, *x* and *y*, which will form the coordinate. A constructor function is included to initialize the *x* and *y* values and provide a default coordinate of (0,0). The *Plot* function will use the *x* and *y* member values to position the cursor at an *(x,y)* coordinate on the screen and display the string "C++". To see how the functions work we need to develop their implementations. Here they are:

```
// CONSTRUCTOR IMPLEMENTATION
Point :: Point(int x, int y)
{
  this -> x = x;
  this -> y = y;
}

// PLOT IMPLEMENTATION
void Point :: Plot()
{
  gotoxy(x,y);                // DOS PLATFORMS ONLY
  cout << "C++";
}
```

The constructor implementation applies the **this** pointer to prevent ambiguity between the *x,y* class members and the *x,y* constructor parameters. The *Plot* implementation uses the *x,y* class members as arguments in the standard *gotoxy()* function to position the cursor at the *(x,y)* position on the monitor. The *gotoxy()* function is part of *conio.h*, which must be included in the program. Be aware that this function might not be available on all platforms.Once the cursor is positioned using *gotoxy()* the *cout* statement displays the string "C++" at the cursor position.

A statement to define an object, *P*, of the *Point* class and initialize *P* to point to the middle of the screen is:

Point P(40,12);

This statement defines *P* and calls the constructor to initialize the *(x,y)* coordinate to (40,12), which is the approximate middle of the screen.

The following statement will call the *Plot* function to move the cursor to the *(x,y)* coordinate position and display the string.

P . Plot();

To call a non-constructor function, you simply list the object, a dot, then the function name with any required arguments. Of course, the *Plot* function doesn't require any arguments, since it operates directly on the private members of the object.

Access Functions

Remember that the only way to access the private members of an object are with a member function. Even if we simply want to examine the private members of an object we need to use a function that is declared within the same object class. Such a function only needs to return the private member(s) to the calling program. Access functions are used for this purpose.

An ***access function*** is a function that only returns the values of the private members of an object.

Let's revisit one of our *Rectangle* class declarations, adding access functions to it as follows:

```
class Rectangle
{
public:
    Rectangle(float L, float W);            // CONSTRUCTOR
```

```
float Perimeter();              // RETURN PERIMETER
float Area();                   // RETURN AREA
float Current_Length();         // ACCESS LENGTH
float Current_Width();          // ACCESS WIDTH
~Rectangle();                   // DESTRUCTOR

private:
  float *Length;                // RECTANGLE LENGTH
  float *Width;                 // RECTANGLE WIDTH
};
```

Two new member functions called *Current_Length()* and *Current_Width()* have been added here to return the *Length* and *Width* private member values, respectively. Since the only purpose of an access function is to return the value of a private member, the implementation only requires a **return** statement as follows:

```
// IMPLEMENTATION OF LENGTH ACCESS FUNCTION
float Rectangle :: Current_Length()
{
  return(*Length);
}

// IMPLEMENTATION OF WIDTH ACCESS FUNCTION
float Rectangle :: Current_Width()
{
  return(*Width);
}
```

When either of these implementations are executed, the respective private member value is returned to the calling program. So, if we define *Box* to be an object of *Rectangle*, you can call either access member using dot notation to examine the private members. For instance, to display the member values of *Box*, the access functions could be called as part of *cout* statements like this:

```
cout << "\nThe length of the box is:  " << Box.Current_Length();
cout << "\nThe width of the box is:  " << Box.Current_Width();
```

Messages

A *message* is a call to a member function.

The term ***message*** is used for a call to a member function with the idea that when we are calling a member function, we are sending a message to the object. The object responds to the calling program by sending back return values. This idea is illustrated in Figure 12-7. As you will see shortly, objects communicate with each other using messages.

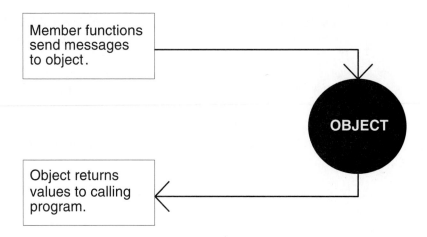

Figure 12-7 Messages are the means of communicating with an object.

To generate a message to an object, you must call one of its member functions. You call a member function by using either the dot operator or the pointer operator. The required formats are:

SENDING A MESSAGE USING THE DOT OPERATOR

<object name> • <function name> (argument listing);

SENDING A MESSAGE USING THE POINTER OPERATOR

<object name> → <function name> (argument listing);

You see that the syntax is very much like that required to access a structure. The pointer operator must be used when the object name is a pointer; otherwise you use the dot operator. Here is our *Rectangle* class again with all the features that we have added up to this point:

```
class Rectangle
{
public:
  Rectangle(float L = 0, float W = 0);      // CONSTRUCTOR
  float Perimeter();                        // RETURN PERIMETER
  float Area();                             // RETURN AREA
  float Current_Length();                   // ACCESS LENGTH
  float Current_Width();                    // ACCESS WIDTH
  ~Rectangle();                             // DESTRUCTOR

private:
  float *Length;                            // RECTANGLE LENGTH
  float *Width;                             // RECTANGLE WIDTH
};
```

Let's define three *Rectangle* objects called *Box1*, *Box2*, and *Box3*. We will define *Box1* as a regular static object, *Box2* to be a static object with a pointer, and *Box3* to be a dynamic object. Here are the required definitions:

```
Rectangle Box1(2,3);              // Box1 IS A STATIC OBJECT

Rectangle Box2;
Rectangle *B2 = &Box2;            // Box2 IS A STATIC OBJECT
                                  // POINTED TO BY B2
Rectangle *Box3 = new Rectangle;  // Box3 IS A DYNAMIC OBJECT
```

Next, let's send messages to all the functions of the three boxes using *cout* statements. We will use a separate *cout* statement for each message so that you can easily observe the required syntax. Here are the messages:

```
cout << "\n\nThe length of Box1 is:  " << Box1 . Current_Length();
cout << "\nThe width of Box1 is:  " << Box1 . Current_Width();
cout << "\nThe perimeter of Box1 is:  " << Box1 . Perimeter();
cout << "\nThe area of Box1 is:  " << Box1 . Area();

cout << "\n\nThe length of Box2 is:  " << B2 -> Current_Length();
cout << "\nThe width of Box2 is:  " << B2 -> Current_Width();
cout << "\nThe perimeter of Box2 is:  " << B2 -> Perimeter();
cout << "\nThe area of Box2 is:  " << B2 -> Area();
```

```
cout << "\n\nThe length of Box3 is:  " << Box3 -> Current_Length();
cout << "\nThe width of Box3 is:  " << Box3 -> Current_Width();
cout << "\nThe perimeter of Box3 is:  " << Box3 -> Perimeter();
cout << "\nThe area of Box3 is:  " << Box3 -> Area();
```

Observe that each group of four *cout* statements deals with a different box object. The first group sends messages to *Box1* via the dot operator. The second and third groups send messages to *Box1* and *Box2* using the pointer operator.

Putting Everything Together in a Complete Program

We now have all the ingredients to build a complete program. Here it is:

```
#include <iostream.h>

// Rectangle CLASS DECLARATION
class Rectangle
{
public:
    Rectangle(float L = 0, float W = 0);    // CONSTRUCTOR
    float Perimeter();                      // RETURN PERIMETER
    float Area();                           // RETURN AREA
    float Current_Length();                 // ACCESS LENGTH
    float Current_Width();                  // ACCESS WIDTH
    ~Rectangle();                           // DESTRUCTOR

private:
    float *Length;                          // RECTANGLE LENGTH
    float *Width;                           // RECTANGLE WIDTH
};

void main()
{
//DEFINE OBJECTS
    Rectangle Box1(2,3);                    // Box1 IS A STATIC OBJECT

    Rectangle Box2(3,4);
    Rectangle *B2 = &Box2;                  // Box2 IS A STATIC OBJECT
                                            // POINTED TO BY B2

    Rectangle *Box3 = new Rectangle;        // Box3 IS A DYNAMIC OBJECT
```

```
// DISPLAY LENGTH, WIDTH, PERIMETER AND AREA OF BOX OBJECTS

  cout << "\n\nThe length of Box1 is:  " << Box1.Current_Length();
  cout << "\nThe width of Box1 is:  " << Box1.Current_Width();
  cout << "\nThe perimeter of Box1 is:  " << Box1.Perimeter();
  cout << "\nThe area of Box1 is:  " << Box1.Area();

  cout << "\n\nThe length of Box2 is:  " << B2 -> Current_Length();
  cout << "\nThe width of Box2 is:  " << B2 -> Current_Width();
  cout << "\nThe perimeter of Box2 is:  " << B2 -> Perimeter();
  cout << "\nThe area of Box2 is:  " << B2 -> Area();

  cout << "\n\nThe length of Box3 is:  " << Box3 -> Current_Length();
  cout << "\nThe width of Box3 is:  " << Box3 -> Current_Width();
  cout << "\nThe perimeter of Box3 is:  " << Box3 -> Perimeter();
  cout << "\nThe area of Box3 is:  " << Box3 -> Area();
}

// CONSTRUCTOR IMPLEMENTATION
Rectangle :: Rectangle(float L, float W)
{
  Length = new float;
  *Length = L;
  Width = new float;
  *Width = W;
}

// IMPLEMENTATION OF Perimeter() FUNCTION
float Rectangle :: Perimeter()
{
  return(2 * (*Length + *Width));
}

// IMPLEMENTATION OF Area() FUNCTION
float Rectangle :: Area()
{
  return(*Length * *Width);
}

// IMPLEMENTATION OF Current_Length() FUNCTION
float Rectangle :: Current_Length()
{
  return(*Length);
}
```

```
// IMPLEMENTATION OF Current_Width() FUNCTION
float Rectangle :: Current_Width()
{
  return(*Width);
}


// DESTRUCTOR IMPLEMENTATION
Rectangle :: ~Rectangle(void)
{
  delete Length;
  delete Width;
}
```

You see that our program includes the *Rectangle* class declaration which includes six public function members and two private pointer members. The functions consist of a constructor with default values, a destructor, two access functions, and two functions that return the perimeter and area of the rectangle. Three objects are defined for the *Rectangle* class, then messages are sent to the objects by calling all their respective functions. Can you predict the output of the program? Here it is:

> The length of Box1 is: 2
> The width of Box1 is: 3
> The perimeter of Box1 is: 10
> The area of Box1 is: 6
>
> The length of Box2 is: 3
> The width of Box2 is: 4
> The perimeter of Box2 is: 14
> The area of Box2 is: 12
>
> The length of Box3 is: 0
> The width of Box3 is: 0
> The perimeter of Box3 is: 0
> The area of Box3 is: 0

This program summarizes most of what has been covered in the last two sections. Before going on, study the program to make sure that you understand everything in it. Many important OOP concepts are demonstrated here.

✔ **Quick Check**

1. In OOP, a class member function is sometimes called a _____.

2. The complete definition of a member function, which includes the function header and body is called the function _____. \

3. Write a header for a member function called *Wheels()* that will return the number of wheels from a class called *Truck*.

4. A member function that is used specifically to initialize class data is called a _____.

5. How do you know which member function in a class is the constructor function?

6. True or False: The return data type of a constructor function is optional.

7. How do you call a class constructor?

8. What is the primary use for a class destructor?

9. All member functions of a class carry with them a built-in pointer to the function called _____.

10. How do you call a non-constructor member function of a class?

11. A member function that only returns the values of the private class members is called a _____ function.

12. Why is the term "message" used for a call to a member function?

12-3 OOP PROGRAM CONSTRUCTION

Up to this point, we have been working with relatively simple C++ programs for learning purposes. Commercial programs, on the other hand, can get very complex involving several thousand lines of code. Remember what to do when tackling a complex problem? You're right, break it down into simpler subproblems, the old "divide and conquer" strategy. The same is true when building a large program. Rather than placing everything into a single source file and compiling/linking this file into an executable file, we place different parts of the program in separate files, edit them separately, compile them separately, then link them all together to create the executable file. This is the way the pros do it!

From the beginning you have included header files in your C++ programs. These header files primarily provide interfaces to the standard functions used in your program. The C and C++ languages were developed around the idea of using many separate files for a programming project and linking them together to create the executable file. There are several reasons for this approach. First, it allows you to create smaller, more manageable files. This facilitates a team approach to software development. Each team member writes, debugs, and compiles his/her own part of the project code independent of the other team members. When all the individual files are completed, they are linked to create a common executable program.

Second, programs made of separately compiled files are easier to maintain. When changes need to be made to the program, only those files affected by the change need to be modified and recompiled. Any unaffected files do not need to be recompiled.

Third, you can hide any important proprietary parts of the program code from the user by only providing the user with the binary object code for those parts. What really makes one C++ program different from another are the member function implementations. So, suppose that you provide the class declarations to the user as a *.cpp* source file and the function implementations as a *.obj* object file. The class declaration provides a listing of all the data members as well as the function prototypes. The function prototypes provide the required interface to an object of that class. This is all the user needs to know to use the class. He or she does not need to know how the functions are implemented. The function implementations can be compiled into a binary object file and supplied to the user. The user can then include the class declaration file in his/her applications program and link it along with the function implementation object file to create the final executable file. This encourages programmers to write object-oriented code that can be reused in other programs and shared with other programmers without compromising confidentiality. This idea is illustrated in Figure 12-8.

You should be aware of the rules for what must be recompiled and linked if things change in the class declaration header file or the function implementation file. If the "*.h*" class declaration header file is modified, then *every* "*.cpp*" source file that includes the header file must be recompiled. On the other hand, if the "*.cpp*" function implementation file is modified, then only this file must be recompiled. In either case, the entire application project must be relinked.

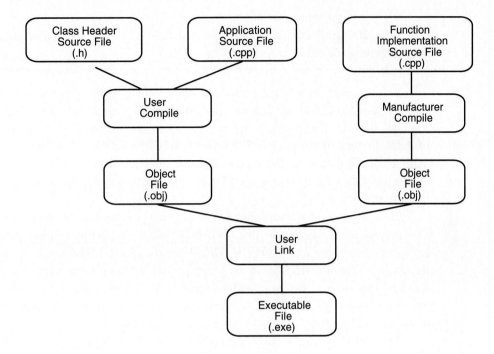

Figure 12-8 Object interfaces can be made public by supplying users with the class header files as source code, while hiding the function implementations in object files.

CASE STUDY: BUILDING A MULTI-FILE C++ PROGRAM

C++ compilers and commercial programs are constructed using the multi-file concept. The software manufacturers provide you with all the standard header files that include the function prototypes as source code, but do not supply you with the source code for the function implementations. Thus, you cannot alter and possibly corrupt the standard function implementations.

Most C++ compilers allow you to build your own multi-file programs. In this case study you will see how the TURBO C++ compiler allows you to build muli-file programs through the use of the ***project manager***. When using the project manager, you specify all the files required to build an application program. This information is kept in a ***project file***.

A ***project file (.prj)*** identifies the files that need to be compiled and linked to create a given executable program.

You can add or delete files to and from your project, view/edit individual files in the project, and set options for a file in the project. When working with program files in the project, the project manager automatically updates the information kept in the project file and identifies those files that need to be re-compiled and linked to produce an executable program. If a given program file is altered, only that file is recompiled by the project manager. This saves program development time.

Let's suppose that you want to develop a C++ project using the TURBO C++ project manager. To do this, you must select the **Project** option from the main menu bar of the TURBO C++ IDE. When the **Project** option is selected, you use the *Insert* key to add files to the project. Once all the program files have been added to the project file, you will **Compile | Make** the project file. When the project file is compiled, the project manager will automatically compile and link all the individual program files to produce an executable file.

As an example, let's build a project out of the *Rectangle* program that we developed at the end of the last section. We will place the *Rectangle* class declaration in a separate file called *rectangl.h* like this:

```
// rectangl.h HEADER FILE

// Rectangle CLASS DECLARATION
class Rectangle
{
public:
    Rectangle(float L = 0, float W = 0);    // CONSTRUCTOR
    float Perimeter();                       // RETURN PERIMETER
    float Area();                            // RETURN AREA
    float Current_Length();                  // ACCESS LENGTH
    float Current_Width();                   // ACCESS WIDTH
    ~Rectangle();                            // DESTRUCTOR

private:
  float *Length;                            // RECTANGLE LENGTH
  float *Width;                             // RECTANGLE WIDTH
};
```

Next, we will place all the function implementations in a separate file called *rectangl.cpp* like this:

```cpp
// rectangl.cpp IMPLEMENTATION FILE

#include "rectangl.h"

// CONSTRUCTOR IMPLEMENTATION
Rectangle :: Rectangle(float L, float W)
{
  Length = new float;
  *Length = L;
  Width = new float;
  *Width = W;
}

// IMPLEMENTATION OF Perimeter() FUNCTION
float Rectangle :: Perimeter()
{
  return(2 * (*Length + *Width));
}

// IMPLEMENTATION OF Area() FUNCTION
float Rectangle :: Area()
{
  return(*Length * *Width);
}

// IMPLEMENTATION OF Current_Length() FUNCTION
float Rectangle :: Current_Length()
{
  return(*Length);
}

// IMPLEMENTATION OF Current_Width() FUNCTION
float Rectangle :: Current_Width()
{
  return(*Width);
}

// DESTRUCTOR IMPLEMENTATION
Rectangle :: ~Rectangle(void)
{
  delete Length;
  delete Width;
}
```

The first executable statement that you see in this file is a preprocessor directive that includes the *rectangl.h* class declaration header file. This directive is required so that the *rectangl.cpp* file can be compiled to produce a *rectangl.obj* file. The file will not compile unless the class header file in included, since without it, the compiler doesn't know the class declaration from which the functions are derived. Notice that double quotes are employed around the header file name so that the compiler will look for the file in the system working directory.

Finally, you will write a separate application file. Let's call this file *myprog.cpp*. Here it is:

```
// myprog.cpp APPLICATION FILE

#include "rectangl.h"
#include <iostream.h>

void main()
{

//DEFINE OBJECTS
    Rectangle Box1(2,3);                    // Box1 IS A STATIC OBJECT

    Rectangle Box2(3,4);
    Rectangle *B2 = &Box2;                  // Box2 IS A STATIC OBJECT
                                            // POINTED TO BY B2

    Rectangle *Box3 = new Rectangle;        // Box3 IS A DYNAMIC OBJECT

// DISPLAY LENGTH, WIDTH, PERIMETER AND AREA OF BOX OBJECTS
    cout << "\n\nThe length of Box1 is:  " << Box1.Current_Length();
    cout << "\nThe width of Box1 is:  " << Box1.Current_Width();
    cout << "\nThe perimeter of Box1 is:  " << Box1.Perimeter();
    cout << "\nThe area of Box1 is:  " << Box1.Area();

    cout << "\n\nThe length of Box2 is:  " << B2 -> Current_Length();
    cout << "\nThe width of Box2 is:  " << B2 -> Current_Width();
    cout << "\nThe perimeter of Box2 is:  " << B2 -> Perimeter();
    cout << "\nThe area of Box2 is:  " << B2 -> Area();

    cout << "\n\nThe length of Box3 is:  " << Box3 -> Current_Length();
    cout << "\nThe width of Box3 is:  " << Box3 -> Current_Width();
    cout << "\nThe perimeter of Box3 is:  " << Box3 -> Perimeter();
    cout << "\nThe area of Box3 is:  " << Box3 -> Area();
}
```

Here is where the objects are defined for the program. In addition, function *main( )* appears here along with any other functions that are part of the application program. This file must also include the *rectangl.h* header file, since it won't compile unless the compiler knows the class declaration for which the objects are being defined.

Now we have three separate files: *rectangl.h*, *rectangl.cpp*, and *myprog.cpp*. At this point, you could compile the *rectangl.cpp* function implementation file to produce a *rectangl.obj* object file. Then, compile the *myprog.cpp* application file and link it with the *rectangl.obj* object file to produce an executable program called *myprog.exe*. This would require separate compiling and linking steps. However, there is an easier way using the TURBO C++ project manager. You simply open a project file by selecting the **Project** option from the TURBO C++ main menu bar. Let's suppose that we call this project *myproj.prj*. Once the project file is open, you can add and delete files to and from the project. For this project you will add the *myprog.cpp* application file and the *rectangl.cpp* implementation file. You *do not* add the *rectangl.h* header file to the project because it is included as part of the other two files. Figure 12-9 depicts the composition of our project file.

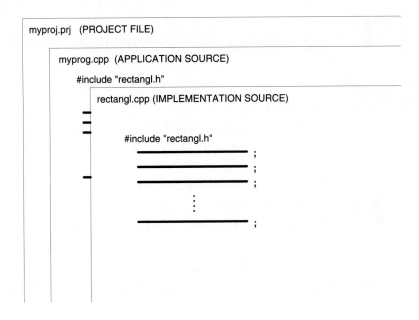

Figure 12-9 A project file includes all the program files needed to create an executable application file.

Once the project is built, you simply **Compile | Make** the project file. When the project file is compiled, it will automatically perform the compiling and linking steps required to produce an executable file called *myproj.exe*. In addition, if there are any errors in any of the files that make up the project, the project manager will open the file in error and place the cursor at the point of the error. Once the error is corrected you can attempt to **Compile | Make** the project again from that point. Furthermore, at any time you can edit and compile any of the component files independently of the project file.

After building a project, you can open the project at any time using the **Project** option. When a given project is opened, TURBO C++ will load the files that are part of that project so that they can be viewed and altered if necessary. In addition, you can obtain a listing of any included header files for a project by selecting the **Include Files** option in the **Projects** menu window. From here, you can also view and edit any of the included files by selecting the **View** option in the header files listing window. When a project is recompiled, the project manager only compiles those files that have been changed, resulting in reduced compile time.

At this point, it might be a good idea to build, compile, and execute your own project using the *Rectangle* program. Refer to your compiler reference manual if you get stuck building your project.

 Quick Check

1. State three reasons for using the multi-file approach for developing software.
2. What file(s) in a C++ software project provide the interfaces to the class objects?
3. Why might a software manufacturer not supply you with the member function implementation source code?

The remaining questions relate to the TURBO C++ compiler.

4. A file that identifies the files that need to be compiled and linked to create an executable program is the _____ file.
5. When building a C++ project, which files must be listed in the project manager?
6. Why don't you list header files in the project manager?
7. How can you view header files that are part of a project?

CHAPTER SUMMARY

Object-oriented programs are developed from the inside out by expanding on simple classes. The fundamental components of any object-oriented program are the class and its objects. At the abstract level, a class can be described as an interface, since it defines the behavior common to all of its objects. At the implementation level, a class is a construct that describes a set of data and related operations that are common to its objects. The abstract level provides an outside view of a class, while the implementation level provides the inside view of the class, disclosing its behavioral secrets. At the implementation level, a class is comprised of private and public members. The private class members are hidden from the outside, since they can only be accessed using the public member functions. This provides for information hiding within the class.

Encapsulation is the idea of packaging things together in a well-defined programming unit. A structure, or struct, in C is encapsulated, since it consists of a collection of data fields. A class in C++ is also encapsulated, since it consists of a collection of data fields and related functions. However, a C struct does not provide information hiding, while a C++ class does provide information hiding through its private declarations.

An object is an instance, or specimen, of a class. Thus, an object of a given class has the structure and behavior defined by the class.

The functions defined for a given class are called member functions. There are various types of member functions including constructor functions, destructor functions, and access functions. The member functions provide a means of communication with the object via messages. Messages are sent to an object by calling the member functions which perform a given task on the hidden object data. The object responds via the values returned by the member functions.

Object-oriented programs are normally constructed using a multi-file approach. Class declarations are placed in separate header files. All the member function implementations for a given class are placed in a separate file that includes the class header file. Finally, the application program is placed in a separate file that includes all the class header files. The individual files are edited and compiled separately then linked together to form an executable file. This facilitates a team approach to software development and makes such programs easier to maintain. Moreover, the user can be supplied the source code of the class header files and the object code of the function implementation files. This encourages reuse of the object-oriented code while protecting the implementation of that code from corruption by the user. Most C++ compilers include a project manager that facilitates the multi-file approach to building programs.

QUESTIONS AND PROBLEMS

Questions

1. Define the following OOP terms:
   Class at the abstract level
   Class at the implementation level
   Encapsulation
   Information Hiding
   Object
   Instance
   Member
   Function Implementation
   Constructor
   Destructor
   Access Function
   Overloaded Constructor
   Message

2. What are the two major sections that make up a class declaration?

3. What is the scope of a private class member?

4. What is the scope of a public class member?

5. The concept of combining data with a set of operations that are dedicated to manipulating the data so tightly that outside operations can not affect the data is called _____.

6. A computer window can be considered an object of a window class. What data and operations might be part of this object?

7. Where are function prototypes normally placed in a class declaration?

8. True or False: The abstract definition for a class provides the inside view of the class.

9. What is meant by the term "behavior," relative to a class object?

10. True or False: A class is an interface.

11. A member function that simply displays the values of class data members is called a _____ function.

12. What is the purpose of a constructor?

13. Suppose that a member function called *Initialize()* is part of a class called *Student*. The prototype for the *Initialize()* function is:

   void Initialize();

   a.   Write a header line for the function implementation.

b. Write a statement to call the *Initialize()* function for the object *Isaac_Newton* of the *Student* class.

Use the following class declaration to answer questions 14–21:

```
#include <stdio.h>
#include <string.h>
#include <iostream.h>

class Student
{
public:
  Student(char Nam[] = "None",
          char Maj[] = "None",
          int Num = 0,
          float GPA = 0);
  void Initialize();
  void Student_Data();

private:
  char Name[25];
  char Major[20];
  int Student_Number;
  float GPA;
};
```

14. What is the name of the constructor function?

15. Write a statement to define John Doe as a student object that will be initialized to the default values in the constructor.

16. Jane Doe (student #456) is a Computer Science major with a GPA of 3.58. Write a statement to define Jane Doe as a student object that will be initialized to the proper data values.

17. Write an implementation for the *Student()* function.

18. Write an implementation for the *Initialize()* function that will allow the user to enter the data values from the keyboard.

19. Write a statement that will allow the user to initialize the Jane Doe object from the keyboard.

20. Write an implementation for the *Student_Data()* function, assuming that this function will display the student data.

21. Write a statement that will display the data in the John Doe student object.

22. True or False: A destructor may or may not have parameters.

23. Suppose that you have a constructor called *Circle()*. What will be the corresponding destructor name?

24. When are destructors normally used in a C++ object-oriented program?

25. Given the following function implementation:

```
Dogs :: Dogs(int Legs)
{
  Legs = Legs;
}
```

    a.   What special type of function is this?

    b.   What problem would the compiler encounter when attempting to compile this implementation?

    c.   Rewrite the implementation using the scoping operator to correct any problems.

    d.   Rewrite the implementation using the **this** pointer to correct any problems.

26. What two operators can be used to send a message to an object?

27. Explain why you should use a multi-file approach when developing C++ programs.

28. Suppose that you want to develop a commercial object-oriented program whereby you provide the user with the function interfaces while hiding their implementations. Explain how such a program would be organized and supplied to the user.

29. Explain the rules for recompiling and relinking when things are modified in a class header file or a function implementation file for a given application.

Problems

Least Difficult

1. Declare a class called *Employee* as part of a header file called *employe.h*. The class is to have data members to store the employee's name, hourly rate, and hours worked. The class is to have member functions to perform the following tasks:

    • A constructor function to initialize the hourly rate to a minimum wage of $4.25 per hour and the hours worked to 0.

    • A function to get the employee's name from the user.

- Three separate access functions to display each of the data members.
- A function to return weekly pay, including overtime pay where overtime is paid at a rate of time-and-a-half for any hours worked over 40.

2. Write the implementations for the functions in problem 1 and place them in a file called *employe.cpp*.

3. Write an application program that defines an object for the class declared in problem 1 and tests the functions in Problem 2. Place this program in a file called *pay.cpp*.

4. Build a project from the files created in problems 1–3. Compile, debug, and run the project file.

More Difficult

Use the multi-file approach when writing programs to solve the following problems.

5. Create an invoice object that contains all the information necessary to process one line of an invoice. Assume that the invoice must include the following data and functions:

Data:	Quantity Ordered
	Quantity Shipped
	Part Number
	Part Description
	Unit Price
	Extended Price
	Sales Tax Rate
	Sales Tax Amount
	Shipping
	Total

Functions:
- A function to initialize all the data items to 0, except the Sales Tax Rate which should be initialized to 5%.
- A function to allow the user to initialize all the data items from the keyboard.
- A function to calculate the Extended Price of the item.
- A function to calculate the Sales Tax Amount of the item.
- A function to calculate the Total amount of the invoice.
- A function to display the invoice data with header information in a business-like format.

Most Difficult

6. A stack is ideal to implement using a class, since it must include the stack data elements as well as the functions that operate on those elements in a tightly bound manner. As a result, object-oriented programming is perfect for implementing stacks. Here is a declaration for a *Stack* class:

```
class Stack
{
public:
  void ClearStack();
  int EmptyStack();
  int FullStack();
  void Push(char Element);
  char Pop();

private:
  char Data[100];
  int Top;
};
```

This stack can hold 100 character elements as seen by the character array declaration within the class. An integer member called *Top* is declared to access the top element of the stack. Thus, *Top* provides the array index of the top element in the stack. The stack is empty when *Top* is −1 and the stack is full when *Top* is 100. Write the stack function implementations according to the following criteria:

- *ClearStack()* sets *Top* to −1.

- *EmptyStack()* tests to see if *Top* = −1.

- *FullStack()* tests to see if *Top* = 100.

- *Push()* first checks to see if the stack is full by calling the *FullStack()* function. Then it must increment *Top* and place *Element* in the array at the index pointed to by *Top*.

- *Pop()* first checks to see if the stack is empty by calling the *EmptyStack()* function. If the stack is not empty, it returns the character element located at the array index pointed to by *Top* and decrements *Top*.

Write an application program to completely test your stack class.

7. Write a 12-hour clock program that declares a *Clock* class to store hours, minutes, seconds, AM, and PM. Provide functions to perform the following tasks:

- Set the hours, minutes, seconds to 00:00:00 by default.

- Initialized the hours, minutes, seconds, A.M., and P.M. from user entries.

- Allow the clock to tick by advancing the seconds by one and at the same time correcting the hours and minutes for a 12 hour clock value of A.M. or P.M.

- Display the time in hours:minutes:seconds A.M./P.M. format.

Write an application program that allows the user to set the clock and tick the clock at one second intervals while displaying the time.

13

CLASS INHERITANCE

INTRODUCTION

One of the most important properties of object-oriented programming is *inheritance*. In fact, a program that doesn't employ inheritance is not an object-oriented program.

> *Inheritance* is that property of object-oriented programming that allows one class, called a *derived class*, to share the structure and behavior of another class, called a *base class*.

The natural world is full of inheritance. All living things inherit the characteristics, or traits, of their ancestors. Although you are different in many ways from your parents, you are also the same in many ways due to the genetic traits that you have inherited from them. In object-oriented programming, inheritance allows newly created classes to inherit members from existing classes. These new *derived*, or *child*, classes will include their own members, but also include members inherited from the *base*, or *parent*, class. So, you can view a collection of classes with common inherited members as a *family* of classes, just like the family that you belong to. Classes are related to each other through inheritance. Such inheritance creates a class hierarchy.

In this chapter, we will first explain why inheritance is important, then illustrate its use via a practical example. Finally, we will discuss the last two important aspects of OOP: *polymorphism* and *dynamic binding*.

13-1 WHY USE INHERITANCE?

One reason to use inheritance is that it allows you to reuse the code from a previous programming project without starting from scratch to reinvent the code. Many times the code developed for one program can be reused in another program. Although the new program might be slightly different from the old, inheritance allows you to build on what was done previously. Why reinvent the wheel?

Another reason for using inheritance is that it allows you to build a *hierarchy* among classes. The classes that include those things that are most commonly inherited are at the top of the hierarchy just like your ancestors are at the top of your genetic family hierarchy. Take a banking situation, for example. A general bank account class is used to define variables, such as an account number and account balance, and member functions, such as deposit, that are common to all bank accounts. Then, classes which define a checking account, super-now account, and savings account, can all be derived from the bank account **base** class. This way they will inherit the account number and balance members as well as the deposit function of the general bank account class. Although the derived classes may all have their own unique members, they all include the bank account base class as part of their structure. Thus, a general bank account class would be at the top of a banking class hierarchy. This idea is illustrated by the hierarchy diagram in Figure 13-1.

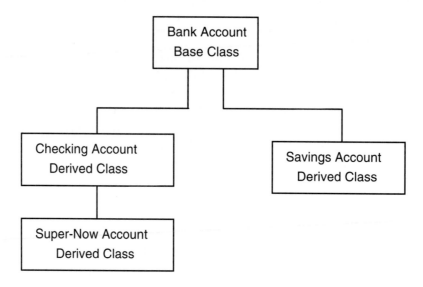

Figure 13-1 The *Checking* and *Savings* classes are derived from the *Bank Account* base class, which has data and function members common to both of these derived classes. The *Super-Now* class is derived from the *Checking* class and will inherit data and function members from both the *Checking* and *Bank Account* classes.

In fact, the left side of the hierarchy diagram in Figure 13-1 shows two levels of inheritance. The *Bank Account* class is inherited by both the *Checking* class and the *Savings* class. In addition, the *Checking* class is inherited by the *Super-Now* class. Notice that the *Super-Now* class inherits the *Bank Account* class indirectly through the *Checking* class. A family of classes related like this is referred to as a **class hierarchy**.

PROGRAMMING NOTE

The important link between a derived class and its base class is the IS-A link. The IS-A relationship must exist if inheritance is used properly. For instance, a checking account IS-A bank account. A super-now account IS-A checking account. However, a savings account IS **NOT** A checking account, it IS-A banking account. Thus, a savings account should *not* be derived from a checking account, but a general bank account class. Always consider the IS-A link when creating inheritance. If there is no IS-A relationship, inheritance should not be used.

 Quick Check

1. A parent class is called a _____ class in C++.

2. A child class is called a _____ class in C++.

3. A collection of classes with common inherited members is called a _____.

4. List at least two reasons for using inheritance.

5. True or False: The proper use of inheritance would allow a line class to be derived from a point class.

6. True or False: The proper use of inheritance would allow a pixel class to be derived from a point class.

7. True or False: The proper use of inheritance would allow a pickup truck class to be derived from a truck class.

13-2 DECLARING AND USING DERIVED CLASSES

A derived class is declared using the following format:

FORMAT FOR DECLARING DERIVED CLASSES

class <derived class> : **public** <base class>
{
  <Derived Class Member Functions>

  <Derived Class Member Data>
};

Let's illustrate inheritance via the classes of bank accounts shown in Figure 13-1. Look at the figure again and you see that the *Checking* and *Savings* classes are derived from the *Bank Account* base class and the *Super-Now* class is derived from the *Checking* class. Here is how we will set up the various account classes:

Bank Account Class

The *Bank Account* class is at the top of the hierarchy diagram and, therefore, will be the base class for the entire family. It will contain member data and functions that are common to all types of bank accounts. The structure of this class will be:

Function Members:
- A function to make deposits.
- A function to access the account number.
- A function to access the account balance.

Data Members:
- An account number.
- An account balance.

Checking Account Class

The *Checking* account class will inherit the *Bank Account* class members. In addition, it will contain the following members.

Function Members:

- A constructor function to initialize the *Checking* account data members.
- A function that will cash a check by receiving a check amount and debit the account balance accordingly.

Data Members:

- A minimum balance value that will dictate when a per-check charge is to be made.
- A value that will be charged on each check cashed when the account balance is less than the minimum required balance.

Super-Now Checking Account Class

A super-now acount is simply an interest bearing checking account. As a result, this class will inherit the *Checking* account class members and, therefore, will also inherit the *Bank Account* class members. In addition, the *Super-Now* account class will contain the following members:

Function Members:

- A constructor function to initialize the *Super-Now* checking account data members.
- A function that will credit interest to the account if the balance is above the required minimum.

Data Members:

- An annual interest rate value that is credited to the account balance on a monthly basis, if the account balance remains above a minimum required level.

Savings Account Class

The savings account class is derived from the original *Bank Account* base class. In addition to the *Bank Account* class members, the *Savings* account class will contain the following:

Function Members:

- A constructor function to initialize the *Savings* account data members.

- A function that will credit interest to the account.
- A function that will debit the account for a withdrawal.

Data Members:
- An annual interest rate value that is credited to the account balance on a monthly basis.

Now, we begin our program construction by declaring our *Bank Account* base class as follows:

// BANK ACCOUNT HEADER FILE (account.h)

```
#ifndef ACCOUNT_H
#define ACCOUNT_H

// BANK ACCOUNT BASE CLASS DECLARATION
class Bank_Account
{
public:
  void Deposit(float Dep);         // ADD DEPOSIT
  int Account_Num();               // RETURN ACCOUNT NUMBER
  float Current_Balance();         // RETURN ACCOUNT BALANCE

protected:
  int Account_Number;              // ACCOUNT NUMBER
  float Balance;                   // ACCOUNT BALANCE
};
#endif
```

First, you see that the class declaration is provided in a header file called *account.h*. Next, you see three preprocessor directives, *#ifndef* and *#define* at the beginning of the file and *#endif* at the end of the file. These directives are required because this header file will be included in several additional files. The specific purpose of these directives will be discussed shortly. Looking at the *Bank_Account* class declaration, you see that it contains three function members and two data members. The three public functions are *Deposit()*, *Account_Num()*, and *Current_Balance()*. The *Deposit()* function will be used to make a deposit to the account. The *Account_Num()* and *Current_Balance()* functions are access functions that are used to retrieve the account number and balance, respectively. You might be wondering why there is no constructor function to initialize the data members of the class. Well, when inheritance is used properly, there are no objects created for the base class. When no objects are created for a class, the class is called an *abstract class*. An abstract class never needs a constructor, since there will be no objects created for it. Only the derived classes will have objects and the constructors will be placed in each of the derived classes. These constructors will be used to initialize the data members inherited from the base class. You will see how this works shortly.

The data members of the *Bank_Account* base class are *Account_Number* and *Balance*. Notice that they are declared as **protected members** using the keyword **protected**.

> A **protected member** of a class is a member that is accessible to both the base class and any derived classes of the base class in which it is declared. Thus, a protected member of a base class is accessible to any class within the class family, but not accessible to things outside the class family.

You could say that a protected member of a base class has accessibility that is somewhere between that of a private member and a public member. If a member is a private member of a base class, it is *not* accessible to a derived class. However, a protected member of a base class is accessible to any derived classes. On the other hand, a protected member is "protected" from being accessed outside of the class family, thereby preserving data hiding within the family. Next, we develop an implementation file, called *account.cpp*, for the base class as follows:

```
// ACCOUNT IMPLEMENTATION FILE (account.cpp)

#include "account.h"

// IMPLEMENTATION FOR Deposit() FUNCTION
void Bank_Account :: Deposit(float Amount)
{
  Balance += Amount;
}

// IMPLEMENTATION FOR Account_Num() FUNCTION
int Bank_Account :: Account_Num()
{
  return (Account_Number);
}
```

```
// IMPLEMENTATION FOR Current_Balance() FUNCTION
float Bank_Account :: Current_Balance()
{
  return (Balance);
}
```

The function implementations shown in this file should be self-explanatory.

Now, let's declare our first derived class. This class, called *Checking,* will be derived from the *Bank_Account* class as follows:

```
// CHECKING ACCOUNT HEADER FILE (checking.h)

#ifndef CHECKING_H
#define CHECKING_H

#include "account.h"

// CHECKING ACCOUNT DERIVED CLASS DECLARATION
class Checking : public Bank_Account
{
public:
  Checking(int Acct_Num = 0000,
          float Bal = 0,              // CONSTRUCTOR
          float Min = 1000,
          float Chg = .5);
  void Cash_Check(float Amt);        // CASH A CHECK

protected:
  float Minimum;                     // MINIMUM BALANCE TO
                                     // AVOID CHECK CHARGE

  float Charge;                      // PER-CHECK CHARGE
};
#endif
```

Again, the *Checking* class declaration is coded as a header file. The header file name is *checking.h.* Looking at the class declaration you see that the *Checking* class is derived from the *Bank_Account* class. This is indicated by the colon between the derived class (*Checking*) and the base class (*Bank_Account*) in the class declaration. The base class header file (*account.h*) must be included in this file to make the declaration. Furthermore, notice the use of the keyword **public** prior to the base class name. This designation makes the *Bank_Account* class a public base class to the derived *Checking* class.

A **public base class** allows all public members of the base class to be public in the derived class.

When a base class is designated as **public** in the derived class declaration, the inherited members of the public base class maintain their access level in the derived class. Thus, inherited private members remain private, protected members remain protected, and public members remain public in the derived class. In our example, the public members of the *Bank_Account* ciass are the *Deposit()*, *Account_Num()*, and *Current_Balance()* functions. The use of the keyword **public** prior to the base class name, *Bank_Account*, in the derived *Checking* class declaration makes all of these functions public to the *Checking* class just as if they were declared as part of the public section of the *Checking* class. Without the use of the keyword **public,** the public functions of the *Bank_Account* class would *not* be accessible to any program using an object of the *Checking* class. In other words, without the base class being public, an application program could not call any of the base class functions via a derived class object.

For example, suppose an application program defines an object called *John_Doe* for the *Checking* derived class like this:

Checking John_Doe;

If the *Bank_Account* base class is not made public, then a message to its *Current_Balance()* function via the *John_Doe* object would cause a compiler error. Thus, the statement

John_Doe . Current_Balance();

would not compile, since *Current_Balance()* is not public for *Checking*.

Now, back to the *Checking* class declaration. Two member functions are declared for the *Checking* class: *Checking()* and *Cash_Check()*. The *Checking()* function is a constructor that is used to initialize all four data members of the class. (Why does this class have four data members, since only two are shown in the foregoing declaration?) Notice that each data member has a default value. The *Cash_Check()* function is used to debit the account balance by cashing a check.

You see that the *Checking* class has two protected members, *Minimum* and *Charge*. The *Minimum* data member will be used to store a minimum balance value, whereby no per-check charge is made if the account balance is above the stored minimum value. The *Charge* data member will be used to store a per-check charge for writing checks if the account balance is less than *Minimum*. Notice that both *Minimum* and *Charge* are designated as protected members, since they will be inherited by the *Super-Now* class (See Figure 13-1).

Of course, since *Checking* is derived from *Bank_Account*, the protected *Bank_Account* class members, *Account_Number* and *Balance*, are inherited by the *Checking* class. Thus, *Checking* actually has four data members, *Account_Number* and *Balance* which are inherited from *Bank_Account*, as well as *Minimum* and *Charge* which are declared in *Checking*.

PROGRAMMING NOTE

You will avoid confusion about when to use the keywords **protected** and **public** relative to inheritance if you remember the following points:

• Use the keyword **protected** in a base class declaration if you want to allow access to private members of the base class by the derived class. The protected members will be accessible within the class family but not outside of the family.

• Use the keyword **public** when declaring a derived class if you want the public members of the base class to be public for the derived class.

The **protected** and **public** options are provided in C++ to provide flexibility during inheritance. With the proper use of these options, you can specify precisely which base class members are to be inherited by the derived classes. If you do not want the private members of a base class inherited, do not protect the private class members of the base class. If you do not want the public members of the base class inherited, do not use the keyword **public** in the derived class declaration.

Next, we need to construct an implementation file for the *Checking* class. Let's call the file *checking.cpp*. Here it is:

```
// CHECKING IMPLEMENTATION FILE (checking.cpp)

#include "checking.h"
#include <iostream.h>
#include <stdio.h>

// IMPLEMENTATION FOR Checking() CONSTRUCTOR
Checking :: Checking (int Acct_Num, float Bal, float Min, float Chg)
{
  Account_Number = Acct_Num;
  Balance = Bal;
  Minimum = Min;
  Charge = Chg;
}

// IMPLEMENTATION FOR Cash_Check() FUNCTION
void Checking :: Cash_Check (float Amt)
{
  if (Amt > Balance)                // TEST FOR OVERDRAW
  {
    cout << "\nCannot cash check, account overdrawn. "
            "Press ENTER to continue";
    getchar();
  }
  else                              // CASH CHECK
     if (Balance < Minimum)            // DEBIT BALANCE WITH
                                       // CHECK AMOUNT
                                       // AND CHARGE

         Balance -= Amt + Charge;
     else                              // DEBIT BALANCE WITH
                                       // CHECK AMOUNT

         Balance -= Amt;

}
```

As you can see, the *Checking()* constructor function sets the values of *Account_Number*, *Balance*, *Minimum*, and *Charge* from values received by the function when an object is defined for the class. Recall that a class constructor is automatically called when an object is defined for the class. Of course, if values are not provided in the object definition, the data members are initialized to their respective default values. The *Cash_Check()* function receives an amount (*Amt*) from the calling object and generates an error message if this amount exceeds the account balance. Otherwise, the check is cashed and the account balance is debited accordingly. Notice that a check cashing charge is applied if the amount of the check is less than the required minimum balance.

Looking back at Figure 13-1 you see that a *Super_Now* class is derived from the *Checking* class. A super-now account is one where you get interest on your checking account if you maintain a minimum balance. In addition, no per-check charge is made if the balance stays above the minimum. This is a perfect place to declare a derived class of the *Checking* class, since the *Super_Now* class can inherit the *Minimum* and *Charge* data members as well as the *Cash_Check()* function of the *Checking* class. So, let's develop a header file for the *Super_Now* class and call it *supernow.h*. Here's one that will work:

```
// SUPER NOW ACCOUNT HEADER FILE (supernow.h)

#include "checking.h"

// SUPER NOW ACCOUNT DERIVED CLASS DECLARATION
class  Super_Now : public Checking
{
public:
  Super_Now(int Acct_Num = 0,
            float Bal = 0,                    // CONSTRUCTOR
            float Min = 5000,
            float Chg = .5,
            float Rate = 12);
  void Add_Interest();                        // ADD INTEREST TO BALANCE

protected:
  float Interest_Rate;                        // ANNUAL INTEREST RATE
};
```

First you see that the *checking.h* header file is included, since the *Super_Now* class is derived from this class. The *Super_Now* class declaration uses the keyword **public** so that the public functions of *Checking* are inherited by *Super_Now*. There are two additional functions declared for this class. The *Super_Now()* constructor function that initializes the data members of the class, and the *Add_Interest()* function that will credit the account balance with interest at a rate specified by the *Interest_Rate* data member.

The only data member unique to this class is *Interest_Rate*, which specifies the annual interest rate to be applied to the account. However, through inheritance there are four additional data members. What are they? Well, *Account_Number* and *Balance* are inherited from the *Bank_Account* class via the *Checking* class, while *Minimum* and *Charge* are inherited directly from the *Checking* class. Here is the implementation file for the class:

```
// SUPER NOW IMPLEMENTATION FILE (supernow.cpp)

#include "supernow.h"

// IMPLEMENTATION FOR SUPER NOW CONSTRUCTOR
Super_Now :: Super_Now (int Acct_Num,
                        float Bal,
                        float Min,
                        float Chg,
                        float Rate)
{
  Account_Number = Acct_Num;
  Balance = Bal;
  Minimum = Min;
  Charge = Chg;
  Interest_Rate = Rate;
}

// IMPLEMENTATION FOR Add_Interest() FUNCTION
void Super_Now :: Add_Interest()
{
  if (Balance >= Minimum)
  {
    float Interest = Balance * (Interest_Rate/12/100);
    Balance += Interest;
  }
}
```

The file is called *supernow.cpp*. As you can see, the *Super_Now()* constructor function initializes all the class data members. The *Add_Interest()* function adds monthly interest to the account if the account balance is greater than or equal to the minimum required balance.

The last class that we need to declare is the *Savings* account class. Here's the declaration:

```
// SAVINGS ACCOUNT HEADER FILE (savings.h)

#include "account.h"
```

```
// SAVINGS ACCOUNT DERIVED CLASS DECLARATION
class Savings: public Bank_Account
{
public:
  Savings( int Acct_Num = 0,
               float Bal = 0,                      // CONSTRUCTOR
               float Rate = 12.0);
    void Add_Interest();                           // ADD INTEREST TO BALANCE
    void Withdraw(float Amt);                      // SUBTRACT WITHDRAWAL

protected:
  float Interest_Rate;                             // ANNUAL INTEREST RATE
};
```

There are three additional functions defined for the *Savings* class. The *Savings()* constructor function is used to initialize the class data members. The *Add_Interest()* function is used to credit the account balance with monthly interest earnings. The *Withdraw()* function is used to debit the account balance when a savings withdrawal is made. Moreover, since the *Savings* class is derived from the *Bank_Account* class, it inherits the *Deposit()* function.

The *Savings* class also inherits the *Account_Number* and *Balance* data members from the *Bank_Account* class. In addition, an *Interest_Rate* data member is defined for this class. The *Interest_Rate* data member will store an annual savings account interest rate value.

Here is the associated implementation file:

```
// SAVINGS IMPLEMENTATION FILE (savings.cpp)
#include "savings.h"

// IMPLEMENTATION FOR Savings() CONSTRUCTOR
Savings :: Savings(int Acct_Num, float Bal, float Rate)
{
  Account_Number = Acct_Num;
  Balance = Bal;
  Interest_Rate = Rate;
}

// IMPLEMENTATION FOR Withdraw() FUNCTION
void Savings :: Withdraw(float Amt)
{
  Balance -= Amt;
}
```

```
// IMPLEMENTATION FOR Add_Interest() METHOD
void Savings :: Add_Interest()
{
  float Interest = Balance * (Interest_Rate/12/100);
  Balance += Interest;
}
```

The function implementations should be self-explanatory by now. Notice, however, that this *Add_Interest()* function differs from the *Add_Interest()* function in the *Super_Now* class. The *Savings* class *Add_Interest()* function does not depend on a minimum balance, whereas the *Super_Now* class *Add_Interest()* function does.

We can use the Venn diagram shown in Figure 13-2 to summarize the bank account class family hierarchy. Notice how the class inheritance patterns can be seen by the intersections between the classes.

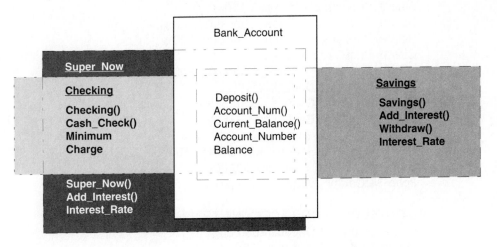

Figure 13-2 A Venn diagram of the bank account class family hierarchy.

Finally, we need an application file to exercise our class family. Here is one that will demonstrate most of the family features:

```
// BANKING APPLICATION FILE (banking.cpp)

#include "account.h"
#include "checking.h"
```

```
#include "supernow.h"
#include "savings.h"
#include <stdio.h>
#include <iostream.h>
#include <iomanip.h>

void main()
{

// DEFINE BANKING ACCOUNT OBJECTS
   Checking Bjarne_Stroustrup_1(0001);
   Super_Now John_McCarthy_1(0002);
   Savings Grace_Hopper_1(0003);
   Checking Grace_Hopper_2(0004);

// MONTHLY CHECKING ACCOUNT TRANSACTIONS
   Bjarne_Stroustrup_1.Deposit(1500);
   Bjarne_Stroustrup_1.Cash_Check (500.00);
   Bjarne_Stroustrup_1.Cash_Check (500.00);
   Bjarne_Stroustrup_1.Cash_Check (700.75);
   Bjarne_Stroustrup_1.Cash_Check (200.00);
   Grace_Hopper_2.Deposit(2500);
   Grace_Hopper_2.Cash_Check(25.75);
   Grace_Hopper_2.Cash_Check(75.25);

// MONTHLY SUPER-NOW ACCOUNT TRANSACTIONS
   John_McCarthy_1.Deposit(2000.00);
   John_McCarthy_1.Cash_Check(200.00);

// MONTHLY SAVINGS ACCOUNT TRANSACTIONS
   Grace_Hopper_1.Deposit(2000.00);
   Grace_Hopper_1.Withdraw(350);

// MONTHLY REPORT OF ACCOUNT BALANCES
   cout << setprecision(2);
   John_McCarthy_1.Add_Interest();
   Grace_Hopper_1.Add_Interest();
   cout << "\n\n\t\t\tAccount Balances\n\n";

   cout << "\nAccount Number:  "
        << Bjarne_Stroustrup_1.Account_Num()
        << "\tBjarne Stroustrup:  $"
```

```
            << Bjarne_Stroustrup_1.Current_Balance();

    cout << "\nAccount Number:  "
            << John_McCarthy_1.Account_Num()
            << "\tJohn McCarthy: $"
            << John_McCarthy_1.Current_Balance();

    cout << "\nAccount Number:  "
            << Grace_Hopper_1.Account_Num()
            << "\tGrace_Hopper: $"
            <<  Grace_Hopper_1.Current_Balance();

    cout << "\nAccount Number:  "
            << Grace_Hopper_2.Account_Num()
            << "\tGrace_Hopper: $"
            <<  Grace_Hopper_2.Current_Balance();

    cout << "\n\nPRESS ENTER TO RETURN TO DOS";
    getchar();
}
```

The application file is called *banking.cpp* and begins by including all of the class header files. The class header files must be included because the respective class objects are defined in this application file. Looking at function *main()* within the file, you see that several objects are defined for the various banking account classes. The object name corresponds to the customer name. A suffix is added to the customer name so that the same customer can have more than one bank account. For instance, you see that *Grace_Hopper_1* is a checking account object, while *Grace_Hopper_2* is a savings account object. Notice also that a unique account number is specified when each object is defined. As a result, the customer account number in the base class is initialized with this value. All other data members will take on their respective default values, since only the account number value is specified during the object definition.

Next, monthly transactions are listed for each type of account. Can you determine what should happen in each transaction? Finally, a monthly balance report of each account is generated on the display monitor. What will be the balance for each account at the end of the month, using the indicated transactions in the order that they appear?

A project file is needed to efficiently develop such a program in C++. For this program the project file would include all the *.cpp* implementation files and the *.cpp* application file as shown in Figure 13-3.

The project data shown in Figure 13-3 is what you would see for this project by viewing the Project Window in TURBO C++. Notice that the header files are not listed as part of the project, since they are included in the various *.cpp* files.

Project: BANKING

File name	Location	Lines	Code	Data
ACCOUNT.CPP		21	54	0
SUPERNOW.CPP	.	29	193	16
CHECKING.CPP	.	34	189	64
SAVINGS.CPP .		26	133	8
BANKING.CPP .		66	858	261

Figure 13-3 The *banking.prj* project as viewed in the TURBO C++ Project Window.

Single Versus Multiple Inheritance

Up to this point, we have been dealing with single inheritance. Actually, there are two types of inheritance possible: *single inheritance* and *multiple inheritance.* Single inheritance occurs when all inherited class members can be traced back to a single parent class. The type of inheritance depicted in Figure 13-1 is single inheritance. Multiple inheritance occurs when the inherited class members can be traced back to more than one parent class. As an example of multiple inheritance, consider the *iostream.h* header file that you have been including in your programs to use the *cout* and *cin* objects. The *iostream.h* header file declares the *iostream* class. This class is derived from two parent classes: *istream* and *ostream.* The *istream* class provides the members necessary for formatted input and the *ostream* class provides the members necessary for formatted output.

As a result of multiple inheritance, the *iostream* class inherits both the required input and output members. In addition, the *istream* and *ostream* classes are derived from a single class called *ios.* The *ios* class provides file operations common to both input and output and maintains internal flags used by *istream* and *ostream.* Single inheritance allows both *istream* and *ostream* to inherit these common members. The diagram in Figure 13-4 illustrates the *ios* family hierarchy. Here, we have single inheritance from *ios* to *istream/ostream* and multiple inheritance from *istream/ostream* to *iostream.*

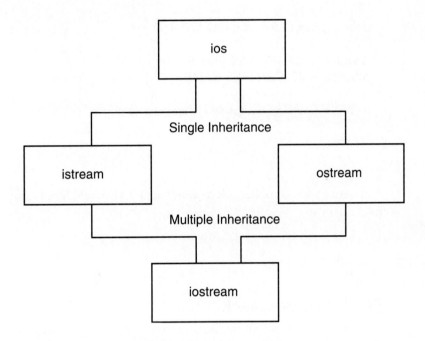

Figure 13-4 Single inheritance exists between the *ios* class and the *istream/ostream* classes. Multiple inheritance occurs between the *istream/ostream* classes and the *iostream* class.

Using #ifndef: An Implementation Detail

To close this section, I need to discuss the *#ifndef* preprocessor directive as promised earlier. You observed the use of this directive along with the *#define* and *#endif* directives in the *Bank_Account* and *Checking* class declarations. Since these classes are base classes, they need to be included as header files in more than one file. For example, *account.h* is included in *checking.h, savings.h,* and *banking.h* files. Since *account.h* provides the declaration for the *Bank_Account* class, the compiler sees multiple declarations for this class via the multiple include directives. It's as if you declared a variable several times in a single source file. Such an oversight causes a "Multiple declaration for ..." compiler error. Since the *Bank_Account* class must be included in multiple files for inheritance purposes, you must tell the compiler that you are only declaring it once. This is the purpose of the *#ifndef* directive. So, always use the following format when declaring base classes in C++:

> ### *DECLARING BASE CLASSES IN C++*
>
> **#ifndef** <HEADER FILE NAME> _H
> **#define** <HEADER FILE NAME> _H
>
> < BASE CLASS DECLARATION>
>
> **#endif**

Consult your compiler reference manual if you need more information on the **#ifndef** directive.

 Quick Check

1. True or False: When declaring a derived class, the derived class is listed first followed by a colon and the base class.

2. True or False: A public base class allows its public members to be used by any of its derived classes.

3. True or False: A protected base class member is protected from any use by the derived classes of that base class.

4. When base class header files are included in multiple implementation and application files, you must use the _____ directive to avoid "Multiple declaration" compile errors.

5. What would be wrong with deriving the *Savings* class from the *Super_Now* class in the program discussed in this section?

6. What type of inheritance occurs when all the inherited members in a family can be traced back to more than one parent class?

13-3 POLYMORPHISM AND DYNAMIC BINDING

In the Chapter 12 introduction, it was stated that there were four concepts central to OOP: encapsulation with data hiding, inheritance, polymorphism, and dynamic binding. We have thoroughly explored the first two. For completeness, we will now briefly discuss the latter two concepts of polymorphism and dynamic binding.

Polymorphism

The term "polymorphic" is Greek meaning "of many forms." Polymorphism can be associated with functions or objects as seen in the following definitions:

> A *polymorphic* function is one which has the same name for different classes of the same family but has different implementations for the various classes.

> A *polymorphic* object is one which has the same name as objects of other classes in a class hierarchy such that each object, although related through a common base class, may have different behavior.

As you can see, polymorphism allows functions of the same name and objects of the same name to behave differently within a class family. You have just seen an example of a polymorphic function in our bank account class family. Can you identify which function it is from the class header files? You're right if you thought the *Add_Interest()* function. Notice that this function is defined in both the *Super_Now* and *Savings* classes. The function interface is identical in both classes, however the implementation is different in each class. In effect, we are hiding alternative operations behind the common *Add_Interest()* interface. This means that the two objects defined for these classes will respond to the common operation, *Add_Interest()*, in different ways. Languages that do not support polymorphism, such as Pascal and C, require large switch/case statements to implement this effect.

Polymorphism allows objects to be more independent, even though they are members of the same class family. Moreover, new classes can be added to the family without changing existing ones. This allows systems to evolve over time, meeting the needs of a changing application. Consider a word processing program where the system is required to print many different types of documents. Recall from Chapter 12 that many such programs employ classes to define the structure and behavior of a given type of document. Each document class will have a *Print()* function to print a specific document in its correct format. Such a function would be a polymorphic function, since it would have a common interface, but behave differently for different document objects.

Polymorphism is accomplished using overloaded functions or ***virtual functions***. Overloaded functions were discussed earlier in Chapters 7 and 12. However, virtual functions are something new. The difference between the two has to do with the different techniques that are used by C++ to call the function. Overloaded functions are called using ***static binding***, while virtual functions are called using ***dynamic binding***.

Dynamic versus Static Binding

Binding relates to the actual time when the code for a given function is attached, or bound, to the function.

> ***Dynamic***, or ***late***, ***binding*** occurs when a polymorphic function is defined for several classes in a family but the actual code for the function is not attached, or bound, until execution time. A polymorphic function which is dynamically bound is called a ***virtual*** function.

Dynamic binding is implemented in C++ through ***virtual functions***. With dynamic binding, the selection of code to be executed when a virtual function is called is delayed until execution time. This means that when a virtual function is called, the executable code determines at run time which version of the function to call. Remember, virtual functions are polymorphic, and therefore have different implementations for different classes in the family.

> ***Static binding*** occurs when a polymorphic function is defined for several classes in a family and the actual code for the function is attached, or bound, at compile time. Overloaded functions are statically bound.

Static binding, on the other hand, occurs when function code is "bound" at compile time. This means that when a non-virtual function is called, the compiler determines at compile time which version of the function to call. Overloaded functions are statically bound, while virtual functions are dynamically bound. With overloaded functions, the compiler can determine which function to call based on the number of and data types of the function parameters. However, virtual functions have the same interface within a given class family. Therefore, pointers must be used during run time to determine which function to call. Any ideas on how this is accomplished? (Hint: Remember that each function has its own unique *this* pointer.) Fortunately, you don't have to worry about how the binding is accomplished, since this is taken care of automatically by the compiler.

You should be aware that virtual functions are most often declared in a base class in C++ using the keyword **virtual.** When a function is declared as a virtual function in a base class, the compiler knows that the base class definition might be overriden in a derived class. The base class definition is overriden by defining a different implementation for the same function in a derived class. If the base class definition is not overriden in a given derived class, then the base class definition is availble to the derived class.

 Quick Check

1. True or False: A virtual function is polymorphic.

2. True or False: All polymorphic functions are virtual functions.

3. True or False: The virtual function interface is identical for each version of the function in a given class family.

4. Overloaded functions are _____ bound.

5. Virtual functions are _____ bound.

6. The implementation code for a dynamically bound function is determined at _____.

CHAPTER SUMMARY

Inheritance is an important property of object-oriented programming that allows one class, called a derived class, to share the structure and behavior of another class, called a base class. The derived class should always be related to its base class via the IS-A relationship. There is both single inheritance and multiple inheritance. Single inheritance occurs when all inherited class members can be traced to a single base class. Multiple inheritance occurs when the inherited class members can be traced back to more than one base class. You control the amount of data member inheritance by designating the members as private, protected, or public in the base class declaration. You control the amount of function inheritance by designating the base class as public or non-public (by default) in the derived class declaration.

Polymorphism has to do with functions and objects which have the same name, but different behavior within a class family. Polymorphism allows functions and objects to be more independent and class families to be more flexible. Overloaded functions and virtual functions are polymorphic. Overloaded functions are statically bound to their code during compile time, while virtual functions are dynamically bound to their code during run time.

QUESTIONS AND PROBLEMS

Questions

1. Define the following terms:
   Base Class
   Derived Class
   Inheritance
   Single Inheritance
   Multiple Inheritance
   IS-A
   Polymorphism
   Dynamic Binding
   Static Binding

2. Suggest several real-world applications for the use of inheritance.

3. What relationship must be considered between a potential derived class and its base class when developing inheritance?

4. Given a base class called *Point*, write the class declaration header line for a derived class called *Pixel*. Assume that the functions in *Point* are to be public in *Pixel*.

5. Explain how a protected class member differs from a private class member and a public class member.

6. When should you use the keyword **public** in a derived class declaration?

7. When should you use the **#ifndef** directive in a class header file?

8. Why is a virtual function polymorphic?

9. Explain the difference between static binding and dynamic binding.

Problems

Least Difficult

1. Determine the output generated by the application program (*banking.cpp*) given in this chapter.

2. Code the class header and implementation files for the banking program given in this chapter. Then, write your own application program to exercise the class family in different ways. See if you can predict the results of your banking transactions.

More Difficult

3. Add a *Credit_Card* class to the *Bank_Account* class family developed in this chapter. The *Credit_Card* class should inherit the *Bank_Account* class directly. Provide functions to debit monthly charges and interest from the account balance. Write an application program to exercise a *Credit_Card* object and report the balance due.

4. Declare a *Resistor_Circuit* class that contains the following members:

   Function Members:

   - A function that will allow the user to enter the resistor values and the number of resistors in the circuit.

   - A function that will display the resistor values along with the equivalent resistance of the circuit.

   Data Members:

   - The resistor values stored in an array.

   - The number of resistors in the circuit.

   - The equivalent resistance of the circuit.

5. Declare two derived classes called *Series_Circuit* and *Parallel_Circuit* that inherit the *Resistor_Circuit* class declared in problem 4. Provide the following functions in these derived classes:

   Series_Circuit():

   A function to calculate the equivalent resistance of a series circuit.

   Parallel_Circuit():

   A function to calculate the equivalent resistance of a parallel circuit.

6. Write an application program that defines a series resistance object and a parallel resistance object from the classes declared in problems 4 and 5. Include statements in the program that will exercise the object functions to calculate circuit resistance of the respective objects.

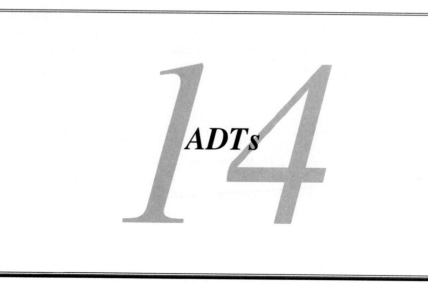

INTRODUCTION

Abstract data types, or ADTs, provide for data abstraction. The idea behind data abstraction is to combine data with a set of operations that are defined for that data in one neat encapsulated package called an ADT. The ADT can then be used by knowing what the operations do, without needing to know the details of how the computer system implements the data or its operations. You have been using data abstraction since Chapter 2 when you learned about the C++ data types. In each case, you learned about the structure of the data type, the operations that could be performed on a given data type, and how to use those operations. You were not concerned about how the computer stores the data or how the operations were implemented. You could concentrate on their use rather than their implementation.

Data abstraction is an important software development and programming tool. When developing software with ADTs you can concentrate on the ADT data and related operations, without worrying about the inner implementation details of the ADT. Data abstraction provides for generality, modularity, and protection when developing software.

We will begin this chapter with a general discussion of ADTs. In the first section, we will discuss all the facets of an ADT so that you completely understand all of its implications. Then, the remaining three sections will use object-oriented programming to build three classic ADTs: the stack, the queue, and the linked list.

14-1 THE CONCEPT OF DATA ABSTRACTION

Let's begin with a definition for an ADT, and then look at some important characteristics of an ADT.

An *abstract data type (ADT)* is a collection of data and related operations.

- *Abstraction*
  The term *abstract* means that the data and related operations are being viewed without considering any of the details of *how* the data or operations are implemented in the computer system. You have been working with abstact data types thoughout this book, without knowing it. For instance, consider the *float* data type used in C++. Have you been

concerned about how floating point values are stored in memory? Have you been concernced about how C++ implements floating point operations? Of course not! All that you are concerned about is the general structure of a floating point value, what operations are available to be used with floating point values, and how to use these floating point operations. The implementation details are left to the C++ compiler designer.

This whole idea of abstraction facilitates the design of modular software and the development of algorithms for software design, because abstraction allows us to hide implementation details thereby facilitating more general thinking.

- *An ADT includes both data and related operations.*

Think of an ADT as a black box that contains *private* data and *public* operations. Sound familiar? You know what the box does and how to use it through its *public* operations, or interface. However, you are not concerned about what goes on inside the box. The ADT black box concept facilitates modular software design.

The Data: An ADT defines the data to be operated upon as well as the operations that can be performed on the data. An ADT is not the same thing as a data structure. A data structure provides a way of structuring, or organizing, data within a programming language. You will be concerned about data structures when you implement an ADT, since you will have to decide how to organize and store the ADT data. However, on the surface you are not concerned with these implementation details in order to access and manipulate the ADT data.. The data in an ADT must be private, which means that it is hidden from any operations that are not defined for the ADT.

The Operations: The ADT includes operations, or functions, that manipulate the ADT data. These operations are public, which means that they are used by outside software to access and manipulate the private ADT data. Again, all you are concerned about at the abstract level is what these operations do and how to use them. As a result, the interface to the operations within the ADT must be complete enough to totally describe the effect that they have on the data. However, you are not concerned about how they do what they do.

- *An ADT provides a means to encapsulate details; whereby the data is completely hidden from its surroundings.*

   Recall that *encapsulation* with *information hiding* allows you to combine data with the operations that are dedicated to manipulating the data so tightly that outside operations can not affect the data. This allows the application program to be oblivious to how the ADT data are stored. In addition, information hiding provides for data protection. Only those operations that are defined for the ADT can operate on the ADT data. As a result, the data cannot be corrupted intentionally or unintentionally by using "unauthorized" operations.

- *ADT operations provide loose coupling to the outside world via a function interface.*

   The operations defined for an ADT provide the interface between the outside world and the ADT. In other words, the only way to gain access to the ADT is through the ADT operation, or function, interfaces. Again, the ADT is like a black box that is connected to its surroundings via its function interfaces. The function interfaces provide the communications channel between an application program and the ADT. This idea is illustrated in Figure 14-1. This figure should look familiar to you, since it is basically the same figure used to illustrate a class in Chapter 12. As you might now suspect, the class in C++ provides an ideal implementation of an ADT.

By using ADTs during software development, we gain modularity, generality, and protection. We gain modularity, since ADTs can be thought of as black box building blocks during software development. We gain generality, since algorithms can be developed that only depend on the function interface to the ADT without considering the implementation details of the ADT. In addition, once an ADT is developed, it is available for general use in many applications without rewriting the ADT code. We gain protection through information hiding. Private data stored within an ADT cannot be corrupted intentionally or unintentionally.

   The definition of an ADT given above completely describes the C++ class that we developed in Chapter 12. Recall that a class includes both data (private members) and related operations (public functions) that are encapsulated. In addition, the private member data is completely hidden from anything outside the class. Finally, the class is coupled to its outside world via the class function interfaces (prototypes). That is, to access the class data from the outside you must invoke the public member functions of the class. This is why C++ is ideal for coding ADTs.

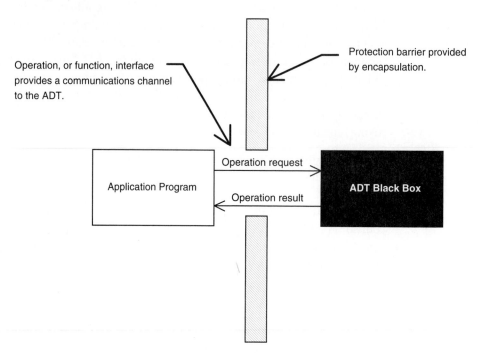

Operation, or function, interface provides a communications channel to the ADT.

Protection barrier provided by encapsulation.

Application Program

Operation request

Operation result

ADT Black Box

Figure 14-1 The ADT is like a black box that is connected to its surroundings via its function interfaces.

The remainder of this chapter is devoted to building some classic ADTs. As you study these ADTs keep in mind the general ideas of data abstraction presented in this section.

 Quick Check

1. What term is used to indicate that data and its related operations are being viewed without considering any of the details of how the data or operations are implemented in the computer system?
2. Give an example of an ADT with which you have been working in the C++ language.

3. The ADT black box concept facilitates _____ software design.
4. True or False: A data structure and an abstract data type are the same thing.
5. Data protection in an ADT is provided by _____.
6. The interface to an ADT is through its _____.
7. Why do you gain modularity through the use of ADTs?
8. Why do you gain generality through the use of ADTs?

14-2 ADT STACK

You have been introduced to the stack ADT via some of the programming problems in previous chapters. Now it is time to take a closer look at this important ADT. Stacks are common in a wide variety of applications in computer science. For example, you observed the use of a stack when you studied recursion in Chapter 7. With recursion, a stack is employed to save information as the recursive function calls are made. Once the primitive state is reached, the stack information is retrieved to determine the final recursive function value.

In general, a stack is used to reverse the order of data placed in it. Now, let's see how a stack works, beginning with a formal definition for a stack:

The *stack* is a collection of data elements and related operations whereby all the insertions and deletions of elements to and from the stack are made at one end of the stack called the *top*. A stack operates on the *last-in*, *first-out*, or *LIFO* principle.

To get the idea of a stack, think of a stack of trays in a spring-loaded bin such as what you might find in a cafeteria line. Such a stack is illustrated in Figure 14-2. When you remove a tray from the stack, you remove it from the *top* of the stack. If you were to add a tray onto the stack, you would place it on the *top* of the stack. All insertions and deletions of trays to and from the stack are made at the *top* of the stack. In other words, the last tray placed onto the stack will be the first tray removed from the stack. This characteristic is commonly referred to as *last-in*, *first-out*, or simply *LIFO*. Examples of the LIFO principle are hard to find in everyday life. For instance, suppose that you enter a grocery store check-out line. If the line is operating on the LIFO principle, the last person in the line would be the first one to be checked out. It might be quite some time until you were able to pay for your groceries, especially if other people keep entering the line. Think about how unfair such a line would be! To be fair, a grocery store line must operate on a *first-in, first-out*, or *FIFO*, principle. This principle is associated with *queues* and will be discussed in the next section. Although the LIFO principle is not very common in everyday life it is very common in many problems that arise in computer science.

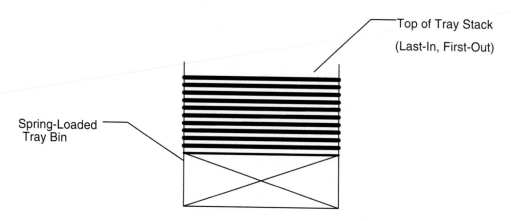

Figure 14-2 A stack obeys the last-in, first-out (LIFO) principle like this stack of cafeteria trays.

Now, let's consider the cafeteria tray stack again. What operations do you suppose could be performed on such a stack? Well, first of all you can move an empty tray bin into position in preparation for adding trays to the bin. Then, you can begin adding trays to the bin to form a stack of trays. When a single tray is added to the stack, it can only be added at the *top* position and no other position. Adding an element to a stack is referred to as a *push* operation. You can remove a tray from the *top* of the stack and, normally, you can't remove a tray from any other position other than the top of the stack. Removing an element from a stack is called a *pop* operation. You could also inspect the *top* tray but no others. You could see if the stack of trays were empty, but if not empty you would not know how many trays were in the stack. Given the situation, you are forced to access the trays from the *top* of the stack. The stack of trays provide a very good analogy to stacks in computer science, since the operations that can be performed on a stack of trays form the basis for the stack ADT in computer science. Here is a summary of legal stack operations:

- CreateStack ⇒ Creates and empty stack.

- Push ⇒ Places an element on the top of a stack.

- Pop ⇒ Removes an element from the top of a stack.

- TopElement ⇒ Inspects the top element of the stack, leaving the stack unchanged.

- EmptyStack ⇒ Determines if the stack is empty.

Now we are ready to define our stack ADT. Remember, to define an ADT we must include both a definition for the ADT data as well as any operations that will be needed to manipulate the data. Consider the following ADT definition:

ADT Stack

Operations, or Interface:

CreateStack()
   Creates an empty stack.

Push()
   Adds a new element to the top of a stack.

Pop()
   Removes the top element of a stack.

TopElement()
   Copies the top element of the stack, leaving the stack unchanged.

EmptyStack()
   Determines if the stack is empty.

Data:

A collection of data elements that can only be accessed at one location, called the *top* of the stack.

Implementing the Stack ADT

The ADT definition given above provides all the information needed to work with a stack. The operations are clearly defined in order to access and manipulate the stack data. Now it is time to consider the implementation details in order to create stacks in C++. Remember, however, that the following implementation details are not part of the ADT definition. We can always change how we implement the stack ADT, but the stack ADT definition will remain constant.

It is perfectly natural to use a one-dimensional array to hold a stack. We must use an existing structure to implement our stack, since there is no inherent built-in stack data type available in C++, or most other high level languages for that matter.

Creating a Stack Using an Array

We will create an array of some arbitrary length and create an integer variable called *Top* to keep track of the top element on the stack. Remember, we only need to keep track of the top element of the stack, since, by definition, access to the stack elements must be through the top of the stack. To initialize the stack, we will set *Top* to the value −1 as shown in Figure 14-3.

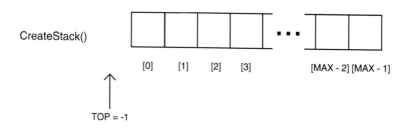

Figure 14-3 Setting *Top* to the value −1 will create an empty stack.

First, look at the array. It is defined with indices ranging from [0] to [*MAX* − 1] and, therefore, can hold *MAX* elements. The array will be used to hold a stack such that the first stack element will be placed at position [0] in the array, the second stack element at position [1], and so on. We will create an integer variable called *Top* that will "point" to the array index that locates the top element in the stack. In Figure 14-3, the value of *Top* is set to −1 to indicate that the stack is empty. The value −1 is used to indicate an empty stack condition, since there is no

−1 index in the array. So, using this idea, all we have to do to create a new empty stack is to define an array and set *Top* to the value −1. How do you know if the stack ever becomes empty when processing the stack data? Of course, the stack is empty if the value of *Top* is −1. The algorithm required to create a stack using our array implementation is straightforward. Here it is:

CreateStack( ) **Algorithm**

BEGIN
    Set *Top* = −1.
END.

Now we are ready to start pushing elements onto the stack.

Pushing Elements Onto a Stack

The first element pushed onto an empty stack will be placed in position [0] of the array. However, before the first element can be placed into the array, the value of *Top* must be incremented to point to position [0]. Let's suppose that we have created a character array to form a stack of characters. Then we execute the following operation:

Push('A')

The push operation causes the value of *Top* to be incremented from −1 to 0, then the character 'A' is placed at position [*Top*], or [0], of the array. Next, suppose we execute another push operation like this:

Push('B')

This push operation causes *Top* to be incremented from 0 to 1, then the character 'B' is placed on the top of the stack which is now array position [1]. Lastly, let's execute a third push operation like this:

Push('C')

Now we are pushing the character 'C' onto the stack. Again, the value of *Top* is incremented and this character is placed into array position [*Top*], or [2]. This sequence of three push operations is illustrated in Figure 14-4.

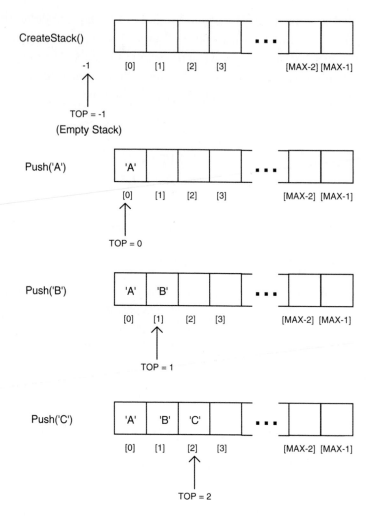

Figure 14-4 The effect of creating a stack and pushing three character elements onto the stack.

It is important to note that the value of *Top* must be incremented *prior* to placing the element on the stack. Thus, we say that the *Push()* operation pre-increments the stack pointer, *Top*. Here is an algorithm for *Push()*:

Push() **Algorithm**

BEGIN
    If the stack is not full
        Increment *Top*.

> Place element at array position [*Top*].
>
> Else
>
> > Display full stack message.
>
> END.

Notice that a test is made to determine if the stack is full, since you cannot push an element onto a full stack. When would our stack be full? Well, the stack is full when the array is full, right? Since the maximum array position is *MAX – 1*, the stack will be full when *Top* has the value *MAX – 1*.

Popping Elements From a Stack

Now we are ready to illustrate several popping operations. Given the stack in Figure 14-4, suppose that we execute a single pop operation like this:

Pop()

What happens to the stack? Well *Top* is pointing to the *last* element placed on the stack (the character 'C') so all we need to do is to remove the element at array position [*Top*], or [2]. However, once the element is removed, the value of *Top* must be decremented to locate the new top of the stack. Thus, in Figure 14-4, the character 'C' at position [2] is removed and the value of *Top* is decremented from 2 to 1 to locate array position [1], which is the new top of the stack.

Next, suppose we execute a second pop operation. This removes the character 'B' and *Top* is decremented to array position [0]. Finally, if we execute a third pop operation the character 'A' is removed from the stack and *Top* is decremented to the value –1, indicating an empty stack. This sequence of events is shown in Figure 14-5.

Remember that the *Pop()* operation decrements *Top* after the element is removed from the stack. Thus, we say that the *Pop()* operation post-decrements the stack pointer. Here is an algorithm for *Pop()*:

Pop() **Algorithm**

> BEGIN
>
> > If the stack is not empty
> >
> > > Remove element at array position [*Top*].
> > > Decrement *Top*.
> >
> > Else
> >
> > > Display empty stack message.
>
> END.

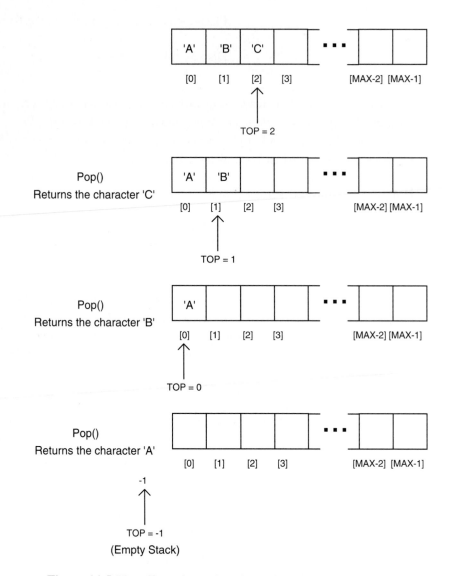

Figure 14-5 The effect of popping three character elements from the stack in Figure 14-4.

Notice that a test must be made to determine if the stack is empty, since you cannot pop an element from an empty stack. How do you know when the stack is empty? Of course, when *Top* has the value −1.

One final point: Although the stack is empty after the three popping operations in Figure 14-5, the array still contains the 'A', 'B', 'C' character elements. These elements could obviously be accessed by reading the array. However, remember that, by definition, an ADT restricts the data access to only those operations defined for the ADT. Therefore, the only possible way to access the elements in the array is through the stack operations, *Push()* and *Pop()*, defined for the stack ADT. Any direct array access would violate the idea of an ADT. This is why object-oriented programming is ideal for implementing ADTs. With object-oriented programming, we can make the array a **private** data member of a class, thereby restricting its access to only those operations defined for the ADT. As a result, the ADT data is completely hidden from the outside world.

Inspecting the Top Element of a Stack

The last operation of our stack ADT that we need to illustrate is the *TopElement()* operation. Recall that this operation makes a copy of the top element on the stack, leaving the stack unchanged. So, let's assume that we start with the stack in Figure 14-4 and execute a *TopElement()* operation like this:

TopElement()

Like the *Pop()* operation, the *TopElement()* operation reads the element at array position [*Top*]. However, unlike the *Pop()* operation, *TopElement()* does not decrement the stack pointer, *Top*. This operation is illustrated in Figure 14-6.

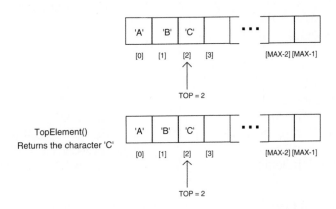

Figure 14-6 The effect of the *TopElement()* operation.

The algorithm for *TopElement( )* is straightforward. Here it is:

TopElement( ) **Algorithm**

```
BEGIN
   If the stack is not empty
            Copy element at array position [Top].
   Else
            Display empty message.
END.
```

Coding the Stack ADT

We are now ready to code our stack ADT. We will code the ADT as a class to enforce encapsulation and information hiding. Here is the stack ADT class coded as a C++ header file called *stack.h*.

```cpp
// STACK CLASS DECLARATION (stack.h)

#ifndef STACK_H
#define STACK_H

const int MAX = 5;                          // MAXIMUM STACK SIZE
enum {EMPTY = -1, FULL = MAX - 1};          // DEFINE EMPTY = -1
                                            // AND FULL = MAX - 1

enum {FALSE, TRUE};                         // DEFINE FALSE = 0 AND
                                            // TRUE = 1

class Stack
{
public:
  Stack();                                  // CONSTRUCTOR FOR CreateStack()
  int EmptyStack();                         // CHECKS FOR EMPTY STACK
  int FullStack();                          // CHECKS FOR FULL STACK
  void Push(char Char);                     // PLACE ELEMENT ON TOP
  char Pop();                               // REMOVE ELEMENT FROM TOP
  char TopElement();                        // INSPECT TOP ELEMENT

private:
  char S[MAX];           // CHARACTER ARRAY TO HOLD THE STACK
  int Top;               // Top LOCATES TOP ELEMENT OF STACK
};
#endif
```

First you see a constant, called *MAX,* defined. This constant will dictate the maximum size of the array, or stack. Next, you see several enumerated data elements defined. We set *EMPTY* to the value −1 to designate an empty stack. Then we set *FULL* to the value *MAX − 1* to designate a full stack. You know why *EMPTY* is set to −1, but why is *FULL* set to *MAX − 1*? Well, theoretically the size of a stack is only limited by the amount of memory available in the system to hold the stack. However, since we are using an array to hold the stack, the maximum stack size is limited by the size of the array. The size of this array implementation is *MAX* which means that the last array index is [*MAX − 1*]. As a result, when the top of the stack is located at array index [*MAX − 1*], the stack is full.

The last two enumerated data elements defined in the header file are *FALSE* and *TRUE*. The element *FALSE* is set to 0 and the element *TRUE* is set to 1. These elements take on the values 0 and 1, respectively, by default according to the way that C++ assigns default values to enumerated data. They will be used as return values when testing the stack for an empty or a full condition.

The stack ADT is defined as a class called *Stack*. The public members of the class include the operations defined for the stack ADT. First you see the *Stack()* constructor. This constructor will take the place of the *CreateStack()* operation. Remember how a constructor works? When an object is defined for a class, the constructor is automatically called to initialize the private members of the class. Here, the constructor function will be coded to set the value of *Top* to *EMPTY*, or −1. Isn't this what the *CreateStack()* operation must do? We could not use the name *CreateStack()*, since a constructor must have the same name as the class.

Next you see the *EmptyStack()* function listed. This function will return the integer 1 (*TRUE*) if the stack is empty, or 0 (*FALSE*) if the stack is not empty. The next function defined is *FullStack()*. This function will be used to determine if the stack is full. The function will return the integer 1 (*TRUE*) if the stack is full, or 0 (*FALSE*) if the stack is not full. (What constitutes a full stack?) You have noticed that in our formal ADT definition we did not have a *FullStack()* operation and, in theory, no such operation is needed for the stack ADT. However, *FullStack()* is required in this implementation, since we are using a finite array to hold the stack.

The last three functions defined for the class are *Push()*, *Pop()*, and *TopElement()*. You already know the purpose of these functions. However, take a close look at each function prototype. The *Push()* function accepts a character, *Char,* to be pushed onto the stack. It does not return any value, since it will simply place *Char* into the array at the top position. The *Pop()* function does not have any formal parameters, since it will read the element at the top position of the stack array. The return type of *Pop()* is a character, since it will return the popped element to the calling program. Likewise, the *TopElement( )* function does not require any formal parameters, since it simply reads the top element of the stack. The return data type is character, since it will return a copy of the top element to the calling program.

The private members of the class are the character array, *S[ ]*, and the integer variable, *Top*. The size of the array is *MAX* which means that the stack can hold *MAX* elements. However, remember that the last array index is [*MAX − 1*]. It goes without saying that array *S[ ]* will hold a stack of characters whose top element is located by *Top*.

PROGRAMMING NOTE

The C++ class fully encapsulates the stack ADT. As a result, only those operations defined in the class can operate on the stack data. Even though the stack is being implemented with an array, the stack array is private and, therefore, cannot be corrupted by any operations outside of the class. When using the stack you are forced to use only those operations defined by the stack ADT. This is why encapsulation and information hiding are so important when creating ADTs. As you can see, the class in C++ inherently provides the encapsulation and data hiding required by ADTs.

Now we need to look at the implementation file for the *Stack* class functions.

```
// STACK IMPLEMENTATION FILE (stackop.cpp)

#include "stack.h"
#include <iostream.h>

// IMPLEMENTATION OF Stack() CONSTRUCTOR
Stack :: Stack()
{
  Top = EMPTY;
}
// IMPLEMENTATION OF EmptyStack()
int Stack :: EmptyStack()
{
  if (Top == EMPTY)
    return (TRUE);
  else
```

```
      return (FALSE);
    }
// IMPLEMENTATION OF FullStack()
int Stack :: FullStack()
{
  if (Top == FULL)
    return (TRUE);
  else
    return (FALSE);
}
// IMPLEMENTATION OF Push()
void Stack :: Push(char Char)
{
  if (!FullStack())
  {
    ++Top;
    S[Top] = Char;
  }
  else
    cout << "\n\nThe stack is full!\n";
}
// IMPLEMENTATION OF Pop()
char Stack :: Pop()
{
  char Character;
  if (!EmptyStack())
  {
    Character = S[Top];
    --Top;
    return (Character);
  }
  else
   {
    cout << "\n\nThe stack is empty!\n";
    return ('#')              // RETURN '#' TO INDICATE STACK EMPTY
   } // END ELSE
} // END FUNCTION
// IMPLEMENTATION OF TopElement()
char Stack :: TopElement()
{
  if (!EmptyStack())
    return (S[Top]);
```

```
   else
   {
     cout << "\n\nThe stack is empty!\n";
     return ('#')                 // RETURN '#' TO INDICATE STACK EMPTY
   } // END ELSE
} // END FUNCTION
```

The file is named *stackop.cpp*. You see that the stack header file, *stack.h*, is included in this file. The first implementation is for the constructor function, *Stack()*. This function simply creates a new stack by setting *Top* to *EMPTY*, or −1. Next, the *EmptyStack()* function returns *TRUE* if the stack is empty or *FALSE* if the stack is not empty. What constitutes an empty stack? Of course, when the value of *Top* is −1. This is the test that is made in the **if/else** statement. Notice how the enumerated data elements defined in the stack header file are used here. Remember that *EMPTY* is defined to be −1, *TRUE* is defined to be 1, and *FALSE* is defined to be 0.

The structure of the *FullStack()* implementation is similar to *EmptyStack()*. However, *FullStack()* checks to see if the value of *Top* is equal to *FULL*. Recall that *FULL* is an enumerated data type defined in the header file as *MAX − 1*. This value is the maximum array index value. When *Top* reaches *MAX − 1* the array is full, thereby making the stack full.

The implementation of the *Push()* function employs an **if/else** statement to check for a full stack condition. You cannot push an element onto a full stack. The condition is checked by calling the *FullStack()* function. If the stack is not full, the value of *Top* is incremented and the character, *Char*, received by the function is stored in the stack array at position *S[Top]*. If the stack is full, an appropriate message is displayed.

The *Pop()* function employs an **if/else** statement to check for an empty stack condition. You cannot pop an element from an empty stack. Here, the *EmptyStack()* function is called as part of the **if/else** statement. If the stack is not empty, the element at array position *S[Top]* is obtained and assigned to the local variable *Character*. (Why is a local variable required here?) The value of *Top* is then decremented and the character, *Character*, is returned to the calling program.

Finally, the *TopElement()* function is similar to the *Pop()* function in that it checks for an empty stack condition and, if the stack is not empty, returns the character at array position *S[Top]*. Notice, however, that the value of *Top* is not altered, thereby leaving the stack unchanged.

Now all we need is an application program to test our stack ADT. Here is one that will do the job:

```
// APPLICATION FILE TO TEST THE STACK ADT (stackapp.cpp)

#include "stack.h"
#include <iostream.h>

void main()
{
    char Character;          // CHARACTER TO BE STACKED
    int Number;              // NUMBER OF CHARACTERS TO BE STACKED
    int Count = 0;           // LOOP COUNTER

    Stack Stk;               // DEFINE STACK OBJECT

// GET NUMBER OF ELEMENTS TO STACK
    cout << "\nYou cannot enter more than " << MAX
         << " elements. \nHow many elements do you have to enter? ";
    cin >> Number;

// PUSH ELEMENTS ONTO STACK
    while (!Stk.FullStack() && Count < Number)
    {
        ++Count;
        cout << "\nEnter a character element:  ";
        cin >> Character;
        Stk.Push(Character);
    }
// INSPECT TOP ELEMENT OF THE STACK
    if (!Stk.EmptyStack())
        cout << "\nThe top element of the stack is:  "
             << Stk.TopElement();
    else
        cout << "\nThe stack is empty!";

// POP AND WRITE STACK ELEMENTS
    cout << "\nThe contents of the stack are:  ";
    if (Stk.EmptyStack())
        cout << "\nThe stack is empty!";
    else
        while (!Stk.EmptyStack())
            cout << Stk.Pop();

    Stk.Pop();                       // ATTEMPT TO POP AN EMPTY STACK

}
```

The program begins by including the stack ADT header file, *stack.h*. There are several local variables declared at the beginning of *main()*. These variables will be used to process the stack information, as you will see shortly. An object called *Stk* is defined for our *Stack* class. The user is first prompted for the number of characters to be entered onto the stack. A **while** loop is used to push the entered characters onto the stack one character at a time. Notice that the **while** loop will execute as long as the stack is not full and the number of characters entered is less than the number dictated by the user. The user is prompted within the loop to enter one character at a time. After the character is read from the user, it is pushed onto the stack by calling the *Push()* function.

The next segment of code inspects and displays the top character on the stack with a call to the *TopElement()* function.

The final segment of code pops the entire stack and displays the stack elements one character at a time. Notice the use of the **if/else** statement to assure that an attempt is not made to pop an empty stack. A **while** loop is used to pop and display the stack elements. The loop is controlled by making a call to the *EmptyStack()* function. As a result, the loop will execute until the stack is empty.

Finally, notice that a single call to *Pop()* is made after the stack is emptied. This call is made to test the *Pop()* function relative to an empty stack. Here is a sample run of the program:

```
You cannot enter more than 5 elements.
How many elements do you have to enter?  3↵

Enter a character element:  A↵

Enter a character element:  B↵

Enter a character element:  C↵

The top element of the stack is:  C

The contents of the stack are:  CBA

The stack is empty!
```

Observe what has happened. The user entered three characters in the order 'A', 'B', 'C'. The program shows that the last character entered, 'C', is on the top of the stack. Then, the contents of the stack are popped and displayed. Notice that the output order is reversed from the input order due to the LIFO principle. Finally, the attempt to pop an empty stack resulted in the appropriate message to the user, thus verifying the integrity of the *Pop()* function.

Quick Check

1. Suppose that the user filled a stack using the application test program in this section. What would happen if a call was made to the *Push()* function after the stack was full?

2. Since we are using an array implementation for a stack, why can't you randomly access the stack elements using array operations, rather than accessing them through *Top*?

3. With our array implementation of a stack, a *Push()* operation requires that the stack pointer be _____.

4. True or False: With our array implementation of a stack, the stack is full when the value of *Top* becomes equal to *MAX*, where *MAX* is the maximum number of elements that the array can hold.

5. With our array implementation of a stack, the stack is empty when the value of *Top* is _____.

6. What is the functional difference between the *Pop()* function and the *TopElement()* function?

7. There is no *FullStack()* operation defined for the stack ADT. Why did we have to include a *FullStack()* function in our implementation?

14-3 ADT QUEUE

A *queue* is another important ADT in computer science. There are more examples of queues in the real world than stacks, since queues have the *first-in, first-out*, or *FIFO*, property. For instance, the grocery store line mentioned in the last section is a queue. Aircraft in a holding pattern waiting to land at a busy airport represent a *queuing* operation. As aircraft approach the airport traffic area, they are placed in a holding pattern such that the first one in the pattern is the first one to land. We say that the aircraft are being *queued* into the pattern. A computer scientist would never say that the aircraft are being *stacked* in the pattern, right? Can you think of other real world examples of queuing operations?

Recall that the LIFO property of stacks reverses the order of the stack elements from input to the stack to output from the stack. Queues, on the other hand, exhibit the FIFO property which preserves the order of the elements from input to output. Now for a formal definition of a queue.

A *queue* is a collection of data elements where all insertions of elements into the queue are made at one end of the queue, called the *rear* of the queue; and all deletions of elements from the queue are made at the other end of the queue, called the *front* of the queue. A queue operates on the *first-in*, *first-out*, or *FIFO* principle.

From the above definition, you see that queue access occurs at one of two ends of the queue. If an element is added to the queue it is added to the rear of the queue just as in a grocery store check-out line. On the other hand, if an element is removed from the queue, it is removed from the front of the queue, as with the grocery store line. Of course, you can't remove an element from an empty queue.

We are now ready to define our queue ADT as follows:

ADT Queue

Operations, or Interface:

CreateQ
   Creates an empty queue.

Insert()
   Adds an element to the rear of a queue.

Remove()
   Removes an element from the front of a queue.

FrontElement()
   Copies the front element of a queue, leaving the queue unchanged.

EmptyQ()
   Determines if the queue is empty.

Data:

A collection of data elements with the property that elements can only be
added at one end, called the *rear* of the queue, and elements can only be
removed from the other end, called the *front* of the queue.

Implementing the Queue ADT

Like a stack, the queue ADT is not predefined in C++ or most other programming
languages. Therefore, we must implement it using something that is predefined in
the language. Again we will use the versatile array to implement the queue.
However, we need to make use a special array called a ***circular***, or ***wrap-around***,
array. Look at the array in Figure 14-7 to see how we can create a queue using a
circular array.

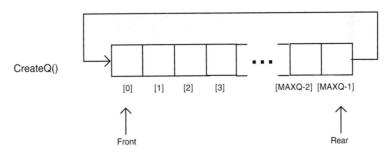

Figure 14-7 Setting *Front* to 0 and *Rear* to *MAXQ − 1* will create a queue
using a circular array implementation.

Creating A Queue Using a Circular Array

You see an array whose size is *MAXQ* and highest index is *MAXQ − 1*. To make
the array hold a queue we need to initialize two integer variables that locate the
front and rear of the queue. Here, *Front* is initialized to 0 so that it locates position
[0] of the array, and *Rear* is initialized to *MAXQ − 1* so that it locates the last
array position. Thus, an appropriate algorithm for *CreateQ()* is:

CreateQ() **Algorithm**

BEGIN
Set *Front* = 0.
Set *Rear* = *MAXQ* − *1*.
END.

Now, here's the idea behind a circular array. When we are using an external integer variable, such as *Front* or *Rear*, to locate elements in the array we will advance the variable through the index range of the array, in our case from 0 to *MAXQ* − *1*. When the variable needs to be advanced past the last array index, *MAXQ* − *1*, we will force it to the first array index, 0. Thus, the variable will be advanced as follows:

0, 1, 2, 3, •••, *MAXQ* − *1*, 0,1,2, 3, •••, *MAXQ* − *1*, 0, 1, 2, 3, •••

This way, the advancing process can continue in a circle indefinitely. All we need to accomplish this task is an **if/else** statement like this:

If *Rear* == *MAXQ* − *1*
Set *Rear* = 0.
Else
Set *Rear* = *Rear* + 1.

Here you see that the **else** statement increments *Rear*, unless the value of *Rear* is *MAXQ* − *1*. If this is the case, *Rear* is set to 0. Of course, we will do the same thing with *Front* to make it wrap around.

Now we are ready to begin inserting and removing elements to and from the queue. Remember, we will insert elements at the rear of the queue and remove elements from the front of the queue.

Inserting Elements Into a Queue

To insert an element into the queue, we must first advance *Rear* then place the element at array position [*Rear*]. Thus, suppose we start with the array shown in Figure 14-7 and execute the following three insertion operations:

Insert('A')
Insert('B')
Insert('C')

The sequence of events created by these three operations is illustrated in Figure 14-8.

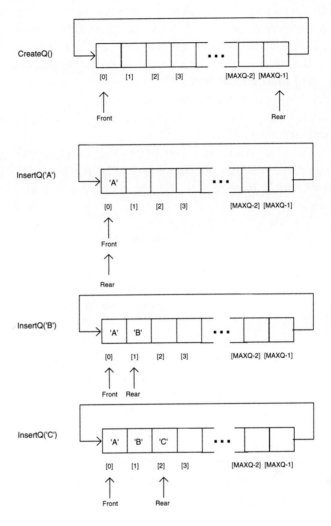

Figure 14-8 The effect of creating a queue and inserting three character elements into the queue.

We begin with the queue being initialized using *CreateQ()*. Remember that *CreateQ()* initializes *Front* with the value 0 and *Rear* with the value *MAX − 1*. When the first character, 'A', is inserted into the queue, the value of *Rear* must be advanced prior to the character being placed in the array. However, since *Rear* locates the last array index, *MAXQ* − *1*, the value of *Rear* is forced to 0 using the wrap-around idea. Once *Rear* is advanced to 0, the character 'A' is placed at array position [*Rear*], or [0]. Notice that both *Front* and *Rear* locate the character 'A'. This is always the case when there is only one element in the queue.

The second character to be inserted is the character 'B'. Again, *Rear* is advanced to locate the next array position. This time, however, the value of *Rear* is **not** *MAXQ* − *1*. Therefore, 1 is added to *Rear* such that it locates the next sequential array position, [1]. The character 'B' is then placed at array position [*Rear*], or [1].

The third insert operation places that character 'C' at array position [2]. Notice that *Front* has not been affected by the insert operations and locates the first character inserted into the queue. Here is an algorithm that reflects the *Insert()* operation:

Insert() **Algorithm**

```
BEGIN
    If the queue is not full
        If Rear == MAXQ – 1
            Set Rear = 0.
        Else
            Set Rear = Rear + 1.
        Place element at array position [Rear].
    Else
        Display full queue message.
END.
```

The first thing that must be done is to check for a full queue. How do you know when the queue is full? Or, for that matter, how do you know when the queue is empty? Well, since we are using an array implementation, the queue is full when the array is full, and the queue is empty when the array is empty, right? But, how can we use *Front* and/or *Rear* to determine when the array is full or empty? Your first thought might be that the queue is full when an element is placed in the last array position, thereby making *Rear* take on the value *MAX* − *1*. But, from Figure 14-7 you see that this condition also reflects an empty queue condition. In fact, because of the circular nature of the array, there is no way to determine a full or empty queue condition using the values of *Front* and *Rear* unless we alter the nature of our implementation. Think about it!

The simplest way to determine an empty or full queue condition is to count the number of elements being inserted and removed from the queue. When an element is inserted into the queue we will increment an element counter. When an element is removed from the queue we will decrement the element counter. This way the queue is empty when the counter value is 0 and full when the counter value reaches the size of the array, *MAXQ*. To do this we must add an additional processing step to our *Insert()* algorithm that will increment the element counter. Here is a modified *Insert()* algorithm that will permit us to determine a full queue condition:

Modified *Insert()* Algorithm

BEGIN
    If the queue is not full
        Increment element counter.
        If *Rear == MAXQ − 1*
            Set *Rear = 0.*
        Else
            Set *Rear = Rear + 1.*
        Place element at array position [*Rear*].
    Else
        Display full queue message.
END.

You should be aware that there is another way to implement a queue using a circular array that doesn't require an element counter to determine the empty/full conditions. However, this implementation requires that you sacrifice one array position by not allowing any queue elements to be placed in this position. This implementation will be left as a programming exercise at the end of the chapter.

Now, back to the algorithm. If the queue is not full, the element counter is incremented and the **if/else** wrap-around statement is executed to advance *Rear*. Once *Rear* is advanced, the element is placed in array position [*Rear*]. Note that *Rear* must be advanced prior to placing the element in the array. Of course, if the queue is full, no action is taken on the queue and an appropriate message is displayed.

Removing Elements From a Queue

Let's remove the three elements that were inserted in Figure 14-8 by executing the following *Remove()* operations:

Remove()
Remove()
Remove()

This sequence of events is illustrated in Figure 14-9.

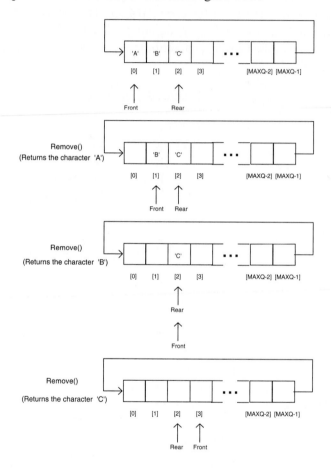

Figure 14-9 The effect of removing three character elements from the queue in Figure 14-8.

Elements are removed from the front of the queue. As a result, the first element to be removed from the queue is the character 'A' at array position [*Front*], or [0]. Once the element is removed, *Front* is advanced to the next circular array position. Now the character 'B' is at the front of the queue. The second *Remove()* operation removes this character and advances *Front* to position [2]. Now the only remaining element in the queue is the character 'C'. Notice that both *Front* and *Rear* locate this character, since it is the only element in the queue. A third *Remove()* operation removes the character 'C', leaving an empty queue. How can it be that the queue is empty, since *Front* and *Rear* are not in their initialized positions? Moreover, *Front* has moved ahead of *Rear*. Is this a problem? No! Remember how we have defined an empty and a full queue? It does not matter where *Front* and *Rear* are located in determining the empty or full queue conditions. All that matters is the value of the element counter. If the element counter is 0, the queue is empty. If the element counter is *MAXQ*, the queue is full. Here is an algorithm for the *Remove()* operation.

Remove() **Algorithm**

```
BEGIN
    If the queue is not empty
            Decrement element counter.
            Remove the element at array position [Front].
            If Front == MAXQ – 1
                    Set Front = 0.
            Else
                    Set Front = Front + 1.
    Else
            Display empty queue message.
END.
```

The algorithm begins by checking for the empty queue condition. If the queue is not empty, the element counter is decremented and *Front* is advanced via the **if/else** wrap-around statement. If the queue is empty, an appropriate message is displayed.

Inspecting the Front Element of a Queue

The next thing we need to do is to develop the *FrontElement()* operation. Suppose we execute the following statement on the queue created back in Figure 14-8:

FrontElement()

The results of this operation are shown in Figure 14-10.

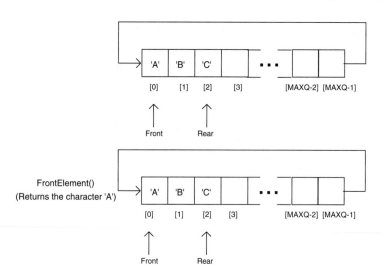

Figure 14-10 The effect of inspecting the queue created in Figure 14-8.

Here you find that neither *Front* or *Rear* are affected by the *FrontElement()* operation. The operation simply returns the front character of the queue. The following algorithm will support this operation:

FrontElement() **Algorithm**

> BEGIN
>   If the queue is not empty
>   Copy the element at array position [*Front*].
>   Else
>   Display an empty queue message.
> END.

If the queue is not empty, the algorithm simply copies the element at the front position of the queue. Comparing this to the *Remove()* algorithm, you find that there is no operation on the element counter or the *Front* position locator.

Coding the Queue ADT

We are now ready to code the queue ADT. To assure encapsulation and information hiding we will code the ADT as a class. Here's the class declaration:

```
// QUEUE CLASS DECLARATION (queue.h)

#ifndef QUEUE_H
#define QUEUE_H

const int MAXQ = 5;                      // MAXIMUM QUEUE SIZE
enum {EMPTY = 0, FULL = MAXQ};           // DEFINE EMPTY = 0 AND
                                         // FULL = MAXQ
enum {FALSE, TRUE};                      // DEFINE FALSE = 0 AND
                                         // TRUE = 1

class Queue
{
public:
  Queue();                     // CONSTRUCTOR TO IMPLEMENT CreateQ()
  int EmptyQ();                // CHECKS TO SEE IF QUEUE IS EMPTY
  int FullQ();                 // CHECKS TO SEE IF QUEUE IS FULL
  void Insert(char Char);      // ADD ELEMENT TO REAR
  char Remove();               // REMOVE ELEMENT FROM FRONT
  char FrontElement();         // INSPECT FRONT ELEMENT

private:
  char Q[MAXQ];        // CHARACTER ARRAY TO HOLD THE QUEUE
  int Front;           // Front LOCATES FRONT ELEMENT OF QUEUE
  int Rear;            // Rear LOCATES REAR ELEMENT OF QUEUE
  int ElementCount;    // ELEMENT COUNTER
};

#endif
```

The above file is coded as an include file called *queue.h*. At the beginning of the file you find the same type of constant and enumerated data definitions as we coded in the stack ADT. Notice, however, that *EMPTY* is defined with a value of 0 and *FULL* is defined with a value of *MAXQ*. These definitions will be used when testing the element counter for the empty and full conditions, respectively.

The public functions that are listed in the class are those defined for the queue ADT, with the exception of the *FullQ()* operation. Why do we need a *FullQ()* operation for our implementation? The same reason that we needed a *FullStack()* operation for our stack implementation. We are dealing with a finite array data structure. Note also that the *CreateQ()* operation is implemented by the class constructor.

The private section begins by declaring a character array called *Q[ ]* as a private member. As a result, this queue will store character elements. The size of the array is *MAXQ*, where *MAXQ* has been defined as the constant 5 for example purposes. There are three private integer variables: *Front*, *Rear*, and *ElementCount*. You should now be aware of their use in this implementation. Again, it is important to stress the hiding of these private class members. No operations outside of the class can affect the contents of *Q[ ]*, or the values of *Front*, *Rear*, or *ElementCount*. As a result, any queue object created for this class cannot be corrupted by intentional or unintentional operations outside of the queue class.

Next we need an implementation file to define the class functions. The file is called *queueop.cpp* and is provided below:

```
// QUEUE IMPLEMENTATION FILE (queueop.cpp)
#include "queue.h"
#include <iostream.h>

// IMPLEMENTATION OF Queue() CONSTRUCTOR
Queue :: Queue()
{
   Front = 0;
   Rear = MAXQ – 1;
   Count = EMPTY;
}

// IMPLEMENTATION OF EmptyQ()
Queue :: EmptyQ()
{
  if (ElementCount == EMPTY)
    return (TRUE);
  else
    return (FALSE);
}

// IMPLEMENTATION OF FullQ()
Queue :: FullQ()
{
  if (ElementCount == FULL)
    return (TRUE);
  else
    return (FALSE);
}

// IMPLEMENTATION OF Insert()
void Queue :: Insert(char Char)
{
```

```
  if (!FullQ())
  {
    ++ ElementCount;
    if (Rear == MAXQ − 1)
      Rear = 0;
    else
      ++Rear;
    Q[Rear] = Char;
  }
  else
    cout << "\n\nThe queue is full!\n";
}

// IMPLEMENTATION OF Remove()
char Queue :: Remove()
{
  char Character;
  if (!EmptyQ())
  {
    --ElementCount;
    Character = (Q[Front]);
    if (Front == MAXQ − 1)
      Front = 0;
    else
      ++Front;
    return (Character);
  }
  else
  {
    cout << "\n\nThe queue is empty\n";
    return ('#')              // RETURN '#' TO INDICATE QUEUE EMPTY
  } // END ELSE
} // END FUNCTION

// IMPLEMENTATION OF FrontElement()
char Queue :: FrontElement()
{
  if (!EmptyQ())
    return (Q[Front]);
  else
  {
    cout << "\n\nThe queue is empty!\n";
    return ('#')              // RETURN '#' TO INDICATE QUEUE EMPTY
  } // END ELSE
} // END FUNCTION
```

In this file, all of the queue algorithms discussed earlier have been coded. Compare each coded function to its algorithm so that you understand what's going on. There were no algorithms developed for the *EmptyQ()* and *FullQ()* operations, since they are so straightforward. Observe that the code for the *EmptyQ()* and *FullQ()* functions simply tests the element counter for an *EMPTY* or *FULL* condition. Recall that *EMPTY* is defined as 0 and *FULL* is defined as *MAXQ*.

     The following application file, called *queueapp.cpp*, has been created to test our queue ADT:

```
// APPLICATION FILE TO TEST THE QUEUE ADT (queueapp.cpp)

#include "queue.h"
#include <iostream.h>

void main()
{
  char Character;       // CHARACTER TO BE QUEUED
  int Number;           // NUMBER OF CHARACTERS TO BE QUEUED
  int Count = 0;        // LOOP COUNTER

  Queue Q;              // DEFINE QUEUE OBJECT

// GET NUMBER OF ELEMENTS TO QUEUE
  cout << "\nYou cannot enter more than " << MAXQ
       << " elements. \nHow many elements do you have to enter? ";
  cin >> Number;

// INSERT ELEMENTS INTO QUEUE
  while (!Q.FullQ() && Count < Number)
  {
    ++Count;
    cout << "\nEnter a character element: ";
    cin >> Character;
    Q.Insert(Character);
  }

// INSPECT FRONT ELEMENT WITHOUT CHANGING QUEUE
  if (!Q.EmptyQ())
    cout << "\nThe front element of the queue is: "
         << Q.FrontElement();
```

```
// REMOVE AND WRITE QUEUE ELEMENTS
   cout << "\nThe contents of the queue are: ";
   if (Q.EmptyQ())
    cout << "\nThe queue is empty!";
   else
    while (!Q.EmptyQ())
      cout << Q.Remove();

   Q.Remove();           // ATTEMPT TO REMOVE FROM EMPTY QUEUE
}
```

The test program defines Q as an object of class *Queue*. Elements are then inserted into Q one at time from user entries via a **while** loop. Notice that the loop executes as long as the queue is not full and the number of elements entered does not exceed the number of elements the user specified for entry. A call is made to *FullQ()* in the loop test to check for the full queue condition and terminate the loop when the queue is full, regardless of how many elements the user attempts to enter. Once the user elements are inserted into the queue, the front element is inspected by a call to the *FrontElement()* function. Here, a call to *EmptyQ()* is made to assure that the queue is not empty prior to the inspect operation. The next segment of code removes and displays the queue elements. If the queue is not empty, a **while** loop is entered to remove and display all of the queue elements one at a time. The termination of the loop is controlled by a call to *EmptyQ()*. As a result, the loop statements will execute, removing and displaying one element with each iteration, until the queue is empty. Finally, a single call is made to *RemoveQ()* in an attempt to remove an element from an empty queue. This call was made to test the *RemoveQ()* function. Here are the results of executing the test program:

You cannot enter more than 5 elements.
How many elements do you have to enter? **3**↵

Enter a character element: **A**↵

Enter a character element: **B**↵

Enter a character element: **C**↵

The front element of the queue is: A

The contents of the queue are: ABC

The queue is empty!

In this test run, the user has entered the characters 'A', 'B', and 'C'. The front character, 'A', is copied and displayed to verify the *FrontElement()* function. Then all of the characters of the queue are removed and displayed. Notice that the characters are displayed in the same order in which they were entered, thereby verifying the FIFO principle. The last line on the display verifies that the *Remove()* function checks for the empty queue condition.

 Quick Check

1. Suppose that the user filled a queue using the application test program in this section. What would happen if a call were made to the *Insert()* function after the queue was full?

2. True or False: With our array implementation of a queue, an *Insert()* operation requires that *Front* be advanced prior to placing the element in the array.

3. Write the pseudocode required to advance *Front* for the circular array implementation of a queue.

4. True or False: With the circular array implementation of a queue, *Front* can never have a higher value than *Rear*.

5. Using the circular array implementation of a queue, how can you tell when there is only one element in the queue?

6. Theoretically, the size of a queue is unlimited. Why did we have to include a *FullQ()* function in our implementation?

7. Explain how to determine when the queue is empty and when the queue is full using our array implementation.

14-4 ADT LIST

You have already been dealing with lists even though we have not made a formal definition of a list, but now is the time to do so.

A *list* is a *sequence* of data elements whose basic operations are insertion and deletion of elements to and from the list.

The arrays, stacks, and queues that you have studied so far are lists. Each of these lists represents a s*equence* of data elements. The term *sequence* implies ordering. This means that the list has a first element, a second element, and so on. In an array, the elements are ordered from the first array position to the last array position. In a stack, the elements are ordered from the top of the stack (last element in) to the bottom of the stack (first element in). In a queue, the elements are ordered from the front of the queue to the rear of the queue. Stacks and queues, however, are special kinds of lists, since the insert and delete operations are defined to be at the end(s) of the list. An array has no such restriction, since you can access the list randomly, inserting and deleting elements from any position in the list. Thus, stacks and queues must be sequentially accessed, while arrays can be randomly accessed.

In each of the lists you have studied so far, the sequencing of the elements is *implicit*. This means that the element sequence is inherent to the structure definition. The sequencing of elements in an array is given implicitly, since the first element is stored in position [0], the second element in position [1], and so on. Thus, given any element in the array, you can always locate its successor element. Given the element at array position [5], you know that its successor is at array position [6]. In a stack, the sequencing of elements is given implicitly from top to bottom. Given the element located at *Top* you know that the next element is located at *Top − 1*. In a queue, the sequencing is from front to rear. Given an element located at *Front* you know that its successor is located at *Front + 1*. In all of these lists, once you locate the first element, you can locate the second, and so on, via the natural ordering of the structure. However, there is one kind of list where the sequencing of elements must be provided *explicitly*. This means that given any element in the list, the location of its successor must be clearly specified, since its location is not inherent within the natural sequencing of the list elements. Such a list is called a *linked list*.

Linked Lists

First, consider the following formal definition of a linked list:

> A ***linked list*** is a sequential collection of data elements such that, given any element in the list, the location of its successor element is specified by an *explicit* link, rather than by its natural position in the collection.

Now, here's the idea: A linked list consists of a sequence of ***nodes***. A node contains two things: an ***element*** and a ***locator***, or ***link***. The element is the information that is stored in the node, and the locator is the link that locates the *next* node in the list. This idea is illustrated in Figure 14-11.

NODE

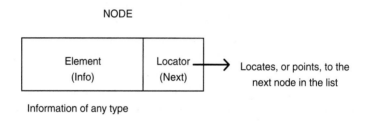

Information of any type

Figure 14-11 A single node in a linked list.

The element part of the node may contain a simple integer, character, or string as well as an entire structure which contains many other data elements. For instance, the element part of a node could be a *struct* that contains your name, address, and telephone number. We will call this the *Info* part of the node. The locator part of the node is the explicit locator, or link, to the next sequential node in the list. We will call this the *Next* part of the node. We say that *Next* locates, or points to, the next node in the list. Now, look at the sample linked list in Figure 14-12.

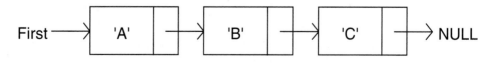

Figure 14-12 A linked list containing three nodes.

The linked list in Figure 14-12 contains three nodes storing character information. The first node is located by a locator called *First*. We must always have a means of locating the first node in the list and will always designate this as *First*. Notice that *First* locates, or points to, the first node in the list. The first node locates, or points to, the second node, and so on. The last node points to *NULL*, since there are no more nodes in the list. We will use the term *NULL* to designate the end of the list. It is easy to see that the list is sequentially ordered from the first to the last node and the ordering is given explicitly via the *Next* part of each node.

Now we need to develop some notation that will be used to discuss linked lists. We will implement our linked list using pointers and, therefore, refer to a node locator as a pointer. Here is some notation and terminology that will be employed when discussing linked lists:

> *Node(P)* refers to the entire node pointed to by *P*.
> *Info(P)* refers to the information part of the node pointed to by *P*.
> *Next(P)* refers to the next, or pointer, part of the node pointed to by *P*.
> The *predecessor node* to *Node(P)* is the node just before *Node(P)*.
> The *successor node* to *Node(P)* is the node just after *Node(P)*.

This linked list notation and terminology is illustrated in Figure 14-13.

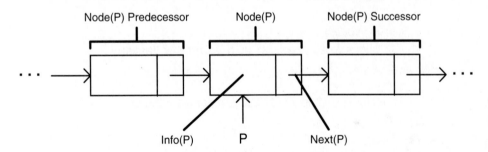

Figure 14-13 Notation and terminology used with linked lists.

Of special interest is *Next(P)*. *Next(P)* is always a pointer and points to *Node(P)*'s successor node, unless *Node(P)* is the last node in the list. If this is the case, *Next(P)* has the value *NULL*.

To get familiar with this notation, consider the following algorithm:

BEGIN
    Set *P = First.*
    While *P ≠ NULL*
        Write *Info(P).*
        Set *P = Next(P).*
END.

Can you determine what the algorithm does? Well, notice that *P* is made to point to the first node in the list by setting *P* to *First.* Then, the **while** loop will execute as long as *P* is not equal to *NULL.* Each time the loop is executed, the information in the node pointed to by *P* (*Info(P)*) is written and *P* is advanced to point to the next sequential node in the list. In other words, the list is *traversed* from the first node to the last. At each node, the information stored in the node is written. Now that you have a general feel for a linked list, it is time to define our linked list ADT as follows:

ADT Linked List

Operations, or Interface:

CreateList()
    Creates an empty list.

InsertNode()
    Adds a data element to the beginning of the list.

DeleteNode()
    Removes a specified data element from the list.

TraverseList()
    Traverses the list, processing the list information as required.

EmptyList()
    Determines if the list is empty.

Data:

A sequential collection of data elements.

Implementing the Linked List ADT

The natural way to implement a linked list is by using pointers. As you can see from the ADT definition, we have defined five linked list operations. We now need to show how pointers can be used to implement these operations. For each of the operations, we will develop an algorithm using the linked list notation given earlier. Then, we will code the algorithms in C++.

Creating an Empty Linked List

The first thing that must be done before building a linked list is to create an empty list. An empty list will be a list with no nodes in it, right? So, to create a list without any nodes, all we need to do is set *First* to *NULL* as shown in Figure 14-14.

$$First \longrightarrow NULL$$

Figure 14-14 An empty list is created by making *First* point to *NULL*.

Remember that 1) we will be using pointers to implement our linked list, 2) *First* will be the pointer that locates the first node in the list, and 3) *NULL* will define the end of the list. So, if we make *First* point to *NULL* we have an empty list. Here's the simple algorithm:

CreateList( ) **Algorithm**

BEGIN
  Set *First = NULL*
END.

Inserting Data Into a Linked List

Next, we need to develop an algorithm to insert a data element into the linked list. Since the linked list data elements are contained in nodes, this operation requires that a node be added to the list. Looking at the ADT definition, you see that we will always add a node at the beginning of the list. To accomplish this task we need to do four things:

1. Create a new node.

2. Fill the node with the data to be stored.

3. Make the new node point to the first node in the list.

4. Make *First* point to the new node.

For example, suppose that we have a linked list of the two characters 'A' and 'B', in that order. Then, we execute the following operation to insert the character 'C' into the list:

Insert('C')

The sequence of events that must be performed to insert a new node containing the character 'C' at the beginning of the list are shown in Figure 14-15.

Initial List

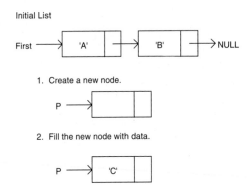

3. Make the new node point to the first node.

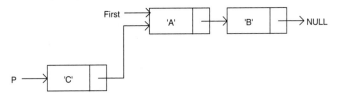

4. Make First point to the new node .

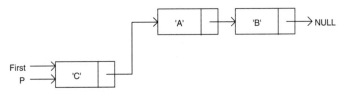

Figure 14-15 Inserting a node at the beginning of a linked list.

To create the new node, we simply make a temporary pointer, *P*, point to an empty node. As you will find out shortly, a node will be coded as a struct that contains a data, or *Info*, member and a pointer, or *Next*, member. The new node struct will literally be created from nothing using dynamic memory allocation and the **new** operator. So, to create a new node and make *P* point to this node will we use the following statement in our algorithm:

Set *P* = new Node.

Next, the information field of the new node is filled with the data element, in this case the character 'C'. To accomplish this task we will place the following statement in the algorithm:

Set *Info(P)* = 'C'.

This statement says to "place the character 'C' in the information part of the node pointed to by *P*."

Once the data is in the new node, we must add the node to the list. Since the node is to be added at the beginning of the list, we make the new node point to the first node in the list. Notice from Figure 14-15 that, prior to this step, *First* is pointing to where the new node needs to point. As a result, all we need to do is to assign *First* to the pointer, or *Next*, part of the new node. The following pseudocode statement will accomplish this task:

Set *Next(P)* = *First*.

The above statement says to "assign *First* to the pointer part of the node pointed to by *P*." Performing this assignment places the new node at the beginning of the list. However, *First* is now pointing to the second node in the list and needs to be moved to point to our new node.

Our new node is currently being pointed to by *P*. Thus, to make *First* point to the new node all we have to do is to set *First* to *P* like this:

Set *First* = *P*.

That's all there is to it. Here's the complete algorithm:

InsertNode( ) **Algorithm**

BEGIN
  Set *P* = new Node.

Set *Info(P)* = Data Element.
Set *Next(P)* = *First*.
Set *First* = *P*.
END.

Make sure that you understand how the four statements in the above algorithm accomplish the four tasks shown in Figure 14-15, especially in light of the notation that is being used. You might have noticed that, since our *InsertNode()* algorithm places the new node at the beginning of the list, the character 'C' is placed out of its natural order, relative to the other nodes in the list. An **ordered linked list** is a linked list whereby all the data elements are in some natural order from the first node to the last node in the list. To create an ordered linked list, our *InsertNode()* algorithm must be changed to search the list for the correct insertion point prior to adding the node to the list. This will be left as an exercise at the end of the chapter.

Deleting Data From a Linked List

Deleting data from a linked list requires that we delete the node containing the data from the linked list. Deleting a node from a linked list is the most difficult operation to be performed. As a result, we will develop several algorithm levels, working up to one that can be coded in C++.

Looking at the ADT definition for *DeleteNode()* you see that we must delete a specified data element from the list. This means that, given an element to delete, we must search for the element in the list. Then, once the element is found, adjust the list pointers to eliminate the node that contains the element to be deleted. So, our first level algorithm becomes:

DeleteNode() **Algorithm (First Level)**

BEGIN
Search the list for the element to be deleted.
Adjust the list pointers to eliminate the node that
contains the element to be deleted.
END.

Searching a Linked List

We will employ a simple sequential search to find the node to be deleted. This means that, beginning with the first node, we must test the element stored in the information part of the node against the specified element to delete and advance to the next node, repeat the testing procedure, and so on until we get to the end of the list. Here is an algorithm that will do the job:

Linked List Search Algorithm

```
BEGIN
  If the list is empty
    Write an appropriate message.
  Else
    Set P = First.
    Set PredP = NULL.
    Set Found = FALSE.
    While (NOT Found) AND (P ≠ NULL)
      If Info(P) == Element
        Set Found = TRUE.
      Else
        Set PredP = P.
        Set P = Next(P).
END.
```

The first thing that must be done is to test for an empty list, since you cannot delete a node from a list that is empty. If the list is empty, an appropriate message is written to the user; otherwise the search process is started.

There are two key pointer variables employed for the search. We will use the pointer P as a pointer to traverse the list, beginning at *First* and ending when P becomes *NULL*. In addition to P, we will employ another pointer called *PredP* that follows P through the list as the search progresses. As a result, the pointer *PredP* will always point to the node just prior to the node to which P is pointing. Recall that this is the predecessor node to *Node(P)*. This idea is illustrated in Figure 14-16

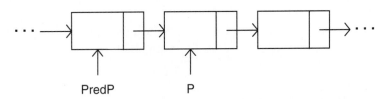

Figure 14-16 During the list search procedure, P will point to the node being tested, and *PredP* will point to the predecessor node to *Node(P)*.

A **while** loop is employed to control the search. Notice that the loop tests for two conditions: (NOT *Found*) and (*P ≠ NULL*). The AND operator requires that both tests be TRUE for the search to proceed. As a result, the search will stop when either the element is found or when *P* becomes *NULL*. Within the loop, we use an **if/else** statement to test the information contained in *Node(P)*. If *Info(P)* is equal to the element being searched for, the Boolean variable is set to TRUE and the loop will break. Otherwise, both pointers are advanced to the next respective node in the list. Do you see how the statement *Set Pred(P) = P* makes *PredP* point to *Node(P)* and the statement *Set P = Next(P)* makes *P* point to *Node(P)*'s successor node?

So, when the search loop is broken, *P* is pointing to the node to be deleted and *PredP* is pointing to this node's predecessor. But, what if the element being searched for was not in the list? In this case, *P* will move all the way through the list and stop when it becomes *NULL*. Also, what if the node to be deleted is the first node in the list? Well, in this case *P* and *PredP* will not be advanced at all, and will have their original values of *First* and *NULL*, respectively.

Deleting a Node in a Linked List

Next, let's develop the pseudocode required to actually delete a node from the list. Since this task follows the foregoing search algorithm we will use the values of *Found, P,* and *PredP* to delete the required node. Here's the delete algorithm:

Delete Algorithm

```
BEGIN
 If (Found)
   If (PredP == NULL)
     Set First = Next(P).
   Else
     Set Next(PredP) = Next(P).
 Else
     Write a message that the element was not
     found in the list.
END.
```

Here, the first thing to do is to check to see if the element being searched for was found during the search. If *Found* is TRUE coming out of the search algorithm, the element was found and the node must be deleted. Otherwise, the element was not found and an appropriate message must be written to the user. If the element was found, a nested **if/else** statement is employed to delete the respective node. If the node to be deleted is the first node in the list, we simply make *First* point to the second node in the list by setting *First* to *Next(P)*. This deletes the first node in the list. How do you know if the node to be deleted is the first node in the list. Of course, *PredP* has the value *NULL* after exiting the search algorithm. If *PredP* does not have the value *NULL,* the node to be deleted is not the first node in the list. In this case, the nested **else** makes the pointer from *Node(P)*'s predecessor jump around *Node(P)* and point to *Node(P)*'s successor. This is accomplished by setting *Next(PredP)* to *Next(P)*. The diagram in Figure 14-17 illustrates this operation:

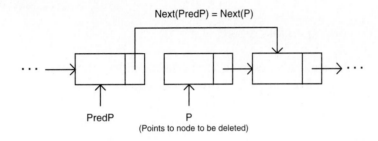

Figure 14-17 Setting *Next(PredP)* to *Next(P)* deletes *Node(P)* from the list.

Now putting the search algorithm together with the delete node algorithm, we get an algorithm for our ADT *DeleteNode()* operation that can be coded in C++. Here is the final algorithm:

DeleteNode() **Algorithm**

BEGIN
  If the list is empty
    Write an appropriate message.
  Else
    Set *P = First.*
    Set *PredP = NULL.*
    Set *Found* = FALSE.
    While (NOT *Found*) AND (*P* ≠ *NULL*)
      If *Info(P)* == *Element*
        Set *Found* = TRUE.

        Else
            Set *PredP = P*.
            Set *P = Next(P)*.
        If (*Found*)
            If (*PredP == NULL*)
                Set *First = Next(P)*.
            Else
                Set *Next(PredP) = Next(P)*.
        Else
            Write a message that the element was not found
            in the list.
    END.

Traversing a Linked List

You have already observed a traversal algorithm. Here is one that is customized to fit our ADT definition for *TraverseList( )*:

TraverseList( ) **Algorithm**

        BEGIN
            If the list is not empty
                Set *P = First*.
                While *P ≠ NULL*
                    Write *Info(P)*.
                    Set *P = Next(P)*.
            Else
                Write a message to indicate an empty list.
        END.

The algorithm begins by checking for an empty list. If the list is not empty a temporary list pointer, *P*, is initialized to the beginning of the list. A **while** loop is then executed to process the information stored in the nodes. In this case, we are simply writing the node information, *Info(P)*. Once the node information is written, *P* is advanced to point to the next node in the list. The loop continues writing the node information and advancing *P* through the list until the value of *P* becomes *NULL*. Of course, an appropriate message is written to the user if the list is empty.

Checking for an Empty List

To complete our ADT implementation, we must develop an algorithm for the *EmptyList()* operation. Recall that this operation simply checks to see if the list is empty. How do you know when the list is empty? Right, when *First* has the value *NULL*. As a result, the algorithm is:

EmptyList() **Algorithm**

```
      BEGIN
       If First == NULL
         return TRUE.
       Else
         return FALSE.
      END.
```

As you can see, *EmptyList()* returns the Boolean value TRUE if the value of *First* is *NULL*; otherwise it returns the value FALSE. We can now call upon this operation in the other operations when we need to test for an empty list.

Coding the Linked List ADT

We are now ready to code the linked list ADT. How do you suppose that we will code it in C++? You guessed it, using a class to assure complete encapsulation with information hiding. First, the class declaration:

```
// LINKED LIST CLASS DECLARATION FILE (list.h)
#ifndef LIST_H
#define LIST_H

#include <iostream.h>          // REQUIRED TO DEFINE NULL POINTER

enum {FALSE,TRUE};             // DEFINE FALSE = 0 AND TRUE = 1

// NODE STRUCTURE DECLARATION
struct Node
{
  char Info;                   // INFORMATION PART OF NODE
  Node *Next;                  // POINTER TO NEXT NODE
};
```

```
class List
{
public:
 List();                                 // CONSTRUCTOR TO
                                         // IMPLEMENT  CreateList()
 ~List();                                // DESTRUCTOR TO
                                         // DEALLOCATE LIST MEMORY
 void InsertNode(char Char);             // FUNCTION TO INSERT A NODE
 void DeleteNode(char Char);             // FUNCTION TO DELETE A
                                         // SPECIFIED NODE
 void TraverseList();                    // FUNCTION TO TRAVERSE LIST
 int  EmptyList();                       // FUNCTION TO TEST FOR
                                         // EMPTY  LIST


private:
 Node *First;                            // DEFINE First AS A POINTER TO
                                         // THE NODE STRUCT

};
#endif
```

The class declaration is placed in a header file called *list.h*. Before the *List* class is declared, a struct called *Node* is declared. Remember that a linked list node has two parts: an information part and a pointer part. As a result, the *Node* struct has two parts. The information part is defined as a character field called *Info*. This means that our linked list will hold character data. The pointer part of the node is defined as a pointer field called *Next*. Notice that the data type pointed to by *Next* is the *Node* struct itself. This means that the *Next* pointer will point to a struct which has the same definition as the *Node* struct in which *Next* is defined. Isn't this what we want to do? The *Next* pointer in a node needs to point to another node of the same structure, right?

Following the *Node* struct declaration we declare a class called *List*. The class must consist of the linked list node structure and the functions required to operate on that structure. All we have to do to define the entire linked list is define a pointer to the first node in the list. From here, each node locates its successor node via its *Next* pointer. So the single private member of the class is a pointer, called *First*, which will locate the first node in the list. Notice that *First* is a pointer to our *Node* struct data type.

The first function declared in the class is the class constructor, called *List()*. This constructor function implements the *CreateList()* operation and will be coded to set *First* to *NULL*.

The second function declared is the class destructor, called *~List()*. This is an ideal application for a destructor! We will be generating new nodes by dynamically allocating memory. When we delete a node, we will deallocate the memory required for that node. So, why not deallocate the memory allocated to the entire list by using a destructor when we are done processing the list? In other words, our *~List()* destructor will delete the entire list by deallocating all memory allocated to the list when we are done processing the list. This function is not part of our ADT definition and is only included due to the use of dynamic memory allocation.

Next you see the remaining four operations required for the *Linked List* ADT. You are now aware of the purpose of these four operations. The task at hand is to code the respective algorithms developed for these operations as part of an implementation file.

The function implementation file is called *listop.cpp*. Here it is:

```
// LINKED LIST IMPLEMENTATION FILE (listop.cpp)

#include "list.h"
#include <iostream.h>

// IMPLEMENTATION OF CONSTRUCTOR List()
List :: List()
{
  First = NULL;
}

// IMPLEMENTATION OF DESTRUCTOR, ~List()
List :: ~List()
{
  Node *P;             // DEFINE P AS A POINTER TO
                       // THE NODE STRUCT
  Node *Temp;          // DEFINE Temp AS POINTER TO
                       // THE NODE STRUCT
  P = First;           // SET P = FIRST
  while (P!= NULL)     // TRAVERSE LIST UNTIL P = NULL
  {
    Temp = P -> Next;  // MAKE Temp POINT TO NEXT NODE IN LIST
    delete P;          // DEALLOCATE NODE(P)
    P = Temp;          // MAKE P POINT TO NEXT NODE
  }
}
```

```
// IMPLEMENTATION OF InsertNode()
void List :: InsertNode(char Char)
{
  Node *P;                          // DEFINE P AS A POINTER TO
                                    // THE NODE STRUCT
  P = new Node;                     // ALLOCATE MEMORY FOR NODE(P)
  P -> Info = Char;                 // PLACE CHAR IN INFO(P)
  P -> Next = First;                // INSERT NODE(P) AT BEGINNING
  First = P;                        // MOVE First TO NODE(P)
}

// IMPLEMENTATION OF DeleteNode()
void List :: DeleteNode(char Char)
{
  int Found = FALSE;                // INITIALIZE Found TO FALSE

  Node *P;                          // DEFINE P AS A POINTER TO
                                    // THE NODE STRUCT

  Node *PredP;                      // DEFINE PredP AS A POINTER TO
                                    // THE NODE STRUCT

  P = First;                        // START P AT FIRST NODE
  PredP = NULL;                     // START PredP AT NULL

// IF LIST EMPTY, WRITE EMPTY MESSAGE, ELSE
// SEARCH FOR ELEMENT TO BE DELETED
  if (EmptyList())
    cout << "\nYou cannot delete a node from an empty list!";
  else
  {
    while (!Found && P != NULL)     // TRAVERSE LIST UNTIL FOUND
                                    // OR P == NULL
    {
        if (P -> Info == Char)      // TEST INFO(P)
          Found = TRUE;
        else                        // ADVANCE POINTERS
        {
          PredP = P;                // CATCH PredP UP TO P
          P = P -> Next;            // ADVANCE P
        }
    } // END SEARCH LOOP
```

```
    // DELETE NODE IF FOUND, ELSE WRITE NOT FOUND MESSAGE
    if (Found)
    {
        // DOES NODE(P) HAVE A PREDECESSOR?
        // IF NOT, DELETE FIRST NODE, ELSE DELETE NODE(P)
        if (PredP == NULL)
        {
          First = P -> Next;            // MOVE FIRST TO SECOND NODE
          delete P;                     // DEALLOCATE NODE(P)
        }
        else
        {
          PredP -> Next = P -> Next;    // MAKE NEXT(PredP) JUMP
                                        // AROUND NODE(P)
          delete P;                     // DEALLOCATE NODE(P)
        } // END IF FIRST NODE
    } // END IF FOUND
    else                                // WRITE NOT FOUND MESSAGE
        cout << "\nThe character '" << Char << "' is not in the list!";
  } // END SEARCH ELSE
} // END FUNCTION

// IMPLEMENTATION OF TraverseList()
void List :: TraverseList()
{
  Node *P;                             // DEFINE P AS A POINTER TO
                                       // THE NODE STRUCT
  P = First;                           // START P AT FIRST NODE

  // IF LIST IS NOT EMPTY, TRAVERSE LIST
  // AND WRITE INFO(P), ELSE WRITE LIST EMPTY MESSAGE
  if (!EmptyList())
  {
    while (P != NULL)                  //TRAVERSE LIST UNTIL P = NULL
    {
      cout << P -> Info << " -> ";     // WRITE INFO(P)
      P = P -> Next;                   // ADVANCE P
    }
    cout << "NULL \n\n";               // WRITE "NULL"
  }
  else                                 // WRITE EMPTY LIST MESSAGE
    cout << "\nThe list is empty!";
}
```

```
// IMPLEMENTATION OF EmptyList()
int List :: EmptyList()
{
  if (First == NULL)
    return (TRUE);
  else
    return (FALSE);
}
```

Now remember, we are implementing our linked list ADT using dynamic pointers. The first implementation that you see in the above code is for the constructor, *List()*. This function simply initializes a new list by setting *First* to *NULL*. Next, the destructor function, *~List()* begins by defining temporary pointers, *P* and *Temp*, to the *Node* struct data type. The pointer *P* is initialized to point to the first node in the list by setting it to *First*. A **while** loop is then executed until the value of *P* becomes *NULL*. Within the loop, *Temp* is set to the next node in the list and the **delete** operator is executed to deallocate the memory being used by *Node(P)*. Once the node memory is deallocated, *P* is advanced to the next node in the list by setting *P* to *Temp*. Why do we need *Temp*?

The remaining function implementations simply reflect their respective algorithms. However, take special note of how dynamic pointers are employed to code the algorithm. For example, notice how the *InsertNode()* function allocates memory for a new node by executing the **new** operator. The statement *P = new Node* allocates memory dynamically for a *Node* struct, then makes *P* point to that struct. In the *DeleteNode()* function, the statement *delete P* deallocates the memory occupied by the *Node* struct to which *P* is pointing. The pseudocode operations used in our algorithms are implemented in C++ using pointers as summarized in Table 14-1.

TABLE 14-1 LINKED LIST PSEUDOCODE
VERSUS C++ POINTER CODE

Pseudocode	C++ Pointer Code
Info(P)	P -> Info
Node(P)	*P
Next(P)	P -> Next

Make a sincere effort to understand how each of the algorithms developed in this section are coded using dynamic pointers in the above implementation file. You now possess all the knowledge required to understand this code.

Last but not least, we need an application file to test our linked list ADT. Here is the one that I used:

```
// APPLICATION FILE TO TEST LIST ADT (listapp.cpp)
#include "list.h"
#include <iostream.h>

void main()
{
  char Character;      // CHARACTER TO BE INSERTED INTO LIST
  int Number;          // NUMBER OF CHARACTERS TO BE INSERTED
  int Count = 0;       // LOOP COUNTER

  List L;              // DEFINE LIST OBJECT

// INSERT SPECIFIED NUMBER OF ELEMENTS INTO LIST
  cout << "\nHow many nodes do you want to insert? ";
  cin >> Number;
  while (Count < Number)
  {
    ++Count;
    cout << "\nEnter a character element:  ";
    cin >> Character;
    L.InsertNode(Character);
  }

// TRAVERSE AND WRITE LIST ELEMENTS
  cout << "\nThe contents of the list are:  ";
    L.TraverseList();

// DELETE A SPECIFIED CHARACTER  FROM THE LIST
  cout << "\nWhich character element do you want to delete? ";
  cin >> Character;
  L.DeleteNode(Character);

// TRAVERSE AND WRITE LIST ELEMENTS
  cout << "\nThe contents of the list are:  ";
    L.TraverseList();
}
```

The application file name is *listapp.cpp*. The code begins by including the *list.h* header file as well as other standard header files that are required. An object, *L*, is defined for the *List* class. The user is then prompted to enter any number of list elements. Is the user restricted to some maximum number of elements as with our stack and queue implementations? No! This is the advantage of using a dynamic pointer implementation. As long as memory is available, we can add as many elements to the list as we want. (Why were we limited with our stack and queue implementations?)

Once a list is constructed, the list is traversed by calling *TraverseList()* to display the list elements. Then the user is prompted to delete a specified character from the list. The character is deleted and the list is traversed and displayed again. Here's a sample run:

How many nodes do you want to insert? **3**↵

Enter a character element: **A**↵

Enter a character element: **B**↵

Enter a character element: **C**↵

The contents of the list are: C -> B -> A -> NULL

Which character element do you want to delete? **B**↵

The contents of the list are: C -> A -> NULL

 Quick Check

1. True or False: In a linked list, the sequencing of the nodes is implicit.
2. The two parts of a linked list node are the _____ and _____.
3. If *Node(P)* is the last node in the list, the value of *Next(P)* is _____.
4. True of False: In a pointer implementation of a linked list, we know that the list is empty when the value of *First* is zero.

5. What happens if you reverse the order of steps 3 and 4 in the insertion process illustrated in Figure 14-15?

6. Will the list search algorithm given in this section detect multiple occurrences of the same element in a linked list?

7. What happens if the statements *Set Pred(P) = P* and *Set P = Next(P)* are reversed in the linked list search algorithm?

8. Write an algorithm using the pseudocode notation developed in this section for the list destructor function, *~List( )*.

CHAPTER SUMMARY

The definition of an ADT includes the following key concepts:

- *An ADT provides for data abstraction.*

- *An ADT includes both data and related operations.*

- *An ADT provides a means to encapsulate and hide information details; whereby the ADT data is completely hidden from its surroundings.*

- *ADT operations provide coupling to the outside world via a function interface.*

Data abstraction is an important software development and programming tool. When developing software with ADTs you can concentrate on the ADT data and related operations, without worrying about the inner implementation details of the ADT. Data abstraction provides for generality, modularity, and protection when developing software.

Three classic ADTs are the stack, queue, and linked list. The stack ADT provides for a collection of data elements whereby elements are always added and removed from one end of the stack called the *Top* of the stack. As a result, stacks operate on the last-in, first-out (LIFO) principle which reverses the ordering of data elements from input to the stack to output from the stack. The queue ADT provides for a collection of data elements whereby elements are always added to the rear of the queue and removed from the front of the queue. Thus, queues operate on the first-in, first-out (FIFO) principle which preserves the ordering of data elements from input to the queue to output from the queue. The linked list ADT provides for a list of data elements whereby elements are always added to the beginning of the list (with the exception of an ordered linked list) and removed from a specified position in the list. Linked lists consist of nodes which contain an information part and a pointer part. The pointer part of any node locates the next sequential node in the list. Arrays, stacks, and queues provide for implicit sequencing of data, while linked lists provide for explicit sequencing of data.

Object-oriented programming is ideal for implementing ADTs due to its data hiding ability. When an ADT is coded as a class, only those operations that are defined for the ADT can be used to access and manipulate the ADT data.

QUESTIONS AND PROBLEMS

Questions

1. Why is data abstraction an important software development tool?

2. What three things are gained by using ADTs during software development?

3. Suppose that we implement a queue using a non-circular array. The queue is initialized such that $Front = Rear = 0$. Then, as we add elements to the queue we increment $Rear$ and insert the element into the array at position $[Rear]$. When we remove elements from the queue, we remove the element at position $[Front]$ and increment $Front$. What problem is encountered with this implementation? Can the problem be corrected? If so, how? What do you suppose the disadvantage is to this implementation versus the one given in this chapter.

4. How do you know that there is only a single element in a queue using the implementation discussed in this chapter?

5. Suggest a way of implementing a queue using a non-circular array. (Hint: Always keep $Front$ at position [0] in the array.)

   What is the disadvantage of this implementation compared to the circular array implementation?

6. Would a compiler use a stack or a queue to keep track of return addresses for nested function calls?

7. Use the stack ADT to write the pseudocode required to remove the element just below the top element of a stack.

8. How must the class header files for the stack, queue, and linked list ADTs given in this chapter be changed to store integers?

9. How must the class header files for the stack, queue, and linked list ADTs given in this chapter be changed to store floating point numbers?

10. How must the class header files for the stack, queue, and linked list ADTs given in this chapter be changed to store structures (structs)?

11. Use the queue ADT to write the pseudocode required to move the element at the rear of the queue to the front of the queue.

12. Suppose that *P* is pointing to some given node in a linked list. What is pointed to by the expression *Next(Next(P))*?

13. Suppose that *P* is pointing to some given node in a linked list. What information is accessed by the expression *Info(Next(P))*?

14. Verify, through desk-checking, that the linked list *DeleteNode()* algorithm developed in this chapter works for the last node in the list.

Problems

Least Difficult

1. Change the stack ADT implementation given in this text to store integers. Write an application program to test your integer stack.

2. Change the queue ADT implementation given in this text to store floating point numbers. Write an application program to test your floating point queue.

3. Code the linked list ADT given in this chapter and write an application program to test the following features:

   • Deleting the first node in the list.

   • Deleting the last node in the list.

   • Deleting a node from an empty list.

4. A palindrome is a word that has the same spelling both forward and backward. Three examples are the words MOM, DAD, and ANNA. Write a program that uses a stack and a queue to determine if a word entered by the user is a palindrome.

5. Write a program that uses only stacks to determine if a word entered by the user is a palindrome. (Hint: You will need three stacks. Why?)

More Difficult

6. A problem with the array implementation of a stack is that the array is finite, thus requiring a *FullStack()* operation. A dynamic pointer implementation of a linked list does not have this limitation. Implement the stack ADT using a dynamic linked list. (Hint: Make the top of the stack point to the first node in the list. In fact, replace *First* with *Top*.

Then always insert and delete at this first node when you push and pop data, respectively.)

7. You can implement a queue in a circular array without using an element counter to determine the empty/full conditions. To do this you must sacrifice an array position such that no element is ever stored in this position. In this implementation *Front* will locate the empty array position and the empty position will always precede the actual front element in the queue. This idea is shown in Figure 14-18.

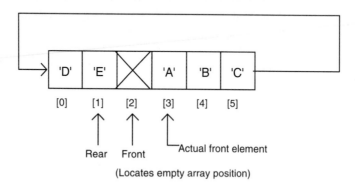

Figure 14-18 An alternative way to implement a queue using a circular array.

With this implementation, the queue is empty when *Front = Rear* and the queue is full when *Rear + 1 = Front*. To insert an element into the rear of the queue you must pre-increment *Rear*. To remove an element from the front of the queue you must pre-increment *Front*. The queue can be initialized to an empty condition by setting *Front = Rear = MAXQ – 1*.

Write a program using object-oriented code for this implementation. Be sure to write a test program to see if the implementation works.

Does it really matter relative to data abstraction which implementation is used for the queue, this one or the one given in the chapter? Both implementations do the same thing relative to the ADT definition, right?

8. A problem with the array implementation of a queue is that the array is finite, thus requiring a *FullQ()* operation. A dynamic linked list does not have this limitation. Implement the queue ADT using a dynamic linked list. (Hint: Make *Front* point to the first node in the list and *Rear* point to the last node in the list.)

9. Change the linked list ADT given in this text to store structs consisting of a name, address, and telephone number. Write an application program to test your linked list.

10. An ordered linked list is one in which the information in the list is ascending or descending from the first node to the last node in the list. To develop an ordered linked list ADT, the *InsertNode()* operation needs to search for the proper insertion point of the information being added to the list prior to inserting the node into the list.

    Develop an ordered linked list ADT to store character data in ascending order, from the beginning to the end of the list. (Hint: You will need to employ two pointers as we did in the *DeleteNode()* operation.) Write an application program to test your ordered linked list.

11. Modify the ADT developed in problem 10 to store a list of address structs, where each struct contains a name (last, first), address, and telephone number. The list should be in ascending order according to the last name. Write an application program to test your address list.

FILE I/O

INTRODUCTION

All the data types and structures you have learned about so far have provided you a means of organizing and storing data in primary memory. However, recall that primary memory is relatively small and, more importantly, volatile. In other words, when the system is turned off or power is lost for any reason, all information stored in primary memory goes to "bit heaven." The obvious solution to this problem is to store any long term data in secondary memory, since secondary memory is nonvolatile.

In this chapter, you will learn how to create files in C++. A file provides you a means of storing information in a convenient and organized manner in secondary memory, such as magnetic disk. There are two basic types of files in C++: character files and binary files. Character files are used to store ASCII data and binary files are used to store numeric data such as integer and floating point values. When you think about it, all information in a C++ program, even complex data entities such as arrays, structs, and objects, can be reduced to either character (ASCII) or numeric binary data. Now, let's complete your learning journey in *Structuring Techniques* with a discussion of files.

15-1 FUNDAMENTAL CONCEPTS AND IDEAS

> A *file* is a data structure that consists of a sequence of components of the same data type.

There are two important aspects to the foregoing definition. First, a file is a *sequence* of components. This means that the data elements, called **components**, are arranged within the file sequentially, or serially, from the first component to the last component. As a result, when accessing files, the file components must be accessed in a sequential manner from one component to the next. A common analogy for a file is an audio cassette tape. Think of the songs on the tape as the file components. How are they stored on the tape? You're right, sequentially from the first song to the last. How must you access a given song? Right again, by sequencing forward or backward through the tape until the desired song is found. Thus, like a cassette tape, a file is a sequential, or serial, storage medium. This makes file access relatively slow as compared to other random access storage mediums. Second, all the components of a file must be the *same data type*, either character (ASCII) or numeric (binary). The default data type for a file in C++ is character. This means that you must specifically designate non-character binary files.

You might be tempted to think of a file as a one-dimensional array, but there are some important differences. First, files provide a means for you to store information within a program run as you do with arrays. But, unlike arrays, files also allow you to store information between program runs. Second, many compilers require you to access the file components in sequence, starting with the first file component. You cannot jump into the middle of a file like you can an array to access a given component. However, C++ does provide a means of semi-random direct access using the *seek* operations. More about this later. Third, files are not declared with a specific dimension as arrays are. Once you declare a file, its size is theoretically unlimited. Of course, the file size is actually limited by the amount of storage space available in secondary memory, such as a disk.

In C++, all file I/O is based on the concept of file streams.

A *file stream* provides a channel for data to flow between your program and the outside world.

In particular, a file stream provides a channel for the flow of data from some source to some destination. Think about what happens when you are typing characters on the keyboard when prompted by a program. You can think of the characters as flowing, or streaming, from the keyboard into the program. Likewise, when your program generates a character display, you can easily visualize the characters streaming from the program to the display.

Classes Provide the Basis for C++ Files

All program I/O is supported by files that operate on predefined classes in C++. The familiar *cin* and *cout* statements that you have been using in your programs for keyboard input and display output are really objects of the *iostream* file class. The *cin* and *cout* objects invoke predefined file streams. Thus we say that standard input is read from the *cin stream* and standard output is written to the *cout stream*. When you include the *iostream.h* header file in your program, the *cin* and *cout* file streams are defined automatically. Of course, the only files that you can access conveniently with *cin* and *cout* are the keyboard and display files that are "attached" to these file streams.

For accessing disk files, you must use one of three classes: *ifstream, ofstream,* or *fstream*. The *ifstream* class is used to perform input, or read, operations from disk files, the *ofstream* class is used to perform output, or write, operations to disk files, and the *fstream* class can be used to perform both read and write operations on disk files. All three of these classes are declared in the *fstream.h* header file.

A hierarchy diagram of the C++ file classes is provided in Figure 15-1. Above the dashed line in Figure 15-1 you find the classes declared in *iostream.h*, while below the line you see the classes declared in *fstream.h*. Notice all the *fstream.h* classes are derived from the *iostream.h* classes. As a result, by including the *fstream.h* header file in your program, you have access to the predefined file streams (*cin, cout*) as well as file streams that you will define for disk I/O. File streams that you will define for disk I/O are referred to as ***named*** file streams.

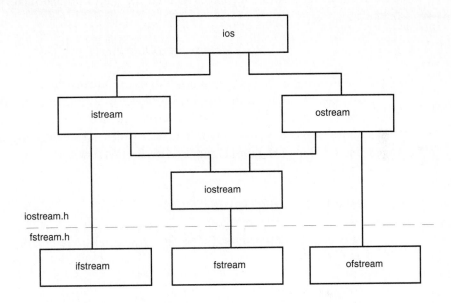

Figure 15-1 The file class hierarchy in C++.

Creating File Streams in C++: The File Stream Definition

To create a named file stream in C++ you must do two things:

1. Define a file stream object for one of the *fstream.h* file classes.

2. Attach the file stream object to a particular disk file to ***open*** the file.

When you create a named file, the first thing you must do is define an object for one of the named file classes. File stream objects that are used exclusively for input are defined as objects of the *ifstream* class. Thus, the statement:

ifstream Input;

defines *Input* as an input file stream object. You use the *ofstream* class to define files stream objects that are used exclusively for output. Thus, the statement:

ofstream Output;

defines *Output* as an output file stream object. Finally, you must use the *fstream* class when defining objects that will be used for both file input and output. The statement:

fstream InputOutput;

defines *InputOutput* as both an input and output file stream object.

Next, you must attach the file stream object to a physical file. When a file stream object is attached to a physical disk file, the disk file is opened for access. This requires the use of the *open()* function which is inherited by all the file stream classes. Here is the format required to call this function:

FORMAT TO OPEN A DISK FILE

<file stream object> • **open** (<disk file name>, <file open mode>,
                                                <file protection mode>);

The first thing that must be specified is the file stream object. The object name is followed by a dot, which is followed by the *open()* function and its required arguments. From your knowledge of OOP, you know that this statement simply calls the *open()* function defined in the respective file stream class.

The *open()* function can have up to three arguments: a disk file name, an open mode designator, and a protection mode designator. The disk file name must adhere to the requirements of the operating system. For DOS systems, the file name cannot exceed eight characters. A three character extension, separated from the file name by a dot, is optional. Thus, DOS file names such as *sample*, *sample.dat*, and *sample12.dat* are all legal file names. The physical disk file name can be specified directly within double quotes (i.e. "sample.dat") or indirectly as a character array variable.

The open mode designator argument defines what type of file access is to be performed. The eight predefined mode designators available in C++ are listed in Table 15-1.

TABLE 15-1 OPEN MODE DESIGNATORS DEFINED IN C++

Mode	Definition
ios :: in	Open file for reading
ios :: out	Open file for writing
ios :: ate	Seek to end of file upon opening
ios :: app	Open for appending to end of file
ios :: nocreate	Open fails if file does not exist
ios :: noreplace	Open fails if file exists
ios :: trunc	Open file and discard existing contents
ios :: binary	Binary file: CRLF pairs not translated

The third argument possible in the *open()* function call is the protection mode designator. The four protection modes defined for C++ files are listed in Table 15-2. You will normally not be concerned with the file protection mode and therefore do not need to list one as an argument in the *open()* function.

TABLE 15-2 FILE PROTECTION MODES DEFINED IN C++

Mode	Access Protection
S_IREAD	Read Only
S_IWRITE	Write Only
S_IREAD I S_IWRITE	Read and Write

As an example of opening a file, suppose that we wish to open a file stream called *InputOutput*. The file stream is defined for the *fstream* class and is to be attached to a disk file called *test.dat*. In addition, the program will both read and write the file. The appropriate open statement would be:

```
InputOutput . open("test.dat", ios :: in  I  ios :: out);
```

As you can see, the file stream object calls the *open()* function using the dot operator. The physical disk file to be opened is placed within double quotes as the first argument in the function call. The first argument could also be a string (character array) variable that holds the disk file name. The second argument provides the file mode designators. Here, two designators are ORed together using the | operator to tell the compiler that the file can be both read from (*ios :: in*) or written to (*ios :: out*). No protection mode is listed for this file.

The read/write mode(s) must always be specified when a file stream object is defined for the *fstream* class, since by definition, this class is used for both input and output (reading/writing) file access. Read/write modes do not need to be specified when opening files defined for the *ifstream* or *ofstream* classes, since such files are input and output files, respectively, by default. For instance, if *Output* is defined as a file stream object of the *ofstream* class, the open statement would simply be:

Output . open("test.dat");

On the other hand, if *Input* is defined as a file stream object of the *istream* class, the open statement would be:

Input . open("test.dat");

The first four mode designators in Table 15-1 are the most commonly used. However, you should take special note of the last designator, *ios :: binary*. By default, all files in C++ are character, or ASCII, files. To designate a file as a non-character file, you designate it as mode *ios :: binary*. You must use binary files to store numeric information, such as integers and floats. Of course, a binary file is *not* an ASCII file, and therefore CRLF patterns are not translated as such.

Example 15-1

Write statements to create the following disk files:
a. A file stream called *Read* that will read from a disk file called *sample.doc*.
b. A file stream called *Write* that will write to a disk file called *sample.doc*.
c. A file stream called *Read_Write* that will read and write a disk file called *sample.doc*.
d. A file stream called *Append* that will append a file whose name is stored in a character array called *FileName[]*.

Solution:

a.   ifstream Read;
                     Read . open("sample.doc");

b.   ofstream Write;
      Write . open("sample.doc");

c.   fstream Read_Write;
      Read_Write . open("sample.doc", ios :: in | ios :: out);

Again, notice that the *ios :: in* and *ios :: out* file modes are ORed together to create a read/write file when the *fstream* class is specified.

d.   ofstream Append;
      Append . open(FileName, ios :: app);

Here, the *ios :: app* mode is specified, since the file is to be appended. To append a file means to add components to the end of the file.

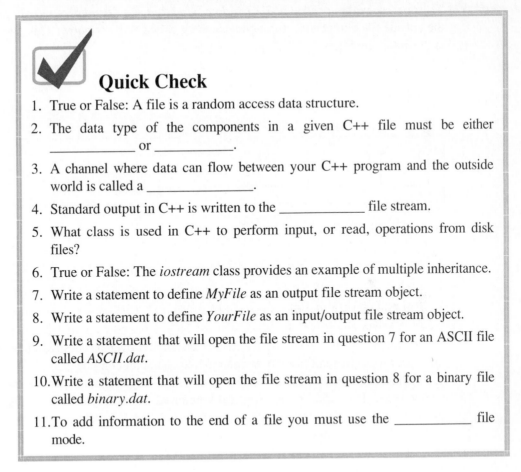

Quick Check

1. True or False: A file is a random access data structure.

2. The data type of the components in a given C++ file must be either _____ or _____.

3. A channel where data can flow between your C++ program and the outside world is called a _____.

4. Standard output in C++ is written to the _____ file stream.

5. What class is used in C++ to perform input, or read, operations from disk files?

6. True or False: The *iostream* class provides an example of multiple inheritance.

7. Write a statement to define *MyFile* as an output file stream object.

8. Write a statement to define *YourFile* as an input/output file stream object.

9. Write a statement that will open the file stream in question 7 for an ASCII file called *ASCII.dat*.

10. Write a statement that will open the file stream in question 8 for a binary file called *binary.dat*.

11. To add information to the end of a file you must use the _____ file mode.

15-2 ACCESSING FILE INFORMATION

Before getting into specific file access routines, let's take a minute to discuss the more important overall concept of file access.

The File Window

Files can be thought of as a means for a program to communicate with the "outside world." Information can be read into the program by placing it in a file and having the program read that file. In the same way, the program can write information to the outside world by writing to a file. As you know, C++ treats the user keyboard as an input file and the display monitor as an output file. Now, the question is: "How does your program communicate with the file?" The answer is: "Through something called a ***file window***." In other words, your program "sees" the outside file components through something called a file window. This concept is illustrated by Figure 15-2.

FILE OF CHARACTERS

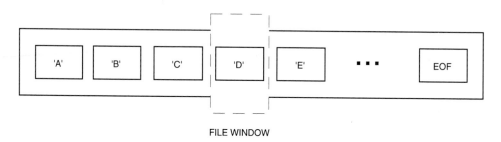

FILE WINDOW

Figure 15-2 File components are accessed through a file window.

In Figure 15-2, the file consists of a sequence of character components. To access a given character, the window must be positioned over that character so that it can be "seen." Once the window is positioned over the desired character, information can be read from, or written to that character component.

When you open a file, a window is automatically created to access the file components. This window is technically referred to as a ***file stream buffer***. Consequently, the file stream buffer, or window, is the link between the program and the file components.

File Operations

Now that you know how a file is created and structured, you need to learn about some general operations that will allow you to work with files. The following discussion will center on C++. I should caution you, however, that file operations in C differ somewhat from file operations in C++, since file operations in C++ are structured around classes. As a result, there are operations available in C++ that are not available in C. Thus, a program written in C++ might not compile in C.

It is probably best to look at a comprehensive example in order to learn how to access C++ files. Let's begin by developing our own class that will be used specifically for file access. We will include member functions in the class that allow us to perform the following common file access routines:

- Initialize a private data member with a disk file name entered by the user.

- Write, or create, a new file.

- Read and display an existing file.

- Append an existing file.

- Change an existing file.

Here is the class declaration:

```
// files.h  CLASS DECLARATION HEADER FILE
#ifndef FILES_H
#define FILES_H

#include <fstream.h>

class Files : public fstream
{
public:
  void GetName();
  void WriteFile();
  void ReadFile();
  void AppendFile();
  void ChangeFile();

private:
  char FileName[13];
};
#endif
```

First, you see that the *fstream.h* header file is included prior to the class declaration. The *fstream.h* header file is included, since it contains the *fstream* class declaration. The *fstream* class forms the base class for our *Files* class as you can see from the class declaration. As a result, our *Files* class will inherit all the members of the predefined *fstream* class.

The declaration provides for a single private data member called *FileName*. This *FileName* character array will be used to store the name of the disk file being attached to our file stream objects. Notice that the array can store up to 13 character elements to provide for an 8 character file name, a dot, a 3 character extension, and a null terminator. Four public functions are part of the class to provide the file access routines that are listed above. Our *Files* class declaration will be stored in a header file called *files.h*.

Next, we need to develop an implementation file for each of the member functions. Let's take them in order, beginning with the *GetName()* function.

Getting A Disk File Name From the User

The *GetName()* function simply gets a physical disk file name from the user and initializes the *FileName* member of our *Files* class to the string entered by the user. Here's the implementation:

```
// getname.cpp IMPLEMENTATION FILE FOR GetName() FUNCTION
#include "files.h"
void Files :: GetName()
{
// GET THE FILE NAME FROM USER TO
// INITIALIZE FILE NAME DATA MEMBER
   cout << "\n\nWhat file name do you want to use?\n"
        << "Note:  Not more that 8 characters with"
        << " a 3 character extension.\n\n";
   cin >> FileName;
} // END FUNCTION
```

The opening comment indicates that the *GetName()* implementation is stored in a file called *getname.cpp*. The *files.h* file must be included in this file, since *files.h* contains our *Files* class declaration, of which *GetName()* is a member. The body of the implementation is straightforward and you should not have any trouble understanding it at this point.

Writing, or Creating, a New File

Next, we need to develop an implementation for the *WriteFile( )* function. This function must accomplish the task of creating a new file if it doesn't already exist, or completely rewriting an existing file with new components. Here are the general file operations required to accomplish this task:

- Define an output file stream object.

- Open the file stream in output mode and attach it to a disk file name.

- Get the new file components from the user and write them to the file.

- Close the file stream.

We will place the *WriteFile( )* implementation in a file called *write.cpp*. Here it is:

```cpp
// write.cpp  IMPLEMENTATION FILE FOR WriteFile()

#include "files.h"
#include <stdio.h>
#include <stdlib.h>
#include <string.h>
#include <conio.h>

void Files :: WriteFile()
{
// DECLARE LOCAL CONSTANTS AND VARIABLES
   const SIZE = 81;
   char Line[SIZE];

// DEFINE OUTPUT FILE OBJECT
   ofstream Output;

// OPEN FILE
   Output.open(FileName);
   if (!Output)
   {
    cerr << "This file cannot be opened.";
    exit(1);
   }
```

```
// GET FILE COMPONENTS AND WRITE TO FILE
  cout << "Enter a file component or DONE when finished:  ";
  gets(Line);
  while (strcmp(Line,"DONE"))
  {
    Output << Line << '\n';
    cout << "Enter a file component or DONE when finished:  ";
    gets(Line);

  } // END FOR

// CLOSE FILE
  Output.close();

} // END FUNCTION
```

First, notice that each of the major operations that need to be performed in this implementation are commented so that they can be easily identified in the code. The code begins by including the header files that are needed in this implementation. Of course, our class header file (*files.h*) must be included, since *WriteFile()* is a member function of our *Files* class. Before anything can be done with a file, a file stream object must be defined and opened. The object is called *Output* and is defined for the *ofstream* class which is inherited via our *Files* class. The *ofstream* class is used here, since *WriteFile()* only writes, or outputs, information to the file. Next, the *Output* stream object is opened by calling the *open()* function. (How does the *Output* object have access to this function?) The only argument needed in the *open()* function is the physical disk file name that will be attached to the *Output* stream object. Recall that our *GetName()* function obtains the disk file name from the user and initializes the *FileName* member of the class to the user entry. The *open()* function has access to this value, since, by inheritance, *open()* is a member of our *Files* class. Observe that *FileName* is provided as the argument for the *open()* function.

After the file stream is opened, an **if** statement is inserted to determine if the file stream can be opened. If, for any reason, the file stream cannot be opened, the file stream object will return a value of zero. If a value of zero is returned, an error message is displayed via a *cerr* statement and the program is aborted via an *exit()* statement. The *cerr* statement does basically the same thing as *cout*. However, the *cerr* statement is usually employed for file operations rather than *cout*, since some programs might attach *cout* to a file other than the standard display monitor file. The *exit()* function causes the program to abort and return to the operating system. In addition, *exit()* closes any files that were previously opened by the program.

The next section of code gets the file components from the user and writes them to the file. By default, the file is a character file. Here, we are obtaining character strings from the user via the *gets()* function and storing them in a local character array called *Line*. The maximum size of *Line* is 81 characters to allow for a maximum string of 80 characters and a null terminator. Recall that the width of a typical monitor screen is 80 characters. Once a string is obtained from the user, it is written to our *Output* file stream object using the familiar << insertion operator. We say that the << operator "inserts" the string into the file stream. In our case, the string contained in *Line* is inserted into the *Output* file stream. Notice that the *gets()* function and file write operation are both part of a **while** loop that iterates once for each component the user has to enter. The loop breaks when the user enters the string "DONE".

The last thing to do is to close the file stream. This is accomplished by a call to the *close()* function. The *close()* function is the counterpart to the *open()* function. Unlike the *open()* function, the *close()* function does not require any arguments. ***Open file streams must always be closed before exiting the program.*** In fact, it is a good idea to close a file stream as soon as you are done accessing it so that you don't forget. For this reason, we will always close any open file streams immediately when we are done accessing them within a file handling routine.

Reading and Displaying an Existing File

The next implementation we need to deal with is the *ReadFile()* implementation. The operations that must be performed here are:

- Define an input file stream object.

- Open the file stream in input mode and attach it to a disk file name.

- Read the file components and display them to the user.

- Close the file stream.

We will store this implementation in a separate file called *read.cpp*. Here it is:

```
// read.cpp IMPLEMENTATION FILE FOR ReadFile() FUNCTION
#include "files.h"
#include <stdlib.h>
```

```
#include <stdio.h>

void Files :: ReadFile()
{
// DEFINE LOCAL CONSTANTS AND VARIABLES
  const SIZE = 81;
  char  Line[SIZE];

// DEFINE INPUT FILE OBJECT
  ifstream Input;

// OPEN FILE
  Input.open(FileName);
  if (!Input)
  {
   cerr << "This file cannot be opened.";
   exit(1);
  }

// READ AND DISPLAY FILE
  cout << "The current file contents are:  \n\n";
  while (!Input.eof())
  {
   Input.getline(Line,SIZE);
   cout << Line << '\n';
  }

// CLOSE FILE
  Input.close();

// PROMPT TO CONTINUE
  cout << "\n\nPress ENTER to continue.";
  getchar();

} // END FUNCTION
```

You see that our *files.h* file is again included in this file, since the *ReadFile()* function is part of our *Files* class. The file stream object is called *Input* and is defined for the *ifstream* class. The *ifstream* class is used, since all we will do is read a file. Next, the file stream is opened and attached to the disk file name stored in *FileName*. Again, an error message is generated and the program aborted if for some reason the file stream cannot be opened. The file components are read as part of a **while** loop. Notice the loop test. There is a standard function available in the *ios* class called *eof()*. (How does our implementation inherit this function?) The *eof()* function returns a 1 (TRUE) when the file window is at the end of file position, otherwise a value of 0 (FALSE) is returned.

The end of file (eof) position is defined as the position just after the last component in the file. Our *Input* object calls the *eof()* function in the loop test via the statement *!Input.eof()*. The test will be TRUE and the loop statements will execute as long as the window is not at the eof position. The first loop statement reads the component at the current file window position via the *getline()* function. Recall that *getline()* reads a string character-by-character and places it in an array. In our case the string is read and placed in a local character array called *Line*. After a given string is read, the file window is at the beginning of the next string in the file in preparation for the next loop iteration unless, of course, the window is at the end of file position. Once a string is read, the second loop statement displays the string via a *cout* statement. Finally, after all the file strings are read and displayed, the loop terminates and the file stream is closed.

Appending an Existing File

Appending a file means to add information to the end of the file. The operations required to perform this task are:

- Define an output file stream object.

- Open the file stream in append mode and attach it to a disk file name.

- Get the additional file components from the user and write them to the file.

- Close the file stream.

This implementation will be stored in a separate file called *append.cpp*. The code required to append an existing file is almost the same as that for creating a new file. The only difference is the open mode argument specified in the *open()* function. Here's the required implementation code:

```
// append.cpp  IMPLEMENTATION FILE FOR AppendFile()

#include "files.h"
#include <stdio.h>
#include <stdlib.h>
#include <string.h>
```

```
void Files :: AppendFile()
{
// DECLARE LOCAL CONSTANTS AND VARIABLES
   const SIZE = 81;
   char Line[SIZE];

// DEFINE APPEND FILE OBJECT
   ofstream Append;

// OPEN FILE
   Append.open(FileName, ios :: app);
   if (!Append)
   {
     cerr << "\nThis file cannot be opened.";
     exit(1);
   }

// GET FILE COMPONENTS AND APPEND TO FILE
   cout << "\n\nEnter new file component or DONE when finished:  ";
   gets(Line);
   while (strcmp(Line,"DONE"))
   {
     Append << Line << '\n';
     cout << "\n\nEnter new file component or DONE when finished:  ";
     gets(Line);
   }

// CLOSE FILE
   Append.close();

} //END FUNCTION
```

Comparing this code to the *WriteFile()* code you find that the only difference is in the name of the object (*Append* versus *Output)* and the open mode argument (*ios :: app* versus *ios :: out)*. Does this tell you anything about how the open mode positions the file window? Well, the *ios :: out* mode positions the window at the beginning of the file, and in addition, erases any information in an existing file. As a result, any write operations to the file create entirely new information in the file. On the other hand, the *ios :: app* mode positions the window at the end of the file and does not erase existing information. Therefore, any write operations to the file add information to the end of the file.

Changing an Existing File

The last function we need to discuss is the *ChangeFile()* function. This function requires the following file operations:

- Define an input/output file stream object.

- Open the file stream in both input and output mode and attach it to a disk file name.

- Get the component to be changed from the user and search the file for the component.

- Seek the old component position.

- Erase the old component information from the file.

- Seek the end of file position.

- Write the new component information to the end of the file.

- Close the file stream.

The idea here is to get the component to be changed from the user, then search the file for that component. Once found, we will erase the old component information from the file and ask the user to provide the new component information. The new component information will then be written to the end of the file. Let's get into the code. By the way, this implementation will be stored in a file called *change.cpp*. Here it is:

```
// change.cpp IMPLEMENTATION FILE FOR ChangeFile() FUNCTION

#include "files.h"
#include <stdlib.h>
#include <string.h>
#include <stdio.h>

void Files :: ChangeFile()
{
// DEFINE LOCAL CONSTANTS AND VARIABLES
   const SIZE = 81;
   char  OldLine[SIZE], NewLine[SIZE], Entry[SIZE];
   int WindowPos;
   int Flag = 0;
```

```
// DEFINE INPUT/OUTPUT FILE OBJECT
  fstream Change;

// OPEN FILE OBJECT
  Change.open(FileName, ios :: in | ios :: out);

// GET COMPONENT TO CHANGE FROM USER AND SEARCH FILE.
// IF COMPONENT FOUND, ERASE AND PLACE NEW
// COMPONENT AT END OF FILE
  cout << "\n\nWhich line do you wish to change?  ";
  gets(Entry);
  while (!Change.eof())
  {
    // SET WindowPos TO FILE WINDOW  POSITION
    WindowPos = Change.tellg();

     // READ A FILE COMPONENT
    Change.getline(OldLine,SIZE);

    // COMPARE FILE COMPONENT TO USER ENTRY
    if (!strcmp(OldLine,Entry))
    {
        Flag = 1;    // SET FLAG TO TRUE IF FOUND

        // SEEK FOUND COMPONENT POSITION
        Change . seekg(WindowPos, ios :: beg);

        // REPLACE COMPONENT WITH *'s
        for (int i = 1; i < strlen(OldLine) + 1; ++i)
            Change <<  '*';

        // GET NEW COMPONENT FROM USER
        cout << "\nLine found, what do you wish to change it to?  ";
        gets(NewLine);

        // SEEK END OF FILE
        Change.seekp(0, ios :: end);

        // ADD NEW COMPONENT TO END OF FILE
        Change << NewLine << '\n';
        break;
    } // END IF
  } // END WHILE
```

```
// WRITE MESSAGE TO USER IF COMPONENT NOT FOUND
  if (!Flag)
  {
     cout << "\nLine not found.  Press ENTER to get back to main menu";
     getchar();
  } // END IF

// CLOSE FIND FILE
  Change.close();

} // END FUNCTION
```

The code begins by including several header files that are required for this file. Several local items are defined at the beginning of the *ChangeFile()* implementation. You will discover their use shortly. A file stream object called *Change* is defined for the *fstream* class. The *fstream* class is required here because we will use this object to both read and write the file. The file stream is then opened and attached to the disk file name stored in *FileName*. In addition, notice that the file stream is opened for mode *ios :: in* and mode *ios :: out*. Recall that you must specify the input/output modes when using the *fstream* class, since no default mode is assumed.

After the file stream is opened, the user is prompted to enter the component information to be changed. The user entry is placed in a local character array called *Entry*. A **while** loop is then executed to search for the entered component. Notice that the **while** loop will execute until one of two conditions occur: 1) when the end of the file is encountered, or 2) when the component being searched for is found. Look at the first statement in the **while** loop. Here, the object is invoking a function of the *istream* class called *tellg()*. (How does this program inherit *tellg()*?) The *tellg()* function returns the current position of the file window. The value returned represents the number of bytes the window is located from the beginning of the file. This value is assigned in the program to a variable called *WidowPos* that will be used later. You should be aware that there is a comparable function, called *tellp()*, defined for the *ostream* class. We are using *tellg()* rather than *tellp()* to be consistent with an input operation. Actually, either could be used in this case, since both *istream* and *ostream* are inherited by our *Files* class via *fstream*.

Now back to the program. After the window position is stored using *tellg()*, a file component is read via the *getline()* function and placed in a character array called *OldLine*. The string compare function *strcmp()* is then called as part of an **if** statement to compare the file component just read (*OldLine*) with the entry from the user (*Entry*). If the two strings are the same, a local variable called *Flag* is set to 1 (TRUE). This variable will be used later to write a message to the user if the component search fails. Next, the *Change* object invokes an inherited function called *seekg()* to position the file window at the beginning of the component which was just read. Recall that the file window was at the beginning of the component to be read just prior to calling *getline()*. However, after the *getline()* function reads the component, the window moves to the beginning of the next sequential file component. Therefore, if the component being searched for is found, the window must be backed up to the beginning of this component so that it can be erased from the file. This is why we stored the window position in *WindowPos* just prior to reading the component. Here is the statement that we are using to call *seekg()*:

Change . seekg(WindowPos, ios :: beg);

This statement places the file window at the beginning of the found component, *OldLine*. The first argument, *WindowPos*, contains the number of bytes that the *Oldline* component is located from the beginning of the file. The second argument, *ios :: beg*, tells the compiler to move the window relative to the beginning of the file. So, the first argument in *seekg()* specifies the number of bytes to move the window, while the second argument specifies the starting point. There are three possible starting points for this second argument: the beginning of the file (*ios :: beg*), the current position of the file window (*ios :: cur*), and the end of the file (*ios :: end*). Thus we can move the file window so many bytes from the beginning of the file, the current position of the file window, or the end of the file. The *seekg()* function recognizes the three possible arguments of *ios :: beg*, *ios :: cur*, or *ios :: end*.

Now that the searched-for component has been found, it is effectively erased by replacing it with asterisks. This is accomplished using a **for** loop that iterates a number of times equal to the length of the found component, *OldLine*. Notice the call to the *strlen()* function in the loop test. The *strlen()* function calculates the length of the *Oldline* component. The resulting length determines when the loop will terminate. With each loop iteration, an asterisk (*) is written to the file such that the *OldLine* component is overwritten with *'s.

The task now is to get the new component information from the user and append it to the end of the file. The user is prompted for the new component information, which is obtained using a call to *gets()* and stored in the character array called *Newline*. To append the new information to the file, the file window must be moved to the end of file position. This is accomplished with a call to the *seekp()* function. The *seekp()* function is analogous to the *seekg()* function used earlier. However, *seekp()* is inherited via *ostream*, while *seekg()* is inherited via *istream*. Thus, the *seekp()* function should be used in conjunction with file write operations and *seekg()* used with file read operations. Actually, either could be used here, since both are inherited by this program. We are using *seekp()* to be consistent with its purpose, since we are about to perform a file write operation. Here is the statement we are using to call *seekp()*:

Change . seekp(0, ios :: end);

Notice the two arguments. The first argument, 0, tells the compiler to move the file window zero bytes from the second argument specification. Thus, the window will be positioned zero bytes from the *end* of the file.

After the window is positioned at the end of the file, the *NewLine* component is written to the file via the statement:

Change << NewLine << '\n';

Once the new component is appended to the file, a **break** statement is executed to break the **while** loop.

The next segment of code checks *Flag* to determine if the component searched for was found during the previous search loop. If the component was not found in the file, an appropriate message is displayed to the user.

The Application Program

Now all we need is an application program to test our *Files* class. Here is one, called *fileio.cpp*, that will exercise all of the file operations that we have just developed:

```
// fileio.cpp  APPLICATION FILE FOR FILE I/O

#include "files.h"
#include <ctype.h>
#include <iostream.h>

void main()
{
// DECLARE MyFile OBJECT AND LOCAL VARIABLES
   Files MyFile;
   char Choice;
```

```
// GET FILE NAME FROM USER
   MyFile.GetName();

// GENERATE FILE ACCESS MENU
   do
   {
     cout  << "\n\n\t\tWrite and create a new file (W)"
               "\n\n\t\tRead and display file (R)"
               "\n\n\t\tAppend file (A)"
               "\n\n\t\tChange file (C)"
               "\n\n\t\tQuit(Q)"
               "\n\n\n\t\t\tENTER CHOICE ---> ";
     cin >> Choice;
     Choice = toupper(Choice);
     switch (Choice)
     {
       case 'W':  MyFile.WriteFile();
                       break;
       case 'R':  MyFile.ReadFile();
                       break;
       case 'A':  MyFile.AppendFile();
                       break;
       case 'C':  MyFile.ReadFile();
                        MyFile.ChangeFile();
                       break;
       default :  cout << "\n\nInvalid choice.";
     } // END SWITCH
   } while (Choice != 'Q');
} // END MAIN
```

Again you see our *files.h* header file included so that we can define an object for our *Files* class. Function *main()* begins by defining an object called *MyFile* of the *Files* class. This object is then used to call our *GetName()* function to obtain a disk file name from the user. A menu is then generated on the screen that allows the user to exercise any of the file operations that are part of the *Files* class. Of course, these are the operations that we just developed. Once the user selects a given menu option, the respective class function is called via the *MyFile* object. Notice in particular that both the *ReadFile()* and *ChangeFile()* functions are called for the Change (C) menu option. The reason for this is to allow the user to examine the existing contents of the file via the *ReadFile()* function prior to entering a component to be changed.

As you might suspect, this program was developed as a project. Here is a copy of the project window screen:

Project: FILEIO

File name	Location	Lines	Code	Data
APPEND.CPP	.	42	215	118
READ.CPP	.	43	198	90
GETNAME.CPP	.	1	57	105
CHANGE.CPP	.	59	318	142
WRITE.CPP	.	41	212	117
FILEIO.CPP	.	47	309	161

The project window shows all of the individual function implementation files as well as the application file. Of course, the required header files are not shown as part of the project, since they are included within those files that are listed.

 Quick Check

1. True of False: File operations in C++ are the same as those in C.

2. List the major operations that are required to create a new file.

3. List the major operations that are required to read an existing file.

4. What is the difference, relative to the position of the file window, between using the *ios :: out* versus the *ios :: app* file modes when opening a file?

5. How does the *change.cpp* program in this section inherit the *tellg()* function?

6. What does the *tellg()* function return to the calling program?

7. True or False: The *tellg()* function should be used with input files, while the *tellp()* function should be used with output files.

8. What function must be used to position the file window for an output file?

9. What three predefined starting points are available to the *seekg()* and *seekp()* functions?

10. The distance to move the file window from the specified starting point when using *seekg()* or *seekp()* must be expressed in _____ units.

CHAPTER SUMMARY

A file is a sequential data structure that consists of components that are all of the same data type. Files provide a means for your program to communicate with the outside world. Any I/O operations performed by your program, even keyboard input and display output, are handled via files. Files in C++ can be either ASCII character files or binary files. The default type of file is the character file. If a file is to be a binary file, the binary file mode must be specified when the file stream is opened.

All file I/O in C++ is in the form of file streams that employ predefined classes. The *ifstream* class is used to create input file stream objects, the *ofstream* class is used to create output file stream objects, and the *fstream* class is used to create file stream objects that will be used for both input and output. All three of these file stream classes are declared in the *fstream.h* header file. File streams that you create are called named file streams. To create a named file stream you must define a file stream object for one of the *fstream.h* file classes, and attach the stream object to a particular disk file using the *open()* function. The *open()* function can have up to three arguments: a physical disk file name, a file mode designator, and a protection mode designator. See Tables 15-1 and 15-2 for a list of the predefined file mode and protection mode designators.

Once a file stream is opened, it is ready for processing. The individual components within a file are accessed via a file stream window. The window must be positioned over the component to be accessed. When a file is opened, the window, sometimes called a file stream buffer, is automatically created to access the file components. Typical tasks that are performed on disk files include writing new files, reading existing files, appending existing files, and changing the information in existing files. The C++ language has various predefined functions to facilitate the coding of these tasks. After a file stream is processed, it must always be closed using the *close()* function.

QUESTIONS AND PROBLEMS

Questions

1. Describe the structure of a file.
2. What is a file stream?
3. What is a file stream window and how is it used during file processing?
4. What three predefined classes provide the basis for C++ files?
5. What header file provides the predefined file class declarations in C++?

6. What two operations must be performed to create a named file stream in C++?

7. The *open()* function can have up to three arguments. What are they? What is the purpose of each argument?

8. True or False: The *ios :: out* file stream mode does not need to be designated for an object defined for the *ofstream* class.

9. When must the *ios :: app* mode be specified when opening a file stream?

10. What mode must be specified to open a binary file stream?

11. Write statements to create the following disk file streams:

    a. A character file stream called *FileIn* that will read a disk file called *mydata.txt*.

    b. A binary file stream called *BinaryIn* that will read a disk file called *mydata.bin*.

    c. A binary file stream called *BinaryI_O* that will both read and write a disk file called *mydata.bin*.

    d. A character file stream called *AddTo* that will append a file whose name is stored in a character array called *Name*.

12. True or False: When a file stream is opened for the *ofstream* class and no append mode is specified, the file stream window is placed at the beginning of the file and all components in an existing file are overwritten by any subsequent write operations to the file.

13 List the major operations that must be performed in order to change the contents of an existing file.

14. Write a statement that will store the current position of the *MyFile* file stream window in a variable called *Position*. Assume that *MyFile* is defined for the *ofstream* class.

15. Write a statement that will move the file stream window in question 14 to a position that is *Position* bytes from the current position of the window.

16. Write a statement that will position the *MyFile* file stream window to the beginning of the file. Assume that *MyFile* is defined for the *ifstream* class.

17. Write a statement that will position the *MyFile* file stream window to the end of the file. Assume that *Myfile* is defined for the *ofstream* class.

18. Write a statement that will write a string called *String* to an output file stream object called *MyFile*.

19. Write a statement that will read a string component at the current window position of an input file stream called *MyFile* and place it in a character array called *String*.

20. Write a loop structure that will search for a string called *String* in a file stream called *MyFile* and set *Flag* to TRUE if the string is found.

Problems

Least Difficult

Perform the following tasks for problems 1–5:

- Add the specified function to the *Files* class developed in this chapter.
- Write an implementation file for the specified function.
- Add the specified function to the application program menu in *fileio.cpp* in order test the function.

1. A function called *Copy()* that will copy an existing file to a new file.

2. A function called *Erase()* that will erase an existing file.

3. A function called *Compare()* that will compare the contents of two files and report to the user if they are the same or different.

4. A function called *CleanUp()* that will clean up a file by removing the asterisks inserted by the *Change()* function developed in this chapter. The cleaned-up file should have no blank lines or fill characters.

5. A function that will read a file, then rewrite it to a new file with every line preceded by a sequential line number. The line number must be left justified on the screen when the file is displayed.

More Difficult

6. Rewrite the file access functions developed in this chapter to handle files of two-digit hexadecimal values.

7. Write a program that will create a new file of integers by multiplying an existing file of integers by 2.

Most Difficult

8. Using the techniques discussed in this chapter, write and test a program that will handle a parts inventory file of the following information:

   - Part Name
   - Part Number
   - Part Price
   - Quantity on Hand

   Develop functions that will allow a user to create the parts inventory file, read and display the file, append the file, and change information in the file.

APPENDIX A
TURBO C++ JUMP START

INTRODUCTION

Borland's TURBO C++ is a full-powered, highly capable C++ compiler that offers programmers an Integrated Development Environment (IDE for short) that is easy-to-learn and easy-to-use even for the beginning programmer.

With TURBO C++ you don't need to use a separate editor, compiler, linker, and debugger in order to create, debug, and run your C++ programs. All of these features are built into TURBO C++ and are all accessible from the IDE.

This appendix is intended to familiarize the beginning programmer, and anyone else not familiar with TURBO C++, with the necessary features of the IDE that will help you get started programming in C++. An introduction to the elements of the IDE Desktop and a "hands-on" approach will allow you to get started quickly with a sample "Hello World" program. You will gain the most benefit from the topics covered in this appendix if you work interactively through Section A-1 while using TURBO C++ on your computer. Hands-on is the best way to become familiar with C++ and the TURBO C++ IDE.

Other topics covered in this appendix are: a more detailed explanation of the components of the IDE Menu system to get you programming with TURBO C++, how to use the on-line Help feature, using the Integrated Debugger, and Hot Key shortcut tips. For in-depth information of all of the features available in TURBO C++ you will need to consult the TURBO C++ users manual.

Hardware and Software Requirements

TURBO C++ runs on IBM and compatible PCs, including 286, 386, or 486 computers. TURBO C++ requires a 286 or higher CPU, DOS 3.31 or higher, a hard disk, a floppy drive, and at least 640K plus 1MB of extended memory. It will run on any 80-column monitor. TURBO C++ also supports, but does not require, a mouse.

What You Need to Know to Use TURBO C++

It is assumed that you have a working knowledge of DOS, (file maintenance and manipulating directories), how to use a mouse, and the use and location of keys on the keyboard.

A-1 GETTING STARTED ⇒ "HELLO WORLD"

Starting TURBO C++

TURBO C++ must be installed on your computer system before you can use it. The directory where TURBO C++ is located also needs to be added to the **PATH** statement in the computer's *autoexec.bat* file so that the computer can locate the program files to run TURBO C++. You can type **PATH** and press **ENTER** (↵) at the DOS prompt to find out if the TURBO C++ directory is in the **PATH** statement. The default directory for these files is **C:\TC\BIN**. If the correct directory is in the **PATH** statement, you can simply type **TC** and **ENTER**, as shown in Figure A-1, to start TURBO C++.

Figure A-1 Enter TC at the DOS prompt.

If simply entering **TC** doesn't work, change to the directory containing the TURBO C++ program files, then type **TC** and press **ENTER**, as shown in Figure A-2 (for example, **CD\TC\BIN** ↵ **TC** ↵).

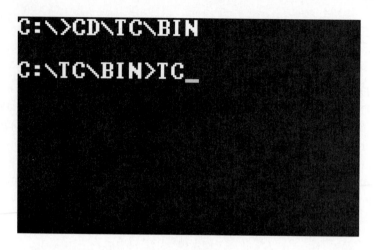

Figure A-2 Change to the TURBO C++ directory and type TC.

Since TURBO C++ is a compiler for both C and C++ programs, there are some important options that you may need to set to prepare for Object Oriented C++ programming. If you are working with a computer system that has already been prepared for C++ programming, check with your instructor or lab supervisor before changing any TURBO C++ options. If your computer has not been configured for C++ programming, Section A-2, **"Important Options to Check Before Using TURBO C++"** has some suggestions for setting options.

Elements of the IDE Desktop

What you will see after starting the TURBO C++ program is the Integrated Development Environment, or IDE, screen. This is the control center and editing environment for TURBO C++. Elements of the IDE are shown in Figure A-3.

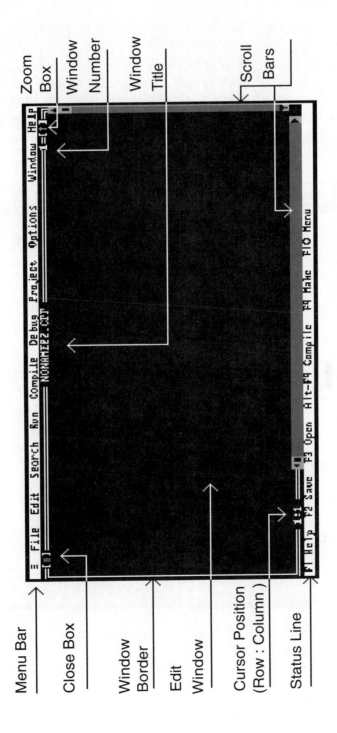

Figure A-3 TURBO C++ Integrated Development Environment (IDE) desktop.

The Menu Bar

The Menu Bar shown in Figure A-4 is the primary access to all the commands available in TURBO C++. It is always at the top of the screen except when you're viewing your program's output in the user screen. The **F10** key activates the Menu Bar and the cursor control arrow keys can be used to move to the menu items needed. You can also click the mouse on any menu item to activate its pull down menu.

Figure A-4 The Menu Bar.

If you choose an item in a pull down menu that is followed by an ellipsis (...), a Dialog box will be displayed allowing you to enter needed information, as shown in Figure A-5. (For details about Dialog boxes see Section A-3, "**Using Dialog Boxes.**")

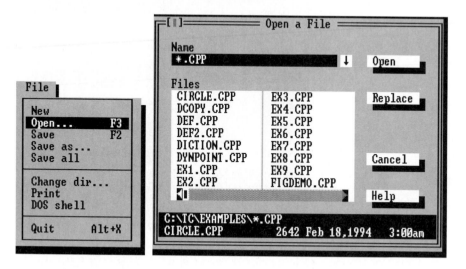

Figure A-5 Before and after choosing a menu item with ellipsis (...).

If you choose an item in a pull down menu that is followed by an arrow (▶) the command leads to another menu, as shown in Figure A-6.

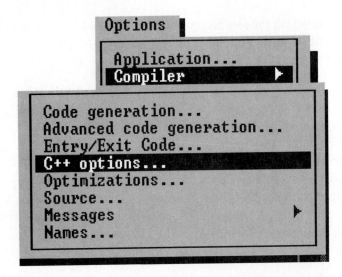

Figure A-6 Before and after choosing a menu item with an arrow (▶).

If you choose an item that doesn't have an ellipsis or arrow, the action will be performed as soon as you choose the command.

Menu items that are not presently available for use will be lighter and cannot be selected until they can be actively applied by the IDE.

To choose a command, simply move the highlight bar to the desired command and press **ENTER** or click the command with the mouse. To cancel an unwanted pull down menu or close an unneeded dialog box, press the **Esc** key.

A Hot Key, or shortcut, method to a menu item is to hold the **ALT** key and press the first letter of the needed item. For example, press **ALT + F** for the **File** menu. An alternate shortcut is to press the **F10** key to activate the Menu Bar, then press the first letter of the needed menu item. For example, press **F10** then **F** for the **File** menu.

Once a pull down menu is selected, pressing the first letter of a command in the pull down menu will activate that command. For example to print the active file, you can simply press **ALT + F** for the **File** menu then press **P** for the print option.

Learning the Hot Keys and shortcuts available in the TURBO C++ IDE can save valuable programming time. It is a good idea to practice them and make a habit of using them.

The Status Line

The Status Line, shown in Figure A-7, is displayed at the bottom of the screen. It shows basic keystrokes and shortcuts, or Hot Keys, that are available at that moment in the active window. The items in the Status Line will change as the active option in the window changes. It tells you what the program is doing. For example, the Status Line will display the message **"Saving** *filename*" when a file is being saved. It offers on-line hints on any selected menu command and dialog box item. Always take note of the information that the status line is displaying, since it will keep you informed as to what is going on.

| F1 Help   F2 Save   F3 Open   Alt - F9 Compile   F9 Make   F10 Menu |

Figure A-7 An example Status Line.

The Edit Window

Most of what you see and do in the TURBO C++ IDE takes place in a window. The Edit window, shown in Figure A-8, will be the one that you use to write and edit your programs.

For a more detailed description of the Close Box, Window Border, Cursor Position, Scroll Bars, Program Title, Window Number, Zoom Box, and how to manipulate TURBO C++ windows, see Section A-3, **"TURBO C++ Window Management."**

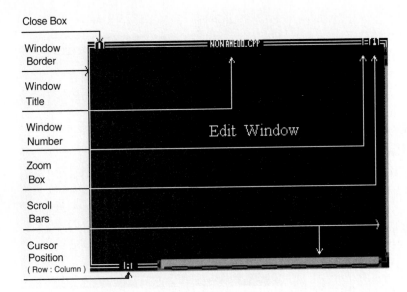

Close Box
Window Border
Window Title
Window Number
Zoom Box
Scroll Bars
Cursor Position
(Row : Column)

Edit Window

Figure A-8 The TURBO C++ Edit window.

Creating Your First Program

Now that you are somewhat familiar with the TURBO C++ IDE, it's time to create your first program. The only way to really learn C++ and the TURBO C++ IDE is to get busy and just do it.

Opening a New File

First you need to open a new file for your program. This can be done, as shown in Figure A-9 , by selecting the **File** menu from the Menu Bar then selecting the **New** menu item from the pull down menu. Pressing **ALT + F** then **N** will also accomplish this task.

Figure A-9 Open a **New** file.

Typing in the Program

After you have a new file window open, you can type in the program. Enter the following program:

```
#include <iostream.h>
#include <conio.h>

// PROGRAM sample.cpp USED TO DEMONSTRATE THE TURBO C++ IDE

void main( )
{
        clrscr( );                      //CLEAR THE SCREEN
        gotoxy(34,12);                  // POSITION THE CURSOR
                                        // AT THE MIDDLE OF THE SCREEN
        cout << "HELLO WORLD";          // DISPLAY MESSAGE
}
```

Once you have entered the program, the edit screen should appear like that shown in Figure A-10.

```
  ≡  File  Edit  Search  Run  Compile  Debug  Project  Options      Window  Help
 ┌─[■]════════════════════════ SAMPLE.CPP ═══════════════════════════1═[↕]─┐
 │#include <iostream.h>                                                    ▲│
 │#include <conio.h>                                                       ▓│
 │                                                                         ││
 │// PROGRAM sample.cpp USED TO DEMONSTRATE THE TURBO C++ IDE               │
 │                                                                         │
 │void main()                                                              │
 │{                                                                        │
 │   clrscr();              // CLEAR THE SCREEN                             │
 │   gotoxy (34,12);        // POSITION THE CURSOR                          │
 │                          // AT THE MIDDLE OF THE SCREEN                  │
 │   cout << "HELLO WORLD";_ // DISPLAY MESSAGE                             │
 │}                                                                        │
 │                                                                         │
 │                                                                         │
 │                                                                         │
 │                                                                         │
 │                                                                         │
 │                                                                         │
 │                                                                        ▼│
 │══ 11:26 ══◄▌                                                          ►▐│
 └─────────────────────────────────────────────────────────────────────────┘
  F1 Help  Alt-F8 Next Msg  Alt-F7 Prev Msg  Alt-F9 Compile  F9 Make  F10 Menu
```

Figure A-10 Enter the "Hello World" program.

Saving the Program

Always save your program to disk once it has been entered. While you are working with a program in the TURBO C++ IDE, it is stored in the computer's primary memory, but not on disk. If the power to the computer should happen to go off, the program would be lost. Saving the program makes a permanent copy of it on disk. If you are entering a long program, you should save it every ten or fifteen minutes. This will keep you from loosing what you have worked so hard to create. Remember, always save and save often!

Saving the program can be done, as shown in Figure A-11, by selecting the **File** menu from the Menu Bar, then selecting the **Save** command from the pull down menu. Another way is to simply press the **F2** Hot Key from anywhere within the IDE.

Figure A-11 Choose the Save command (**F2**).

When you save a program for the first time, you will need to give it a file name, as shown in Figure A-12. Remember that you are working with DOS and must follow DOS's file naming rules. The most important of these are that a file name can be up to eight characters in length and cannot contain any spaces. When programming in C++, your source program files should have a *.cpp* extension. Give our "Hello World" program the name *sample.cpp*.

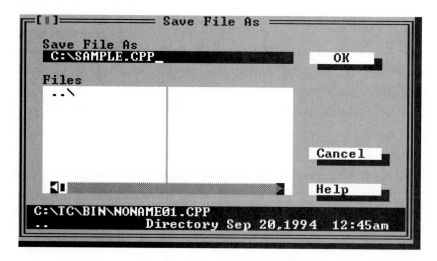

Figure A-12 Naming a C++ file.

Compiling the Program

Now that you have entered and saved the program, it is time to compile it. You can compile the source code program, as shown in Figure A-13, by selecting the **Compile** menu from the Menu Bar then selecting the **Compile** command from the pull down menu. Or press the **ALT + F9** Hot Key combination without having to access the Menu Bar. Compiling a source code program creates an object (*.obj*) file that the CPU can understand.

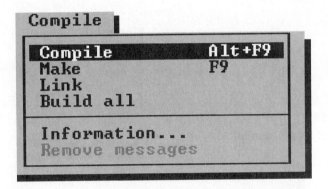

Figure A-13 Choose the **Compile** command (**ALT + F9**).

Figure A-14 shows the status box that you will see as your program compiles. Notice the message at the bottom of the box, **"Ctrl-Break to quit."** This means that if you need to terminate the compile process at any time, you can hold the **CTRL** key and press the **BREAK** key. This will terminate the compile process immediately.

```
══════════════════ Compiling ═══════════════════
Main file: SAMPLE.CPP
Compiling: \TC\INCLUDE\IOSTREAM.H

                        Total       File
    Lines compiled: 192         192
          Warnings: 0           0
            Errors: 0           0

    Available memory: 1871K
           Ctrl-Break to quit
```

Figure A-14 Compiling a program.

If there were no errors in the program, the message **"Success : press any key"** will be displayed, as shown in Figure A-15. It's always a great feeling to see this message, since it means that you typed in the program correctly and the compiler found all the files necessary to compile the program.

Figure A-15 Success!

Errors

If there were any errors in the program, the message, **"Errors : press any key"** will be displayed, as shown in Figure A-16, and you will have to fix the errors before you can link and run the program.

```
╔════════════════ Compiling ════════════════╗
║  Main file: SAMPLE.CPP                     ║
║  Compiling: EDITOR → SAMPLE.CPP            ║
║                                            ║
║                        Total      File     ║
║        Lines compiled: 1035       1035     ║
║              Warnings: 0          0        ║
║                Errors: 1          1        ║
║                                            ║
║  Available memory: 1911K                   ║
║  Errors              :      Press any key  ║
╚════════════════════════════════════════════╝
```

Figure A-16 Errors!

If the compiler has detected an error, pressing any key will produce an Errors Message window. A highlight bar will then show where any errors are located in your program. A simple statement about the nature of the error and its line number is displayed in the Errors Message window.

TURBO C++ also offers Help screens with a more detailed explanation of a particular error. To activate a Help screen, position the highlight bar on an error in the active message window that you need more information about, then press the **F1** key. For example, look at Figure A-17.

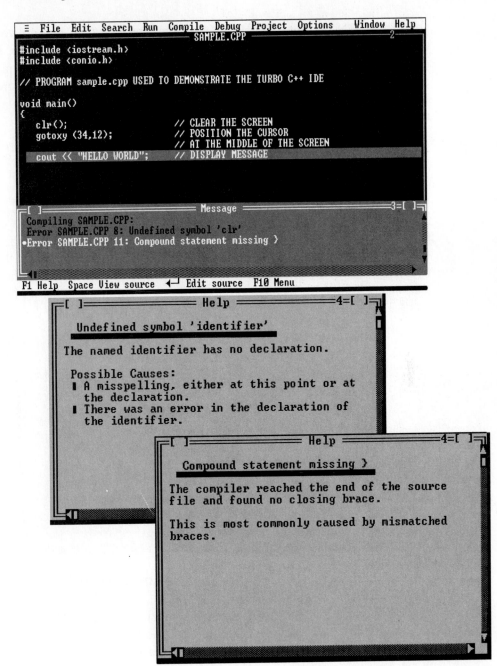

Figure A-17 Error messages and **Help** screen example.

The Errors Message window indicates that two errors have been detected in the *sample.cpp* program. The figure shows that *clrscr()* needs to be spelled correctly and that a closing brace (}) needs to be placed at the end of the program to correct the errors. A Help screen like the ones shown in the second portion of Figure A-17 will be displayed when you position the highlight bar on an error in the active message window and then press the **F1** key.

When an error is highlighted in the Errors Message window, pressing **ENTER** will position the cursor in the Edit window just after the error. You can then correct the error. After correcting all errors, you must compile the program again.

Linking the Program

Once the program is successfully compiled, you need to link it. Linking the object file creates an executable (*.exe*) program that is a combination of all the files needed to run the program properly. Select the **Compile** menu from the Menu Bar, then select the **Link** command from the pull down menu, as shown in Figure A-18. The Hot Key combination for this action is **ALT + C** then **L**.

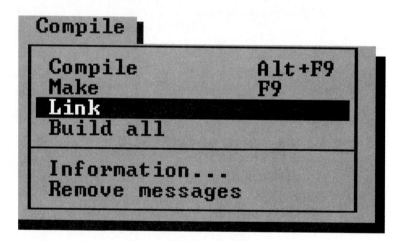

Figure A-18 Choose the **Link** command.

The compiler will link your object file and any needed TURBO C++ library files to produce an executable (*.exe*) file that is ready to run. See Figure A-19 for a look at the status box that is displayed while a program is linking. Notice the **"Ctrl-Break to quit"** message. Use this key combination if you need to terminate the linking process.

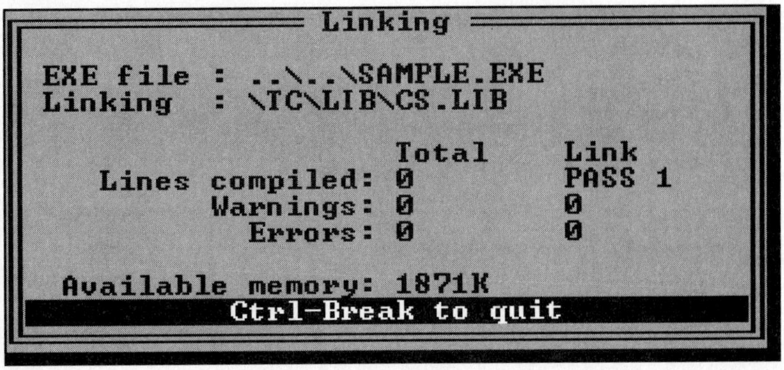

```
┌══════════════════ Linking ══════════════════┐
│                                              │
│  EXE file  : ..\..\SAMPLE.EXE                │
│  Linking   : \TC\LIB\CS.LIB                  │
│                                              │
│                        Total      Link       │
│      Lines compiled:   0          PASS 1     │
│             Warnings:  0          0           │
│               Errors:  0          0           │
│                                              │
│     Available memory: 1871K                  │
│ ████████████ Ctrl-Break to quit ████████████ │
└══════════════════════════════════════════════┘
```

Figure A-19 Linking a program.

Running the Program

When the program is successfully compiled and linked, you can run it to make sure that it does what it is supposed to do. Select the **Run** menu from the Menu Bar, then select the **Run** command from the pull down menu, as shown in Figure A-20. The Hot Key combination of CTRL + F9 will also perform this action. By the way, pressing CTRL + F9 will also compile, link, and run the program from the Edit window, so that you don't have to do each step separately.

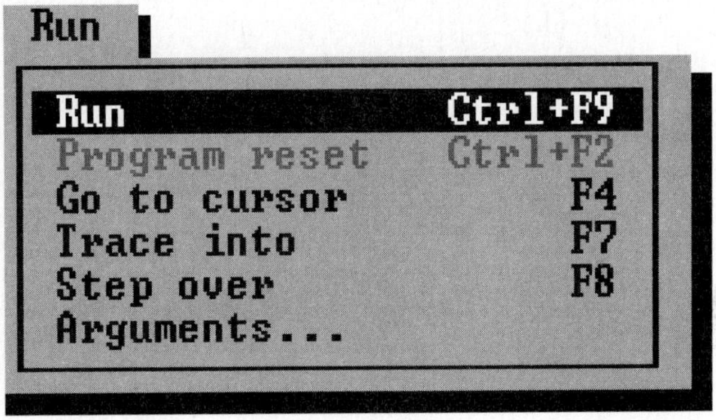

```
 Run
┌─────────────────────────────┐
│ Run              Ctrl+F9     │
│ Program reset    Ctrl+F2     │
│ Go to cursor          F4     │
│ Trace into            F7     │
│ Step over             F8     │
│ Arguments...                 │
└─────────────────────────────┘
```

Figure A-20 Choose the **Run** command (CTRL + F9).

When you run the program, you will notice that the screen flashes and returns to the TURBO C++ Edit Window. The message that was sent out by the program is on the User Screen.

Checking the User Screen

To see the results of the program run you must check the User Screen. To do this you can select the **Window** menu from the Menu Bar and then select the **User screen** menu item from the pull down window, as shown in Figure A-21. Or you can use the Hot Key combination of **ALT + F5** without having to access the Menu Bar.

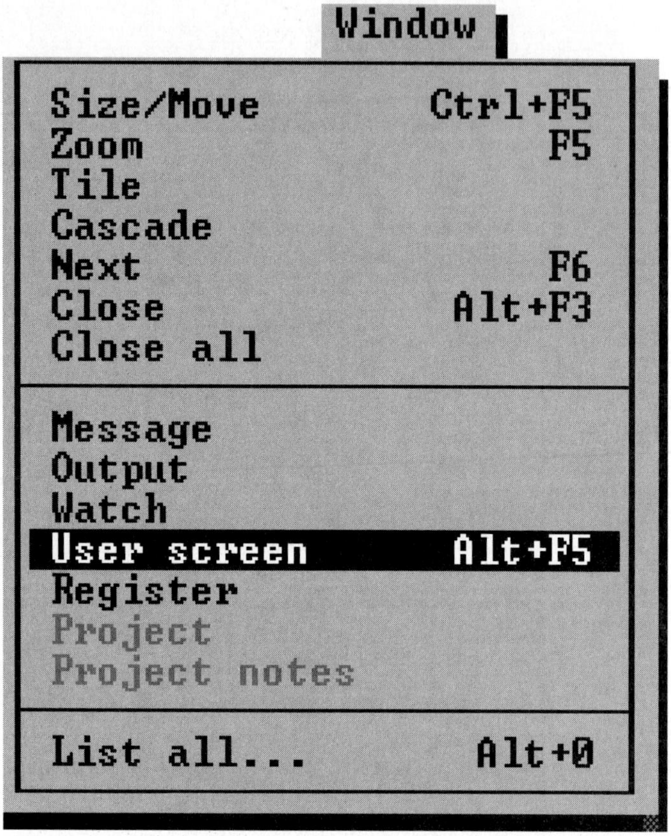

```
                              Window

        Size/Move                Ctrl+F5
        Zoom                          F5
        Tile
        Cascade
        Next                          F6
        Close                     Alt+F3
        Close all

        Message
        Output
        Watch
        User screen               Alt+F5
        Register
        Project
        Project notes

        List all...               Alt+0
```

Figure A-21 Choose the **User screen** option (**ALT + F5**).

The output of our "Hello World" sample program is shown in Figure A-22. You will notice that the message **HELLO WORLD** is displayed in the center of the screen. This is exactly what the program is supposed to do. So if your screen looks like Figure A-22, congratulations, it worked! From the user screen, you can press any key to return to the TURBO C++ Edit Window in the IDE.

Figure A-22 The User screen from the "Hello World" program.

Closing the File

When you are finished with a program file make sure that you have saved any final changes (**F2**) and then close the file. Select the **Window** menu from the Menu Bar, then select the **Close** command from the pull down menu to close the active window, as shown in Figure A-23. Alternatively, you can use the Hot Key combination of **ALT + F3** without having to access the Menu Bar. Clicking the Close Box in the upper left corner of the window will also close the window. If you are ready to close all the windows that you have open, you can select the **Close all** command in the **Window** menu.

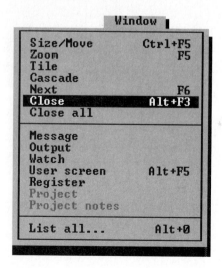

Figure A-23 Close the **File** window (**ALT + F3**).

If you leave any file window open when you exit from TURBO C++, that file window will open when you start TURBO C++ again. So it is good programming practice to close a file window when you are finished with it.

Exiting TURBO C++

When you are finished using TURBO C++, select the **File** menu from the Menu Bar, then select the **Quit** command from the pull down menu to exit TURBO C++, as shown in Figure A-24. Or you can use the Hot Key combination of **ALT + X** without having to access the Menu Bar.

Figure A-24 Choose **Quit** to exit TURBO C++ (**ALT + X**).

A-2 IMPORTANT OPTIONS TO CHECK BEFORE USING TURBO C++

There are some important options that you may need to set to prepare for object-oriented C++ programming. *If you are working with a computer system that has already been prepared for C++ programming, check with your instructor or lab supervisor before changing any TURBO C++ options.* If your computer has not been prepared for C++ programming, this section contains some suggestions for setting compiler, directories, and editor options. Refer to your TURBO C++ users manual for more information about other options that you can set to customize the TURBO C++ compiler and IDE.

Compiler Options

Since TURBO C++ is a compiler for both C and C++ programs, there are some compiler options you need to set to prepare for C++ programming. When you select the **C++ Options** in the **Compiler** menu choice of the **Options** Menu Bar item, shown in Figure A-25, a Dialog box is displayed that gives you the choice of having the compiler compile for **C++ Always**.

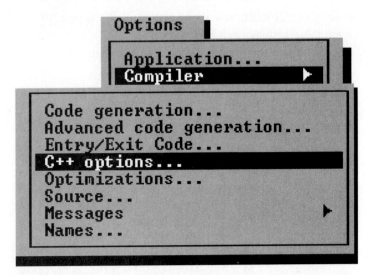

Figure A-25 The **Compiler** choice of the **Options** menus.

The **C++ Always** button should have the dot beside it, as shown in Figure A-26. This option must be on to allow you to compile and run the C++ object-oriented programs presented in this book.

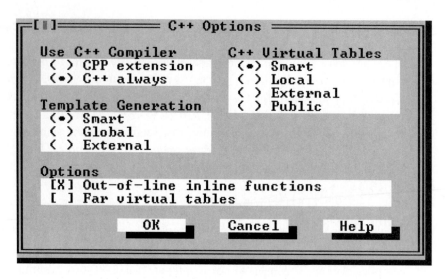

Figure A-26 The **C++ Options** Dialog box.

Directories Options

Choosing the **Directories** menu choice of the **Options** Menu Bar item, shown in Figure A-27, displays a Dialog box that will allow you to instruct the compiler which directories to use and where they are located on your computer.

Figure A-27 The **Directories** choice of the **Options** menu.

The **Include Directories** should be where the TURBO C++ include files are located. The **Library Directories** should be where the TURBO C++ library files are located. The **Output Directories** should indicate where you want your programs to be saved. The **Source Directories** should be where your program files are located. See Figure A-28 for example directory settings. As you can see, the **Output Directories** and **Source Directories** are the same, in this recommended configuration.

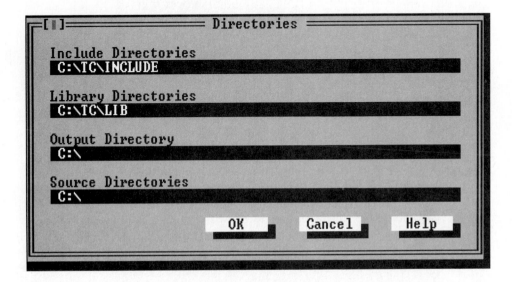

Figure A-28 TURBO C++ directory settings example.

Editor Options

A new feature beginning with TURBO C++ 3.0 is syntax highlighting. With this feature, the Edit Window is syntax-sensitive. When the option turned on, keywords, identifiers, symbols, integers, comments, and any other part of the syntax of the C++ code is identified by a different foreground and background color. This feature is on by default when TURBO C++ is installed. If you do not want to use this feature you can select the **Options** item on the Menu Bar, then the **Environment** item in the pull down menu. Then, select **Editor** from the next sub- menu, as shown in Figure A-29.

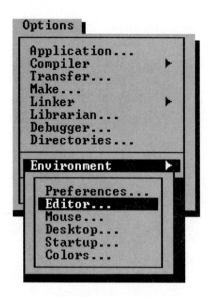

Figure A-29 Select the **Editor** option.

To turn off the syntax highlighting feature, make sure that there is NOT a check by the **Syntax Highlighting** option in the Dialog box that is displayed when you choose the **Editor** option, as shown in Figure A-30. To remove the check in the box, move the highlight bar to **Syntax Highlighting** and press the space bar.

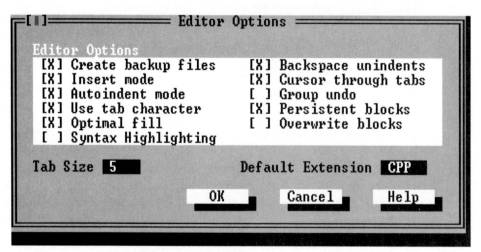

Figure A-30 Turning off the **Syntax Highlighting** option.

A-3 IDE DETAILS

This section provides a closer look at Dialog boxes, some of the TURBO C++ IDE menu items, window management, and a summary of Hot Keys. Because TURBO C++ is a professional programming tool, it has some options that won't be covered in this section of the appendix. For complete details of items not covered, refer to your TURBO C++ users manual.

Using Dialog Boxes

Since a menu item that has an ellipsis (...) after it opens a Dialog box, you will need to know how to use Dialog boxes and their components. A Dialog box is the way that TURBO C++ allows you to view and set options. When you are working with Dialog boxes, there are five basic types of controls: action buttons, radio buttons, check boxes, list boxes, and input boxes. Figure A-31 shows an example Dialog box that includes these items.

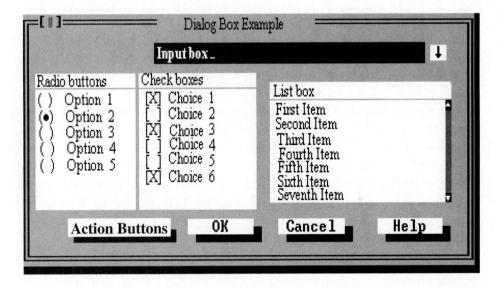

Figure A-31 A sample Dialog box.

Action Buttons

The Dialog box in Figure A-31 has three **action buttons**: **OK, Cancel,** and **Help.** If you choose **OK**, the choices in the Dialog box are made; if you choose **Cancel,** nothing changes and no action is made and the Dialog box is cleared from the screen; if you choose **Help**, a Help window about this Dialog box will open.

The **Esc** key can be used to close a Dialog box even if a **Cancel** button is not displayed in the box.

There are several methods that can be used to select a desired item in a Dialog box:
- Click on the item with the mouse
- Press **ALT +** the highlighted letter of the item .
- Press the **TAB** key or **SHIFT + TAB** to move forward or backward to make the item active, then press **ENTER.**

Any item becomes active when it is highlighted.

Radio Buttons

The Dialog box also has **radio buttons**. They are called radio buttons because, like the buttons on a car radio, only one can be active at any time. If you activate, or "push," a new one, the one that was active deactivates, or "pops out". To activate a radio button, click it or its text with the mouse. Or, from the keyboard press **TAB** until the group is highlighted and then use the arrow keys to choose a particular radio button. Press the **SPACE BAR** to toggle the button on or off.

Check Boxes

The Dialog box also has **check boxes**. When you select a check box, an **X** appears in it to show that it is selected. An empty box shows that that option is not selected. To turn a box on or off, click it with a mouse or TAB to it and press the SPACE BAR. You can have any number of check boxes on at any time.

List Boxes

A **list box** allows you to scroll through and select an item from a list of choices. The list is often comprised of file names. You can choose an item from a list box by clicking the scroll bar to move the needed item into view and then clicking it with the mouse. Or, an item can be chosen with the keyboard by pressing the TAB key until the list box is highlighted and using the arrow keys to move the highlight bar to your choice and pressing ENTER.

Input Boxes

Some Dialog boxes also contain **input boxes** that allow you to type in text. To enter text into the input box, make the box active by either clicking it with a mouse or using the TAB key to highlight it. Once the box is highlighted, enter the needed text.

Menu Bar Details and Hot Keys

This portion of the appendix is arranged in the order that the items appear on the Menu Bar at the top of the IDE screen. Figure A-32 shows a complete break down of the Menu Bar.

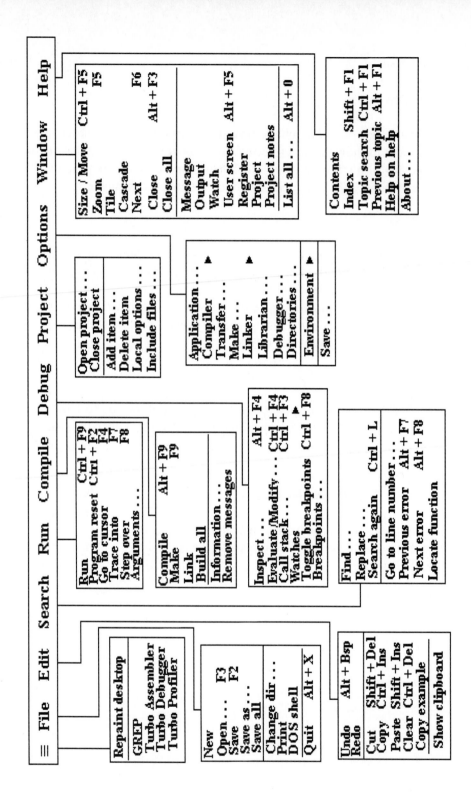

Figure A-32 TURBO C++ IDE Menu Bar components.

Remember that there are several ways to access the menu items. You can:

- Press the **F10** key to activate the Menu Bar, then move the highlight bar to the needed menu item and press **ENTER**. You can then make a selection from the pull down menu by moving the highlight bar to the needed command, then press **ENTER**.

- Click the needed Menu Bar item with the mouse, then click the command of your choice in the pull down menu.

- Hold the **ALT** key down and press the first letter of the needed Menu Bar item to activate its pull down menu, then press the highlighted letter of the command that you need.

- Use the Hot Key or Hot Key combination without having to access the Menu Bar first. (If you learn the Hot Keys, they will save you a lot of time!)

Be sure to take note of the Hot Keys displayed on each pull down menu.

The ≡ **System** Menu

The first item on the Menu Bar is the ≡ **System** menu, shown in figure A-33. The Hot Key combination for accessing this menu is **ALT + SPACE BAR**.

The **Repaint desktop** command will redraw the screen. This is sometimes necessary if a program leaves unwanted characters on the screen.

You can run programs shown in the Transfer portion of this pull down menu by selecting them. When you exit a selected program you will be returned to TURBO C++. Programs can be added to this list with the **Transfer** command in the **Options** menu. See the TURBO C++ users manual for the details.

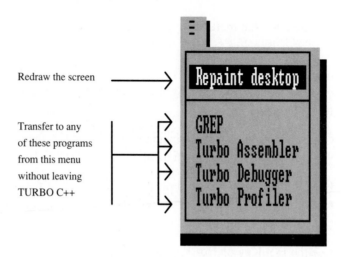

Redraw the screen ————————→

Transfer to any
of these programs
from this menu
without leaving
TURBO C++

Figure A-33 The ≡**System** menu (ALT + SPACE BAR).

The **File** Menu

The **File** menu, shown in Figure A-34, allows you to create, open, save, and print your program files. It also lets you perform other file functions, such as change the working directory, exit to the DOS shell, and quit TURBO C++. The Hot Key combination for accessing the **File** menu is ALT + F.

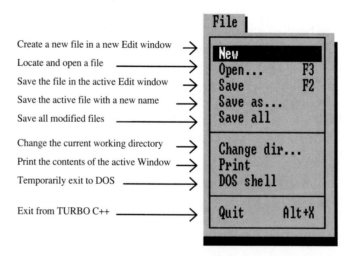

Create a new file in a new Edit window →
Locate and open a file ————————→
Save the file in the active Edit window →
Save the active file with a new name →
Save all modified files ————————→

Change the current working directory →
Print the contents of the active Window →
Temporarily exit to DOS ————————→

Exit from TURBO C++ ————————→

Figure A-34 The **File** menu (ALT + F).

Choose the **Open** command when you need to bring a previously saved C++ source code program into an Edit window. Figure A-35 shows the Dialog box that is displayed when you activate the **Open** command.

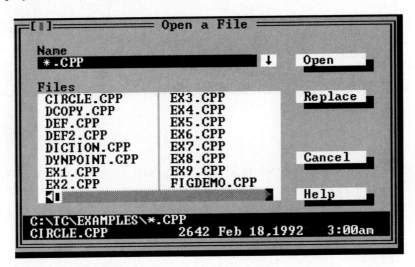

Figure A-35 The Open a File Dialog box.

A list of files is displayed in the **Files** list of the **Open** Dialog box. You can select a file from the list or type in the name of the file you want to open in the **Name** portion of the box. Press the **ENTER** key when you have made your selection or click the **Open** button.

The **Save** command saves the file in the active Edit window to disk. Refer to Section A-1, **"Saving the Program"** for more details about saving and naming a program.

The **Print** command is also one that you will use quite often from the **File** menu. It lets you print the contents of the active Edit, Output, or Message window. The file is sent to the DOS print handler, which sends the file to the printer. Make sure the printer is on-line and ready before you choose the **Print** command.

If you only want to print selected text instead of the entire file, highlight the text first, then press **CTRL+K** then **P**.

The **Quit** command exits TURBO C++, removes it from the computer's memory, and returns you to the DOS command prompt. For more about exiting TURBO C++, refer to Section A-1, "**Exiting TURBO C++.**"

The easiest way to exit from TURBO C++ is the Hot Key combination of **ALT + X**.

The **Edit** Menu

The **Edit** menu, shown in Figure A-36, lets you cut, copy, and paste text in the Edit Windows. You can **Undo** changes or reverse the effect of the most recent undo with **Redo**. You can also open a Clipboard window to view or edit its contents and copy text from the Message and Output windows. The Hot Key combination to access the **Edit** menu is **ALT + E**.

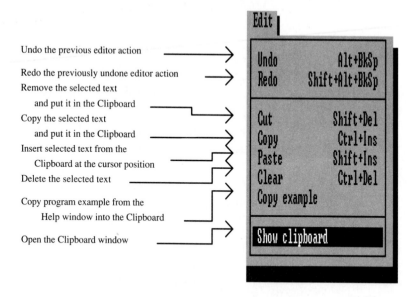

Figure A-36 The **Edit** menu (**ALT + E**)

Before most of the commands in the **Edit m**enu can be used, you have to select the text that is to be edited. The commands apply to the selected text only. You can select text with either the keyboard or a mouse. The easiest method for selecting text from the keyboard is to hold down the **SHIFT** key and press any of the arrow keys until the desired text is highlighted or "selected." Release the arrow and **SHIFT** key when all the text to be selected is highlighted.

To select text with a mouse, position the cursor where you want to start, hold the left mouse key down, and drag the mouse pointer over the text to be selected.

Once the desired text is selected, the commands in the **Edit** menu become available.

Using **Copy** and **Paste** can save you typing time when entering a program that has sections of code that are similar. Simply select **Copy**, then **Paste** the code to the new location and make any necessary changes to the copied code.

When you **Cut** or **Copy** text, it is placed in the **Clipboard**. The Clipboard is a special window in TURBO C++. It holds the cut or copied text so that you can **Paste** the text somewhere else.

Take note of the Hot Keys for the **Copy** and **Paste** operations, **CTRL + INS** for **Copy** and **SHIFT + INS** for **Paste**. These can be used without having to access the Menu Bar.

The **Search** Menu

The **Search** menu, shown in Figure A-37, lets you search for text, function declarations, and error locations in your programs. You can also replace specific text with new text. The Hot Key combination for accessing the **Search** menu is **ALT + S**.

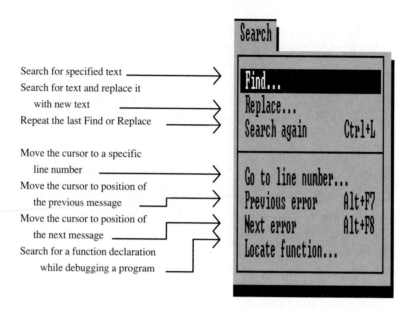

Search for specified text ⎯⎯⎯⎯⎯⎯⎯⎯⎯⎯→
Search for text and replace it
   with new text ⎯⎯⎯⎯⎯⎯⎯⎯⎯⎯→
Repeat the last Find or Replace ⎯⎯⎯⎯⎯→

Move the cursor to a specific
   line number ⎯⎯⎯⎯⎯⎯⎯⎯⎯⎯⎯⎯→
Move the cursor to position of
   the previous message ⎯⎯⎯⎯⎯⎯⎯→
Move the cursor to position of
   the next message ⎯⎯⎯⎯⎯⎯⎯⎯⎯⎯→
Search for a function declaration
   while debugging a program ⎯⎯⎯⎯⎯

Figure A-37 The **Search** menu (ALT + S).

The **Find** command displays the **Find Text** Dialog box, shown in Figure A-38. This is where you type in the text to search for and set the options that affect the search.

Figure A-38 The Find Text Dialog box.

The **Replace** command displays the **Replace Text** Dialog box, shown in Figure A-39. This box lets you type in the text you want to search for and the text you want to replace it with. The **Prompt on replace** option should be checked to avoid errors in replacing text. If you want the specified text to be replaced in the entire file, TAB to the **Change All** button and press ENTER or click it with the mouse.

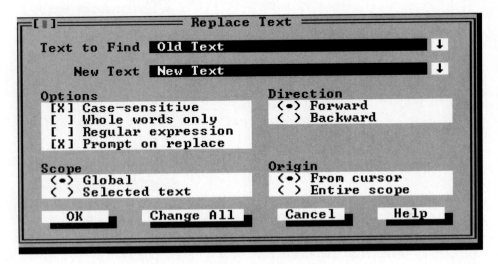

Figure A-39 The Replace Text Dialog box.

The **Run** Menu

The **Run** menu, shown in Figure A-40, has commands to run your finished programs and step commands to use while debugging a program. The Hot Key combination for accessing the **Run** menu is **ALT + R**.

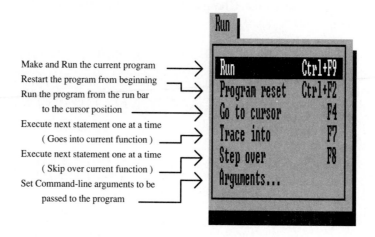

Make and Run the current program ⟶

Restart the program from beginning ⟶

Run the program from the run bar
to the cursor position ⟶

Execute next statement one at a time
(Goes into current function) ⟶

Execute next statement one at a time
(Skip over current function) ⟶

Set Command-line arguments to be
passed to the program ⟶

Run	Ctrl+F9
Program reset	Ctrl+F2
Go to cursor	F4
Trace into	F7
Step over	F8
Arguments...	

Figure A-40 The **Run** menu (**ALT + R**).

The **Run** command runs your finished program. If you have made any changes to the source code since it was last compiled, the **Run** command will compile and link your program before running it.

The **Go to cursor**, **Trace into**, and **Step over** commands are discussed in the debugging section of this appendix, A-5, "**Single Step and Tracing.**"

If you need to stop the program run before it is finished, you can press **CTRL+BREAK**. This terminates the run and returns you to the IDE.

The **Compile** Menu

The commands on the **Compile** menu, shown in Figure A-41, are used to compile and link your program, and to make or build your project. To use these commands you have to have a file open in an active Edit window or a project defined. The Hot Key combination to access the **Compile** menu is ALT + C.

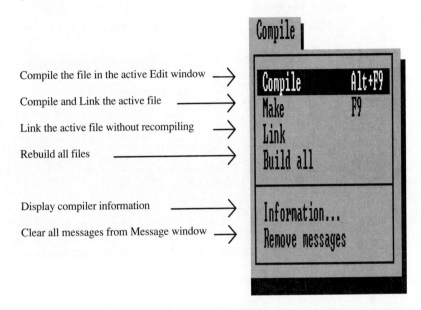

Compile the file in the active Edit window ⟶

Compile and Link the active file ⟶

Link the active file without recompiling ⟶

Rebuild all files ⟶

Display compiler information ⟶

Clear all messages from Message window ⟶

Figure A-41 The **Compile** menu (ALT + C).

The **Compile** command compiles the active source code file to an object (*.obj*) file. A status box, shown in Figure A-42, will be displayed while the program is being compiled. When the compiling process is finished, you can press any key to remove the box. For more information on compiling a program, see Section A-1, **"Compiling the Program."**

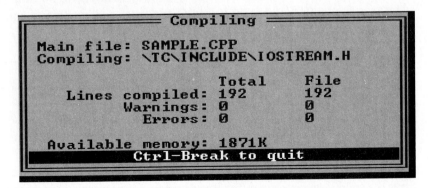

Figure A-42 The Compile status box.

The **Link** command takes the current object (*.obj*) file and necessary library files and links them in memory to produce a new executable (*.exe*) file. A status box, shown in Figure A-43, will be displayed as the files are being linked. For more information on linking, see Section A-1, **"Linking the Program."**

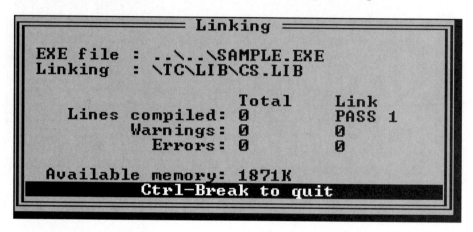

```
══════════════════ Linking ══════════════════

  EXE file  :  ..\..\SAMPLE.EXE
  Linking   :  \TC\LIB\CS.LIB

                         Total       Link
     Lines  compiled:  0           PASS 1
            Warnings:  0           0
              Errors:  0           0

  Available  memory:  1871K
            Ctrl-Break  to  quit
```

Figure A-43 The Linking status box.

The **Debug** Menu

The **Debug** menu, shown in Figure A-44, contains the commands that control all the features of the TURBO C++ Integrated Debugger. The Hot Key combination for accessing the **Debug** menu is **ALT + D**.

The **Inspect** command opens an Inspector Window that allows you to view and modify values in a data item. You can inspect **integers**, **floating point values**, **characters**, **pointer contents**, **array contents**, and **structure contents** just to mention a few.

The easiest way to open an Inspector window is to place the cursor on the data item you want to inspect, then press the Hot Key combination of **ALT + F4**.
You close an Inspector Window by making it active and using the Hot Key combination of **ALT + F3**. Of course, **ALT + F3** closes any active window.

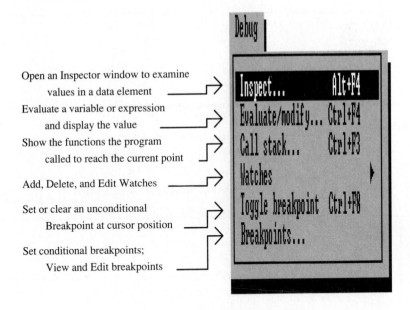

Open an Inspector window to examine
values in a data element ⟶

Evaluate a variable or expression
and display the value ⟶

Show the functions the program
called to reach the current point ⟶

Add, Delete, and Edit Watches ⟶

Set or clear an unconditional
Breakpoint at cursor position ⟶

Set conditional breakpoints;
View and Edit breakpoints ⟶

Figure A-44 The **Debug** menu (**ALT + D**).

Selecting the **Watch** command activates the sub-menu shown in Figure A-45. From this sub-menu you can **add** an expression to, **delete** an expression from, and **edit** the current expression in the Watch window. For more about Watches, see Section A-5, **"Using the Watch Window."**

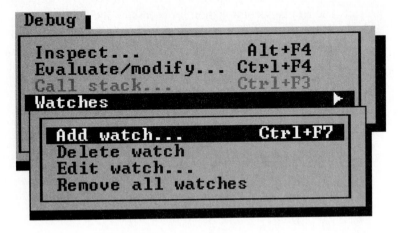

Figure A-45 The **Watch** sub-menu.

The easiest way to **Add** an expression or variable to the Watch Window is with the Hot Key combination of CTRL + F7.

The **Toggle Breakpoints** command lets you set or clear an unconditional breakpoint on the line where the cursor is positioned. The breakpoint is marked by a highlight bar. You can use breakpoints in the debugging process. For more about their use, see Section A-5, **"Setting a Breakpoint."**

The easiest way to set or remove a breakpoint is to position the cursor where you want to add or remove the breakpoint, then use the Hot Key combination of CTRL + F8.

The **Project** Menu

The **Project** menu, shown in Figure A-46, contains all the project management commands to create a project, add or delete files to or from your project, set options for a file in the project, and view included files for a specific file in the project. The Hot Key combination for accessing the **Project** menu is ALT + P.

The **Open project...** command displays a Dialog box, shown in Figure A-47, that allows you to select and load a project or create a new project by typing in a project name in the **Name** box.

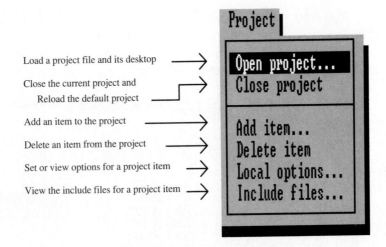

Load a project file and its desktop → **Open project...**

Close the current project and
    Reload the default project → **Close project**

Add an item to the project → **Add item...**

Delete an item from the project → **Delete item**

Set or view options for a project item → **Local options...**

View the include files for a project item → **Include files...**

Figure A-46 The **Project** menu (**ALT + P**).

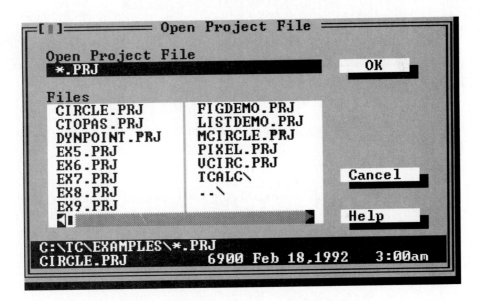

Figure A-47 The Open Project File Dialog box.

The **Add item...** command displays a Dialog box, shown in Figure A-48, that allows you to add a file to the project list. Choosing the **Add** button puts the currently highlighted file in the **Files list** into the Project Window. You can also type in a file name and press **ENTER** to add a file to a project.

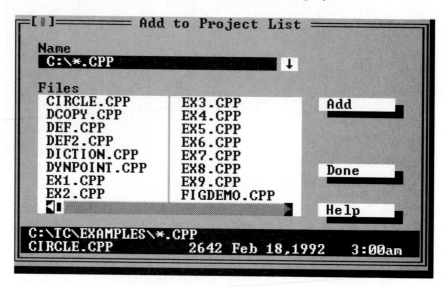

Figure A-48 The Add to Project List Dialog box.

For more information about how to build a project, see Chapter 12, Section 3.

The **Options** Menu

The **Options** menu, shown in Figure A-49, contains commands that let you view and change the default settings of almost every feature of TURBO C++. The commands in this menu either lead to a Dialog box or sub-menu. The Hot Key combination to access the **Options** menu is **ALT + O**.

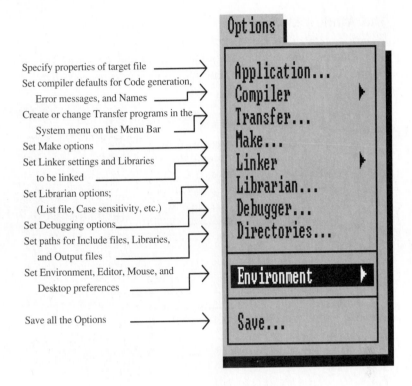

Specify properties of target file ⟶

Set compiler defaults for Code generation,
Error messages, and Names ⟶

Create or change Transfer programs in the⟶
System menu on the Menu Bar ⟶

Set Make options ⟶

Set Linker settings and Libraries
to be linked ⟶

Set Librarian options;
(List file, Case sensitivity, etc.) ⟶

Set Debugging options ⟶

Set paths for Include files, Libraries,
and Output files ⟶

Set Environment, Editor, Mouse, and
Desktop preferences ⟶

Save all the Options ⟶

Figure A-49 The **Options** menu (**ALT + O**).

The options that you need to check before programming in C++ are covered in detail in Section A-2, **"Important Options to Check Before Using TURBO C++."**

The **Save...** command displays a Dialog box, shown in Figure A-50, that allows you to save changes that you have made to the TURBO C++ options.

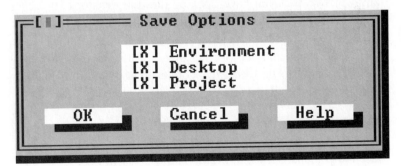

Figure A-50 The Save Options Dialog box.

The **Window** Menu

The window management commands are found in the **Window** menu, shown in Figure A-51. The Hot Key combination to access the **Window** menu is **ALT + W**.

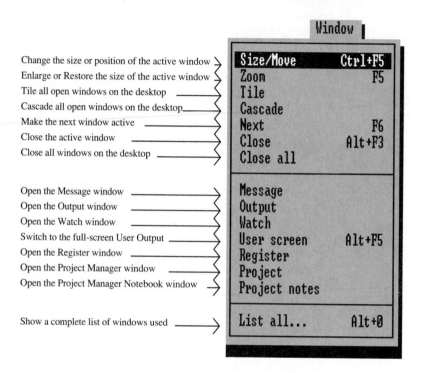

Figure A-51 The **Window** menu (**ALT + W**).

The first portion of the **Window** menu contains commands to manipulate any windows that you have open on the IDE desktop. The second portion of the menu contains commands that allow you to open special windows used in different TURBO C++ features. Refer to Figure A-51 for a short description of each of these commands and see Section A-3, **"TURBO C++ Window Management"** for more details. The **List all...** command at the bottom of the menu shows a list of all windows used.

The **Help** Menu

The **Help** menu, shown in Figure A-52, gives you access to the TURBO C++ on-line Help feature. There is Help information on almost all aspects of the IDE and

TURBO C++. The status bar at the bottom of the IDE screen also provides helpful on-line menu and Dialog box hints whenever you highlight a command. The Hot Key combination to activate the **Help** menu is ALT + H.

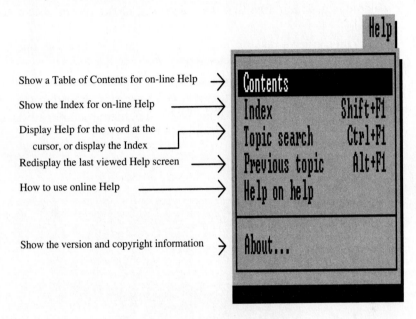

Show a Table of Contents for on-line Help

Show the Index for on-line Help

Display Help for the word at the
cursor, or display the Index

Redisplay the last viewed Help screen

How to use online Help

Show the version and copyright information

Figure A-52 The **Help** menu (ALT + H).

The **Contents** command opens the Help window and displays the main table of contents. You can select and branch to an item from this list.

The **Index** command opens a Dialog box that displays a full list of Help items.

The **F1** key can be used to access on-line Help. For Help on a particular IDE item, place the cursor or highlight bar on that item and press **F1**. For Help on a C++ keyword, place the cursor on that word and press **CTRL** + **F1**. For Help on how to use Help, press the **F1** key when any Help window is open.

The **Esc** key can be used to close any open Help window. See Section A-4, **"HELP ?!"** for more details about how to use Help.

TURBO C++ Window Management

There is a window for almost everything you do in the TURBO C++ IDE. A window is a screen area that you can open, close, move, resize, zoom, tile, and cascade.

You can have many windows open in the IDE, but only one window can be active at any time. The active window is the one that you are currently working in. It is the one on the "top of the stack" if you have more than one window open. Any command you select or text that you type in is applied to the active window. The active window will have a double-lined border around it, a title, a close box, a zoom box, and scroll bars like the one in Figure A-53.

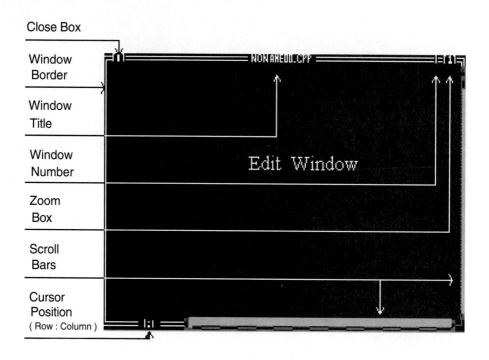

Figure A-53 TURBO C++ window components.

Each component of a window has a special function for window management. A mouse is required to use most of these components.

Click the Close Box with the mouse to close the window.

To make the window smaller or larger, click-and-drag the Corners of the Window Border.

The Title Bar contains the Window Title and Window Number. Click-and-drag the Title Bar to move the window around on the IDE desktop. The Window Title contains the name of the window. If you are using the **Edit Window**, the Window Title will be the name of your program file. The first nine windows that you open in the IDE will have a Window Number in the upper right corner. Pressing ALT + the number of the window will make that window active.

The window's Zoom Box is also in the upper right corner. If the Zoom Box contains an up arrow (⇧), click it to enlarge the window to its maximum size. If the Zoom Box contains a double-headed arrow (⇕), the window is already at its maximum and clicking it will return the window to its original size.

The Scroll Bars are vertical and horizontal bars along the right side and the bottom of the window. Use a mouse to scroll through the window contents by clicking on the arrows at the scroll bar ends.

The Cursor Position shows the current line and column location of the cursor in the **Edit** window. An asterisk * will be displayed by the Row:Column numbers if you have modified your file since the last time you saved it.

Choosing the **Open** command in the **File** menu will open a new **Edit** window, or you can use the **F3** Hot Key. Other windows can be opened by selecting their menu items in the **Window** menu.

TURBO C++ provides two ways to view all of the windows you have open. Choosing the **Tile** command in the **Window** menu will arrange the windows on the screen so that you see them all. Figure A-54 shows our *sample.cpp* program in an **Edit** window, an **Output** window, and a **Message** window. These windows are tiled so that we see a portion of each. To bring any one of the tiled windows to full screen, make it active first by pressing ALT + the window number, and then press the **F5** key to enlarge it, or click on the zoom box (⇧). You can restore the window's size by pressing the **F5** key again, or by clicking on the zoom box (⇕).

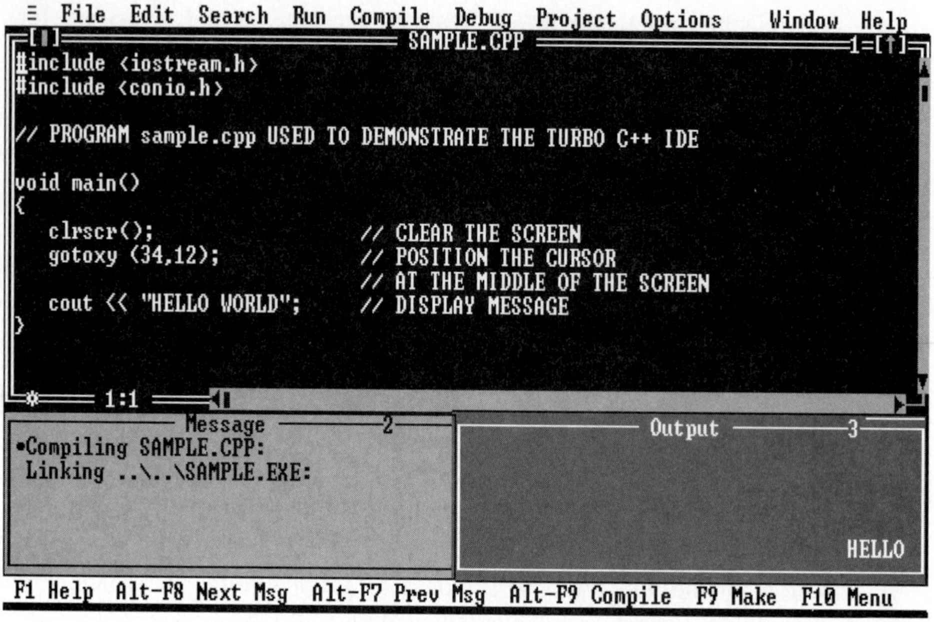

```
  ≡  File  Edit  Search  Run  Compile  Debug  Project  Options     Window  Help
┌─[■]══════════════════════════ SAMPLE.CPP ══════════════════════1═[↑]═┐
│#include <iostream.h>                                                  ▲│
│#include <conio.h>                                                     ■│
│                                                                        │
│// PROGRAM sample.cpp USED TO DEMONSTRATE THE TURBO C++ IDE             │
│                                                                        │
│void main()                                                            │
│{                                                                       │
│   clrscr();                     // CLEAR THE SCREEN                     │
│   gotoxy (34,12);               // POSITION THE CURSOR                  │
│                                 // AT THE MIDDLE OF THE SCREEN          │
│   cout << "HELLO WORLD";        // DISPLAY MESSAGE                      │
│}                                                                       │
│                                                                       ▼│
└─※══ 1:1 ══◄■────────────────────────────────────────────────────────►┘
┌──────────── Message ───────────2─┐┌──────────── Output ────────────3─┐
│•Compiling SAMPLE.CPP:            ││                                   │
│ Linking ..\..\SAMPLE.EXE:        ││                                   │
│                                  ││                                   │
│                                  ││                                   │
│                                  ││                             HELLO │
└──────────────────────────────────┘└───────────────────────────────────┘
 F1 Help  Alt-F8 Next Msg  Alt-F7 Prev Msg  Alt-F9 Compile  F9 Make  F10 Menu
```

Figure A-54 Tiled TURBO C++ windows.

Choosing the **Cascade** command in the **Window** menu will arrange the open windows in an overlapping manner. When viewed this way, the active window will be in the foreground and have a double border. Figure A-55 shows the three windows from the tiled example arranged in a cascade fashion. The **Output** window is the active window, since it has a double border and is located in the foreground.

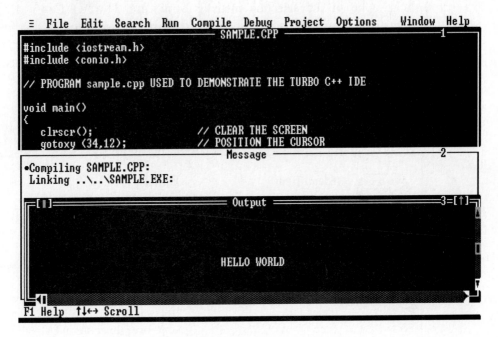

Figure A-55 Cascaded TURBO C++ windows

Summary of Hot Keys and Shortcuts

TURBO C++ offers several methods for selecting commands, options, and features. One of the selection methods is to use TURBO C++'s Hot Key combinations. This section contains reference lists of Hot Keys for use from the keyboard. The Hot Keys immediately activate a command or Dialog box without having to access the Menu Bar first. Table A-1 lists the most commonly used Hot Keys.

TABLE A-1 GENERAL PURPOSE TURBO C++ HOT KEYS

Hot Keys	Menu Item	Action
F1	Help	Displays a Help screen
F2	Save	Saves the file in the active Edit Window
F3	Open	Opens a file
F4	Go to Cursor	Runs the program to the cursor position
F5	Zoom	Zooms to the active window
F6	Next	Cycles through the open windows
F7	Trace Into	Traces into functions in Debug mode
F8	Step Over	Steps over functions in Debug mode
F9	Make EXE	Makes an executable (.EXE) file
F10	(none)	Activates the Menu Bar
ALT + X	Quit	Exits TURBO C++ to DOS

Table A-2 lists the Hot Keys used to access the items on the Menu Bar. You can also select a Menu Bar item's pull down menu by activating the Menu Bar with the **F10** key and then pressing the first letter of the needed item.

TABLE A-2 TURBO C++ MENU BAR HOT KEYS

Hot Keys	Menu Item	Action
ALT + SPACEBAR	System Menu	Activates the System Menu
ALT + C	Compile Menu	Activates the Compile Menu
ALT + D	Debug Menu	Activates the Debug Menu
ALT + E	Edit Menu	Activates the Edit Menu
ALT + F	File Menu	Activates the File Menu
ALT + H	Help Menu	Activates the Help Menu
ALT + O	Options Menu	Activates the Options Menu
ALT + P	Project Menu	Activates the Project Menu
ALT + R	Run Menu	Activates the Run Menu
ALT + S	Search Menu	Activates the Search Menu
ALT + W	Window Menu	Activates the Window Menu

Table A-3 lists the Editing Hot Keys that can be used while you are typing or editing your programs in the **Edit** window. Remember that some of the editing commands require that you select the text to work with before using the command.

TABLE A-3 TURBO C++ EDITING HOT KEYS

Hot Keys	Menu Item	Action
CTRL + DEL	Clear	Removes selected text
CTRL + INS	Copy	Copies selected text to the clipboard
SHIFT + DEL	Cut	Removes selected text to the clipboard
SHIFT + INS	Paste	Pastes text from the clipboard
ALT + BACKSPACE	Undo	Restores text to the previous condition
CTRL + L	Search Again	Repeats the last Find or Replace
F2	Save	Saves the file in the active window
F3	Open	Lets you open a file
HOME	(none)	Moves to the beginning of a line
END	(none)	Moves to the end of a line
CTRL + PAGE UP	(none)	Moves to the beginning of a file
CTRL + PAGE DN	(none)	Moves to the end of a file

Table A-4 lists the Hot Keys available for managing the various windows that you will be using in the TURBO C++ IDE.

TABLE A-4 TURBO C++ WINDOW MANAGEMENT HOT KEYS

Hot Keys	Menu Item	Action
ALT + (NUMBER)	(none)	Makes window (number) active
ALT + 0 (ZERO)	List	Lists all open windows
ALT + F3	Close	Closes the active window
ALT + F4	Inspect	Opens an Inspector window
ALT + F5	User Screen	Displays the User Screen
F5	Zoom	Zooms or unzooms the active window
F6	Next	Cycles through the open windows
CTRL + F5	(none)	Changes the window size or position

Table A-5 lists the Hot Keys that make accessing TURBO C++'s on-line Help fast and easy.

TABLE A-5 TURBO C++ ON-LINE HELP HOT KEYS

Hot Keys	Menu Item	Action
F1	Contents	Opens a context-sensitive Help screen
F1 F1	Help on Help	Brings up Help on Help
SHIFT + F1	Index	Brings up the Help Index
ALT + F1	Previous Topic	Displays the previous Help screen
CTRL + F1	Topic Search	Calls up Help on selected C++ syntax and functions in the Editor only

Table A-6 lists the Hot Keys available while running or debugging your programs.

TABLE A-6 TURBO C++ RUNNING AND DEBUGGING HOT KEYS

Hot Keys	Menu Item	Action
ALT + F4	Inspect	Opens an Inspector window
ALT + F7	Previous Error	Takes you to the previous error
ALT + F8	Next Error	Takes you to the next error
ALT + F9	Compile to OBJ	Compiles the active file to .OBJ
CTRL + F2	Program reset	Resets the running program
CTRL + F3	Call Stack	Brings up the stack of used functions
CTRL + F4	Evaluate/Modify	Evaluates an expression
CTRL + F7	Add Watch	Adds a watch expression
CTRL + F8	Toggle Breakpoint	Sets or clears a conditional breakpoint
CTRL + F9	Run	Runs the active program
F4	Go to Cursor	Runs the program to the cursor position
F7	Trace Into	Runs one step at a time, tracing into functions
F8	Step Over	Runs one step at a time, stepping over functions
F9	Make EXE	Makes (compiles and links) the active program

TURBO C++'s Hot Keys are often the easiest and fastest method to activate a command or function of the IDE. Most of them are listed on the right side of their command in the pull down menus. So if you forget one, you can look it up in the menus.

A-4 HELP ?!

On-line context-sensitive help is available for almost every item in the TURBO C++ IDE and C++ language.

Using TURBO C++ Help in General

You can get Help at any point, except when your program has control of the computer, by pressing the **F1** key.

Selecting **Help on Help** in the **Help** menu, or pressing **F1 F1**, will display the Help screen shown in Figure A-56.

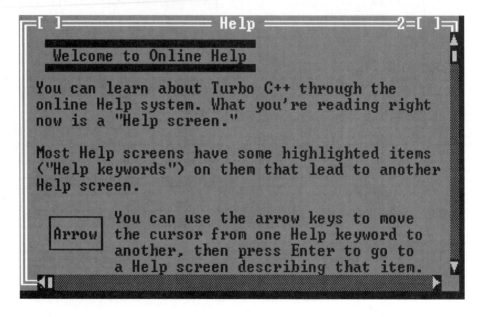

Figure A-56 Help on Help screen.

This is a good place to get started. Use the scroll bars or down arrow key to scroll through the text. **Help on Help** has good tips and information about how to make the best use of TURBO C++ on-line help.

Selecting the **Contents** command in the **Help** menu displays the **Help Contents** box shown in Figure A-57.

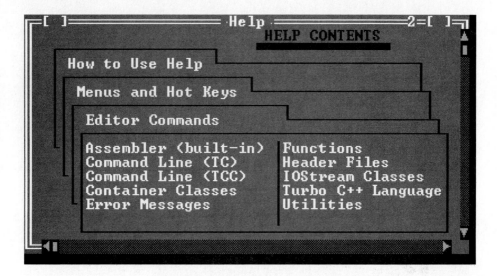

Figure A-57 Help Contents.

To choose an item from this box, move the cursor to the item and press **ENTER** or click the item with a mouse. You can branch to any other part of the Help system from the **Help Contents** window.

Selecting the **Index** command in the **Help** menu will display a complete list of items for which TURBO C++ has on-line help, as shown in Figure A-58. Alternatively, you can use the Hot Key combination of SHIFT + **F1** to bring up the **Help Index** from anywhere within the IDE.

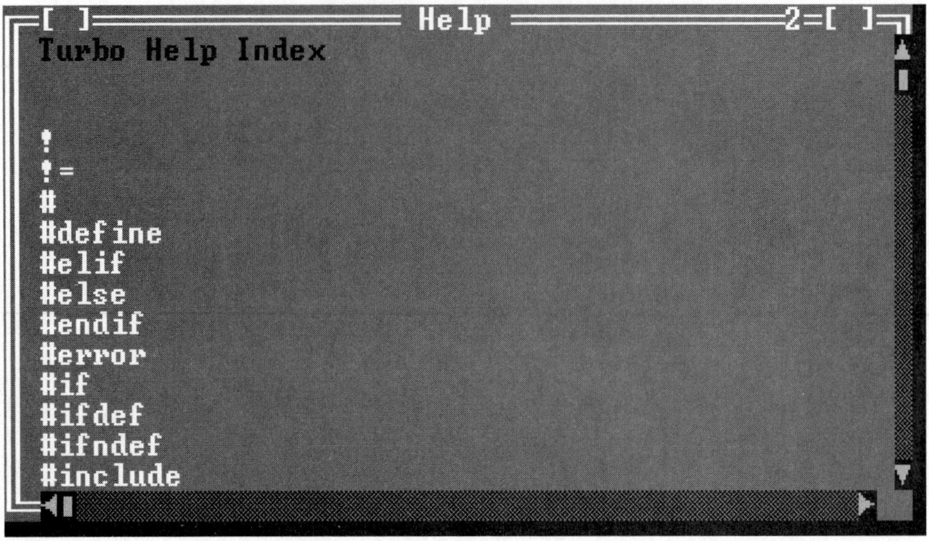

Figure A-58 The Help Index.

Use the scroll bars or arrow keys to view the index list. Highlight your choice and press **ENTER** to make a selection.

Help on Specific Keywords and Built-in Functions

For help and information on specific keywords and built-in TURBO C++ functions, position the cursor on the word and select the **Topic search** command in the **Help** menu, or use the Hot Key combination of CTRL + F1. You can use **Topic search** while you are working in the Edit Window. A Help screen will be displayed with information about the specific keyword or function. Figure A-59 shows the Help screen for the keyword **void**.

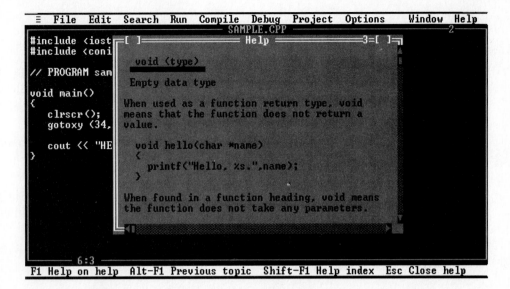

Figure A-59 An example Help screen.

The Help screens tell what the keyword or function is used for, examples of their use, and the header files that need to be included in your program in order to use the function.

If you have a question about how to use a TURBO C++ keyword or function, just type it in the Edit Window and press **CTRL + F1** for a help screen about the item.

A-5  BUGS?

Bugs are errors in your programs that are due to the incorrect use of the C++ language (syntax errors) or incorrect programming logic (logic errors). Since we are all human and make mistakes, a program that doesn't contain an error of some sort is a rare occasion.

Testing and debugging are two very important, but sometimes overlooked, steps in the programming process. Testing is making sure that your program is behaving the way that you want it to and that it is producing the correct results. Debugging is the process of finding and correcting errors, or "bugs," in your programs. It often takes more time finding and fixing bugs than writing the program.

When to Debug

There is no absolute correct procedure to debug a program, but a systematic approach can help make the process easier. Some basic steps of debugging are:

- Realizing that you have an error.
- Locating the error.
- Determining the cause of the error.
- Fixing the error.

First of all you have to realize that you have an error. Sometimes, this is very obvious when your computer freezes up or crashes. At other times, the program might work fine until certain unexpected information is entered by someone using the program. The most subtle errors occur when the program is running fine and the results look correct, but when you examine the results closely, they are not quite right.

The next step in the debugging process is finding the error. Isolating the location of the error is sometimes the most difficult part of debugging.

Syntax errors will be found and displayed in an **Error Message** window when you compile your program. These errors must be fixed before you are able to run and test your program. For more information about using the messages in

the **Error Message** window, see Section A-1, **"Compiling the Program -
Errors."** Your TURBO C++ reference manual contains a complete list of error
messages and suggestions of how to fix the errors. You can also get on-line help
by highlighting the error message in the **Error Message** window and pressing the
F1 key.

Logic errors are a little more difficult to find. Your program may be running
fine and producing results, but if the results are not correct, the cause must be
found. If you have used a structured, modular approach in writing your program,
the job of finding the error will be easier. The TURBO C++ Integrated Debugger
allows you to step over functions that you know are working properly and trace
into functions that you need to examine more closely as you run and test your
program.

Finding the cause of the error is the next step in debugging. After finding the
error, it is usually easier to determine what is causing the program to not perform
correctly. Using a **Watch** window to monitor variables and display their changing
values during debugging will help show you when the error occurs and what kind
of input causes the program to misbehave.

Fixing the error is the final step in debugging. Knowing where the error is,
your knowledge of the C++ language, this book, TURBO C++ on-line help, the
Integrated Debugger, and the TURBO C++ reference manuals are all valuable
tools in fixing the error and removing the "bug" from your program.

Using the Integrated Debugger

The TURBO C++ Integrated Debugger is one of the best tools to deal with bugs
that creep into your programs. It allows you to do source-level debugging without
leaving the convenience of the IDE. It helps with the two hardest parts of
debugging: finding the error and finding the cause of the error. It does this by
allowing you to trace into your programs and their functions one step at a time.
This slows down the program execution so that you can examine the contents of
the individual data elements and program output at any given point in the
program. You can also set breakpoints that allow you to run your program up to
the place where you have determined that an error has occurred, then step through
and inspect the portion of the program that isn't producing correct results. The
commands for the TURBO C++ debugging features are found in the **Debug** and
Run menus on the Menu Bar, as shown in Figure A-60.

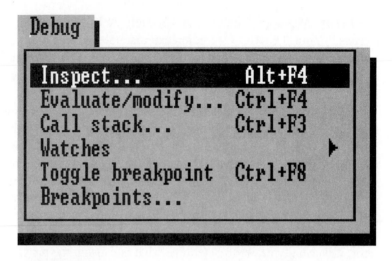

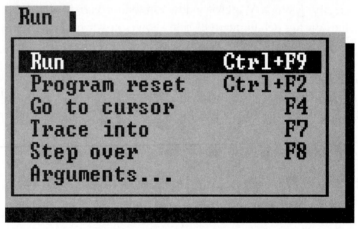

Figure A-60 The **Debug** and **Run** menus.

It would be a good idea to highlight the items on these menus and press the **F1** key to read the on-line description of what each does and how to use them.

We will use the following program from Chapter 3 Section 3-2, **"Reading String Data,"** to show how to use the **Watch** window, single step through program execution, reset the program, and set a breakpoint. At this time, enter and save the program listed in Figure A-61.

```
// THIS PROGRAM SHOWS HOW THE DEBUGGER DISPLAYS DATA

#include <iostream.h>
#include <conio.h>

void main()
{
  char Name[30];                              // DEFINE  ARRAY
  clrscr();                                   // CLEAR THE SCREEN
  cout << "Enter a name --> ";                // PROMPT THE USER
  cin >> Name;                                // READ THE NAME
  cout << "\nThe name is " << Name;           // DISPLAY THE NAME
}
```

Figure A-61 shows the example program in the **Edit** window.

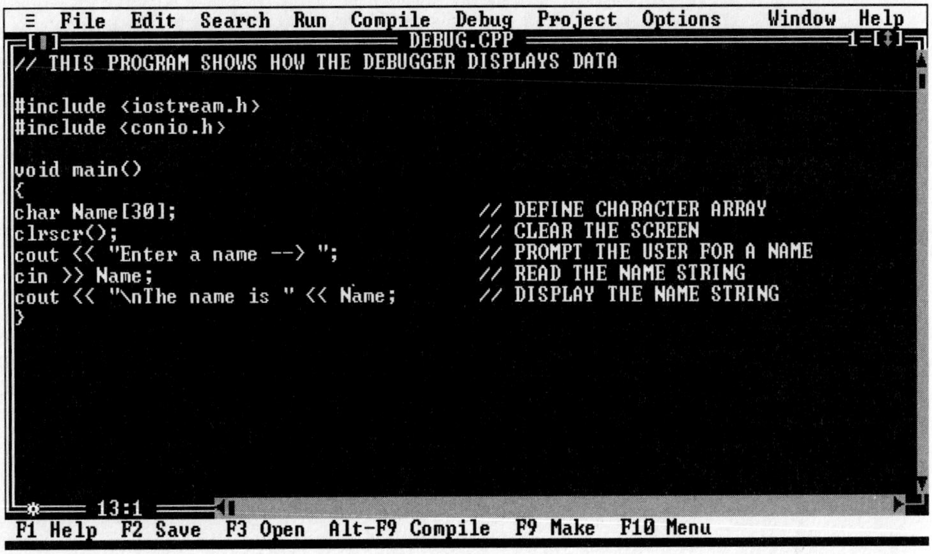

```
≡  File   Edit   Search   Run   Compile   Debug   Project   Options      Window   Help
┌[■]══════════════════════════ DEBUG.CPP ══════════════════════════1=[‡]┐
// THIS PROGRAM SHOWS HOW THE DEBUGGER DISPLAYS DATA

#include <iostream.h>
#include <conio.h>

void main()
{
char Name[30];                      // DEFINE CHARACTER ARRAY
clrscr();                           // CLEAR THE SCREEN
cout << "Enter a name --> ";        // PROMPT THE USER FOR A NAME
cin >> Name;                        // READ THE NAME STRING
cout << "\nThe name is " << Name;   // DISPLAY THE NAME STRING
}



└══ 13:1 ═══◄┃
 F1 Help  F2 Save  F3 Open  Alt-F9 Compile  F9 Make  F10 Menu
```

Figure A-61 An example program.

Using the Watch Window

Watch windows show the contents of the expressions or variables that you want to watch. This allows you to see what is happening inside of your program as it executes. Open a **Watch** window at this time.

To open a **Watch** window and add an expression to examine, select the **Watches** from the **Debug** menu, then select the **Add watch ...** command from the sub-menu, as shown in Figure A-62, or press the Hot Key combination of CTRL + F7.

```
 ≡  File  Edit  Search  Run  Compile  |Debug|  Project  Options      Window  Help
┌[■]══════════════════════════════ DE ┌───────────────────────────────┐─1=[↕]┐
║// THIS PROGRAM SHOWS HOW THE DEBUGG │ Inspect...            Alt+F4  │      ▲
║                                     │ Evaluate/modify...  Ctrl+F4   │      ■
║#include <iostream.h>                │ Call stack...       Ctrl+F3   │
║#include <conio.h>                   │ Watches                     ▶ │
║                                     ├───────────────────────────────┤
║void main()                          │ Add watch...        Ctrl+F7   │
║{                                    │ Delete watch                  │
║char Name[30];                       │ Edit watch...                 │
║clrscr();                            │ Remove all watches            │
║cout << "Enter a name --> ";         └───────────────────────────────┘
║cin >> Name;                            // READ THE NAME STRING
║cout << "\nThe name is " << Name;       // DISPLAY THE NAME STRING
║}


├─*═══ 13:1 ═══◄■                                                        ▼
└══════════════════════════════════════════════════════════════════════►■┘
 F1 Help   Insert a watch expression into the Watch window
```

Figure A-62 Adding a Watch window.

Figure A-63 shows the **Add Watch** Dialog box that allows you to type in the variable name of the data element to watch. Be very careful that you enter the variable name *exactly* as it is in the program. C++ is case-sensitive, so upper or lowercase does matter.

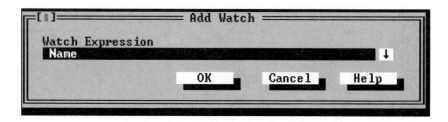

Figure A-63 Adding an expression to watch.

In this example, we will watch the *Name* array. Type *Name* in the **Watch Expression** input box. Click **OK** or press **ENTER** to add the specified expression to the **Watch** window.

Since only one window is active at a time in TURBO C++, it is a good idea to tile the windows so that you can view the program in the **Edit** window and the variable expressions in the **Watch** window. Select the **Tile** command from the **Window** menu, as shown in Figure A-64.

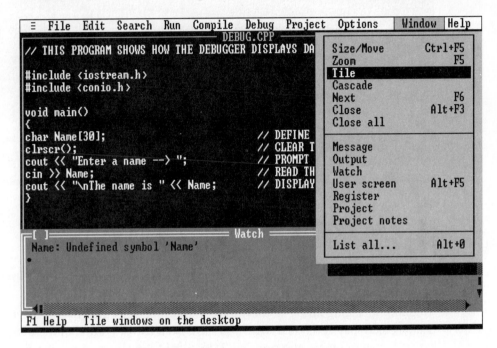

Figure A-64 Choose the **Tile** command.

The windows are shown tiled in Figure A-65. Notice that before the debugger is activated, the message in the **Watch** window shows that the variable *Name* is undefined. TURBO C++ doesn't recognize a variable until after it has been declared within the program execution.

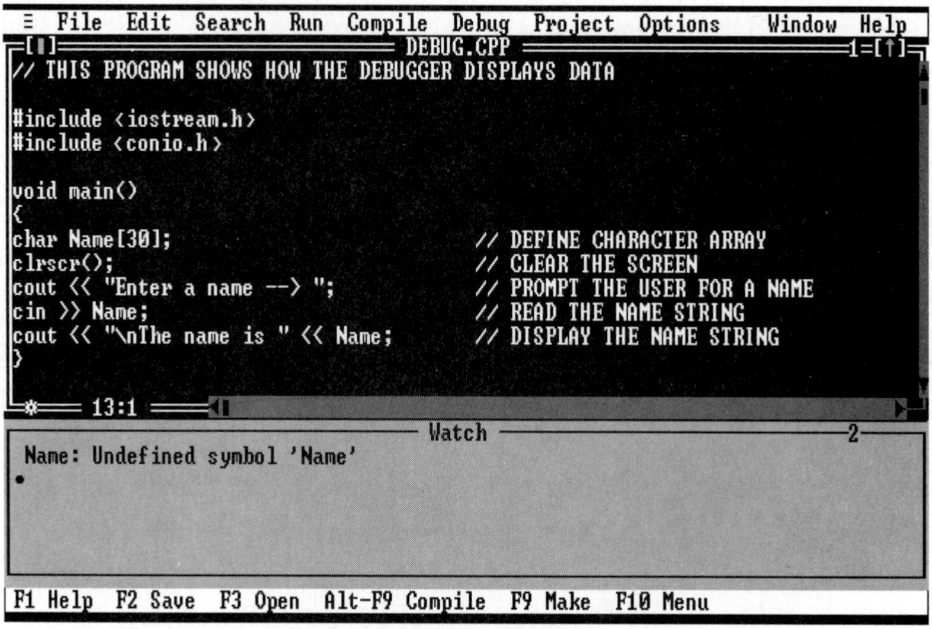

```
 ≡  File  Edit  Search  Run  Compile  Debug  Project  Options    Window  Help
┌─[■]═══════════════════════════ DEBUG.CPP ═══════════════════════1=[↑]═┐
│// THIS PROGRAM SHOWS HOW THE DEBUGGER DISPLAYS DATA                    ▲
│                                                                       ▓
│#include <iostream.h>                                                  ▓
│#include <conio.h>                                                     ▓
│                                                                       ▓
│void main()                                                            ▓
│{                                                                      ▓
│char Name[30];                    // DEFINE CHARACTER ARRAY            ▓
│clrscr();                         // CLEAR THE SCREEN                  ▓
│cout << "Enter a name --> ";      // PROMPT THE USER FOR A NAME        ▓
│cin >> Name;                      // READ THE NAME STRING              ▓
│cout << "\nThe name is " << Name; // DISPLAY THE NAME STRING           ▓
│}                                                                      ▓
├─※═══ 13:1 ═══◄▌────────────────────────────────────────────────────►▌┘
┌─────────────────────────────── Watch ─────────────────────────────2──┐
│ Name: Undefined symbol 'Name'                                         │
│ ●                                                                     │
│                                                                       │
│                                                                       │
│                                                                       │
│                                                                       │
└───────────────────────────────────────────────────────────────────────┘
 F1 Help  F2 Save  F3 Open  Alt-F9 Compile  F9 Make  F10 Menu
```

Figure A-65 The windows tiled.

Single Step and Tracing

There are two options for single stepping the program execution, **Trace into (F7)**
and **Step over (F8)**. **Trace into** single steps and executes each line of your
program, including all of the functions and include files that your program calls.
This method may be needed when you have isolated the portion of the program or
function that contains an error. To **Trace into** functions, press the **F7** key for
each line of code to execute. **Step over** traces the high-level flow of your
program by single stepping and executing each line of code in the function *main ()*,
stepping over the details of the other functions. To **Step over** functions, press the
F8 key for each line of code to execute. The **Step over** and **Trace into**
commands are in the **Run** menu shown in Figure A-66. Press **F8** at this time to
start single stepping through the program.

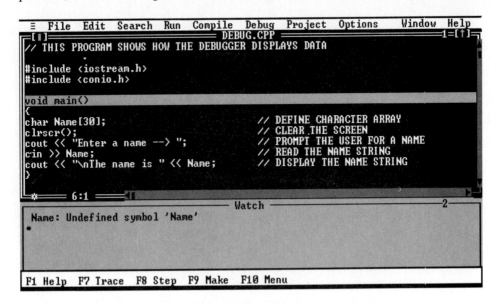

```
  ≡  File  Edit  Search  Run  Compile  Debug  Project  Options  Window  Help
┌[■]────────────────────────────────────────────────────────────────────1=[↑]┐
│// THIS PROGRAM SHOWS │ Run              Ctrl+F9 │a                           │
│                      │ Program reset    Ctrl+F2 │                            │
│#include <iostream.h> │ Go to cursor         F4  │                            │
│#include <conio.h>    │ Trace into           F7  │                            │
│                      │ Step over            F8  │                            │
│void main()           │ Arguments...             │                            │
│{                     └──────────────────────────┘                            │
│char Name[30];                          // DEFINE CHARACTER ARRAY             │
│clrscr();                               // CLEAR THE SCREEN                   │
│cout << "Enter a name --> ";            // PROMPT THE USER FOR A NAME         │
│cin >> Name;                            // READ THE NAME STRING               │
│cout << "\nThe name is " << Name;       // DISPLAY THE NAME STRING            │
│}                                                                             │
├──── 6:1 ────◄▌──────────────────── Watch ─────────────────────────────2────┤
│ Name: Undefined symbol 'Name'                                               │
│ ●                                                                           │
│                                                                             │
│                                                                             │
└─────────────────────────────────────────────────────────────────────────────┘
 F1 Help   Execute next statement; skip over the current function
```

Figure A-66 Choose Step over (**F8**)

After selecting **Step over** (**F8**), the highlighted run bar is positioned at the beginning of the function *main ()* in the **Edit** window. This marks the execution position, as shown in Figure A-67, indicating the *next* statement to be executed.

```
  ≡  File  Edit  Search  Run  Compile  Debug  Project  Options  Window  Help
┌[■]═══════════════════════════ DEBUG.CPP ═══════════════════════════════1=[↑]┐
│// THIS PROGRAM SHOWS HOW THE DEBUGGER DISPLAYS DATA                          │
│          ·                                                                   │
│#include <iostream.h>                                                         │
│#include <conio.h>                                                            │
│                                                                             │
│void main()                                                                  │
│{                                                                             │
│char Name[30];                          // DEFINE CHARACTER ARRAY             │
│clrscr();                               // CLEAR THE SCREEN                   │
│cout << "Enter a name --> ";            // PROMPT THE USER FOR A NAME         │
│cin >> Name;                            // READ THE NAME STRING               │
│cout << "\nThe name is " << Name;       // DISPLAY THE NAME STRING            │
│}                                                                             │
├──── 6:1 ────◄▌──────────────────── Watch ─────────────────────────────2────┤
│ Name: Undefined symbol 'Name'                                               │
│ ●                                                                           │
│                                                                             │
│                                                                             │
└─────────────────────────────────────────────────────────────────────────────┘
 F1 Help  F7 Trace  F8 Step  F9 Make  F10 Menu
```

Figure A-67 The run bar positioned at the function *main()*.

Press **F8** to execute each line of code to bring the highlighted run bar to the
cin >> *Name;* line shown in Figure A-68. Before pressing **F8** to execute this line,
notice that the message in the **Watch** window now shows that the *Name* array is
defined and contains garbage. Now, press **F8** again to execute the *cin* statement.

```
 ≡  File  Edit  Search  Run  Compile  Debug  Project  Options   Window  Help
 [■]                              DEBUG.CPP                            1=[↑]
// THIS PROGRAM SHOWS HOW THE DEBUGGER DISPLAYS DATA

#include <iostream.h>
#include <conio.h>

void main()
{
char Name[30];                        // DEFINE CHARACTER ARRAY
clrscr();                             // CLEAR THE SCREEN
cout << "Enter a name --> ";          // PROMPT THE USER FOR A NAME
cin >> Name;                          // READ THE NAME STRING
cout << "\nThe name is " << Name;     // DISPLAY THE NAME STRING
}

    11:1
                                 Watch                                  2
  Name: "⌐\x40"
  •


 F1 Help  F7 Trace  F8 Step  F9 Make  F10 Menu
```

Figure A-68 Ready to execute the *cin* statement.

Figure A-69 shows the user screen that is displayed after pressing **F8** to
execute the *cin* statement.

Figure A-69 The *cin* user screen.

Type in your name on the user screen and press **ENTER**. After typing your
name and pressing the **ENTER** key, you are returned to the **Edit** window and the
run bar is on the next statement ready to execute it, as shown in Figure A-70.

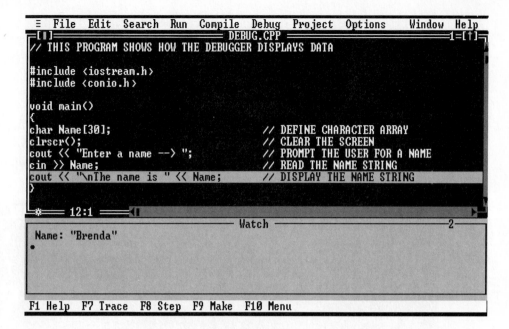

Figure A-70 Ready to execute the *cout* statement.

Notice that the message in the **Watch** window now shows that the contents of the *Name* array are the characters entered from the user screen. This means that this portion of the program is working correctly. If the contents of the *Name* array did not match what was entered, we would know that there was an error, or bug, at this point. Always check to make sure that the variable contents are what you expect them to be when debugging your programs. Press **F8** again to execute the *cout* statement.

Figure A-71 shows the user screen that is displayed upon pressing the **F8** key to execute the *cout* statement.

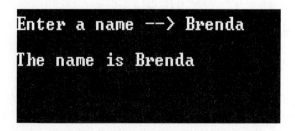

Figure A-71 The *cout* user screen.

This completes your debugging exercise. Read over the remaining sections on **Resetting the Program** and **Setting a Breakpoint** and experiment with them using the example program.

Resetting the Program

There may be times that you need to start single stepping a program from the beginning before you have reached the end. The **Program reset** (CTRL+F2) command in the **Run** menu will reposition the run bar back at the beginning of the program for you, as shown in Figure A-72

```
 ≡  File   Edit   Search  Run  Compile   Debug   Project   Options      Window   Help
┌─[■]══════════════════════════════════════════════════════════════════1═[↑]═┐
│// THIS PROGRAM SHOWS     Run               Ctrl+F9    ▐                    ▲│
│                          Program reset     Ctrl+F2                          │
│#include <iostream.h>     Go to cursor           F4                          │
│#include <conio.h>        Trace into             F7                          │
│                          Step over              F8                          │
│void main()               Arguments...                                      │
│{                                                                           │
│char Name[30];                              // DEFINE CHARACTER ARRAY        │
│clrscr();                                   // CLEAR THE SCREEN              │
│cout << "Enter a name --> ";                // PROMPT THE USER FOR A NAME    │
│cin >> Name;                                // READ THE NAME STRING          │
│cout << "\nThe name is " << Name;           // DISPLAY THE NAME STRING       │
│}                                                                           ▼│
│══ 6:1 ═══◄▌                                                               ►▐│
├──────────────────────────── Watch ─────────────────────────────2───────────┤
│  Name: Undefined symbol 'Name'                                             │
│  ●                                                                         │
│                                                                           │
│                                                                           │
│                                                                           │
├───────────────────────────────────────────────────────────────────────────┤
│ F1 Help    Restart the program from beginning                             │
└───────────────────────────────────────────────────────────────────────────┘
```

Figure A-72 Resetting the program (CTRL + F2).

Setting a Breakpoint

If you have determined that your program is running correctly up to a certain point, a breakpoint can be set so that you can run the program and then start single stepping at the portion of the program that needs closer inspection. A breakpoint is a place in your program that you want execution to run to, then stop or "break" at. To set a breakpoint, move the cursor to the line of code to stop at, then select the **Toggle breakpoint** (CTRL + F8) command in the **Debug** menu, shown in Figure A-73, or press CTRL + F8.

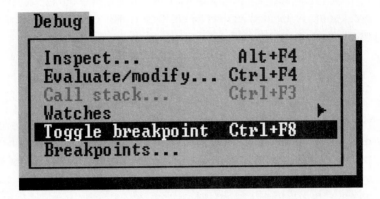

Figure A-73 Set a breakpoint (**CTRL + F8**)

A breakpoint bar, like the one shown in Figure A-74, will be placed on the line where the cursor is currently located in the program. Once a breakpoint is set, running the program (**CTRL + F9**) will cause the program to stop executing at the breakpoint and return you to the debugger. At this point you can single step the remainder of the program.

```
=[■]=================== DEBUG.CPP ===================1=[↑]=
// THIS PROGRAM SHOWS HOW THE DEBUGGER DISPLAYS DATA

#include <iostream.h>
#include <conio.h>

void main()
{
char Name[30];                    // DEFINE CHARACTER ARRAY
clrscr();                         // CLEAR THE SCREEN
cout << "Enter a name --> ";      // PROMPT THE USER FOR A NAME
cin >> Name;                      // READ THE NAME STRING
cout << "\nThe name is " << Name; // DISPLAY THE NAME STRING
}.
=■= 11:1 ==◄|                                              ►
=================================== Watch ===================2=
 Name: Undefined symbol 'Name'
 •

F1 Help  F2 Save  F3 Open  Alt-F9 Compile  F9 Make  F10 Menu
```

Figure A-74 The breakpoint position.

A breakpoint can be removed by placing the cursor on the line where the breakpoint is located and pressing CTRL + F8 again, since CTRL + F8 toggles a breakpoint on or off.

TURBO C++ also offers other debugging features not covered in this appendix. Refer to your TURBO C++ reference manuals for more information about these other features.

Remember that debugging is an ongoing process, since it sometimes seems that you think you have all the bugs fixed and then another one shows up. If you use the systematic approach described in this appendix, the job of removing the bugs will be easier. Good luck finding and removing those "bugs"!

APPENDIX B
QUICK CHECK SOLUTIONS

CHAPTER 1:

SECTION 1-1

1. The three major sections of a microcomputer's architecture are the CPU, MEMORY, and I/O.

2. A CPU contained within a single integrated circuit is called a *microprocessor*.

3. Arithmetic and logic operations performed by the ALU section of a CPU are:

Arithmetic Operations	Symbol	Logic Operations	Symbol
Addition	+	*Equal to*	==
Subtraction	–	*Not equal to*	!=
Multiplication	*	*Less than*	<
Division	/	*Less than or equal to*	<=
		Greater than	>
		Greater than or equal to	>=

4. Three things that might be found in a CPU are *internal registers*, the *arithmetic and logic unit (ALU)*, and the *control unit*.

5. A 4M system has *4 × 1024 × 1024 = 4,194,304 (or just over 4 million)* bytes of RAM.

6. Programs stored in ROM are often called *firmware*.

7. After a program is loaded into primary memory, compiled, and linked, the machine instructions are fetched from primary memory, decoded, executed, and the resulting data is stored back in primary memory.

SECTION 1-2

1. C++ is referred to as a mid-level language because it provides low-level access to system hardware and software while having the advantages of a high-level language.

2. The steps that must be performed to translate a C++ source code program to an executable program are:

   • Write the source code.

   • Compile the source code into object code.

   • Link the object code to other required routines to form the executable program.

3. An object file (*.obj*) is produced by the compile step.

4. An executable file (*.exe*) is produced by the linking step.

5. The purpose of the linking step is to integrate the program with any additional routines that are required for proper program execution.

6. The major difference between the C language and the C++ language is that C++ allows for object-oriented programming while C does not.

SECTION 1-3

1. English-like statements that require less precision than a formal programming language are called *pseudocode* statements.

2. Some questions that must be answered when defining a computer programming problem are:

   • What outputs are needed?

   • What inputs are needed?

   • What processing is needed to produce the output from the input?

3. To test and debug a program you can desk-check, compile, and run it.

4. Commenting is important within a program because it explains what the program does and makes the program easier to read and maintain.

SECTION 1-4

1. It is important to use an algorithm in the planning of a program to define what steps are needed to produce the desired final result. An algorithm keeps you from "spinning your wheels."

2. The three major categories of algorithmic language operations are sequence, decision, and iteration.

3. Three decision operations are *If/Then, If/Then/Else,* and *Switch/Case.*

4. Three iteration operations are *While, Do/While,* and *For.*

CHAPTER 2:

SECTION 2-1

1. A set of data elements that more or less belong with each other is called a *data type*.

2. Data types that are predefined within a programming language are called *standard* data types.

3. User-defined data types defined to meet a given application are called *enumerated* data types.

4. The three major data type categories in a structured programming language are the *scalar, structured ,* and *pointer* data categories.

SECTION 2-2

1. The range of values that can be provided via the standard *int* data type is –32,768 to +32,767.

2. An overflow error occurs when, as a result of a calculation, a value exceeds its predefined range.

3. The two ways that floating point values can be represented in a C++ program are using either *decimal* or *exponential* format.

4. The following values will be returned when these functions are executed:

    toascii('B') = 66

    toascii('?') = 63

5. The extended character set defined for the IBM PC must use the **unsigned char** data type.

6.   A character string is stored in a data structure called an *array*.

7.   Twenty-nine bytes of storage are required to store the string "The United States of America". Remember that you must include room for the null terminator character.

SECTION 2-3

1.   The two reasons for declaring/defining constants and variables in a C++ program are:
   - The compiler must know the value of a constant before it is used and must reserve memory locations to store variables.
   - The compiler must know the data type of constants and variables.

2.   The following will declare a constant called *PERIOD* that will insert a period wherever it is referenced in a program.

      const char PERIOD = '.' ;

3.   The following will declare a constant called *BOOK* that will insert the string "Structuring Techniques: An Introduciont Using C++" wherever it appears in a program.

      const char BOOK[ ] = "Structuring Techniques: An Introduction Using C++";

4.   Given a string variable that must store a string of up to 25 characters, an array size of 26 must be defined to store the string variable.

5.   The following will define a string variable called *Course* that will be initialized to a string value of "Data Structures".

      char Course[ ] = "Data Structures" ;

SECTION 2-4

1.   Enumerated data types allow the programmer to define a problem more clearly and make the program more readable than standard data types.

2.   The following will define an enumerated data type called *Automobiles* which consists of 10 popular automobile brands.

      enum Automobiles {Ford, BMW, Geo, Chrysler, Volvo, Nissan, Mazda, Porsche, Cadillac, Toyota};

3.   The compiler assigns the numeric value of 0 (zero) to the first element in an enumerated data type.

SECTION 2-5

1.   Any C++ program consists of two sections called the *preprocessor* and *main function* sections.

2.   The following is an *#include* directive to include a standard header file called *stdlib.h* into a program, assuming that the header file is located in the system default directory.

```
#include  <stdlib.h>
```

3.   The following is a *#define* directive to substitute the string "PROGRAM 2-3" every place that the identifier *Prog* appears in the program.

```
#define Prog "PROGRAM 2-3"
```

4.   A subprogram that returns a single value, a set of values, or performs some specific task in C++ is called a *function.*

5.   Global constants and variables must be declared/defined before the main function identifier, *main().*

6.   Local constants and variables can be declared/defined anywhere in the program as long as they are declared/defined before their use.

CHAPTER 3:

SECTION 3-1

1.   The file that must be included to use *cout* is the *iostream.h* header file.

2.   The operator that must be employed to send information to the *cout* object is the << *(double left angle bracket)* operator.

3.   The following is a *cout* statement to display my name as a fixed string of information.

```
cout << "Brenda";
```

4.   The following is a *cout* statement to display my name when it is stored in a string variable called *Name.*

```
cout << Name;
```

5.   The escape sequence that must be used to generate a CRLF is \n.

6.   The file that must be included to use the *setw()* field width manipulator is the *iomanip.h* header file.

7.   The following is a *cout* statement that will display the value of a variable called *Number* with a field width of 10 columns.

```
cout << setw(10) << Number;
```

SECTION 3-2

1.   The operator that must be employed to send information to the *cin* object is the >> *(double right angle bracket)* operator.

2.   The following statements will prompt the user to enter a value for an integer variable called *Number* using *cin* to read the user entry.

```
cout << "Please enter an integer :  ";
```

cin >> Number;

3.   Blanks, tabs, new lines and form feeds are all considered whitespace.

4.   True: When reading character data, *cin* will read only one character at a time.

5.   When using the >> operator to read string data, the *cin* statement will terminate when whitespace is encountered.

6.   The *getline()* function can be used as *cin.getline()* to include whitespace when reading string data.

7.   *gets()* or *fgets()* should be used in lieu of *cin* when reading string data after reading numeric or character data.

8.   The following employs the *gets()* function to read a string of up to 25 characters and stores it in a variable called *Name*.

     char Name[26];

     gets(Name);

9.   The function *gets()* converts the CRLF to a null terminator.

10. The function *fgets()* reads and stores the CRLF then adds a null terminator.

SECTION 3-3

1.   In order to make a program more user friendly you can include a program description message to tell the user what the program does, include prompting messages for any read operations, and have well formatted output information.

2.   The I/O manipulator, *flush*, should be used after a printer output operation to assure reliable printed information.

3.   The symbol used to insert comments in your program is the // *(double forward slashes)* symbol.

4.   Four places where your program should include comments are:

   •   At the beginning of the program, stating the program's purpose.

   •   At the beginning of each block of code, explaining what the block does.

   •   At individual program lines if their purpose is not clear.

   •   At major subprograms (functions), describing what they do.

CHAPTER 4:

SECTION 4-1

1.   The order in which C++ performs arithmetic operations is as follows:

     . ( )   *   /   %   +   −

Any operations inside of parentheses are performed first, then (from left-to-right) multiplication, division, and modulus, then (from left-to-right) addition and subtraction.

2. The statement --x; is equivalent to the statement x = x - 1;

3. The statement, "The division operator will produce an integer result when either of the operands is an integer," is false because this happens only when both the numerator and denominator operands are integers.

4. True: The modulus operator is only defined for integers.

5. The difference between using the pre-increment operator versus the post-increment operator on a variable is that a pre-increment operator increments the variable before any expression involving the variable is evaluated and a post-increment operator increments the variable after any expression involving the variable is evaluated. It is important to be careful which one you use, especially when the variable is used as part of a compound expression because undesirable results can be produced if the wrong incrementing operator is used.

SECTION 4-2

1. The statement x += 5; is equivalent to the statement x = x + 5;.

2. The statement x /= y; is equivalent to the statement x = x/y;.

SECTION 4-3

1. Operators that allow two values to be compared are called *relational* operators.

2. In C++, a logical FALSE is equated to the value *0 (zero)*.

3. The difference between the = operator and the == operator in C++ is that the = operator assigns the statement on the right to the variable on the left and the == operator compares two quantities to determine if they are equal.

4. The value 1 (TRUE) is generated as a result of the operation 4 > 5 – 2, since 4 is greater than (5 – 2) or 3.

5. The value 0 (FALSE) is generated as a result of the operation (5 != 5) && (3 == 3), since (5 != 5) is FALSE, making the entire AND statement FALSE.

SECTION 4-4

1. In order to use a standard function in your program, you must include its *header file*.

2. To get an on-line description of a standard function using the TURBO C++ compiler while working in the edit mode, press *CTRL+F1* and select the function from the on-line help index. An alternative way is to place the cursor on the desired function name in the edit mode and press *CTRL+F1*.

3. The *strcpy()* function must be employed to assign string data to a string variable in a C++ program.

4. The statement strcpy(Compiler,"C++"); will assign the string "C++" to a string variable called *Compiler*.

5. The *strcmp()* function should be used instead of Boolean relational operators when comparing string values because Boolean relational operators do not give correct logical results when comparing strings.

CHAPTER 5:

SECTION 5-1

1. True: A test expression that evaluates to any non-zero value is considered TRUE.

2. True: When a test expression in an **if** statement evaluates to zero the related **if** statements are bypassed.

3. The correct **if** statement reads as follows:
    ```
    if (x == y)
        cout << "There is a problem here";
    ```
    The test expression needs to be a comparison, not an assignment.

4. The && (AND) Boolean operator must be employed to test if two conditions are TRUE.

5. The !&& (NOT AND) Boolean operator must be employed to test if one of two conditions is FALSE.

6. The || (OR) Boolean operator must be employed to test if one of two conditions is TRUE.

7. When x is zero, since $!x = !0 = 1$ = TRUE.

SECTION 5-2

1. True: When the test expression in an **if/else** operation evaluates to zero, the **else** statements are executed.

2. The following pseudocode needs an **else** statement because without an **else** statement, both statements "It's payday" and "It's not payday" would be written when the **if** test is true.
    ```
    If Day == Friday
        Write("It's pay day").
    Write("It's not pay day").
    ```

3. True: Framing with curly braces can be eliminated when an **if** or **else** statement section only has a single statement.

SECTION 5-3

1. Indentation is important when operations are nested for code readability and to be able to see at a glance which statements belong to which **if** or **else** statements.

2. True: Any given **else** always goes with the closest **if**.

Consider the following pseudocode for questions 3–5:

```
If Value < 50
  If Value > -50
    Write ("Red").
  else
    Write ("White").
else
  Write ("Blue").
```

3. "Red" will be written when the value is greater than −50 and less than 50.

4. "White" will be written when the value is less than or equal to −50.

5. "Blue" will be written when the value is greater than or equal to 50.

SECTION 5-4

1. The selection of a particular case in a **switch** statement is controlled by a *matching* process.

2. If that you have *n* cases in a **switch** statement and there are no **break** statements in any of the cases, all of the cases will be executed sequentially when a match is made on the first case.

3. The statement, "There are never any times when a case should not contain a **break** statement" is false, because there may be times when several subsequent cases need to be executed as the result of a match to a given case.

4. A statement that can be inserted at the end of a **switch** statement to protect against invalid entries is the **default** statement.

5. A common application for **switch** statements is *menu-driven programs.*

CHAPTER 6:

SECTION 6-1

1. True: A **while** loop breaks when the test expression evaluates to zero.

2. False: The **while** loop is a pretest loop not a posttest loop.

3. The **while** loop statements need to be framed, since without the framing, the value of *x* is never changed and you will have an infinite loop.

4. The correct the code for question 3 is:

```
x = 10;
while (x > 0)
{
  cout << "This is a while loop";
  --x;
}
```

5. The loop will never execute, since the loop test is FALSE. Notice that x is initialized to 1 and is never $< = 0$.

6. This is an infinite loop. Notice that x is initialized to 1 and is incremented with each loop iteration. Thus, the **while** test of $x > = 0$ is always TRUE.

SECTION 6-2

1. True: A **do/while** loop breaks when the test expression evaluates to zero.

2. True: A **do/while** loop is a posttest loop.

3. The value of x is never changed within the loop, thereby creating an infinite loop.

4. The correct code for question 3 is:

```
x = 10;
do
{
  cout << "This is a do/while loop";
  -- x;
}
while (x > 0);
```

5. The loop will execute once, since a **do/while** loop is a posttest loop.

6. Without the limitations of the computer, the loop will execute infinitely, since x starts out greater than 0 and is incremented inside of the loop. But, considering the physical limitations of the computer it will execute 32,768 times before wrapping around to $-32,768$ and causing the test to be FALSE.

SECTION 6-3

1. The three things that can appear in the first line of a **for** loop structure are:

    • The loop counter initialization

    • The loop test expression

    • The increment/decrement of the counter

2. True: The loop counter in a **for** loop is altered after the loop statements are executed in a given iteration.

3. True: A **for** loop can always be replaced by a **while** loop, since they are basically the same looping structure, just coded differently.

4. The loop will execute zero times, since the test condition x is 0 (FALSE) on the first test.

5. The loop will execute 11 times.

6. The **for** loop statements must be framed when there is more than one statement to be executed within the loop.

7. If you have two nested loops, with the inner loop executing 5 times and the outer loop executing 10 times, there will be 50 total iterations. The inner loop will execute 5 times for every outer loop iteration. (5×10).

8. In a down-to loop, the loop counter is always *decremented*.

SECTION 6-4

1. The statement that will cause only the current iteration of a loop to be aborted is the **continue** statement.

2. The **break** and **continue** statements are normally used as part of an **if** statement within a loop structure.

3. The loop will execute twice. When x is incremented to 1 at the end of the first iteration, the **if**(x) statement will be TRUE (non-zero) in the second iteration, causing the **break** statement to execute to abort the loop structure.

CHAPTER 7:

SECTION 7-1

1 The role of a function in a C++ program is to eliminate the need for duplicate statements. The use of functions allows you to solve large complex problems by breaking the problem down into smaller more easily manageable subproblems (top/down approach).

2 The three main sections of a function are the *function header*, *local variables or constants*, and *statement* sections.

3. The function header in a C++ program is the data interface for the function. It forms a common boundary between the function and its calling program.

4. The three parts of a function header are:
   - The data type of the value to be returned by the function, if any.
   - The name of the function.
   - A parameter listing.

5. A function variable, waiting to receive a value from the calling program is called a *parameter*.

6. A **return** statement in a function is used when a single value must be returned to the calling program.

7. The difference between an actual argument in a calling program and a formal parameter in a function header is that the actual argument contains the value passed to the formal parameter in the function header. In other words, the formal parameter receives the value from the actual argument in the calling program.

SECTION 7-2

1. **void** must be used as the return data type when a function does not return a single value to the calling program

2. The two things that must be considered when developing a function header are:

    *   What the function must accept to perform its task.

    *   What the function must return.

3. One-way communication of data from the calling program to a function is provided via *value* parameters.

4. Two-way communication of data between the calling program and a function is provided via *reference* parameters.

5. To specify a reference parameter in a function header you must use the & *(ampersand)* symbol prior to the parameter identifier.

6. The body of a function is normally located after the closing brace of *main()*.

SECTION 7-3

1. The primary purpose of a function prototype is to allow the compiler to check for any mismatches between the actual arguments in a function call and the formal parameters that the function expects to receive.

2. A function prototype is normally located after the preprocessor directives and before function *main()* in a C++ program.

3. True: Parameters listed in a function prototype can be listed only by data type, without any corresponding identifiers.

4. True: Default parameters can appear on either the function prototype or function header, but not both.

5. True: Once a default parameter is specified in a function prototype, the remaining parameters in the parameter listing must be default parameters.

6. When overloading a function, the return data type as well as the number and data types of the function parameters will determine how the function will perform.

SECTION 7-4

1. A global variable that has file scope must be placed *outside and prior to* function *main()* in a C++ program.

2.   A local variable has *block* scope.

3.   The altering of a global variable by a function is referred to as a *side effect*.

4.   To retain the value of a local function variable from one call of the function to the next the keyword **static** must be used in front of the variable declaration.

SECTION 7-5

1.   The statement: "There is no way that a C++ function can call itself" is false, because C++ supports recursion which allows a function to call itself.

2.   We can describe recursion as a "winding" and "un-winding" process, because recursion "winds" values onto a stack and when the primitive state is reached it "un-winds" the values to calculate the final result.

3.   When the primitive state is reached a recursive function call is terminated.

4.   The pseudocode required to find *N!*, where *N* is any integer is:

   If N = 0 Then
   　　　Factorial = 1.
   Else
   　　　Factorial = N * Factorial (N – 1).

5.   The statement: "An advantage of recursion is that it does not require a lot of memory to execute" is false because recursion uses large amounts of memory to keep track of each recursive call.

6.   True: All recursive problems can also be solved using iteration.

CHAPTER 8:

SECTION 8-1

1.   The two major components of an array are the *index* and *element*.

2.   The statement, "The elements within a given array can be any combination of data types" is false, because the elements within a given array must all be of the same data type.

SECTION 8-2

1.   An array definition initialized with the integer values –3 through +3 is:

   int Numbers[7] = { -3,-2,-1,0,1,2,3 };
   　　　　　　　OR
   int Numbers[] = { -3,-2,-1,0,1,2,3 };

2.   The dimension of the above array is 1×7.

3.   The contents of the array char Language[5] = {'C','+','+'}; are:

   ['C'] ['+'] ['+'] ['\0'] ['\0']

4. The contents of the array char Language[] = "C++"; are:

    ['C'] ['+'] ['+'] ['\0']

5. A null terminator character (\0) is placed in each array position of a globally defined character array without any initializing values.

SECTION 8-3

1. The **for** loop required to fill the array char Characters[15]; is:

    for (int Index = 0; Index < 15; ++ Index)
                cin >> Characters [Index];

2. The **for** loop that will display the contents of the above array is:

    for (int Index = 0; Index < 15; ++ Index)
                cout << Characters [Index] << '\t';

SECTION 8-4

1. The statement, "An array name is in the address of index [1] of the array" is false, because the array name locates index [0] of the array.

2. A prototype for a function called *Sample()* that must alter the array
    char Characters[15]; is:

    void Sample (char Characters [15]);

3. A prototype for a function called *Test()* that will alter a single array element in the above array is:

    void Test (char &Element);

4. A statement that will call the above function to alter the element stored at index [5] of the array in question 2 is:

    Test (Characters [5]);

CHAPTER 9:

SECTION 9-1

1. Given the two-dimensional array definition, float Sample [10][15]; , the maximum row index is 9 and the maximum column index is 14.

2. The statement cout << sizeof(Sample)/sizeof(float); will display the number of array positions in the array *Sample[]*, or 150.

3. A statement that will read a value from the keyboard and place it in the first row and last column of the array defined in question 1 is:

    cin >> Sample [0] [14];

4. A statement that will display the value stored in the second row and third column of the array defined in question 1 is:

cout << Sample [1] [2];

5. The code, using **for** loops, that will display the elements of the array defined in question 1 is:

    ```
    for (int Row = 0; Row < 10; ++Row)
    {
        for (int Col = 0; Col < 15; ++Col)
            cout << Sample [Row] [Col];
        cout << '\n';
    }
    ```

6. A prototype for a function called *Display()* that will display the contents of the array defined in question 1 is:

    void Display (float Sample [10] [15]);

7. A statement to call the *Display()* function in question 6 is:

    Display (Sample);

8. A two-dimensional array in C++ is *row* major order.

SECTION 9-2

1. A problem that might be encountered when defining large multidimensional arrays is the "array size too big" error. This means that you are attempting to set aside more memory for the array than a particular computer system can allocate.

2. A three dimensional array in C++ is *plane* major order.

3. A definition for a three dimensional array of integers that has 10 planes, 15 rows, and 3 columns is:

    int Integers [10] [15] [3];

4. To determine how many bytes of storage is occupied by the above array you can use:

    sizeof(Integers)

    If your compiler stores an integer in two bytes this calculation becomes

    $(10 \times 15 \times 3) * 2 = 900$ bytes.

5. The code, using **for** loops, to display the contents of the array defined in question 3, one plane at a time is:

    ```
    for (int Plane = 0; Plane < 10; ++ Plane)
    {
        for (int Row = 0; Row < 15; ++ Row)
        {
            for (int Col = 0; Col < 3; ++ Col)
                cout << Integers [Plane] [Row] [Col];
            cout << '\n';
        } // END ROW FOR
    } // END PLANE FOR
    ```

CHAPTER *10*:

SECTION 10-1

1. Suppose that *pchar* is a pointer to a character and *Character* is a character variable. A statement to make *pchar* point to the character stored in *Character* is:

   pchar = &Character;

2. A statement that will make an integer pointer called *p1int* point to the same integer to which an integer pointer called *p2int* is pointing is:

   p1int = p2int;

3. The statement, "If *Character* is defined as a character variable, then &*Character* can be altered at any time" is false because &*Character* represents a constant pointer and cannot be changed by the program.

4. True: If *pchar* is defined as a character pointer, then *pchar* can be altered at any time.

SECTION 10-2

1. A definition for a static character pointer called *pchar* and a character variable called *Character* is:

   char *pchar;
   char Character;

2. A statement to make *pchar* point to the variable *Character* defined in question 1 is:

   pchar = &Character;

3. A statement to initialize *pchar* defined in question 1 to the character 'A' is:

   *pchar = 'A';

4. The statement, "The assignment *pchar* = 'Z' is legal, as long as *pchar* is defined as a character pointer" is false, since *pchar* must be assigned to another pointer, not a character type. The correct assignment would be:

   *pchar = 'Z' .

5. When a pointer is initialized dynamically, the **new** operator must be used in the pointer definition.

6. The statements required to initialize a dynamic character pointer called *pchar* to the value 'B' are:

   pchar = new char;
   *pchar = 'B';

7. A statement that will deallocate the memory allocated in question 6 is:

       delete pchar;

8.   The statement, "When you deallocate pointer memory using the **delete** operator, the respective pointer is deleted" is false, because the pointer remains and only the memory space that was used by the pointer is deallocated.

SECTION 10-3

1.   A statement that defines a string pointer called *pstring* and initializes it to the string "C++" is:

      char *pstring = "C++";

2.   A statement to display the entire string in question 1 is:

      cout << pstring;

3.   A statement to display just the first character of the string in question 1 is:

      cout << *pstring;

           OR

      cout << pstring[0];

4.   A statement to display just the last character of the string in question 1 is:

      cout << pstring[2];

           OR

      cout << *(pstring + 2);

5.   A statement to display the last two characters of the string in question 1 is:

      cout << *(pstring + 1) << *(pstring + 2);

               OR

      cout << pstring[1] << pstring[2];

6.   Suppose that *p1* is a pointer which points to index [5] of an array of double floating point values, and *p2* is a pointer pointing to index [15] of the same array. Then $p2 - p1$ will yield the value 10.

SECTION 10-4

1.   True: An array name is always a constant pointer.

2.   A definition for a constant pointer called *pstring* to point to the string "Zane" is:

      char * const pstring = "Zane";

3.   Rewriting the definition in question 2 so that the pointer will be variable and the string will be constant:

      const char * pstring = "Zane";

4.   Rewriting the definition in question 3 so that both the pointer and string will be constant:

const char * const pstring = "Zane";

SECTION 10-5

1.   A definition for an array of pointers called *Courses* to point to the strings "Calc", "Assembler", and "C++" is:

   char * Courses[] = {"Calc", "Assembler", "C++", NULL};

2.   "Calc" is located at *Courses* using the array in question 1.

3.   The *address* of the string "C++" is located at *Courses[2]* using the array in question 1.

4.   "lc" is located at *Courses* + 2 using the array in question 1.

5.   The single character 'e' is located at *(Courses[1] + 3)*.

6.   The concept of using several levels of addressing to access data is known as *indirection*, or *indirect addressing*.

SECTION 10-6

1.   True: When a pointer is used in a function call, any operations on the pointer data within the function will affect the pointer data in the calling program.

2.   True: A pointer argument in a function call must have a corresponding pointer parameter in the function prototype.

3.   A prototype for a function called *MyFunc()* that will receive a pointer to a string is:

   void MyFunc(char *);

4.   A prototype for a function called *MyFunc()* that will receive an array of pointers to strings is:

   void MyFunc(char **);

5.   Assuming that *MyNames* is defined as an array of pointers to strings, a statement that will call the function in question 4 is:

   MyFunc(MyNames);

SECTION 10-7

1.   True: A function name is a constant pointer.

2.   A prototype for a variable function pointer called *My_Func_Ptr* that can be used to point to functions that receive a single integer value and return a single integer value is:

   int (* My_Func_Ptr) (int);

3.   Given the following function prototypes:

   int Square(int);
   int Cube(int);

A statement to make the function pointer defined in question 2 point to the *Square()* function is :

My_Func_Ptr = Square;

A statement to make the function pointer defined in question 2 point to the *Cube()* function is:

My_Func_Ptr = Cube;

4. True: When a function pointer is created, the parameter data types and return data type must match those of any function to which it must point.

CHAPTER 11:

SECTION 11-1

1. The statement, "All the members of a given structure must have the same data type" is false because a structure can have members of different data types.

2. A declaration for structure called *Account* that has four floating point members named *Deposits*, *Withdrawals*, *Interest_Rate*, and *Balance* is:

```
struct Account
{
  float Deposits;
  float Withdrawals;
  float Interest_Rate;
  float Balance;
}
```

3. A definition for an un-initialized variable called *Checkbook* for the structure declared in question 2 is :

Account Checkbook;

4. The following is a definition for a variable called *Passbook* for the structure declared in question 2 and initialized to the stated values:

```
Account Passbook = {1500.00,
                    500.00,
                    0.1,
                    2345.49};
```

SECTION 11-2

The following structure definition is used to answer questions 1–9:

```
struct Account
{
  float Deposits;
```

```
      float Withdrawals;
      float Interest_Rate;
      float Balance;
    } Checkbook, Pass, *Passbook;

      Passbook = &Pass;
```

1. The structure variables are a non-pointer variable called *Checkbook* and a pointer variable called *Passbook*.

2. A statement to assign a value of $250.00 to the *Deposits* member of the *Checkbook* structure is:

    ```
    Checkbook.Deposits = 250.00;
    ```

3. A statement to assign a value of 12% to the *Interest_Rate* member of the *Passbook* structure is:

    ```
    Passbook -> Interest_Rate = 0.12;
    ```

4. A statement to allow the user to input a value for the *Withdrawals* member of the *Checkbook* structure is:

    ```
    cout << "\nEnter amount of withdrawals: ";
    cin >> Checkbook.Withdrawals;
    ```

5. A statement to allow the user to input a value for the *Deposits* member of the *Passbook* structure is:

    ```
    cout << "\nEnter amount of deposits: ";
    cin >> Passbook -> Deposits;
    ```

6. A statement to display the account balance in the *Checkbook* structure is:

    ```
    cout << "\nThe Account Balance is: " << Checkbook.Balance;
    ```

7. A statement to display the account balance in the *Passbook* structure is:

    ```
    cout << "\nThe Account Balance is: " << Passbook -> Balance;
    ```

8. The header for a function called *Input()* that would obtain user entries for the *Checkbook* structure is:

    ```
    void Input (Account Checkbook)
    ```

9. A header for a function called *Output()* that would display the contents of the *Passbook* structure is:

    ```
    void Output (Account *Passbook)
    ```

SECTION 11-3

The following structure definitions are used to answer questions 1–6.

```
    struct Address
    {
      char Street[25];
      char City[25];
```

```
        char State[2];
        char Zip[10];
      };
      struct Employee
      {
        char Name[25];
        int ID;
        Address Addr;
        float Salary;
      };
      Employee  JD;
```

1. The *Address* structure is nested inside of the *Employee* structure.

2. A statement to assign "John Doe" for the employee name is:

   ```
   JD.Name = "John Doe";
   ```

3. Statements to allow the user to enter the employee's state of residence are:

   ```
   cout  <<  "\nEnter the employee's state of residence:  ";
   gets (JD.Addr.State);
   ```

4. Statements to allow the user to enter the employee's salary are:

   ```
   cout  <<  "\nEnter the employee's salary:  ";
   cin  >>  JD.Salary;
   ```

5. A header for a function called *Display_Employee( )* that will display the data stored in the *Employee* structure is:

   ```
   void Display_Employee (Employee Employ)
   ```

6. Statements required for the function in question 5 to display the employee data are:

   ```
   void Display_Employee (Employee Employ)
   {
     cout << "\nEmployee Name:  " << Employ.Name
          << "\nEmployee ID:  "  << Employ.ID
          << "\nEmployee Address:  " << "\n\t\t" << Employ.Addr.Street
          << "\n\t\t" << Employ.Addr.City << ", " << Employ.Addr.State
          << ' ' << Employ.Addr.Zip
          << "\nEmployee Salary:  " << Employ.Salary;
   }
   ```

CHAPTER *12:*

SECTION 12-1

1. By a class defining the behavior of its objects, we mean that the class defines how its objects act and react when they are accessed.

2. False: Data hiding is not ensured by encapsulation, since encapsulation only dictates that the data and/or functions are packaged together in a well-defined unit.

3. True: Private class members can only be accessed via public member functions.

4. Combining data with the functions that are dedicated to manipulating the data such that outside operations cannot affect the data is known as *information or data hiding*.

5. True: A struct is an encapsulated unit.

6. Information hiding is provided by the *private* section of a class.

7. The behavioral secrets of a class are revealed at the *implementation* level.

8. A definition for a static object called *Pick_Up* for a class called *Truck* is:

    ```
    Truck  Pick_Up;
          OR
    Truck PU;
    Truck *Pick_Up = &PU;
    ```

9. A definition for a dynamic object called *Station_Wagon* for a class called *Automobile* is:

    ```
    Automobile  *Station_Wagon = new Automobile;
    ```

SECTION 12-2

1. A class member function is sometimes called a *method*.

2. The complete definition of a member function, which includes the function header and body is called the function *implementation*.

3. A header for a member function called *Wheels()* that will return the number of wheels from a class called *Truck* is:

    ```
    int  Truck :: Wheels(void);
    ```

4. A member function that is used specifically to initialize class data is called a *constructor*.

5. You can tell which member function in a class is the constructor, since the constructor has the same name as the class and has no return data type.

6. The statement, "The return data type of a constructor function is optional" is false because a constructor cannot have a return data type.

7. A class constructor is called automatically when an object is defined for that class.

8. The primary use for a class destructor is to deallocate memory allocated dynamically by a constructor.

9. All member functions of a class carry with them a built-in pointer to the function called *this*.

10. You can call a non-constructor member function of a class by listing the object name, a dot, and the function name with any required arguments.

11. A member function that only returns the values of the private class members is called an *access* function.

12. The term "message" is used for a call to a member function because when an object function is called, we are sending information to the object and the object sends back information.

SECTION 12-3

1. Three reasons for using the multi-file approach for developing software are:
   - It allows the creation of smaller, more manageable files.
   - Programs are easier to maintain.
   - The programmer can hide important program code from the user.

2. Header files in a C++ software project provide the interfaces to the class objects.

3. A software manufacturer might not supply you with the member function implementation source code to keep the user from altering and possibly corrupting the function implementations, or to hide the function implementations for proprietary reasons.

4. A file that identifies the files that need to be compiled and linked to create an executable program is the *project* file *(.prj)*.

5. When building a C++ project, the *.CPP* files such as application and implementation files must be listed in the project manager.

6. You don't list header files in the project manager since the header files are already included in the *.CPP* files as *#include* preprocessor directives.

7. You can view header files that are part of a project by selecting the **Include Files** option in the **Projects** menu and then select the **View** option in the header files listing window.

CHAPTER 13:

SECTION 13-1

1. A parent class is called a *base* class in C++.

2. A child class is called a *derived* class in C++.

3. A collection of classes with common inherited members is called a *family of classes*.

4. Two reasons for using inheritance are:

- Inheritance allows you to reuse code without having to start from scratch.
- Inheritance allows you to build a hierarchy among classes.

5. False: The proper use of inheritance would not allow a line class to be derived from a point class, since a line IS NOT A point.

6. True: The proper use of inheritance would allow a pixel class to be derived from a point class, since a pixel IS-A point.

7. True: The proper use of inheritance would allow a pickup truck class to be derived from a truck class, since a pickup truck IS-A truck.

SECTION 13-2

1. True: When declaring a derived class, the derived class is listed first followed by a colon and the base class.

2. True: A public base class allows its public members to be used by any of its derived classes.

3. The statement, "A protected base class member is protected from any use by the derived classes of that base class" is false since the derived classes of a base class have access to the base's protected members.

4. When base class header files are included in multiple implementation and application files, you must use the *#ifndef* directive to avoid "Multiple declaration" compile errors.

5. The main reason that *Savings* should not be derived from *Super_Now* is that a savings account is *not* a checking account. Such an inheritance would not be natural.

6. *Multiple inheritance* occurs when all the inherited members in a family can be traced back to more than one parent class.

SECTION 13-3

1. True: A virtual function is always a polymorphic function.

2. False: All polymorphic functions are not virtual, since an overloaded function is polymorphic, but not virtual.

3. True: The virtual function interface is identical for each version of the function in a given class family.

4. Overloaded functions are *statically* bound.

5. Virtual functions are *dynamically* bound.

6. The implementation code for a dynamically bound function is determined at *run time*.

CHAPTER *14:*

SECTION 14-1

1. The term *abstract* is used to indicate that data and its related operations are being viewed without considering any of the details of how the data or operations are implemented in the computer system.

2. *Float*, *int*, or any of the other data types are examples of ADTs that we have been working with in the C++ language.

3. The ADT black box concept facilitates *modular* software design.

4. The statement, "A data structure and an abstract data type are the same thing" is false, since a data structure provides a way of structuring or organizing data and an ADT defines the data to be operated on as well as the operations that can be performed on the data.

5. Data protection in an ADT is provided by *encapsulation and information hiding*.

6. The interface to an ADT is through its *function interface*.

7. You gain modularity through the use of ADTs, since ADTs are building blocks for use in software development.

8. You gain generality through the use of ADTs, since algorithms can be developed that depend only on the ADT function interface without concern for the implementation details of the ADT.

SECTION 14-2

1. If the user filled a stack using the application test program in this section and a call was made to the *Push()* function after the stack was full, *FullStack()* would return a value of TRUE and the message, "The stack is full!" would be displayed on the screen.

2. You can't randomly access the array holding the stack, since the array is a private member of the *Stack* class and can only be accessed via the stack operations defined for the class.

3. With our array implementation of a stack, a *Push()* operation requires that the stack pointer be *pre-incremented*.

4. The statement, "With our array implementation of a stack, the stack is full when

the value of *Top* becomes equal to *MAX*, where *MAX* is the maximum number of elements that the array can hold" is false, since the array begins at 0. Thus, *Top* must equal *MAX – 1* when the stack is full.

5. With our array implementation of a stack, the stack is empty when the value of *Top* is –1.

6. The functional difference between the *Pop()* function and the *TopElement()* function is that the value of *Top* is not changed with the *TopElement()* function and it is with the *Pop()* function.

7. We had to include a *FullStack()* function in our implementation of a stack because of the finite storage capacity of an array.

SECTION 14-3

1. If the user filled a queue using the application test program in this section and a call was made to the *Insert()* function after the queue was full, *FullQ()* would return a value of TRUE and the message "The queue is full!" would be displayed on the screen.

2. The statement, "With our array implementation of a queue, an *Insert()* operation requires that *Front* be advanced prior to placing the element in the array" is false, because *Rear* must be advanced not *Front*.

3. The pseudocode to advance *Front* for the circular array implementation of a queue is:

    If *Front* == MAX – 1
        Set *Front* = 0.
    Else
        Set *Front* = *Front* +1.

4. The statement, "With the circular array implementation of a queue, *Front* can never have a higher value than *Rear*" is false because, for example, after the last element is removed, the value of *Front* can be greater than the value of *Rear*.

5. Using the circular array implementation of a queue, *Front* == *Rear* when there is only one element in the queue.

6. We had to include a *FullQ()* function in our implementation of a queue because of the finite storage capacity of the array used to hold the queue.

7. Using our array implementation of a queue, the element counter is equal to 0 when the queue is empty and the element counter is equal to *MaxQ* when the queue is full.

SECTION 14-4

1. The statement, "In a linked list, the sequencing of the nodes is implicit" is false. The sequencing of nodes in a linked list is explicit, since the location of the successor of any given node must be clearly specified in the node.

2. The two parts of a linked list node are the *element* and *locator (or pointer)*.

3. If *Node(P)* is the last node in the list, the value of *Next(P)* is *NULL*.

4. The statement, "In a pointer implementation of a linked list, we know that the list is empty when the value of *First* is zero" is false, because the list is empty when the value of *First* is NULL.

5. If you reverse the order of steps 3 and 4 in the insertion process illustrated in Figure 14-15, the linked list will be los,t since the pointer to it will be reassigned to the single new node.

6. The list search algorithm given in this section will not detect multiple occurrences of the same item in a linked list. It could be made to detect multiple occurrences by placing the search in a **while** loop and searching for the item until the end of the linked list is reached.

7. If the statements *Set PredP = P* and *Set P = Next(P)* are reversed in the linked list search algorithm, *P* and *PredP* would be pointing to the same node.

8. An algorithm for the list destructor function, *~List( )* is:

    ~List( ) **Algorithm**
    BEGIN
        Set P = First
        While P ≠ NULL
            Delete P.
            Set P = Next (P).
    END.

CHAPTER *15:*

SECTION 15-1

1. The statement, "A file is a random access data structure" is false , since a file is a sequential access data structure.

2. The data type of the components in a given C++ file must be either *character* or *binary*.

3. A channel where data can flow between your C++ program and the outside world is called a *file stream*.

4. Standard output in C++ is written to the *ofstream* file stream.

5. The *ifstream* class is used in C++ to perform input, or read, operations from disk files.

6. True: The *iostream* class provides an example of multiple inheritance.

7. A statement to define *MyFile* as an output file stream object is:

    ofstream MyFile;

8. A statement to define *YourFile* as an input/output file stream object is:

    fstream YourFile;

9. A statement that will open the file stream in question 7 for an ASCII file called *ASCII.dat* is:

    MyFile.open ("ASCII.dat");

10. A statement that will open the file stream in question 8 for a binary file called *binary.dat* is:

    YourFile.open ("binary.dat" , ios :: binary, ios :: in I ios :: out);

11. To add information to the end of a file you must use the *ios :: app* file mode.

SECTION 15-2

1. The statement, "File operations in C++ are the same as those in C" is false, since file operations in C++ are centered around classes and classes are not available in C.

2. The major operations that are required to create a new file if it does not already exist are:

    *   Define an output file stream object.
    *   Open the file stream in output mode and attach it to a disk file name.
    *   Get the new file components from the user and write them to the file.
    *   Close the file stream.

3. The major operations that are required to read an existing file are:

    *   Define an input file stream object.
    *   Open the file stream in input mode and attach it to a disk file name.
    *   Read the file components and display them to the user.
    *   Close the file stream.

4. The difference, relative to the position of the file window, between using the *ios :: out* versus the *ios :: app* file modes when opening a file is that the *ios :: out* mode

positions the file window at the beginning of the file and the *ios :: app* positions the file window at the end of the file.

5. The *change.cpp* program in this section inherits the *tellg()* function from the *fstream* class..

6. The *tellg()* function returns the current position of the file window to the calling program.

7. True: The *tellg()* function should be used with input files, while the *tellp()* function should be used with output files.

8. The standard function, *seekp()*, must be used to position the file window for an output file.

9. The three predefined starting points available to the *seekg()* and *seekp()* functions are:

    • *ios :: beg* (for the beginning of a file)

    • *ios :: end* (for the end of a file)

    • *ios :: cur* (for the current position of the file window)

10. The distance to move the file window from the specified starting point when using *seekg()* or *seekp()* must be expressed in *byte* units.

GLOSSARY

Abstract data type (ADT)	A structure that includes both data and related operations with a means to encapsulate the structure details; whereby the structure data is completely hidden from its surroundings and the structure operations provide loose coupling of the structure to the outside world via a function interface.
Access function	A function that only returns the values of the private members of an object.
Actual argument	A value passed to a function during a function call.
Algorithm	A series of step-by-step instructions that produce a solution to a problem.
Array	An indexed data structure which is used to store data elements of the same data type.
Base class	The parent class of a derived class.
Block scope	The accessibility, or visibility, of a local variable defined in a given block of code, such as a function.
Calling program	The program that calls, or invokes, a function.
Class (abstract level)	An *interface* that defines the behavior of its objects.
Class (implementation level)	A syntactical unit that describes a set of data and related operations that are common to its objects.
Components	Data elements in a file form components.
Compound statement	Several statements framed by curly braces.
Constructor	A special class function that is used to initialize the data members of an object automatically when the object is defined.

Control structures	A pattern for controlling the flow of a program module.
Data type	A set of data elements that more or less belong with each other. Examples include *int, char, float, enum.*
Declaration	A declaration specifies the name and attributes of a value, but does not reserve storage. We declare constants.
Default parameter	A function parameter that is assigned a default value in the function prototype or the function header, but not both.
Definition	A definition specifies the name and attributes of a variable and also reserves storage. Variables are defined.
Delete operator	The delete operator is used to deallocate memory created dynamically by the **new** operator.
Derived class	An inherited, or child, class that will include its own members and also include members inherited from the base class.
Destructor	The counterpart of a constructor that is used to "clean up" an object after it is no longer needed. Normally used to deallocate memory allocated to an object by the object constructor.
Dynamic binding	Dynamic binding occurs when a polymorphic function is defined for several classes in a family but the actual code for the function is not attached, or bound, until execution time. A polymorphic function which is dynamically bound is called a *virtual* function.
Encapsulation	To package data and/or operations into a single well-defined programming unit.
Enumerated data types	A set of data elements that the programmer defines for a particular application.

Field	An item of meaningful data.
FIFO	First-in, first-out; FIFO is associated with queues.
File	A data structure that consists of a sequence of components of the same data type, usually associated with program I/O. A means by which the program communicates with the "outside world."
File scope	The scope of a global variable defined prior to *main()* that is accessible to any block in the same file.
File stream	A file stream provides a channel for data to flow between the program and the outside world.
File stream buffer	The link between a program and the file components.
File window	The means for a program to communicate with a file. The file window locates components within the file for processing.
Fixed repetition loop	A loop that will be executed a predetermined number of times.
Formal parameter	A variable used in a function header that receives the value of the respective actual argument in the function call.
Function	A subprogram that returns a single value, a set of values, or performs some specific task such as I/O.
Function header	A statement that forms a common boundary, or interface, between the function and its calling program.
Function prototype	A model of the interface to the function that is used by the compiler to check calls to the function for the proper number of arguments and the correct data types of the arguments.

Global variable	A variable, defined prior to *main()*, that can be used by all functions of a given program, including *main()*. Global variables have file scope.
Identifier	A unique name associated with a constant, variable, function, data structure, class, object, etc.
Information hiding	Information hiding is accomplished when there exists a binding relationship between the information, or data, and its related operations such that operations outside of an encapsulated unit can not affect the information inside the unit.
Implementation	The definition of the function for a class that includes the function header and the body of the function.
In-line function	A function whose implementation is coded within curly braces, following the function prototype.
Indirection	Indirection has to do with the levels of addressing it takes to access data.
Inheritance	That property of object-oriented programming that allows one class, called a *derived class*, to share the structure and behavior of another class, called a *base class*.
Instance	In object-oriented programming, an example, or specimen, of a class. We say that an object is an instance of a class.
IS-A	The link between a derived class and its base class.
Iteration	A control structure, also called looping, that causes the program flow to repeat a finite number of times.

LIFO

Last-in, first-out;. LIFO is associated with stacks.

Linked List

A sequential data structure where, given any element in the list the location of its successor element is specified by an *explicit* link, rather than by its natural position in the structure.

List

A *sequence* of data elements whose basic operations are insertion and deletion of elements to and from the list.

Local variable

A variable that is defined within a given block of code, such as a function. Local variables have block scope.

Member

Any item declared in a structure or class.

Message

A call to a member function.

Method

A function that is a part of a structure or class.

Microprocessor

A single integrated circuit (IC) chip that contains the entire central processing unit (CPU).

Multiple inheritance

Multiple inheritance occurs when the inherited class members can be traced back to more than one parent class.

Nested looping

Looping structures that are located within other looping structures..

Nested structure

A structure within a structure.

new Operator

The **new** operatar is used to dynamically allocate memory.

Object

An instance, or specimen, of a given class. An object of a given class has the structure and behavior defined by the class which is common to all objects of the same class.

Object-oriented programming	A form of programming whereby data and related operations are specified as classes whose instances are objects. The data and related operations are so tightly bound such that only those operations defined for a class can affect the class data. This idea of encapsulation and information hiding allows the easy formation of ADTs.
Object program	The binary machine language program generated by a compiler and usually has a file extension of *.obj*.
Overloaded constructor	A constructor that performs different tasks depending on the number and/or type of arguments that it receives. An overloaded constructor is statically bound at compile time.
Parameter	A data item that is received by a function in order for it to perform its designated operation.
Pointer	A pointer is used to represent an actual machine addresses.
Polymorphism	Polymorphism occurs when functions or objects have the same name for different classes of the same family but behave differently.
Posttest loops	Testing a condition after each loop execution as in the **do/while** loop structure.
Pretest loops	Testing a condition each time before a loop is executed as in the **while** and **for** loop structures.
Primitive state	A known condition that terminates a recursive function call.
Project file (*.prj*)	A file that identifies the files that need to be compiled and linked to create a given executable program.

Protected member   A member of a class that is accessible to both the base class and any derived classes of the base class in which it is declared. Thus, a protected member of a base class is accessible to any class within the class family, but not accessible to things outside the class family.

Pseudocode   An informal set of English-like statements that are generally accepted within the computer industry to denote common computer programming operations. Pseudocode statements are used to describe the steps in a computer algorithm.

Public base class   A base class that allows all of its public members to be public in its derived classes.

Queue   A primary memory storage structure that consists of a list, or sequence, of data elements. All insertions of elements into the queue are made at one end of the queue, called the *rear* of the queue and all deletions of elements from the queue are made at the other end of the queue, called the *front* of the queue. A queue operates on the *first-in*, *first-out*, or *FIFO* principle.

Reading   Reading is obtaining data from something such as an input device or a data structure; a copy operation. A read operation is usually a non-destructive operation.

Recursion   A process whereby an operation calls itself until a primitive state is reached.

Recursive function   A function that calls itself.

Reference parameters   Parameters that provide two-way communication between the calling program and the function.

Run-time error   When the program attempts to perform an illegal operation as defined by the laws of mathematics, logic, or the particular compiler in use.

Scope   Scope refers to the largest block in which a given constant or variable is accessible, or visible.

Selection

A control structure where the program selects, or decides, between one of several routes depending on the conditions that are tested.

Sequence

A control structure where statements are executed sequentially, one after another, in a straight-line fashion.

Single inheritance

Single inheritance occurs when all inherited class members can be traced back to a single parent class.

Source program

The program that you write in the C++ language which normally has a file extension of *.cpp*.

Stack

A primary memory storage structure that consists of a list, or sequence, of data elements where all the insertions and deletions of elements to and from the stack are made at one end of the stack called the *top*. A stack operates on the *last-in*, *first-out*, or *LIFO* principle.

Standard function

A predefined operation that the C++ compiler will recognize and evaluate to return a result or perform a given task.

Star, *

In front of a pointer variable denotes the contents of the memory location where the pointer is pointing.

Static binding

Static binding occurs when a polymorphic function is defined for several classes in a family and the actual code for the function is attached, or bound, at compile time. Overloaded functions are statically bound.

Structure

A collection of data members, or data fields, and function members. Also called a struct.

Structured design

A methodology that requires software to be designed using a top/down modular approach.

Structured programming

Structured programming allows programs to be written using well-defined control structures and independent program modules.

Syntax error	An error created by violating the required syntax, or grammar, of a programming language.
Value parameters	Parameters that allow for one-way communication of data from the calling program to the function.
Virtual function	Functions which have the same name but different implementations for various classes within a class family. A virtual function is dynamically bound.
Whitespace	Blanks, tabs, new lines, form feeds, etc. are all forms of whitespace.
Writing	Writing is often associated with the output of data to a display monitor, printer, or file. In addition, data can be "written" to data structures such as arrays, structs, or objects. A write operation is usually a destructive operation.

INDEX

A

Abstract class, 523
Abstract data type (ADT), 543–46, 730
  data, 544
  encapsulation, 545
  information hiding, 545
  interface, 545
  linked list, 579–99
    implementation, 582–99
    operations, 582–91
  operations, 544
  queue, 563–78, 736
    implementation, 602
    operations, 565–72
  stack, 550–63, 737
    implementation, 550–63
    operations, 548–49
Abstraction, 463, 543
Access function, 494, 730
Actual argument, 730
Algorithm, 19, 730
  effective, 27
  elegance, 347
  operations, 28
  well-defined, 27
Alias, 400
Arithmetic and logic unit (ALU), 5
Arithmetic operations, 6
Arithmetic operators, 130
Array, 307, 730
  access, 316–22, 359–72
  circular, 565
  definition format, 310, 356
  dimension, 309
  elements, 308–9
  holding a stack, 550–51
  holding a queue, 565–66
  indices, 309
  initialization of, 311–15

more than two dimensions, 372–76
one-dimensional, 307–22
plane major order, 374
row major order, 356
searching
  binary search, 341–48, 351
  sequential search, 331–35
size of, 359
sorting
  bubble sort, 351
  insertion sort, 335–41
  selection sort, 352
structure of, 307–8
two-dimensional, 355–72
wrap-around, 565
ASCII
  code table, 48
  files, 610
Assembler, 15
Assembly language, 14–15
Assignment operators, 135

B

Base class, 517, 730
  public, 526, 736
Behavior, 463, 465
Binding, 538
  dynamic, 538, 731
  static, 538, 737
Block scope, 730
Boolean operations, 136–41
  logical, 139–41
  relational, 137–39
break statement
  in loops, 238–40
  in **switch** statements, 196
Bulk storage, *see* Secondary memory
Bus, 6